CROSSLINES Essential Field Guides to humanitarian and conflict zones

Afghanistan

SECOND EDITION – FULLY REVISED

Edward Girardet
Co-editors: Charles Norchi and Mirwais Masood

Media Action International

Published for Media Action International by ***CROSSLINES*** *Publications*
Geneva, Switzerland

First published in Geneva, Switzerland by *CROSSLINES Publications*

Cover Photo: Jonathan Walter © 2002 (Shrine of Hazrat Ali, Mazar-e-Sharif)
Design and layout: Nikki Meith, *Maximedia Ltd.*

Please address all enquiries to:

CROSSLINES Essential Field Guides
c/o Media Action International
PO Box/Case postale 2638
CH-1211, Geneva 2
Switzerland
Email: editor@crosslinesguides.com Website: www.crosslinesguides.com

ISBN: 297001761X
Printed in France at Imprimerie Sadag, Bellegarde

Contents

CONTENTS

Maps

Preface

This fully revised and updated edition of the *CROSSLINES Essential Field Guide to AFGHANISTAN* represents our response to the exceptional interest shown in the first publication of this book in 1998. The original edition came out at a time when no one was particularly interested in Afghanistan apart from the usual bastion of Afghan *aficionados*, aid workers, journalists and occasional travellers. For the media and human rights groups, the Taliban, who were in power at the time, were always a good subject because of their repression of females and their peculiar penchant for banning everything from kite-flying, music and dancing to chess playing and the loud clicking of ladies' shoes.

For many aid workers during the 1990s, however, continued foreign assistance to Afghanistan became something of a duty, if only because basic human decency prevented one from abandoning this magnificent but war-wracked country and its increasingly exhausted population as a lost cause. The events of 11 September 2001 had not yet precipitated that flood of instant international attention on Afghanistan from the media. In fact, in the summer of 2001, less than two months prior to the terror assaults in America, the United Nations was struggling with how to project Afghanistan's dire humanitarian predicament – driven by two decades of war and four years of drought – onto the radar screen of global concern.

One of the original reasons for producing the *Essential Field Guide to Afghanistan* in the late 1990s was to provide anyone interested (or who should be interested) in Afghanistan with a handy reference book of analysis and background resources critical for a better understanding of this country. The *EFG* was also designed as a template for similar field guides on countries in crisis elsewhere. Our principal goal remains to promote more well-informed humanitarian interventions in conflict and post-conflict zones as well as to encourage greater and more balanced media coverage in these regions.

Our target audience for this field guide continues to be a broad range of players both inside and outside the country, from reporters, aid workers, local NGOs, human rights advocates and environmentalists to donors, diplomats, academics and business representatives. Numerous international agencies and donors rapidly included the first edition as an indispensable part of their Afghanistan briefing kits. This firmly demonstrated the urgent need for accurate, impartial background analysis to be made available to every aid worker or diplomat, regardless of focus. As Anders Fange, director of the Swedish Committee for Afghanistan, one of the most experienced of the international agencies working in the region, noted: "The Essential Field Guide is useful for both the old Afghan hand and the newcomer. It is not the sort of book that I would read in one go, but it's an excellent information resource that anyone dealing with Afghanistan should have." Even Unocal, the American oil consortium which sought to obtain rights from both the Taliban and the United Front (also known as the Northern Alliance) for building a pipeline across Afghanistan, acknowledged the usefulness of the book. "I've just got your book for 25 bucks and it's saved us tens of thousands of dollars in information," one company official told us. We wished that Unocal would at least make a humanitarian contribution in return for such cheap information, but they never did.

Sales of the 1998 edition were proceeding modestly until the events of September 11, 2001, which prompted a striking surge in demand among journalists, aid workers and the military. Bookshops in Islamabad, where most of the news organizations were based for the covering of the US-led intervention in Afghanistan, quickly ran out of their few remaining copies, obliging television networks, such as *ABC News* and *Fox Television*, to have the book hand-carried or couriered out. The International Committee of the Red Cross immediately bought several dozen – claiming that it was the best handbook available on Afghanistan, or on any humanitarian situation worldwide for that matter. The British NGO Oxfam insisted that all those leaving for Afghanistan should have the *EFG* as part of their briefing kits. One American aid agency coordinator complained that "every time we order copies for our field people, they disappear at headquarters." Various aid workers told us they did not care whether their own organizations bought the book or not; they had purchased their own copies.

One unplanned for – but not unexpected – interested party was the US armed forces. A San Diego-based naval officer called our Geneva office in disgust to say that he had had to purchase his copy of the *EFG* on the Ebay internet auction site for US$ 250 because Amazon.com and other suppliers had run out. Various intelligence organizations also ordered their own copies and immediately queried when a new and revised version would come out. One Afghan engineer spent almost the entire night reading a loaned copy of the *EFG* from cover to cover. "Every Afghan professional should have a copy of this copy," he blurted incredulously. "Why haven't Afghans got this information? This must be made available in Dari." We assured him that we would try to produce an Afghan edition. Finally, one German officer of the International Security Assistance Force (ISAF) in Kabul told us that "every single soldier should be issued a copy before they go out." He added that peacekeeping is not just a matter of providing security but also understanding the country where you are working. He pleaded with us to come out with a new version as soon as possible and to ensure that we informed all participating countries within ISAF the moment it came out. "This is where the EFG is such an excellent asset, and could even save lives," he maintained.

It has taken us nearly two years to produce this fully revised edition of the *Essential Field Guide to Afghanistan*. One of the reasons for the delay was purely financial. It took an inordinate amount of time to put together the funding package, and for this we particularly thank our sponsors. Another was that it was not worth doing a new version until the dust had settled somewhat. The euphoria following the toppling of the Taliban has now been replaced by a more sober view of Afghanistan's long-term prospects. Furthermore, much of the information available in 2002 was either old or unreliable, often dating back to the 1990s, even late 1970s. Many aid or donor organizations were constantly re-quoting outdated or unreliable information as fact. The past two years has allowed agencies to consolidate much information. However, some essential data – such as population estimates (which range from 18 to 26 million) and ethnic representation – will remain highly contentious until a full census is conducted.

As with the first edition, the editors have tried to furnish the best assessments and information possible. Several new overview essays have been commissioned, to reflect new realities in the spheres of security, humanitarian aid and reconstruction. Most of the original essays and briefs have been completely re-written, while the remainder have been updated with new data and situation assessments. In many respects, the 2004 Essential Field Guide is a completely new handbook. It is with some regret that, owing to shortage of space, we have been forced to leave out some of the first edition's essays and briefs.

We have sought to provide the sort of reliable on-the-ground information, critical analysis, practical advice and background resources that will help those reporting the story or those involved in the humanitarian and recovery process to gain a better grasp of the situation. Our aim is to help integrate knowledge across a range of different sectors. We hope, for example, that the health worker will be sufficiently stimulated to read about the environmental impact of the war on Afghanistan or to demonstrate an interest in the cultural background of the country. All too often, aid workers tend to remain caught up in their specialized domains without seeking to grasp the bigger picture. It is also exceptionally worrying to note how quickly so-called 'experts', whether journalists, aid coordinators or intelligence officers, pick up on clichés and pass them off as part of their own assessments.

Overall, the *EFG* has taken a 25-year perspective (since the first fighting of summer 1978) to stress the need to fully understand the background behind the country's years of destruction and war – and why there is still chronic insecurity, particularly in southern and eastern provinces. As well as background analysis on every sector of interest, the *EFG* offers a detailed travel guide for getting around; practical advice on how to stay safe and healthy while working and living in Afghanistan; contact lists of key agencies; phrasebooks; and pointers to where you can find out more, whether books, websites or research facilities.

The creation of the *Essential Field Guide* series emerged out of personal experience. As many colleagues from the *BBC*, the *New York Times*, *Le Monde*, *El Pais*, or *Der Spiegel* covering wars and humanitarian situations will agree, this is the sort of information that journalists and producers could have used on many occasions, especially when covering areas where information is scattered and one has no special contacts. The same goes for numerous relief coordinators, frontline doctors or human rights lawyers, who suddenly find themselves thrust into conflict zones with scarcely 24 hours' notice.

Equally, the *Essential Field Guide* is designed for those who know the region well, but who may wish to expand the breadth of their overall knowledge. We hope to encourage all those visiting Afghanistan to explore new areas which directly or indirectly affect their own fields of expertise. But, as with the 1998 edition, we are not trying to create the complete guide to Afghanistan with this revised handbook. If the guide succeeds in serving as an essential information tool which can help make a difference, then we have succeeded in what we have set out to do. Obviously, such information is only useful so long as it remains accurate. For this reason, the editors appeal to those involved in Afghanistan, particularly aid organizations, journalists and peacekeepers, to keep us updated on their activities and contact changes. The establishment of the *CROSSLINES Afghanistan Monitor* is another way for us to keep up with events by publishing regular insights, opeds and briefs – which will also be made available on the *CROSSLINES* website: www.crosslinesguides.com.

The Editors, December 2003

Acknowledgements

The Editors, CROSSLINES and Media Action International would like to thank the following sponsors and co-sponsors for their generous support.

Principal Sponsors and Co-Sponsors

The Smith Richardson Foundation
60 Jesop Road, Westport, CT. 06880, USA
Website: www.srf.org

The Embassy of the Royal Government of the Netherlands in Kabul, Afghanistan
The initial principal sponsor of the *CROSSLINES* Essential Field Guide to Afghanistan in 1998, the Foreign Ministry of the Netherlands is one of the most active donors involved in supporting media and public information in humanitarian, conflict and recovery situations. Contact:

Kabul Office of the Netherlands Mission to the Islamic State of Afghanistan
House no. 2 and 3, Street no. 4, Ansari and Ghiyassuddin Watt, Shahr-e-Naw, Kabul
Tel: +93 70 286640, 286641, 286847
Website: www.minbuza.nl

The Swiss Development Corporation, Kabul, Afghanistan and Bern, Switzerland
The SDC provides mainly humanitarian aid to Afghanistan with an emphasis on the integration of refugees, including internally displaced, secondments to UN agencies and to the International Committee of the Red Cross, health services, and natural disaster support, notably the impact of drought on local communities. Contact:

SDC Head office, Freiburgstrasse 130, 3003 Berne, Switzerland
Tel: +41 31 322 3475, 324 1348

Swiss Cooperation Office Afghanistan
Wazir Akbar Khan, Street no. 13 (side lane, 3rd right), House 485, Kabul
Website: www.sdc.admin.ch

The Swedish Committee for Afghanistan, Kabul, Afghanistan
Founded in 1980, the Swedish Committee for Afghanistan (SCA) is one of the largest and most experienced of the non-governmental organizations working in Afghanistan. Focusing on primary education, health, disability and agriculture, SCA was among the first agencies to provide crossborder aid in time of war, primarily health, educational and agricultural support. SCA seeks to help the poorer sections of Afghan society, including vulnerable groups such as

women, children and people with disabilities. Covering 18 provinces in the eastern half of the country, SCA and its 9,000 Afghan staff support more than 400 primary schools and 150 health clinics in under-served areas, providing basic services and work opportunities where little else is available. While the overall aim remains the same nearly a quarter of a century later, namely to fight poverty and promote rehabilitation and development, this pioneering agency has constantly adapted its programmes to the changing needs of Afghan society.

Sarah Lawrence College
1 Mead Way, Bronxville, New York 10708-5999, USA
Tel: +1 914 337 0700
Website: www.slc.edu

Media Action International (MAI), Geneva, Switzerland and Kabul, Afghanistan
A not-for-profit foundation focusing on media and public information support in humanitarian, conflict and post-conflict situations.
***CROSSLINES Publications,* Geneva, Switzerland**
An independent production group of journalists, producers and media consultants.

We would like to thank all the aid agencies and their representatives, journalists, donor organizations, peacekeepers, human rights lawyers, academics and private citizens, including numerous Afghan friends and colleagues, who have assisted with suggestions, ideas, critiques, a bed at night, food and tea at the most unexpected moments, transport, protection, and other forms of more than welcome support and hospitality. While we cannot even begin to name all those who have gone beyond the call of duty to assist, and we apologise in advance for not including everyone (without intent), we would like specifically to thank the following for their help and guidance in putting this fully revised edition together: Ali Wardak, Andrew Wilder, Ascension Martinez, Bahram Barzin, Dan Kelly, Dawn Greene, Desmond Charles, Farhana Faroukhi, Firoten Ghausuddin, Ian McClellan, Jan-Erik Wänn, Jim Williams, Jo de Berry, Lala Gul, Mark Rowland, Tim Winch. We would like to thank Jeff Danziger for sharing with us his great cartoons, Joe Crowley of AIMS for supplying maps, the International Federation of Red Cross and Red Crescent Societies for the use of Thorkell Thorkelsson's wonderful photographs, and Wolf Marloh for his slide scanning services. We'd also like to thank the tireless and largely voluntary efforts of Bethan Montague-Brown, Isabelle Lehouck, Katja Flueckiger, Kristen Eichensehr, Mohammed Shuaib, Nora Geiger, Sue Pfiffner, Smruti Patel, Todd Biffard, Voltaire Casino. As ever, Nikki Meith has excelled herself in her design, layout (and patience). And particular thanks must go to MAI's programme coordinator Amaury Coste in Kabul and MAI's administrator Marilu D'Onofrio in Geneva. Many thanks, too, to Charles Norchi for having obtained the initial funding to kick off this new edition.

Edward Girardet would like to thank, once again, his darling wife, Loretta Hieber-Girardet, for her enduring patience and understanding, even when times were difficult. Lori finally visited Afghanistan on numerous occasions from 2001 onwards and has come to appreciate this extraordinary place and its people. And why, as an outsider, one has no choice but to embrace this staggeringly beautiful country with fascination and awe but also incredible frustration. This is dedicated to Lori and the children, Elisa and Alexander.

Jonathan Walter would like to dedicate his share of the book to his wife Charlotte and two children, Lila and Wilfie, with big hugs all round.

The Editors

Edward Girardet is a journalist, writer and broadcast producer who has reported widely from humanitarian and conflict zones in Africa, Asia and elsewhere since the late 1970s. As a foreign correspondent for the *Christian Science Monitor, US News and World Report* and *The MacNeil-Lehrer NewsHour* based in Paris, he first began covering Afghanistan several months prior to the Soviet invasion in 1979. As a journeyman reporter, he has travelled throughout much of the country making well over 50 trips to the region, many of them by foot and clandestinely. He has written and edited several books, including *Afghanistan – The Soviet War* published in 1985. An avid outdoorsman, he has worked on numerous television current affairs and documentary segments on subjects ranging from the war in Angola to lost tribes in Western New Guinea and environmental issues in Africa for major European and North American broadcasters. Since the mid-1990s, Girardet has been a co-founding director of Media Action International (formerly International Centre for Humanitarian Reporting) operating in Pakistan, Kosovo, Rwanda, West Africa and Indonesia. Most recently, he has written for *National Geographic* magazine, the *Christian Science Monitor* and other publications. Living with his family in Cessy, France near Geneva, Girardet is currently writing a personal book on a quarter of century of reporting in Afghanistan.

Jonathan Walter is a freelance writer and editor specializing in humanitarian issues. Since 1998, he has edited the *World Disasters Report*, published by the Geneva-based International Federation of Red Cross and Red Crescent Societies, and he is author of *The End of Development,* published by the New Economics Foundation in London. Apart from hitch-hiking through Afghanistan three times to research for this field guide, he has worked in Nepal as community aid director for a leading NGO, in Kosovo on media projects for returnees, and in Kenya as a volunteer among the Samburu people. For four years, Walter served in south-east Asia as an officer in the British Army's Brigade of Gurkhas. A keen mountaineer, he has led expeditions to the Alps, Himalayas and Borneo. He holds masters degrees in comparative religions from Cambridge University and philosophy from St. Andrew's University.

Charles Norchi has worked as a journalist, human rights lawyer and consultant in Afghanistan from the Soviet occupation of the 1980s to the present. He has published in major newspapers and contributed to books on foreign affairs, international law and Afghanistan. Norchi has travelled widely on various human rights, reporting and advisory initiatives ranging from the Indian subcontinent to Southern Africa, notably Zimbabwe, Namibia and South Africa. He has lectured or otherwise participated in fora in Geneva, Switzerland for Media Action International and other organizations with particular emphasis on democracy building, communications and security in conflict and post-conflict situations. Norchi is a consultant to the World Bank; a Fellow at Yale Law School; a director of the Policy Science Center, Inc.; Fellow of the Explorers Club; and a professor at Sarah Lawrence College in the United States.

Mirwais Masood began his career teaching English for Afghan refugees in Islamabad, Pakistan in 1996. Five years later, Masood, who is originally from Kabul, became head of the English Language Programme (ELP) in Islamabad. In early 2002, he joined Media Action International (MAI) as assistant programme coordinator for Afghanistan. Masood worked on a number of different projects, notably the *CROSSLINES Essential Field Guide to Afghanistan.* He helped establish various MAI projects, such as the Novice Journalism Training Programme in conjunction with the universities of Kabul, Herat and Balkh, and is also editor of the Dari-Pashto edition of the *Afghanistan Monitor.* Aside from his MAI activities, Masood has reported for the Institute for War and Peace Reporting (IWPR) plus researched for National Geographic.

OVERVIEWS

J. Hartley/UNICEF

Introduction: a new beginning?

By Edward Girardet

The collapse of the Taliban in late autumn 2001, coupled with a more committed international involvement in the recovery of Afghanistan, brought with it a new hope that its beleaguered people might finally witness real peace following nearly a quarter of a century of war. Nevertheless, notwithstanding large-scale pledges of donor support at the January 2002 Tokyo conference – which quickly led to a major rehabilitation of many urban areas, especially Kabul – it remains questionable whether most Afghans, particularly those in rural areas, are really that much better off today than they were during the late 1990s, when the first edition of this guide was published. The return of four million boys and girls to 'school' (often classes in a tent or under the shade of a tree) is undeniably an important step forward. But reconstruction has been very slow, due to donor delays in transferring funds, diversions of aid to short-term needs and threats to the security of aid operations. According to the US NGO, Care International, after 18 months of international aid, just one percent of Afghanistan's reconstruction needs had been met (SEE AID & RECOVERY).

By mid-2003, the central government of President Hamid Karzai was still too weak to assert itself over most provincial warlords. Nor could many parts of the country, notably in the Pashtun-dominated east and south, claim the same level of security as that achieved by the Taliban during their years of influence (1994-2001). Almost daily attacks on Afghans and foreigners alike by suspected pro-Taliban or Islamic extremist groups, as well as by renegade *mujahideen* and bandits, have prompted even some of the most dedicated aid agencies, such as Médecins sans Frontières (MSF) and the International Committee of the Red Cross (ICRC), to reduce if not halt their operations in some regions. The vast majority of international aid agencies and non-government organizations (NGOs) tend to focus on more easily (and safely) implemented initiatives in the Afghan capital rather than serving a more equitable slice of the recovery cake to remoter rural areas, such as Hazarajat in central Afghanistan, Nuristan in the northeast, or Helmand and Nimruz to the southwest.

The cultivation of opium poppies – pruned by a Taliban ban to under 200 tonnes in 2001 – has sprung back stronger than ever. The 2002 harvest amounted to 3,400 tonnes – 75 percent of world supply – despite international efforts to curb the problem. The IMF calculates that the crop was worth US$ 2.5 billion to Afghanistan, roughly half of the country's annual GDP, while 2003's crop was larger still. The country's finance minister has warned of the dangers of an emerging 'narco-mafia'. Meanwhile, abuses of human rights – especially those of women – continue largely unchecked. Despite the fall of the Taliban and the establishment of a Ministry of Women's Affairs, fundamentalist attitudes towards women persist throughout much of the country. Forced marriages, domestic violence and rape remain all too common, while the country's criminal justice system has proved inadequate to protect Afghan women (SEE HUMAN RIGHTS, WOMEN).

At the root of Afghanistan's problems is the ongoing crisis of insecurity, armed attacks and terrorism. The United States-led military Coalition has failed to fully quash anti-government elements, despite its initial success in helping the rival United Front faction (also known as the Northern Alliance) to power. The US's ongoing 'war on terror' relies on paying off and supporting numerous Afghan military commanders, many of whom are implicated in serious human rights abuses – the very warlords whose militias are supposed to be disarming. This has led to criticisms that international military and political agenda are working at cross purposes (SEE US POLICY). While the US army continues to take casualties, attacks on aid workers shot up to around 20 per month during the year to September 2003. 'Neo-Taliban' elements – aligned with the disaffected warlord Gulbuddin Hekmatyar – have encouraged attacks against anyone seen to be supporting the US-backed Karzai administration. Aid workers, private sector contractors, policemen and soldiers – whether Afghan or foreign – have all become targets. Meanwhile, the disarmament of warring factions has barely begun – in large part because of the perceived dominance over the defence ministry of ethnic Tajiks from the Northern Alliance.

Of enormous concern has been the reluctance of the international community to broaden the UN-mandated peacekeeping force beyond the environs of Kabul – despite the constant urging of the Afghan government, the UN and numerous aid agencies. While the now NATO-headed International Security Assistance Force (ISAF) readily acknowledges the urgent need for better security outside the capital, it regards such enforcement as primarily the responsibility of the fledgling Afghan National Army. Yet even the most optimistic ISAF officials consider it unlikely that an Afghan force can ever fully assume such a task in the present environment. Meanwhile, the deployment of Provincial Reconstruction Teams (PRTs) to various urban centres during 2003 is not expected to be sufficient to spread peace across the country. In October 2003, NATO agreed in principle to extending the 5,500-strong ISAF beyond Kabul – but in practice this depends on the UN agreeing to a broader mandate and on NATO powers providing more troops.

The failure of ISAF – or anyone else – to take on the peacekeeping job outside Kabul, even if only by providing security in the country's main towns, has severely threatened the recovery process and condemns much of Afghanistan to greater volatility in the years ahead. Many fear that two Afghanistans will emerge – or have indeed begun to emerge. One is based on an internationally-supported Kabul (plus other select urban zones), much like during the Soviet occupation of the 1980s; while the other comprises a patchwork of fiefdoms controlled by warlords, drug traffickers and Pashtuns not

Jeff Danziger

prepared to accept the dominance of their country by other Afghan ethnic groups or foreigners (SEE SECURITY). While the agreement of a new Constitution in January 2004 is a major step forward, it is likely to remain a paper exercise until security improves nationwide.

Ever since the first revolts erupted against the communist regime of the People's Democratic Party of Afghanistan (PDPA) in the summer of 1978, well over one million Afghans have been killed. This does not include the countless men, women and children who have succumbed to disease, malnutrition, exposure and other indirect effects exacerbated by war conditions. Some six million Afghans were forced to flee the country as refugees, most of them during the decade-long Soviet occupation (1979-1989) when over five million left. With the departure of the Soviets in February 1989, many refugees managed to return to their homes, but renewed bouts of fighting and shelling continued to produce fresh waves of misery during the 1990s and early 2000 as civilians sought to flee the sheer horror inflicted on them by rival Afghan factions (SEE REFUGEES). At various points, too, during Afghanistan's wars, another two million or more have found themselves displaced as 'internal refugees' within their own homeland. Since the late 1990s, a series of earthquakes and the worst drought in living memory have impoverished Afghans further by destroying their homes and forcing them to flee their lands and sell their livestock.

Afghanistan has been seized by various different kinds of conflict over the past 25 years. During the growing civil strife from mid-1978 to the end of 1979, much of the destruction – such as the bombing of Herat in retaliation for the March 1979 uprising or the massacre at Kerala (Kunar province) on 20 April 1979, when over 1,000 men and boys were brutally gunned down – was conducted by communist-led Afghan government forces supported by Soviet advisors. Within weeks of taking power in April 1978, the new regime of President Nur Mohammed Taraki of the PDPA's Khalq ('Masses') faction had begun imposing social reforms with a ruthlessness that angered many, including potential reform-minded supporters. Purges, arrests and the assassination of dissidents from all segments of Afghanistan's political and religious spectrum soon followed. Such actions quickly provided the beginnings of a nationwide uprising. For their part, the rebels (or *mujahideen* as they became known) began – at first sporadically – to launch attacks against PDPA symbols such as police stations, army posts and government officials, including teachers. These soon spread to include schools, administrative offices, highways and even development projects – in fact, anything perceived to be a product of the PDPA regime. By Christmas 1978, at least a dozen provinces were in revolt.

When Soviet troops invaded Afghanistan on 27 December 1979, the war turned into a national resistance struggle. During a decade of occupation (1979-1989), Red Army forces, in conjunction with Afghan regime troops, were responsible for massive destruction of the countryside. They also severely damaged numerous disputed urban areas, ranging from the suburbs of Kandahar in the south to the northern town of Anawa in the Panjshair Valley. The Soviets regularly conducted large-scale offensives involving as many as 12,000 troops supported by helicopter gunships, MiG jetfighters and tanks against towns and villages believed to be affiliated with the guerrillas. These operations involved the deliberate destruction of houses, irrigation systems and fruit orchards as well as the planting of landmines and booby traps (SEE LANDMINES).

Such actions constituted a policy designed to force civilians either to accept government control, or to leave the country. Referred to as "migratory genocide" during the 1980s by many observers, at least one third of the Afghan population (estimated in the early 1980s at 14-17 million) fled the Soviet war. This policy caused whole regions to be abandoned by most of their inhabitants, leaving ghost settlements in their wake. The effects are still painfully evident today with numerous villages and hamlets abandoned or marked by shattered buildings, dead trees and crumbling irrigation ducts.

Following the departure of the Soviets in February 1989, the conflict reverted once again to that of a civil war. However, it was a war that continued to involve outside players, including the Americans, Pakistanis, Iranians and Saudis. Arab-backed Islamic fundamentalist groups, such as the *Wahabi* headed by the likes of Osama Bin Laden (first encountered by this writer in February 1989 in Kunar Province), also sought to establish themselves among the Afghans. Heavily supported by private and government interests in Saudi Arabia, Algeria and Egypt, for example, the *Wahabi* had become increasingly involved during the latter days of the Soviet occupation. As Ahmed Rashid illustrates in his contribution to this guide, to describe Afghanistan as being a country caught up only in an "internal conflict" – as legalists citing international law would define it – shows little understanding of the situation (SEE WAR WITHOUT BORDERS).

After the Soviet withdrawal, Pakistan's military Inter Services Intelligence organization (ISI) was particularly keen to ensure a quick Pashtun-led *mujahed* takeover of Kabul. ISI pressured the guerrilla factions to take Jalalabad by military means before moving on to the Afghan capital. This proved a disastrous mistake for the *mujahideen*. Even worse, the Pakistanis pushed their Pashtun favourite, former Afghan resistance politician Gulbuddin Hekmatyar into a position of artificial leadership which had little to do with his influence among Afghans on the ground. (Hekmatyar was also heavily supported by the Americans during the Soviet war. The Bush administration recently branded their former protégé a 'terrorist' following his declaration of *jihad* against the United States in early 2002). The ISI's policy heralded a new turn in the Afghan war. There was a rise in attacks against the major towns which, until then, had remained relatively unscathed by the direct effects of war. Seeking to dislodge the PDPA regime of Mohammed Najibullah, which much to the surprise of many was able to hold on for almost three years following the Soviet pullout, the *mujahideen* became involved in a more conventional form of warfare rather than the guerrilla tactics at which they had been relatively successful. There was also a dramatic increase in fighting amongst the *mujahideen* themselves. Inter-factional strife had always existed in Afghanistan, but as some observers correctly pointed out during the late 1980s, there was an acute danger of it turning into a Beirut-style conflict.

As a result, Kabul began to suffer growing damage from *mujahed* attacks with rising casualties among civilians. Remarkably little damage had actually occurred during the Soviet occupation given that their focus had been on the countryside. Following the capture of Kabul in 1992, the struggle for control among the different groups disintegrated into a nonsensical mad dogs' war with little regard for its inhabitants. During the period leading up to the fall of the Najibullah government, the *Wahabi* and other foreign Islamic elements had sought to retain their influence amongst the *mujahideen*, but more or less pulled out of Afghanistan – temporarily – when Hekmatyar's Hezb-e-Islami and other Pashtun fundamentalist factions failed to assert themselves.

The large-scale destruction one can see today in Kabul is overwhelmingly the result of bitter internecine strife during 1992-94, particularly between the forces of the largely Pashtun Hezb-e-Islami, the Hazara Hezb-e-Wahdat, the Tajik-dominated Jamiat-e-Islami (led by Ahmed Shah Massoud) and the mainly Uzbek Jumbesh-e-Melli (led by Abdul Rashid Dostum). Incessant, indiscriminate shelling, rocket assaults and aerial bombing by Afghans against Afghans destroyed whole areas of the city. An estimated 50,000 civilians were killed plus countless others wounded. Tens of thousands had to flee, losing everything they possessed in the process, particularly during the brutal assaults in late 1993 and early 1994.

Eventually, however, the conflict became more directed against the Taliban who had been sweeping the south of the country, primarily through buy-offs of commanders rather than military means (SEE TALIBAN). But the Taliban's capture of Kabul in September 1996 did not bring the conflict to an end. Bitter fighting ensued as the United Front (an alliance between Jamiat, Jumbesh and Wahdat forces created in 1996) sought to stave off further Taliban advances in the central and northeast highlands. The battle to control Mazar flared fiercely during 1997, before the city fell to the Taliban in August 1998. Meanwhile, the Taliban employed deliberate scorched earth tactics against the 'rebel-held' plains of Shomali, north of Kabul, and starved the people of Bamiyan by a blockade of food aid. By the summer of 2001, the Taliban dominated well over 80 percent of the country, with Massoud's United Front forces pushed back to the northeastern province of Badakhshan and the Panjshair Valley.

During this same period, the Arab-backed Al Qa'eda led by Osama Bin Laden and other *Wahabi*-influenced groups returned. Massoud had consistently warned the West of the rising establishment of Arab and other foreign-backed, particularly Pakistani, terrorist training camps inside Afghanistan in the late 1990s and early 2000 – but to little avail. While travelling to Europe for the first time in the spring of 2001, he repeated his warnings in Brussels and Paris with specific allegations against Bin Laden. The French provided him with some support, such as weapons and ammunition, as did other Europeans, the Russians and the Iranians. The Americans reportedly also provided some backing but only seemed to wake up to Massoud's warnings following the events of September 11, 2001 and the Afghan leader's assassination by suspected Al Qa'eda operatives two days earlier. On October 7, 2001, the US and its British Coalition allies stepped in to support the United Front against the Taliban by launching a bombing campaign, which ultimately ended with the collapse of the Taliban regime in Kabul and across the rest of Afghanistan in late November.

Afghanistan's wars have set the country back decades. Despite considerable advances in education, health and other forms of development during the 1960s and 1970s, any sense of nationwide improvement has been on hold since the early days of the Soviet occupation. Until the collapse of the Taliban and the wholescale return of the international community in early 2002, most of the aid to Afghanistan had been in the form of emergency relief. While humanitarian support since the early 1990s did much to ameliorate conditions in many areas, only limited forms of reconstruction, such as the rebuilding of homes or the rehabilitation of irrigation networks, were undertaken. It was never possible for ordinary Afghans or aid agencies to undertake longer-term initiatives such as the establishment of an urgently needed primary health care system or the replanting of the country's devastated forests.

As at the end of 2003, much of Afghanistan still lies in a state of ruin or neglect. Military assaults, indiscriminate shelling and looting – as well as the destitution caused by uncontrolled deforestation, drought, poverty and the abandonment of whole villages – have all played their part in destroying or severely damaging many of this country's once thriving urban and rural areas, cultural sites and natural resources. Since the end of 2001, internationally-supported reconstruction projects and local initiatives have begun to make a difference in some parts. Yet the bulk of Afghanistan's basic infrastructure, such as roads, power grids or hospitals, is in dire need of repair or outright overhaul. Major road reconstruction (or even temporary grading) only began towards the end of 2002, while progress on the flagship Kabul-Kandahar trunk road was seriously hampered by poor security. Most of the international support for improving the country's shattered health facilities has so far been focused on the capital, leaving over 60 percent of Afghans without regular access to even the most basic form of qualified medical treatment. Four years of drought have added another fatal ingredient to the cocktail of conflict and economic collapse. *Kuchi* nomads have lost millions of head of livestock, resorting to aid handouts at refugee camps. Farmers who have struggled to make ends meet growing wheat have turned to opium, which makes 20-40 times more profit and thrives in dry conditions. Much of Kabul remains without regular electricity because its reservoirs are parched of water. Sewage disposal is non-existent.

As a journalist who has covered Afghanistan since September 1979, less than three months prior to the Soviet invasion, I have always found it exhilarating to travel in this extraordinary country. Since undertaking the writing and research of the first edition of the *Essential Field Guide* in 1997 and 1998, I returned with National Geographic in the summer of 2001 and left only days before the events of September 11. In fact, I found myself staying at the same guesthouse with the two Arab assassins of Ahmed Shah Massoud, who was murdered on September 9. Even before the fall of the Taliban, I was struck by how tired Afghans were from so many years of war. Yet it was – and still is – this 'conflict fatigue' that I regard as possibly the most positive force for resolving Afghanistan's quarter century of crisis.

For the newcomer to Afghanistan, but also for the veteran aid *afficionados* or reporter *wallahs* who have wandered in and out of this semi-arid land of mountains and deserts since the early years, it is crucial to maintain a historical and cultural perspective on its various wars. We need to understand not only the reasons behind the civil conflict of the late 1970s, followed by the Soviet occupation of the 1980s, but also why fighting is still ongoing – and growing – between anti-government groups and Coalition Forces (including their Afghan allies). And why, just as the British and the Soviets discovered during the 19th and 20th centuries, there can be no military solution to Afghanistan's problems or insecurity (SEE HISTORY).

Admittedly, Afghanistan is a difficult place to grasp. As many of us have found, Afghanistan grows on you with a passion. It is a defiant and often contradictory nation whose people exhibit an array of characteristics ranging from touching hospitality, warmth and even tolerance, to shameless opportunism and selfishness. To say the least, it is a frustrating country. And as the British, Russians, Pakistanis, Americans and other outsiders have discovered, Afghans are also an impossible people to control. Nevertheless, journalists and aid workers need to make a greater effort to fathom the Afghan way of thinking and the circumstances that have caused this extraordinary nation to be ravaged with such vehemence. This is crucial if the recovery process, which may take decades and cost billions of dollars (US$ 30 billion, according to the government), is to succeed. While many of us, including this writer, tend to use over-simplistic language, such as "Afghans believe that...", it does little justice to the extreme complexity of this society to talk in generalizations, or even worse, to ignore the issues at hand. One French nurse in Kabul adamantly insisted that she did not consider it vital to know anything about Afghan politics nor its tribal and ethnic background as it would only interfere with her humanitarian work. Such attitudes, and above all, ignorance, can lead to disastrous consequences not only for the way aid is implemented but potentially for the security of relief workers themselves.

The new and fully revised overview essays and information briefs in this *Essential Field Guide* seek to help readers deepen their grasp of what is happening in Afghanistan today, while maintaining the historical context of our first edition – vital in order to be able to interpret current events. Ahmed Rashid's revised essay on regional players, for example, will help readers better grasp the continuing internationalization of the Afghan conflict. Christine Johnson's new overview on aid and recovery clarifies the nature of international aid to Afghanistan. Charles Norchi has expanded his essay to provide one of the first analyses of Afghanistan's fledgling Constitution; while Ali Wardak's overview charts a course through the complex waters of Afghanistan's different ethnic and tribal groups. As editors, we are seeking to provide a book that contains a 25-year perspective, combined with fresh data on recent developments. The idea is to help the doctor, the agricultural engineer, the diplomat or the journalist not only to understand why certain things have happened in Afghanistan and the region, but also why it is critical to pay attention to every aspect of Afghan life, from the impact of war, shattered irrigation canals or deforestation to cultural looting, human rights abuses or even the need to drink tea as a preliminary to any discussion.

With ongoing international support, Afghanistan may finally emerge as a real country again. But numerous hazards remain, originating both from home and abroad. Many players, whether outside governments, local warlords or drug traffickers, still regard this land as a playground of strategic or personal ambition. For those of us who remembered the extraordinary sense of warmth, congeniality and culture of this people prior to the outbreak of war, but also during much of the national resistance against the Red Army occupation, many Afghans still come across as tired and depressed by the prospects of renewed war if the recovery fails. Yet ordinary people, it appears, want to have a say in their own future. Many seem determined to do so, regardless of the dangers – for example, the group of women health workers and teachers I met in Herat province during the days leading up to the June 2002 *Loya Jirga,* or the growing ranks of young Afghan journalists (Tajiks, Uzbeks and Pashtuns alike) who wish to monitor developments in Afghanistan for the public good (SEE MEDIA).

But there are many in power, whether provincial warlords in western and eastern regions, or Kabul-based faction chiefs among the so-called Panjshairi mafia, who are just as determined to ensure that ordinary Afghans do not have the say they deserve. As a result, numerous Afghans still regard themselves as being held hostage by an array of interest groups, ranging from gun-toting politicians and drug traffickers to outside powers such as Pakistan, Turkmenistan and Iran. Despite the utter war-weariness of most ordinary people, these groups persist in their threats to peace as a result of their own greed and self-interest – be they political, regional, economic or religious.

For an outsider with a long-term empathy for this country and its people, it is clear to me that Afghanistan can only move forward through proper reconciliation amongst Afghans themselves, whether Tajik, Uzbek, Hazara or Pashtun. Every man and woman must have the right to consider him or herself a *Watandar* (countryman) of the Afghan nation on an equal basis with an equal stake in the future. For their part, the former *mujahideen*, particularly the dominant Tajiks and the Panjshairis, need to accept that the war is over. As a nation of poets, their tales and exploits will certainly not be forgotten, but Afghanistan has neither the means nor the time to grant winners' spoils as a right. Without the involvement of Pashtuns – the largest ethnic group and principal opponents to the northerners – in the new Afghanistan, there can be no peace. The feuding factions need to overcome their differences, while foreign interests, particularly Pakistan, need to halt their interference. As an extraordinarily resilient people, Afghans can probably survive on an *ad hoc* basis in an ongoing environment of volatility and insecurity for years to come. But this is neither what Afghans deserve nor what the international community should want. As a region, Central Asia and the Indian subcontinent would fare far better, both politically and economically, with a peaceful and vibrant Afghanistan within its midst.

***Edward Girardet** is a journalist and writer who has reported on Afghanistan and other conflicts since 1979 for the Christian Science Monitor, American Public Television and National Geographic. He is author of* Afghanistan: The Soviet War *and other books. Girardet is director of Media Action International, a Geneva-based humanitarian organization focusing on credible and independent public information initiatives.*

Aid and recovery

By Christine Johnson

Foreign aid to Afghanistan has a long history. By 1963, 49 percent of state expenditure was funded in this way, and at the time of the communist coup in April 1978, the figure was still over a third. The coup and the Soviet invasion that followed in December 1979 changed the pattern as Western organizations began making aid available for refugees and for cross-border activities. Dependence on Afghan resistance leaders, however, compromised much of the humanitarian response of the 1980s, giving rise to widespread diversion of resources, and strengthening the new, armed elite at the expense of more traditional structures. This was true not only inside the country but also in the refugee camps of Pakistan, where registration with a *mujahed* party was a prerequisite for receiving aid.

The Soviets left in 1989, but President Najibullah's government was to last nearly three more years. Its demise in 1992 led to a period of confusion as to how the international community should respond to the needs of Afghans. As rival factions ripped apart the city of Kabul, other parts of the country were effectively left to their own devices. With no government to relate to, aid largely worked at a local level with a multiplicity of organizations all making their own decisions. This was far from satisfactory, and the impasse in political efforts to solve Afghanistan's problems – combined with a wider questioning of the role that international assistance could play in conflict situations – led, in 1997, to the United Nations developing a new approach: the Strategic Framework for Afghanistan (SFA).

The Strategic Framework was to provide "...a more coherent, effective and integrated political strategy and assistance programme" based on "shared principles and objectives". The aim was that political and aid initiatives would reinforce each other and facilitate "the transition from a state of internal conflict to a just and sustainable peace". At the heart of the SFA was the conceptualisation of Afghanistan as a "failed state", a place of "collapsed public services, fragmented social infrastructure and non-existent political legitimacy". It was a reasonable description of the mid-1990s, but as the Taliban gained control of over 80 percent of the country they increasingly began to assert some of the functions of a state, albeit a repressive one that was recognised by very few countries and which had a very different view of its role from that held by Western liberal democracies.

As the 1990s drew to a close, the discriminatory policies of the Taliban and the issues of drugs and terrorism – in particular the provision of sanctuary for Osama Bin Laden – brought about a progressive hardening of political attitudes on the part of the international community. This in turn led to an increasing level of aid conditionality, as the withholding of assistance was used to try and bring about changes in the behaviour of the Taliban. The policy met with a notable lack of success. Establishing 'bottom lines' for negotiations proved difficult in practice for both donors and agencies. The gap, too, between 'principled' positions and actual humanitarian practice was often considerable. Most of all, the problem was how to make progress when the Taliban were really not very interested in the West's idea of principles, and did not care enough for Western aid to be forced into them.

To Western governments, any use of assistance that might be seen to be giving legitimacy to the Taliban became unacceptable, so working directly with government departments was off limits. Yet there was a humanitarian crisis in the country and ignoring the emergent authorities was not an option – so agencies fudged and compromised. In crucial areas such as health services, government employees continued to get 'incentives' despite discriminatory policies against women; various activities were defined as 'health programmes' so that women could continue working in them despite Taliban restrictions; and ongoing development needs became 'emergencies' so that they might receive funding.

In some ways September 11th changed everything for Afghanistan. In others, however, it changed little or nothing. The destruction of the country's infrastructure, the poverty and the drought remained the same; the politics and the international community's relationship to Afghanistan altered radically. After an initial hiatus caused by the evacuation of international staff, the focus of Western agencies shifted to mounting a massive food relief operation. The numbers deemed at risk from severe food shortages suddenly tripled from three million in August 2001 to nine million in November, although it was never clear how these figures had been arrived at. By the end of the year USAID chief, Andrew Natsios, publicly claimed that the international community had averted starvation in the country. A lot of food was certainly delivered, but only some of it got to where it was most needed and many Afghans survived – as in the past – through their own ingenuity.

Parallel to the humanitarian response, moves were started to assess the cost of reconstruction. The World Bank, Asian Development Bank and UNDP conducted a Preliminary Needs Assessment, providing for a donor conference in Tokyo in January 2002 the calculation that it would cost US$ 10.2 billion over five years to reconstruct Afghanistan. Donors pledged around half this amount, but the consequent publicity raised hope amongst the Afghans that they were entering a new era. It was a hope that was to ebb away as two years later the visible fruits were little other than more white faces and white Land Cruisers on the streets of Kabul.

Donors insisted that the money they had pledged had indeed been turned into reality; but too little of it got beyond the capital and too much of it was consumed in agency start-up costs for it to have made much difference to the lives of ordinary people. The UN reported that in March 2002, around three million children returned to rudimentary primary school classes, of which one third were girls. This figure climbed to four million in 2003. Meanwhile, by mid-2003 over two million refugees had returned home in the world's largest repatriation for 30 years. But many aid projects looked like the old humanitarian response and, two years after the fall of Kabul, the aid effort had yet to shift gear into major reconstruction and development. The short-term nature of the early funding also created problems for NGOs, many of which expanded rapidly and then found themselves struggling without the funds to sustain what they had begun.

In early 2002, the United Nations created a new integrated mission – the UN Assistance Mission to Afghanistan (UNAMA), under the leadership of Lakhdar Brahimi – in order to fulfil the tasks assigned to it under the Bonn Agreement signed the previous December. In many ways, however, the new structure was oddly reminiscent of the old. Although as overall mission head Brahimi was responsible for the entire UN operation, below him the structure split into two, a political pillar and an assistance pillar, and the distrust between the two that had been a feature of the past continued. Human rights were supposed to be integrated throughout, but with an international community that for the most part seemed to have lost its commitment to human rights, and a mission chief who publicly stated that one could not yet achieve both justice and peace in Afghanistan, it appeared that the importance of human rights had been downgraded. Human rights organizations struggled to get any action on abuses which would have caused outrage had they happened under the Taliban.

Meanwhile, the emergency *Loya Jirga* – a traditional council of delegates from across the country which met in Kabul in June 2002 to elect a new Afghan Transitional Authority (ATA) – was marred by violence and intimidation. Perhaps the most damage was caused by Brahimi's buckling under pressure from warlords, such as Herat's Ismail Khan, to allow them to participate – as well as his decision to grant entry to the northern-dominated Amniat (secret police). Many grassroots delegates complained that they were threatened or physically beaten. Furthermore, US meddling in favour of its United Front allies (also known as the Northern Alliance) prevented the popular former King from becoming a lead figure at the *Jirga*, which might have helped neutralize some of the warlords. The failure of the *Loya Jirga* to achieve the transition promised in the Bonn Agreement, namely to a broad-based government, should have raised a fundamental question for the UN: should it simply be supporting the ATA as the government, or should it be trying to bring about a transition to something more genuinely broad based and democratic? The question was, however, largely buried in the relentless pressure for short-term stability.

From the beginning the coordination effort struggled. It took months to establish the assistance pillar of UNAMA and the large UN agencies, such as WFP, UNICEF and UNHCR, continued to be responsible to their respective headquarters rather than to the Kabul mission. Outside Kabul, the UN continued to run coordination offices in the key regional centres, but distrust between the political and assistance wings remained prevalent in many places. The influx of money attracted hundreds of new NGOs (an estimated 800 were operating in and out of Kabul by mid-2003) and with it came further problems of coordination, along with a lack of quality and problems of inappropriate behaviour. Rents in

Thorkell Thorkelsson/International Federation

Kabul soared, driving some local Afghan NGOs from their premises and making accommodation for hundreds of thousands of returning refugees unaffordable. Meanwhile, the inflated salaries offered by international organizations for Afghan staff undermined efforts to retain or attract the skilled labour vital for rebuilding the country's shattered public sector. In autumn 2002, for example, an advertisement in the local Kabul paper for a driver in the US Embassy offered a salary of over US$ 500 a month (at current exchange rates), while a doctor in a government clinic was receiving about US$ 45 per month.

All of these problems were well known from Kosovo and other post-conflict countries that had seen high profile responses, yet the assistance community seemed incapable of avoiding them. Whether it was the UN or the NGOs, agency pressure for visibility and for funds seemed to be driving the aid agenda forward more relentlessly than the objectively assessed needs of ordinary Afghans. One significant change was the attempt by the ATA to assume control of humanitarian and development assistance. In a country where aid agencies were accustomed to working under minimal restrictions, this shift proved difficult for many to come to terms with. Discomfort at change was compounded by feelings of unease at an administration that remained dominated by the Panjshairi faction of the former Northern Alliance.

For most Afghans security remains the number one priority. "Unless you get rid of the guns", many will tell you, "you can kiss goodbye to free and fair elections". Yet in many parts of the country the security situation has deteriorated since the collapse of the Taliban. The agreement signed at Bonn in December 2001 was less a peace agreement than a deal brokered by the international community in the wake of a war won largely by an external power. This victory has laid bare all the old power struggles that devastated the country in the pre-Taliban years, and at the same time the fight against Al Qa'eda has brought new weapons into the country. Afghanistan remains under the control of a patchwork of warlord militias and the President does not command a military force strong enough to control even one of them. On June 17, 2003, a large group of 79 aid agencies publicly expressed their concern by co-signing a declaration maintaining that "in the past six months, security has deteriorated and violence against civilians has increased…the security spiral is downward, and the people of Afghanistan are now speaking of the 'days of better security under the Taliban'."

Disarmament is seen as a priority, yet traditional disarmament assumptions do not really apply in Afghanistan. The problem is less one of demobilising an army than dealing with a society where guns are commonplace and their use often unrelated to any command structure. While there are those who could be seen as the regular forces (men who are uniformed and/or under clear command and control structures and with livelihoods tied to the military establishment) these are a relatively small group. In addition to the full-time soldiers there are those who are conscripted into the regular forces for short periods of time, thereafter returning to their communities, and finally there are those who are part of irregular militias. The line between all of these and those who use the gun for banditry or other criminal activity is often blurred. In addition, and in part in reaction to this environment, there are many people who simply keep guns in self-defence.

Most Afghans believe that the majority of those under arms would be prepared to give them up if conditions were right. However, this requires that people feel confident about their individual security, about representation as a group, and about the possibility of solving conflict through peaceful means. It also requires that they have an economic alternative to the gun. To date the situation in Afghanistan offers none of these. As a result, what has been collected are mainly old guns or weapons left behind by the Taliban, and they have remained at district or provincial level rather than being given to the central authorities. In addition, enormous caches of weapons uncovered by US-led Coalition Forces, including anti-tank guns and rockets, have been turned over to local forces working with the Coalition – precisely the groups that will most urgently need to be disarmed.

The formation of a genuinely national army and police force has been an urgent priority from the beginning, yet progress has been painfully slow and a year on from Bonn it was publicly admitted that it would be a much longer process than originally envisaged. Amongst the many problems are questions of size, command and pay. Efforts by Defence Minister Fahim to base the national army on his own forces continue to undermine progress, as commanders are unlikely to give up arms to someone who is perceived as another faction leader. There is also the critical issue of moving responsibility for the maintenance of internal security from the army to the police – a transition that will not be easy after a quarter century of war. All of this is made more difficult by the fact that many of the commanders are heavily bound up in the war economy, making substantial profits from smuggling consumer goods and from the drugs trade.

Since the fall of the Taliban, Afghanistan has reclaimed its place as the world's biggest opium producer. In 2002, the country produced about 3,400 tonnes – some 75 percent of world production. Record crops were reported in many areas and poppy was grown in districts where it was previously unknown. The crop was worth about US$ 1.2 billion to its farmers and a further US$ 1.3 billion to its traffickers – accounting for about 50 percent of Afghanistan's GDP. In 2003 the planting of opium poppy spread into more new districts resulting in an even greater harvest (3,600 tonnes). The web of those involved in the trade is extensive, with links into key figures in the Afghan Transitional Administration (ATA). Although President Karzai has committed his administration to the eradication of the poppy, it is hard to see how he can put this ban into practice.

It is unlikely that any of these difficult shifts necessary to bring about security stand a chance of taking place unless an independent international force remains in Afghanistan for a considerable time. Yet despite continued requests by both President Karzai and the UN, the International Security Assistance Force (ISAF) still remained confined to Kabul two years after the Taliban's collapse. Meanwhile, the security role of Coalition Forces is blurred by the continuing prosecution of the war against Al Qa'eda.

Reconstruction – whether physical or institutional – has been very slow to take effect. It has been well recognized that the years of war, and more recently of drought, have decimated the livelihoods of Afghans. Many people have lost most of their assets and just getting enough to feed their families continues to be an endless struggle. Being seen to produce tangible benefits for the people remains crucial to the legitimacy of the ATA. Yet there are clearly questions as to the extent to which they can undertake the activities needed.

The question of civil service reform has been on the agenda since December 2001, yet so far there has been little visible progress. Many staff lack the skills to undertake the jobs now required, most are paid pitifully little. Some departments have dealt with this problem by bringing in a small number of very highly paid staff on special contracts – hardly a sustainable solution. Others, most notably the Ministry of Public Health, have used incentives provided by NGOs and the UN to supplement salaries; the amounts involved are more realistic but the problems of sustainability remain. The international community continues to talk of 'capacity building', but without a resolution of the salaries problem their efforts will achieve little. Those whose capacity is built will simply leave for employment which provides better opportunities for them and their families.

In addition to the longer-term issues of economic recovery, there are the pressing issues of short-term support to the very poor. While the administration's National Development Framework and accompanying National Development Budget view economic recovery as the prerequisite for any poverty reduction strategy, the poorest cannot wait for economic recovery. Traditionally most support for the poor has come in the form of food assistance. But while there are pockets of the country where this is still required, the bulk of assistance to livelihoods needs to come from programmes providing cash wages. The supply of free wheat through assistance programmes has depressed prices for farmers, further encouraging them to shift into poppy production. The ATA clearly signalled its wish to move away from food assistance in 2002, but the scale of projects providing cash wages is as yet far from adequate and it is not at all clear how resources might be provided on the scale required. The situation is made more critical by the pressure on large numbers of refugees to return home from Pakistan and Iran.

Service provision in a large country with difficult terrain and limited resources, both human and financial, is an enormous challenge for both the ATA and the assistance community. There is an understandable urge to attempt to achieve too much in order to compensate for the years of neglect. Yet everything cannot be accomplished at once and trying to do so wastes time and energy planning for events that are simply not going to occur. The key to utilising limited capacity is to make clear priorities. Two constraints will set the boundaries to what is possible: finance and capacity. There are hard decisions about the extent to which the government wants basic services accessible to all, and the extent to which it will allow inequality to develop. If it wishes to have the resources to implement universal access to basic services, for example, then it will be necessary to say no to some higher level service development at the centre, services for which there will undoubtedly be political pressure. Unless clear decisions are taken there will be an inevitable drift to better quality services in urban areas at the expense of the rural.

Since many people simply cannot get to district centres, basic level services will have to be provided at the community level. As remote areas offer little incentive for the private sector, and it is unlikely that the state will be able to provide them with services, communities themselves will need to be involved in service provision. The planning framework needs, however, to be set by the state. It should have a role as a guarantor of an equitable distribution of resources. Grants to communities cannot replace planned and properly supported services. Nor should construction programmes be allowed to displace planning in determining where resources go; it is easy to find the money to build a clinic or a school, harder to staff it for year after year. There need to be countrywide policies and targets, and donor funding should be strictly tied to these rather than to the current historic patterns. Yet so far there is little sign of this happening.

Last but not least there are the issues of accountability and transparency. Already, many Afghans have noted with dismay the levels of corruption that have arisen in government services. They come, as in so many parts of the world, with the pressures to hand out jobs and the need for bribes to get things done.

All of these challenges are interlinked and it is likely that progress will be made by a slow process of edging forward rather than any great leap into the future. This will require the long-term support of the international community, not just in funding but in political engagement. Whether that commitment will be forthcoming has yet to be seen, and there are many who fear that the elections scheduled for summer 2004 will signal a reduction in the international community's support to Afghanistan. Such a move would only open the way for further conflict.

Chris Johnson has worked in Afghanistan since 1996, first for Oxfam and then as Director of the Strategic Monitoring Unit (now AREU). She currently works as a consultant.

War without borders

By Ahmed Rashid

After nearly quarter of a century of warfare, conflict and unparalleled bloodshed, no country in the modern era has been the victim of such outright foreign interference by superpowers and its regional neighbours as Afghanistan. From the Soviet invasion of Afghanistan in December 1979, to Pakistan's interference in backing the Taliban and, most recently, the United States-led military intervention from October 7, 2001 onwards, there has been a continuous flow of arms from neighbouring countries to all the warlord parties. For this reason, numerous ordinary Afghans feel fully justified when they claim that the civil war has been fuelled as much by their uncompromising power-hungry commanders as by foreign powers.

The resurgence of pro-Taliban and other anti-government groups since late 2002 has resulted in almost daily armed attacks against Coalition and Afghan government forces. Nearly 400 Afghan civilians, soldiers and aid workers were killed by Taliban raids during August-September 2003 alone, suggesting that outside involvement is continuing in a similar manner as before, including trans-frontier operations out of Pakistan. In Quetta, the capital of Pakistan's Baluchistan province, thousands of Taliban fighters are living in mosques and *madrassas* with the full support of a provincial ruling party and militant Pakistani groups.

As a consequence, Afghanistan's civil war (which is arguably continuing) has been not merely a complex history of social, political and ethnic conflict but also a litany of the shifts and strategies of neighbours as they arm, fund and influence their various proxies inside the country.

The former Soviet Union dragged Afghanistan into the front line of the Cold War after its invasion, leading the United States to forge a broad coalition of Islamic and Western states to back the Afghan *mujahideen.* The United States alone provided an estimated six billion dollars worth of military and humanitarian aid to the Afghan resistance during the decade-long Soviet-Afghan war (1979-1989). Nearly two dozen countries backed the *mujahideen* with some form of military aid, channelled to them through Pakistan, which emerged as a temporary home for the *mujahed* leadership and some three million Afghan refugees. The Soviet Union meanwhile grouped together the countries of Eastern

Europe and the Soviet Socialist Republics of Central Asia to back the communist regime of the People's Democratic Party of Afghanistan (PDPA) in Kabul.

The withdrawal of Soviet troops in February 1989 did not lead to an immediate cessation of superpower involvement. Both the Soviet and Western blocs pumped in even more military hardware to both sides of the Afghan political divide, in an attempt to preserve the *status quo*. After Kabul fell to the *mujahideen* in April 1992, just months after the break-up of the Soviet Union, the US and Russia finally cut off their military aid. For a brief moment, Afghanistan's western and northern neighbours – Iran, Russia and the five newly-independent Central Asian Republics (CARs) – let the Afghan warlords fight out their power struggles on their own.

However, Pakistan continued military support to the main Pashtun factions, especially the Hezb-e-Islami faction led by Gulbuddin Hekmatyar, which attempted to capture Kabul from the largely Tajik forces under President Burhanuddin Rabbani and Ahmed Shah Massoud. As the civil war intensified, other countries played a greater role inside Afghanistan. Russia and the CARs, especially Uzbekistan, supported the Afghan Uzbek forces of General Rashid Dostum in his attempt to maintain a buffer state in the north between the fundamentalist Pashtuns in the south and Central Asia.

The emergence of the Taliban at the end of 1994 created the most widespread consternation among Afghanistan's northern neighbours since the withdrawal of Red Army troops in 1989. The Taliban brought a new factor into the equation: a messianic and uncompromising message of Pashtun-based Islamic fundamentalism and expansionism, the like of which the region had never witnessed before. It gave rise to accusations from Central Asian leaders and Iran that the Taliban would try and extend their influence to Central Asia. Moreover, the fact that the Taliban movement was Pashtun-driven and backed by Pakistan and Saudi Arabia rekindled the same suspicions amongst the CARs and Iran as had existed in the 1980s.

Pakistan's Afghan policy for the past two decades has been to back the major Afghan Pashtun parties. The Pashtun tribes straddle the porous Afghan-Pakistani border (imposed by the British as the Durand Line in 1893 but never recognized by Afghanistan). Islamabad's fears that Pashtun nationalism or fundamentalism might advocate a future Pashtun state carved out of the two countries has dominated its concerns. At the same time, Pashtuns play an influential role in Pakistan's military, bureaucracy and the intelligence services. The fact that the Afghan capital was under the Tajik domination of Rabbani in the early 1990s for the first time since the short-lived reign of Bacha Saqao (a Tajik from the Shomali plains north of Kabul) in 1929, and that the divided Afghan Pashtuns had lost their historically dominant role in Afghanistan, created considerable unease amongst Pakistani Pashtuns in high office. A Pashtun regime in power in Kabul was not just a source of pride for Pakistani Pashtuns, but also an assurance that the Afghan Pashtuns would not consider other territorial options. These factors prompted Pakistan to switch support from Hekmatyar to the newly emerging Taliban in 1995.

Pakistan persuaded Saudi Arabia to do the same. Riyadh's major policy concern was the containment of Iranian and Shi'a influence in Afghanistan. The Saudis, wary of Iran's growing support to the non-Pashtun ethnic groups and supportive of the Taliban's anti-Shi'a stance, backed the Taliban with finances and other material aid. For its part, Iran was convinced that the US and Saudi Arabia were backing the Taliban as part of a strategic plan to encircle Iran. Until the Taliban capture of the western city of Herat, just 70 miles from the Iranian border, Iran along with Pakistan had supported the anti-Rabbani alliance in which Tehran's proxy, the Shi'a-based Hezb-e-Wahdat drawn from the minority Hazara group, played a major role. However, the defeat of Wahdat outside Kabul at the hands of Massoud's forces, combined with Iran's historic mistrust of the Pashtuns and the perceived US and Saudi backing for the Taliban, forced Iran to open a serious dialogue with Rabbani. This resulted in military support for the United Front, also known as the Northern Alliance.

The Taliban's capture of Herat and Persian-speaking western Afghanistan in September 1995 dramatically altered the strategic balance of the region. As perceived by Iran, it gave the Pashtuns outright control of western Afghanistan for the first time. Herat was once part of the Persian Empire and remained closely linked culturally, linguistically and economically to the Persian court for centuries. Iran considered that its strategic backyard had been taken over by an ethnically alien and virulently anti-Shi'a force. Russia, which faced the burden of a continuing civil war in Tajikistan, believed that it must contain both Pashtun domination of Afghanistan and the spread of Islamic fundamentalism to Central Asia. Russia could not easily forget that the exporters of fundamentalism into Central Asia during the 1980s were Pashtun *mujahideen* rather than their Tajik or Uzbek counterparts.

In 1996, even before the Taliban's capture of Kabul, Iran, Russia and Uzbekistan had begun sending considerable military and financial aid to Rabbani. Russian planes arrived in Kabul regularly from Tajikistan, Russia and Ukraine with Russian arms, ammunition and fuel but also brand-new banknotes. Iran, meanwhile, had developed an air bridge from Mashad in eastern Iran to Kabul, flying in armaments and fuel to the Rabbani government. Iran also set up five training camps south of Mashad and along the Afghan border for some 7,000 fighters belonging to Ismail Khan, the former ruler of Herat who had been ousted by the Taliban. These fighters, re-equipped by Iran, would be used in late 1996 to open a new front against the Taliban in Badghis province, north of Herat. India also allied itself with Rabbani, largely as an attempt to undermine its old enemy Pakistan. Overall, however, Indian support for Rabbani remained minimal. Uzbekistan, the strongest military power in Central Asia, stepped up support for General Dostum's buffer mini-state. Dostum was a fellow Uzbek, who had developed close personal links with Uzbek President Islam Karimov. Uzbekistan's perception was that as long as the Taliban posed no threat to northern Afghanistan, they posed no threat to Central Asia either. Uzbekistan's attitude changed dramatically following the Taliban conquest of Kabul in 1996 and its move northwards.

Turkmenistan, a self-declared neutral state that shares some 300 kilometres of border with western Afghanistan, had developed excellent working relations with Ismail Khan. His defeat and the arrival of the Taliban on their borders initially created great unease, but the Turkmen quickly established a working relationship with the Taliban in Herat where they maintained a Consulate. Turkmenistan was the only Central Asian state which refused to attend the extraordinary summit of the Commonwealth of Independent States (CIS) after the Taliban capture of Kabul. Despite considerable Russian pressure, they refused to condemn the Taliban. As fighting intensified across the country, however, the Turkmen were faced with serious threats. For the first time ever in July 1997, some 9,000 Afghan Turkmen crossed the border into Turkmenistan seeking shelter from the fighting. Although the refugees soon returned home, the continuing war was now affecting Turkmenistan's frontier border regions.

The situation in Tajikistan has been far more complicated. Since 1991, both Hekmatyar and Massoud had backed various factions of the Tajik Islamic opposition trying to overthrow the Dushanbe government. But in 1995, Rabbani established working relations with Dushanbe in order to line up more support for his government. Rabbani visited both Moscow and Dushanbe and urged all sides in the Tajik civil war to step-up peace negotiations. Tajikistan was thus deeply disturbed by Rabbani's ousting from Kabul. The arrival of the Taliban in the north had a major salutary effect on the Tajik civil war. It forced all sides in the conflict and Russia to quicken the pace of negotiations out of fear of the Taliban. A settlement between the Tajik government and the opposition was finally reached in Moscow on 27 June 1997. This allowed Rabbani's forces to use Tajikistan as a receiving point for the military aid Russia and Iran were providing. Massoud was granted Kulyab airbase in southern Tajikistan so as to supply his forces at the front.

The extent of this outside interference worried the Americans who, after a lapse of four years, once again began to take an interest in trying to resolve the Afghan conflict. The US Assistant Secretary of State for South Asia, Robin Raphael, launched an initiative in the spring of 1996. Raphael visited the three power centres of Kabul, Kandahar, Mazar-e-Sharif and three Central Asian capitals. During a United Nations Security Council debate on Afghanistan on 10 April – the first to be held for seven years – the US led an initiative, along with other states, in supporting the idea of an international arms embargo on Afghanistan. The Americans wanted to use the embargo as a lever to persuade all the involved regional countries to agree to a common platform for non-interference in Afghanistan. At the same time, they wanted to lend greater weight to UN efforts to convene a conference attended by all the Afghan factions.

But in an election year, Washington's aims in the quagmire of Afghanistan remained limited. Its principle policy concern – the containment of Iran's growing involvement in Afghanistan and Central Asia – was too obviously transparent to disguise. Despite US attempts to keep Iran out, Tehran was accepted as a major player by all neighbouring states including Pakistan. The US was also concerned about the support given by various Afghan factions to Islamic terrorist groups who were active in the US and Saudi Arabia and the growing drugs trade emanating from Afghanistan. These issues, however, were still not important enough on the US foreign policy agenda to create a major US peace initiative for Afghanistan.

The climax of the regional opposition to the Taliban came immediately after their forces swept into Kabul in September 1996. Iranian President Al Akbar Rafsanjani explicitly warned the Taliban to restrain themselves. "This is a disaster and we strongly regret it. We have repeatedly advised the Afghans that war is not the right way to solve their problems but unfortunately they don't let go. Afghanistan has turned into a complicated and un-solvable issue in the region," Rafsanjani said. Iranian newspapers were even more vehement. "The Taliban capture of Kabul was designed by Washington, financed by Riyadh and logistically supported by Islamabad," said the *Jomhuri Islami* daily newspaper.

Russia immediately galvanised support from all the Central Asian states. "Russia notes with alarm the danger that this conflict poses to the international community and its destabilizing effect in the region. The Taliban victory only aggravates the crisis for Afghanistan," said a Russian Foreign Ministry statement. In Tajikistan, the 25,000 Russian troops on the Tajik-Afghan border were placed on high alert. President Karimov of Uzbekistan warned the Taliban not to attempt to cross the Amu Darya (Oxus River) which divides Afghanistan from Central Asia. Publicly, he announced that Uzbekistan would offer material support to the ousted Rabbani government and General Dostum. At an emergency summit meeting in Almaty on 4 October 1996, Russia and the Presidents of Kazakhstan, Kirghizstan, Tajikistan and Uzbekistan warned the Taliban to stay away from northern Afghanistan or face a severe response. The Taliban defiantly dismissed the threat.

The second climax in less than a year for the neighbouring states was the Taliban's brief capture of Mazar-e-Sharif on 24 May 1997. Virtual paranoia swept through Central Asia. The bloodshed on their doorstep (Mazar is just 70 kilometres from the border) created the spectre of war and thousands of Afghan refugees crossing into their territory. Military security was heightened throughout the region. Iran appealed to the UN to intervene and openly urged Russia, the Central Asian Republics and India to help the anti-Taliban alliance. The Taliban's lack of diplomatic understanding of how the real world works increased regional fears. Rather than appeasing their concerned neighbours, the Taliban remain deliberately provocative. They made no effort to moderate their social policies to win greater support in the West. Instead, they deliberately made them harsher and rather than succumb to some of the demands of their allies such as Pakistan, who urged them to talk to the opposition, they rejected any suggestion of compromise. The Taliban's foreign policy was thus marked by the extremism that symbolised their social policies and radical views on Islam. Concessions and compromise were impossible.

Pakistan continued to support the Taliban, ensuring that Islamabad became increasingly isolated in the region as Afghanistan's other neighbours stepped up their backing of the anti-Taliban alliance. At the same time, however, Pakistan undertook extensive diplomatic forays to try and convince the Taliban to negotiate. The lack of any real response from the Taliban signalled to the international community and the regional states that Pakistan appeared to be losing any influence it had once enjoyed, or thought it had, over the Taliban. The Taliban's attitude towards foreign policy – or its lack of one – became a major cause for worry amongst Afghanistan's neighbours. Regional leaders such as Uzbekistan's President Islam Karimov publicly stated that the Taliban sought to conquer Central Asia. The question of whether the Taliban intended to carry their revolution beyond Afghanistan's borders remained the principle issue of concern for Central Asia and Russia.

Some Taliban leaders in Kandahar, fighters at the frontline and administrators in Kabul did espouse, in varying degrees, an expansionist foreign policy. The Taliban's highly idealistic view of the new Islamic regime that they wanted to bring about was reinforced by the simple if naïve belief that people across the region were just waiting to receive them with open arms. But this idealism – of wanting to recreate a strong Muslim *umma* or community guided by a

Taliban ideology – was not tempered with any knowledge about the history, geography and complex social structures in the region. And judging by the Taliban handling of the Uzbeks, Hazaras and Tajiks in Mazar, they appeared hardly prepared to deal with the complexities posed by ethnicity in Afghanistan and Central Asia.

The Taliban generation of *mujahideen*, or fighters for Islam, were brought up on the 1980s' diet of Islam's fight against communism and the Soviet Union, which the Afghans spearheaded. It came replete with the conviction that the collapse of the Soviet Union was solely caused by the Afghan *jihad*. Since then, the West and the rest of the Muslim world have betrayed Afghanistan and not given Afghans their due. For the Taliban, educated only in *madrassas*, or Islamic schools, the end of the Cold War created more enemies and more conspiracies. These included the convictions that US and Russian imperialism and secularism were destroying Palestine, Chechnya and Bosnia; Hindu India was suppressing the Kashmiris; the dictators in Central Asia were refusing to let their people follow the Islamic path; and the UN was refusing to recognise the Taliban and thereby conspiring against Islam. This somewhat paranoid world picture for the Taliban was compounded by the latent anti-Shia'ism inculcated from their Deobandi *madrassas* in Pakistan, which pitted the Taliban directly against Iran.

Other, economic, interests have also created differences between Afghanistan's neighbours. The idea of a gas pipeline between Turkmenistan and Pakistan that would cross Taliban-controlled southern Afghanistan at first created intense competition between two oil company consortia – one led by the American giant Unocal, the other led by the Argentinian company, Bridas. Both companies spent considerable time, effort and money in wooing the Afghan factions but particularly the Taliban. The pipeline issue also pitted Iran and Russia against Pakistan. Iran feared that such a pipeline would be an American attempt to dominate its border region and avoid the more logical exit route for the energy-rich Central Asian states which was through Iran rather than Afghanistan. Russia wished to maintain its dominance over Central Asia's energy resources. In 2002, however, the Kabul authorities formally agreed on the establishment of such a pipeline with Pakistan and Turkmenistan, although not directly involving the original oil consortia.

The enormous trade in weapons across Afghanistan and into neighbouring states, and the sanctuary given by Afghan warlords for terrorists and militant Islamic opposition groups from the regional countries were equally destabilizing. Increasingly contentious, too, was the vast smuggling trade that developed across Afghanistan and fed into the entire region. Landlocked Afghanistan was allowed to import duty-free goods via the Pakistani port of Karachi, but this permission was hugely abused as smuggled goods traversed back into Pakistan before being smuggled into Central Asia and Iran. The shattered Afghan economy has been, and, to a degree, still is, predominantly dependent on smuggled foodstuffs, fuel and other consumer goods from the regional states. In all these states, the Afghan smuggling trade has led to large-scale loss of customs revenues and created periodic shortages of essential goods, especially foodstuffs. Another factor threatening destabilisation has been drug trafficking. All the countries in the region fear the disruptive effects caused by the increased production of heroin in Afghanistan, which has helped finance warlord armies and created drug Mafiosi in all these states, as the heroin is smuggled through Iran, Pakistan and Central Asia to Europe.

The US-led war that defeated the Taliban in December 2001 produced an immediate acceptance by regional countries of America's dominant position in Afghanistan. The Bonn Agreement, which installed Hamid Karzai as the interim President and set out a three-stage political timetable for Afghanistan, had the unprecedented support of all of Afghanistan's neighbours including Pakistan and Iran. However the US appear to have no clear political strategy for the country and seem only intent on pursuing the remnants of Al Qa'eda. As before, many Afghans perceive such outside involvement as being one of self-interest rather than responding to the interests of Afghans themselves.

By the end of 2002, much of the promised international funding to help reconstruct the country had still not arrived in adequate sums. As a result, Afghanistan has seen a slow down in the reconstruction process, an intensification of internal ethnic problems and by the winter of 2002-03 the revival of the Taliban who have begun to attack US and Afghan army posts closer to the border with Pakistan. In many areas, security is considered far worse than prior to the overthrow of the Taliban. Pashtuns, too, have seen relatively little of the pledged international support implemented in their own regions of eastern and southern Afghanistan.

At the time of writing, in autumn 2003, all the neighbouring states are once again openly interfering in the country. Pakistan is giving covert support to the Taliban and the US are playing a delicate balancing act. One US army officer in Afghanistan reported, with some frustration, the sight of Pakistani army posts on the border waving Taliban groups in and out. But while Washington may want to rein in the Pakistani military, at the same time it wants Pakistan to deliver 9,000 troops to Iraq and wants President Musharraf's help in capturing Osama Bin Laden – ideally before the US presidential elections in 2004.

Iran, meanwhile, is supporting Ismail Khan, the warlord of western Afghanistan, despite claims of wishing to help the Kabul authorities as its priority; and Uzbekistan is providing aid and bodyguards to General Rashid Dostum, the Uzbek warlord in the north. Meanwhile, India and Russia have strengthened their alliances with and aid to the leaders of the former United Front, in particular the Defense Minister General Mohammed Fahim. Foreign interference in Afghanistan can be expected to continue until the country has the capacity to develop national institutions such as a multi-ethnic army and police force, to invest rapidly in infrastructure development and to ensure the political process succeeds.

Ahmed Rashid is a British-Pakistani journalist and writer for the Far Eastern Economic Review, *the* Wall Street Journal *and the* Daily Telegraph. *He is also author of* The Taliban *and other books dealing with Central Asia and the subcontinent. Rashid is founder of the Media Support Fund aimed at helping start-up Afghan print publications.*

Security and keeping the peace

By Jonathan Walter

> *"We have offered all Afghans, warlords or no warlords, to be part of the nation-building in Afghanistan. And there is an opportunity for them to come and participate, and go down in Afghan history as good people...What I don't want is fighting in this country."*
>
> *Hamid Karzai, June 2002*

Of all the countries in the world, Afghanistan is one of those least associated with keeping the peace. For more than three millennia, armies of invading Aryans, Persians, Greeks, Huns, Arabs, Mongols, Moghuls and British have sought to subjugate the region's people and plunder its treasures. More recently, a decade fighting the Soviet invasion and another decade of vicious factional feuding brought Afghanistan to its knees. The Taliban imposed a repressive peace on much of the country, with ongoing military clashes limited mainly to the north. Paradoxically, however, the US-led war against Al Qa'eda and its Taliban hosts in late 2001 – which aimed to liberate Afghanistan from years of terror – has led to greater insecurity for ordinary Afghans across much of the country. At the end of 2003, UN Secretary General Kofi Annan warned: "We need to deal with the security issue and if we do not deal with that, we may lose Afghanistan."

More than 18 months after the Taliban fled, no international peace-keeping forces operated outside the capital – despite endless requests from the Karzai administration, the UN, NGOs and prominent US analysts. Meanwhile, attempts to train and equip a new Afghan national army have foundered on the rocks of ethnic rivalries. During 2003, security across Afghanistan was so bad that around one third of the country was off-limits to international aid workers. In August-September 2003, nearly 400 Afghan civilians, aid workers and soldiers were killed in Taliban raids, mainly in the east and south of the country. Ironically, when the Taliban were in power, aid agencies were able to access around 80 percent of the country. Meanwhile, continuing war and lawlessness have helped catapult Afghanistan's production of opium poppies back to record levels – 3,600 tonnes in 2003, around three quarters of global production.

This compares to a crop of just 185 tons in 2001, following a Taliban crackdown. Narco-criminality is on the rise.

The consensus among most analysts and aid workers is that since 2002, security has got worse, not better. Worse still, they believe this is largely because of the US-led Coalition's policy of supporting powerful regional warlords – in the hope of gaining their support to combat Al Qa'eda – rather than disarming them. This could prove self-defeating. According to a report published in June 2003 by the influential US Council on Foreign Relations, "failure to stem deteriorating security conditions and to spur economic reconstruction could lead to a reversion to warlord-dominated anarchy and mark a major defeat for the US war on terrorism."

Military operations within Afghanistan following the US-led campaign to oust the Taliban have fallen into two distinct and at times contradictory categories: continuing the 'war on terror' and keeping the peace – carried out by different troops under separate command structures. During 2002-03, the US military, with some support from the British Army, concentrated on offensive operations aimed at hunting down 'remnants' of the Taliban and Al Qa'eda. Although the US headquartered its forces at the old Soviet airbase at Bagram, an hour's drive north of Kabul, the two main theatres of operations have been in the mountainous provinces of Khost, Paktia and Paktika along the Pakistani frontier, and in the hills and deserts around Kandahar and Uruzgan in the south-west. Around 11,500 troops are involved, but their search – while uncovering various arms caches – has proved largely fruitless in terms of rounding up key Taliban or Al Qa'eda leaders. Their presence on Afghan soil has, however, attracted almost daily attacks from various armed groups. By late 2003, the US was spending nearly US$1 billion per month on military operations in Afghanistan – dwarfing the amount spent by the US Agency for International Development on relief and reconstruction (which totalled around US$1 billion for the whole of 2002).

Some analysts have argued that the US military presence across the country – and in particular the ability of US forward air controllers to call in massive bombardments at short notice from huge B-52 warplanes – has so far helped prevent any major clashes between opposing Afghan factions. Indeed, one official in the Afghan administration said in January 2003 that if the US were to withdraw, there would be a 'bloodbath'. This, however, is a fragile basis for peace, and depends upon US forces not becoming distracted by other theatres in the 'war on terror'. Throughout 2002-03, several volatile regions of Afghanistan boiled over into armed conflict. Around Gardez, in Khost province, the Karzai-appointed governor traded gunfire for months with a local warlord, Badshah Khan Zadran (paid, armed and trained by the US until late 2002). In the far west, around Shindand airbase, forces loyal to Ismail Khan – self-styled Amir of Herat – rained artillery shells on the Pashtun forces of Amanullah Khan. And in the north, a smouldering feud between the troops of Uzbek General Dostum and the Pashtun Atta Mohammed kept crackling into life, even as their leaders were holding disarmament talks with the UN in Mazar.

The ongoing Coalition campaign has been heavily criticised by aid agencies and analysts, who accuse the US of undermining peace in Afghanistan through its policy of paying off local warlords like Badshah Khan to help in the hunt for Al Qa'eda. As well as cash donations, the US military have routinely allowed their Afghan militia allies to help themselves to arms caches found on operations. Yet the UN's agenda is to disarm these very militia forces and build up a single national army answerable only to Kabul. Rather than being demobilised, the warlords have used the influence and resources gained by association with Coalition Forces to impose themselves as local governors – despite being hated by many ordinary Afghans.

Human rights have suffered as a result. In particular, the gains made in women's rights have been reversed in some parts of the country. Armed robbery, extortion, kidnapping and the rape of women, girls and boys have been documented – often with the complicity or involvement of local government officials, police and commanders. According to a report published by the US-based NGO Human Rights Watch in July 2003: "Human rights abuses in Afghanistan are being committed by gunmen and warlords who were propelled into power by the United States and its coalition partners after the Taliban fell in 2001. These men and others have essentially hijacked the country outside of Kabul." The report names various leading government ministers and regional commanders whose troops or officials are responsible for human rights abuses.

American forces have at times made themselves very unpopular with some Afghans, particularly in the conservative Pashtun belt of the south, through heavy-handed tactics towards civilians in their 'war on terror'. They have damaged personal property during house searches and body-searched Afghan women – gravely offending Pashtun family honour. One of the most notorious incidents involved the airborne strafing of a wedding party in Uruzgan in June 2002, after US troops reported coming under fire. Over 50 Afghan men, women and children were killed. It was subsequently thought that high-spirited wedding guests firing AK-47s into the air had been mistaken for terrorists.

A major threat to security in central, eastern and southern Afghanistan has become the resurgence of violent Islamist extremism. A dangerous mix of Al Qa'eda, Taliban and troops loyal to former *mujahed* Gulbuddin Hekmatyar have regrouped across the border in Pakistan's mountainous tribal agencies, aiming to channel rising Pashtun discontent against both the US forces and against the ethnic Tajik domination of the defence, foreign affairs and intelligence ministries in Kabul. In 2002, extremists tried, unsuccessfully, to assassinate President Karzai while he was visiting Kandahar; but they succeeded in killing over 30 Afghan civilians by detonating a car bomb in Kabul. Early in 2003, Hekmatyar declared a *jihad* against Coalition Forces and their collaborators (i.e. the Karzai government and anyone who supports them). The elusive Taliban leader, Mullah Omar, called on Afghans to "fight like the Iraqis to rid your country of foreign oppressors". Countless attacks have been launched at Coalition Forces, employing rockets, grenades and small arms. More disturbingly, they have targeted aid offices and killed aid workers, both Afghan and foreign, in an apparent attempt to disrupt and discredit relief and reconstruction in the south of the country. Moderate Afghan clerics in the same region, who had expressed support for Karzai or who had condemned the Taliban's tactics, have also been attacked and killed.

Both Afghans and Americans have pointed the finger at Pakistan. While President Musharraf has succeeded in rounding up some high-profile Al Qa'eda leaders, Pakistan's Inter Service Intelligence (ISI) appears to be turning a blind eye to the Taliban. According to the US military, 90 percent of the attacks on US

Leaving the Loya Jirga

forces have been launched from Pakistan, leading some analysts to accuse Musharraf of playing a 'double game'. Trouble flared up in July 2003, when Afghan and Pakistani forces exchanged fire along their common border in Nangarhar and Kunar provinces. Pakistan said they were simply supporting US forces in anti-terror operations. But Afghans accused Pakistani troops of digging in positions 20 miles inside the disputed border as part of a land-grab. Tensions flared in Kabul over the issue, when a mob ransacked the Pakistani embassy. By late 2003, Taliban leaders were openly operating in Quetta, capital of Pakistan's Baluchistan province, with the acquiescence of the province's hardline fundamentalist government.

Other neighbours continue to interfere in Afghanistan's affairs too – Russia has pledged US$100 million in military aid to Defence Minister Fahim; Iran gives money and military hardware to Ismail Khan who controls most of western Afghanistan; and Uzbekistan supplies Dostum in Mazar-e-Sharif with aid and bodyguards.

Keeping the peace in Kabul has proved to be the great success story of military operations following the fall of the Taliban. An International Security Assistance Force (ISAF), established under a UN Security Council resolution in December 2001, has been mandated to run until at least the end of 2004. Around 30 countries have contributed troops and the force, which began in early 2002 under British command, totalled around 5,000 troops during 2002-03. However, that compares with 45,000 troops keeping the peace in Kosovo in 2001 – a territory of just two million people. In August 2003, NATO assumed command of ISAF in its first ever deployment outside Europe.

As well as keeping Kabul safe, ISAF's three main tasks are: aiding the Afghan authorities in developing national security structures; assisting in the country's reconstruction; and helping develop and train future Afghan security forces. Controversially, however, ISAF's role has been strictly limited to Kabul city. This has exasperated pretty much the entire aid and diplomatic community, as well as many locals. "We feel this is a great handicap," Afghanistan's UN Ambassador Ravan Farhadi is reported as saying. In June 2003, 79 aid agencies signed a petition pleading the UN and NATO to spread ISAF's security blanket across the whole country. The agencies warned that: "the people of Afghanistan are now speaking of the 'days of better security under the Taliban'."

Poor security, especially in the north around Mazar and in the south from Khost to Kandahar, has greatly compromised relief and reconstruction operations, and undermined Hamid Karzai's credibility as the man who could deliver ordinary Afghans a peace dividend. Work on the country's flagship infrastructure project – reconstructing the shattered trunk road from Kabul to Kandahar – was held up for months as workers became the targets of Taliban raids. Aid agencies shelved operations across a third of the country as both their Afghan and international staff suffered gun attacks, rape and robbery. In the year to September 2003, attacks on aid workers rocketed from two or three per month to around 20 per month. The World Food Programme warned that cancelling humanitarian aid projects in the south would put the lives of 1.3 million Afghans at risk.

The usual reason given for not expanding ISAF outside the capital has been that no countries are willing to contribute the extra troops necessary. Some commentators argue that the US's war planning for Iraq meant they were reluctant to commit extra peacekeepers to Afghanistan. For their part, the US argues that other countries must play a larger role. Meanwhile, the US's combat troops in-country would not do peacekeeping on the grounds that it is bad for morale and distracts from their anti-terror mission. But, as Lakhdar Brahimi, head of the UN mission, points out: "Even from the narrow angle of the war against terrorism, you have got to do a little bit more than trying to damp down threats from Al Qa'eda." In October 2003, NATO indicated it was happy to expand ISAF beyond Kabul – although this would be dependent on a new UN mandate and, crucially, the willingness of NATO members to provide extra resources.

The role of soldiers in humanitarian aid and reconstruction has raised major concerns with aid workers. Across the country, teams of military operatives, plain-clothed but often armed, have engaged in rebuilding schools, bridges and hospital facilities – under the guise of the Coalition Joint Civil-Military Operations Task Force (CJCMOTF). These operations concern aid workers for several reasons: principally, they fear that disaffected Afghans will associate all Westerners – including aid workers – with the military agenda of the 'war on terror'. Some aid workers refuse any contact with CJCMOTF operatives. As one NGO worker explained to a British journalist in August 2002: "When there is a backlash against the Americans, we want a clear definition between us and them." Tragically, this definition was lost on the Taliban gunman who executed an international Red Cross delegate in cold blood in March 2003 near Kandahar – part of Afghanistan which has suffered heavy-handed military interventions by US forces. The incident is seen as exemplifying the dangers of blurring the boundaries between neutral aid and politically-motivated war.

Furthermore, while the overriding principle of humanitarian aid is to ensure that the most needy get priority, the kind of aid carried out by military forces is inspired by more political motives. 'Force protection' is one reason – since commanders believe their occupying forces will be more accepted by the local community – and therefore safer – if they are seen to be helping out. Another reason may be that humanitarian activities provide a good cover for intelligence-gathering. The Mazar-based Coalition Humanitarian Liaison Centre (CHLC), for example, listed among its tasks "rebuilding public facilities" and acting as a "channel of communication to coalition commanders, the US embassy and USAID". Aid workers are very concerned that their own neutral, impartial humanitarian principles are being undermined by more political and military agenda.

Far from being put off by these concerns, the Coalition intends to expand its military-civilian activities by establishing Provincial Reconstruction Teams (PRTs) in 12 regional centres, including Kunduz, Bamiyan, Gardez, Mazar, Herat, Jalalabad and Kandahar. By August 2003, four PRTs were deployed, numbering 50-100 troops plus civilian aid and political advisors. Their objectives, according to the US Department of Defense, are "security, reconstruction, strengthening the influence of the central government and monitoring and assessing the local regional situations". However, the PRTs only have enough soldiers to safeguard their own limited operations, rather than acting as a wider regional stabilization force. Their mandate prevents them not only from intervening in 'green-on-green' inter-factional fighting, but also from curbing human rights abuses or opium production.

The PRTs' hybrid nature hybrid nature further blurs the important boundary between humanitarian and military operations, putting neutral aid workers at risk of attack. Furthermore, the PRTs have been criticised for wasting precious resources on small-scale reconstruction (of schools for example) – a job which could be done far more cheaply by NGOs with lower overheads. NGOs have called on PRTs to concentrate their efforts on security, disarmament and protection of human rights – areas where they have a comparative advantage. There is a residual suspicion that PRTs are an attempt to create 'security on the cheap' for Afghanistan.

The long-term solution to Afghan security, envisaged by the Bonn Agreement of December 2001, is that private, regional militias are disarmed and a national Afghan army and police force are built up, answering only to the President in Kabul. But this process has got off to a slow and inauspicious start. The German-backed police academy is geared up to train 1,500 students every three years – but with more than 80,000 officers to train, it will be decades before an effective force is ready. Meanwhile, plans for the disarmament, demobilization and reintegration (DDR) of former militiamen lack the incentives and enforcement necessary to work. There are thought to be as many as 10 million guns in circulation, and most Afghans have proved very reluctant to hand in any except the oldest and most useless firearms. As Karzai's brother, Ahmed Wali, put it: "every family will keep at least one Kalashnikov and some pistols for itself. Afghans always have weapons in the house – it's part of the culture". As long as Afghanistan remains a dangerous and lawless place, this culture is unlikely to change.

More seriously, the DDR plans fail to tackle the thorny issue of when or how powerful, rival commanders, such as Herat's Ismail Khan or Defence Minister Fahim, will surrender control of their private armies. Furthermore, while Fahim and his United Front faction maintain control over the Ministry of Defence, rival warlords are highly unlikely to demobilise their forces. Analyst Mark Sedra draws a parallel with Northern Ireland: "if you don't deal with the political grievances, if you don't deal with issues of reconciliation, disarmament will be impossible." Added to which, viable employment alternatives have to be found for the tens of thousands of militiamen who won't find a job in a new national army.

The aim of international donors is to create a relatively small but well-trained national army representing all ethnic groups. Only a small proportion of its projected 70,000 troops would be drawn from regional militias, to avoid recreating factional divisions within the national army. But by late 2003, just 5,000 troops had been trained. Why? Willing recruits have not been forthcoming, while 40-50 percent have dropped out either during or after the 10-week basic training course. Many were lured in by exaggerated promises of wages and conditions of service which did not materialise. Food and living conditions were said to be poor. The First National Guard Battalion, trained by the British, numbered 550 men at the end of training in April 2002 – nine months later, the unit had shrunk to just 200. Furthermore, warlords who were invited to put recruits forward for the national army have often sent their worst, least fit men to Kabul. Given that efforts to build an Afghan army are led by the Defence Ministry, those warlords opposed to Fahim's dominant United Front faction have no incentive to support the formation of such a national army.

Afghanistan's regional warlords still control between 100,000 to 200,000 fighting troops. They are funded by private taxes, drug money or contributions from foreign governments, and answer not to Karzai but to the wishes of their regional, and ethnically diverse, masters. For example, Ismail Khan in Herat funds his private army and police force through siphoning off hundreds of millions of dollars in customs revenues from the Iranian border crossing at Islam Qala – cash which should theoretically be submitted to Kabul. Meanwhile, according to *The Guardian* newspaper, in the east, British taxpayers subsidise Hazrat Ali, the warlord (but not governor) of Nangarhar province; Ali's troops "specialise in arresting people on the pretext that they are Taliban supporters and torturing them until their families pay up".

Even Defence Minister Fahim – who has inherited command of tens of thousands of Panjshairi troops from the late Ahmed Shah Massoud – has been conspicuously reluctant to embrace the Afghan National Army (ANA). He is widely regarded as running the Ministry as a personal fiefdom – 90 of the 100 generals whom he appointed in early 2002 belonged to his United Front faction. EFG editors travelling up the Panjshair Valley in 2002 saw substantial stockpiles of Russian tanks, armoured fighting vehicles, APCs, rocket launchers and lorry-loaded surface-to-air missiles, tucked away in the fold of the mountains. Is Fahim also hedging his bets?

As long as this situation continues, the ANA will lack influence, credibility and morale. Soldiers in regional militias have little incentive to join such an army – which in any case entails being posted far from home – while their commanders have no incentive to lose their power base through demobilisation or by providing troops for a national army so obviously dominated by one faction. There are signs of some slow progress – in June 2003, Karzai succeeded in extracting US$ 20 million from Ismail Khan, which helped pay long-overdue salaries to thousands of soldiers and policemen. In October, Karzai appointed three deputy defence ministers from the Pashtun, Hazara and Uzbek ethnic groups. However, in the same month, ISAF reported its concern at 300 illegal heavy weapon systems (artillery, rocket launchers, missiles, tanks and APCs), which were still positioned within Kabul (and in range of the presidential palace) – against the provisions of the Bonn Agreement. The weapons belong mainly to United Front commanders loyal to Fahim, and not to the new Afghan army.

Time is not on the side of those seeking a democratic peace. In June 2004, a new permanent government of Afghanistan is due to be elected – but UN officials have warned that this deadline may slip. A drastic increase in the size and capability of the national army – relative to regional militias – will be needed if this new government is to exercise effective authority outside the capital. The US military will prove key to achieving this aim, argues the report by the US Council on Foreign Relations. As well as training more soldiers for the Afghan army, America must commit its combat troops to peacekeeping, to supporting Karzai's bid to control defiant warlords, and to actively disarming and reintegrating regional militias – otherwise this vital task will probably fail. Meanwhile, says the report, the US administration must encourage reform within the Ministry of Defence, to ensure it becomes a more representative entity under the full control of the central government.

Without a secure operating environment, progress in political, legal, economic and physical reconstruction cannot take place. Donors and aid agencies alike are hesitant to commit to major rebuilding projects while lawlessness prevails. Meanwhile, one prominent Afghan analyst, Barnett Rubin, has warned that the creation of a new constitution may prove a "meaningless exercise" if security does not improve. With warlords controlling the countryside, the prospect of free and fair elections slated for 2004 seems to be receding like a mirage in the desert. Yet progress in recovery and reconstruction is critical not only for the welfare of ordinary Afghans, but also for boosting the credibility of Afghanistan's fledgling, civilian government – the country's best chance of casting aside years of factional fighting.

Jonathan Walter is editor of the World Disasters Report *and co-author of this field guide. For five years he served as an officer in the British Army.*

The Taliban phenomenon

By the Editors, with background historical analysis by John Butt

Following the Taliban's collapse as the ruling faction of over 80 percent of Afghanistan in November 2001, the movement quickly receded into hiding. From late 2002 onwards, however, the Taliban began to re-emerge, largely from Pakistan's tribal areas, launching ever-bolder armed attacks against US-led Coalition and Afghan government forces. By mid-2003, these attacks were occurring on an almost daily basis in eastern and southern Afghanistan. Assaults and bombings have been on the rise in the cities too, including Kabul. Soldiers are not the only targets – aid workers (both Afghan and foreign) and Afghan clerics unwilling to endorse the return of the Taliban have also been attacked and in some cases killed. Girls' schools in both the south and north of the country have burned down, allegedly by Taliban arson attacks. In September 2003, one Taliban 'intelligence official' was quoted as saying: "all those working in Afghanistan for the interests of America and the Crusaders deserve to be killed."

While the Taliban movement's ability to fight as a unified force may have been fragmented by Coalition Forces, it is clear that it will prove exceedingly difficult for the internationally-backed Kabul authorities to contain anti-government activities by small armed groups operating in the mountainous regions of the southeast, bordering Pakistan. There are many mountains and desert areas for such groups to hide in on the Afghan side of the Durand Line, and they have also found welcome sanctuary among the Pashtun tribesmen of Pakistan's North West Frontier Province (NWFP), who are not only strongly sympathetic to the Taliban but also bitterly anti-American. 'Neo-Taliban' indoctrination in *madrassas* around Peshawar is reported to be encouraging *jihad* against the West. The victory in NWFP's 2002 elections of an alliance of Islamic extremist parties, the Muttahida Majlis-e-Amal (MMA), has further emboldened the Taliban. Even if Islamabad's armed forces adopted a stronger hand in containing pro-Taliban operations on its side of the border, the tribal agencies have never proved easy to control – and the MMA will make it harder still.

Meanwhile, in Quetta, capital of neighbouring Baluchistan province, Taliban leaders have been openly reorganising their comeback, recruiting new fighters and issuing orders to armed groups within Afghanistan by satellite phones. Baluchistan's ruling coalition includes the Jamiat-e-Ulema Islam (JUI), which publicly supports the Taliban. In October 2003, the JUI's leader (and Baluchistan's information minister) said: "Karzai's time is finished. Only the Taliban can constitute the real government in Afghanistan". The Taliban also remain highly popular among numerous non-tribal Pakistanis, including key elements of the Pakistani armed forces – especially the powerful Inter Services Intelligence (ISI) organization, a traditional backer of Pashtun nationalist and radical groups in Afghanistan.

During most of their years in power (1994-2001), the Taliban enjoyed broad popular support in the Pashtun-dominated southern and eastern provinces of Afghanistan. Their ranks were swollen by legions of Islamic volunteers from Pakistan, Saudi Arabia, Indonesia and elsewhere, including Britain and other European countries. However, as early as 1999 or 2000, the movement's leadership was beginning to implode, with splits between the Kandahar-based Taliban and other factions in Jalalabad, Khost and elsewhere. As has often happened in Afghan history, one group sought to monopolize its control by not consulting with its counterparts. Later, as the West cracked down on Arabic and other *Wahabi*-inspired terror elements, or pressured traditional backers (notably Pakistan) to withhold their support, the Taliban found their financial resources severely reduced. Equally crucial was their loss of access to the funding produced by a highly lucrative border trade of goods crossing over from Pakistan, Iran and the Central Asian Republics.

In the autumn of 2001, the Taliban were unable to resist heavy military pressure by the United Front (also known as the Northern Alliance) supported by massive US bombing. They were further thwarted by the CIA's strategy of paying off local commanders in the hope of attracting their backing. Although the US-led Coalition succeeded in toppling the regime, many of the Taliban's leaders and supporters simply slipped over the border into Pakistan, or went into hiding in Afghanistan's Pashtun belt. They took with them money looted from the central bank before the fall of Kabul and have since augmented their finances through drug trafficking.

While initially successful in their conventional military actions, Coalition Forces have been inadvertently contributing to the re-emergence of the Taliban and other anti-government groups through often heavy-handed operations against the local Afghan population. The airborne attack of a wedding party in Uruzgan province in June 2002, which killed over 50 Afghan civilians, is one of many examples. Civilian casualties have been high, possibly 3,000 or more deaths since the October 2001 intervention. The US military has tended to regard anyone with a gun as a supporter of the Taliban or Al Qa'eda, whether justified or not. Similarly, too, Afghan commanders collaborating with the Americans have often branded their political or commercial rivals as pro-Taliban to serve their own purposes.

Another factor in the re-emergence of the Taliban is a rising sense of grievance among Pashtuns in the south and east of the country, who feel politically and militarily marginalized by the Karzai administration. Although Karzai is himself a Pashtun, he has failed to build a base of Pashtun support in the south, and is perceived as vulnerable to the influence of ethnic Tajiks who control the defence, interior and foreign ministries. Karzai has tried to engage more moderate elements of the Taliban in dialogue – a strategy thought to be unpopular with his Tajik ministers. Nevertheless, at least 50 former Taliban officials took part in December 2003's Constitutional Loya Jirga.

Pashtun resentment is further fuelled by a perception that both foreign military forces and international aid agencies are pro-Kabul or focus their attention on Kabul at the expense of the east and south. Numerous Afghans, particularly in rural areas, are increasingly nostalgic about the Taliban, who reined in abusive armed groups (including former *mujahideen*) and brought peace to much of the country, even if their methods proved harsh.

Some players are seeking to benefit from the Taliban movement's legacy. These include fundamentalists such as former resistance politician, Gulbuddin Hekmatyar, who declared *jihad* against the United States in 2002 (ironically, the Americans and Pakistanis were among his staunchest supporters during the Soviet war of the 1980s).

Islamic specialist John Butt now examines the origins of the Taliban and how it came to emerge as one of the country's most powerful factions in the late 20th Century.

When the Taliban – the Islamic Students Movement – appeared on the Afghan scene in late 1994, they took the world by storm. There was little understanding of where the Taliban came from, what they represented, who they were and where their appeal lay. Even following their overthrow in late 2001, they were not much better understood than they were when they first emerged.

One thing is clear: November 1994 does not represent the birth of the Taliban. They were on the scene well before then. "Do you remember when you came to Kandahar in April 1992?" the Governor of Kandahar province, Mawlawi Mohammed Hassan – widely considered number two in the Taliban movement – asked me in the course of a conversation we had early in 1997. He mentioned my visit then to the village of Mullah Pasanay, elevated to Chief Justice of Kandahar province by the Taliban and a leading light behind the Taliban movement. "Well, we were organized then. We thought we would give the 'gun-slingers' (the term used in Kandahar to describe the *mujahideen*) a chance to get their act together. We did not make our move until we had lost all hope."

What Mullah Hassan said is consistent with evidence of Taliban organizations existing throughout Afghanistan, at least since the late 1980s and even before then. These were usually organized on a provincial level. Though the majority of Taliban are from the Pashto-speaking areas of Afghanistan, there were also organizations of Talibs from predominantly non-Pashtun provinces such as Takhar, Badakhshan and Baghlan.

Nevertheless, the bulk of the Taliban came from the Pashtun provinces, and particularly the Pashtun strongholds of Greater Paktia (Khost, Paktia and Paktika), Wardak, Ghazni and Kandahar. The predominantly, but not exclusively, Pashtun nature of the Taliban is evident in their name. 'Taliban' is the Pashto plural for 'Talib.' In Arabic and Persian, the plural of the same word is 'Tulaba.' 'Talib' is originally an Arabic word meaning 'seeker.' The Prophet of Islam urged believers to 'seek' knowledge, even if it meant going to China. The word has thus become commonly used for a seeker of religious knowledge – a religious student.

The tradition of travelling in order to gain knowledge can also be traced to the above statement of the Prophet. It is because of this tradition that Afghan students have become used to travelling, first to India and then to Pakistan, for acquiring knowledge of religion. Prior to the partition of India in 1947, students of religion used to travel to the centres of learning in Deoband (Darul Uloom, Deoband) and to a lesser extent Delhi (Darul Uloom Aminiyya).

Deoband and Afghanistan

The affinity of the Deobandi school of learning, in particular, to Afghanistan goes back to the early 20th Century. The Taliban are heirs to this traditional affinity. Not only has there been a steady stream of scholars from Afghanistan receiving education at Deoband; "freedom fighters" – among them independence-minded scholars of the Deobandi school – have also been regular visitors to Afghanistan.

Foremost of these was Mawlana Ubaidullah Sindhi, a leading Indian religious scholar who remained in Afghanistan from 1916 to 1923. Despite his own progressive nature, the Deoband school from which Mawlana Sindhi hailed has always been associated with traditional thinking in Afghanistan. Deoband represented the wing of Indian Muslim thinking which was suspicious of Western education, and sought to strengthen traditional Islamic education in the face of what was seen as an onslaught from the secular West. It was this same mentality which came up with the slogan, at the time of the introduction of secular education in Afghanistan under Amir Amanullah Khan in the 1920s:

> *"Those who go to school,*
> *Do so just for money.*
> *They will have no place in heaven,*
> *But will flay around in hell."*

Until the independence of India and Pakistan, the "Afghan connection" of the Deobandi school was synonymous with anti-British sedition. In its efforts to keep British imperialism at arms-length, Afghan rulers always treated Deobandi figureheads with at best grudging respect, sometimes bordering on disdain.

Even before Mawlana Sindhi moved to Afghanistan, the head of the royal *madrassa* (religious school) in Kabul – a Deoband graduate by the name of Abdul Razzaq – tried to mount anti-British operations on the Frontier. He was prevented from doing this by Amir Habibullah (1908-1919), who did not wish to unduly aggravate the British rulers in India.

This same policy was followed by Amir Amanullah Khan (1919-29), who actually banned any religious scholars with a foreign education – including Deoband – from teaching in Afghanistan. This decision followed considerable pressure on the Amir from British rulers in India, to expel Mawlana Sindhi and his group of Indian rebels from Afghanistan. This he did in 1923, but not before Mawlana Sindhi and his companions had played a crucial role – on the Afghan side – in the fighting leading up to the independence of Afghanistan in 1919.

It was at this time that a chain of religious schools – the *madrassas* – started operating in the northwest frontier regions of British India. These same schools, some eighty years on, have spawned the Taliban. Still, until 1947, the ultimate aim of Afghan religious students was to receive their education at the main centres of learning in Deoband and Delhi. Following the independence of India and Pakistan, leading scholars of the Deobandi school opted to open *madrassas* in Lahore, Karachi and Akora Khattak in Pakistan's North West Frontier Province. With the establishment of these *madrassas*, there was a gradual increase in the number of students from Afghanistan crossing the Durand Line to receive Islamic education.

After 1947, as the centre of learning for Afghan religious students moved from India to Pakistan, there was a sea-change in the political focus of the Deobandi movement in the frontier regions of Pakistan and inside Afghanistan itself. While the British had remained in India, there were two main aims of the movement: the more scholastic and spiritual minded aimed to consolidate Islamic learning in the face of British-sponsored Western education, while on a political level, some Deobandi scholars sought to assist the anti-British forces struggling for independence. When the British left the subcontinent, the Deobandis focused their attention on the secular forces in Pakistan and later in Afghanistan itself.

During the 1970s, there was a continuing flow of religious students travelling from Afghanistan to Pakistan to receive religious knowledge. Many of these studied in the main centres of learning, in Karachi (New Town Darul Uloom and Darul Uloom Karachi), Lahore (Jamiya Ashrafiyya), Peshawar (Jamiya Ashrafiyya and Darul Uloom Sarhad), as well as various smaller institutions spread around the frontier provinces of Pakistan and Baluchistan. The number of these *madrassas* increased dramatically with the beginning of the Afghan war in 1978, and the Islamization policies followed by the President of Pakistan, Mohammed Zia-ul Haq.

Traditionalists and Islamists

The Taliban movement represented the return of the traditional, *madrassa*-based Islamic scholar to the Afghan political scene. Until the Taliban came to prominence, it was the Islamists who combated the rising forces of secularism and, later, communism in Afghanistan. It is important to understand the distinction between *traditionalists* – epitomised by the Taliban – and *Islamists* – represented by such parties as the Jamiat-e-Islami of Professor Burhanuddin Rabbani (the former alliance president of Afghanistan ousted from Kabul by the Taliban in September 1996) and Hezb-e-Islami of Gulbuddin Hekmatyar. The Taliban were educated in religious schools – *madrassas* – while the Islamists are generally products of the state education system.

The Taliban are traditionalists – seeking to return to the purity of the teachings of the Koran and the *Sunnah*, the practice of the Prophet. The Islamists, meanwhile, are modernists in that they are seeking a contemporary, albeit political, interpretation of Islam. The Taliban, being products of religious *madrassas* in Pakistan, are more inclined towards that country, while the Islamists have mostly received higher religious education in Al-Azhar University in Egypt, where they have been influenced by the political thinking of the Muslim Brotherhood. The Islamists – particularly the Hezb-e-Islami of Gulbuddin Hekmatyar – have been able to form highly organized political parties whereas the Taliban are still not organized along party lines.

However, there is evidence of the Taliban being organized on a provincial basis from the time of the *jihad* (holy war) against the Soviet army and Communist government in Afghanistan. Organizations of Taliban took the form more of regional associations than political parties. For example, the Jamiat-e-Tulaba-e-Paktia-wa-Khost was a rough association comprising those religious students pursuing studies in Pakistan, originally hailing from the provinces of Paktia and Khost in south-eastern Afghanistan. Every now and then, these students would come from their various *madrassas* in Pakistan and gather in their native provinces of Afghanistan. One such gathering was held in Khost shortly after the capture of that province by the *mujahideen* in 1991. The gathering attracted many thousands of religious students from *madrassas* in Pakistan, who came to their native province for a "turban-tying" *(dastar bandi)* ceremony – their official initiation into the ranks of the *ulama*, the scholars of Islam.

This gathering of Taliban was symptomatic of similar organizations existing elsewhere in the country which represented a huge, and, at that time, latent force. In Khost, the Taliban were represented in the administration which ruled the province during the *mujahed* interregnum, between the fall of Najibullah's government in the province and the Taliban takeover in late 1994. A leading light in the Taliban movement, Abdul Hakim Sharai, was Chief of Security in the province during this time. Later, he was to become Governor of Zabul province under the Taliban.

Taliban were also influential in the administration of Mawlawi Mansur in Paktia. Mawlawi Mansur, belonging to the Harakat-e-Inqilab-e-Islami (Revolutionary Islamic Movement) of Mohammed Nabi Mohammedi, was murdered in Hezb-e-Islami controlled territory in 1993. Later, the party of Mohammedi, a leading scholar of the Deobandi school of thought, was to defect almost entirely to the Taliban. However, for the most part, Taliban throughout Afghanistan remained isolated from power until the Kandahar Taliban made their move in late 1994.

Tribals and non-tribals

Following the takeover of Kabul in September 1996, the Taliban advanced towards the Shomali plain, stretching towards the Hindu Kush north of Kabul. It was here that their advance was halted. The resistance they met in the Shomali plain came from ordinary villagers, as well as from supporters loyal to Ahmed Shah Massoud. In a way, this resistance was surprising. The Shomali plain had produced Bacha Saqao, a Tajik who in 1929 led a regime remarkably similar in its religious hue to the Taliban themselves. One might have thought that the people of Shomali would have rallied to the support of the Taliban. That they did the opposite was because the Shomalis did not see the Taliban as a religious movement. Instead, they saw in the Taliban shades of the tribal confederation which, under the future king Nadir Shah, had unseated Bacha Saqao. (Subsequently, the Taliban ruthlessly destroyed the Shomalis' homes and deliberately devastated their agricultural infrastructure by ordering press-ganged young men from Kabul and the region to uproot vineyards and fruit orchards and wreck irrigation systems.)

For non-tribal fundamentalism, represented by Bacha Saqao, the transition to the Islamism of Burhanuddin Rabbani was more logical than a reversion to the traditional, more tribal Islam of the Taliban. To a certain degree, by the time of the fall of Kabul, the Taliban movement had been hijacked by tribal, ethnic and even nationalist elements. Yet it still had considerable support from the Islamic scholars who had earlier in the century provided the ground-swell of support for Bacha Saqao. Such is the complex alignment of conflicting forces which makes for the extraordinarily entangled state of Afghan politics today. If the Taliban had been able to project a more purist Islamic image, they might have been acceptable to the people of the northern plains. By projecting a tribal image, or being projected as such, they became totally unacceptable.

When the Taliban launched their takeover of the north of Afghanistan in May 1997, among the first to recognise them was the government of Saudi Arabia. For two reasons this might have seemed a strange decision. The Saudis had spent much of the 1980s trying to spread their own particular puritanical brand of Islam – *Wahabiism* – in Afghanistan. Why then should they have promoted a different brand – that of the Taliban?

Secondly, the Taliban were continuing to give shelter to the most famous of Saudi dissidents – Osama Bin Laden. Why should they have recognised a regime that was giving refuge to its sworn enemy? There is a degree of conjecture in one's answer to both these questions. It may be that Saudi support for the Taliban should be seen more in geopolitical than in religious terms, and was part of the continuing rivalry with Iran for influence in Afghanistan. (The Iranian government was one of the main supporters of the anti-Taliban coalition). One may speculate that, as far as the Saudi regime was concerned, Osama Bin Laden was relatively harmless in the care of the Taliban. The Saudis may well have received assurances from the Taliban that he would not pose a threat to Saudi interests while living under their protection.

Regarding the Taliban's approach and beliefs, it is true that in the past the Saudi government provided support to *Wahabiite* tendencies in Afghanistan. This may well have proven a chastening experience for the Saudis. It was clear that the people of Afghanistan were opposed to *Wahabiism* as such. The vast majority of Afghans had no time for a brand of Islam which renounced the *Hanafi* school of thought, to which all *Sunni* Afghans adhere. Many Afghans, however, became affiliated to *Wahabi* groups but usually for opportunist reasons, such as money.

From this point of view, the puritanical Deobandi interpretation of Islamic teachings may have appeared as an acceptable compromise to the Saudis. On most questions of dogma, the position of the Deobandis is quite similar to that of the *Wahabis*, though with considerable concessions to Afghan tradition and custom. Most importantly, the Deobandis strictly adhere to the *Hanafi* school of thought to which Afghans swear allegiance.

On the question of the Islamic status of shrines, for example, the Taliban adopted a more cautious approach than the *Wahabis*. While the *Wahabis* insist that the building of shrines, and visits to them, are un-Islamic and polytheistic practices, the Taliban showed more deference to age-old Afghan traditions on this question. Not wishing to disturb a hornet's nest, they did not stop people from visiting shrines. However, as they consolidated their hold on areas, they began imposing what they considered to be a more Islamic code of conduct at shrines, particularly as far as praying to God, and not to the shrine itself, was concerned. The reverence of relics, particularly the cloak of the Prophet, which they used to sanction the position of their leader Mullah Omar as Commander of the Faithful, was even more liberal in comparison to strict interpretation of the *Wahabis*.

As for the seemingly extreme measures of the Taliban, which attracted considerable publicity in the West, they were understandable in the context of

Tali-*bans*

During 1996-97, the Taliban's Department for the Promotion of Virtue and the Prevention of Vice issued various decrees, aimed to prevent:

- **Girls going to school**
- **Women working for or visiting foreign aid agencies**
- **Women participating in politics**
- **Women revealing any part of their body (even ankles) in public**
- **Young women washing clothes by the river**
- **Men shaving or cutting beards**
- **Men growing long hair**
- **Men measuring for and tailoring ladies' clothes**
- **Music or drumming in any buildings or vehicles**
- **Music and dancing at weddings**
- **Displaying any representations of the human face**
- **Shopping during prayer time**
- **Keeping pigeons or playing with birds**
- **Kite flying and selling**
- **Drug pushing and addiction**
- **Gambling**
- **Interest charges on loans and money changing**
- **Sorcery**
- **Homosexuality**

Punishments were harsh: beating with whips and imprisonment for minor offences; amputation of hands for theft; burial alive for homosexuality; execution for murder; and death by stoning for adultery or "multiple intercourse" (sleeping with two men in one month) if witnessed by at least four people. *JW*

the *Hanafi* school of thought. Without going into each particular measure, it might be enlightening to see where the thinking behind such measures as the confinement of women, and their cloaking in the all-enveloping *burqa*, came from. In the principles of *Hanafi* jurisprudence there are two fundamental tenets, both of which are extremely important in understanding Taliban thinking. The first is that an action may not be *haram* – 'forbidden' – in itself, but it becomes so if it is likely to lead to an *haram* action. The concealment of women can be seen in the light of this principle. Women are expected to cover themselves, not because this is desirable in itself, but in order to prevent immorality.

Such approaches, however, were not accepted by many Afghan women of urban background who viewed the various Talib edicts as a means of control or reinforcement of a traditionally male dominated society. During the Taliban regime, women were not allowed out of their homes without their faces concealed. Less than a year after the fall of the Taliban, an estimated one in five women in the busy bazaars of central Kabul was walking around without face cover – despite the presence of highly conservative elements within the Northern Alliance's own supposedly pro-Western government. To a lesser extent, the same thing was happening in Jalalabad. In rural communities, however, women rarely emerge without face cover – unless they are educated professionals, such as teachers, journalists, doctors or nurses.

Another principle which lay behind many of the edicts of the Taliban is that of an action being 'permissible' (*ruskhah*) and 'honourable' (*azeemah*). It is 'permissible', for example, to take a life for a life, but the 'honourable' thing to do is to forgive. In Afghan tribal tradition, this principle has often been turned upside down. For example, taking a life for a life has come to be considered honourable. Often, the Taliban imposed an action which they saw as honourable – as opposed to permissible – though it might be arguable whether this is seen from a strictly Islamic, or from a tribal, point of view.

One may argue with many measures of the Taliban, even from an Islamic point of view, but it is quite clear that the phenomenon of the Taliban was not artificially created. The Taliban have deep roots in Afghan society. Because these roots were indigenous to Afghan society, others may have decided that they were a force worth supporting. Even within the Northern Alliance, there are similar traditional beliefs that have proved no different from those propagated by the Taliban. As a movement, the Taliban also provided mainly rural Afghans – exhausted by so many years of war – with a sense of peace and security that the *mujahideen* were not able to offer.

John Butt*, founder editor of the BBC's radio soap opera for Afghanistan,* "New Home, New Life", *is an expert in Islamic theology with long experience of Afghanistan. Parts of this essay have been updated by the editors.*

Human rights: the struggle for dignity

By Charles Norchi

"Killing you is a very easy thing for us."

— Human Rights Watch report, July 2003

Human rights in Afghanistan have been a story of deprivation, misery and violence. The country ranks at the bottom of international development indicators, while its people rank at the top of populations that have suffered torture, executions, displacement, bombing and oppression. Human rights declined precipitously with the Soviet occupation, continuing through the *mujahideen* and Taliban periods. But Afghanistan has never had a human rights culture. Protection of individual and collective dignity was traditionally achieved through customary or Islamic practices. Secular legal codes protected some fundamental freedoms in certain urban areas at certain times, but provincial elites largely rejected the authority of those laws. The new Afghanistan now faces the formidable challenge of weaving customary practices, conflicting religious interpretations *and* secular laws – including a new Constitution that meets international legal obligations – into a functioning human rights culture.

Afghans suffered immeasurably in the final hot contact of the Cold War. At its apex in the mid-1980s, 200,000 Soviet troops were in Afghanistan. Initially, aerial bombardments and joint Soviet-Afghan regime ground operations were used against the growing Afghan resistance. Helicopter gunships became the Soviet military's workhorse. They ferreted out mountain-based guerrillas, but were increasingly used against villages and refugee caravans. Civilians became targets of attacks. Troops in a position to distinguish between *mujahideen* and civilians attacked non-combatants, including women and children. When Mikhail Gorbachev came to power, special forces (*Spetznaz)* were used. These units were directly deployed into villages and were responsible for some of the most notorious atrocities. Human rights organizations collected evidence suggesting three patterns of situations in which civilians found themselves the object of attack. The first was directed to the depopulation of areas of strategic value. The second was the killing of individual civilians as part of a general attack on the civilian population of a village. The third situation was that of attacks on individual civilians, such as village elders or religious leaders, usually as a form of punishment or warning.

The Soviets used terror as a tactic. Heavy firepower was used indiscriminately, massacring many thousands of civilians. Crops were destroyed and villages razed, in an effort to drive Afghans into the refugee camps of Pakistan and Iran. The aim was to remove support for the *mujahideen* and to pacify the country. Anti-personnel mines were used extensively across the country – the smaller 'butterfly' mines being scattered indiscriminately by air. They were intended to maim rather than kill. Their victims were mostly civilians and often children.

For many in the West during the 1980s, Afghanistan conjured up romantic images of a land of Kipling and Kim, where turbaned freedom fighters crossed deserts, mountains and Central Asian steppes to fight the Soviet Red Army. In fact, the human rights reality was horrific. Five years after the last Soviets left in 1989, the country was still engulfed in war. From 1992-94, *mujahideen* factions brutally competing for power committed massive human rights violations, particularly in urban areas such as Kabul. Afghans were still victims of indiscriminate bombing, torture and mutilation. Some of those implicated in the abuses of the mid-1990s have now found their way into Afghanistan's new government.

When the Taliban emerged from the chaos in 1994 to impose order, they cracked the whip in the name of Allah. Afghanistan became a captive nation. There was no future, only a nightmarish present. Women were banned from the workforce – 30,000 families headed by war widows had no means of support other than begging. Girls' schools and colleges were shut. Music, television and flying kites were among banned activities. The soccer stadium was used for weekly lashings and executions. For most Afghans, especially women, human dignity took a holiday.

When American and British forces dislodged the Taliban regime in 2001, Afghanistan's human rights history entered a new chapter. Subsequent United Nations-brokered talks in Bonn, Germany on 5th December 2001 resulted in the Bonn Agreement, which acknowledged "the right of the people of Afghanistan to freely determine their political future in accordance with the principles of Islam, democracy, pluralism and social justice." The Agreement was intended as a road map to peace, security, reconstruction and the protection of human rights. But the road to better human rights has proved bumpy.

Recent mass graves containing victims from every major ethnic group dot Afghanistan. They were filled by the Taliban and its enemies, notably the United Front (also known as the Northern Alliance). Thirteen mass graves have been discovered in the north and in Bamiyan. The NGO Physicians for Human Rights has received tips of many more. When the northern towns of Kunduz and Taloqan collapsed in late 2001, 5,000 Taliban surrendered and 2,000 remain unaccounted for. The mass grave at Dasht-e-Leili holds at least a thousand bodies of pro-Taliban prisoners who suffocated while being transported to General Dostum's headquarters in Shibarghan in sealed shipping containers.

Even after the formal fighting finished, human rights trends remained worrisome. At the Emergency *Loya Jirga* in June 2002, by which Afghans selected

an interim government, delegates reported extensive intimidation from military commanders and secret police. Outside Kabul, warlords have ruled by the power of the gun rather than the authority of laws such as the Bonn Agreement. Threats by United Front thugs loyal to Abdul Rasul Sayyaf, Younis Qanooni and defence minister Fahim have continued. Many Pashtuns in the north have been attacked or targeted, and forced to flee to camps in the south or into Pakistan. The situation for women in most of the country has remained especially grim. During 2003, personal insecurity remained the overwhelming human rights complaint of individual Afghans. The trend of impunity for human rights violations has been reinforced because no formal inquiries have been conducted and some alleged perpetrators hold government positions. Most of the northern mass graves were filled by troops under the command of General Dostum, who was later appointed to President Karzai's National Defence Commission.

Despite the trends, the UN Assistance Mission in Afghanistan (UNAMA) has been reticent about putting human rights at the top of their agenda. The belief has been that securing fundamental rights can only follow peace and the establishment of an independent formal government. The logic is that human rights activity and formal inquiries into past abuses could have a destabilizing effect. However, as a result, many human rights opportunities have been missed.

The Bonn Agreement mandated that: "The Interim Administration shall, with the assistance of the United Nations, establish an Independent Human Rights Commission, whose responsibilities will include human rights monitoring, investigation of violations of human rights and development of domestic human rights institutions." The nascent Afghan Human Rights Commission has received international support from the wider human rights community, including the UN, governments and NGOs. Its first chair was Ms Sima Samar, who had been the minister of women's affairs in the Afghan Interim Administration. The inaugural Commission comprised eleven members, including five women, with all major ethnic groups represented. The role of the Human Rights Commission has been evolving slowly. However, in June 2002, it received strong impetus from a Presidential Decree which endowed the Commission with important transitional justice powers to address past abuses, including the capacity to document crimes against humanity that have been committed in Afghanistan over the past quarter century. To implement this would be a courageous step, one which UNAMA has been unwilling to take. Under the Presidential Decree, the Commission would also have the responsibility to ensure that national laws are consistent with international human rights obligations and to advise on Afghanistan's monitoring of human rights treaty obligations. The Independent Commission was established as a state organ by the draft Constitution submitted to the Constitutional *Loya Jirga* in December 2003.

Afghanistan's Independent Human Rights Commission will only have teeth when it receives the international support to build effective central and regional offices, to process complaints and over time to build a reputation among ordinary Afghans for obtaining remedies for claims. A member of the UN's High Commission for Human Rights was seconded to Kabul to help train Afghan Commission members; and a former member of New Zealand's Human Rights Commission was assisting the Commission organize its work, including establishing systems to process claims. As the UN Special Rapporteur for Afghanistan declared: "The Afghan National Human Rights Commission should be enabled, through the provision of adequate resources, to develop its capacity at an accelerated pace in order to be able to build a progressively more effective role in investigation and monitoring of human rights violations."

But as long as warlords terrorize wide swathes of the country, the Commissioners' work will be impeded. People have been hampered in their efforts to convey human rights information to the Commission, the UN and the media. In February 2003, a UN report noted that individuals have been "arbitrarily detained, intimidated, threatened, brutalized or tortured, or have reportedly disappeared for having shared information regarding human rights violations with reporters or the United Nations Assistance Mission in Afghanistan (UNAMA), or because they were relatives of witnesses."

Agreeing to a new Constitution has been a major hurdle. The Bonn Agreement committed the transitional government of Afghanistan to an interim legal framework based on the Constitution of 1964, which confirmed international legal obligations to which Afghanistan has been a party. But a new Constitution had to be in place as a precondition for holding free and fair elections in late 2004, so drafting began in earnest during 2003. Vice-president Professor Ne'amatullah Shahrani chaired the drafting commission, while a second Constitutional commission was created to consult broadly with the people of Afghanistan and produce a final draft for submission to the Constitutional *Loya Jirga* (CLJ). The full CLJ was to be formally convened in October 2003 and by the end of that month it was to publish and widely disseminate the Constitution – but this deadline slipped to December 2003. From the beginning, there were divisions in the commission among those who favoured conservative interpretations of Islamic law and the progressives who looked to the 1964 Constitution and international human rights standards.

Can there be peace without justice?

The north of Afghanistan has seen some of the worst violence of recent years. Until the late 1990s the area was relatively stable and prosperous, under the command of General Rashid Dostum, although scant regard was paid to human rights. This stability was shattered in March 1997, when General Malik Pahlawan, Dostum's number two, mutinied, allied himself with the Taliban and ousted Dostum from Mazar. The Taliban's victory was, however, short-lived. As they disarmed local forces, resistance broke out. Malik then turned against the Taliban, who found themselves trapped in the city. Hundreds of them were killed in the streets and 2,000 taken prisoner, later to be executed and dumped down wells or in the desert. This sparked a series of massacres. The second, of Hazara civilians, happened when the Taliban attacked Mazar the following September. Then, when the Taliban finally took the city in 1998, thousands of civilians were killed, along with Hazara forces trapped in the city.

So it was not surprising that, when the Northern Alliance (including Dostum) captured the north with the aid of Coalition Forces in 2001, further massacres occurred. Hundreds of Taliban and other combatants who surrendered after the fall of Kunduz are believed to have died by summary execution or by suffocating in the containers in which they were transported.

Bodies from all these massacres lie in mass graves across northern Afghanistan. What to do about these sites, particularly Dasht-e-Leili near Shibarghan (believed to be the site of the 2001 atrocities), has polarised the international community. Although many believe a proper investigation of the graves and a dignified burial of the remains are essential to any accountability and reconciliation process, so far little has been done. The UN conducted preliminary investigations in May 2002, but said the decision to investigate lay with the Afghan authorities and the Human Rights Commission.

There was concern that witnesses could not be protected and that responsibility to the living should take precedence over justice to the dead. International human rights groups disagreed, as did the UN Special Rapporteur on Extra-judicial Executions, who visited Afghanistan in October 2002 and called for an international inquiry into past human rights violations, including the graves in the north. Finally, the UN authorised an official investigation into the sites but said it should be limited to "finding and preserving evidence" and should have a "low profile" since systematic and full investigations "would seriously disrupt the fragile peace that the Government and international community are striving to foster and reinforce." Since then a number of witnesses to Dasht-e-Leili have allegedly disappeared or been tortured. As one human rights worker noted: "Every time someone comes and looks, someone disappears".

A longer version of this box appeared in the World Disasters Report 2003

Selection to the CLJ would be key. That process would either build national consensus or exacerbate divisions.

A preliminary draft Constitution was completed in spring 2003. There was criticism that it was not debated and reviewed in a sufficiently broad-based way. The Constitution-making exercise was intended to engage all segments of Afghan society to achieve a consensus document. But participation became an issue, especially for women. Close observers termed the public consultations a fig leaf to satisfy the commission's mandate. Not surprisingly, there was internal division over the drafts. Changes sought by the president were not implemented and he appointed a working group tasked with revision. Still, between conflicting claims and inevitable compromises, the process (which concluded with the CLJ agreeing on a final draft in January 2004) may well have produced a document which Afghans feel they own. And that is much more than can be said of earlier constitutions. The question is: will it protect fundamental rights?

The preliminary draft contained laudable and even progressive provisions, but a number of its articles were confusing. These were addressed in the final drafting stages and in the Constitutional *Loya Jirga*. There were some key issues as the document moved towards finalization. The draft submitted to the CLJ proclaimed: "In Afghanistan national sovereignty belongs to the nation and the nation enforces it directly or through its representatives." That is noteworthy, as some Islamic constitutions place sovereignty squarely in the hands of Allah. The draft provided for a presidential system with a bicameral National Assembly and a traditional *Loya Jirga* to be convened in extraordinary circumstances. An earlier draft provided for a prime minister to satisfy former Northern Alliance leadership. Would the preliminary formulation survive to the final draft?

Surprisingly for an Islamic constitution, the draft referred to international human rights early in the preamble ("Observing the United Nations Charter and respecting the Universal Declaration of Human Rights") and stipulated the "creation of a civil society free of oppression, atrocity, discrimination and violence, based on rule of law, social justice, protection of human rights and dignity, and ensuring fundamental rights and freedoms of the people". A later clause asserted: "The State of Afghanistan is obligated to create a prosperous and progressive society based on social justice, protection of human dignity, the realization of democracy and the maintenance of national unity and equality among all ethnic groups and tribes and to provide for balanced development in all areas of the country".

In an earlier draft, a clause in a chapter on "The Fundamental Rights and Duties of Citizens" provided that: "The citizens of Afghanistan whether female or male are equal before the law and have equal rights and duties regardless of language, tribal and clan affiliation, religion, place of residence and social position." This explicit gender equality in that draft was especially noteworthy. However the language did not survive internal debate and was redrafted in the version submitted to the CLJ to read, simply: "The citizens of Afghanistan have equal rights and duties before the law".

There were tensions between the secular and the sacred in all the drafts, reflecting similar tensions throughout much of Afghan society. The document naturally established that: "The religion of Afghanistan is the sacred religion of Islam", while stating: "The followers of other religions are free to perform their religious ceremonies within the limits of the provisions of the law". This was hardly an endorsement of unfettered religious freedom. The third article of the document then stipulated: "In Afghanistan, no law can be contrary to the sacred religion of Islam and the values of this Constitution". Analysts worried that the vagueness of that provision could be a dangerous instrument in the hands of extremists.

Another issue is reference to the Hannafi School of Jurisprudence. It is the dominant school, but is not accepted by all Afghans. In a section on the judiciary, the draft stated: "When there is no provision in the Constitution or other laws regarding ruling on an issue, the court's decisions shall be within the limits of this Constitution in accord with the Hannafi jurisprudence and in a way to serve justice in the best possible manner". Would the Hannafi School be invoked in the final draft as the default source of law for judicial review?

After multiple drafts and at times acrimonious debate, the 502 delegates to the Constitutional *Loya Jirga* approved a new Constitution for Afghanistan on 4 January 2004. Observers criticised the *Jirga* as scripted, with the majority belonging to voting blocks controlled by powerful warlords. Still, the outcome was a document which if applied, might provide the new beginning Afghans sorely need. The new Constitution balances the goals of an Islamic state with a promise to abide by the United Nations Charter and the Universal Declaration of Human Rights. It provides for a presidential system with a directly elected president, a bicameral national assembly, and an independent judiciary. Notably, it names all of Afghanistan's ethnic groups as part of the nation, allowing all groups to use and teach their languages in areas where they are the majority. Certain freedoms, such as the right to publish and to form social organizations, are limited. Equal rights for women are affirmed and two Parliament seats for each province are reserved for women. The document does not address the relationship between Islam and international human rights law, nor does it provide for muscular institutions to protect those rights, except through the currently weak Afghan Independent Human Rights Commission. As the *Loya Jirga* drew to a close, its Chairman Sibghatullah Mujaddedi reflected: "If this Constitution is not put into practice and not implemented, then it would not be given the respect that we have all promised." The true challenge now is for every Afghan to own the new Constitution.

There is a lesson from Afghan history. The country's first Constitution was promulgated by King Amanullah in 1923. He established new courts, introduced secular legal codes and reformed traditional customs and wearing of the veil. It did not go well. By 1928 Amanullah faced tribal uprisings and before long fled to India, while a fundamentalist Tajik bandit proclaiming himself Habibullah II of Afghanistan occupied Kabul. Thus began a trend in the country's constitutive processes: a clash between the urban centre's exercise of power, based on narrow secular authority, and the power bases of religion and custom wielded by elites in the rest of the country. These tensions have affected Afghan constitutions and laws from the time of Amanullah to the present.

Without security, human rights cannot be secured. Even with a Constitution that proclaims to secure human dignity, the reality is that in Afghanistan the most fundamental right – well-being – is in short supply. Numerous reports from the NGO Human Rights Watch during 2002-03 have documented incidents of intimidation, harassment, kidnapping and death threats. According to one report: "The atmosphere of violence, along with resurgent religious fundamentalism in parts of the country, is endangering the most important human rights improvement since the end of the Taliban – the ability of girls to go back to school." The situation is worse in the rural areas than the towns, but even in the cities human rights gains since the fall of the Taliban are being lost. Once again, the Afghan population is at risk.

Afghanistan's achievement of legitimate statehood will turn on the ability to secure fundamental human rights. This will require the support of the international community – both in terms of improving security and in strengthening the country's criminal justice system. Security nationwide remains the number one human rights problem and the international community must address it. The hope is that the situation will improve with NATO taking over the International Security Assistance Force (ISAF) command. Patrols and operations must be extended across the country and not limited to Kabul. In a positive move in October 2003, NATO said it was open to expanding ISAF's presence across the country. Furthermore, an intense nationwide demobilization of every non-authorized military unit must occur, since warlord entrenchment is a serious risk. This is an essential precondition to free and fair elections. Arms caches must be returned to the authority of the central government. The UN should implement a highly visible human rights programme, which entails public monitoring and reporting. The capacity of the Afghan National Human Rights Commission to reach communities across the country must be strengthened.

Afghans want the world community to take their human rights seriously. Afghanistan is party to the major international human rights treaties and it has reconfirmed its commitment to those obligations. It has signed the convention establishing the new International Criminal Court and in early 2003 it ratified the Convention on the Elimination of Discrimination Against Women (CEDAW). One of Afghanistan's great human rights challenges is coming to terms with the past. But the long shadow of impunity for massacres and past human rights violations could fall across the new state. More than two decades of conflict and chaos amount to a grim record of massacres, rapes, abductions of women and children and destruction of property. A national accountability policy must be formulated and it must be reflected in the new constitutive order. This will be delicate so long as perpetrators of past offences remain in positions of authority.

Dr Komal Hossain, the UN Special Rapporteur on Afghanistan in 2003, declared to the UN Human Rights Commission: "The tragic events of 11 September in an extraordinary way set in motion events presenting once again an opportunity for change. This opportunity has created the Bonn framework for transition. The international community cannot fail this time to fulfil its responsibility. It cannot once again let down the Afghans." Afghanistan is still real estate trying to become a nation state and human rights are at the core of the process. If the country slips towards the chaos of insecurity, many may yearn for the return of Taliban-style law and order – and that would be a disaster for human rights.

Charles Norchi *is an international lawyer and professor who has worked in Afghanistan as a journalist and human rights advocate since 1981.*

Exile for a cause: the plight of refugees

By Peter Marsden

Over the past quarter of a century, Afghanistan has produced one of the largest refugee movements since the end of World War II, sending over five million refugees to the neighbouring countries of Pakistan and Iran as well as to Europe, North America and India. The first Afghans began fleeing communist repression within weeks of the 1978 coup d'etat by the Khalq ('Masses') faction of the People's Democratic Party of Afghanistan (PDPA), the overwhelming majority heading for Pakistan's North West Frontier Province. By the time of the December 1979 Soviet invasion, some 400,000 had crossed the border into Pakistan and another 200,000 into Iran. The exodus quickly became a flood; an estimated 1.9 million had fled by the end of the first year of the occupation, constituting the largest single group of refugees in the world.

By the early 1980s, Soviet counter-insurgency methods were leading to what many observers at the time saw as a deliberate form of "migratory genocide." From 1985 to 1990, according to estimates of the United Nations High Commissioner for Refugees (UNHCR), a staggering 6.2 million Afghans – including children born in exile – were living in Pakistan and Iran alone: just under half the world's refugee population. When the pro-communist regime of President Najibullah fell in 1992, millions of refugees flooded back, believing that the *jihad* was finally over. But the flood soon slowed to a trickle during the mid-1990s, as civil war tore Afghanistan apart once more. By the end of 1997, 2.7 million refugees remained in Pakistan, Iran and other regional countries. This number crept up in response to ongoing drought and conflict to the point where, by the beginning of 2001, both Pakistan and Iran were claiming to have two million refugees each – still the single largest refugee caseload in the world.

In the year following the fall of the Taliban regime in late 2001, between 1.5-1.8 million Afghan refugees returned home – mainly from Pakistan, whose police forces began harassing and evicting refugees from border camps. Refugees were also spurred on to return by media reports that the international community was bringing peace and a massive reconstruction programme. Despite the evidence that this mass return was a consequence of media-induced optimism and police harassment in both Pakistan and Iran, the international community has consistently presented the return as a vote of confidence in the new Afghan government and as a key indicator to present the US-led military intervention and the Bonn Agreement as a success. The reality, however, is that many have returned to find their homes destroyed, their property ownership in dispute and no means of earning a living off the land, after losing vital agricultural skills during decades in exile. An independent report on Afghan repatriation in 2002 concluded: "many returnees found themselves in a worse position after their return than before."

The rate of return during the first half of 2003 was very much less than the corresponding period in 2002. UNHCR surveys indicate that many refugees fear they will not find housing or jobs, while continuing unrest in Afghanistan is seen as another key deterrent.

The origins of the refugee situation in Afghanistan can be traced as far back as the early part of the 20th Century when King Amanullah, who ruled from 1919-1929, attempted to introduce a process of reform aimed at improving the position of women and girls. He failed, however, to consult with and involve the traditional tribal and religious leadership of the country. He also failed to ensure the necessary military support to secure a degree of compliance. His reforms were barely introduced before he met with armed opposition and had to abdicate. Amanullah's successors immediately cancelled his reforms and adopted a more conservative approach, taking their lead from the religious establishment of *ulama* and *mullahs.*

It was not until the 1950s that the reform movement resurrected itself under Prime Minister Mohammed Daoud. Backed by the Soviets, Daoud strengthened his government's armed forces, while at the same time he engaged in debate with the religious leaders. As a result, he was able to secure certain concessions through a combination of force and persuasion before falling from office in 1963. Nevertheless, his efforts culminated in the 1964 Constitution which was agreed by a large assembly, representing all parts of Afghanistan and, among other provisions, accorded legal equality to both women and men.

The reform process proceeded steadily during the 1960s and 1970s within a climate of growing political ferment and radicalism, inspired by student movements elsewhere in the world. Two particular movements emerged: one, socialist, looked to Moscow for guidance; the other, radical Islamist, drew on the thinking of the Muslim Brotherhood and of Islamic thinkers from the Indian subcontinent.

When Daoud ousted King Zahir Shah in 1973, and proclaimed himself President, he initially sought the backing of the socialist movement, which had formed the PDPA. He also leaned heavily on Moscow and encouraged an accelerated process of Soviet political, economic and military engagement in Afghanistan. Tensions, however, soon arose between Daoud and the PDPA over the pace of reform and his attempts to suppress the movement finally resulted in the April 1978 Saur Revolution.

The communist PDPA was quick to impose land reforms and to introduce a female literacy programme but used excessive force in the process. They demonstrated an arrogant and gross insensitivity to societal religious and cultural norms. There was an immediate backlash from all sections of rural society, with very clear echoes of the response to Amanullah's reforms.

But this time, the level of armed conflict was considerably more acute. The communists brutally put down the wave of armed insurrections which manifested themselves throughout the country, provoking a call for holy war or *jihad*. The existence of the *jihad* justified not only the taking up of arms against the PDPA but also a process of migration, on the religious grounds that the believers had been wronged. This followed the example of a migration which Mohammed and his followers had undertaken.

The military actions of the PDPA provoked an early exodus of refugees in 1978 and 1979 to the neighbouring Islamic countries of Iran and Pakistan, which regarded it as their Islamic duty to provide hospitality to those seeking exile. They also provided active support to the *jihad* by supplying arms to men of fighting age and by facilitating their regular transit across borders to engage in attacks on communist forces. The radical Islamist parties, which had emerged in Kabul in the 1960s, were quick to capitalize on the Islamic dimension to the conflict and assumed an increasingly leading role from bases in Pakistan and Iran.

This situation fed into the paranoia of the Soviet Union over the possibility of encirclement along its southern borders. The Islamic Revolution in Iran of 1978 had deprived the United States of a strategically important base in the region. Moscow may have speculated that the armed uprising could be exploited by the US to establish a military presence in Afghanistan. This and other factors led to a chain of events which culminated in the Soviet invasion of Afghanistan in December 1979. Both the invasion and the repression inflicted by the Red Army and Afghan government forces provoked the population further, resulting in a rapid intensification of the conflict. Growing numbers sought exile in Pakistan and Iran, to the point where by the mid-1980s, Pakistan accommodated 3.3 million refugees and Iran 2.9 million.

Some Afghans attempted to remain in their villages but found it increasingly difficult to withstand the bombardment and armed entry into their homes by Soviet forces. It was common for families to flee to the mountains, where they would reduce their food intake to the absolute minimum in order to survive, while the men returned to fight as *mujahideen* and to keep the land under cultivation as best they could. Some villages fared worse than others. Within the same district, certain areas of strategic importance would be reduced to rubble while others were barely touched and life could continue with a degree of normality.

Only a small handful of primarily French and British humanitarian organizations provided a trickle of clandestine crossborder assistance during the early 1980s to civilians seeking to survive inside Afghanistan. The overwhelming majority of aid organizations and donors preferred to offer so-called 'official' assistance to refugees only, mainly in Pakistan. United Nations agencies, for example, refused to become involved in any form of crossborder relief. According to some observers, this lack of international assistance to help civilians withstand the impact of war inside Afghanistan actually contributed to the refugee exodus as many people had little option but to leave.

When the Soviet Union announced its decision to withdraw its forces by February 1989, much of the international community expected the Soviet-backed regime of President Najibullah to fall almost immediately. They also anticipated, not unreasonably, that this would result in the immediate return of the six million refugees in Pakistan and Iran, with the ending of the *jihad*. The UN geared itself up for a massive relief operation in support of the returnees.

However, the government did not fall until three years later, when the Soviet Union itself collapsed and the flow of arms and other resources supplied by Moscow came to an end. In the meantime, the UN, working closely with NGOs, sought to prepare the ground for the eventual return of refugees through programmes aimed to rehabilitate the agricultural base of Afghanistan. This resulted in a trickle of refugees, mostly men, returning to their villages from Pakistan for the summer to rebuild their homes and get the land working again before wintering in the refugee camps. Meanwhile, the families who had spent the war in the mountains of Afghanistan returned home as soon as the Soviet troops left. They started the process of reconstruction long before the aid agencies arrived to offer assistance. At this stage, however, there was no return from Iran.

When the Soviet-backed government was replaced by the *mujahed*-led Islamic State of Afghanistan in April 1992, the *jihad* was finally over. The summer of 1992 saw a return of refugees from the North West Frontier Province of Pakistan on a massive scale, tempered only by the gradual realization that disunity within the *mujahideen* was going to result in further conflict.

The ending of the *jihad* was a trigger for Iranian authorities to put pressure on refugees to go home, particularly those who had fled from the villages of Farah province to the desert camps on the other side of the frontier. In summer 1992, Iran began bulldozing these camps and by December the government had agreed a repatriation programme with UNHCR aimed at returning all its 2.9 million refugees by the end of 1995. The stability created in Herat by the rule of the *mujahed* leader Ismail Khan encouraged people to return. By the end of 1993, much of Herat's exiled population had come home. Those who remained in the desert camps had little choice but to return when their temporary homes were destroyed.

Continuing conflict, however, inhibited further return from Iran in 1994 and 1995. The capture by the Taliban of the whole of western Afghanistan in September 1995 brought the return process to a halt. Efforts by UNHCR to assist refugees from northern Afghanistan to return via Turkmenistan met with a total lack of interest. Refugees from the north indicated that the chronic level of insecurity across the northern and central provinces represented a major deterrent to their return. Instead, people started to go back to Iran in their thousands to escape the restrictions imposed by the Taliban and the deteriorating economic situation following the takeover.

There was also a substantial flow of migrant workers from 1993 onwards, as younger members of returnee families left Afghanistan to look for work in Iran, while their elders continued the long process of reconstruction. A significant population growth among Afghans brought on by improved healthcare in Iran made it difficult to achieve self-sufficiency in spite of substantial progress in restoring the agricultural base in western Afghanistan, as in many other parts of the country.

The advent of the Taliban in 1994 had a positive effect, however, on the return of refugees to Kandahar and the Pashtun belt of southern Afghanistan. Prior to the capture of Kandahar in October 1994, the city and surrounding

Thorkell Thorkelsson/International Federation

region had been subject to chronic instability. The Taliban brought absolute security to a wide area. People started returning in large numbers to revitalise the urban economy and work on the land. However, the initial failure of the Taliban to take Kabul in 1995-1996 led to fears that the Islamic movement might not be able to maintain their hold. As a result, the return process became more cautious.

Meanwhile, in September 1995, aid agency rations and free services for the refugees living in Pakistani camps were finally curtailed. When the refugees had first arrived towards the end of the 1970s, they had been accommodated in camps along the length of the border and provided with tents, various food items, kerosene and kitchen equipment. They had quickly built their own mud homes and compounds, with or without assistance, and had gradually found work to supplement their rations. Schools, clinics and water supply systems were established in the camps. Over time, the rations were reduced to the point where only wheat and kerosene were provided. The ending of free rations in 1995 coincided with a decision to require refugees to contribute towards the costs of water, education and health services.

The decision to wind down and then end the rations and free services was based on the premise that the refugees were in a position to be self-sufficient, at least at the level of the poorest among the population of Pakistan. The UN sought to minimize hardship for disadvantaged groups by providing an allocation of cooking oil for women attending clinics and children attending school. But a December 1996 study of refugee camps near Peshawar indicated that a significant proportion of the population were living at a very marginal level. Many had to look for work on a daily basis and some would go for long periods without finding work. The allocation of free cooking oil did not appear to prevent large numbers of refugees from being dependent on the charity of their neighbours.

In spite of the difficulties that refugees in Pakistan faced in their daily efforts to survive, the pace of return remained very low over the following years (around 100,000 per year until 1999). It was not until the Taliban capture of Taloqan, in September 2000, that there was a significant change in the underlying patterns. This new Taliban conquest provoked large-scale displacement from the province of Takhar. Around 170,000 people fled into Pakistan, while many more remain displaced within north-eastern Afghanistan. The Pakistan government housed the initial outflow in existing refugee camps but took a harder line with non-Pashtun refugees (Pashtuns formed the majority of the Afghan refugee population in Pakistan). These were housed in a makeshift camp on the edge of the major refugee settlement of Jalozai near Peshawar.

International journalists visited in droves to witness the full horror of people living under plastic bin liners. Neither the UN's World Food Programme (WFP) nor UNHCR were able to provide aid for this group in the face of Pakistan's refusal to permit registration. Finally the government agreed to register the refugees if they were relocated to new camps in the tribal territories, away from urban centres where they could secure employment.

From early 2001 onwards, Pakistan's previous hospitality towards Afghan refugees began to ebb away, reflecting growing public opposition to the Afghan presence and changes in key personnel within the Pakistan government. Pakistan's response to the Jalozai influx in late 2000 was an early manifestation of a clear change of policy, both to encourage refugees to return and to discourage any further arrivals of Afghans into Pakistan. Afghan refugees were increasingly harrassed by the Pakistan police and some young Afghan men were arbitrarily picked up by the Pakistan authorities and deported to Afghanistan. The closure of a major camp at Nasir Bagh, near Peshawar, sent an important signal that now was the time to think of returning.

In the wake of the 11 September attacks, UNHCR persuaded Pakistan to accept Afghan refugees fleeing any US-led military action against the Taliban. However, UNHCR found the new camps designated by the authorities to be problematic because of security and other concerns. So when the US-led invasion started on 7 October 2001, UNHCR was unprepared. Fortunately, the scale of the outflow was very much less than had been planned for, in part because of pressure on Pakistan from the US government to police the border and prevent the Taliban and other radical elements from fleeing.

UNHCR coped, at least in the short term, by establishing temporary 'holding' camps just inside the Pakistan border at Chaman. However, Pakistan then called a halt to any further influx, following agreement with the Afghan government and UNHCR to embark on a repatriation programme with effect from 1 March 2002. The 40,000 people left in the holding camp then became a potentially

Afghan refugees become political pawns

Nearly six million Afghans fled the fighting of the 1980s and 1990s and sought sanctuary in Iran, Pakistan and further afield. But since the US bombed the Taliban out of power in late 2001, Afghan refugees have come under increasing pressure from the countries hosting them to return home. During 2002-03, Afghans applying for refugee status in Western countries were routinely refused asylum. And refugees in Pakistan's camps were threatened with eviction and camp closure to force them back over the border.

Media publicity about the reconstruction of Afghanistan encouraged many refugees to return home. President Bush spoke of a 'Marshall plan' to rebuild the country, and donors queued up to pledge US$ 4.5 billion in aid. During 2002, around 1.8 million refugees returned, way in excess of estimates. When asked why, one returnee in the Shomali Plain replied simply: "the whole world told us they were rebuilding Afghanistan".

Yet for most who return, there are few prospects for making a living – except by growing opium poppies. After years of living in an urban refugee environment, their farming skills are rusty. The country remains devastated by war and drought. Landmines will take a decade to clear. Shattered infrastructure lies waiting to be rebuilt. Warlords control large swathes of territory – insecurity for most Afghans is worse than under the Taliban.

According to a report commissioned by the Kabul-based Afghanistan Research and Evaluation Unit, the mass repatriation was driven by political pressures. While the US and its allies – including the new Afghan government – were keen to show the benefits of their campaign to oust the Taliban, the Pakistan and Iranian authorities seized the chance to offload two decades worth of refugees. But this was in the interests neither of those returning nor of Afghanistan's long-term recovery. "Many returnees found themselves in a worse position after their return than before", says the report, while "the scale and speed of the return helped to divert yet more of the limited funds available for reconstruction into emergency assistance."

Rehm-u-din's story is typical. His family of 10 have lived in Pakistan's Katcha Garhi camp since 1981. In March 2003, he was served an eviction notice. "It is not the time", he said. "When I left Afghanistan, we were five brothers and my father owned a small piece of land. Now I have two sons who are married, and five daughters. I do not have a house or job to go back to. The land is under dispute. My sons do not know anything about farming." It's not that he doesn't want to return. "My country is heaven to me. I will definitely go back," he says. "But I am waiting till I am sure that we will not die of hunger at home."

A longer version of this box appeared in the World Disasters Report 2003

permanent population, along with a similar number camped in Spin Boldak just across the border inside Afghanistan. These two populations comprised mainly *kuchi* nomads, affected by the drought, and Pashtuns fleeing persecution for being ethnically associated with the Taliban. In August 2002, UNHCR established new camps for these unfortunate people in the desert to the west of Kandahar. But relocation proved very unpopular because of the area's barrenness and lack of job opportunities.

Further police harassment put considerable pressure on Afghans living in Pakistan's urban areas to take advantage of the repatriation programme initiated in March 2002. This programme provided returnees with wheat, cash, household utensils and, for some, building materials. By the end of September 2002, around 1.5 million refugees had returned – partly because of the repatriation programme and partly because the media coverage of January 2002's donor conference in Tokyo created high expectations of international investment and well-paid jobs. A high proportion of returnees settled in Nangarhar province, which had recovered reasonably well from the drought of 1999-2001. An estimated 400,000 returnees travelled to Kabul where, UNHCR reported, they had no choice but to live in destitute conditions in ruined houses because rents had soared with the arrival of international organizations. There were indications that many of those who had returned to claim the assistance package might have slipped back into Pakistan to continue their lives there, in spite of difficulties with the Pakistan authorities.

Far fewer refugees returned from Iran during 2002. A repatriation agreement drawn up between Iran, Afghanistan and UNHCR in April 2002 had, by the end of September 2002, resulted in the return of 270,000 refugees. Although the Iranian authorities employed a sustained media campaign to put considerable pressure on Afghan refugees to return, police action has been primarily targeted at those without documentation. The low rate of return from Iran relative to Pakistan reflects two factors. For those refugees planning on returning to farm, agricultural conditions in eastern Afghanistan, bordering Pakistan, were far better than in Afghan provinces bordering Iran. Secondly, the porous border with Pakistan enabled refugees to return home but keep their options open to re-enter Pakistan illegally in search of work. Those leaving Iran faced far greater difficulty in seeking to re-enter Iran illegally.

When refugees originally fled to Iran, most were sent to live in major cities, particularly Mashad, where they were expected to find their own housing and gain employment within designated menial occupations. However, they were given access to free medical and education services, plus entitlements to generous subsidies on basic food and other items available to the Iranian population. Some refugee camps were established along the desert border with Afghanistan and supported by the Iranian government as bases for insurgency operations against the Soviets.

Once the repatriation programme started in 1992, the Iranian government began to place restrictions on the Afghan population, particularly in relation to their right to operate businesses and to work in certain occupations. A worsening economic situation forced Iran to reduce subsidies and to demand contributions from the refugees towards the costs of education and health services. The economically marginal position of many Afghans led to acute suffering. Those who fled in the mid-1990s in response to the Taliban occupation, flooding in central and south-western Afghanistan and the fighting in Kabul, had to survive without access to subsidies or services and without the limited protection which refugee documentation accords. A study undertaken in July 1996 of refugees in Mashad and Tehran revealed a highly marginal level of existence, much as in Pakistan, in which intermittent daily labouring was the principle source of income. From 1995 onwards, the Iranian authorities took steps to reduce the Afghan population of Mashad, through a combination of deportations and spontaneous returns. But the pace of return from 1997-2001 was extremely slow, due to tensions between the (Shi'a) Iranian government and the (Sunni) Taliban.

The experience of exile has markedly changed attitudes within the population. Women have been compelled by circumstances to take on an economic role, even though this may not have been part of their lives prior to exile. In the cities of Iran, women have often had to fend for themselves without family support in a difficult and sometimes hostile urban environment, making them more assertive and independent. Many of them have had to engage in tailoring, embroidery and other forms of piecework at a fraction of the very low rates of pay which men receive. In the refugee camps of Pakistan, women have found themselves subject to greater restrictions on their mobility than had been the norm in their villages.

The presence of aid agencies among Afghan refugee populations in both Iran and Pakistan has led to female education and preventive health care becoming more highly valued. One consequence of this has been that refugee children are now more likely to survive infancy – further increasing the population in exile. The value placed by returning refugees on healthcare and education may lead them to expect more in the way of public services once back in their home communities.

In addition to the millions of refugees who have fled across international borders, conflict and drought during the 1990s displaced over one million Afghans within their own country. As the conflict shifted from a rural-based *jihad* against the Soviets to the more urban-based civil war of the 1990s, so huge numbers of city-dwellers were forced to flee. Some were allowed across international borders as refugees, but hundreds of thousands ended up as "internally-displaced persons" (IDPs). Since they do not qualify as refugees, many have had to fend for themselves while some have become the responsibility of the ICRC, UNHCR and other aid agencies.

The first major movement of IDPs was to Mazar-e-Sharif, following the rocketing of Kabul in August 1992. The rockets which rained on the capital in January 1994 drove many more Kabulis from their homes. When Pakistan closed its borders, they had to be accommodated in two enormous IDP camps near Jalalabad. From January 1997 onwards, the Taliban capture and scorching of the Shomali plains north of Kabul forced whole villages to flee. Some fled to the Panjshair Valley while around 200,000 sought refuge in the slums of Kabul itself. From 1999-2001, the worst drought in living memory forced hundreds of thousands of Afghans in northern provinces to flee their land and seek refuge in Herat and Mazar-e-Sharif or in IDP camps outside the cities. Enormous numbers of *kuchi* nomads – whose flocks and grazing lands were decimated by drought – descended on Kandahar. Meanwhile, many victims of the Taliban's capture of Taloqan in 2000 had nowhere to flee when Pakistan closed its borders. Some 9,000 of them set up camp on islands along the river bordering Tajikistan. By 2000-01, around one million Afghans were displaced within their own country.

The US's military action against Afghanistan in late 2001 made access to drought-affected areas almost impossible for humanitarian agencies. As a result, even more Afghans – desperate for food and water – flooded into IDP camps in Herat and Mazar. The numbers in Maslakh camp near Herat swelled to over 100,000. At the same time, people fled to the countryside as cities such as Kandahar and Jalalabad sustained heavy bombing. The collapse of Taliban power in the north led to reprisals against Pashtuns and forced many to flee, even though their descendants had lived in the region for over a century.

As access for humanitarian agencies to drought-affected areas eased after December 2001, migration slowed down and the summer of 2002 saw people returning to their villages in large numbers, particularly from Maslakh camp. Those who left Kandahar and Jalalabad have also largely returned, as have those stranded on islands on the Tajik border. However, the Pashtun settlers who fled from the north have found that not only is Pakistan unwilling to receive them, but fellow Pashtuns in the south of Afghanistan are also unwilling to offer hospitality. Throughout 2003, Pashtuns were continuing to arrive in southern Afghanistan to escape harassment and insecurity in the north – swelling the IDP population of the south to 350,000. UNHCR has had to take responsibility for this population in the absence of any other governmental or non-governmental organizations willing to accept this mandate.

Peter Marsden *is Information Coordinator for the British Agencies Afghanistan Group, based at the Refugee Council in London.*

The ethnic and tribal composition of Afghan society

By Ali Wardak

Afghanistan is a mosaic of different ethnic and tribal groups, most of whom have lived together for centuries. These include Pashtun, Tajik, Hazara, Uzbek, Turkmen, Aimaq, Baluch, Brahui, Nuristani, Pashai, Pamiri, Kirghiz, Qizilbash, Mongols (also referred to as Moghuls), Arabs, Gujars, Kohistanis, Wakhis and Jats. In addition, a large population of nomads and small numbers of Hindus, Sikhs and Jews also live in Afghanistan. These ethno-linguistic groups are referred to as *qawm* (tribe, people), *wolas* (tribe, people) or *taifa* (ethno-linguistic group, tribe). Group members are generally distinguishable by their distinct language or accent, ethnic origin, and sometimes by their specific cultural and religious practices and physical features. Some groups form the majority in specific regions – for example, the Pashtuns to the south and east, the Tajiks and Uzbeks to the north and the Hazaras in central Afghanistan. Linguistic, cultural and geographical characteristics all play an important role in forming the ethnic/tribal identities of Afghan people.

However, the opportunities offered by trade, employment, universities and government or military service have pulled generations of Afghans from different ethnic/tribal backgrounds into urban areas to live and work side by side. Inter-marriages and shared religious and social activities have further strengthened the multi-cultural Afghan identity at the expense of ethnic/tribal affiliations, at least in urban centres. Many people from different ethnic backgrounds see themselves first as Afghans and only second as, for example, Pashtuns, Tajiks, Hazaras or Uzbeks. In Kabul, Herat and other urban centres, where intermarriages among members of different ethic/tribal groups are common, tribal identities have been absorbed by new 'metropolitan' identities such as *Kabuli* and *Herati*.

As there has never been a systematic and complete census in Afghanistan, little reliable data exist regarding the total population and its various ethno-linguistic groups. This is one reason why the subject has become highly controversial and politicized in recent years – in particular among the various Afghan factional groups and warlords who have exploited ethnicity and religion for their own political and economic gains. After nearly a quarter century of war, the Bonn Agreement of December 2001 authorised the Afghan Transitional Administration (ATA) and the United Nations Population Fund (UNFPA) to conduct the first systematic national census in time for the national elections in 2004. However, as the ATA is presently dominated by warlords associated with one faction, the UN authorities along with many Afghans fear that the census may be influenced by those with guns, money and political power – as happened during the 2001 emergency *Loya Jirga*. Therefore a preliminary 'pre-census household listing' has been planned, to count every household and collect basic information about the number of residents and their age and gender. The issues of ethnic/tribal affiliation – plus more detailed data on occupation, household income and education – will be left to a more complete census to be conducted in 2005. The collection and compilation of this data is likely to take a few years.

To understand Afghanistan's ethno-linguistic make-up, it is crucial to look at the geographic distribution of its various tribal groups. While the map below indicates the locations of these groups, it does not reveal the more complex picture of inter-tribal mixing and coexistence in many urban centres. The description which follows is organized according to the relative size of each ethnic/tribal group, starting with Pashtuns, the largest such group in Afghanistan.

Pashtun

The majority of Afghan Pashtuns have traditionally lived in the south and east of Afghanistan. Large communities of Pashtuns have also settled in the north and west of the country, and several hundred thousand live a fully nomadic life. However, after the collapse of the Taliban regime in late 2001, Pashtuns – particularly in the north – became the victims of targeted violence, murder, extortion and looting at the hands of warlords associated with the United Front (also known as the Northern Alliance). This forced tens of thousands of Pashtuns to flee to the south in search of safety – often ending up in rudimentary camps for displaced people.

Tribal Pashtuns constitute the largest ethnic group in Afghanistan. Estimates from the 1960s and 1970s (when the total Afghan population was around 13-14 million) suggested that settled Pashtuns constituted roughly half of the country's population. According to a 1981 projection by the former-USSR's Academy of Sciences, based on the Afghan government's incomplete 1979 census, Pashtuns formed 55 percent of Afghanistan's settled – as opposed to nomadic – population. Working on these figures, American anthropologist Louis Dupree estimated the Pashtun population at 6.5 million in 1980, while British writer Anthony Hyman put the figure at seven million two years later. However figures from the 1990s vary more widely. According to T. Eighmy's 1990 report on the subject, Pashtuns form just 38 percent of the Afghan population – a figure reflected in the CIA Factbook of 2002. Meanwhile, the Wak Foundation put the total number of settled Pashtuns in Afghanistan at 63 percent in 1998. In the same year, the experienced German Afghanologist, B. Glatzner, concluded: "Pashtuns are estimated to account for between 40 percent and 60 percent of Afghan nationals."

Around 12 million Pashtuns live across the border in Pakistan, mainly in the North West Frontier Province. Also known as 'Pathans', they were artificially

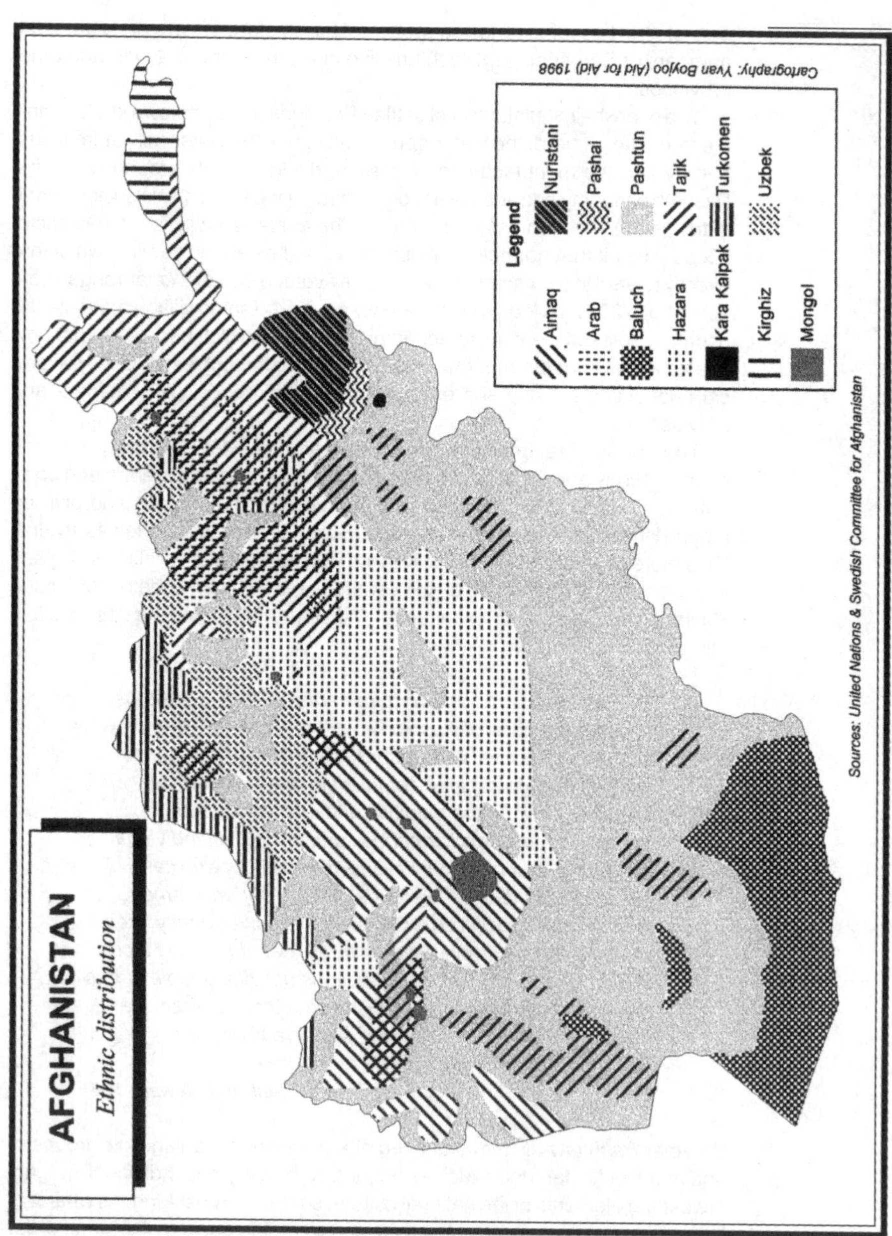

cut off from their Afghan cousins by the 'Durand Line', drawn up by the British in 1893 to mark the Afghan border but never recognized by successive Afghan governments. Afghanistan's Pashtuns are generally divided into *Durrani* and *Ghilzai* branches, with further sub-branches whose names are often suffixed with *zai* or *khil*. Pashtuns are mostly *Sunni* Muslims and speak *Pashto* –

one of the two official languages of Afghanistan. However, significant numbers of Dari-speaking Pashtuns live in Kabul, Herat, Parwan and other provinces.

The overwhelming majority of settled Pashtuns are farmers. And it is mainly the farm, the orchard, the water-spring and canal, the water-mill, animal husbandry and the manufacturing of basic agricultural tools around which the Pashtun economy and society are organized. At the heart of this social organization is the Pashtun *kalay*, or village. The average *kalay* is a small socio-economic unit that normally consists of several extended families which are directly related to a common ancestor. The average size of a *kalay* ranges from about 50 to 200 individuals who normally attend the same village mosque. It is usually a self-sufficient socio-economic unit within which people are not only related to one another through blood ties, but also through established reciprocal relationships. They share agricultural tools, goods, gifts, favours and services.

The norms of reciprocity are governed at a local level by *trabgani* – the code of behaviour within which members of each *kalay* cooperate and compete with one another. *Trabgani* is a source of both cohesion and division among kin in different circumstances, but should not be interpreted as 'rivalry'. On a more general level, reciprocity in the Pashtun *kalay* and individual behaviour in society are governed by the centuries-old Pashtun code of behaviour, *Pashtunwali*. One pair of experienced Western Afghanologists describe it in this way:

> *"In addition to the basic requirements of Islam, Pashtuns observe the code of Pashtunwali. It is simple but demanding. Group survival is its primary imperative. It demands vengeance against injury or insult to one's kin, chivalry and hospitality toward the helpless and unarmed strangers, bravery in battle, and openness and integrity in individual behaviour. Much honour is given to Pashtuns who can successfully arbitrate the feuds that are endemic among them. Fines and blood money are devices frequently used to limit violence among rival families. Pashtunwali is a code that limits anarchy among a fractious but vital people. It has influenced other groups within the country who must deal with similar environmental and social realities"*
>
> *Newell and Newell, 1981*

Whether *Pashtunwali* has influenced other Afghan ethno-linguistic groups or not, many of its demands such as hospitality, bravery and individual integrity are central elements of the national culture, shared by most Afghans whatever their ethnic background. Such values constitute the basis of the moral order and of (informal) social control in Afghan villages and tribes, which have historically resisted the penetration of successive governmental mechanisms of (formal) social control.

Pashtuns have contributed significantly to Afghan culture and society. They have historically resisted the attempts of foreign military powers to subjugate them. For two centuries, from Ahmed Shah Durrani in 1747 to President Daoud who was overthrown in 1978, Pashtuns ruled Afghanistan as *Amirs* and Kings. Alongside other Afghan tribes, many Pashtuns fought with considerable success against Soviet forces in the 1980s. According to some observers, however, clan loyalties prevented resistance fighters from adopting more effective regional tactics against the Soviets, with some Pashtun groups preferring to operate in a more localized (and limited) manner. Nevertheless, leading Pashtun commanders such as Abdul Haq of the Hezb-e-Islami's Younis Khalis faction managed to overcome such parochialism by organizing highly mobile guerrilla groups operating inside Kabul itself as well as throughout the eastern region.

Other key Pashtun personalities, past and present, include: Mir Wais Hotak, Nazo Ana, Malalai, Sayed Jamaloddin Afghani, Mahmud Tarzi, Mohammad Zahir Shah, Gulbuddin Hekmatyar, Mullah Mohammad Omar and Hamid Karzai.

Tajik

Afghan Tajiks are predominantly settled in the north and northeast of Afghanistan. Estimates from the 1970s – reflected in the work of Dupree and Hyman – suggested that the total number of Tajiks in Afghanistan was around 3.5 million (approximately 25 percent of the population in the 1970s). The Soviet Academy of Sciences' 1981 projection put the figure at 19 percent. More recently, Tajiks have been reported as forming anything from 12 percent (Wak Foundation, 1998) to 25 percent (Eighmy 1990; CIA Factbook, 2002) of the Afghan population. It is important to mention that the estimated 600,000 Persian-speaking inhabitants (*Farsiwan*) of the western city of Herat and its surrounding areas are sometimes incorrectly referred to as Tajiks. A much larger number of Tajiks (around six million) live in neighbouring Tajikistan. Afghan Tajiks are predominantly *Sunni* Muslims and speak *Dari* (Afghan Persian) – one of the two official languages of Afghanistan.

Working mainly as farmers in fertile mountainous valleys and foothills, the social organization of the Tajik economy and society resembles that of the settled Pashtuns of Afghanistan: the largely kinship-based Tajik *deh* (village), the basic unit of collective action, is socially organized around the agricultural farm, vineyard, orchard, water-mill, canal/spring, and the processing of agricultural products. Within the *deh*, Tajik villagers are not only tied to one other through kinship relationships, but also through the institutionalized reciprocity which their agricultural economy requires. They exchange favours, services, gifts, agricultural products and tools, which create strong mutual obligations among donors and recipients.

The rules of reciprocity are spelled out by *abdurzadagi* – the established code of behaviour which guides members of the village-based kin-group on whom to cooperate with, whom to compete with, whom to marry, and – in short – how to live as an individual in the community. The moral and social values associated with *abdurzadagi* often coexist in a symbiotic relationship with religious values expressed in the village mosque, itself an important part of the moral and social order of the *deh*.

Tajik inhabitants of valleys and villages often trace their roots to one or more common ancestor(s). However, unlike the Pashtuns, they refer to themselves by their regional name (e.g. *Panjshairi*, *Ghorbandi*) rather than an ancestral name. Social boundaries are not very rigidly drawn – whoever lives in the region may assume its regional identity. Some scholars categorize this form of social formation as 'peasantized' rather than 'tribalized'.

Despite the fact that Tajiks are mainly farmers, many migrated to and settled in urban areas during the 1950s-70s, particularly in Kabul. They benefited from modern educational and technical facilities and achieved very high standards of educational and professional qualification. Many educated Tajiks occupied high-ranking positions in government and played a very important role in running the bureaucratic machinery of successive administrations. As one writer put it:

> *"Because they [Afghan Tajiks] make up the bulk of the educated elite and possess considerable wealth in Kabul and Herat, they have significant political influence. Their influence lies predominantly in the government ministries, public services, and trade bodies."*
>
> *Javad, 1992*

The development of modern Afghanistan's economic, cultural and educational institutions prior to the Soviet invasion owed much to the dedication of many talented Tajiks, and their contribution to Afghan culture and society has been tremendous. Moreover, Tajiks contributed very significantly to the Afghan resistance movement against the Soviet invading forces. Some of Afghanistan's best-known and most effective guerrilla commanders, such as Ahmed Shah Massoud, were Tajik. Other key past and present Tajik personalities include: Abdullah Ansari, Rabi'a Balkhi, Habibullah Kalakani (known as Bacha-e-Saqao), Burhannudin Rabbani, Mohammad Qasim Fahim.

Hazara

Hazaras live predominantly in the central mountainous region of Afghanistan known as Hazarajat. Until recently they constituted a significant part of the population of Kabul, but a large number have now settled permanently in the Pakistan city of Quetta. Estimates of Afghanistan's Hazara population from the early 1980s range from 800,000 (Dupree, 1980) to around 1.5 million (Hyman, 1982). The USSR's Academy of Sciences' 1981 projection calculated they formed eight percent of the Afghan population. However, Eighmy put this figure at 19 percent in 1990. Hazaras speak *Hazaragi*, which is a distinct dialect of *Dari*. As predominantly *Shi'a* Muslims, they are mostly followers of the *Ja'faria* ('Twelver') school. They are divided into various sub-tribes and large kinship-based social units and their names are usually prefixed by *Dai*, in the way that Pashtuns use the suffixes *khil* and *zai*.

As predominantly herders and farmers, the social and economic organization of the Hazara *qaria/deh* (village) is similar to that of the Tajik *deh*. It is usually a geographically bounded area that comprises a number of extended families with members of various villages tracing their common ancestral roots to a sub-tribe or clan. As among Pashtuns and Tajiks, clan leaders (*maliks, khans* and particularly *sayeds*) exercise a considerable amount of authority in Hazara society. Despite attempts by Hazara warlords to undermine *sayeds* (who are considered to be descendants of the Prophet and are usually religious scholars), they remain the centre of authority at the local level. In practice, the *sayed* is a preacher, teacher, spiritual leader and interpreter of religious laws and doctrines. Often based at the *takia khana* (*Shi'a* mosque), he also plays an important role in the resolution of disputes.

However, the social organization of the Hazara economy and society is also closely related to the consolidation of Afghanistan as a centralized state, which led to the forced subjugation of all the state's internal opponents. Amir Abdur Rahman Khan, who in 1880 became King of Afghanistan, was obsessed with the centralization of government power in an era of widespread anarchy, when local *khans, mirs, pirs* and *mullahs* controlled different parts of the country and continually fought with one another. To achieve this goal, the King used all possible means of repression. These included deportation of his *Ghilzai* Pashtun rivals to the remote areas of *Turkistan* (now the northern region of Afghanistan), inciting negative religious sentiments between *Sunnis* and *Shi'as*, and the brutal killing of all rivals.

During Abdur Rahman's two decades of tyrannical rule, Hazaras were the most severely affected. The government employed its predominantly *Sunni* subjects to forcibly repress the Hazaras' resistance to the King's emerging central government. This resulted in large-scale violence against the Hazaras, including looting of houses and the killing of numerous men and women. Furthermore the Hazaras were discriminated against as *Shi'as* (often having to perform the most menial jobs) and were largely excluded from the social, cultural and political life of wider Afghan society. This state of affairs gradually became institutionalized, while successive Afghan governments (with the exception of Amanullah Khan and Dr Najibullah) looked on. They did little or nothing to put an end to the discrimination and exclusion practised against this sizeable minority of Afghans.

Such discrimination has led to the gradual emergence of a communal Hazara consciousness of being a distinguishable cultural and religious community, supported by the hard work and social solidarity of its members. Many Hazaras in Kabul and other cities became successful entrepreneurs, businessmen and merchants. They also proved to be effective fighters, both against the communist PDPA regime as well as against the Soviets. According to outside observers who have travelled with Hazaras, their military and economic performance in recent years has almost certainly allowed them to rise up from their previous position as underdogs to adopt a strong identity of their own.

Those Hazaras living in the central mountainous region of Hazarajat, with its harsh weather and terrain, have steadfastly struggled against the cruelty of man and nature. They have mixed farming, herding and skilful crafting in wool, fur and wood to survive, self-sufficiently, in extreme climatic conditions. However, recent drought and blockades of Hazarajat by Taliban forces in the late 1990s created serious shortfalls in basic food commodities. Tens of thousands of Hazaras became increasingly reliant on the international aid community to avoid starvation during winter months. In Kabul, ethnic tensions with the Taliban – exacerbated after the May 1997 debacle in Mazar-e-Sharif – forced many Hazaras to flee the capital. Since the collapse of the Taliban regime in late 2001, many Hazaras have returned from exile to Kabul and to other parts of Afghanistan. Key past and present Hazara personalities include: Faiz Mohammad Katib, Sayed Ismail Balkhi, Sayed Husain Anwari and Abdul Karim Khalili.

Uzbek

Afghanistan's Uzbeks live in the northern plains of the country, separated from Uzbekistan by the Amu Darya (Oxus River) and cut off from much of Afghanistan by the high snow-topped Hindu Kush mountains. Only in the 1960s was this part of Afghanistan linked to the rest of the country through the building of the Salang tunnel. These fertile northern areas, also known as *Turkistan*, form a naturally-bounded homeland for the Afghan Uzbeks. Estimates from the early 1980s put the total number of Uzbeks between one million (Dupree, 1980) and 1.3 million (Hyman 1982). The Soviet Academy of Sciences' 1981 projection estimated that Uzbeks formed nine percent of the Afghan population, while in 1990, Eighmy put this figure at 6.3 percent. Far larger numbers of Uzbeks (approximately 23 million) live in neighbouring Uzbekistan. The Uzbeks of Afghanistan are *Sunni* Muslims and speak *Uzbeki*.

Similar to the Pashtuns, Afghanistan's Uzbeks mix farming with herding. The vast northern plains represent some of the most fertile farming land in the country and, with irrigation from the Amu Darya, are particularly suitable for growing rice and cotton. Cotton production, processing and trade used to be one of the main sources of national income, and played an important role in the economic development of the northern cities of Mazar-e-Sharif and Kunduz. In addition, the Uzbeks produced high quality *karakul* lamb fleeces and hand-woven rugs. The *karakul* wool was exported to Europe and soon became another important source of income, despite growing competition from countries such as Namibia.

Similarly, the rugs and carpets which were produced mainly by Uzbek (and Turkmen) women found a lucrative outlet in European markets, particularly Germany, Britain and the former USSR. Moreover, the production of gas, oil and fertilizer in northern Afghanistan created hundreds of jobs in the 1960s-70s. The economic resources of the north made its predominantly Uzbek population relatively self-sufficient and attracted labourers, traders and skilled professionals from all over the country.

The self-sufficiency of the Uzbeks, alongside the geographical remoteness from Kabul of their northern region, has traditionally played an important role in their limited interaction with central governments and national institutions. Although successive governments have been represented in northern provinces by governors, judges, magistrates and the military, the centre of Uzbek authority, economy and social organization has always been the *qishlaq* or Uzbek village. Similar to the Pashtun *kalay* and the Tajik and Hazara *deh,* the *qishlaq* is usually situated in a demarcated geographical area that comprises more than one extended family, the members of which have a common ancestor.

The organization of the *qishlaq* is unique and it provides the fundamental context for political and social action. It is the traditional structure of authority and its main figure is the *arbab* (landlord). Social relationships revolve around the ways that peasants in the *qishlaq* relate to the *arbab.* Members of the Uzbek *qishlaq* are generally peasants who work on the *arbab's* land. The former are not only economically dependent on the *arbab*, but also socially and politically dependent, since the *arbab* is usually an influential figure who has links with government institutions. The peasants thus need the *arbab's* help both in community matters and in dealing with officials. The social organization of the *qishlaq* and the *arbab* are in turn closely linked to the local mosque – an important agency of social control within the village.

The Uzbeks have contributed outstandingly to the Afghan economy, culture and society: their rugs, *karakul* goods, cotton and other agricultural products constituted the backbone of the economy particularly in the 1960s-70s. The majority of ordinary Uzbeks were active in fighting against the invading Soviet forces. They have also produced strong military and political personalities, including Abdul Rashid Dostum and Ne'amatullah Shahrani.

Turkmen and Aimaq

Afghan Turkmen share a close Turkic cultural and linguistic affinity with Afghan Uzbeks. They live in the northern and north-western provinces of the country which border Turkmenistan. Estimates from the early 1980s put the total number of Afghan Turkmen between 125,000 (Dupree, 1980) to 600,000 (Hyman 1982). The Soviet Academy of Sciences' 1981 projection estimated that Turkmen formed three percent of the Afghan population, while in 1990, Eighmy put this figure at 2.5 percent. Some 3.5 million Turkmen live in neighbouring Turkmenistan. Afghan Turkmen are *Sunni* Muslims and speak *Turkmeni* – a Turkic language which is closely related to *Uzbeki.*

The Turkmen are a semi-nomadic people who mix herding with farming. The raising of lambs for *karakul* fleece used to be a major source of income. *Karakul* pelts and the very fine rugs and *gelims*, which Turkmen women produced, represented some of the most important Afghan exports to Europe and the USA. Although Turkmen are more geographically mobile than Uzbeks, the social organization of both groups is very similar.

Afghan Aimaq are scattered throughout the northwest and central regions of the country. *Aimaq* means 'nomad' in Turkic, but the mobility and power of their chiefs was curtailed by Amir Abdur Rahman, who put them under the control of the Governor of Herat in the 1880s. Their total number was estimated to be around 800,000 in the early 1980s. Traditionally the Aimaq are herders and carpet weavers. Several thousand also live in Iran, where they are referred to as *Berberi.* Since the Aimaq in Afghanistan live in close proximity with other Afghan groups, notably the *Farsiwan* of Herat and the Turkmen, Uzbeks and Hazaras, they have generally adopted the culture of the group that is immediately their neighbour. Aimaq are predominantly *Sunni* Muslims and most speak *Dari.*

Baluch and Brahui

Divided, like the Kurds, between three countries – Pakistan, Iran and Afghanistan – the Baluch have a tradition of rebellion against central governments and harbour ambitions to create a separate state of Baluchistan. Since the mid-1970s some 2,500 Baluch guerrillas, fighting for autonomy in Pakistan, took refuge in southern Afghanistan. But their struggle for independence has seldom received international support and has faded after political repression by all three countries.

Afghan Baluch and Brahui live predominantly in the south-western provinces of Nimruz, Helmand and Kandahar. Their total number in Afghanistan was estimated at around 300,000 in the early 1980s. A larger number of Baluch inhabit Baluchistan, a province of Pakistan, and several thousand more live in Seistan province of Iran.

Although the majority of Baluch are semi-sedentary, some live as caravaneers and nomads. Their social and economic organization is not significantly different from other Afghan ethnic/tribal groups who survive on small-scale farming and herding. However, since the Baluch live on Afghanistan's porous borders with Pakistan and Iran, and can travel between the three countries without bothering about frontier regulations, some are involved in small-scale crossborder trade. Although Afghan Baluch speak their native *Baluchi* tongue, many also know *Dari* and/or *Pashto*. They are *Sunni* Muslims.

The Brahui, who live in the south-western region of Afghanistan, resemble the Baluch both culturally and in their general lifestyle. In fact, many Brahui consider themselves a subgroup of the Baluch. Some work as tenant foragers and herders for Pashtun or Baluch landlords. Although Brahui is the native language of this Afghan group, most of its members also speak either *Pashto* or *Baluchi*. They are *Sunni* Muslims.

Nuristani, Pashai, Pamiri and Kirghiz

The Nuristani, whose total number was estimated at 100,000 in the early 1980s, live in the mountains of eastern Afghanistan. They maintained their ancient paganism until 1896, when they were forcibly converted by the sword to Islam by Amir Abdur Rahman. With the change of religion, the name of their traditional homeland (Kafiristan – Land of the Infidels or non-believers) was changed to Nuristan (Land of Light – Islam). It is with this new cultural identity – Nuristani – that they now strongly identify, even creating their own government during the Soviet-Afghan war, including a foreign ministry to issue visas to visiting journalists and aid workers, and a finance ministry to tax passing caravans. On a local level, however, the Nuristani refer to themselves by the name of the valley or area in which they live.

Nuristan is located in the middle of the Hindu Kush mountain range, in the provinces of Kunar and Laghman. It occupies four valleys, each with its own distinct dialect – Kati, Waigali, Ashkun and Parsun. Due to the rugged topography of the region (Nuristan contains some of Afghanistan's few remaining forests) it has limited arable land. Terraced farming is mixed with goat-herding and forestry, but the economy is very much one of subsistence. As settled farmers/herders, the social organization of Nuristani society does not appear to be significantly different from most other Afghan ethnic/tribal groups, with one notable exception: women are considered of equal importance to men in the daily life and work of the community.

As with other groups, the extended family and clan networks constitute the basis of social order. Despite Islam, Nuristanis have retained various elements and institutions, including clandestine wine-making, from their ancient culture, which make them stand out as an unique Afghan social group. Traditionally they leave their dead exposed to the elements for a whole year before burying them and planting over the grave a carved wooden effigy, which the spirit of the deceased occupies. They normally wear their traditional clothes even outside Nuristan and speak a distinct language – *Nuristani*, containing elements of Indian, Greek, and Iranian tongues. Some Nuristanis also speak *Pashto*, while all are *Sunni* Muslims. They were the first tribal group to declare rebellion against the communist PDPA government in October 1978. Subsequently the area became an important transit base for *mujahideen* operations and has remained largely autonomous ever since.

Towards the eastern mountains of Nuristan lives another ethnic/tribal group, the Pashai. While their social and economic organization is very similar to that of the Nuristanis, they speak their own language – *Pashai.* Due to their proximity to the Pashtuns in Kunar province, most Pashai also speak *Pashto.* They are *Sunni* Muslims.

Further to the north of Nuristan live two relatively small ethnic/tribal groups – the Pamiri and the Kirghiz. While the Pamiri are generally settled farmers and herders in and around Badakhshan province, the Kirghiz are a largely nomadic people who live in huts very close to the Chinese border. The total number of each group is estimated to be several thousand. However, hundreds of Kirghiz families migrated to Turkey after the occupation of the Wakhan Corridor (the 'panhandle' of north-eastern Afghanistan) by the Soviet forces in 1980. While all Kirghiz are *Sunni* Muslims, some Pamiris are followers of *Shi'a* (Isma'ili) Islam. The Pamiri speak the *Pamiri* dialect of *Dari,* while the Kirghiz speak a *kipchak Turkic* dialect.

Other settled ethnic and tribal groups

Several smaller groups further add to the cultural richness of Afghan society, including Qizilbash, Mongols/Moghuls, Arabs, Gujars, Kohistanis, Wakhis and Jats. The total number of all these groups in 1980 did not exceed several thousand, according to Dupree. Although some of them, such as the Jats, have retained their distinct lifestyle and language, the rest have largely adopted the culture of the dominant, neighbouring ethnic group. However, the urbanite Qizilbash (*Shi'a* Muslims) have held very important professional and bureaucratic positions in national institutions. Isma'ilis – who follow the Aga Khan – are another group, living in northern areas.

Afghanistan has also been home to several thousand Hindus, Sikhs and some Jews. These groups lived and worked mainly in urban centres such as Kabul, Kandahar and Herat. They greatly contributed to Afghan trade and business, but many left after the Soviet invasion in 1979.

Nomads

Afghan nomads – *kuchis* – are an important feature of Afghan society and culture but do not represent a specific ethnic/tribal group. Instead, it is their unique fully-nomadic lifestyle that separates the *kuchis* from the rest of Afghanistan's settled populations. Afghan nomads are mainly comprised of Pashtuns (up to 80 percent) along with some Baluch and Kirghiz. Estimates of the numbers of *kuchis* range from 500,000 to three million.

Most *kuchis* have traditionally been herders and traders, with sheep and camels constituting their main property. Baluch and Pashtun nomads generally spend winter in Pakistan and move to Afghanistan in spring when the weather is warmer. Their tradition of widespread grazing lands has occasionally led to conflicts between nomads and villagers. Some villagers complained that the surrounding grassland was overgrazed and exploited by the nomads, who were seen as aliens. Some non-Pashtuns also saw the seasonal presence of the predominantly Pashtun nomads as a form of Pashtun expansionism.

However, most settled local populations established enduring economic relationships with the nomads. In exchange for locally-produced grain, fruit and vegetables – as well as grazing rights – the nomads traded tea, sugar, mutton and goat meat, wool and dairy products. This exchange was particularly extensive between the nomads and the populations of remote and isolated villages, where *kuchis* were often used as a means of communication and transportation to the outside world. According to Louis Dupree, writing in 1980, the nomads' huge animal stock also fertilized the deserts and hillsides which would have otherwise remained barren. He argued that, far from being a burden to the land, nomads "...live in a symbiotic, not parasitic, relationship with man and nature in Afghanistan."

Whatever the effect of nomads on the rest of society, a quarter century of war has had serious implications for the nomadic population of Afghanistan. Most *kuchis* were unable to continue their traditional existence after the Soviet invasion. Many remained as herders or traders (often in the transport sector) in the North West Frontier region of Pakistan, or fought alongside the *mujahideen* inside Afghanistan.

Although travellers and locals have witnessed the presence of large numbers of nomads during 2002 in the southern and eastern regions of Afghanistan, tens of thousands have ended up in camps for displaced persons. The presence of millions of landmines has severely limited the scope of their traditional migration patterns. By 1997, Afghan *kuchis* were believed to have lost about 35,000 animals to mines, which works out at 25 beasts (worth around US$ 3,000) per household. Furthermore, as a result of five years of almost continuous drought, *kuchis* have lost even more animals and income.

Effects of war on the ethnic and tribal groups of Afghanistan

The past 24 years of war have devastated both Afghanistan's infrastructure and the social, political and economic organisation of Afghan society. An estimated one and a half million Afghans were killed and six million more fled to other countries. Equally seriously, the conflict deprived a generation of young people from gaining educational qualifications and other useful skills. Instead, fighting for rival warlords provided these young men with a source of income, social status and a way of channelling their energy.

Warlords maintained their own ethnically-based armies that fought against one another. A key factional tactic was to 'divide and rule' by propagating ethnic and religious hatred. They attempted to turn the Afghan conflict into an ethnic war. Examples of this included: the aerial bombing of Hazaras and looting of their houses in the Karte Seh quarter of Kabul by the Tajik-dominated Jamiat-e-Islami faction in 1994-95; the massacre of the predominately Pashtun Taliban by Uzbek and Hazara militias in Mazar-e-Sharif and surrounding areas in 1997; the massacre of Hazaras in Yakaolang by Taliban forces in 2000-2001; and the suffocation of hundreds of Taliban prisoners by joint Tajik, Uzbek and Hazara forces in northern Afghanistan in late 2001.

In addition to the six million refugees who fled Afghanistan, conflict also displaced at least one million Afghans within the country during the 1980s-90s. These internally-displaced persons (IDPs) have been forced to flee from Badghis to Herat, from Shomali to Kabul, from Kabul to the Panjshair Valley and more recently from northern Afghanistan to Kandahar and surrounding areas. The IDPs in Herat were predominantly Pashtun and Baluch, whereas those in Jalalabad were largely Tajik or non-Pashtun. Significantly, aid workers and visitors reported that non-Pashtuns in predominantly Pashtun Jalalabad and the Pashtuns and Baluch in predominantly *Farsiwan* Herat were received as fellow Afghans and enjoyed considerable assistance from the local population. In some cases, locals in 'host' cities even shared their own homes with displaced Afghans.

These observations are very important. They would seem to indicate that despite the apparent division of the country along ethno-linguistic lines, ordinary Afghans still feel that they are bonded to one another in different ways. Indeed, shared religion, customs and moral values, inter-marriages, economic interdependence, clothing, lifestyle and, more importantly, a shared interest in the establishment of peace and social order are all common grounds that unite ordinary Afghans.

The collapse of the Taliban regime and the establishment of the Afghan Interim Authority in December 2001 raised hopes among many Afghans that there was an opportunity to end Afghanistan's warlord culture and rebuild the country's social, political and economic institutions. Consequently during 2002, over 1.5 million Afghan refugees returned home. However, the reinstatement of some warlords as key political and military leaders in the post-Taliban administration – plus the US government's emphasis on the 'war against terrorism' rather than on rebuilding Afghanistan – has spread disillusion among many Afghans about the prospects of lasting peace. The US's military and financial support for warlords, who may cooperate in hunting down remnants of the Taliban and Al Qa'eda, continues to be a major source of ethnic tension in the country.

However, despite the exploitation of religion and ethnicity as vehicles for reaching positions of power by various factional leaders, the forces of unity between ordinary Afghans remain strong. The long-term prospects of unity, peace and stability lie in a multi-cultural Afghanistan in which its ethnic and tribal diversity is a source of strength, progress and cultural richness. Only then can Afghanistan rebuild itself, take its place in the international community, and face the challenges of the 21st Century.

***Dr Ali Wardak** – an Afghan specialist – is a senior lecturer in criminology at Glamorgan University, U.K.*

For a bibliography on Afghanistan's ethnic and tribal composition, SEE INFORESOURCES.

Media coverage: frontline, fringe or propaganda?

By Edward Girardet

In an editorial on 1 June 1982, the *New York Times* wrote that the world's attention span for conflicts and humanitarian crises was estimated at 90 days. Commenting on the continued Soviet occupation of Afghanistan nearly two-and-a-half years after the December 1979 invasion, the newspaper noted that Afghanistan had all but slipped from sight. "But still the war goes on," the paper observed. "The Russians, incredibly, are no nearer victory than at the start, when experts blandly forecast that their modern army would subdue primitive tribesmen in months. It is bigger news than a bored world realizes."

Looking back to when the first edition of the *Essential Field Guide* appeared in 1998, this assessment appeared both sad and ironic. The Soviets, who had pulled out finally in February 1989, were once again involved – this time as Russians – in another war, Chechnya. There they began using the same brutal methods against the civilian population as they had in Afghanistan. But they also suffered similarly horrendous setbacks at the hands of Chechen partisans as they had with the *mujahideen*. Clearly, the Russians, who in mid-2003 were still involved in Chechnya, had learned few lessons from their Afghan experience except in the domain of media. As during the 1980s with Afghanistan, the Moscow authorities are doing everything possible to deny the press – both Russian and international – access to a war that it prefers to designate an 'internal affair' and of no concern to the outside world. Chechnya remains heavily under-covered despite the efforts – often at great risk – by a small number of journalists to undertake more candid reporting of this brutal conflict. Immediately following the events of September 2001, and the US intervention in Afghanistan, the Kremlin leapt at the chance to characterize its repression of Chechen civilians as part of the same international struggle against 'terrorism'. The Russians are now using this *rationale* to justify their continued human rights abuses without the first-hand coverage of nosy reporters. The last thing they want is to have journalists provide the sort of reporting that prevented the Red Army in Afghanistan from waging an unnoticed war.

Also at the time of the *Essential Field Guide's* first edition, Afghanistan was a country well into its 20th year of war. Fighting had become a civil conflict between two major factions, the Taliban and the United Front, also known as the Northern Alliance. Afghanistan in 1996-97 witnessed periods of relatively good coverage with major European and American news organizations ranging from French television and *CNN* to the *Süddeutsche Zeitung*, *The Times* and the *New York Times* lending prominent coverage to the humanitarian plight, the continuing war, and the Taliban phenomenon. Much of the coverage, however, sometimes sensationalist, was focused on repression by the Taliban, particularly against women. Other real, substantive issues, notably the sheer and utter exhaustion of many Afghans with regard to war, tended to be ignored. The 90 days proposed by the *New York Times* suddenly seemed a generous timeframe given the media's obsession with nine-second sound bites and highly competitive 'live' saturation coverage of events. On coming to power in 1996, the Taliban had simply institutionalized what other fundamentalist groups and individuals had been doing or advocating for years. Talib abuses were often not much different from those that Afghans had long since been forced to endure under many *mujahideen*, including elements of the United Front, during the post-Soviet period. Nor were such excesses that dissimilar to the forms of repression later imposed by various factions and warlords operating since the fall of the Taliban. This has led some analysts to wonder whether things outside the Afghan capital are really that much better under the new internationally-backed Kabul authorities headed by President Hamid Karzai than their Taliban predecessors.

The murder of United Front commander Ahmed Shah Massoud on 9 September 2001, followed by the terrorist assaults in the United States two days later, suddenly thrust Afghanistan back into the media limelight. With the launching of the US bombing against Taliban and Al Qa'eda targets on 7 October 2001, it was the turn of the American military to be directly involved in Afghanistan. This brought with it massive media coverage, particularly television. Although the US and its Coalition partners succeeded in ousting the ruling Taliban in support of the United Front, they too, like the Soviets, appeared to be underestimating this country and its people. By intervening with such an unsubtle hand, the Americans found themselves – like the sorcerer's apprentice – inadvertently scattering the 'sources' of terrorism to the wind and creating in their place a whole new (and uncontrollable) arena of Islamic resentment against the West, both inside and outside Afghanistan. By spring 2003, there were almost daily armed attacks by anti-Western Islamic groups (many of them former Taliban) against the US-led Coalition and Afghan government forces. Since then, such attacks have grown steadily worse, with extremist or Pashtun nationalist groups stepping up their assaults against international aid agencies, civilian targets and journalists. These have assured that parts of southern and eastern Afghanistan remain even more insecure today than prior to the US intervention. The dangers involved have prevented many journalists from seeking a broader picture of the situation other than in the company of Coalition Forces or well-connected aid agencies.

For the first year or so of the Bush administration's military intervention in Afghanistan, broad public support was accomplished with the help of a largely compliant and jingoistic media, particularly mainstream US television. There was little questioning as to whether heavy-handed aerial bombardment of the country as a means of countering terrorism was advisable or whether it made sense to support local warlords, or even create new ones, to fight the Taliban or track down Al Qa'eda operatives. Some journalists, particularly the more experienced Afghan hands, expressed deep concern that Washington was once again implementing policies that were failing to take long-term considerations into account. And this was not the first time. During the Soviet war of the 1980s, both aid workers and reporters had warned that Pakistani and American backing of Islamic extremists – such as Gulbuddin Hekmatyar and, indirectly, Arab *Wahabi* like Osama Bin Laden – would come back to haunt them in the future.

Nevertheless, major American networks, such as *Fox Television*, *CNN Domestic*, and *NBC* were reluctant to even consider the warnings of the past. "The American people are not interested in history," proclaimed one *Fox TV* show host, drowning out the reservations raised by one of his guests in the weeks that followed September 11. Much of America's coverage of the 2001-02 US intervention was often more reminiscent of Soviet-style propaganda of the 1970s than the quality reporting standards many Americans like to imagine their press embodies. The lack of serious assessment by leading news organizations shocked even the most cynical punter. The networks – but also some of the mainstream print media – jostled to outdo each other with their patriotism by cheering on Washington's new 'war on terror' regardless of the consequences. *TIME* magazine, for example, demanded that all reports referring to Afghan casualties be 'balanced' by incorporating a reference to those killed at the World Trade Center. Even at the time of writing in mid-2003, the Pentagon strives to minimize Afghan casualty figures by declaring current estimates of 3,000-4,000 dead as 'way off the mark.'

The events of September 11 paralysed the American media's ability to provide critical, informed and above all, balanced, reporting of Afghanistan. For some, the 2001-02 intervention proved even harder to report than the Soviet-Afghan war of the 1980s. The Pentagon has gone out of its way to manipulate and control open reporting of its war. Key press conferences during the fighting were often held well away from the frontlines, in Florida for example, to ensure that those attending did not have close knowledge of on-the-ground conditions. This encouraged a distinct laziness among many journalists who failed to undertake the necessary legwork for a better understanding of what was going on. Some also confused their role as reporters with that of supporters of the American or Coalition military by referring to 'us' or 'our forces' and 'them' or 'the enemy' in their dispatches. Even worse, they relied on the Coalition as their principal source of information. The fact that much of the Pentagon's intelligence, particularly during the early months, was based on poor data or was part of an overall propaganda or disinformation effort did little to perturb them. Journalists operating out of the former Soviet airbase at Bagram – used by the Americans, one of the belligerents, as their headquarters – had to sign waivers agreeing not to report certain military activities. To a degree, they were also dependent on the Coalition for security, food, accommodation and transport – hardly an impartial approach to independent news coverage.

On the whole, European and other international coverage of Afghanistan since September 11 has been of a far higher standard than that provided by the mainstream US media. However, even the BBC, which normally seeks to distance itself from UK policy, skirted dangerously close to compromise by presenting Coalition interpretations at face value. This said, a healthy number of US journalists and broadcast producers have persisted in their efforts to furnish quality coverage despite their own organizations' bids to outdo each other with 'America First' approaches. In the end, however, it was mainly the American print and Internet press (but also *National Public Radio*), which saved the day for their country's journalistic pride. Publications such as *The Nation, The Sentinel, New York Times, Christian Science Monitor, Washington Post*, and *Dallas Morning News* have pushed hard to provide credible and balanced reporting of the intervention. Some of these have continued to provide quality coverage of developments in Afghanistan by reporting consistently on the international recovery process in Afghanistan well into 2003.

As with most conflicts, Afghanistan has always suffered from hot and cold bouts of interest. When fighting first erupted in the summer of 1978, with local factions opposed to communist rule staging increasing attacks against the government, it marked the beginning of a devastating series of conflicts that have now dragged on for almost a quarter of a century. It also signalled the start of a mass exodus of civilians that would quickly snowball into the world's largest refugee crisis since World War II. The early stages of the fighting received relatively little international press coverage. Only the occasional news reports referred to police stations being hit, party officials assassinated, or hippie buses taking the odd sniper bullet from bearded *mujahideen* hiding out in the mountains. It was only when Adolphe Dubs, the American ambassador in Kabul, was killed in February 1979, followed by the lynching of a large group of Soviet advisors in Herat, that events in Afghanistan began to have international repercussions. A growing trickle of stories started to emerge about a new Central Asian war.

It was the December 1979 Red Army invasion, however, that first caused the world media to focus its attention *en masse* on Afghanistan – and then, over the years, only in intermittent bursts. As Soviet occupation forces moved in, journalists, producers, photographers and cameramen, both male and female, flocked by the hundreds to Kabul and other parts of the country to report the incursion. Others travelled to Peshawar and Quetta or to the rapidly expanding refugee camps along the Pakistan-Afghan frontier. For several months, it was possible to cover both sides of the story. This became steadily more difficult as the Soviet-backed Afghan regime cut back on visas, particularly to those who had reported with the *mujahideen.* Such one-sidedness has always been a drawback in the coverage of the Afghan war. While some newspapers sought to include reports from Moscow or from the Afghan capital by other correspondents, it was virtually impossible for one journalist to cover both the Soviets and the guerrillas. A similar situation developed during the Taliban period with the difficulty of reaching – for both logistical and security reasons – certain opposition areas in the northern and central parts of the country.

Another problem was that journalists representing partisan interests in the United States or Europe assumed blatantly anti-communist stances paying little attention to the faults of the so-called 'freedom fighters'. Most of the more reliable information about what was happening inside Afghanistan was provided by Western journalists and humanitarian relief workers operating crossborder. Many, including Americans, strongly criticised the way US aid, both military and humanitarian, was being delivered. Others preferred to ignore it as it skewed their image of freedom-loving Afghans determined to throw off the Red Army yoke. At Pakistan's behest, huge amounts of weaponry and ammunition were directed to Pashtun fundamentalist groups such as Hekmatyar's Hezb-e-Islami faction. Much of this was stockpiled, to be later deployed in Afghanistan's new civil war following the collapse of the Najibullah regime in 1992. Some well-informed US State Department and USAID officials concerned by the detrimental effects of such policies had sought to encourage more outspoken reporting of what was happening but were threatened or transferred elsewhere.

Most Western journalists during the Soviet war reported clandestinely with the *mujahideen*, while the bulk of the Soviet and East European press corps operated on the Red Army side. It was with the collapse of the Soviet Union that both sides were able to compare notes of their respective coverage. It soon emerged that Eastern and Western journalists suffered similar frustrations with their Afghan subjects, whether government *askari* or resistance *mujahideen*. Unlike Vietnam, journalists – except those East Bloc correspondents reporting with the Red Army – could not simply fly in and out of conflict areas by helicopter. For a small but significant portion of the Western press corps, it was often a matter of trekking for days, weeks, even months across mountains and deserts to report the story. Many, however, simply did not have the time to undertake serious crossborder trips. As a result, the majority of journalists during the 1980s and early 1990s based their coverage on short visits to Peshawar with 'in-out' excursions to *mujahed* bases inside Afghanistan in order to obtain 'frontline' bylines. Mobile satellite television and telephone units, just beginning to make an appearance during the late 1980s, did not really figure in reporting from the field. Television networks such as *CBS, BBC, NBC, ITV, ZDF* and *Antenne 2* (now *France2)* had to rely mainly on freelance cameramen and women for the bulk of their footage.

As a correspondent for *The Christian Science Monitor* and American public television's *MacNeil-Lehrer NewsHour,* for example, this writer often travelled with a freelance crew for six weeks at a time. Unable to file from the mountains, one had to wait until back in Peshawar or Paris to produce a series of lengthy articles plus two or three television reports. Correspondents for *Le Monde, The Washington Post, TIME, The Guardian, The New York Times, Der Spiegel, Corriere della Sera, El Pais* and other newspapers and magazines all did the same. Ironically, such trips probably provided far better informed reporting than much of the 'live' coverage during the Gulf Wars I and II, Somalia or Rwanda. One had time to talk to people and assess the situation from the field while combining it with information obtained from various embassies, relief agencies and other sources based in Pakistan, India, Paris or London. During much of the Soviet occupation, media coverage from inside Afghanistan was provided by a small clutch of European, American, Australian, New Zealand, Japanese and other correspondents, probably no more than 100 throughout the year.

The increased US involvement in the war against the Soviets prompted a renewed surge of interest among American media from 1986 onwards. Not unlike the coverage of the 2001-02 US intervention, however, there was often

Voice of Peace

Zakia Zaki has a strong chin and a warm smile. She meets the gaze of strangers confidently beneath her black *chador*. Once headmistress of the local school, now she is director of Afghanistan's first independent radio station. *Radio Solh* (literally, 'Radio of Peace') operates out of Jebel-us-Saraj – a small but strategically located town two hours north of Kabul, where the main road to the Salang tunnel crosses the Ghorband river.

The station lies on the edge of town, above the fortress once controlled by Ahmed Shah Massoud. Green flags flutter above shallow mounds of earth: the graves of the *shahid* – soldiers martyred in battle, whose souls escape judgement and live on for eternity. A 20-foot antenna sticking out of a walled garden gives Radio Solh away. Inside are rose bushes, a pond filled with carp and the green shade of two huge sycamore trees.

Zakia greeted us with green tea and raisins. "During the US bombing, this was an anti-Taliban station", she said. "Now we broadcast news, politics, music, literature, as well as special programmes for women and children." They reported on the progress of the *Loya Jirga* – to which Zakia went as an elected representative.

"Are the people turning against the old *mujahideen* commanders now?" I asked. "We have no hard feelings against them", said Zakia, "as long as they support democracy. But some of the local commanders are not happy that a woman is in charge of this radio station." Were women respected under Massoud? "Yes", she replied, "Massoud said women had rights to education and health. He paid for girls' schools and female teachers. He even said he would only agree to this radio station if it was independent and run by a woman!"

Massoud's murder in September 2001 sealed his already high reputation. His portrait now adorns private homes and public buildings across the country, from the Pashtun east to the Uzbek north. His finely-featured face acts as a talisman, guaranteeing security for those who put their faith in him. He is *shahid*. His soul lives on.

A small toad plopped into the pond. The north wind tugged at the sycamore leaves. Beyond, the sun beat down mercilessly. I asked how the *Loya Jirga* had gone in Jebel-us-Saraj. "It was great. But the participation of women was not so good. News about the vote didn't reach them in time. And many of the officials did not let women participate. Of the 1,500 places in the final *Loya Jirga* in Kabul, only 180 are for women. That's not enough." But aren't there female ministers in the new Afghan government? "Yes", said Zakia with a smile. "But they are in Kabul – they have not visited here. They don't understand the problems of women in this country because they have spent so long living abroad." *JW* a lack of critical reporting. Too many American journalists visiting the region, or writing from Washington and New York, relied too heavily on what they were being told by the State Department, the Central Intelligence Agency, the Pentagon, the White House, the US Agency for International Development (USAID) and other sources, including various 'Beltway Rat' think-tanks in Washington. The reporting was often poorly informed, sometimes the result of disinformation. Some of the relief agencies in Peshawar, especially those which had no operations inside Afghanistan, cultivated curious links with the US government and were equally uninformed about the situation or knowingly contributed to the disinformation process. USAID was particularly anxious that a united front be maintained by the press *vis à vis* the Soviets. The agency bitterly resented any outspoken reporting of its operations, many of which were little more than fronts to support the mainly fundamentalist *mujahed* groups, such as Hekmatyar's Hezb-e-Islami, in the name of anti-Soviet political expediency. Hekmatyar, the former Peshawar-based resistance politician, who has now been branded a terrorist by Washington, recently declared *jihad* against his former backers. He is also seeking to assume the Taliban mantle with pledges to throw out the American non-believers from Afghan soil.

Washington's increased commitment during the late 1980s to the *mujahideen,* coupled with more humanitarian support by European and other Western countries, prompted a significant rise in the number of aid agencies in Peshawar, Quetta and among the refugee camps. In turn, this engendered greater coverage for the aid story by encouraging journalists from Sweden to Mexico to visit local operations supported by their own governments or aid agencies. But once the Soviets left in February 1989, so did most of the journalists. They only returned in droves again when the *mujahideen* took Kabul in 1992. Months later, most were gone again when it became clear that the war was not going to end cleanly. Instead, as forecast by some observers, a Beirut-style civil conflict erupted. There was too much stored weaponry and too many unresolved factional interests ranging from a blatant thirst for power to lucrative drug and arms trafficking activities to allow Afghans to return to their homes in peace. And so Afghanistan became 'yet another war' with sporadic media coverage. This was interspersed by bouts of saturation coverage such as 'Afghanistan revisited' documentary films or newspaper reports on drug wars or Islamic extremism.

Under the Taliban, too, it became increasingly difficult for camera teams and photographers to work. Afghanistan was in danger of becoming a 'closed' or inaccessible conflict, at least in certain parts of the country. But at least the Taliban's repressive actions against both women and journalists attracted attention. So did the destruction by the Taliban and their foreign Islamic backers of much of the country's cultural heritage, such as the blowing up of the Bamiyan Buddhas in 2001 or the ongoing looting by Pakistani-backed groups and individuals of the Hadda stupas outside Jalalabad and other cultural sites throughout the 1990s and early 21st Century.

Much of the Western media's reporting of Afghanistan, whether during the Soviet occupation or during the more recent US intervention against the Taliban, has embraced a strong element of frontline romanticism. For those reporting the resistance against the Red Army, it was a matter of coping with often harsh 19th Century conditions, trekking with horse caravans across the Hindu Kush and drinking tea with desert nomads. There was also the need to operate clandestinely with foot guerrillas seeking to ward off attacks by helicopter gunships and MiGs. Afghanistan had its fair share of 'war cowboys', and not just amongst the journalist community. Many aid workers and Afghan *wallahs* were enthralled by the excitement of trekking 'inside.' The Soviet war further attracted journalists who appeared more interested in the 'Great Game' itself. Some dabbled with Western intelligence services or even took part in the fighting. Others had themselves photographed brandishing kalashnikovs or aiming anti-aircraft guns, a real no-no if you don't want to be accused of being a mercenary or a spy.

Today, such frontline intrepidness still intrigues. One American gem dealer, regularly travelling into Afghanistan, unabashedly advertised himself as the "Indiana Jones of the '90s." During the US intervention in late 2001 and early 2002, journalists from the United States but also Europe often turned up in battle fatigues, some even boasting of carrying guns – "to kill Bin Laden" as one pompous American TV presenter asserted – because that was clearly the sort of garb 'war' journalists were supposed to wear.

Overall, however, throughout the past 25 years, many among the foreign press corps, particularly the freelancers, have proved both conscientious and professional in their reporting. They have furnished a coverage that is as accurate and as balanced as can be expected under often exceptionally difficult circumstances. As a key conflict, Afghanistan never quite made it. The fighting had simply dragged on for too long. And despite the current recovery process, the conflict continues. Nevertheless, not unlike Vietnam in the 1960s and early 1970s, Afghanistan was, and still is, a poignant landmark for journalists. It is a conflict that has managed to move, despite all odds, with the times, in terms of both how it is fought and how it is reported. While the 2001 terror attacks drew renewed media attention to Afghanistan, it had less to do with the plight of ordinary Afghans than the impact of the Taliban, Al Qa'eda and global terrorism on Western security. Only days prior to the assaults, UN aid officials in Islamabad were complaining about the lack of coverage of Afghanistan's humanitarian crisis resulting from the effects of both war and drought.

With the fall of the Taliban there has been a surge of new and independent Afghan media. By the end of 2002, some 200 Afghan magazines, newspapers and newsletters had emerged, albeit some only to survive one or two editions. Media groups, both local and international, such as AINA, the Open Media Fund, UNESCO and the Afghan Media Resource Centre have been seeking to help develop the print sector, while other organizations, notably Media Action International and the Institute for War and Peace Reporting, have stepped in to provide professional training of both young and experienced journalists. The BBC Trust and Internews have also been helped with the restructuring, training and equipping of Afghan radio and television, including a number of non-state stations. In many respects, critical and independent journalism in Afghanistan has had to start from scratch as Afghans who had learned their craft prior to the Soviet war tended to focus more on un-sourced opinion rather than straight reporting. And those, particularly among younger Afghans, who want to become journalists, lack the experience.

Yet the crucial role of independent media and public information as a key component to Afghanistan's recovery process still fails to inspire most donors. Media support remained limited in 2003 – and primarily directed at the broadcast media – compared to other sectors. The donor argument is that given the country's high illiteracy rate (over 70 percent) the majority of Afghans listen to radio. Most still depend on the *BBC*, *VOA*, *Deutschewelle* and, more recently, *Radio Free Afghanistan*, for their primary information. Independent radio stations, mainly FM, are growing in number – and there is a strong argument for developing community radio – but reception is difficult in the mountains. Television, particularly satellite, is having an expanding impact but largely only on those who can afford the equipment or have access to regular power supplies. "Who is going to read newspapers if most people cannot even read?" asked one senior Western European diplomat, while a World Bank representative maintained that "information is not exactly a priority given all of Afghanistan's reconstruction needs."

Such donor reasoning fails to take into account that not only do Afghans have the need – and the right – to credible information as to what is going on but that most independent reporting comes from print. As in other countries, the broadcast media rely largely on newspapers and magazines for stories and ideas. *Radio Television Afghanistan*, despite its significant international support in the form of equipment and training, has already come under pressure from various ruling political and religious factions to curb its content and reporting. There have even been attempts to forbid cable and satellite reception although this may have more to do with business monopolies than with editorial perception. Regardless, this does not bode well for Afghan broadcasting. It will also assure that – as before – many Afghans will continue to rely on foreign broadcasters, such as the *BBC*, for their principal information, resulting from a mistrust of local media.

Media advocates stress the need to adopt a more long-term approach that regards support for the print media as an investment for recovery. This includes better management training enabling newspapers and magazines to become more viable on their own through advertising and better distribution. The print media, even if costly by Afghan standards, could also play a crucial role in reducing the nation's very high illiteracy rate. One way would be to distribute specially tailored print media to high schools and village community centres. Not only would this offer local populations and school children a readily accessible information resource but would also serve as an effective educational tool for aid agencies. Assessments by Media Action International and National Geographic have shown an acute shortage of reading material in Afghan schools, particularly in rural areas, where children's and youth magazines could provide quick impact by helping to improve reading skills while at the same time putting across health and other recovery messages. As numerous aid agencies have still to understand, credible public information initiatives supported by media can dramatically help reduce disease, improve mother-child health care, and develop agriculture – Afghanistan's principal industry.

More crucially, however, the Afghan print media has a significant role to play in the monitoring of the current recovery and peacekeeping process, while keeping tabs on human rights and other key developments. This accountability role is already causing discomfort to warlords such as Ismail Khan and General Atta Mohammed, as well as powerful political protagonists within the Kabul government such as defence minister Fahim, whose agents have threatened or beaten up Afghan journalists for their critical reporting. Such actions can

only stress the need for the international community to encourage the building of a more effective and outspoken independent local media. Up till now, however, support for print publications has had to rely largely on non-donor backing, such as the Open Media Fund started by Pakistani-British writer Ahmed Rashid. A long-time Afghan hand, he has sought to help independent Afghan start-up publications, such as *Takhassos* monthly, published by the professional *shura* in Herat. For its part, Media Action International with support from the German government has been helping Afghan student journalists from Kabul, Herat and Balkh universities set up their own independent magazine, *Youth Voice*, to keep high school and university students informed of recovery, human rights, cultural and other issues. It also seeks to provide young journalists with an open and critical forum within which to report. With USAID backing, these young journalists are in the process of setting up their own campus radio stations in Herat and Mazar.

Of particular concern, however, is the unwillingness of many international donors to help assure appropriate public accountability of Afghanistan's massive reconstruction process, already heavily weighted by corruption and other forms of abuse. While certain institutions have been established by the international community to promote greater transparency, such monitoring needs to become part of the public domain. Together with NGOs such as the International Crisis Group, Amnesty International and Human Rights Watch, it is up to a vibrant and independent watchdog media to ensure that the public is constantly informed. It does not help to have long and well-researched 'after-the-fact' evaluation reports exploring what has gone right or wrong. The donors need to recognize that, more than anything else, Afghanistan – as with other conflict and post-conflict situations such as Ivory Coast, Somalia or Liberia – requires credible media, both local and international, to help prevent the situation from being hijacked once again by outside powers. An effective Afghan media can also serve as a crucial tool for critically assessing – on an ongoing basis – the actions of local or regional warlords as well as sectors such as drugs, oil, timber and other licit or illicit commercial interests.

Edward Girardet is director of Media Action International and co-author of *The Essential Field Guide*. He has reported on Afghanistan as a journalist since 1979 for the *Christian Science Monitor, National Geographic* and other publications.

Landmines: an enduring legacy

By Timothy Weaver and Jonathan Walter

Pattern I. Someone steps on a buried anti-personnel mine. The blast blows off the foot, shredding the bone and tissues of the leg up to and often above the knee. The other leg, genitals, buttocks and arms are lacerated. Fragments from the mine itself, and dirt, gravel, clothing, skin and bone are blasted up into the body. The unlucky ones are killed outright.

Pattern II. A ground-level fragmentation mine is set off by a person tripping a wire. Metal fragments are blown out in an arc that can tear a body to shreds. The victim suffers multiple puncture wounds, superficial or deep, depending on how far they are from the mine. The unlucky ones are killed outright.

Pattern III. Farmers planting rice, children playing, and deminers clearing fields have their hands blown off and are blinded when they inadvertently touch or pick up anti-personnel (AP) mines. The unlucky ones are killed outright.

Mine injuries are not always fatal. It depends on the nature and purpose of the mine. Many AP mines are designed to maim rather than kill; others such as the bouncing mines that spring up to waist height before detonating, have a 100 percent 'kill ratio' when set off. Meanwhile, unexploded ordnance (UXO) – such as stray anti-tank rockets, artillery rounds or the "cluster bombs" dropped by US forces in late 2001 – can prove even more deadly and dangerous than landmines.

The International Committee of the Red Cross (ICRC) estimates that 200,000 Afghans have been killed or wounded by mines since 1979. Half the fatalities are thought to be due to lack of access to medical treatment immediately after the blast. According to UNICEF, children represent half of all injuries and deaths from landmines in Afghanistan – many of them fall victim while playing, tending animals or collecting firewood. Meanwhile, the US-led bombing campaign during late 2001 scattered thousands of UXO which caused many more civilian casualties. When the border with Pakistan was closed, many internally displaced people tried new routes to get out of Afghanistan – routes which were often still mined from previous conflicts. According to the UN, between 150-300 Afghan civilians continue to be killed or injured by mines and UXO every month.

Since 1979, Afghans have had to live with the fear that the next step they take could be their last. As the war has gone through successive phases, the danger posed by mines has been ever-present. During the 1980s, the invading Soviets and their Afghan 'Regime' allies used mines extensively to subdue the local population and to cut off *mujahed* supply routes. They mined outposts defensively, border regions and supply routes. Irrigation canals, fields, roads and residential areas were mined to deprive the *mujahideen* of the support of local populations. The Soviets mapped defensive minefields, but the AP 'butterfly' mines dropped from the air were by their very nature impossible to control. In return the *mujahideen* also laid mines – including many anti-tank varieties.

The withdrawal of Soviet forces in 1989 led to a worsening of the situation. The Soviets left behind large stockpiles of arms and ammunition, including landmines. All the combatants used and reused them – often wildly, crudely and cruelly – over the years since 1989. After the fall of President Najibullah in 1992, weapons and ammunition, including mines, continued to find their way into Afghanistan through Iran, Pakistan and the former Soviet republics to the north, supplied by various countries seeking to influence the balance of power in the future Afghanistan.

At the end of the 1980s Afghanistan was already tagged as the most heavily mined country in the world. That was before the fighting spread to the towns, which became the battlegrounds for the warring factions. As frontlines shifted rapidly, control of minefields changed hands several times. This led to confusion about the exact size, content and position of many minefields. The civil war of the 1990s led to ever more indiscriminate mine-laying, with little central control over deployment and scant effort made to map or mark minefields, or to clear areas no longer of tactical value. During the civil war, cities became battlegrounds. Mines laid in urban streets and buildings continue to have an impact today. Families are made homeless. Children are blown up while playing or searching for firewood.

Afghanistan was the first conflict in which mines were regarded as a weapon of terror. The horribly mutilated men, women and children who arrived at the border hospitals of Pakistan, sometimes after days of travelling, made the point eloquently that civilians were now more at risk from mines than combatants. They were also easier targets. Medical resources have always been meagre and the war cut into them heavily, leaving them woefully inadequate. Treatment of the injured has drained the medical system, while the fighting destroyed medical facilities and disrupted supply lines.

Twenty four years of war have broken down communities and family groups. In many areas the rural pattern of life has changed irrevocably. Families with mine victims suffer poverty: as breadwinners and labourers are lost to mines, so the fields are then lost to the families. They are unable to tend them. The cities provide the only alternative, and families move from rural to urban areas where they may enjoy marginally better access to health services and employment opportunities.

Treatment for mine victims does not stop when the doctor sews up the wound. There is a long process of rehabilitation. Artificial limbs have to be made and fitted. Physiotherapy sessions must be organized. Trauma counselling may be necessary. All this places further burdens upon the health services

J. Hartley/UNICEF

– the average cost of rehabilitating a mine victim was estimated at US$ 5,000 in 1993. People have to learn to live with permanent disability. They face the prospect of being a burden to their family. Many families are forced into debt to meet the costs of medical treatment for mine victims.

The immediate effects of landmines may be seen on the streets of Afghanistan – men, women and children hobbling around on crutches. The long-term effects have been to turn a country that was once self-sufficient in food production into one that is dependent on foreign food aid. Mines have prevented farmers from returning to work on the land. They have blown apart the migratory patterns of the *Kuchi* nomad traders. They have helped keep refugees in foreign camps, idling their lives away far from home and depending on aid donors' compassion.

Demining programmes began after the withdrawal of the Soviet Army in 1989, and have made some progress. The task of mapping and clearing was first taken up by international agencies. Teams of army engineers arrived in Pakistan in 1989 to teach refugee Afghans the principles of mine awareness, mine detection and mine-clearing. Nearly fifteen years later, numerous non-governmental organisations (NGOs) are still labouring at the same Herculean task, coordinated by the United Nations' Mine Action Programme for Afghanistan (MAPA). MAPA focuses on four aspects of mine and UXO action: survey, clearance, awareness and technical training. Fifteen NGOs numbering over 7,000 Afghan staff implement the programme. From 1989-2002, the programme cleared (or declared safe) 754 square kilometres of minefields and battlefields, and taught 2.4 million people how to identify and avoid mines and UXO. Even so, during 2000-2001, MAPA's budget was nearly halved as donors tired of Afghanistan's ongoing war. Most field staff had to be sent on unpaid leave for several months. According to the UN's demining office in Mazar, the combination of lack of funding, natural disasters, bad weather and security problems meant they hardly cleared any mines during 2001.

MAPA's immediate aim is not to clear Afghanistan of every single landmine – rather it is to clear 'high impact areas' (of which well over 300 square kilometres remain) and to map and physically mark off low priority areas. High impact areas are those where civilians face the greatest risk: residential and commercial areas, agricultural and grazing land, tracks connecting villages to main roads, irrigation canals, schools, mosques and graveyards.

Surveying remains an enormously dangerous but critical process. Typically, a local landowner or commander will ask a mine action NGO to clear their land. A general survey team will recce the area, talk to local people and assess what kind of minefield it is likely to be. Then a technical survey team will have to establish the limits of the field on foot with metal detectors. Mine detection dogs – trained to sniff out explosives up to a metre underground – have also proved very effective in surveying and clearance.

As better access enables more widespread surveying, so new minefields are uncovered and the demining task becomes greater. In 1996, for example, the UN identified 252 new mined areas in Kabul. Following the fall of the Taliban in late 2001, the total area contaminated by minefields and UXO grew further still. By the end of 2002, the UN estimated that 850 square kilometres of land were still contaminated – 126 square kilometres more than in 2001. There are two reasons for this: bombs dropped during the 'war on terrorism' re-contaminated land once cleared; and, as the Taliban retreated, more contaminated areas which were previously inaccessible were surveyed. These areas included the Shomali plain, Taloqan and Kunduz.

Mine clearance has become far more mechanized in the past five years. A range of mechanical devices, from a three-tonne armoured roller, which explodes AP mines, to the 'dead fish' bulldozer which ploughs up anti-tank mines, are now being employed. However, manual mine clearance teams are still the

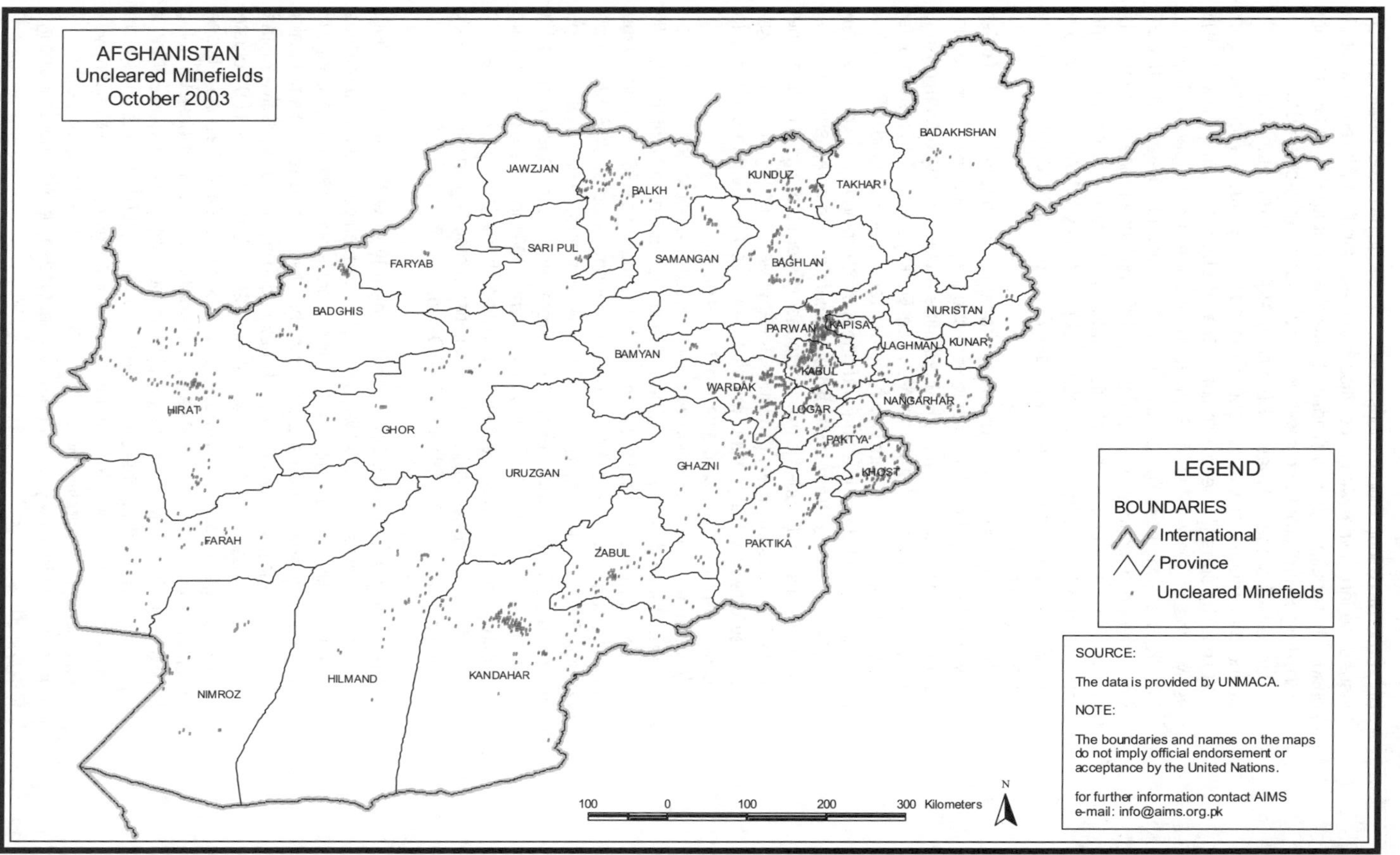
AFGHANISTAN
Uncleared Minefields
October 2003
BADAKHSHAN
JAWZJAN
BALKH
KUNDUZ
TAKHAR
SARI PUL
SAMANGAN
BAGHLAN
FARYAB
BADGHIS
NURISTAN
PARWAN
KAPISA
LAGHMAN
KUNAR
BAMYAN
KABUL
WARDAK
NANGARHAR
LOGAR
HIRAT
GHOR
PAKTYA
GHAZNI
URUZGAN
KHOST
FARAH
ZABUL
PAKTIKA
KANDAHAR
HILMAND
NIMROZ
100 0 100 200 300 Kilometers
N
LEGEND
BOUNDARIES
International
Province
Uncleared Minefields
SOURCE:
The data is provided by UNMACA.
NOTE:
The boundaries and names on the maps do not imply official endorsement or acceptance by the United Nations.
for further information contact AIMS
e-mail: info@aims.org.pk

only option in difficult, mountainous terrain. Once land has been cleared, the UN issues the landowner with a 'certificate of clean land' which requires him to ensure that opium poppies will not be grown there in future. The plan is that the UN's drug control programme will monitor the use of mine-cleared land.

Up to half of the estimated 1.5 million Afghans who returned from exile during 2002 made their way to Kabul. Clearing built-up areas, where mines and UXO may be buried beneath piles of rubble, has become a major priority, with its own challenges. As Rae McGrath, founder of the survey agency MCPA and the UK-based Mines Action Group, puts it: "In many urban areas where earth walls have collapsed through bombing, the clearance process can best be equated to the work of archaeologists, with mines often located two or more metres deep." Since half of all victims fall prey to UXO, MAPA increased its capacity for explosive ordnance disposal (EOD) during 2002 and carried out a post-conflict contamination survey.

Mine awareness has been developed to target Afghans in a range of different ways, from child-to-child sessions to special programmes for wandering *Kuchi* nomads. The BBC has included mine awareness programming in its ongoing radio drama, *New Home New Life*. During 2002-03, the UN targeted school children and teachers with mine awareness and worked to build it into the education syllabus. The huge numbers of returning Afghan refugees are particularly in danger. With many of them impatient to re-establish their homes and cropland after decades in exile, persuading them of the risks of landmines and UXO has become a key challenge. Meanwhile, some Afghans are so poor that they often try dismantling mines to remove the paraffin explosive for cooking fuel – despite being aware of the risks.

The benefits of mine action were calculated in a socio-economic impact survey conducted by the UN in 2000. The survey estimated that the benefits from clearing irrigated cropland amounted to as much as US$ 1.5 million annually per square kilometre (based on an economic loss of US$ 12,000 per fatality). The cost of clearing one square metre of contaminated land was put at around US$ 0.60. However, demining remains a deadly task. Around 100 deminers have lost their lives since 1989, while 500 more have been injured, according to the UN. The accident rate declined from 70 per year before 1998 to just seven accidents in 2001. But casualties climbed again following the US air campaign against the Taliban and Al Qa'eda.

US bombing during late 2001 created deadly new threats for civilians and deminers alike. The UXO left behind has proved particularly hazardous. Airfields, frontline troop positions and military compounds were all pounded by US bombers. In several cases, 2000-pound bombs targeted Taliban ammunition compounds and scattered debris and unexploded ordnance over a five kilometre radius. In total, the UN counted at least 234 areas hit by BLU-97 cluster bombs during the Coalition's campaign. Each bomb contains 202 bomblets and, according to the UN, a conservative estimate of the failure rate of these bomblets is 10 percent. The British-based NGO, Landmine Action – working on Pentagon sources – estimated that the US dropped around 125,000 bomblets on Afghanistan by December 2001. In their unexploded state they are hugely sensitive – even touching them lightly can set them off. Worse still, since they are dropped from a great height, they can penetrate, unexploded, up to 30 centimetres into the ground.

Nomads in no-mans land

"I was enjoying throwing the sugar-boxes on the fire. They exploded in the flames," explained a tall young Afghan to the crowd of avid listeners, "but then I trod on one. It was buried in the earth. I didn't see it." Bair Khan is a member of the *Kuchi*, a tribe of Pashtun nomads which has driven its sheep, goats and camels across the grasslands of the southern Hindu Kush since the beginning of time.

His family was nearing the end of a three-month march from the mountains of Zabul province down to the plains of Kandahar for the winter. When 19-year old Bair went on alone to prepare a camp for the night, an anti-personnel mine took his left leg off above the knee. He wrapped the bleeding stump in his turban and hobbled off in search of help. His family took him by truck to Quetta, over the border in Pakistan, where his leg was amputated. He was one of the lucky ones. Thousands of mine victims die from loss of blood or septicaemia before they make it to hospital.

I met Bair Khan in a *Kuchi* encampment east of Kandahar. He was taking part in an innovative community-based mine awareness programme started by the NGO Handicap International. As Nuri, the Afghan director of the project, explained, their aim is to build mine-awareness from the grassroots up. So his team advertises for community volunteers, trains them for two weeks, and sends them out on a motorbike and a full-time salary to run their own awareness sessions. Nuri makes random checks on his trainers and encourages them to form Mine Committees in the communities they visit. Sessions take place in mosques or, for the *Kuchis*, around a tent. "We train our trainers to tell stories, to act out the drama of an accident. They must involve the victims and learn the lessons," said Nuri.

About 50 nomads had gathered for the mine-awareness session, accompanied by half a dozen scruffy fat-bottomed sheep, a chicken and two donkeys. Waving models of mines, the trainer explained: "This one's a PMN-2. We call it the 'sugar-box.' And that's a 'butterfly' – it comes out of the sky." He tested the crowd. How do you recognise a minefield? What do you do if you see a mine? Or tread on one? Or see someone else tread on one?

Most of the nomads joined in enthusiastically, but there were dissenters too. "We don't care about mines," shouted one man, "we just want someone to feed us – we are hungry." He had a point: *Kuchis* have been the worst hit, losing about 35,000 animals to mines by 1997 – or 25 beasts per household, with a market value of US$3,000. No wonder they are worried about what to eat. *JW*

PFM-1, Soviet-made, was nicknamed the Green Parrot by Afghan guerrillas. This low-metallic plastic weapon is also called the butterfly mine. It has killed and maimed Afghan children who mistake it for a toy. *Illustration by Pamela Blotner*

The bomblets are far deadlier than a regular anti-personnel mine. On detonating, they can puncture 125 millimetres of armoured steel – enough to penetrate the underside of a tank. Their yellow casing is also a fragmentation bomb, deadly to any human within a 50 metre radius. And they act as an incendiary device which can burn houses and cropland. With their yellow casing and mini-parachute, unexploded bomblets are also a deadly new attraction to unsuspecting Afghan children. By early January 2002, 30 civilians were reported killed and 25 injured by cluster munitions in Herat alone. Heavy US bombing around the Taliban stronghold of Kandahar and along the Kunduz/ Taloqan frontline also resulted in civilian casualties and ongoing problems with UXO which set back mine clearance activities by at least one year.

Afghanistan's team of deminers had no training to deal with cluster bombs before they were dropped, although the US subsequently helped with training. The technique of prodding the ground with a bayonet or metal rod, employed by deminers in the past to find AP mines, has proved fatal with buried cluster bomblets. The entire mine action system has had to retrain its survey and clearance teams to deal with what the UN calls a "significant new threat". In the six months following US bombing, half a dozen deminers lost their lives trying to defuse cluster bombs and UXO left behind by the 'war on terrorism'. Earlier, four Afghan deminers and their dogs were accidentally killed by a US bombing raid on Kabul. Meanwhile, US$ 13 million of UN demining equipment was destroyed and looted during the US bombing.

However, one positive result of the international attention focused on Afghanistan is that donor contributions to UN-led demining operations leapt from US$ 26 million in 2001 to US$ 66 million in 2002, and MAPA's workforce swelled from 5,000 to 7,200 over the same period.

In July 2002, Afghanistan agreed to become the 144th state to sign the 1999 United Nations Convention on the Prohibition of the Use, Stockpiling, Production and Transfer of Anti-Personnel Mines and on their Destruction – otherwise known as the Ottawa Landmine Convention. This was a courageous decision given that the US, Russia, China and most of Afghanistan's neighbours have not signed the treaty.

Cluster bombs are not technically banned under the Ottawa Convention because they are designed to explode on impact (even though not all do). The ICRC is supporting an initiative to tackle the problem of "explosive remnants of war" under the Convention on Conventional Weapons. But there is considerable governmental resistance to this idea as it would force states to clear up the mess left by bombing campaigns.

Whatever else donors choose to fund, demining will have to continue. The UN-coordinated mine action programme has shown that Afghans are willing to do this for themselves. But they are not yet in a position where they can do it without the support of international funding. In 2003, the UN estimated it would take 10 years and US$ 500 million to make Afghanistan free from the threat of mines and UXO – as long as clearance operations and international funding continue at current levels. Five years work would be enough to clear high impact areas, followed by another five years to mark off and clear low priority areas. However, progress slowed during the first half of 2003 when the UN suspended mine-clearing work in many southern and south-eastern provinces due to poor security – including armed attacks on demining teams.

While the immediate issue is the clearing of minefields and battlefields, the problem will not end when they have lifted the last mine. One in eight of the population has been involved in a mine-blast incident – Afghanistan will pay the personal, economic and social costs of these weapons for decades to come.

Timothy Weaver *has worked as a journalist and cameraman with Frontline Television.* ***Jonathan Walter*** *is co-author of this guide.*

Defiance and oppression: the situation of women

By Christine Aziz, with updates by Smruti Patel and the editors

From her throne in Herat, Queen Gawhar Shad ruled an empire that stretched from the Tigris river to the borders of China. Historians acknowledge that her husband, Shah Rukh, was a weak man, and that she was the ruling force. Queen Gawhar led a cultural renaissance with her lavish patronage of the arts, attracting artists, architects, poets and philosophers to her court. Shah Rukh died in 1447, but his wife continued to rule for a further decade until she was murdered in her eightieth year.

For the women of Herat, Queen Gawhar Shad is a powerful reminder of a time when women in the region were able to command power and influence the destiny of men. Through the centuries they have made regular pilgrimages to her tomb, leaving gifts for their Queen who has become part of Afghanistan's folklore which celebrates women's strength and courage. But few visit the tomb these days.

When the Taliban took control of Herat in September 1995, the city's women, used to a history of emancipation, fell effectively under house arrest. Schools and universities were closed to them and they were forced to leave their jobs. If they went outside they had to wear the *burqa*, which covered their bodies from head to toe.

Six years later, when the Taliban were ousted from power, the international community was quick to insist that women's issues would go to the top of the agenda. "The recovery of Afghanistan must entail a restoration of the rights of Afghan women", said US Secretary of State Colin Powell in November 2001, adding: "The rights of women in Afghanistan will not be negotiable." However, as examined at the end of this chapter, the situation for most Afghan women has barely improved.

For the past century, Afghan women have been used to demonstrate the ideological and religious whims of successive governments and ruling warlords. This has been made visibly apparent to the world's onlookers through the symbolism of the veil. Afghan women have slipped in and out of it from one decade to another according to the male dictates of the day.

The beginning of the 20th Century saw the role of women in Afghanistan expanding beyond the home. Between 1919 and 1929, Amanullah Khan ruled as King. His desire to modernize the country included the gradual emancipation of women. "Religion does not require women to veil their hands, feet and faces, or enjoin any special type of veil. Tribal custom must not impose itself on the free will of the individual," he said.

Female emancipation accelerated under General Mohammed Daoud, who became Prime Minister of Afghanistan in 1953. Women were encouraged to play an active part in government and join the workforce. In 1959, women were able to enrol as students at Kabul University. This increased visibility of women did not weaken the long-held Afghan tradition that women are at the heart of the family, the most important institution in Afghan society. The honour and status of the family lie with the women, who are controlled and protected by men. The extent to which they are allowed to participate in society beyond the family is determined largely by which ethnic group they belong to and where they live. For example, Hazara and Tajik women traditionally enjoy more freedom than Pashtun women.

In 1973, Daoud ousted his cousin King Zahir Shah and became President of Afghanistan. The issue of a woman's place in society went to the very heart of the Afghan civil war in 1978. One of the main reasons for the outbreak of the fighting was the new communist government's insistence on forced literacy and mixed education for women. The invasion of Afghanistan by Soviet troops the following year led to the increased emancipation of many Afghan women. The ten-year Soviet occupation offered them greater opportunities in education, professional training and work – especially to middle-class and urban women. While thousands of women took advantage of these opportunities, there were many others who helped in the formation of the *mujahideen* in June 1979 – just months before the arrival of the Red Army. These women and later recruits would play an important role in the successful attempt to free their country from Soviet occupation.

Nooria Jehan was one such *mujahed*. In her forties and mother of seven children, she contradicts the West's cliché of the passive Muslim woman. Forceful and expressive she begins to tell her story in Farsi. No doubt her companions have heard it many times before, but they sit spellbound. Nooria was one of the many women who fought against the Soviet occupation and helped oust the pro-Soviet Kabul regime of President Najibullah in 1992 in favour of President Burhanuddin Rabbani and his military commander, Ahmed Shah Massoud. Two of her seven children were killed resisting the Soviets. "The Russians came to occupy our land, and there was a mission for all of us as parents to train and bring up our children to resist the occupation," she said. "They came to play with the dignity of women so we had to protect ourselves and children and other women. If they are occupying our land it means we have no right to do what we want with our land, our property, our country, with our children, with education, with economy, military resources. When I say 'dignity' for women, it goes with all things rooted in our country."

Until the arrival of the Soviets, Nooria had been a young mother concentrating on bringing up her children. She first became involved in the *jihad* (holy war) by distributing "night letters" – resistance pamphlets to civil servants.

"These people had no access to the activities of the *mujahideen*," Nooria recalled. "After one year, the *mujahideen* asked me to take part in terrorist activities and gave me a gun, but I found it difficult to go out and just shoot people. So I learned explosive techniques and began supervising and teaching the younger men. I was leading them into Ministries, like the Ministry of Defence, aiming directly at Russian offices. We would stick explosives under the Russians' tables and chairs." Early one morning, the Soviets came to her house and arrested her. "They said I was a leader and sentenced me to 18 years' prison," she said; but after two years, she was released in exchange for an Afghan communist and a Soviet who had been held by Massoud.

While women like Nooria were fighting alongside the *mujahideen*, there were others, particularly urban educated and working women, who although not supportive of the communist regime, were fearful of losing their new-found freedoms in the event of a *mujahed* victory. In 1989, hundreds of women were enlisted in the militia and regular army units. Horror stories of what happened to women like them at the hands of Islamic fundamentalists were circulating through the towns. One fundamentalist leader had sprayed acid in the faces of women university students in Kabul and a woman driving a minibus to a village had been dragged from the vehicle and knifed to death by Islamic traditionalists.

Sofia is younger than Nooria, and admits to feeling very sad when she looks through photographs taken when she was a school girl during Communist rule. "We used to wear socks with skirts. Look!" she said incredulously, "We were free to go out in the streets. There was more freedom for girls then. You could wear trousers and socks as well, at the university. We never wore anything too short though. We were modest and loved to adapt Western fashions to our tastes from magazines. It was fun."

The ousting of communist President Najibullah in 1992, and the takeover by Rabbani, heralded a return to traditional values. The *mujahideen* declared an Islamic Republic of Afghanistan in Kabul and once more the female population became the initial target of change to illustrate the Republic's Islamic reforms. Women's rights were no longer part of the constitution. "In the beginning it was very strict," recalled Shazia, an aid agency secretary at the time. "They put out a message on the television that we should cover our hair, not use lipstick or stand in groups laughing in public. They said it was not good for us to work. They stuck flowers over the faces of women on the television, so we couldn't see them. We were frightened and stayed in doors. I didn't go to work. But it was very difficult because my family rely on my salary. Then we started coming out, and we were defiant. We wore lipstick and would let our scarves slip and flirted with men on purpose. Some women were attacked, but slowly things began to get better and we went back to our work and to our education."

The Rabbani government always acknowledged the support of women in the fight against the Russians, and was quick to realise that unless women were allowed to work thousands of families would starve. Afghan women have borne the brunt of 24 years of war and internecine strife. In Kabul alone, 30,000 women were left as widows and sole providers of food for their families. Most of them were dependent on relief handouts provided by NGOs, the international Red Cross and Red Crescent movement and the UN. According to Amnesty International, during the early 1990s, thousands of unarmed

J. Isaac/UNICEF

civilian women were killed by unexpected and deliberate artillery attacks on their homes – the vast majority in Kabul. Most Afghan women took no active part in the fighting yet their homes and neighbourhoods were constantly bombarded. During the fighting between rival *mujahed* factions in 1992 and 1994 women became innocent targets. Women related to men sought by various *mujahed* groups, or who resisted abduction or rape, were deliberately and arbitrarily killed. Scores of young women were taken as wives for commanders or sold into prostitution. Others 'disappeared' or were stoned to death. One family in the old Microrayon area of Kabul told how members of General Dostum's faction entered their home in March 1994: "There were 12 of them all carrying kalashnikov rifles with their faces covered. They asked us to give them our daughter. We refused. One of them lifted his gun and shot our daughter in front of our eyes. She was only 20 and had just finished her high school," the mother said.

During this period, women working in professional jobs in government offices were targeted by various *mujahed* groups who considered that education under the Russians had poisoned women's minds and turned them against Islamic principles. These women's offices and homes were raided and women were abused and raped. Hundreds of professional women joined the mass exodus from Afghanistan in 1994. Those who remained had to cope silently with post-traumatic stress and dealing with the everyday struggle to feed their families and keep them warm in freezing winters. They were – and still are – regular victims of landmines. If they are lucky they will find themselves being treated at a Red Cross hospital; if not they will endure amputation without painkillers and little possibility of false limbs. Many Afghan men do not see the need for their wives to have a prosthesis fitted because they say it does not matter if they have to stay at home.

In September 1996, the capital fell to the Taliban. Prior to this, an estimated 8,000 women students had enrolled at Kabul University. Seventy percent of the teachers in Kabul were estimated to be women but were ordered to stay at home. Forty percent of the 150,000 children attending school in Kabul were girls. But to the women of Afghanistan, the Taliban were yet another regime which used them as ideological tools, destroying whatever rights they had managed to hang on to. As citizens of Rabbani's former Islamic Republic of Afghanistan, women had been able to work and study alongside their brothers. They were not allowed to travel abroad, had to cover their heads in the streets and could not drive cars. "These were small prices to pay for the right to work and be educated," said Dr Ester, a former surgeon at Kabul's largest hospital.

However, in every region overrun by the Taliban, their first act was to issue a decree banning all women from public places, jobs and institutions. "Women, you should not step outside your residence," warned a notice issued to the women of Kabul by Mawlawi Rafiullah Moazin, general president of the Religious Police. "If you go outside the house you should not be like women who used to go with fashionable clothes wearing much cosmetics and appearing in front of every man before the coming of Islam...If women are going outside with fashionable ornamental and charming clothes to show themselves, they will be cursed by the Islamic *shari'a* and should never expect to go to heaven."

What would the head of the Taliban's Religious Police have thought of the Afghan heroine, Malalai, who (unveiled) in July 1880 carried the Afghan flag into battle, after her fellow soldiers were killed by the British? Her spirit has been echoed in the defiant voices of many Afghan woman. In Bamiyan, for example, Hazara women organized themselves into militia groups to fight Muslim extremists. They saw what happened to their sisters in Taliban-run areas and did not want the same fate. The region in which they lived was poor and cut off in the winter by heavy snows, but the women were defiant. They also set up a university, despite a severe lack of resources.

In the same spirit, a passionate and courageous appeal was made to the Taliban by a female academic to let women go to work and school. Sidiqa Sidiq, a professor of archaeology in her fifties, quoted extensively from the Koran to tell the newly-arrived Taliban leaders that they were wrong to order women to stay at home. "Based on the orders of the Holy Koran, I am requesting all the concerned brothers and individuals to release us from this detention and these chains and let us continue our education and our jobs. Under the Islamic law that is the prime need for the development of our ruined homeland," she said, adding an appeal to Afghan women to fight for their rights: "Oh sisters, we have to be determined and must not be like our grandfathers expecting assistance from our compatriots abroad and from foreign organizations and countries, because they are shouting only for political propaganda."

Sidiqa's cynicism regarding the foreign response to the plight of women of Afghanistan may well be justified. The human rights abuses committed by the Taliban against women were ignored by the world's media until the militia's arrival in Kabul, where Western journalists witnessed the public whipping of women with bicycle chains because they had not worn their *burqas* correctly. The female populations of Kandahar and Herat had been living under the same conditions for at least two years beforehand.

The Taliban clearly flouted the United Nations declaration which calls for the universal application to women "of rights and principles with regard to equality, security, integrity and dignity of all human persons." But UN officials in Afghanistan consistently failed to take up the issue of female rights with Taliban leaders. The pressure group, Equality Now, reported that several UN agencies operating in Jalalabad suspended all female Afghan employees in early 1997 under pressure from government and rebel forces, thus contravening the UN Covenant on Civil and Political Rights to which Afghanistan is a signatory.

In August 1997 the Taliban instructed medical NGOs in Kabul to stop treating female patients in existing hospitals and transfer them to the partially destroyed Rabi'a Balkhi health centre where they would be treated separately. "The centre was not fit for patients, and for two months while we argued with the Taliban, there was nowhere for the women to be treated," said one aid worker whose agency refused to cooperate with the Taliban request, along with other health agencies. Only the World Health Organization (WHO), whose Saudi representative had congratulated the Taliban on taking power, agreed to comply with their request and offered funds to refurbish the centre. "We finally convinced the authorities to allow women into Kabul's hospitals. But it was a very serious situation as some women could not be treated for two months," the aid worker said.

In the main, it was left to individual agencies to voice support for women. During the Taliban years, approximately 75 percent of women's programmes were affected because skilled Afghan women were needed to access, run and monitor assistance. Save the Children Fund (UK), for example, withdrew from Herat, and British agency, Oxfam, suspended its water and sanitation programme in Kabul, citing operational difficulties concerning access for both expatriate and local women as the problem. It was a slow process among international agencies to unite under standard international rights for women.

Following the fall of the Taliban in the autumn of 2001, many Afghan women were hopeful. The promise of peace and legitimate governance raised expectations of greater freedom and rights for women and girls. UN Security Council resolution 1325 called for the broad participation of women in peace-building and post-conflict reconstruction. The Bonn Agreement of December 2001 laid out guidelines for the development of women's roles, including a pledge for their participation in the *Loya Jirga* and the creation of a Ministry of

Women's Affairs in the new Afghan Interim Administration. An EU resolution called for "granting of international aid for the reconstruction of Afghanistan to be made conditional on the participation of women in decision-making and in the use of such aid" and "the EU to ensure that Afghan women are the direct beneficiaries of between 25% and 30% of the economic aid provided for reconstruction of Afghanistan". Meanwhile, the inter-agency working group for the rights of Afghan women also made recommendations to ensure that the voices of women be heard and their rights and needs be systematically addressed in the reconstruction and development of Afghanistan.

Eleven percent of the seats in the *Loya Jirga* were reserved, resulting in the election of 200 women. For the first time in Afghanistan's history, there is a Ministry of Women's Affairs, with a woman in charge. Another female cabinet minister is responsible for Public Health. And an Afghan woman heads the new Human Rights Commission. Officially women are permitted to work outside the home again and schools are once more open to girls. Female teachers and lawyers who had no choice but to work undercover during the Taliban regime are now openly practising their profession. For the first time in at least five years, 1,000 women took part in university examinations. Primary education is also a success story, with around one million girls (one third of all pupils) returning to school during 2002. Meanwhile, in early 2003, the Afghan administration took a big step forward by ratifying the Convention on the Elimination of All Forms of Discrimination against Women (CEDAW).

All this, however, is only the beginning – with a large gap opening up between rhetoric and reality. In the run-up to the *Loya Jirga* for example, many educated women in western Afghanistan had been told of their rights only days prior to the vote. They were angered that they had not been given more time to prepare or allocated numbers of seats more commensurate with their share in the overall population (over 50 percent). Meanwhile, most women's rights guaranteed on paper remain widely abused on the ground.

Several reports on the situation in Herat in late 2002 by the NGO Human Rights Watch described a city where women live in fear. Under the command of the regional ruler and warlord, Ismail Khan (a former *mujahed* commander who was backed by the US and Iran), Herat is once again subjected to a fundamentalist vision of Islam. While women are no longer openly beaten in the streets – as happened under the Taliban – their every move is strictly policed. Taliban-style laws and policies continue to apply – women and girls who break the rules risk being harassed, threatened or arrested. If caught outside their homes with a man suspected of being unrelated to them, women are forced to go to hospital for a physical 'chastity test'. They are forbidden from speaking publicly or to journalists about women's rights, and they are routinely excluded from decision-making bodies. Khan, of whom Human Rights Watch was especially critical, is said to have pressured women not to work with international NGOs or the United Nations – Herati women are even forbidden from meeting foreign men alone or travelling by car with them. One lady told researchers: "the leadership here is very bad for us. It is not much different than the Taliban".

Nationwide, ongoing insecurity and injustice continue to threaten the rights of women. Banditry and lawlessness are rife not only outside Kabul but in some parts of the capital. Most women continue to fear physical violence and threats to their personal security, which in turn discourages them from participating in reconstruction and public life. Sima Samar, former Minister for Women and now head of the Human Rights Commission, herself became a target of abuse and threats of violence.

In a report dated October 2003, Amnesty International raised serious concerns about the ability of the international community or the Afghan administration to protect women. "The risk of rape and sexual violence by members of armed factions and former combatants is still high", said the report, adding that forced marriage of girls and violence against women in the home are widespread across the country. Even more chilling, Amnesty maintained that: "these crimes of violence continue with the active support or passive complicity of state agents, armed groups, families and communities". If and when the perpetrators of such violence are caught, the prospects of justice remain remote: "The criminal justice system is too weak to offer effective protection of women's right to life and physical security, and itself subjects them to discrimination and abuse." Meanwhile, according to the human rights group, donor governments supporting the reform of the police and judiciary have failed to ensure the support of women's rights.

Despite widespread international rhetoric about women's rights during the Taliban years – and despite claims that their rights would be at the centre of a new post-Taliban Afghanistan – the international community has remained largely deaf and blind to the ongoing threats to women's security and rights happening under the nose of the country's Western-backed government. The rights gained by a small, educated elite have not extended to the millions of rural women who have yet to see much change in their status. And rights may mean little to those without resources to cope: there are two million war widows, many of whom struggle to feed their families as they have no opportunity to earn their own living.

No one expects the situation to change overnight. The rights of women and girls have been a contentious issue in Afghan politics and society for the last hundred years. Women's rights have been used to polarize political and ideological conflicts, and reforms directed at women have often led to political instability. Afghan women are no strangers to exploitation, but in recent years their exploitation has taken new forms, as various international actors, driven by their own political agendas, have sought to make capital out of championing their rights. The main issue is whether Afghan women will now be able to set their own agendas as opposed to adopting those of well-meaning outsiders.

Meanwhile, for rights on paper to be upheld in practice, much needs to change. Better security is a crucial first step, along with reform of the criminal justice system. Better healthcare is equally urgent, as Afghanistan's women suffer catastrophic levels of maternal mortality – as high as 6,500 per 100,000 in Badakhshan according to a recent UN survey. The aid community has a responsibility to ensure that Afghan women are fully involved in planning and implementing reconstruction programmes. Better public education – of men as well as women – is essential to ensure that initiatives promoting women's rights do not backfire in the face of male resistance.

In December 2003, one fifth of the 500 delegates taking part in the Constitutional Loya Jirga (CLJ) were women. As Afghan expert Barnett Rubin pointed out, this is a higher proportion of women than in the US Congress. However, when a young female delegate, Malalai Joya, stood up during the CLJ to criticise the *mujahideen* for dragging her country into war, she caused uproar, received threats and had to seek protection under the United Nations. Nor is Joya alone – women in eastern Afghanistan received death threats after putting their names forward as delegates to the CLJ, while others have complained that their husbands and fathers would not let them leave home to register as voters in 2004's elections. Meanwhile, the new Constitution fails to explicitly recognise women's equality with men, but simply states: "all Afghans have equal rights and duties before the law".

Perhaps the greatest source of hope remains the resilience and courage of Afghan women themselves, which manifests itself every day: the welcoming smile from a woman who wants to invite you into her home to share what little she has; the determination of so many young women to continue their studies in makeshift buildings and despite threats of violence, so they can acquire skills to rebuild their country; the quiet defiance of women in the face of tyranny. These are the qualities that cannot remain hidden behind the *burqa*.

Christine Aziz *is a freelance journalist working out of Amsterdam and London. The editors would like to acknowledge the assistance of Smruti Patel in updating this overview.*

Blowing hot and cold: 20 years of US policy

By William Dowell

Ever since the US-led bombing of Afghanistan in October 2001, there has been a great deal of talk in Washington about Afghan reconstruction – talk that, by mid-2003, was only beginning to be matched by firm action on the ground. Elizabeth Kvitashvili, formerly of the United States' Agency for International Development (USAID) in Kabul, was recently quoted in the *New York Times* as saying that the ability of the Kabul authorities under President Hamid Karzai not only to handle reconstruction funds, but also to account for them, remained uncertain. According to a September 2003 report by New York University's Center on International Cooperation, after 18 months of aid, less than one percent of Afghanistan's reconstruction needs had been met. This, despite promises by President Bush of a new 'Marshall Plan' for Afghanistan.

The joke going around Kabul is that Afghanistan's two greatest sources of foreign currency are narcotics and foreign aid. Only it is not a joke. Afghanistan's production of raw opium has returned to near the peak levels of the late 1990s and is not only reshaping the country's economy but providing a source of revenue (estimated by the UN Drug Office in Vienna at US$ 2.5 billion for 2002-03) that enables organized crime groups to compete effectively with the transitional government for political and military power. While the drug lords are building formidable empires, many fear that very little of the US$ 1.8 billion in aid given to Afghanistan during 2002 has any hope of actually reaching the Afghan public. As much as 75 percent is reportedly going towards purchasing equipment from foreign countries, paying US-based contractors and employees and supporting the mushrooming international aid infrastructure of offices, 4x4 vehicles and expatriate salaries for a wide assortment of NGOs and UN agencies based in Kabul. As attacks by pro-Taliban, Al Qa'eda and other anti-government elements against foreigners and Afghans increase, there is a strong incentive for everyone and everything to stay clustered in the capital.

Reconstruction has been seriously hampered by the lack of a commercial banking system, although one was expected to be established during 2004. Most aid agencies have to carry cash in by hand from Dubai, Islamabad and elsewhere, or deal with local money dealers who, despite their extraordinary efficiency in procuring funds quickly, charge handsomely for it. Yet for many ordinary Afghans, this is the only way to bring money into the country. Neither does Afghanistan have a credible legal system, or for that matter, lawyers to run a commercial economy. Corruption is rampant. Transportation is regularly shaken down by various warlords for exorbitant 'customs duties', little of which ever reaches the transitional administration. Lest anyone doubt that the current government is a fiction created by Washington, President Hamid Karzai is kept alive by a praetorian guard of hulking American guards, provided by a private security firm. Karzai, disdainfully referred to by some as the mayor of Kabul, has struggled to persuade provisional governors to turn over the revenues that his administration desperately needs to function.

Afghanistan has always been poor by the global standards established by the United Nations – it does not even figure on the UN's 2003 Human Development Index (SEE ECONOMICS). The Afghan government estimated its GDP for 2002-03 at around US$ 4 billion (excluding the vast sums generated by drug trafficking), which works out at US$ 180 per capita based on a population of 22 million (the figures used by a September 2003 report by the International Monetary Fund). But it cannot be more than an educated guess, as no comprehensive nationwide population census or reliable economic assessments have been undertaken since the late 1970s. Since then, a quarter of a century of war has killed 1.5 million people, not including the toll wrought by preventable diseases and starvation. Countless more have been wounded or turned into refugees. Through commission and omission, foreign governments including the US, have had a hand in Afghanistan's miseries.

From the December 1979 Soviet invasion onwards, the common denominator across multiple US administrations has been a general lack of interest in the Afghan people themselves. There have been moments of intense concern, but that was usually focused on geopolitical objectives that had little or nothing to do with the people of this rugged Central Asian nation. Afghanistan was seen as an opportunity for increasing pressure on the Soviet Union, or for projecting American influence in the Central and South Asian region, particularly with regard to oil and natural gas resources, or for striking at international terrorism. Despite the rhetoric, the future of the people actually living there seemed secondary, or well beyond the limits of American interest or available resources. In fact, reconstructing Afghanistan was never beyond American resources. Washington was quite content to spend US$ 10 billion on ousting the Taliban and Al Qa'eda, plus one billion dollars per month since then chasing them across the mountains and deserts of Afghanistan. But reconstructing the country's shattered society and infrastructure has only attracted a fraction of that amount.

The Afghans expected the Americans to be more like the British in the 19th Century, the extension of US imperial power to be just another version of the British Empire. But the British had compelling reasons for maintaining a strategic interest in the region. Before World War II, Britain considered India to be the most important source of its colonial wealth. There was a constant fear that the Russians might someday try to overthrow the British Raj in India. Afghanistan was considered a crucial buffer. Britain did not need much from Afghanistan in

a material sense, but it did need to know what was happening there. And it fielded intrepid intelligence officers who spoke the language and were willing to disappear incognito inside the country for months, even years, on end. Besides, a major portion of the United Kingdom's foreign policy establishment was focused on the region. The US never saw the importance of the area in quite that way. After World War II, India became independent and promptly positioned itself with the non-aligned movement to be as annoying as possible to Washington's foreign policy objectives. With not much to gain, the US saw little reason to bother with the region. "The British attached quite a bit of importance to this part of the world," a high-level US State Department official casually informed this writer in the early 1980s. "We don't see it."

The Soviet takeover of Afghanistan shocked and appalled most Americans, but it was not clear what the US could, or should, do about it. In fact, the US Central Intelligence Agency (CIA) was determined not to get involved. All that changed when a maverick Texas congressman, Charlie Wilson, fell under the influence of a vivacious Houston socialite, who was close to Pakistan's President Zia ul-Haq. Swept up in the romanticism of the *mujahideen's* struggle against the Soviets, Wilson eventually picked up a swashbuckling ally inside the CIA, Gust Avrakotos, a renegade known for challenging the conventional wisdom of his superiors. Together, Wilson and Avrakotos influenced the CIA to mount one of its biggest covert operations in history, and to provide the Stinger missiles the *mujahideen* needed to counter the Soviet Union's highly destructive Hind Mi-24 helicopter gunships.

By 1986, US involvement in Afghanistan was changing rapidly. An estimated US$ 600 million a year of military and humanitarian aid was being channelled towards the *mujahideen*, primarily via the Zia dictatorship and the resistance politicians based in Peshawar in Pakistan's North West Frontier Province. As Marin Strmecki, a frequent commentator on Afghanistan, has pointed out, Zia had his own agenda – to turn Pakistan into a dagger pointed at the heart of India. To accomplish that, the country's dictator dreamed of creating a pan-Islamic alliance financed by Saudi Arabia's oil money, armed by a Pakistani nuclear weapon, driven by religious fervour, and manipulated and ultimately managed by Pakistan's equivalent to the CIA, the military's Inter-Services Intelligence organization (ISI). The invasion of Afghanistan by atheistic communists provided an almost perfect growth medium for the strategy.

With the US opponents to intervention in Afghanistan out-manoeuvred by Charlie Wilson's band, the CIA now turned to Pakistan's ISI for its local expertise. The ISI directed the sudden flow of American support to four Islamic fundamentalist groups it felt would best help in Zia's greater strategic plan. The groups were Gulbuddin Hekmatyar's Hezb-e-Islami, Younis Khalis' Hezb-e-Islami, Burhanuddin Rabbani's Jamiat-e-Islami and Abdul Rasul Sayyaf's Ittihad-e-Islami. The bulk of this aid went to Hekmatyar, despite his relatively poor showing on the battlefield inside Afghanistan. Hekmatyar was known to have collaborated with the Soviets on various occasions in a bid to undermine other resistance groups and to strengthen his own position. He was also responsible for severe human rights abuses, including the murder of numerous political opponents and journalists. (In 2002, Hekmatyar was branded a 'terrorist' by Washington, following his declaration of *jihad* against the United States for intervening in Afghanistan.)

Hekmatyar's unsavoury reputation, however, did not appear to faze Wilson or the CIA operatives now managing the operation. They ignored the warnings of experienced journalists and aid workers, many of whom had witnessed first hand some of Hekmatyar's excesses, and insisted that he was the most effective of all the resistance leaders. To its credit, Hekmatyar's party did possess an extremely efficient public relations apparatus. Hekmatyar also spoke English, which for some of the Americans involved made a significant difference. Indirectly, but knowingly too, the United States cooperated with or otherwise supported foreign Islamic groups, such as the Arab *Wahabi* headed by the likes of Saudi terrorist Osama Bin Laden, who sought to co-opt the Pashtun *mujahideen* in the eastern provinces with money and weapons in a bid to create a new and purist Islamic Afghanistan. While there is no evidence establishing formal links between the US and Bin Laden, the Americans were certainly aware of his presence and considered him a useful tool in their efforts to give the Soviets a hard time. Bin Laden, who had funding of his own (and a lot of it, by Afghan standards) had first come to Pakistan and Afghanistan during the early 1980s and established what he called the "Services" office in Peshawar in 1984.

On the other hand, the more effective commanders of the so-called "Resistance of the Interior", such as Ahmed Shah Massoud, Ismail Khan and Abdul Haq, were largely ignored or only supported half-heartedly by the Americans, mainly because they were far too independent for the Pakistanis. While numerous proponents of Afghanistan regarded this as an admirable project in support of a nation fighting for its freedom, it eventually unleashed a chain of events hardly anyone one in Washington could have predicted.

In the United States, offices were set up to recruit Muslims to fight against the Soviets in Afghanistan. Training in special operations was provided to Afghans and Pakistanis through the special forces' John F. Kennedy Special Warfare Center. From the beginning of Charlie Wilson's campaign, it was obvious that the US objective in Afghanistan was to cause pain to the Soviet Union. As one CIA representative told EFG author Edward Girardet in 1987 at a "Beltway Rat" think tank seminar on Afghanistan: "our role is to make the Soviets bleed with their own Vietnam." There was little or no thought about what would happen to the Afghans once the Soviets left. The fact that Afghanistan's pre-war evolution towards a functional secular and technocratic state had been replaced by religious frenzy and ethnic hatreds was simply allowed to fall between the cracks, dismissed as someone else's problem – until the problem boomeranged.

As soon as the Soviets withdrew from Afghanistan in 1989, US support for the *mujahideen* began to wind down. The Red Army had been defeated, or at least, forced to withdraw, so there was no longer any reason to continue supporting the Afghans. Many observers warned that simply abandoning Afghanistan would only create conditions for an even more brutal civil war, Beirut-style, among the *mujahideen*, who had been heavily armed and supported by outside players such as the Americans. The fact that the United States might have a responsibility for continued war in Afghanistan appeared to fall on deaf ears within the US administration. The Americans felt further justified for disassociating themselves when it became clear that the communist Najibullah regime was not going to collapse immediately – this despite a major push by the Pakistanis to have the *mujahideen* with Hekmatyar at the helm take over Jalalabad and then move on to the Afghan capital. In fact, it took over three years for the government of the People's Democratic Party of Afghanistan (PDPA) to fall in April 1992 at the hands of the resistance forces, who were by now bickering amongst themselves at the barrel of a gun.

From 1990 onwards, US money to Afghanistan virtually dried up, yet Pakistan's ISI pushed on as best it could with its original strategy. While the US was effectively out of the picture, Saudi money was still there. Throughout the 1980s and early 1990s, the Saudis were more than generously aiding Afghan education in Pakistan's refugee camps by funding Islamic schools known as *madrassas*, everywhere. Such support was also directed towards areas held by *mujahideen* inside Afghanistan, particularly in rural eastern areas. What the Americans failed to notice was that the schools were promoting a carefully concocted vision of the world in ferocious conflict with Washington's global vision. This should not have been surprising. When Egyptian presidents Nasser and Sadat cracked down on the Muslim Brotherhood from the 1950s onwards, and drove the most radical activists in the movement out of Egypt, many of these political refugees ended up in Saudi Arabia and took jobs as radical teachers. Subsequently, the best students of the new *madrassas* in Pakistan and Afghanistan became prime candidates for the upcoming anti-Western *jihad*.

By the mid-1990s, Osama Bin Laden, who had previously been helpful and even friendly to the CIA, was beginning to be recognised as a potentially dangerous terrorist who was anything but friendly to the US. He was obsessed with the presence of American troops in Saudi Arabia (which acts as custodian of the Holy sites in Mecca and Medina). He was also obsessed that Saudi Arabia had immense oil wealth, yet remained subservient and even obsequious in front of infidels and non-believers, most of whom seemed to be directed by Washington and financial interests in New York. Osama was operating from Sudan, but Khartoum was coming under increasing pressure from Washington to force him to leave. Afghanistan was a natural choice for an alternative safe haven.

In the meantime, Pakistan's ISI had switched its support from Hekmatyar, who had failed to garner the support they had hoped inside Afghanistan, to a new and potentially more effective Islamic movement, the Taliban. From 1994 onwards, if not before, it began funnelling supplies and providing discreet military support to these militants, many of whom had emerged from the Afghan refugee camps and *madrassas* in Pakistan. The ISI introduced Osama Bin Laden to the Taliban's leader, Mullah Omar, and Bin Laden finally made the move from Sudan to Afghanistan during the mid-1990s. Regardless of Pakistan's longer-range objectives, Bin Laden had his own vision. His movement, Al Qa'eda, originally founded to organize Saudi help to the Afghan resistance during the 1980s, now had offices in 68 countries. Al Qa'eda would deliver both a wakeup call to Washington and a message to the increasingly secular rulers of the Islamic world.

On the morning of September 11, 2001, a coordinated attack using four hijacked passenger airliners brought down the World Trade Center's twin towers in New York and destroyed a wing of the Pentagon building, while the fourth en route to a target in Washington crashed in a field in Pennsylvania. The death toll of close to 3,000 people, nearly all civilians, exceeded that of the Japanese attacks on Pearl Harbor that had spurred America into World War II.

Amidst public shock and a national outcry, the White House National Security Council and Pentagon planners scrambled to prepare a response. Secretary of State Colin Powell embarked on a swift and public tour of diplomatic coalition-building. The CIA, meanwhile, prepared the ground by dropping covert agents into the mountains of Afghanistan, equipped with suitcases containing several million dollars in cash to buy the allegiance of United Front[1] commanders for the battle ahead. The ferocious effectiveness of the assault on the Taliban took even the Pentagon by surprise. From October 7 to December 17, 2001, the US dropped 24,000 bombs on an estimated 40,000 to 60,000 Taliban troops (as many as half of them Pakistanis) and another 10,000 foreigners fighting for Al Qa'eda. Fifty-four percent of the munitions were precision-guided 'smart bombs'. The US dropped an average of 100 JDAM 'smart bombs' a day at a cost of US$ 14,000 each. The overall cost of the assault – including munitions, transportation and support – was estimated at US$ 10.2 billion.

The war's rapid success gave Defense Secretary Donald Rumsfeld a bureaucratic advantage in Washington, and cleared the way for a radical redesign of US defence policy. Instead of overwhelming troop strength, backed by massive, conventional firepower, Rumsfeld favoured smaller, highly mobile special forces operations supported by high-tech computer-guided munitions. Another strategic consequence concerned US influence over Central Asia and its vast oil and gas fields. The need to pre-position forces for the war cleared

[1] *Also known as the Northern Alliance – a term coined by the ISI to characterise Massoud's organization as a primarily northern military front that did not include Pashtuns, a premise that was not entirely true given the late commander's constant efforts to involve key Pashtun allies, such as Abdul Qadir of Jalalabad.*

the way for the US to establish logistical bases in the region, particularly in Uzbekistan. A number of key officials of the Bush administrative had been involved with the efforts of US oil company UNOCAL and its efforts to develop a pipeline from Turkmenistan's huge gas fields across Afghanistan to the Arabian Sea during the 1990s. Meanwhile, the Caspian Sea's recently discovered oil reserves have been estimated at a colossal 75 billion barrels. The presence of US military power in the region could provide America with an extra bargaining chip in future energy negotiations.

The speed of the victory in Afghanistan left Washington off guard about how to proceed next. To complicate matters, it was hard to tell who within the US administration was really in charge. While USAID was given the mandate for reconstruction in the south, the Pentagon still had authority for reconstruction in the north. ISAF, the international security force for Kabul, was under the nominal control of the UN Security Council. Although the US had been a key player in the Security Council, it virtually stopped talking to the UN after other members of the Council refused to support the war in Iraq in early 2003. Moreover, the US used its position on the Security Council to block any efforts to increase the size of ISAF beyond 5,000 troops, a view shared by other contributors such as the British, Germans and Dutch. Washington didn't want to be drawn into another Vietnam, and in any case needed to keep as many troops as possible free for the assault on Iraq. But without international security outside Kabul, significant reconstruction was all but impossible.

In late-2003, Rumsfeld softened his stance on expanding ISAF and NATO (which had taken command of ISAF in August 2003) agreed to expand the force beyond Kabul – initially by sending 450 German and Belgian troops to Kunduz, a northern town not considered a major security risk and endowed with an easily defendable airstrip. Ironically, Kunduz was where the Pakistanis were secretly allowed by the Americans to remove planeloads of Pakistani military personnel, who had supported the Taliban and Al Qa'eda following the October 2001 intervention, to avoid embarrassment.

In order to raise local support for the war, the US had funnelled money and equipment to the various warlords of the United Front . When the Taliban regime fell, the United Front – which now consisted mainly of ethnic Tajiks, Hazaras, Uzbeks and Turkmen – were supposed to wait outside Kabul, rather than entering the capital in victory. But America's new allies were not to be prevented from enjoying the moment for which they had been fighting the Taliban for five years. By late 2003, two years after the fall of Kabul, tens of thousands of United Front troops – along with hundreds of heavy weapons systems – remained within firing range of the presidential palace, undermining the authority of the transitional Afghan government and its fledgling national army.

Once the war was over, Washington eventually threw its support behind Hamid Karzai, a moderate Pashtun from Kandahar, as interim president. Already well known among international aid and diplomatic circles in Pakistan during the late 1980s, Karzai had been part of the so-called Rome Group, a collection of ethnic Pashtuns centred around Afghanistan's former king. While engaged in the actual war, the CIA had bypassed the Rome group and dealt directly with various tribal warlords. Subsequently, the CIA acknowledged that Karzai was the best man for the job, primarily because Afghans have always liked their Kabul leaders to command respect but to remain relatively weak. The

US continued to rely heavily on its own 'insider', Zalmay Khalilzad, an Afghan-born American who became President Bush's security advisor on Islamic affairs. Khalilzad, however, had his own vision of what should happen in Afghanistan, a fact which further undercut Karzai's authority.

The obvious reason for picking Karzai, who is urbane, charming and speaks excellent English, was that he is a Pashtun, Afghanistan's largest ethnic group. The Pashtuns, rulers of Afghanistan for two centuries, quite naturally resented the attempts of the United Front to claim leadership of the country as part of the spoils of war. But unfortunately no clear decision was made in the beginning as to who should really be in control. Mohammed Fahim, an ethnic Tajik, who was appointed as Karzai's defence minister, was not only a key Massoud man and member of the United Front, but also a Panjshairi, who fought tooth and nail against having any international peace keeping troops in Afghanistan at all. Fahim finally agreed to allow 5,000 troops to be stationed in Kabul, on the condition that he could keep his own personal troops – which greatly outnumber ISAF – on the outskirts of the city. Fahim, who was made vice-president and could succeed Karzai, has insisted on appointing mostly Tajiks to key defence posts. He also maintained a heavy arsenal of firepower in the Panjshair Valley. Meanwhile, ethnic Tajiks from the United Front were appointed to head the powerful foreign and interior ministries. Despite minor reshuffles during 2003, the idea of an all-inclusive, multi-ethnic government – demanded by the Bonn Agreement of December 2001 – has yet to penetrate.

Other key figures within the Karzai administration are still manoeuvring for what they see will be the final showdown that will reveal who actually can hold on to power. Afghanistan remains an unresolved civil war in slow motion. In that context, whatever reconstruction does succeed could be undone at almost any time. Without a more powerful international peacekeeping presence (particularly in the more volatile regions of the north, south and southeast) coupled with more effective reconstruction initiatives in the provinces, Afghanistan will continue to remain unstable. By mid-2003, the security situation was already considered to be far worse in many areas than prior to the fall of the Taliban, with one third of the country off limits to international aid workers.

Pakistan is still trying to shape Afghan politics, but it is less than clear who calls the shots. While President Musharraf, under pressure from the US, dismissed the top leadership of the ISI after the events of September 11, 2001, many lower ranking members of the organization still sympathize with the Taliban. Pakistan has succeeded in arresting various members of Al Qa'eda – most notably the capture in Rawalpindi of Khalid Sheikh Mohammed, the movement's operations chief, in March 2003. And during the year, the Pakistani military began stepping up its operations – with the support of ISI – against Al Qa'eda elements in select border areas, such as Waziristan. But Pakistan has failed to take similar action against resurgent Taliban elements, which by late 2003 were operating openly in Pakistan's border provinces of Baluchistan and the North West Frontier, areas whose people are sympathetic to the Taliban cause. Meanwhile on Afghanistan's western border, Iran is believed to be hedging its bets by providing some support to former Taliban and Al Qa'eda in frontier areas.

While many Afghans were happy to see the Taliban go, the way America has treated Taliban and Al Qa'eda prisoners since the war has not helped the

US cause. The incarceration at Bagram airbase and Cuba's Guantanamo Bay of suspected Taliban and Al Qa'eda fighters (conveniently classified as 'enemy combatants' rather than 'prisoners of war') has been widely criticised as 'above the law' by organizations such as the International Committee of the Red Cross and by legal experts such as Justice Goldstone, former head of the International Tribunal at The Hague. The dozens of suspects who have been released as innocent, most of them following more than a year in detention in conditions unacceptable under international law, have received no apology or compensation. Some, it appears, were fingered by Afghan rivals as Al Qa'eda or Taliban in return for bounties with no evidence whatsoever of a terrorist affiliation. Some, according to the BBC, were even kidnapped by US, Pakistani and other operatives outside Afghanistan for transportation to Bagram and Guantanamo. Two prisoners in US detention at Bagram were killed as the result of homicide, according to US military pathology reports. Increasingly, the United States is being perceived by Afghans and Pakistanis alike as acting arrogantly and with little consideration for the local population. For Goldstone, the decisions of the US government to persist with such incarcerations, as well as to use torture, kidnapping and other methods contrary to international conventions, can only undermine current efforts to protect democracy against terrorism.

As a number of analysts, such as Anthony Cordesman at Georgetown's Center for Strategic and International Studies, have pointed out, the US-led intervention has dispersed rather than destroyed the Taliban and Al Qa'eda fighters. The danger is that, like a self-transforming virus, the survivors are learning to adapt their tactics to take advantage of American weaknesses. Taliban groups are now operating in the tens, even hundreds, in the border regions between Pakistan and Afghanistan, launching deadly daily attacks against not only Coalition and Afghan government forces, but against civilians, aid workers and religious figures. It has become asymmetric warfare with a vengeance. The other early lesson from Afghanistan is that although American force is lethal in a head-on confrontation, the US is weak when it comes to intelligence. It has shown itself vulnerable to manipulation by duplicitous Afghan tribal chiefs. For example, when the US tried to depend on Afghan groups to surround Al Qa'eda at Tora Bora in November 2001, Al Qa'eda forces were able to bribe their way out and slip through the Americans' fingers.

At the root of the problem has been the American administration's ongoing attempt to buy the loyalty of Afghan warlords with both money and weapons, coupled with promises of eventual political power. In the north, for example, the forces of Uzbek General Dostum and Tajik Atta Mohammed have continued to clash – leading to dozens of deaths and creating an atmosphere of lawlessness in which reconstruction cannot get started. According to the prominent US-based Afghan analyst, Barnett Rubin, speaking in October 2003, these northern factions "are actually groups that were armed by the United States and funded by the United States, and are still considered by the United States as our allies in the war on terrorism, and this shows the basic contradiction in US policy in Afghanistan. We claim to be supporting the government of Hamid Karzai, and yet, we have been allied with these factions that are undermining it and alienating people from it and driving them into the arms of the Taliban."

Now that the pattern of supporting local strongmen has been set, it is difficult to introduce the notions of civic responsibility as an afterthought. Yet, what most ordinary Afghans want is an end to the reign of the warlords, in particular the so-called *jihadists*, and a government that they can claim as theirs. Hence the bitter criticism by local populations of the former *mujaheds* such as Herat's Ismail Khan, who claim to be acting in the interests of the people, but who are in fact only ensuring their own continued power, through a combination of Taliban-era restrictions and intimidation.

Although the situation appears to be fundamentally grim, there are policy options that do make sense. Spreading an international security blanket across the entire country – and not just Kabul – is a crucial first step. According to the US-based Henry Stimson Center, a peacekeeping force of 18,000 troops (far less than was sent to the Balkans) could secure Afghanistan's borders and main roads, while suppressing factional fighting, for a cost of around US$ 1.6 billion per year. Tackling the disarmament of different armed groups and demobilizing the country's estimated 100,000-200,000 militia fighters would be the next key step. The move towards forming a stable government requires a political process, which cannot succeed while ordinary people feel intimidated to vote in a particular way by local strongmen. Getting vital public services up and running – clean water, sanitation and primary healthcare – is essential in a country where one in four children dies before the age of five. Reconstruction needs considerably more resources – at least US$ 20 billion over the next four years, according to the US-based NGO CARE International.

Most observers feel that the transitional administration of Hamid Karzai is not bad – it merely lacks credibility and authority outside Kabul. That can be changed gradually by funnelling resources through the transitional government's own development budget, rather than by distributing aid directly to ministries, individuals and private contractors. The US administration is beginning to realise that the money and arms it has channelled to regional warlords has had the effect of weakening the Kabul administration. These warlords eventually have to be confronted, their private armies disbanded, and their tax revenues delivered to Kabul. Only then will the government's influence extend throughout the country. That will require patience, understanding and subtlety from the US. What is really needed is a longer-term strategic vision which puts ordinary Afghans at the top of the list of priorities.

Is Afghanistan worth the expense and trouble for America? Common sense says that it is. A failure to act effectively this time around will encourage the development of drug-fuelled criminals and terrorist organizations that will be extremely costly to take on – particularly if they link up with the resources of Islamic extremists in Pakistan or Iran. At the very least, the US can no longer permit the country to become a safe haven for the next asymmetric attack against the West. During 2003, the estimated cost to the US of the military occupation was roughly US$ 1.2 billion a month. Yet US investment in reconstruction totalled less than a billion dollars for the whole of 2002. It is a question of priorities, of longer-range vision and of putting resources into strategies that will create stability rather than more dislocation.

William Dowell *is a former TIME magazine correspondent who has covered conflict situations in Southeast Asia, Afghanistan, Africa and Europe. He is currently editor of Global Beat at New York University's Center for War, Peace and the News Media.*

A brief history of Afghanistan

By Chris Bowers

> *"If you do not wield a sword, what else will you do? You, who have suckled at the breast of an Afghan mother!"*
>
> *Afghan couplet*

Afghanistan lies at the crossroads of South and Central Asia; its northern plains an extension of the steppes of Turkistan, the Hindu Kush mountains an adjunct to the Himalayas, its southern deserts a prelude to the Persian Gulf. Linguistically, culturally and ethnically Afghanistan's northern Uzbeks, Turkmen and Tajiks look northwards to Central Asia, the centrally-located Hazaras look westwards to Iran, and the southern and eastern Pashtuns and Baluch find more resonance to the south-east in Pakistan. Although distinct from them, each group and region has more in common with its neighbours over the border than with each other.

A few rulers, most notably Abdur Rahman Khan at the cusp of the 19th Century, have managed to bind the Afghans into rule from Kabul, but arguably none left behind a reliable, coherent governing state system. With the mixture of lofty disdain and sharp perception often evident in British Imperial commentary, Sir Henry Rawlinson wrote, "the nation consists of a mere collection of tribes, of unequal power and divergent habits, which are held together more or less closely, according to the personal character of the chief who rules them. The feeling of patriotism, as known in Europe, cannot exist among Afghans, for there is no common country." One might almost add that there has not been much of a state either.

One of the foremost authorities on Afghanistan, the late Louis Dupree, suggests that Palaeolithic Man probably lived in the caves of what is now northern Afghanistan as long as 50,000 years ago. Afghanistan provided the backdrop to the emergence of two of the world's religions. Legend has it that Zoroaster, the founder of the modern Parsee religion, was born in the north of the country. Historians seem surer, however, with the story that Zoroaster (or Zarathustra as he was also called) was killed either in or near Balkh in around 522 BC. Zoroaster is thought to have converted to his religion the parents of Darius the Great, the ruler of the Achaemenid Empire at its height. From the south of Afghanistan, Greek and Indian influences merged to create the rich Gandhara Buddhist culture. Surfacing first in the Afghan region, it spread (as Mahayana Buddhism) through much of the Far East.

Scholars have identified 25 ruling dynasties which have swept through Afghanistan. Alexander the Great and his armies passed through on the way to India from Persia. Cyrus the Great, Genghis Khan, Tamerlane and Babur all rampaged through Afghanistan on the way to somewhere else. A few patterns emerge. Few, if any, of the invaders stayed for any length of time, nor did they attempt to establish colonies. Less surprisingly, several left behind traces of their passage. Some fair-skinned, blue-eyed Nuristanis claim their features as evidence of descent from Alexander's soldiers. The Mongoloid features of the Hazara people suggest descent from Genghis Khan's soldiers. ('Hazaar' translates as one thousand in Persian: it is widely believed in Afghanistan that Genghis Khan left behind detachments of troops one thousand strong to defend various outposts and that these soldiers were the ancestors of the Hazara people.)

The Uzbeks and Turkmen in the north see their history in terms of a much broader Turkic identity. The ancient khanates of Maimana, Shibarghan and Andkhoi, south of the Oxus River (Amu Darya) were the poorer, smaller relations to the grander Uzbek power centres of Khiva, Bokhara and Samarkand north of the river. Buddhism took root about 1,800 years ago in modern-day Nangarhar, Kabul and Bamiyan provinces. The ancient Buddhist site at Hadda, just outside Jalalabad, is a testament to the indiscriminate nature of the Afghan-Soviet war and the wanton vandalism and looting that sometimes accompanied it. The statues of the Buddha have long since succumbed to the effects of history, treasure hunters or the odd artillery shell.

In the 16th Century three empires emerged, sporadically fighting each other: the Safavids from Iran, who ruled parts of western Afghanistan; the Moghuls from India, who made Kabul their capital; and the Shaibanid Uzbeks, whose kingdom stretched from the plains north of the Hindu Kush far into Transoxiana. In 1747, Nadir Shah of Persia was assassinated and the three empires lapsed into decline. One of Nadir Shah's lieutenants, Ahmed Shah Durrani, seized his chance and became the first ruler whom the Afghans can claim as their own: he controlled – or perhaps *influenced* is a better word – territory which loosely corresponds to modern-day Afghanistan. He was able to seize some bounty and used it to enrich and augment the forces at his disposal. Opportunism, paying off tribesmen and mercenaries with loot, and holding out the prospect of more have pretty much guaranteed success to a whole succession of Afghan warlords over the centuries. Short-term success, that is. Ahmed Shah Durrani was a Pashtun from the Abdali tribal grouping, the bitter rivals of the Ghilzai Pashtuns. For all but a few years, the Durrani provided the rulers of Kabul until 1978, to the exclusion of not only the Ghilzai, but also all other ethnic groups. Some authors date 1747 as the beginning of an Afghan political entity, but it is an argument hard to sustain. Ahmed Shah Durrani, whose base was in Kandahar, was essentially a *primus inter pares*, who by a combination of charisma and circumstance held swathes of territory under his sway. But in no real sense did he have any governing structures. His personal bodyguards were Turkic-speaking Qizilbash (literally 'redheads') rather than Pashtuns.

After his death, Ahmed Shah's empire disintegrated as warring branches competed for the succession: a swirling and ever-changing confusion of broken and remade alliances set the political scene, and to some extent, still form an important undercurrent to Afghan governance. At the beginning of the 19th Century, Afghanistan had no legal existence and no formal borders. These were finally drawn up in the last decade of the century and were contested throughout the preceding decades, principally in reaction to the advances of foreign powers. As Ludwig Adamec puts it, "Modern Afghanistan was born as a result of foreign occupation." Its terrain and the existence of two imperialistic neighbours defined its borders.

Throughout much of the 19th Century, various dusty, isolated Afghan fortresses – Herat, Kandahar or Ghazni – were dubbed the "Key to India" by British military strategists. Britain feared that the steady march south-eastwards of the Russian armies through Central Asia was designed not only to subjugate the people there but also to open up invasion routes towards India. Even resurgent Afghans posed problems to India's defences. Ahmed Shah Durrani, among others, made frequent incursions into the fertile north Indian plains. The British efforts to forestall the Russian advance by intrigue, sorties by intelligence officers, diplomacy, straight bribery and direct military intervention were dubbed the "Great Game" by the British writer Rudyard Kipling, and taken up with almost missionary zeal by some of the most flamboyant adventurers of British and Russian history.

The lack of a state structure or system of formal governance cost Afghanistan dear during this period. Abdur Rahman Khan at the end of 19th Century described Afghanistan as a goat between the two lions of Russia and Britain. But as Lord Lytton, a Viceroy of India, put it, "Afghanistan is a state far too weak and barbarous to remain isolated and wholly uninfluenced, between two great military empires such as England and Russia." Russian soldiers never crossed the Oxus in earnest, but it is not surprising that British military planners should have succumbed to something resembling paranoia. While the borders of British India remained reasonably stable, the Russians moved south capturing Novo Alexandrovsk on the north-eastern shores of the Caspian Sea in 1834, Tashkent in 1865, Samarkand three years later, Krasnavodsk in 1869 and Tekke Turkoman in 1881. By 1885 they had arrived along most of the northern banks of the Oxus River through a combination of conquest and treaty. As the British became increasingly nervous, the two countries almost went to war over the demarcation of a small village of just a few hundred souls called Panjdeh, north of Herat.

In an effort to bring the unruly Afghans under control and to shore up the western approaches to India, British armies twice invaded Kabul within the space of forty years. Both times to no avail: the first ended in spectacular military defeat, the second in fruitless intervention. After capturing Kabul in 1839 and returning the hated Shah Shuja to the throne, the British retreated to Jalalabad in January 1842. Of more than 16,000 troops and camp followers who left Kabul only one doctor (and, later, some escaped prisoners) made it the one hundred miles back to Jalalabad, after some of the most disastrous

leadership ever seen from a British general and constant harrying ambushes through the snowy mountain passes led by Wazir Akbar Khan. (For a colourful, humorous but semi-fictional account of this episode see the 'Flashman' novel, by the British writer George MacDonald Fraser).

Another British army invaded later that year and by way of revenge blew up Kabul bazaar. In 1878, the British returned when, as British author Jan Morris writes, "another presumptuous Amir embarked on a flirtation with the Russians, another British Resident was murdered, another British army was defeated and another punitive force stormed back to Kabul in revenge." By now, the Afghans, although poorly equipped with ancient rifles, had developed a fearsome fighting reputation, a ferocious antipathy to foreigners who tried to rule them and a disdain for any Afghan rulers who came to power on their backs. The Afghans valued their independence above all else. The war and skirmishes against the British and Russians served to knit together the nation. From the aggressor's point of view, the interventions proved less than worthless; in the words of a British report: "as a result of two successful campaigns, of the employment of an enormous force, and of the expenditure of large sums of money, all that has yet been accomplished is the disintegration of the State which it was desired to see strong, friendly and independent."

Whether by design or accident, Afghanistan became a buffer between the Russian and British empires, albeit with Britain guiding its foreign policy. Towards the end of the 19th Century both sides accepted it as such, and saw their interests in it remaining so. Between Abdur Rahman Khan's coming to power in 1880 and his death in 1901, Afghanistan took recognisable shape. Its crucial northern and eastern borders were drawn up and a process of nation-building was started, although in a ruthless fashion. Abdur Rahman Khan established a formative cabinet and developed the framework of a civil administration. He pacified the interior, although how much actual control he exerted is not clear. In an inspired move, he expelled some rival Pashtun tribes *en masse* to the north of the country. Once there, well away from their centres of power and outnumbered by Uzbeks and Persian-speaking 'Tajiks', they had little option but to serve the interests of Kabul by policing the north. Abdur Rahman Khan was clearly more ready to depend on his erstwhile, but Pashtun, enemies rather than on Uzbeks and Persian-speakers native to the north who fell more under the aegis of their local khans – even though the latter had officially been defeated by Abdur Rahman. (Interestingly, when Afghan Uzbek forces revolted against President Najibullah in 1992, one of the reasons given was resentment that a Pashtun, whose family had been resettled in the north by Abdur Rahman Khan, was in command of the government garrison of Mazar-e-Sharif.) In 1893 the eastern border was clarified between British India and Afghanistan. Known as the Durand Line, after the principal cartographer, it was to become much more controversial than its northern counterpart, drawn up three years later. Suffice to repeat the words of Sir George Macartney, surveying the scene from Kashgar: "So fiercely independent and jealous were the Afghans and so turbulent in their domestic politics, that their borders," which he describes elsewhere as being so ambiguous and contradictory as to be almost incomprehensible, "offered unlimited scope to intrigue and aggression by a foreign power." The division, particularly of Pashtun tribes – and even families – in the east, was to prove of great significance for Afghanistan in the 1960s and still has a ripple effect on Afghan-Pakistani relations today.

With its borders finally set and a rudimentary governing system in place, Afghanistan joined the community of nations at the turn of the 19th Century very much as an isolated backwater on the world stage. Its collision with the modern world did not go very smoothly. It was one of the few countries in the world, and probably the only in Asia, which during World War II was neither occupied nor belligerent. It was not considered important enough. There was no all-weather road connecting the north with the south, until Nadir Shah built one in the 1930s. There was no University until the 1930s. The first formal school in Kabul was constructed by Habibullah Khan at the beginning of the 20th Century. There was no railway. Up to today, the only railway ever built in the country was a few miles of track near Zahir Shah's palace in Kabul. It was never connected to any other railway.

In his book *Age of Extremes*, the British historian Eric Hobsbawn wrote that, "the destruction of the past, or rather of the social mechanisms that link one's contemporary experience to that of earlier generations, is one of the most characteristic and eerie phenomena of the late 20th Century." If for one country in the world this was less true then surely it was Afghanistan. History and tradition still ruled the roost. Amanullah Khan, who ruled Afghanistan from 1919 (Independence from Britain) until 1929, tried to drag the country kicking and screaming into the modern world, only to be ejected from power by a scandalised *ulama*. Amanullah had travelled to Western capitals where the gulf between an ever-developing Europe and his backward and remote kingdom was brought home to him in the starkest of manners. Afghanistan was virtually untouched by industrial development. Upon his return he incited widespread outrage when he unveiled his wife, Surraiya, in public, after forcing the tribal elders to abandon their *shalwar kameez* and turbans for morning suits and black ties. Amanullah was influenced by his contemporaries Kemal Ataturk of Turkey and Reza Khan of Iran. While all three were trying to bring in broadly similar reforms, the Turkish and Iranian leaders only ventured to do so once they had consolidated the state's (and their personal) power by building up strong armies. Amanullah, a man ahead of his time and naïve in equal measure, did not and was chased from power by a ragtag group of bandits led by Bacha Saqao, a Tajik, after a tribal uprising. Later Afghan rulers, Babrak Karmal and Najibullah in particular, tried to portray themselves as the modernizing but more pragmatic heirs of Amanullah Khan.

Bacha Saqao was the first non-Pashtun to rule Kabul since 1747. He lasted less than one year. In 1933, Zahir Shah inherited the throne after his father, Nadir Shah, was killed in a blood feud. He ruled for 40 years and, after three decades in exile, returned to Afghanistan in 2002. He attained the throne at 18. Power rested with his uncles for 20 years. But, again, Afghanistan was to be buffeted by foreign factors largely beyond its control.

The British withdrawal from India in 1947 and the consolidation of communism in the Soviet Union changed forever the delicate balance on which Afghanistan's status as a buffer state depended. With the creation of Pakistan, the scales tipped inexorably north. The demarcation of the eastern border back in 1893, resented at the time by a powerless Kabul, now came back to sour relations between Afghanistan and Pakistan. Kabul considered that the demise of British India in effect abrogated the Durand Line. Afghanistan's was the only dissenting voice in the vote which admitted Pakistan to the United Nations.

But what did Afghanistan actually want? Many Pashtuns harked back to the days of Ahmed Shah Durrani when Afghans controlled Peshawar. For them, the border should have been pushed back to include all of the Pashtuns in Pakistan's North West Frontier Province and entailing the creation of 'Pashtunistan' – in fact, little short of the dismemberment of Pakistan. Kabul understood 'Pashtunistan' to mean annexation; others saw it as a new independent country; others still, some sort of autonomy. Daoud Khan, King Zahir's cousin, became Prime Minister in 1953 and took a hardline stance pro-Pashtunistan. Daoud's policy caused untold damage to Afghanistan in the short- and longer-term. In the early 1960s, relations became so bad that the border with Pakistan was closed for a time. The immediate effects of the border closure in 1961 were easy enough to predict: a sharp rise in border tension and a cut in trade. Eastern Afghanistan depended then as it does now on exchange with Pakistan. However, within ten days of the border closing, the Soviet Union offered to buy the harvest that would have gone to Pakistan. Daoud took them up on that.

Since the departure of the British and the end of its empire heyday, the United States had stepped in to try to redress the balance with the Soviet giant to the north. But, from Afghanistan's point of view there was little equality between the two. The closure of the border led to a reduction in American aid to Kabul due to Washington's increasing closeness to Pakistan.

Already America was being outspent in aid terms three-to-one by Moscow. The Soviet Union was also the only customer for one of Afghanistan's few mineral assets: its natural gas fields in the far northwest. Afghanistan totted up a large debt to the Soviet Union which, in turn, was in a position to dictate the price it would pay for the gas coming out of the pipeline that Moscow had paid for and built. Throughout the 1950s, 1960s and 1970s, Afghanistan was drawn ever closer economically to the Soviet Union. Politically, there was no great affection for communism in Afghanistan; the 1917 Revolution of the proletariat held no resonance whatsoever for Afghans. A significant number of people in the north had fled there from Soviet attacks against the Basmachi rebels in the 1920s and were familiar with the ruthlessness of the Red Army. Nevertheless, from the mid-1960s onwards, the Soviet Union tried to draw Afghanistan into its political orbit. It had no real competition.

Despite the personal dynamism of Daoud, Afghanistan was as weak a state as can be imagined and ripe for the picking. Zahir Shah was weak and was expected to be weak. The traditional troika of authority in rural Afghanistan – the *khan*, the *malik* and the *mullah* – only had use or need for a King who would adjudicate when a dispute arose. They did not wish the King to intervene in their business, nor did the King go out of his way to challenge this view. The royal family, meanwhile, kept a stranglehold on positions. Those cousins and distant relatives who were not governors would become generals. The Durrani Pashtuns kept things to themselves. Daoud tried to liberate the political class, but his Pashtun chauvinism gave it nowhere to go but north. He created some of the conditions for 'equal opportunities', but failed to create an actual meritocracy. Kabul's attempts to deal with a famine in 1971 in the far west of the country were tragically ineffective. To many Kabuli intellectuals, frustrated by their antiquated regime, it underlined the need for urgent reform and a decisive step forward. A slow-burning fuse was lit in the early 1960s and smouldered beneath the hopelessly outdated royal system of governance. It would lead to some dramatic and ultimately explosions. The pace of change accelerated unrecognisably: in the space of thirty years from 1964, when Zahir Shah brought in some limited democratic reforms (which in effect made him a constitutional monarch), Afghanistan became a Republic (1973), a Democratic Republic (1978), a Soviet client (1979) and an Islamic state (1992). Yet, despite the speed of change – or perhaps because of it – the political class was tiny and based almost exclusively in the capital. Kabul was an island politically divorced from the countryside.

At its peak prior to the Soviet invasion and while it was in power, the pro-Moscow People's Democratic Party of Afghanistan (PDPA) is thought to have had fewer than 7,000 members. Kabul University, the country's first, was greatly enlarged in 1964. Most of the key figures of the 1980s and 1990s were former classmates. Moscow sought to build up its influence in Kabul through two main channels: the army and the PDPA. Between 1956 and 1977, up to one third of the entire officer corps of the army was trained and educated in the USSR. Many were recruited into the KGB or the GRU, the military intelligence wing. The Americans tried half-heartedly to keep pace with the growing Soviet influence. Daoud used to joke that he would light his American cigarette with a Russian match, but any idea of a happy balance was an illusion. Washington seemed to acknowledge that Afghanistan had a much closer natural relationship with its northern neighbour.

Unfortunately for the PDPA, the two branches of Soviet espionage seemed to be in competition and had sharply different, even conflicting, approaches. Virtually at its birth, the PDPA split into two factions: the Khalq ('Masses') and the Parcham ('Banner'). The two were at times separate parties rather than factions and, given the chance, persecuted and at times tortured each other mercilessly. American analyst Anthony Arnold argues persuasively in his book *Two Party Communism* that the Khalqis owed their allegiance to the GRU and the Parchamis to the KGB. The Khalqis, led by Nur Mohammed Taraki and

Hafizullah Amin, concentrated their recruitment among the armed forces. The Parchamis focused on teachers and social intellectuals. Both saw the need for a dramatic step forward to bring Afghanistan out of a 'museum.' With Soviet help, the Khalqis had already taken part in the palace coup of 1973 in which Daoud overthrew his cousin Zahir Shah and established a Republic. By April 1978, they had the field to themselves.

Although it seems clear that the Soviets had taken part in the planning of the 1978 coup, its precise timing seems to have taken them by surprise. Moscow felt that Daoud had double-crossed them by ditching members of the PDPA from his inner cabinet. The April 1978 coup (also known as the 'Saur Revolution') was an accidental and somewhat botched affair. The shooting to death of a prominent Parchami by unknown gunmen led to demonstrations in Kabul orchestrated by the PDPA.

Somewhat alarmed, Daoud arrested Taraki and Amin a few days later. Remarkably, Amin was not kept under close control and was allowed to receive several visitors. To these people, he reportedly issued the pre-arranged instructions to start the coup on the morning of 27 April. The palace was shelled and confused fighting broke out between various factions and divisions, but by the next morning the Khalqis had won. Daoud and his family were shot to death in the palace, so bringing to an end more than 230 years of almost unbroken Durrani Pashtun rule.

Taraki, a Ghilzai Pashtun, was declared the head of the Revolutionary Council of the Democratic Republic of Afghanistan, after several days of internal dispute and wrangling. Places were given to Parchamis but the facade of unity was not to last. Within a few months, the leading Parchamis were sent abroad as ambassadors – a communist form of exile. In much the same way as Amanullah had done decades before, the Khalqis attacked the centuries-old traditions of rural Afghanistan head on and with as little sensitivity. One government minister caused outrage by offering public prayers to the souls of Marx and Lenin. With just a few decrees, the new authorities took land away from landowners and redistributed it to peasant farmers, totally disrupting the rural and social relationships that had been unchanged for generations.

The countryside was in uproar. Women were forced to take part in literacy campaigns that consisted of reciting party propaganda slogans. A personality cult was built around Taraki. The first major rebellion occurred in the western city of Herat in the spring of 1979. Government buildings were attacked and Soviet advisers lynched. The Soviets were unhappy with the way things were being run by their wayward and inexperienced charges in Kabul. Defections from the Afghan army were becoming increasingly frequent. Relations between Amin and Taraki were becoming increasingly strained, as the regime became more and more vicious in the treatment meted out to foes, real or potential. In February 1979, in an incident which has yet to be fully explained, the US Ambassador, Adolph Dubs, was taken hostage in Kabul and then shot dead by Afghan police forces while apparently trying to free him.

The opposition to the Khalqis was uncoordinated and diverse but became increasingly disruptive. The revolt against the Khalqis in the countryside is seen by many as being as much a reaction to an administration in Kabul trying to impose its will in areas where it was not welcome and where it was not usually present, as against a specific ideology in itself. In other words, the rebellion was against governance *per se*, unwarranted interference as far as many rural Afghans were concerned, as much as it was against communism. Most Afghans in the provinces simply wanted to be left alone. Only in Kabul had the 20th Century had a belated impact.

The Taraki-Amin split became worse. The Soviets seemed to have sided more with Taraki and persuaded him to rid himself of Amin. The plan was betrayed to Amin who got his blow in first, and the life of the first Communist leader of Afghanistan was snuffed out ingloriously by a pillow pressed to the face. Amin assumed power and the Soviets found themselves with a serious problem. A few months later, on 27 December 1979, the Soviets invaded, killing Amin in the process and installing Babrak Karmal, the leader of the Parcham faction.

Chris Bowers *is a former BBC correspondent in Kabul.*

INFOBRIEFS

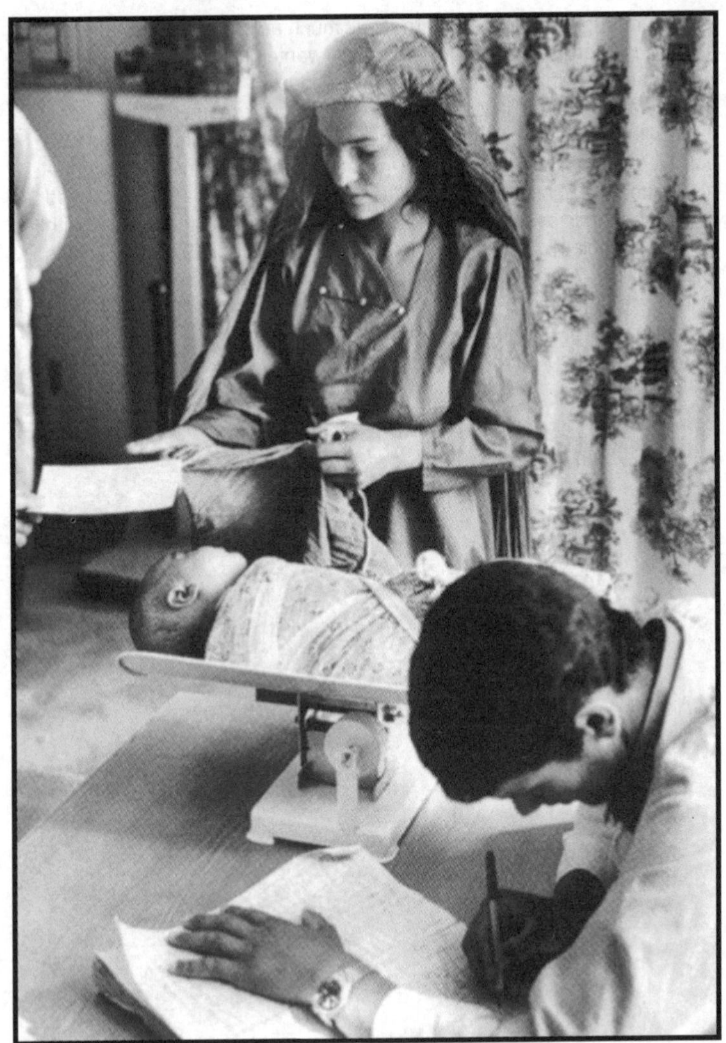

J. Hartley/UNICEF

Afghan data

"There are three types of lies: lies, damn lies and statistics."
Mark Twain

Land:	
Area	**652,225 sq. km**
Borders	**China, Iran, Pakistan, Tajikistan, Turkmenistan, Uzbekistan**
Population:	
Size	**22.5 million** *(UNICEF, 2003)* **to 27.2 million** *(World Bank, 2003)*
Annual growth rate	**2.6%** *(World Bank, 2003)* **to 4.5%** *(UNICEF, 2003)*
Ethnic groups:	
Pashtun	**38%** *(Eighmy, 1990)* **to 63%** *(Wak Foundation, 1998)*
Tajik	**12%** *(Wak Foundation, 1998)* **to 25%** *(Eighmy, 1990)*
Hazara	**8%** *(USSR Academy of Sciences, 1981)* **to 19%** *(Eighmy, 1990)*
Uzbek	**6.3%** *(Eighmy, 1990)* **to 9%** *(USSR Academy of Sciences, 1981)*
Turkmen	**2.5%** *(Eighmy, 1990)* **to 3%** *(USSR Academy of Sciences, 1981)*
Plus Aimaq, Baluch, Brahui, Nuristani, Kuchi and others	
Religion *(Source: National Geographic, 2002)*:	
Sunni Muslim	**84%**
Shi'a Muslim	**15%**
Human Development Indicators *(Source: UNICEF, 2003)*:	
Under five mortality rate	**257/1,000**
Infant mortality rate	**165/1,000**
Maternal mortality rate	**1,600/100,000 – rising to 6,500 in Badakhshan** *(UNICEF/CDC, 2002)*

Life expectancy at birth	43 years
Total fertility rate (average children per healthy woman)	6.8
Under-5s suffering stunting	52%
Population undernourished (1998-2000)	70% *(IMF, 2003)*
Population using improved drinking water	11% (rural), 19% (urban)
Population using adequate sanitation	8% (rural), 25% (urban)
Adult literacy (% over-15s who can read & write)	21% (female), 51% (male)
Net primary school attendance (1992-2001)	11% (female), 36% (male)
Children registered in schools in 2003	3.8 million (37% girls)

Economic indicators (2002-03) *(Source: IMF, 2003)*:

GDP (excluding opium)	US$ 4.05 billion
Value of opium exports	US$ 2.54 billion
Share of opium in the economy	40%-60%
Per capita GDP (excluding opium)	US$ 186
Per capita GDP (including opium)	US$ 302
Real growth rate in GDP (excluding opium)	28.6%
Rise in wheat production from 2001 to 2002	80%

Opium production *(Source: UNODC, 2003)*:

	2002	2001	2000	1999
Total production in tonnes	3,422	185	3,276	4,565
Cultivated area (in hectares)	74,045	7,606	82,171	90,983
Gross revenue to farmers from opium production (US$ m)	1,200	56	128	251
Share in world production	76%			
Estimated number of farmers cultivating poppy	200,000			

Donor contributions (in US$ millions) *(Source: CARE/AACA, 2003)*:

	Spent and pledged (Jan 02-Mar 04)
USA	1,470
EU	1,295
Japan	500
Canada	166
World Bank	103
Norway	93
Iran	88
Saudi Arabia	76
India	72
China	60
Russia	60
TOTAL *(covering over 95% of all pledges)*	3,983

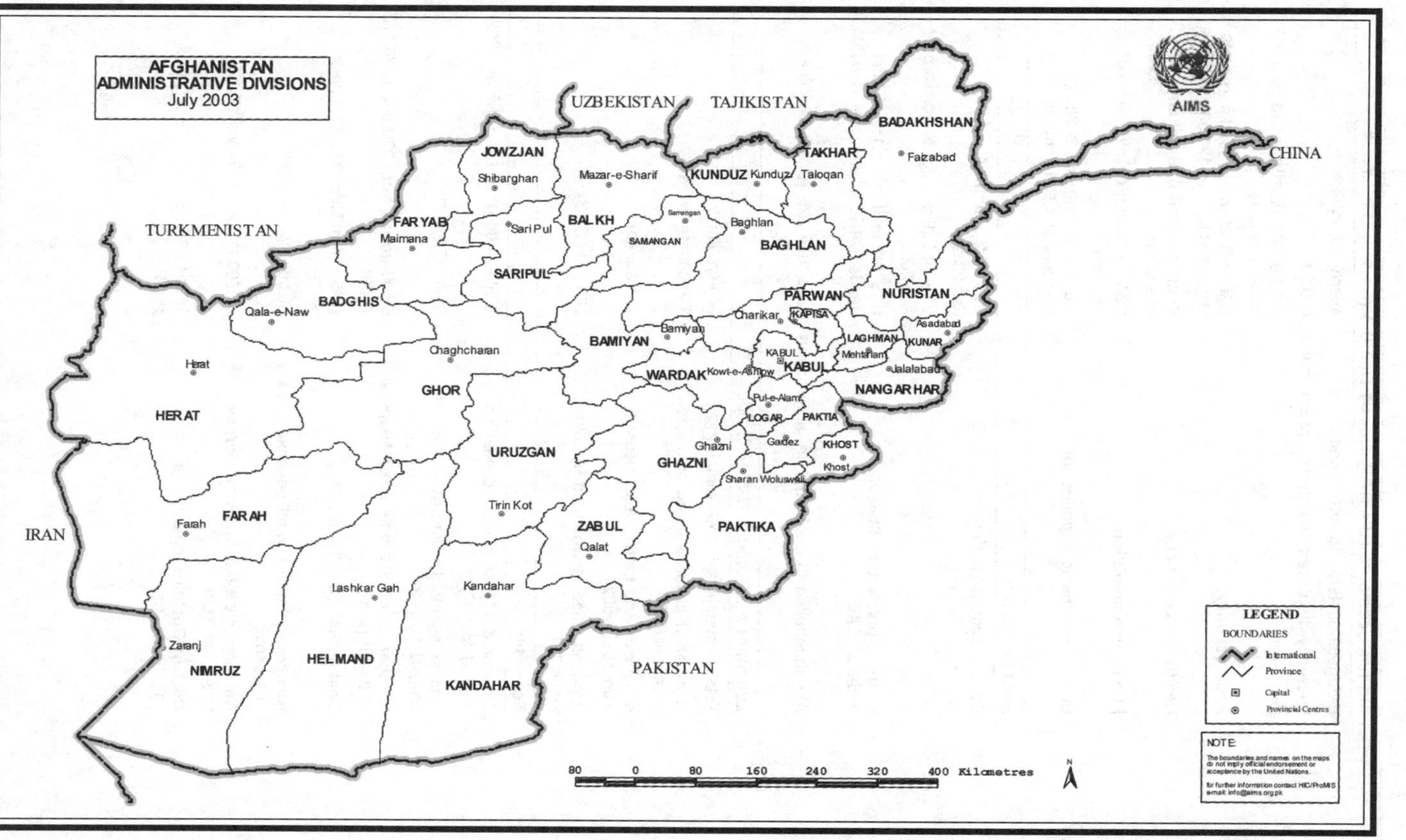
AFGHANISTAN
ADMINISTRATIVE DIVISIONS
July 2003
AIMS
UZBEKISTAN
TAJIKISTAN
TURKMENISTAN
CHINA
IRAN
PAKISTAN
BADAKHSHAN
Faizabad
TAKHAR
Taloqan
KUNDUZ
Kunduz
JOWZJAN
Shibarghan
Mazar-e-Sharif
BALKH
FARYAB
Maimana
Sari Pul
SARIPUL
Samangan
SAMANGAN
Baghlan
BAGHLAN
BADGHIS
Qala-e-Naw
PARWAN
Charikar
KAPISA
NURISTAN
Asadabad
KUNAR
LAGHMAN
Mehtarlam
Jalalabad
NANGARHAR
Bamiyan
BAMIYAN
KABUL
WARDAK
Kowt-e-Ashrow
Pul-e-Alam
LOGAR
PAKTIA
Gardez
KHOST
Khost
Ghazni
GHAZNI
Sharan Woluswali
PAKTIKA
Chaghcharan
GHOR
Herat
HERAT
URUZGAN
Tirin Kot
ZABUL
Qalat
Farah
FARAH
Lashkar Gah
Kandahar
Zaranj
NIMRUZ
HELMAND
KANDAHAR
80 0 80 160 240 320 400 Kilometres
N
LEGEND
BOUNDARIES
International
Province
Capital
Provincial Centres
NOTE:
The boundaries and names on the maps do not imply official endorsement or acceptance by the United Nations.
for further information contact HIC/ProMIS
email: info@aims.org.pk

Aid achievements (UN ITAP, Oct 01-Dec 02) *(Source: IMF, 2003)*:	
Refugees assisted to return home	**nearly 1.8 million**
Internally-displaced assisted to return home	**400,000**
Food aid	**250,000 MT distributed to over 8 million people**
Food security	**5,300 MT of wheat seed and 8,000 MT of fertiliser to 120,000 farmers**
Health – vaccinations	**6 million (polio), 9 million (measles)**
Public administration	**US$ 50 million of civil service salaries**
Education – basic supplies for	**1.8 million children & 70,000 teachers at 4,500 schools**

Reconstruction	
Cost of reconstruction	**US$ 10.2 billion** *(World Bank, Jan 2002)*
	US$ 30 billion *(Afghan government, Aug 2003)*
Value of projects completed by mid-May 2003	**US$ 192 million – c.1% of total needs** *(CARE International, Sep 2003)*
Aid channelled through Afghan government	**Less than 20%** *(CARE International, Oct 2002)*

Landmines *(Source: UN MAPA, 2003)*:	
Total contaminated area remaining	**840 sq. km**
Number of civilians killed or injured by mines/UXO	**150-300 per month**
Minefields and battle areas cleared from 1989-2002	**754 sq. km**
Afghans killed or wounded by mines since 1979	**200,000** *(ICRC)*

Security:	
Estimated Afghan civilian casualties (Oct 01-Mar 02)	**3,000-3,400** *(Prof. Marc Herold, 2002)*
Attacks against UN and NGO workers (Sep 02-Aug 03)	**93** *(CARE, 2003)*
Number of international peacekeepers in Kabul (ISAF)	**5,500 troops from 33 nations** *(NATO, 2003)*
Cost of ISAF (Oct 01-Oct 02)	**US$ 540 million** *(The Economist, 2003)*
Number of international peacekeepers in Kosovo	**50,000** *(NATO, 1999)*
Number of US-led Coalition Forces in Afghanistan	**11,500** *(New York Times, 2003)*
Cost of Coalition operations (Oct 01-Oct 02)	**US$ 10.2 billion** *(The Economist, 2003)*

Afghan timeline

100,000-2,000 BC:	Stone Age
5,000-1,000 BC:	Bronze Age – trading with Mesopotamia and Indus Valley
1,500 BC:	Aryans warriors invade N Afghanistan
500 BC:	Persians invade – rise of Zoroastrianism
330 BC:	Alexander the Great creates Afghan kingdom
250 BC:	Buddhist Emperor Ashoka – edicts carved in stone
300 BC-50 AD:	Bactrian Greeks rule N Afghanistan
50-300:	Kushan Empire. Rise of Silk Route
100-700:	Flourishing of Buddhism and Gandhara art
650-850:	Arabs spread Islam through west and north
1000-1100:	Ghazni and Bost flourish under Sultan Mahmud
1150:	Ghorid dynasty flourishes under Alauddin. Minaret of Jam built
1220:	Genghis Khan devastates much of west and north Afghanistan
1369-1530:	Timurid empire, centred on Herat, lasts from Tamerlane to Babur
1749:	Ahmed Shah Durrani, a Pashtun, begins creation of modern Afghanistan
1839-42:	British occupy then disastrously retreat from Kabul
1878:	Second British invasion, as part of the 'Great Game'
1880-1901:	More nation-building under Amir Abdur Rahman
1893:	Durand Line plotted, dividing Afghanistan from British India
1919:	Third Anglo-Afghan war ends, with Afghanistan gaining independence
1919-29:	Amanullah Khan becomes king, but his progressive reforms backfire
1932:	Kabul University established

INFOBRIEFS

1933-73:	Zahir Shah rules as king. Rise of Soviet influence
1953-63:	Gen Mohammed Daoud becomes prime minister. Abolishes *purdah*
1964:	Creation of constitutional monarchy
1973:	Daoud overthrows king and establishes Republic
1978:	Saur Revolution – Afghan communists assassinate Daoud. Their reforms backfire
1979-80:	Soviets invade and install Babrak Karmal as leader
1980-85:	*Mujahideen* – supported by US, Pakistan, China, Iran & Saudi Arabia – fight Soviets
1985:	*Mujahideen* form alliance against Soviets, based in Peshawar
1980-1989:	Six million Afghan refugees flee as Soviet forces target civilians
1986:	US supply *mujahideen* with Stinger missiles. Najibullah replaces Karmal
1988-89:	Peace accord. Soviet troops pull out. *Mujahideen* fight Najibullah
1992:	*Mujahideen* forces, led by Ahmed Shah Massoud, overthrow Najibullah regime
1993:	Najibullah replaced by Tajik *mujahed* leader, Burhanuddin Rabbani
1992-94:	Devastating civil war between *mujahideen* factions
1994:	Rise of Taliban, who take Kandahar and Herat
1996:	Taliban capture Kabul, execute Najibullah, exile Rabbani, offer refuge to Osama Bin Laden and impose strict Islam. Northern Alliance formed to fight Taliban
1997:	Taliban recognised by Pakistan, Saudi Arabia and UAE. Fierce fighting for control of Mazar-e-Sharif, which Taliban capture in 1999
1998:	Two major earthquakes kill thousands. US fires missiles at suspected Bin Laden camps in retaliation for bombing of US embassies in East Africa
1999-2001:	UN imposes sanctions in failed attempt to force Taliban to hand over Bin Laden
2001:	Taliban destroy Bamiyan Buddhas. Massoud assassinated. Taliban ousted by US forces and Northern Alliance. Bonn Agreement signed
2002:	5,000 foreign peacekeepers arrive in Kabul. Hamid Karzai elected leader by *Loya Jirga*. Vice President Hajji Qadir assassinated. 3 million children go back to school
2003:	Security deteriorates as US forces hunt Taliban/Al Qa'eda remnants. Third of country off-limits to international aid workers. New Constitution drafted and debated

Agriculture

> *"Without our land, there is no food; without our water, there is no life; without our trees and flowers, there is no soul; and without our country, there is no poetry, no music...for then we are not Afghans."*
>
> *– Tribal elder from Nangarhar province, 1989*

Afghanistan's economy is based primarily on farming. And yet barely one-tenth of the country's land area is agricultural. Half of this is rain-fed, the other half irrigated. According to pre-war figures (and current estimates), nearly 80 percent of Afghans live in rural areas and rely on farming for income or subsistence.

To grasp the essentials of farming in Afghanistan, and the effects of war on the land, one needs to appreciate the enormous differences in productivity between various land types. Three-quarters of the country supports only sparse but extensive grazing in the mountains and deserts. A mere five percent of the land area, mainly in the irrigated valleys, produces 85 percent of overall agricultural output.

Since the early 1950s, billions of dollars of international assistance – Soviet, American, German, French and other – have been spent in Afghanistan, much of it directed towards upgrading agriculture and increasing production through the development of large-scale infrastructure, and the expansion of forestry and natural resource management. Some of this aid was shockingly misguided – and primarily for show – such as the large-scale orange and olive tree farms on the eastern outskirts of Jalalabad, established at massive cost by the Soviets during the 1970s. According to the French agency Madera, not a single marketable olive ever emerged from these farms because the Soviets had planted the wrong type, while the oranges were mainly sour rather than sweet and thus not appropriate for local markets. Furthermore, the plains of Nangarhar are not suitable to olives – yet only slightly further up the Kunar Valley to the north, the somewhat cooler semi-arid terrain is excellent for Mediterranean-style tree produce, including olives.

By 1978, the year anti-communist resistance first erupted, Afghanistan was largely self-sufficient in food. It was also a significant exporter of high quality fruit, silk, cotton and other products. Between 1978 and 1989, international assistance, mainly from the Soviet bloc, focused on bringing government-controlled land into production through large-scale development and state farms. However, many programmes totally collapsed with the war; numerous state farms, irrigation and forestry projects were either damaged or destroyed. Others were simply abandoned to the *mujahideen* by the former Soviet-backed regime. When the various guerrilla groups moved in, they frequently looted the facilities, gutted buildings and made off with any equipment that could be resold in Pakistan (anxious that it not fall into the hands of rivals).

Similarly, once magnificent forests, formerly managed by donor-funded programmes, have been ruthlessly cut down for timber by Afghan and Pakistani entrepreneurs, often with the connivance of Pakistani military and government officials who have made small fortunes from the trade. Today, the trafficking of lumber continues, resulting in further destruction of Afghanistan's once resplendent eastern forests (SEE ENVIRONMENT).

During the decade-long Soviet occupation, much of Afghanistan's agricultural infrastructure was ruined. An estimated 22,000 villages in the country's (then) 29 provinces (there are now 32) were destroyed or severely damaged. In many areas, Soviet and Afghan government troops cut down vineyards, orchards, ornamental trees and shrubs for security reasons. The Soviets also destroyed some 3,000 ancient irrigation systems as a means of deliberately disabling the local economy, particularly in parts known to support the *mujahideen*. The mass exodus of one-third of all Afghans to Pakistan and Iran during the 1980s – the majority from rural areas – also severely affected the agricultural situation. Whole regions, including much of the Panjshair Valley and parts of Ghazni and Kandahar provinces, were almost completely depleted of their inhabitants. Most agricultural programmes and support services collapsed as trained professionals – from agricultural advisors to veterinary officers – left. Hundreds of thousands of cattle, camels, sheep and other livestock were killed in the bombing or from landmines; many, too, were stolen or sold off by their owners for survival. As a result, once thriving farms, fields, fruit orchards and pastures were abandoned to the mercy of the wind, rain, snow and drought. Roughly half of the country's irrigation systems were wrecked not only by direct war damage but also through lack of maintenance. And as if this were not enough, countless agricultural areas have been rendered unusable by landmines for years, possibly decades to come; these will need to be cleared before they can again be put to the plough or returned to grazing (SEE LANDMINES).

Following the Red Army's departure in 1989, Afghanistan suffered further destruction during inter-factional fighting in the early and mid-1990s, but this was responsible more for destroying Kabul and other urban areas than for destroying the countryside.

Under the Taliban (1994-2001), there was further destruction of the countryside, particularly in areas held by opposition Hazara groups and the United Front (also known as the Northern Alliance). Whole areas – villages, fruit orchards, and irrigation systems – inhabited by the *Shi'a* Hazara minority in Wardak and Bamiyan provinces, for example, were deliberately destroyed during the late 1990s, while disputed zones with the United Front such as the mainly Tajik Shomali plains north of Kabul were likewise laid waste by the

E. Girardet

Taliban prior to their overthrow in the autumn of 2001. The Pashtun-dominated Taliban went as far as to order the uprooting of vineyards, the razing of houses and the mining of fields as part of their strategy to punish and weaken their opponents.

Overall, the lack of cultivation and soil erosion has resulted in badly degraded agricultural land in many parts of the country (SEE ENVIRONMENT). By the early 1990s, agricultural production had dropped by up to 70 percent (compared to 1978). Humanitarian assistance aimed at rehabilitating agriculture and restoring the national food supply. While this contributed towards a significant growth in crop (notably wheat) and livestock production, as significant numbers of refugees returned during the 1990s, this collapsed again with the onset of a four-year long drought in 1998-99 that only came to an end following good rains and heavy snowfalls in the winter of 2002-03.

In 2003, agricultural production increased dramatically, accounting for 50 percent of the country's GDP. There were excellent harvests in many areas, not only due to increased rain but also better access to quality seeds, fertilizers and other inputs provided mainly by aid agencies such as the Swedish Committee for Afghanistan, Madera, Afghanaid and others. Wheat production rose by nearly 50 percent from 2002 levels, with 5.37 million tonnes harvested in 2003, according to the United Nations Food and Agriculture Organization (FAO) and the World Food Programme (WFP). For its part, the 2002 harvest represented an 80 percent growth (nearly 3.59 million tonnes) over 2001 levels, prior to the US-led military intervention against the Taliban. The production of fruit and vegetables as well as livestock related products, such as dairy, meat, wool and hides, also increased substantially. However, aid agencies note that it may still take several years before such production can expect to reach pre-war (1978) levels.

Emerging from the war: an ability to adapt

Today, despite the overwhelming devastation, much of Afghanistan's basic production pattern remains both simple and robust. The system's simplicity – it has changed little over the past 2,000 years – has proved a major strength in the rapid re-establishment of agricultural production where fighting has stopped. Yet Afghan farmers, many of whom still work with beasts of burden, have shown a remarkable ability to adapt to sophisticated technology, such as high-yielding crop varieties, inorganic fertilizers and agricultural and veterinary chemicals.

The FAO, the leading UN agency for the rehabilitation of Afghanistan's agricultural sector, helped ease the way for the return of nearly three million refugees to their homes during the 1990s. Many fled from their homes again under the Taliban, only to return once more in 2002 and 2003. Nevertheless, village communities have been re-established in many areas, while abandoned land has been brought back into cultivation, providing food and employment for the returnees. Short-term rehabilitation efforts have involved removing landmines from access roads and farmland, distributing seed and planting materials to farmers, implementing disease and pest-control programmes, and restoring abandoned irrigation systems to some degree of functionality. Such rehabilitation continued in areas held by both the Taliban and the United Front. With the collapse of the Taliban and the arrival of major donor resources, the rehabilitation process has speeded up. While the FAO has played a far smaller role in the post-2001 period (for most of 2002-03, it was virtually non-existent on the ground), the rehabilitation of the countryside has pushed ahead under various other aid groups.

Nevertheless, effective, long-term rehabilitation, such as rebuilding irrigation systems, could take decades. The lack of reliable information is one hindering factor. The last comprehensive agricultural survey of Afghanistan was conducted in 1978; much of the information available is out of date and misleading.

While various agricultural surveys have been attempted by aid agencies over the last 25 years, they have been limited to specific regions.

In January 1997, FAO developed an open-ended strategy (*Afghanistan Agricultural Strategy*) aimed at fully developing the country's farming potential. The strategy sought to operate as much as possible through NGOs, supported by simple interventions at the local level. This is what now appears to be happening, yet much will depend on how effective donors are in ensuring the appropriate amount of backing. Another factor, particularly for the poor regions of the south, is the worsening security problem. Increasingly regular raids by anti-government groups during 2002-03 have seriously hampered international aid efforts directed at populations in Helmand, Kandahar, Uruzgan and Zabul provinces. The FAO's strategy, now absorbed into the UN's current rehabilitation strategy, has four principal objectives:

- to create national food security
- to increase economic and social development
- to raise the levels of skills and knowledge
- to protect scarce natural resources

During the 1990s, donor aid to Afghanistan was primarily humanitarian. Current approaches are now shifting from quick-impact activities to longer-term development. As the cash economy expands, pressures will grow for greater capital accumulation and investment. While long periods in refugee camps have made many farmers aware of new technology, they often lack the capital and labour to raise productivity. Many post-Taliban returnees have brought with them tractors and other forms of modern equipment not previously seen in many rural areas. In Kunar, for example, where numerous farmers still work the land with oxen, freelance tractor and combine-harvester crews now tour the farms, hiring themselves out on a daily basis. As one farmer noted, even though this costs him hard cash to harvest the wheat or to plough the land, it does free up resources to undertake other improvements such as the rehabilitation of irrigation canals. What he did not say is that he has available cash from cultivating opium poppies, a relatively easy – and far more lucrative – crop compared to wheat. At the same time, many villagers simply do not have the means to pay for proper rehabilitation of major irrigation ducts, causing much good land to remain arid and fallow.

Outbreaks of animal disease, such as foot and mouth, threaten food security and risk crippling the recovery of Afghanistan's fragile rural sector. According to FAO in early 2003, an estimated US$ 6.89 million is needed over a five-year period to fund projects to help the Afghan government monitor and prevent outbreaks of diseases in cattle, sheep, goats and poultry – and to support some 200 proposed veterinary field clinics providing vaccinations and treatments.

In addition, aid groups have been stressing the need to focus on more remote and poorer rural areas, particularly those traditionally ignored by previous governments and donors. In October 2003, the British government finally agreed to provide US$ 6 million to assist more than 430,000 farmers in the mountains of eastern Hazarajat in central Afghanistan. Designed to support sustainable livelihoods development, the project – to be run by FAO – will seek to improve farm production and generate income opportunities in the provinces of Bamiyan, Wardak, Ghor and Ghazni, where many people struggle to survive at altitudes of 2,000-3,200 metres, with summer grazing extending over 4,000 metres.

Various aid groups maintain that increasing overall food supply and creating saleable surpluses will provide the greatest potential access to food for all Afghans. With better quality seeds and improved agricultural methods, coupled with more marketable new crops, there is no reason why Afghanistan should not become a significant food exporter. As Alain de Bures of Madera points out, Afghanistan has the potential to be a major fruit basket for Central and South Asia, including the Gulf countries, by producing apples, pears and other fruits that cannot be readily grown in India or the Middle East. These can easily be marketed – by road or air – as fresh produce or as jams and juices. However, this would entail better quality production to attract outside markets. As it is, one is already witnessing the effectiveness of new methods such as the planting of wheat between rows of fruit orchards to ensure better quality multiple crops. Similarly, some agencies have been establishing nurseries in northern Afghanistan to introduce more varied cultivation, such as fast growing fuel trees, more appropriate fruit trees requiring only limited irrigation, and deep-rooted trees to protect watersheds.

As a primarily agricultural country, Afghanistan boasts a maximum of 3.5 million hectares of irrigated land and up to four million hectares of rain-fed land. Of the latter, only one million hectares can be used at any one time. Scattered farming communities, long distances and rugged terrain make the delivery of any form of services or transportation of crops problematic. Such drawbacks may encourage poor farmers in remote areas to focus on more easily-grown – and transportable – narcotic crops, such as opium poppies (SEE DRUGS). In Helmand province (which until the late 1990s produced 40 percent of Afghanistan's opium), government authorities have been trying to persuade donors to provide more aid to counter rising poppy production. For lack of international funding and will, however, this has not been forthcoming. As a result, local farmers have stuck to planting poppies. Since the fall of the Taliban, "nothing significant in reconstruction has been done in Helmand, even though it is most strategic for the country's stability", complained governor Sher Mohammed Akhunzada in early October 2003. "While the Taliban are paying their fighters US$ 1,000, I only have promises to offer people, not aid." In 2002, Afghanistan produced 3,400 tonnes of opium, representing 76 percent of world production. The 2003 figures were higher still (3,600 tonnes), with even more expected in 2004 unless similarly lucrative crop alternatives can be found.

Despite efforts by the Karzai government to improve the attractiveness of Afghanistan for market development, the security situation continues to present a major barrier to domestic and external investment (SEE ECONOMICS). Much will depend on the ability of donors, aid agencies and private enterprise to provide local communities with inputs such as fertilizers, chemicals and veterinary medicines – plus micro loans to help improve basic infrastructure. Roads, too, need to be built or rehabilitated to bring farmers nearer to their markets. In July 2002, the Asian Development Bank presented their vision for developing Afghanistan's natural resources and agriculture sector (SEE BOX).

Asian Development Bank's vision, July 2002

(i) A "bottom-up" community based approach to the determination of development priorities, using the micro-watershed as the planning unit;

(ii) A natural resources management and regulatory mechanism, which ensures that the use of natural resources by communities, in aggregate, does not exceed the capacity of natural systems to sustain themselves.

(iii) The critical natural resource is "water" whose availability must be maximized and whose use must be effective and efficient. In doing so, ecosystems will be sustained while agricultural output is maximized. It is essential that all communities and agencies become aware that the abstraction of water incurs a cost over and above the delivery of the water;

(iv) The transfer of modern dryland farming technologies to rainfed areas with a view to producing at least half the country's cereal needs from rainfed farming;

(v) Rehabilitation of small, medium and large irrigation systems managed by their communities/beneficiaries and growing predominantly high value cash crops capable of supporting the cost of the infrastructure;

(vi) A traditional integrated livestock economy based on sustainable rangeland management and crop by-products, plus commercial peri-urban livestock enterprises serving the main urban communities;

(vii) Private sector led provision of agriculture services including seed, fertilizer, farm machinery, agro-chemicals and animal health products;

(viii) Agricultural marketing in the hands of the private sector, but with a significant farmer based marketing organization segment;

(ix) A thriving off-farm income generating sub-sector primarily targeted at and organised/operated by women;

(x) A lean, reformed set of sector institutions performing an agreed set of public sector functions

(xi) An appropriate policy framework conducive to a thriving private sector.

Source: Afghanistan Natural Resources and Agriculture Sector Comprehensive Needs Assessment, Final Draft Report, Asian Development Bank (July 2002)

Irrigation

Agricultural irrigation in Afghanistan dates back more than 4,500 years, with the oldest vestiges found in an ancient settlement near Kandahar. The establishment of permanent settlements and irrigation development went hand-in-hand, as cultivation was largely impossible without some form of water conduit. Water and land allocation have always been closely linked to the customs of local populations. Maintenance work of irrigation systems, such as the regular cleaning of *karezes* (underground irrigation tunnels), remains a traditional activity in the farmers' seasonal calendar.

Nearly 85 percent of the country's water resources come from the Hindu Kush mountains, whose winter snows provide a natural water store. Spring and summer snowmelt supports the perennial flow of all major rivers in Afghanistan. The remaining 15 percent comes from alluvial groundwater aquifers and springs. Ground water from deep wells counts for less than 0.5 percent.

Most of the water for irrigation comes from three major river basins: the Amu Darya (Oxus) Basin to the north; the Desert Basin to the south and southwest; and the Indus Basin (including the Kabul River) to the east and southeast. Reliable data regarding water resources from rainfall and river flow are not available. All measuring stations operational in 1978 (over 140) have been destroyed or their equipment looted. Currently, none works.

The war has had a devastating impact on irrigation. Some 3.5 million hectares of Afghanistan's farmland, producing nearly 80 percent of all wheat and 85 percent of other crops, were irrigated in 1978. Today, barely one-third (1.02 million hectares) of this area is being properly watered. The remaining 70 percent of irrigated land suffers from poor water management, damage due to lack of maintenance and destruction as a direct result of war.

Irrigation can be divided into two main categories: traditional and modern. Traditional irrigation systems include the *arhad* (ground water lifted from shallow wells) and *karez* (a free flow of water from alluvial aquifers through specially-constructed underground tunnels). There are also small-, medium- and large-scale surface water systems supplied by nearby streams and rivers. Modern irrigation schemes involve formal surface water operations (often previously run by the government or state farms) such as dams and pumped water sprinkler systems from wells. As in many countries, the overall efficiency of such systems is poor, no more than 25-30 percent for both traditional and modern irrigation schemes. Labour shortages often result in poor canal maintenance and cleaning. In areas with high ground water tables, over-irrigation, bad drainage and water-logging often cause salination of the soil, forcing fields to lie fallow for one or two years.

Agricultural specialists believe that available water resources are capable of supporting the irrigation of up to 5.3 million hectares. Rehabilitation, however, can be a long process. Lack of maintenance can cause canals and *karezes* to become silted and blocked, often resulting in the river or water supply changing course. This in turn can destroy existing farmland through flooding. Meanwhile, erosion removes thin layers of topsoil which take decades to rectify, if ever.

Another problem is that the traditional *mirab/vakil* system of distributing water rights has been seriously affected, if not abused, by local commanders and armed groups. In many areas, former *mujahideen*, warlords or Taliban fighters have regulated water supplies at whim, or based on contacts, bribes and corruption. This has often resulted in chaos, with some areas denied regular access to water.

According to the FAO, the complete cost per hectare for rehabilitation comes to US$ 300 for traditional schemes and US$ 500 for modern ones (1997 prices). While perhaps a quarter of the cost could be covered by locally organized food-for-work programmes, donors would have to provide the balance in cash to pay for materials, professional staff and operational costs.

In the late 1990s, some observers warned that unless more effective attention was placed on water resources, it would take 200 years for all existing schemes to return to full production. Under present aid commitments, the situation today is not much different. Even if sufficient funding were made available, observers say, it would still require a whole generation to bring Afghanistan back to pre-war production levels. More than food and water are at stake: according to an August 2003 article in the *Economist:* "Drought was an ally of the Taliban. They could not have pushed north without picking up farmers along the way who, having lost their wheat and goats to drought, thought to earn something by shouldering a gun."

Livestock

Since the outbreak of fighting in mid-1978, the effect of Afghanistan's dragging war has had a devastating impact on much of the country's livestock, mainly cattle, sheep, goats, horses, donkeys and camels. While reliable figures regarding livestock populations do not exist, the 1991 *Agricultural Survey of Afghanistan* (ASA) by the Swedish Committee for Afghanistan estimated that losses amounted to as much as half of all draft oxen and two-thirds of sheep and goats. The recent four-year drought (1998/99 to 2002/03) also had a disastrous impact. Apart from killing thousands of livestock, the drought forced many farmers to sell what animals remained in order to survive.

Livestock populations suffered particularly heavy losses in Soviet bombing raids, ground assaults and other forms of military action. But landmines and scattered ordnance have affected animals since the early days of the war (SEE LANDMINES). Not only have livestock been killed while grazing, but villagers often use them to walk through suspected minefields as a form of impromptu clearance. *Kuchi* nomads, who traditionally graze their animals on both sides of the frontier with Afghanistan and Pakistan, are believed to have suffered the most from landmines: by 1995 an estimated 35,000 of their animals had been killed by mines, with each household losing an average of nearly 25 animals (worth about US$ 3,000). This continuing scourge promises to kill and injure both humans and livestock for generations to come.

Numerous animals, too, succumbed as refugees made their way to Pakistan and Iran during the height of the fighting. Once in exile, many were forced to sell their animals for lack of grazing or for much-needed cash. Throughout the war, horses, donkeys, camels and mules were used by the *mujahideen* and aid agencies for supply caravans across the mountains and through the deserts, often with livestock casualties of 10 percent or more per trip. Farming too has suffered from the loss of livestock. For example, apart from milk and other dairy products, oxen are essential for tilling and fertilizing the soil.

Another problem was the collapse of veterinary services, the flight of trained personnel and the destruction of government facilities such as the state farms at Kabul, Jalalabad and Lashkar Gah. Exotic bulls used for cross-breeding, for example, were killed or removed as war booty. Apart from traditional medicines, livestock had little or no access to veterinary services, vaccination programmes and other drugs to combat anthrax, blackleg, sheep pox and enterotoxemia. This has been partially remedied by a relatively effective system of donor-sponsored Veterinary Field Units (VFUs), which began operating in some 244 districts throughout the country in the 1990s.

Following the end of the Soviet war, headcounts indicated that in nearly all provinces, livestock numbers, particularly cattle, were recovering and might reach pre-war levels by the end of the 20th Century. Even the poorest farmers tended to keep at least one cow to cover basic sustenance requirements. Sheep and goat numbers were nearly back to normal. In the northern provinces, an estimated five million Karakul sheep once represented a major export for Astrakhan pelts. Although the war and low demands for pelts brought the industry into crisis, Karakul flocks were returning to their former strength. During the 1990s, Afghanistan was still among the biggest producers of Astrakhan pelts in the world. However, the recent drought has devastated herds once again, leaving many smallholders destitute.

The rains in winter 2002-03 could be expected to increase livestock populations. Further expansion, however, will depend on more good rains plus sufficient grazing and fodder crops, such as lucerne (Medicago sativa), shaftal (Trifolium resupinatum) and berseem (Trifolium alexandrinum). Fodder crops already represent five percent of arable land. Any further growth will have to depend on extra production or the increase of other field crops.

ESSENTIAL DATA

- **80% of Afghans lived in rural areas in 1979**
- **22,000 villages in 29 provinces were destroyed or severely damaged during the Soviet war (1979-1989)**
- **The Soviet war destroyed 3,000 irrigation systems**
- **75% of the country only supports sparse grazing in the mountains and deserts**
- **5% of the land area, mainly irrigated, produces 85% of agricultural output**
- **3.5 million hectares of land were once irrigated – but only 30% was irrigated in 1997**
- **4 million hectares of land are rain-fed, of which only 1 million hectares can be cultivated at any one time**
- **85% of water resources originate from the Hindu Kush**
- **15% of water resources come from groundwater aquifers and springs**
- **Less than 0.5% of groundwater comes from deep wells**
- **Available water supplies could irrigate 5.3 million hectares**
- **Agricultural production dropped by 70% from 1978 to the early 1990s**
- **Wheat production rose by 80% from 2001-02 and by 50% from 2002-03**

Sources: FAO, Swedish Committee for Afghanistan (SCA), UNDP

ESSENTIAL AGENCIES

AACA, ADA, AFGHANAID, DACAAR, FAO, MADERA, OXFAM, SCA, SOLIDARITES, UNDP, UNHCR, UNICEF
Ministries of Rehabilitation and Rural Development (MRRD), Irrigation and Water Resources (MIWR), Agriculture and Animal Husbandry (MAAH)

ESSENTIAL READING

Afghanistan Poppy Survey, UNODC (2003)
Afghanistan Natural Resources and Agriculture Sector Comprehensive Needs Assessment, Final Draft Report, Asian Development Bank (July 2002)
Afghanistan Agricultural Strategy, FAO (Rome, 1997)
A review of the livestock production systems of Afghanistan, N. Cossins, FAO (Rome, 1994)
Agricultural Survey of Afghanistan, Swedish Committee for Afghanistan (Peshawar, 1991)
Afghanistan, Louis Dupree, Princeton University Press (2nd Edition, 1980; reprinted by Oxford University Press, 1997)

Aid in the 1980s: reaping what you sow

For the first half decade of the Soviet occupation, the overwhelming proportion of outside humanitarian aid to Afghans was directed towards the estimated three million refugees based in Pakistan. Much of this was channelled through the Islamabad government and the Afghan resistance parties, despite considerable abuse of aid resources by both Pakistani officials and the Afghan parties in Peshawar. (Iran preferred to deal with its refugees on its own and did not allow outside agencies to assist). The Afghan parties, particularly those closely supported by the Pakistanis, also used aid as a means of influence over the refugees. As the war dragged on, control of outside military and humanitarian aid, as well as funding, became a crucial factor for trying to guarantee allegiance among the numerous resistance fronts inside Afghanistan.

For the estimated eight million Afghans living in the mainly resistance-controlled rural areas, healthcare and education systems had collapsed. Soviet efforts to root out the guerrillas meant a deliberate policy to destroy the economic infrastructure. Such tactics, among other things, resulted in a sharp decline of agricultural production and a consequent food deficit as shown in the first *Agricultural Survey Report* by the Swedish Committee for Afghanistan (SCA) in May 1988.

Only an extremely limited amount of international relief, primarily medical, went to those Afghans seeking to survive in resistance-held areas. This was provided by a small handful of European, American and Muslim NGOs, most of whom transported their aid clandestinely by horse caravan across the mountains. Some, too, provided funding to needy civilians for the purchase of food, fertilizers and seed from government-controlled bazaars – a much cheaper form of aid than smuggling it inside.

For the hundreds of thousands of "internal refugees", who had fled to Kabul and other government-controlled towns, the relief situation was not much better than for many of those facing dire humanitarian predicaments in the countryside. Numerous victims were ignored by the communist government and by the UN agencies still operating officially in Afghanistan. The only international aid (excluding the Eastern bloc countries) that was available tended to be restricted to a few small health projects, such as those run by the World Health Organization (WHO) and UNICEF, plus some highly questionable UNESCO-supported education programmes. At the time, it was UN policy to operate only in government areas, thus limiting themselves to the capital and a few other large towns.

The crossborder NGOs, on the other hand, worked only in the rural areas controlled by the resistance, where the majority of the population lived. Organizations such as the Swedish Committee for Afghanistan (SCA), Médecins Sans Frontières, AFRANE, Afghanaid, Aide Médicale Internationale and a few others sought to alleviate the plight of civilians seeking to remain in the country, despite the risk of further military onslaught. These same NGOs were among the only international agencies providing assistance to remote areas such as Nuristan and Hazarajat in 2003. Several European governments, while reluctant to acknowledge their involvement in crossborder relief, helped back some of these groups. Even the European Economic Community (as the European Union was then called) provided funds for small in-country projects.

Certain major aid agencies clearly were restricted by their mandates. The United Nations High Commissioner for Refugees (UNHCR), for example, technically could deal only with refugees. On the other hand, some of the larger agencies had the means to assist civilians inside Afghanistan but consciously refrained from doing so for political and fund-raising reasons. They preferred to restrict their operations to 'official' sectors only. US-backed organizations, in particular, were expressly forbidden from dealing with any forms of crossborder humanitarian assistance. The US government, which was providing huge quantities of arms to the *mujahideen* but denying its involvement in the war, was terrified of having American nationals captured by the Soviet or Afghan government forces. As one American official working with CARE International noted at the time: "We are not into clandestine relief."

Such policies by both the UN and most donor countries actually may have contributed towards aggravating the refugee situation by placing such an enormous emphasis on humanitarian assistance outside Afghanistan. For their part, the Pakistanis did everything possible to assure that as much aid as possible passed through their own channels. Not only did international aid represent a *milch* cow of growing proportions every year, but also a means of promoting Pakistani policy inside Afghanistan – and Pakistan on the world stage.

From 1986 onwards, the international aid situation, particularly with regard to military assistance, began to change dramatically. Washington decided to support openly the *mujahideen* in their efforts to resist the Soviets. Over US$ 600 million a year worth of military and humanitarian aid began to pour in. Coordinated by the Central Intelligence Agency (CIA) and the US Agency for International Development (USAID), this was distributed largely in collaboration with Pakistan's military intelligence organization, Inter Services Intelligence, or ISI (SEE WAR WITHOUT BORDERS). Other aid sources, both official and private, ranging from the Saudi Arabians to the Chinese also became increasingly involved.

The rise in US aid resulted in a flood of NGOs, many of them desperately seeking projects for projects' sake. Even the UN was scavenging for projects to justify increased amounts of spending. Some NGOs, such as SCA, deliberately turned down USAID funding on the grounds that even if they wished, they could not spend much more money responsibly within the time constraints demanded by the American annual aid budget.

However, much of this humanitarian aid went astray. NGO coordinators and experienced observers estimated that no more than 20-30 percent of US aid actually reached intended beneficiaries inside Afghanistan. The rest ended up in the pockets of Pakistani government and Afghan party officials. This blatant corruption undermined the credibility amongst ordinary Afghans of the very people American policy was seeking to sustain – the exiled resistance leadership.

The failure of the USAID approach was largely the result of Washington's political efforts to establish an Afghan shadow government while remaining heavily dependent on the Pakistanis for implementing this policy, notably via the Peshawar parties. Many of the independent NGOs, however, preferred to cultivate direct links with the resistance fronts or 'local authorities' inside Afghanistan. According to Anders Fänge of the Swedish Committee, whose organization was involved in crossborder relief since the early days of the war: "The most effective humanitarian aid given by the Americans was the Stinger [ground-to-air missile]. It meant that the gunships disappeared and the farmers could start cultivating their fields again. It also meant that the door was opened for more development-oriented activities [as compared to relief] in NGO and USAID programmes."

A significant proportion of international aid, both humanitarian and military, was directed by the Pakistanis (with full knowledge of the Americans) towards the mainly Pashtun Afghan fundamentalist groups such as Gulbuddin Hekmatyar's Hezb-e-Islami faction (SEE KEY PLAYERS). Indirectly, such assistance also benefited the likes of Al Qa'eda leader Osama Bin Laden. While relatively small amounts of aid did succeed in reaching non-Pashtun groups such as Commander Ahmed Shah Massoud's northern Jamiat-led alliance, the Americans ironically did much to arm the very extremists they later blamed for promoting international terrorism. Various Arab and other Muslim fundamentalist groups, such as the *Wahabi*, also stepped up their assistance both to the refugees and inside guerrilla fronts willing to accept their money and support.

On the military side, vast proportions of this military aid were stockpiled and later used against rival *mujahed* groups following the overthrow of the communist regime in Kabul in April 1992. Despite warnings by some international aid coordinators, journalists and diplomats, including American, during the second half of the 1980s that US policy would only lead towards an even more disastrous Lebanon-style situation in the years ahead, American conservative elements preferred to continue with their support in order to "make the Russians bleed," as one US official noted. Or as another former US policy-maker under President Ronald Reagan added: "It was of no concern to us what would happen once the Soviets left." Today, some analysts directly attribute much of the bitter civil strife and post-Soviet devastation of Afghanistan as well as the rise of the Taliban and Al Qa'eda to this extremely myopic policy.

With the withdrawal of the Soviets in February 1989, attention was turned more intensely towards repatriation and reconstruction inside Afghanistan, with the UN assuming a more decisive role. The departure of the Soviets, however, meant a rapidly diminishing interest – and drop in funding – from the Americans. It became quickly apparent (as some observers had pointed out years earlier) that under the Reagan and Bush (senior) administrations, the plight of the Afghans themselves had never been the issue. What had mattered most of all was getting the Soviets out. By 1993, USAID had halted virtually all its funding for humanitarian and development projects. For Washington, Afghanistan was no longer on the radar screen.

Excluding its dismal activities earlier in the war, the UN started up its Afghanistan programmes in 1988, shortly after the Geneva accords. These were in full swing by the beginning of 1989. Many of the earlier approaches were plagued by poor coordination and misguided efforts to encourage the creation of Afghan NGOs. The UN also adopted a big brother attitude with a tendency not to listen to the international NGOs which had already been operating in-country for seven or eight years.

The UN's main problem was that Afghanistan was one of the first cases of a 'complex political emergency' – also described as a 'society in crisis and transition', i.e. a country in war and without a functioning central authority. During the 1990s, such crises became more common with the collapse of the Soviet Union and the end of the Cold War. As one leading independent aid coordinator recently noted: "The UN agencies have their tradition and experience in working with governments; they could never really understand what the absence of a government and a state administration actually meant for an aid programme. They still do not understand it, although they at least are aware of the problem today."

Aid post-Taliban

Since the fall of the Taliban in late 2001, Afghanistan has played host to an enormous influx of aid agencies and resources. In 1999, there were 46 international NGOs registered with the Afghan ministry of planning. By November 2002, this had shot up to 350 registered agencies, plus some 500 more 'passing through'. International staff working for the UN numbered nearly 700. In all, expatriate aid workers, journalists and business people in Kabul and elsewhere totalled around 3,000 by mid-2003. The factional roadblocks which plagued Kabul during the 1990s were replaced by traffic jams of white 4x4 aid vehicles. As Afghanistan climbed to the top of the media and political agenda, so the amount of international aid climbed to keep up. Emergency relief from rich country donors rose from an average of US$ 100 million per year, during 1995-2000, to over US$ 300 million during 2001. Then, in January 2002, donors pledged US$ 4.5 billion over five years to meet both relief and development needs. While this seemed a dizzy amount, compared to what the country had received before, some analysts pointed out that in the grand scheme of post-conflict reconstruction, it didn't amount to much. Aid allocations for Afghanistan in 2002 totalled around US$ 75 per person, compared to US$ 325 per person in Bosnia (1996-99) or nearly US$ 200 per person in Rwanda (1994) and East Timor (1999-2001). When aid money is compared to cash spent on the ongoing military operations in Afghanistan, it looks skimpier still (see Fig. 1).

FIGURE 1: Funds spent in Afghanistan (October 2001-October 2002)

	US$ billions
Reconstruction:	**0.37**
Humanitarian aid:	**1.16**
International Security Assistance Force (ISAF):	**0.54**
Coalition Forces:	**10.20**

Source: The Economist, August 2003

Meanwhile, the amounts of aid pledged are only part of the story – what matters more is the *impact* the aid has. According to Afghan analyst Chris Johnson, "most estimates are that two-thirds of the money pledged at the donor conference in Tokyo in January 2002 was for humanitarian assistance, much of it as food aid." Certainly, millions of Afghans were suffering severe food insecurity after the worst drought in living memory. Then there were the 1.5-1.8 million refugees who returned – far more than anticipated – with various short-term needs. Food aid is cheaper for donor governments to hand out than cash – often they may buy up surplus grain to shore up their own domestic markets. But during 2002, the Afghan government raised concerns that excessive amounts of foreign food aid were distorting the agricultural economy, pushing down crop prices and preventing Afghan farmers from working their way out of crisis. Opium poppies have proved a tempting alternative crop for many farmers struggling to survive.

As for reconstruction, the situation is worse still. Armed attacks by pro-Taliban groups rose sharply during 2003. In order to discredit the reconstruction efforts of the US-backed Karzai administration, they widened their targets to include aid workers and their offices and projects. In March, a foreign delegate working for the International Committee of the Red Cross was executed in cold blood near Kandahar. According to a September 2003 report by CARE International and New York University's Center on International Cooperation, attacks against UN and NGO workers shot up from between 1-3 per month during late 2002 to around 20 per month by late summer 2003. A great swathe of southern Afghanistan, from Khost and Paktia to Uruzgan and Helmand, became virtually off-limits to international aid workers. Work on the reconstruction of the flagship Kabul to Kandahar trunk road slowed to a crawl, as private contractors, road workers and their 700-strong security team became targets. Insecurity and delays have sent the cost of reconstruction soaring. In January 2002, the World Bank estimated the cost of reconstruction at US$ 10 billion. By mid-2003, the Afghan government put it at US$ 30 billion.

According to the CARE report, "the gap between needs and pledges is one concern, but the gap between promised support and actual reconstruction is more troubling". By May 2003, US$ 6.7 billion of aid had been paid or pledged. Yet of this sizeable sum, just US$ 192 million worth of projects had been completed. Pegging Afghanistan's needs at around US$ 20 billion, that means that 18 months after the fall of the Taliban, just one percent of reconstruction needs had been met. Nor can the delays be blamed on the Afghan government. According to CARE: "Despite repeated requests by the Afghan government to give it the financial authority to lead the reconstruction process, donors refused." There is a paradox at the root of all this: the weak capacity of the Afghan government is used as an excuse to bypass their authority during reconstruction; yet, unless donors help build local capacity to manage the recovery process, the government will remain weak and aid resources will continue to flow into the pockets of highly paid consultants and foreigners. Ironically, there is a further danger that, over the next few years, aid flows will decrease at just the time when the Afghan government becomes more capable of absorbing them.

Security, however, remains the overriding issue. Without it, reconstruction will grind to a halt. Yet without reconstruction, popular disaffection with the transitional government and aid agencies alike may grow, playing into the hands of anti-government forces and leading to greater insecurity. The refusal of the international community to extend peacekeeping forces (ISAF) beyond Kabul has frustrated aid agencies and Afghans alike – although in October

2003, NATO, which now commands the peacekeepers, said it was prepared to consider broadening their area of operations. In the meantime, a handful of Provincial Reconstruction Teams (PRTs) – combining lightly armed soldiers and reconstruction experts – have deployed to key urban centres. But, as the *Economist* pointed out in August 2003: "PRTs will at best be only a catalyst. They are too small to effect much change by themselves: the 72-man British one in Mazar-i-Sharif is charged with an area the size of Scotland".

A bewildering variety of different relief and development priorities, programmes, roles and funding structures have been established by the Afghan government, the United Nations, World Bank and NGOs since the departure of the Taliban.

Up to September 2001, the UN used to issue annual consolidated appeals for Afghanistan and other 'complex emergencies'. This changed in early 2002, with the presentation of the **Immediate and Transitional Assistance Programme for the Afghan People (ITAP).** The ITAP aimed to outline a comprehensive international aid strategy to meet relief, recovery, reconstruction and reintegration needs. It spanned the period October 2001-December 2002 and asked for a total of US$1.78 billion. Its programmes covered three main areas: 1) Quick-impact recovery projects; 2) Urgent recurrent costs of the Afghan government; and 3) Critical, unmet and continuing humanitarian needs. In all, the ITAP attracted around US$1.2 billion – with over two-thirds of this money going on food aid and repatriating refugees (see Fig. 2). The United States was the most generous donor by far, accounting for more than one third of total humanitarian assistance to Afghanistan over this period (see Fig. 3).

FIGURE 2: ITAP aid allocations, per sector (October 2001-December 2002)

	US$ millions
Agriculture:	61.3
Coordination and support services:	58.1
Economic recovery & infrastructure:	34.1
Education:	65.7
Family shelter and non-food items:	33.9
Food:	498.5
Health:	76.1
Mine action:	27.8
Multi-sector (mainly refugees)	317.3
Protection/human rights/rule of law:	12.2
Water and sanitation:	11.9
Total:	1,196.7

Source: OCHA, August 2003

FIGURE 3: Total humanitarian assistance for Afghanistan, by donor (October 2001-December 2002)

	US$ millions	% of funding
United States	538.0	35.1
Japan	182.9	11.9
Private/NGO/International	141.3	9.2
European Commission	108.3	7.1
United Kingdom	104.6	6.8
Netherlands	68.4	4.5
Germany	60.5	4.0
Italy	49.6	3.2
Sweden	41.0	2.7
Norway	26.7	1.7
Denmark	25.8	1.7
Australia	25.5	1.7
Canada	22.5	1.5
Saudi Arabia	22.1	1.4
Finland	13.6	0.9
Others	102.6	6.7
Total	1,533.5*	

** Includes contributions both within and outside the UN Consolidated Appeal Process*
Source: OCHA, August 2003

During the course of 2002, the Afghan government developed a **National Development Framework (NDF),** resting on three pillars:

- Humanitarian, Human and Social Capital
- Physical Reconstruction and Natural Resources
- Private Sector Development

Cutting across these three strategic areas are the key issues of security, administrative and financial reform, and gender. This framework became the basis for Afghanistan's National Development Budget (NDB), endorsed by donors in October 2002.

In December 2002, the ITAP was replaced by the UN's **Transitional Assistance Programme for Afghanistan (TAPA)**, which covers the period January 2003-March 2004. Introducing the appeal, the UN secretary-general's special representative to Afghanistan, Lakhdar Brahimi, says: "humanitarian needs will increasingly be met by addressing their underlying causes, as part of a broader strategy linked to recovery and reconstruction". He adds that the appeal intends "to underscore the transition from the independent UN appeals of the past to one that reflects international partnership with the new national authorities and civil society." To reflect this new spirit of partnership, the TAPA is organised according to the three pillars of the NDF. The TAPA appeals for a total of US$ 815.3 million, with 70 percent of the funds going on three main areas: helping refugees and the displaced to return home, strengthening livelihoods and social protection for the critically vulnerable, and promoting education and vocational training.

During 2002, the return of nearly 1.8 million refugees and 400,000 'internally displaced persons' (IDPs) put enormous pressure on the already shattered infrastructure and economies of Afghanistan's towns and villages. A further 1.2 million refugees and 300,000 IDPs were expected to return during 2003. Aid agencies' focus is on providing transport, food and non-food items (e.g. shelter and cooking kits) to help those wishing to return. To ensure that returnees can reintegrate permanently, agencies are working to improve shelter, water, education and health services in communities to which Afghan exiles return. The UN also aims to protect the rights of those who return and to enhance the capacity of government departments involved in repatriation. The budget for refugees and IDPs – which includes aid to camps outside Afghanistan – totals US$ 283 million up to March 2004.

The second largest sector in the TAPA is livelihoods and social protection, for which the budget is US$ 195 million. Twenty-four years of war and five years of drought have destroyed both the national economy and household livelihoods. Rain-fed crops and levels of livestock have been decimated. The UN identified eight highly vulnerable groups in need of assistance: 1) Critically poor (est. six million) – who need food aid or cash for work; 2) Urban poor (216,000 vulnerable in Kabul alone) – who need jobs; 3) Cold season vulnerable (est. two million) – who need 'winterization' (e.g. shelter materials, blankets); 4) Returnees (1.8 million in 2002, est. 1.2 million in 2003) – who need help with reintegration; 5) Internally displaced people (est. one million remain in camps) – who need ongoing humanitarian assistance; 6) Kuchi nomads (est. 1.3 million, of which 50-75 percent are vulnerable) – who need jobs and livestock; 7) Disabled people (est. one million, most critically poor) – who need humanitarian assistance; 8) Poppy growers threatened by opium ban – who need income diversification. A dedicated livelihoods and vulnerability analysis unit (LVAU) has been established in the ministry of rural reconstruction and development to promote cross-sectoral assessments and action to help the poorest Afghans.

The third largest sector in the TAPA is education and vocational training, with a budget of US$ 124 million. According to the ministry of education, by late 2002, although three million children were enrolled in school, a further 1.5 million eligible children were being deprived of educational opportunities. Furthermore, two thirds of those enrolled for education were studying in the open air or in tents, with virtually no learning materials or furniture. To meet present needs, 2,500 new schools need to be built and as many again are in need of major repairs. Other priorities include: 'food for education', teacher salaries and training, developing and printing 16 million textbooks, early childhood development and literacy (especially for women), vocational education (especially for ex-combatants), higher education and strengthening the ministry of education.

Thorkell Thorkelsson/International Federation

Health and nutrition attracts a budget of US$ 89 million in the TAPA, although the appeal points out that overall national needs in the sector are US$ 240 million per year. Health indicators in Afghanistan are among the worst in the world: 257 children out of every 1,000 die before their fifth birthday; maternal mortality is 1,600 per 100,000 live births; life expectancy is 43 years. Priorities within the sector include: primary health care, nutrition, women's health, strengthening institutions and dealing with infectious diseases.

Other major sectors addressed by the TAPA are: mine action (US$ 78 million budget); natural resources management (US$ 42 million); culture, heritage and media (US$ 21 million); public administration (US$ 18 million); security and rule of law (US$ 13 million); status of women (US$ 10 million); drug control (US$ 8 million); and, urban management (US$ 4 million).

The World Bank's latest estimate for the costs of reconstruction runs to US$ 15 billion over the next decade – on top of emergency aid. The Bank set up office in Kabul in February 2002, to provide financing and technical assistance in the areas of public administration and government capacity building, rural and urban infrastructure (especially roads), education and health. During 2002-03, the Bank granted US$ 120 million to target: water, sanitation, electricity and waste disposal in urban areas; labour intensive rehabilitation in hundreds of rural communities; improvements on the Salang road tunnel;

increasing the efficiency of the ministry of finance; assisting higher education and distance learning; and repairing rural roads and bridges. The Bank is also lending money to Afghanistan: in March 2003, it approved an interest-free loan of US$ 108 million to improve the country's highways (principally the Kabul-Salang-Kunduz-Faizabad route) and to improve safety at Kabul international airport (including reconstructing the runway). The credit was the Bank's first loan to Afghanistan since 1979.

The Bank administers the **Afghanistan Reconstruction Trust Fund (ARTF),** which was set up in May 2002 to meet: the government's recurring costs (e.g. salaries of 200,000 teachers, health workers and police); investments in capacity building, feasibility studies and technical assistance; and financing the return of skilled expatriate Afghans. By August 2003 the ARTF had attracted US$ 430 million of pledges from 22 different donors, of which US$ 188 million had been disbursed to the Afghan government. The ARTF is jointly managed by the Asian Development Bank, the Islamic Development Bank, the UN Development Programme and the World Bank. The fund is there to support programmes prioritised by the Afghan government from within its national budget. In August 2003, for example, at the government's request, US$ 10 million was granted from the fund to rehabilitate telecommunications systems, repair Kabul's roads and drains, and provide micro-credit for poor Afghans to meet emergency needs or invest in businesses.

Afghanistan will need substantial external funding for many years. For the financial year March 2003-March 2004, the Afghan government estimates its budget requirements at US$ 550 million. Of this, US$ 200 million is expected to come from domestic revenues, with the remainder being met by international donations (US$ 250 million from the ARTF and US$ 100 million from bilateral donations and other trust funds). Improving Kabul's ability to collect customs revenues from the provinces will prove crucial in bolstering the country's financial independence. Private sector-led recovery is a key part of the Bank's long-term strategy for Afghanistan. To that end, Afghanistan took a major step forward in July 2003, when it secured membership of the multilateral investment guarantee agency (MIGA), which provides political risk insurance for investments going into and out of Afghanistan.

ESSENTIAL READING AND WEBLINKS

Afghanistan Policy Brief, September 15, 2003, CARE International and Center on International Cooperation (Kabul and New York, 2003)

Afghanistan Reconstruction Trust Fund, Report to Donors, March 21-June 20, 2003, World Bank 2003

Humanitarian Assistance, Reconstruction and Development in Afghanistan: A Practitioners' View, Alastair J. McKechnie, World Bank CPR Working Paper No. 3, March 2003

Transitional Assistance Programme for Afghanistan, January 2003-March 2004, United Nations (New York and Geneva, December 2002)

Reuters Foundation AlertNet: www.alertnet.org
UN OCHA's financial tracking system: www.reliefweb.int/fts
UN ReliefWeb: www.reliefweb.int
World Bank: www.worldbank.org

Children

"Only the person who has been poor and unhappy can understand what it is to have nothing."

– Fawad, street-working child, Kabul, September 2001

A quarter of a century of war has killed, injured and displaced enormous numbers of Afghan children. They have witnessed scenes of violence no child should ever see. Their family security has been threatened or shattered. Their opportunities to develop healthy, well-educated lives have been denied. An estimated 300,000 children lost their lives due to the conflict, and over half a million have lost one parent. Health indicators are among the worst in the world: one in four Afghan children will die before their fifth birthday. Four years of severe drought made matters worse: by 2001, more than half of under five year-olds were malnourished, with up to 59 percent showing high levels of stunting. But despite these terrible statistics, many of those who work with Afghan children are surprised by their resilience against all odds.

Children in Afghan society

Afghans traditionally have large families – recent surveys suggest Pashtun women aspire to produce between seven and 10 children. While at least half the population is under the age of 18, childhood ends much earlier than this for most Afghans. Girls are free to play with boys until the age of nine or 10, but are then kept within the household to learn domestic skills. By the time they are 14-17 years old, most girls in rural areas will have entered arranged marriages. The groom's family must pay a 'bride-price' (which can range from US$ 500-US$ 2,500 – up to ten times annual per capita income) while the bride's family offers a dowry in return. During the intense drought of 1998-2001, there were reports that families 'sold off' their daughters into marriage younger than usual in order to raise money.

Boys, meanwhile, are considered adults by the time they are 14 or 15, and will then be expected to start providing for and protecting the family. As Shon Campbell points out, in her overview *Lost Chances – the changing situation of children in Afghanistan, 1990-2000:* "Significant in the childhood of Afghans is the lack of adolescence…life in Afghanistan is too short and resources too scarce to allow such a luxury."

Impact of the conflict

Armed conflict has not only cost the lives of hundreds of thousands of Afghan children, it has deeply affected the physical and emotional development of millions more who have survived. Research conducted in 1998 for the Save the Children group of agencies and UNICEF, reported in *The impact of conflict on children in Afghanistan,* found that nearly 60 percent of children interviewed spoke of a close relative who had died because of the war. Landmines and UXO (unexploded ordnance) have killed or wounded an estimated 130,000 Afghan children. Many of the ruined buildings in and around Kabul and Afghanistan's other major towns have still not been cleared of mines or UXO, posing an ongoing threat to children playing or gathering scraps of metal and paper to earn a living for their families. Data gathered from Kabul's 10 main hospitals from January to June 1997 revealed that 55 percent of all landmine victims and 85 percent of all UXO victims were children. In rural areas, older boys working the fields, clearing irrigation channels or tending livestock are particularly at risk. Nevertheless, landmines account for a minority of children's disabilities – other causes include birth defects, disease and cerebral palsy.

Over half those interviewed for the 1998 research said that their homes had been damaged or destroyed by war, depriving children of their safe haven. Two and a half decades of conflict created the largest caseload of refugees since the second world war. Nearly six million Afghans – one third of the population – were forced to flee to Pakistan, Iran and further afield. Over a million more were displaced within Afghanistan – by war and more recently by drought. Many children survived direct attacks, only to die on the arduous journeys their families were forced to make to reach safety. One 10 year old boy from a camp near Herat told researchers: "When we left Morghab we fastened my brother, who was one year old, on the back of a donkey. On the way he got cold, and by the time we arrived in Herat he was dead." Repeated displacement not only threatened the shelter and safety afforded to children – it exposed them to disease and prevented them from attending school. Meanwhile their parents, cut off from work, possessions and the support of extended family networks, often encouraged their children to scavenge or find menial labour to help support the family.

In the mid-1990s, much was made of psycho-social trauma among the child victims of conflicts in Bosnia and Rwanda. An entire generation of Afghan children have known nothing but war all their lives, and the impact on them in terms of role models and attitudes will be felt for decades to come. However, some past research conducted into trauma among Afghan children is now considered unreliable. It overstated the problem in a context where Afghan children are shown high levels of care and protection by extended family networks, which help them cope with the suffering they have experienced. Nor are attempts to counsel individual children now considered appropriate in Afghanistan, since existing coping mechanisms – based on family and social life – offer more effective solutions for their recovery and development. Agencies working with Afghan children believe that these coping mechanisms should

Are Afghan children traumatized?

What has been the impact of twenty four years of war on children's mental health? How can they be healed when there are so few psychiatrists? Is Afghanistan now burdened with a generation of children who know only what it is to kill and take revenge? These questions – frequently asked by international journalists and aid workers alike – spring from assumptions which only reflect a fraction of the reality in Afghanistan.

Of course, Afghan children have lived through events that most of us would not wish upon any child. There is something about children which makes us want to protect them and assume that any harm will affect them negatively. But, as I work with Afghan children I am constantly amazed at their resilience and fortitude. They have experienced terrible suffering but are still able to live as children, to play, to learn and to laugh. I do not, generally, find children overwhelmed by trauma but children who have come through suffering with their humanity and hope intact. Much of the credit must go to Afghan parents. They bear the brunt of difficult events to shield their children, while teaching them how to cope when bad things do happen. Research among children and their families in Kabul during 2002 revealed that children are taught several key qualities to help them cope.

First is courage. Children are expected to learn how to overcome fear – by confronting their fears and by being reassured when they are afraid. Second, they are taught how to be thankful – for still being alive after an attack, or for being better off than others around them. Third, children are encouraged to be happy through playing, joking, picnicking, going to school, being with friends. Afghans understand that if children have happiness in their life, they are much more able to cope with sadness. Fourth, children are expected to have religious faith. They are taught prayers to say when they are scared. They are encouraged to understand that everything which happens to them is in the hands of God, beyond their control and therefore to be accepted. Finally, children are taught morality. As parents in Kabul note, it is one thing to be exposed to bad events but it is another to know right from wrong. Children need not automatically follow the paths of the wrong.

Afghans know that children who have such qualities will be affected by violence but not permanently scarred by it. Exposure to war might even enhance these positive traits. Certainly in Afghanistan, the thirst for peace, the hunger for knowledge, the strength and motivation among young people will prove to be a major resource in a country struggling to get back on its feet for many years to come.

Jo de Berry, Save the Children (USA), Kabul

be supported and repaired, in order to offer the best psycho-social care to children.

Educational opportunities for Afghan children have been hit hard by both war and Taliban restrictions. By the end of the 1990s, 12 out of 20 boys and just one in 20 girls of schooling-age were going to school. Conflict destroyed much of the infrastructure and drove away tens of thousands of qualified teachers. Meanwhile, Taliban control from the mid-1990s until late 2001 led to strictly-enforced bans both on girls attending school and on female teachers.

In March 2002, UNICEF reported that its 'back to school' initiative resulted in around three million children and 70,000 teachers returning to school. The proportion of schoolchildren who were girls rose from five percent in 2001 to 30 percent in 2002 and 37 percent in 2003. By mid-2003, around 3.8 million children were registered in schools across the country. The experience of refugee families has contributed to higher school enrolment levels. Many rural Afghans, who had previously not known education, came to understand its importance in exile when their children were introduced to schooling in refugee camps and cities such as Peshawar and Quetta. As EFG editors discovered in the spring of 2003, while travelling in traditionally conservative or remote areas ranging from Nuristan to the Hazarajat, most villages now have their own co-educational schools (although reading materials are desperately lacking) and parents are insisting that as many children as possible, including girls, attend. For more information on primary, secondary and tertiary education, SEE EDUCATION.

Child health

The threats posed by poor health are even more deadly than armed conflict. According to UNICEF, Afghanistan's under-five mortality rate is 257 per 1,000 live births – that means one in four children die before their fifth birthday. By comparison, the rate in the US is eight deaths per 1,000 live births. Leading causes of mortality among Afghan children include diarrhoeal diseases, acute respiratory infections, vaccine-preventable diseases and chronic malnutrition.

The Expanded Programme on Immunization (EPI) – implemented by UNICEF and the World Health Organization (WHO) through the Ministry of Public Health (MoPH) and NGOs – has successfully vaccinated millions of children since it was introduced in Afghanistan in 1985. However, during the 1990s immunization levels fell steeply, with coverage against all six vaccine-preventable childhood diseases averaging just 40 percent. Around 30,000 children were thought to be dying of measles each year – the second highest mortality rate from the disease in the world. Since July 2001, the UN and Afghan authorities have vaccinated over nine million children against measles, slashing the number of reported cases by 75 percent. Meanwhile, the UN's quest to eradicate polio worldwide saw over six million Afghan children being immunized during 2002.

Diarrhoeal disease is responsible for over half of all deaths among Afghan children under the age of five. Save the Children-US has reported that 85,000 children die of diarrhoea each year. While health educators stress the need to improve personal hygiene and food preparation, the problem is likely to remain as long as nearly 90 percent of all Afghans lack access to safe drinking water or adequate sanitation facilities.

Thorkell Thorkelsson/International Federation

Over half of Afghanistan's children suffer from stunted growth, while a 2002 survey carried out in Badghis province revealed that 58 percent of under-5s were suffering from chronic malnutrition. One in three suffers from iodine deficiency, which can cause goitres, learning problems and even mental impairment. Agencies are trying to meet these challenges through supplementary and therapeutic feeding projects, distributing vitamin A supplements and adding iodine to national salt supplies.

For more information on mother and child health, SEE HEALTH.

Child exploitation

In mid-2003, UNICEF warned of a serious problem with child abduction in Afghanistan. Many abducted children are thought to be sold as sex slaves or child labourers. There have been reports of Pakistanis buying young boys from poor Afghan families, then smuggling them into religious schools over the border.

From March to May 2002, a survey conducted by the Swiss-based NGO Terre des Hommes (TdH) observed 37,284 children working on the streets of Kabul alone – more than one third of whom were just 8-10 years old. But this number represents only a fraction of the children involved in all types of labour across Afghanistan, such as carpet-making, mining and cross-border smuggling. Alarmingly, 30 percent of children surveyed had only started working on the streets in the past six months. This points to increasing poverty among the city's residents, due to the impacts of four years of drought plus the enormous numbers of very poor refugees returning to Kabul rather than to their original villages after the fall of the Taliban. This trend will put extra pressure on already inadequate infrastructure and economic opportunities in Afghan cities and may increase the trend of street working children further. Nevertheless, the great majority of children surveyed were not homeless, but lived with at least one parent or guardian. TdH attributes this to the strong sense of social responsibility fostered by Islam.

Typically, parents send their children out to polish shoes, burn incense for prayers, act as porters in the markets, wash cars, or simply beg for money – the UN and NGO quarters of Kabul providing particularly rich pickings. They also search wasteland and ruins for firewood, scraps of food, plastic, metal or paper – anything that can be used in the home or sold. In January 1997, AFP reported that Afghan children desperate to earn a few *Afghanis* were stealing human bones from graveyards, which were mixed with animal bones and exported to Pakistan to be turned into cooking oil, soap and chicken feed. The skeleton of an average Afghan reportedly fetched up to 7,000 *Afghanis* (50 US cents at the time).

But not all work by children is so unacceptable: most Afghan boys who take paid apprenticeships, or their sisters who take up carpet weaving, are proud of the contribution this makes to the family's finances. Problems arise when such work becomes exploitative. So far, the shattered state of the Afghan economy means that bonded child labour is on nothing like the scale of that seen in the carpet industries of, for example, northern India. However, one-year bonded contracts for Afghan children working in Pakistan's carpet-weaving industry have been reported since 1999. Meanwhile, the strong family structures of tribal Afghan society, combined with Islam's inherent sexual conservatism, mean that commercial sexual exploitation of children is rare in Afghanistan.

As Shon Campbell reported in 2001: "remarkably, children are not living on the streets and few are unaccompanied, dependent on drugs, forced into prostitution or as participants in armed combat in comparison to other countries experiencing conflict. The social fabric of Afghan society may have been brutally torn, but traditional mechanisms of caring for children are among the last elements to be compromised."

Children's rights

The Convention on the Rights of the Child (CRC), which came into effect in 1990, marked a change in the world's approach to children. In UNICEF's words, "the idea that children have special needs has given way to the conviction that children have rights, the same full spectrum of rights as adults: civil and political, social, cultural and economic." The core of the Convention is to promote the right of every child to survival, to protection from exploitation and abuse, and to the fulfilment of his or her potential as a human being. Today the CRC is the most widely ratified human rights convention in history. Every country in the world – including Afghanistan – has signed it, except for the United States (SEE HUMAN RIGHTS).

Although Afghanistan was a signatory in 1994, the Taliban did not recognise any UN Conventions ratified by previous governments. This, combined with the Taliban's rigid interpretation of Islamic *shari'a* law, had serious implications for the rights of Afghan children. In particular, the severe restrictions on medical care and training for women exacerbated the maternal mortality rate. This in turn threatened the right of children to survival (CRC, Article 6), and potentially their right to health (CRC, Article 24). The Taliban prohibition on both girls' education and female teachers clearly denied the right of all children to receive free primary education (CRC, Article 28), and made judgement by sex, violating Article 2 of the Convention. Furthermore, the Taliban ban on women earning a living outside the home had a serious impact on the children of widow-headed households, forcing particularly those living in towns and cities onto the streets in search of money, food and firewood. This exposed them to the dangers of exploitation, abuse and landmines, violating Articles 9,18 and 19 of the Convention.

Some argue that the Taliban's hard line simply institutionalized the informal values of rural Afghan – and specifically Pashtun – culture. While the departure of the Taliban has improved children's rights in theory, it will take many years to turn these rights into reality, particularly in rural areas. Nevertheless, the Afghan Transitional Authority (ATA) has shown commitment to mainstreaming children's rights. Progress includes the drafting of a new juvenile justice code, the inclusion of child protection as a designated project in the National Development Budget, and the initiation of a comparative study to ensure that Afghan law is modified so as to be compatible with the Convention.

ESSENTIAL DATA

- 300,000 children have lost their lives due to the conflict, and over 500,000 have lost one parent
- One in four children die before their fifth birthday
- On average each year, an estimated 85,000 children die of diarrhoea while 30,000 die of measles
- More than half of under-fives are chronically malnourished, while up to 59 percent of all children suffer stunted growth
- In 2002, over nine million children were vaccinated against measles and six million against polio
- In May 2003, 3.8 million children were registered in schools (37% girls, 63% boys)
- Over 37,000 children are working and begging in the streets of Kabul – earning 30-90 cents per day

ESSENTIAL READING AND WEBLINKS

The Children of Kabul: Discussions with Afghan Families, Jo de Berry et al, Save the Children USA and UNICEF (June 2003)

UNICEF Humanitarian Action, Afghanistan Donor Alert, 17 March 2003

Afghanistan's Children Speak to the UN Special Session, Save the Children Alliance (September 2001)

INFOBRIEFS

Lost Chances – the changing situation of children in Afghanistan, 1990-2000, Global Movement for Children in Afghanistan Working Group (June, 2001)
The impact of conflict on children in Afghanistan, Patricia Sellick for the Save the Children Alliance and UNICEF (May 1998)
First Call for Children: World Declaration and Plan of Action from the World Summit for Children, Convention on the Rights of the Child, UNICEF (1990)
State of the World's Children (annually), UNICEF

www.savethechildren.net
www.tdhafghanistan.org
www.unicef.org

ESSENTIAL AGENCIES

Aschiana, CCA, CiC, SCF-UK, SC-S, SC-US, TdH, UNICEF, UNHCR

Culture

> *"The sand of the desert is lightly blown away by a breath; still more lightly is the fortune of man destroyed."*
>
> *– Turkmen proverb*

Afghanistan's cultural heritage is among the richest in the world. Over the past 6,000 years the region has played host to the earliest Bronze Age civilizations, the birth of fire-worshipping Zoroastrianism, the collision of East and West which generated the first ever representations of the Buddha as a human, and generations of brilliant Islamic architects, miniature artists and calligraphers. By virtue of its geographical position straddling the trade routes between Mediterranean Europe, the Middle East, the Indian subcontinent and China, it has throughout history been a cultural, ethnic and linguistic cross-roads. A vast number of cultural influences – Persian, Sino-Siberian, Hellenistic, Roman, Indian, Turkish, Arab and Mongol – have all contributed to the material, literary and musical inheritance of Afghanistan.

However, a quarter of a century of war, fanaticism and greed have shattered this precious cultural vessel. Many rural sites of great historical importance were damaged or destroyed during the Soviet war, and continue to be looted. The unique Kabul Museum was virtually destroyed by factional fighting and rocket attacks between 1992-1996. Priceless Bagram ivories and Greco-Buddhist sculptures were stolen from the Museum and sold off to unscrupulous international collectors and dealers. Then in 2001, the Taliban sledgehammered most remaining artefacts bearing human or animal features. Meanwhile, the fifteenth century minarets and mausolea of Herat have been shelled and illegal excavations continue around the 12th Century Minaret of Jam, the ancient Greek settlement of Ai Khanum and elsewhere. Most infamously of all, in March 2001, the colossal Bamiyan Buddhas were blown up by the Taliban and Al Qa'eda. Only the mosques (unless they were Shi'ite) have survived the onslaught.

Following the departure of the Taliban in late 2001, the new Ministry of Information and Culture, supported by the United Nations Educational, Scientific and Cultural Organization (UNESCO) and others, tried to piece together what remained. During 2002-03, a debate raged about whether to spend millions of dollars on rebuilding the Buddhas. Meanwhile, in June 2002 the Minaret of Jam became Afghanistan's first World Heritage Site. Numerous rehabilitation projects got underway, including one to rebuild the shattered Kabul museum. However, the illegal smuggling of artefacts continued unchecked, and became almost as lucrative as the opium trade.

One of the best historical and cultural overviews is Nancy Hatch Dupree's book, *An Historical Guide to Afghanistan* (2nd Edition, 1977), still available from bookshops and street-sellers in Peshawar and Kabul. The following summary, which draws material from Dupree's book as well as from first hand investigation, highlights some of the most significant cultural remains and what has happened to them. For more details on individual sites and how to visit them, SEE TRAVEL.

Prehistoric era (c. 100,000-1,000 BC)

The Prehistoric era stretches from Stone Age times (c. 100,000-2,000 BC) to the Bronze Age (c. 5,000-1,000 BC). A number of key sites in Afghanistan have been revealed since the Second World War: Palaeolithic quartzite tools 100,000 years old were found west of Ghazni, and stone tools excavated from Neanderthal rock shelters in Badakhshan and Faryab are thought to be 50,000 years old.

However, it was in the caves of Aq Kupruk, beside the Balkh River in northern Afghanistan, that the most remarkable finds were made. As well as flint tools created so finely that their makers have been dubbed the "Michaelangelos of the Upper Palaeolithic", archaeologists found a human head sculpted, around 20,000 years ago, in light relief from a pebble – one of the oldest representations of man in the world. This pebble is currently missing, possibly stolen from Kabul Museum. At Neolithic sites (c. 2,000 BC) in Darra-e-Kur, Badakhshan, pottery, stone vessels, shell ornaments and human burials were discovered, including goats' and children's skulls buried together.

The Bronze Age (c. 5,000-1,000 BC) saw man move from mountain caves into village and urban communities and begin regional trading with Mesopotamia, Central Asia and the Indus Valley. The Tepe Fullol Hoard of five gold and 12 silver vessels, discovered east of Baghlan, dates from around 2,500 BC and includes a gold beaker with bull motif. Religious shrines discovered at the urban mound of Mundigak and at Deh Morasi, near Kandahar (c. 2,000 BC) contained figurines of pagan mother goddesses. At Shamshir Ghar some bone seals, one depicting a winged camel, were discovered dating from the second millennium BC. It was also around this time that lapis lazuli trading began in Badakhshan and Baghlan. Archaeological evidence suggests that Afghan lapis was used for decorative and medicinal purposes in the three great Bronze Age civilizations of Harappa on the Indus river, Mesopotamia, and beside the Nile in modern-day Egypt.

Aryans and Zoroastrians (c. 1,500-330 BC)

Around 1,500 BC Vedic Aryan warriors, initiators of Hinduism, invaded northern Afghanistan riding two-horsed chariots and settled in the fertile plains of

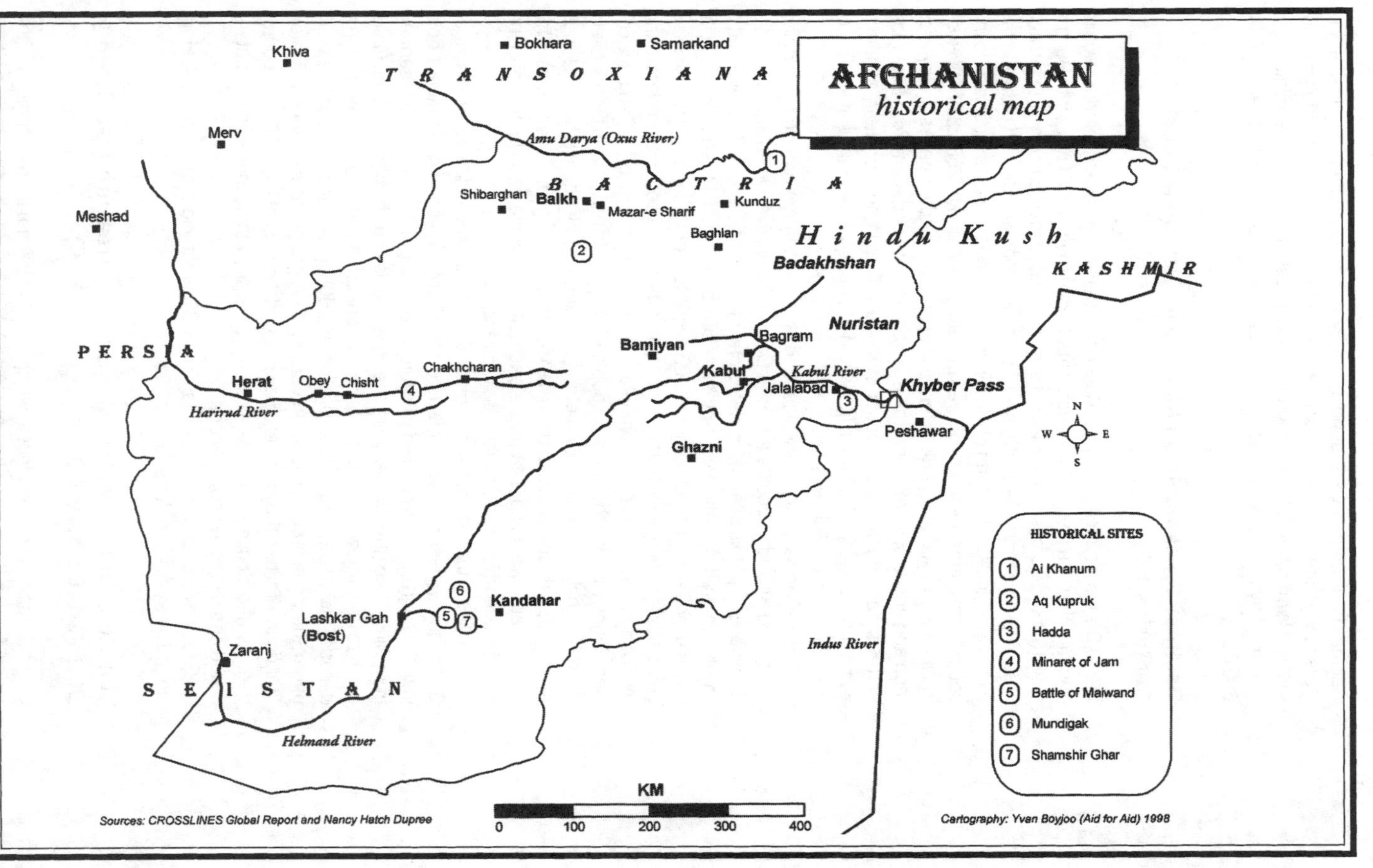
AFGHANISTAN
historical map
Bokhara
Samarkand
Khiva
TRANSOXIANA
Merv
Amu Darya (Oxus River)
BACTRIA
Shibarghan
Balkh
Mazar-e Sharif
Kunduz
Baghlan
Meshad
Hindu Kush
Badakhshan
KASHMIR
Nuristan
Bamiyan
Bagram
PERSIA
Kabul
Kabul River
Jalalabad
Khyber Pass
Herat
Obey
Chisht
Chakhcharan
Harirud River
Peshawar
Ghazni
N
W
E
S
Kandahar
Lashkar Gah
(Bost)
Zaranj
SEISTAN
Helmand River
Indus River
HISTORICAL SITES
1 Ai Khanum
2 Aq Kupruk
3 Hadda
4 Minaret of Jam
5 Battle of Maiwand
6 Mundigak
7 Shamshir Ghar
KM
0 100 200 300 400
Sources: CROSSLINES Global Report and Nancy Hatch Dupree
Cartography: Yvan Boyjoo (Aid for Aid) 1998

Bactria. In time they were supplanted by the Achaemenid King Darius I of Persia, who invaded the Afghan area in 522 BC and who worshipped Ahur Mazda. Worshippers become known as Zoroastrians, when the religion was reformed by Zoroaster, probably born near Balkh sometime between 1,000-600 BC.

Bactrian Greeks and Buddhist Mauryans (4th to 1st Centuries BC)

In 330 BC Alexander the Great of Macedonia destroyed the Achaemenid empire and marched via Herat, Kandahar, Kabul, Panjshair and Kunduz into Bactria (Balkh), before crossing the Hindu Kush with 30,000 men to invade Punjab and Sind. After Alexander's death, his Afghan kingdom was divided between the Greek Seleucids to the north of the Hindu Kush, and the Indian Mauryans to the south, whose most famous king was the Buddhist Ashoka (268-233 BC). Rock inscriptions of Ashokan edicts, encouraging piety and compassion towards men and animals, were found carved in both Greek and Aramaic in Laghman and Kandahar. The whereabouts of these edicts is now unclear, although some are reported to be buried in the mined old city of Kandahar, at the foot of the *Chihlzina,* or 'Forty Steps.'

Greco-Bactrian culture continued to flourish, centred around the fortified town of Ai Khanum, beside the Amu Darya (Oxus River) in Takhar province. Excavations at this site, which dates back to the 3rd Century BC, revealed a highly cultured society living further east than in any Greek-influenced city previously discovered. During 2002-03, experts reported that Ai Khanum was being systematically looted of its treasures through a series of underground excavations. In Kunduz, 627 remarkable coins from the 3rd to 1st Centuries BC were found (the 'Kunduz Hoard') depicting the busts of Bactrian Greek rulers in profile, including one of Demetrius I wearing an elephant's head helmet. Among this hoard, discovered in 1946, were the largest Greek coins ever discovered – weighing 3.4 ounces each. All have since been looted from the Kabul Museum and sold on the black market.

In 1978, Russian archaeologists digging in ancient burial sites near Shibarghan, west of Mazar, discovered 20,000 pieces of magnificent gold jewellery and ornaments inlaid with turquoise and precious stones. Unearthed from Tillya Tepe (the 'Golden Hill'), the collection is known as the Bactrian Gold, and has never been exhibited outside Afghanistan. Feared lost for more than a decade, the treasure resurfaced in August 2003. It had been hidden in a vault under the presidential palace. According to Afghanistan's finance minister, "during the Taliban they tried to open this and the staff of the bank very courageously had blocked the code. They were beaten almost senseless...but resisted and did not reveal the code".

Greek rule ended in Afghanistan in 48 BC when Hermaeus, the last king, signed away his rule in Kabul.

The Kushan Empire and the Bagram Treasure (1st Century BC to 3rd Century AD)

Originating from nomadic tribes, which invaded Bactria from Central Asia, the great Kushan King, Kanishka (c. 78-144 AD), established an empire which

Masjid-e-Jami, Herat *J. Walter*

extended its influence from the Ganges Valley to the Gobi Desert. Centred in the summer on Kapisa, north of Kabul, and Peshawar in the winter, he promoted and hugely benefited from perhaps the richest trade of luxury goods the world has ever seen. Wines, ceramics, glass and gold were shipped east from Imperial Rome and Alexandria, in exchange for silks from the Han dynasty in China, and perfumes, spices and gems from India. In 1939, French archaeologists discovered a magnificent 2nd Century AD Kushan treasure trove at Kapisa. According to Nancy Dupree, this trove, known as the Bagram Treasure, "represents, in capsule form, the extent and richness of the commercial activity along the Silk Route. Here are Chinese lacquers, Greco-Roman bronzes, plaster plaques, and vessels of porphyry and alabaster, Roman glassware and exquisite ivories from India. Together they form the most spectacular archaeological find of the twentieth century". The Bagram ivories (1st to 3rd Centuries AD) were used to decorate various objects, and depict mainly scantily-clad women and goddesses in a style typical of the art of the Indian subcontinent. The Hellenistic bronzes, which date no later than the 1st Century AD, include a statue of Hercules, a bust of Mars, and a mask of Silenus. Many of the ivories have been looted from the Kabul Museum, broken up and sold on the international art market. Kanishka created a magnificent acropolis for himself at Surkh Kotal, near Pul-e-Khumri, north of the Hindu Kush – the heavily looted remains can be seen to this day (SEE NORTHERN REGION).

Buddhism and the art of Gandhara (2nd to 8th Centuries AD)

King Kanishka called a great council of Buddhist scholars in Kashmir, which decided to humanize Buddhism in order to gain popularity over militant Brahmanism. This new school of Mahayana Buddhism placed more emphasis on the miraculous life and compassionate personality of the Buddha. It promised all worshippers universal salvation with the help of enlightened individuals who returned from the brink of nirvana as *bodhisattvas.* This directly resulted in the artistic representation of the Buddha (and his *bodhisattvas*) in human form for the first time. Previously he had been symbolised by devices such as a wheel, footprint or umbrella. Buddhist art flourished under the Kushans. Particularly remarkable was the Gandhara school, centred around Peshawar and Jalalabad, famous for its sculptures representing the Buddha with the physiognomy of a Greek god and the robes of a Roman emperor (SEE BOX). Although Kanishka did not confine his faith to any one religion, during his reign the Buddhist resurgence swept rapidly from India and Afghanistan along the Silk Route into China, Tibet and the Far East where it is far more widespread today than in the Buddha's native subcontinent.

Buddhist sites abound in all but far-western Afghanistan. The focal point of these sites are *stupas*, hemispherical domes containing burial relics. The *stupas,* originally surmounted by a series of umbrellas, were richly decorated with stone, stucco (lime, marble dust and sand) or mud sculptures depicting the life of the Buddha, to inspire the faithful as they walked around them in a clockwise direction. Hadda, near Jalalabad, was one of the most significant sites (2nd to 5th Century AD), featuring more than a thousand *stupas* and famous for expressive faces of visiting pilgrims, artists and merchants sculpted out of stucco. Much of Hadda was destroyed by Russian bombs in the 1980s when the *mujahideen* were sheltering there, and its precious Gandharan sculptures were looted from the Kabul Museum and sold off.

The most famous of all Buddhist sites in Afghanistan is Bamiyan, once home to two colossal Buddha statues, carved out of the rock face around 1,700 years ago (SEE HAZARAJAT). The Big Buddha towered 55 metres high (180 feet), while its companion was around 38 metres high (120 feet). In 1997

Bamiyan Buddhas: rebirth on hold

"Upright in his niche like a whale in a dry dock" was how the writer Bruce Chatwin once described Bamiyan's biggest Buddha. Now, only the dry dock remains. The colossal 55 metre high statue – carved out of a rockface 1,700 years ago – was blown up by the Taliban, along with his 38 metre companion, in March 2001. UNESCO, which proved powerless to prevent this act of cultural vandalism, declared the Bamiyan valley a World Heritage Site in July 2003 – in the hope of preserving what remains.

The Buddhas symbolised a philosophy which maintains that attachment to physical objects and desires is the root of all suffering. So it is ironic that their departure has provoked a heated argument over whether to rebuild them. Afghan authorities and cultural experts who gathered for a UNESCO conference in Kabul in 2002 decided that rebuilding the Buddhas was not a priority. The news came as a disappointment to Paul Bucherer-Dietschi, director of the Bibliotheca Afghanica museum in Switzerland, who has been arguing in favour of reconstruction. The work would take four years and could cost between US$ 30-50 million.

Many experts disagree with Bucherer-Dietschi. Nancy Hatch Dupree, a leading author on Afghan culture, told EFG editors: "it would be a great mistake to rebuild the Buddhas – we don't want to turn them into a fun park. I do not think you can recreate the inspiration of so many centuries ago." Asked if the area would benefit economically from rebuilding the Buddhas, she responded: "The stumps are just as poignant. I think tourists will still come to Bamiyan."

Meanwhile, UNESCO's goodwill ambassador, Ikuo Hirayama, argued that the site should stand as a witness to human barbarity. This suggestion enraged Karim Khalili, leader of the Hazaras (Bamiyan's main ethnic group) and one of the country's vice-presidents. "If you give this as a reason", said Khalili, "you should leave the Twin Towers as they were, as a monument to what terrorism did."

Japan has donated US$ 700,000 to stabilize Bamiyan's crumbling cliffs and protect the 600 monks' caves and mural paintings they harbour. A small museum will be built, and new excavations are planned to unearth a large reclining Buddha statue believed to be buried somewhere in the Bamiyan valley. However, security concerns have delayed restoration work. *JW* a local Taliban commander threatened to blow up the Bamiyan Buddhas, which he considered to be idols. Consequently Mullah Omar, the Taliban leader, stated that the Buddhas would not be touched since "the statues are not worshipped." By March 2001, he had changed his mind – under the influence of Al Qa'eda – and pursued a deliberate campaign to erase all signs of pre-Islamic culture. According to Nancy Dupree: "The smashing of the Bamiyan Buddhas was the final bid for power by the Arabs, because it was their way of diminishing the essence of the separate Afghan identity." The demolition took several weeks to complete. Locals reported that all the plaster comprising the Buddhas' massive bodies was removed by lorries to Pakistan and sold as paperweights.

Until their destruction at the hands of Al Qa'eda and the Taliban, the Buddhas were the largest statues of their kind in the world. Hundreds of monks' cells remain, hollowed out of the rock face beside the site of the Buddhas. Their once magnificent wall paintings are now defaced by military graffiti or blackened by the cooking fires of nomads and Taliban tyre-burning. While reconstruction of the Buddhas remains controversial, the cliffs and caves are the subject of a major restoration project. In July 2003, UNESCO made the Bamiyan Valley a World Heritage Site (SEE BOX).

The earliest known examples (8th Century AD) of the cosmic *mandala* – which subsequently became the key symbol of tantric worship in the Buddhism of Tibet and Nepal – were discovered in the side valley of Kakrak. Other significant Buddhist remains include Tepe Maranjan and Guldara near Kabul; Shotorak near Bagram, famous for its rare imported-schist bas reliefs; Tepe Sardar in Ghazni; and Fondukistan in the Ghorband Valley, which in the 7th Century AD enjoyed the last, elegant blossoming of Buddhist art heavily influenced by the sensuous and languid Indian Gupta school.

The rise of Islam (7th to 12th Centuries)

Afghan history from the 3rd to 7th Centuries AD is a confusion of competing influences, unleashed upon the Kushan empire as it waned in the wake of Roman and Han decadence. Sasanians from Persia, followed by nomadic Hephthalites (White Huns) from Central Asia, descended on the region and for several centuries both Buddhism and Hinduism were practised in Afghanistan. However, in the mid-7th Century Arabs under the banner of Islam took Herat and, two centuries later, the Saffarids from Seistan (south-western Afghanistan) spread Islam as far as Kabul and Balkh. Under the exuberant 9th Century Samanid dynasty from Bukhara, Balkh rose to prominence as an Islamic centre. The *No Gumbad* ('nine domes') mosque, remains of which still stand near Mazar, dates from this period (SEE NORTHERN REGION).

However, under the formidable Sultan Mahmud, son of a slave-turned-general, Ghazni was to become one of the most glittering cities of the Islamic world. A great patron of the arts, Mahmud (998-1030) dominated Afghanistan and western Persia, and carried Islam into India, returning with fabulous booty with which to adorn his palaces in Ghazni and Bost (Lashkar Gah). Many of the splendid bronzes, marble reliefs, ceramics and frescoes from this period were looted or melted by a rocket attack on Kabul Museum in 1993. However, the two early 12th Century minarets, which stand on the outskirts of Ghazni, and the great arch and citadel at Bost, still testify to the power and sophistication of this empire.

Kanishka's acropolis at Surkh Kotal *J. Walter*

The Ghaznavids were overwhelmed in the 12th Century when the Ghorid dynasty, led by Alauddin the 'World Burner,' gutted Ghazni and Bost. He then established his capital at Firozkoh and built victory towers out of Ghazni's soil, reportedly carried there "on the backs of captives whose blood served as mortar." Some historians believe that Firozkoh was situated at Jam in Ghor province where a magnificent minaret 65 metres high still stands (SEE BOX). The minaret's bold geometric designs and Persian-blue Kufic inscriptions are similar to those of the Ghorid portal of the great Friday mosque in Herat. Both structures are the only surviving creations of the late 12th Century Sultan Ghiyathuddin.

Mongol interlude (13th Century)

Genghis Khan, 'sovereign of the sunrise,' became offended when a goodwill gift of 500 camels laden with gold, silver, silks, furs and sable, which he sent to his neighbours in Balkh, went missing. He decided to pay the region a visit with 200,000 of his finest mounted troops, whom he likened to a 'roaring ocean.' By 1221 he had utterly devastated every town and murdered almost every living thing from Balkh and Herat to Ghazni and Bamiyan. So terrible was the destruction that the hilltop citadel of the Shansabani empire, near Bamiyan, is still known today as Shahr-e-Gholghola, or 'City of Screams.'

Timur and the Moghuls (14th to 17th Centuries)

Timur was next to arrive. Known to history as Tamerlane – meaning Timur-e-Lang or 'Timur the Lame', because of an old war wound – he captured Balkh in 1369, Herat in 1381 and proclaimed himself emperor from Kabul to Samarkand (his home town) and the Aral Sea. Timur's youngest son, Shah Rukh, and the latter's amazing wife Gawhar Shad, inherited this huge kingdom on Timur's death in 1405. Under them the arts flourished. Only five minarets and the mausoleum of Gawhar Shad in Herat – described by British writer Robert Byron in the 1930s as "the most beautiful example in colour in architecture ever devised by man to the glory of his God and himself" – still stand today. They are being restored with the help of international agencies. The colourful and exuberant floral patterns of the tiles covering the Friday Mosque in Herat have been restored through a recent UNESCO tile workshop and food-for-work programme. In addition to this architectural heritage, philosophers, poets and the renowned miniaturist artist Bihzad also enjoyed lavish patronage in Herat (SEE WESTERN REGION).

In 1504 Kabul fell to the last of the Timurids, Babur, descended from Genghis Khan and Tamerlane. Babur had been kicked out of his kingdom in Ferghana, east of Samarkand, and headed south in search of adventure. He had intended to destroy Kabul, but was so charmed by the city that he showered its citizens with money instead. After taking Herat and Kandahar in 1507, he turned his attention in 1525 to Delhi and Agra where he founded the Moghul Empire and where he died in 1530. Kabul, however, had claimed a special place in his heart and he asked to be brought back to his favourite garden on the western slopes of Sher-e-Darwaza in Kabul to be buried. Babur's tomb, rebuilt in the 1930s, the Queen's palace and terraced garden of flowerbeds, fountains and avenues of trees were badly damaged during the factional fighting of the 1990s. Both palace and garden are being brought back to life with the help of the Aga Khan Foundation and the UN.

For the 170 years following Babur's death, Afghanistan was the fulcrum between the two great empires of the Indian Moghuls, who controlled Kabul (and occasionally Kandahar) and the Persian Safavids who held sway in Herat. The main Moghul monument dating from this period is the *Chihlzina*, a stone chamber at the top of 40 steps carved out of a cliff on the western edge

Gandhara

Gandhara was both an ancient land and a style of art famous for first representing the Buddha as a human, dressed in robes inspired by classical Greece and Rome. Most Gandharan art dates from the 1st to 5th Centuries AD, when the region bounded by the Oxus and Indus rivers thrived under the peaceful reign of the Kushan kings. Gandhara became the prosperous hub of the Silk Route and a major destination for Buddhist pilgrims.

Buddhism first reached Gandhara in the 3rd Century BC when the Emperor Ashoka built a *stupa* at Taxila, near Rawalpindi. Greek influence began with Alexander the Great's invasion in 329 BC, and was sustained by local Greek kings centred on Ai Khanum in Bactria, now northern Afghanistan. As well as Greek influences, Gandharan art incorporates Indian, Iranian and Zoroastrian motifs.

Early artistic representations of the Buddha were limited to symbols such as the parasol, throne, footprints or begging bowl. But Gandharan art initiated his personification as a human. Theories abound for why this happened. Perhaps artists were inspired by images of the Greek god of knowledge Apollo. More likely, as Buddhism emerged from a narrow sect of monastic wanderers into a broader religion seeking new converts, the need for a divine saviour grew. The *bodhisattva* ('being of wisdom') – an incarnation of the Buddha who out of compassion postpones *nirvana* to help suffering devotees towards salvation – became the focus of a new-found deism within Buddhism and anthropomorphism within Gandharan art.

The *bodhisattvas* are represented as teachers and gods. Their divinity is revealed by a bulge in the skull representing wisdom and concealed by a tuft of hair between the eyebrows (which may represent the yogic third eye of spiritual insight), webbed fingers and toes, elongated earlobes, a halo (inspired by Zoroastrianism) and monastic robes (influenced by Graeco-Roman statuary).

Relics of the Buddha inspired great devotion (his skull bone found its way to Hadda, near Jalalabad). They were stored in *stupas*, which became the architectural focus for generations of pilgrims. As the region prospered, its wealthy inhabitants sought to salve their consciences and gain merit by commissioning statues of *bodhisattvas* or carved reliefs which encircled the *stupas* and related the Buddha's lifestory.

An invasion of White Huns, followed by the arrival of Islam in the 8th-9th Centuries, dealt a death-blow to Gandharan culture and commerce, but the region's artistic influence spread as far as China, Korea and Japan. *JW* of Kandahar. Inside is a carved Persian inscription recording the conquests of Babur.

The emergence of Afghanistan as a nation (18th to 20th Centuries)

In 1709 a Ghilzai Pashtun called Mir Wais Hotak secured the independence of Kandahar from the Persians, but his successors were themselves superseded in 1738 by a Turkoman warrior who had taken the throne of Persia and titled himself Nadir Shah. Nadir continued into India and ravaged Delhi, thereby ending the Moghul Empire, but on his return in 1747 he was poisoned. An Abdali Pashtun, who had led Nadir's personal bodyguard, then assumed control of Kandahar, and was crowned Ahmed Shah Durrani.

By 1749 he had captured Kabul, Herat and Badakhshan, as well as Kashmir, Sind and Punjab. In creating the last genuine Afghan empire he became known as Ahmed Shah Baba, 'Father of Afghanistan.' His blue-domed mausoleum is still in perfect condition in Kandahar, and next to it is one of the holiest shrines in Afghanistan, the Shrine of the Cloak of the Prophet Mohammed. Ahmed Shah received the Prophet's cloak from the Amir of Bukhara in 1768 as part of a treaty to settle northern boundaries, and the shrine is covered in fine tile decorations above a foundation of green marble from Lashkar Gah. The cloak, which had not been seen in public since the 1930s, was taken out by the Taliban leader Mullah Omar in 1994 and shown to a crowd of several thousand *mullahs* to substantiate his claim to be Mullah Al-Momineen, or Leader of all Pious Muslims (SEE SOUTHERN REGION).

The period following Ahmed Shah's death in 1772 is characterized by fratricidal and internecine struggles between the Pashtun Sadozai and Barakzai brothers, not helped by the fact that Ahmed Shah's son Timur left 23 sons and no appointed heir. The 19th Century saw the rise of British and Russian interference in the region and was generally inauspicious from a cultural point of view. In retribution for what they saw as Afghan treachery, the British demolished Kabul's famous covered bazaar in 1842 and then the Bala Hissar fortress in 1880. It was with British military advice that Amir Abdur Rahman razed to the ground most of the 15th Century buildings of Queen Gawhar Shad's *musalla* complex in Herat in 1885, to deny any attacking Russian forces cover within range of the citadel.

Kabul Museum

The Kabul Museum, which opened in 1931, is situated at Darulaman six miles south of the city centre. As the only museum in the region devoted to the culture of Central Asia, covering 100,000 years of human history, its collection was unique. As a leading Pakistani academic and archaeologist, Professor Hasan Dani, said: "The collection of ivories, statues, paintings, coins, gold, pottery, armaments and dress from the prehistoric period to the Bactrian, Kushan and Gandhara civilizations, through to the Hindu, Buddhist and Muslim periods, was unimaginable."

From 1992 to 1996 it was on the frontline between warring factions and received two direct rocket hits, which destroyed many priceless artefacts. What remained was ruthlessly looted by successive waves of soldiers from

Minaret of Jam – World Heritage Site

In June 2002, the 12th Century Minaret of Jam, located in the remote western province of Ghor, became Afghanistan's first World Heritage Site. Soaring to 65 metres, it is the highest minaret in the world after the Qutb Minar in Delhi, which was directly inspired by its Afghan predecessor. Constructed in three brick tiers, the Minaret is adorned with geometric patterns and inscriptions in brick and stucco. Some scholars believe it stands on the site of the capital of the Ghorid dynasty, which ruled Afghanistan from 1148-1214. At that time, towers were used across the region to symbolize the triumph of Islam. The minaret's strategic use as a watchtower may explain why it was left standing by Genghis Khan's invading forces in 1221.

But 800 years on, the Minaret of Jam is in danger of collapsing. Leaning at a precarious angle towards the Hari River, its foundations were perilously undermined during 2001 when winter floods washed away 120 metres of the riverbank. Worse still, recent travellers to the area have described thousands of local Afghans working on illegal excavations around the minaret and selling the artefacts to Herati dealers. The workers are thought to have discovered one half of an enormous gilt wood door, which could form part of a palace complex still hidden at the minaret's foot. Meanwhile, a road being built nearby is in danger of damaging archaeological remains. *JW*

whichever faction held Darulaman at the time. During the winter of 1993 UNCHS (Habitat) and the Society for the Preservation of Afghanistan's Cultural Heritage (SPACH) worked with museum staff to weatherproof the building and secure doors and windows, but treasure-hunters continued to break in, shooting off padlocks and even trying to ram an armoured personnel carrier through the main entrance.

Only the highest quality pieces were stolen from the museum, mostly in 1992-1993 when *mujahed* forces took control of Darulaman from government regime troops. This selective discrimination suggests that, in the words of Nancy Hatch Dupree, "the museum was not plundered by rampaging gangs of illiterate mujahideen" but by people working for middlemen who knew exactly what they were looking for. Najibullah Popal, curator of the Museum adds: "When the Kabul Museum was looted so many times, there must have been specialists showing the *mujahideen* which things to rob. There were thousands of books in the museum library. Most of the *mujahideen* can't read, yet all the books which had illustrations of the museum's best pieces were stolen."

Then in September 1996 museum staff, with support from SPACH, completed six months' work in registering what remained of the collection and removing it to the Kabul Hotel, a magnificent achievement under very difficult circumstances. To their credit the Taliban, after taking Kabul in the same month announced over Radio Shariat that "all people are called on to give back items from the Kabul Museum in their possession. It is illegal to have such items and Shariat law will apply to those who violate this rule." Subsequently, the Taliban hardened their attitude towards non-Islamic art. In March 2001, Taliban officials broke into the Museum and systematically smashed every single artefact depicting human or animal forms. Most of the remains were irreparable. Casualties included the great statue of King Kanishka and an image of the Sakyamuni Buddha.

Museum staff estimate that three-quarters of the collection has been lost, including 40,000 coins ranging from the 8th Century BC to the 19th Century, and the very valuable Bagram ivories – many of which have appeared on the international art market. In September 1995 General Babar, Pakistan's Federal Interior Minister, was quoted as saying that he had purchased one Bagram ivory for US$ 100,000, and intended to give it back to Afghanistan when peace returned. A London antiquities dealer claimed to have been offered several dozen of the ivories in Peshawar for US$ 10 million. Nevertheless several thousand looted artefacts have been recovered through police confiscations, donations and purchases by SPACH, the Foundation for Cultural Heritage in Japan and the Afghanistan Museum in Switzerland. During 2003, international efforts to rehabilitate the museum began with the construction of two new rooms in which to restore surviving fragments.

Art smuggling

> *"For centuries the Afghans have been smuggling. They love the challenge of it. It doesn't matter to them whether they're bringing in Bukhara rugs or AK-47s"*
>
> *– John Butt*

The ravaging of Afghanistan's cultural heritage must rank as one of the greatest artistic tragedies of the past century. The immoral acquisitiveness of Western art collectors, the greed of local Afghan commanders and the corruption of diplomats, customs officials and academics are combining to exploit the country's instability and strip it bare of internationally significant artefacts. Since 1993, around 75 per cent of the Kabul Museum's unique collection has been stolen or destroyed. Now it is the turn of rural areas.

During the Soviet war, numerous archaeological sites were exposed by indiscriminate Russian bombing of rural areas; but now the looting is more organized. Peshawar-based antiques dealers are organizing and paying groups to dig illegally. Corrupt academics with a detailed knowledge of the location of key archaeological sites are directing local military commanders to the choicest sites. Tanks and landmines are used to keep out unwelcome guests. Bulldozers, pickaxes and shovels gouge into soil rich with historical remains. But the art mafia are only interested in the most highly prized items: silver and gold, sculpture or coins.

Artefacts are smuggled through a complicated chain of middlemen before reaching the antiquities salerooms and private collectors of London, New York, Kuwait or Tokyo. Often the objects are first photographed and buried. Rich Western buyers or Pakistani dealers, prospecting in the bazaars of Peshawar, are then tempted into purchases by blurred photographs of looted items. The more experienced dealers disguise themselves as Pashtun tribesmen and are driven up to inspect priceless antiquities kept under armed guard inside the fortified houses of warlords in the tribal territories towards the Khyber Pass. Once the deal is cut, falsified export permits are granted and the artworks are then smuggled back via Afghanistan through the porous borders of Central Asia and Russia into the markets of the West.

Art smuggling is now big business in Afghanistan and the North West Frontier Province of Pakistan. According to one senior Western diplomat, "the trade in Afghan antiquities has become the biggest money-earner after the heroin trade, and it is often the same mafias who are doing both." A Kushan coin from the time of Christ could fetch US$ 20,000; a stone Buddha in the Gandharan style of the 1st to 5th Century AD three-quarters of a million dollars or more. Meanwhile the dealers justify their own greed and the acquisitiveness of their millionaire clients with arguments reminiscent of those of the 19th Century Lord Elgin when he pilfered the marble sculptures of the Parthenon in Athens for the British Museum: we are saving these objects from being destroyed, they say. But whereas the treasure-hunters of the past at least put their booty on public display, today's thieves are concealing artworks of international significance in their penthouses and private collections, forever hidden from the gaze of professional art historians or curious passers-by alike.

The presence of international peacekeepers in Afghanistan has done nothing to stem the tide of smuggling. In June 2003, UNESCO reported that artefacts from thousands of archaeological sites were being looted "by the lorryload". The agency is so concerned it has proposed that governments fund a 'heritage army' to protect key sites from further pillaging. Meanwhile, a lively trade in fakes has sprung up.

Cultural survival depends on local communities

> *"When the longed-for day comes when the fighting stops, the precious cultural heritage of Afghanistan will be one of the foundations on which a peaceful society can be constructed."*
>
> *– Federico Mayor, Director-General of UNESCO, September 1997*

Despite an enormous amount of interest in restoring Afghanistan's cultural heritage, there is little to show for it. In May 2002, an international seminar set priorities and allocated US$ 27 million for cultural activities up to 2005. But a year later, only US$ 3 million had been committed. Restoration of Timur Shah's 18th Century mausoleum and Babur's Garden in Kabul are proceeding. But work on stabilizing the Bamiyan Buddha niches has been delayed by security problems, and other priceless monuments from Bost to Balkh continue to crumble away. Meanwhile, illicit excavations and river erosion threaten the nation's first World Heritage Site – the Minaret of Jam.

Some people question whether it is right to waste valuable resources addressing cultural issues while millions of Afghans are threatened by hunger, landmines and preventable diseases. But by neglecting Afghan culture, one would fail to understand the complex series of forces which have shaped this troubled country's history and which will continue to shape its future course.

Furthermore, the ancient archaeological sites, the priceless artefacts and the cultural monuments, which continue to exist despite two decades of war, represent a unique and universal inheritance for the Afghan people. This legacy stands beyond and above differences of tribe or politics. In a country where political and ethnic fragmentation threatens to shatter any sense of nationhood, this material cultural heritage common to all may yet prove to be emblematic of a national identity for future generations.

While it is easy to focus on what is lost, more treasures undoubtedly still lie buried. In 2002, an ancient Kushan city – perhaps the largest Buddhist settlement ever unearthed in Afghanistan – was discovered by smugglers in Logar province. It too is being systemically looted. Protection for this and other valuable sites seems an unlikely prospect, when neither the government nor the international community seem capable of guaranteeing security beyond Kabul's city limits. As Nancy Dupree has pointed out, the future of the nation's rich cultural heritage lies in the hands of ordinary Afghans: "The local communities are the key. If they have feeling for their monuments, they will survive. Unless we get the local communities fired up, we will see the same cycle of destruction over and over again." The courage of the Afghans who concealed from the Taliban the true whereabouts of the Bactrian Gold is testimony to that.

ESSENTIAL AGENCIES

Aga Khan Foundation, Fondation Bibliotheca Afghanica, SPACH, UNESCO, World Monuments Fund
Ministry of Information and Culture

ESSENTIAL READING AND WEBLINKS

A treasure hunt, The Economist (London, December 18th, 2003)
History of Civilizations of Central Asia, Vols. 1-6, UNESCO (Paris, 2003)
The New Courier, UNESCO (Paris, October 2002)
The Looting of Turquoise Mountain, Rory Stewart, New York Times (August 25, 2002)
Afghan Cultural Heritage in Peril, UNESCO/CEREDAF (2001)
Art of Gandhara, John Eskenazi, London (1998)
Les Nouvelles d'Afghanistan (No. 41-42, Mars 1989) – contains numerous articles on Herat plus a bibliography of books, newspaper articles and video films.
Bactrian Gold, Victor Sarianidi, Aurora Art Publishers (Leningrad, 1985)
A Catalogue of the Toponyms and Monuments of Timurid Herat, Terry Allen, Massachusetts Institute of Technology (Boston, 1981)
Afghanistan, Louis Dupree, Princeton University Press (2nd Edition, 1980; reprinted by Oxford University Press, 1997)
An Historical Guide to Afghanistan, Nancy Hatch Dupree (2nd Edition, Kabul 1977)
The National Museum of Afghanistan, a pictorial guide, Nancy Hatch Dupree (Kabul, 1974)

The Road to Oxiana, Robert Byron, Macmillan (London, 1937; reprinted by Picador, 1981)
Afghanistan Info, Swiss Committee for the Support of the People of Afghanistan (SCSPA), Neuchatel, Switzerland
SPACH newsletters

www.akdn.org/agency/aktc.html
www.archaeology.org/
www.asiasource.org/culturalheritage/
www.developmentgateway.org/node/134111/
www.lib.unc.edu/art/afghanart.html
www.unesco.org/opi2/afghan-crisis/index.htm
www.wmf.org/

Disability

When the word 'disability' is mentioned in connection with Afghanistan, most people automatically think of landmine victims and artificial limbs. It is true that over two decades of war have disfigured tens of thousands. Amputees, however, represent about one-quarter of all disabled Afghans. As many again suffer restricted mobility through polio, and nearly half of the country's disabled are blind, deaf, mentally retarded, or multiply impaired. Disabled women form one of Afghanistan's most vulnerable groups.

No national survey has ever been conducted but observers work on a figure of 700,000-1,000,000 people, or around four percent of the total population who need help because of their disability. A 1999 survey found that just 10-15 percent of these people had access to assistance and treatment – with girls at a particular disadvantage in accessing services. Many disabled Afghans die before they ever receive the care they need and so fail to become even a statistic. The presence of disabled people affects the whole family, which means up to 15 percent of the population is affected, directly or indirectly, by disability.

Amputees are more frequently seen than other disabled because they are the most mobile; but many other handicapped Afghans tend to be hidden from view, owing perhaps to a sense of cultural shame. Inherited mental illness, for example, is often regarded as a punishment for sinfulness. Mental disability, particularly cerebral palsy, can be caused by birth complications such as obstructed labour or oxygen starvation of a baby at birth. These complications could be significantly reduced by better maternal nutrition, more midwives, and better prenatal and mother/child healthcare (SEE HEALTH).

The causes of disability are varied, but many are preventable. One solution is offered by the ongoing work of the UN's Mine Action Programme for Afghanistan (MAPA), which combines surveying, clearance and mine-awareness training (SEE LANDMINES). Immunization against polio, being spearheaded by UNICEF, the World Health Organization (WHO) and health sector NGOs, is another. But the 'cold chain' (refrigeration), which is required to keep vaccines at the right temperature, presents considerable logistical problems.

Some argue that the words 'disabled' or 'handicapped' are in some senses pejorative: the 'disabled' person simply suffers from a physical or mental *impairment*, and is only *disabled* by society's prejudices against them. Hence much rehabilitation work focuses on the issue of impaired people's *rights* (and

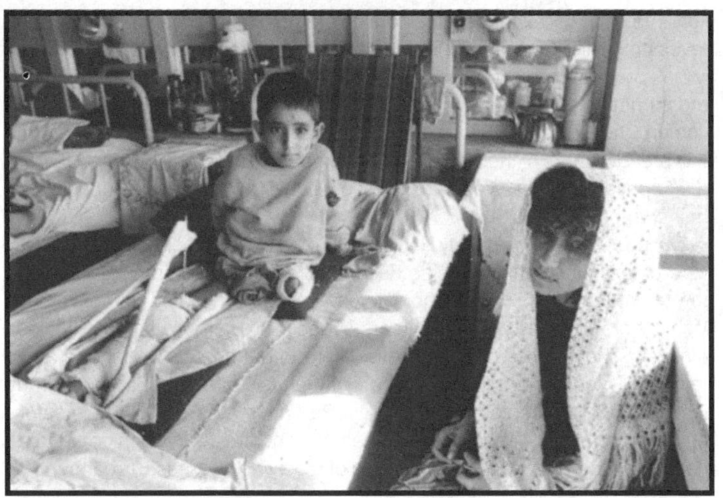

J. Hartley/UNICEF

not simply their individual medical problems), on combating society's ignorance and prejudice and on encouraging communities to take responsibility for the rehabilitation and integration of impaired people.

The Comprehensive Disabled Afghans Programme (CDAP), which began in January 1995, is a joint UN/NGO approach which aims to help disabled Afghans integrate within their own communities, by encouraging them to play a full and constructive role in mainstream services such as health, education and development. CDAP's programme operates through a policy of Community Based Rehabilitation (CBR) – a strategy which promotes the rehabilitation, social participation, equal opportunities and integration of all disabled people. CDAP is a project of the United Nations Development Programme (UNDP), implemented by the UN Office for Project Services (UNOPS), which in turn subcontracts NGOs – principally the Swedish Committee for Afghanistan (SCA) – to carry out programme activities in the field.

CDAP aims to apply the principles of CBR by training locally-based Afghans as mid-level rehabilitation workers. Their responsibilities include: surveying the number of disabled people in their area; integrating impaired children where possible into ordinary schools; developing home-based training in practical solutions with the families of the disabled; seeking out local craftspeople willing to take on impaired adults as apprentices for skills training; referring those who need it to health and other services; and support in creating local CBR committees and disabled people's organizations. Rehabilitation workers also recruit and train volunteers, supply them with training materials, and thus create a cascade effect that maximizes access to local communities.

One of CDAP's overriding aims is to avoid institutionalizing the disabled. By educating and involving family members in the training and integration process, entire communities become more aware of disabled people, their difficulties and the fact that they can act as contributing members of the community. In

April 1998, CDAP expanded its efforts to promote greater self-sufficiency and development in Afghan family life by starting a Vulnerable Women and Children (VWC) programme. This provides vocational skills training – such as tailoring and carpet weaving – and income-generation support for highly vulnerable women who look after their children and disabled husbands, and who are the only breadwinners of their families. Interest-free micro-credit loans of US$ 50-100, repayable within a year, are made available to help disabled people start their own businesses.

During 2001, 60 Community Rehabilitation and Development Centres (CRDC) were established, which provide decentralized education in disabilities and how to prevent them. For example, to prevent cerebral palsy, trainers advise Afghans not to marry before 15 years of age and to avoid unions with close relatives. They advise prospective mothers to eat a healthy diet and avoid heavy work during pregnancy. Greater emphasis is being placed on early detection of the symptoms of disability. Parents may wait 3-4 years before reporting their child's impairments to health authorities. If this can be cut to six months, children stand a better chance of receiving successful treatment.

Numerous NGOs run orthopaedic centres which provide devices such as prosthetic limbs for amputees and braces (orthoses) for polio and tuberculosis victims. Since 1988, the International Committee of the Red Cross (ICRC) has provided 60,000 Afghans with artificial limbs through six orthopaedic centres across the country. Some NGOs specialize in making off-road wheelchairs. In 1998, the Institute of Medical Education (part of the Afghan Ministry of Public Health) agreed on the curriculum for a two-year training course to qualify Afghan physiotherapists. The course trained 85 Afghans for the CDAP programme between 1999 and 2001.

Reported cases of blindness and deafness among Afghans are on the increase. The causes are either warfare (rocket, shell and mine explosions), insufficient basic healthcare, or genetic disorders arising from the widespread tradition of marrying close relatives. Some NGOs provide training for the blind in orientation, mobility and daily living skills, and produce braille or tape-recorded books and stories. In June 2003, the International Assistance Mission (IAM) reopened the country's only high school for the blind in Kabul, 10 years after it had been destroyed by factional fighting. Other NGOs teach deaf children sign language to counteract the social isolation which may result when not even parents can communicate with their offspring. Deaf adults are taught sign-language and vocational skills under local apprenticeships.

Since the fall of the Taliban in late 2001, however, some agencies report that donor support for disability has slackened – partly because it is perceived as less visible than other more high profile interventions. The Afghan minister for martyrs and the disabled said his offices had been looted of all their contents by the Taliban and he barely had enough funds to pay his staff, let alone support hundreds of thousands of disabled people. Foreign aid has not flooded in to alleviate the situation. In April 2002, the 77-year old Kabul Assistance Centre – home to 220 physically and mentally impaired Afghans – was turning away over 100 people a day for lack of international assistance. A conference in September proposed new legislation and a database of the disabled. But by the end of the year, the patience of Kabul's disabled community – many of whom are destitute – had run out. Hundreds of them demonstrated against the government, complaining they hadn't received their meagre monthly benefits, had no way of earning a living and felt neglected.

ESSENTIAL DATA

- **Of Afghanistan's disabled, 25% are amputees, 25% are impaired by polio, and 50% suffer from TB, blindness, deafness, mental retardation and cerebral palsy.**
- **Around 700,000-1 million Afghans are disabled, but up to 15% of the population is affected by disability directly or indirectly**
- **Blindness affects an estimated 1.5-2% of Afghans – one of the highest rates in the world**

ESSENTIAL AGENCIES

AARBRAR, HI, IAM, ICRC, MAPA, SCA, SERVE, SGAA, UNOPS/CDAP
National Disability Commission (NDC) – part of the Ministry of Martyrs and Disabled (MMD)
National Union of the Disabled of Afghanistan

ESSENTIAL READING

CDAP Annual Report and publicity material (available through UNOPS/CDAP)
CDAP Sign Language Dictionary for Dari and Pashto, CDAP (2002)
Disabled Village Children, David Werner (translated into Dari and Pashto, 2001)
Disability in Afghanistan, Peter Coleridge, CDAP (1999)
Self care for spinally injured persons, Nick Clarke (available through Motivation)

Drugs and drug trafficking

"Opium! Dread agent of unimaginable pleasure and pain!"
– Thomas de Quincey, 1821

In 2002, Afghanistan once again became the world's leading supplier of opium, producing 3,400 tonnes out of an estimated world total of 4,600 tonnes. In 2003, production climbed to 3,600 tonnes – representing an average annual income of US$ 3,900 per opium-growing family. The International Monetary Fund (IMF) valued Afghanistan's opium exports for 2002-03 at US$ 2.54 billion, which represented "between 40-60 percent" of the country's GDP. Around half of this gross revenue went to farmers, while the rest went to local traders. However, international drug dealers make more still – the United Nations estimate that the annual turnover of international trade in Afghan opium and its derivatives (including morphine and heroin) totals US$ 30 billion.

Between 70-90 percent of heroin seized in Western Europe – and almost 100 percent in Iran, Pakistan, Turkey, the CARs and Russia – originates from Afghanistan. Some 10 million people, two thirds of the world's opiate abusers, now rely on Afghan-produced opium and heroin for their consumption. In turn, the cultivation of opium poppies directly contributes to the livelihoods of around 1.7 million rural Afghan men, women and children. More Afghans still are involved in trading, refining and trafficking the drug.

According to the UN Office on Drugs and Crime (UNODC) in Vienna, "the total collapse of law and order" in the country during the American military campaign in the autumn of 2001 contributed overwhelmingly towards the increase. Internationally supported anti-narcotics campaigns have failed to curb the planting of poppy, and Kabul's lack of effective control during 2002-03 over the provincial areas where poppies are grown has also contributed to the rise in production.

Over the past decade, the area of land cultivated with opium poppies has ranged from 53,000 to 91,000 hectares, with yields per hectare on average three times higher than in Burma. The provinces of Helmand and Nangarhar between them accounted for two thirds of all production during 2002. The rest was cultivated in the northern regions, in the eastern mountain valleys of Kunar and in the areas around Kandahar to the south. The latest reports from

2003, however, suggest that poppy is now being planted in more and more remote districts. According to the UNODC's opium survey of October 2003, 28 out of Afghanistan's 32 provinces were cultivating opium poppies during 2003. Large declines were registered in Helmand and Kandahar provinces, due in part to government eradication measures, leaving Nangarhar as the country's top drug producer.

The world illicit drug market is changing, according to the UN. Global cultivation appears to be going down, particularly in countries such as Burma and Laos, which means that illicit production is now more focused on Afghanistan. Meanwhile, heroin abuse among Central Asian populations is increasing, with Tajikistan registering a seven-fold rise over the past seven years. Heroin abuse is also rising in Pakistan and Afghanistan itself. The former Soviet Central Asian Republics (CARs) are emerging as a favoured narcotics transit route for Russia and Europe. Some analysts fear that Central Asia could develop into an even greater hub of narcotics production and use in the years ahead, particularly if Afghanistan's insecurity persists. In September 2003, the IMF warned: "a dangerous potential exists for Afghanistan to progressively slide into a narco-state where all legitimate institutions become penetrated by the power and wealth of traffickers."

Opium production is a relatively recent cash crop for Afghanistan. Poppy cultivation on a large scale began in the early 1980s, in response to bans on production in Iran, Pakistan and Turkey. The years between 1990 and 1994 witnessed a relentless and unchecked annual increase in poppy cultivation. Afghanistan's share of world production grew from around 20 percent in 1980, to 50 percent in 1995, to 79 percent under the Taliban in 1999. Afghanistan first overtook Burma as the world's top producer during the 1990s.

In 1999, as part of the so-called 'Golden Crescent' (including Pakistan, Iran and increasingly the Central Asian 'stans') Afghanistan produced a record 4,565 tonnes of opium, compared to just 200 tonnes in 1978. The higher yields of 1999 were attributed to favourable weather, improved cultivation techniques and the shifting of some farmland to poppy cultivation (SEE AGRICULTURE). Farmers were using urea fertilizer and new tractors from Pakistan to expand their production. More irrigated land was – and still is – being turned over to poppy cultivation, producing higher yields.

In July 2000, the Taliban, desperate to avoid international sanctions, issued a complete ban on poppy cultivation which was so successful that production fell by 95 percent during 2001. According to UN figures, the prohibition meant that just 7,606 hectares were cultivated and only 185 tonnes of opium harvested in 2001, mainly from northern provinces outside Taliban control. Antinarcotics officials concluded, however, that the Taliban's ban may have had more to do with marketing than with a determination to prevent opium poppy cultivation. The ban pushed prices up 20 times, from an average of US$ 30 per kilo in 2000 to US$ 700 per kilo in 2001. Surplus opium stocks were then sold off at enormous profit to both traffickers and Taliban coffers – and prompted a huge surge in cultivation in 2002.

During 2001, northern provinces (controlled by the United Front, also known as the Northern Alliance) took advantage of the ban in Taliban areas and expanded their production, with Badakhshan alone representing 83 percent of the year's cultivation (6,342 hectares) compared to 2,458 hectares the previous year. Despite the much-heralded boasts of the United Front regime under President Rabbani that opium production was against the tenets of Islam, even his capital, Faizabad, was surrounded by fields of poppies openly cultivated by local farmers and trafficked by drug lords operating in connivance with the United Front.

The fall of the Taliban in late 2001 brought a collapse in law and order across the country which coincided with the poppy-planting season. So, although the new Afghan Interim Administration – heavily encouraged by Western donors – issued a decree in January 2002, banning all opium cultivation and trading, it was too late. By early 2002, barely four months after the fall of the Taliban, white and mauve-coloured poppies were once again being grown openly, even along the main roads between Kabul and the Pakistan border.

Nevertheless, with Britain as the leading donor, the Kabul authorities launched a much-publicized campaign to persuade farmers through a combination of force and financial incentive – US$ 350 per *jerib* (nearly 0.3 hectares) – not to harvest their crops. By mid-2002, the British government declared that almost one third of the country's production had been destroyed. The Afghan government put the figure even higher. However, it soon emerged that a more accurate estimate was probably less than 10 percent. Subsequently, the UN estimated that production during 2002 had shot up ten times to 74,000 hectares, compared to 2001. During 2003, the area under cultivation climbed further, to 80,000 hectares.

What went wrong with the eradication campaign? In many cases, the local authorities and commanders never forwarded the compensation money. Sometimes they paid after the resin had been harvested. Often, too, results were falsified. Some farmers took the money but still sold their harvest to the traffickers. Others planted even more poppy to qualify for more payments to pull it up. Kabul lacked influence over the provinces to enforce the ban, while international donors failed to provide sufficient funds or alternative livelihoods to ensure that eradication efforts would succeed.

Opium – as the IMF points out in its September 2003 report – remains a highly attractive crop for hundreds of thousands of Afghan farmers desperately impoverished by 24 years of war and drought. Poppy is a weather-resistant crop which requires less attention than wheat while providing much higher average returns per acre. It has a short growing season, and the early harvest enables farmers to reap other crops later or even to plant a second opium crop. Furthermore, opium is easy to store, transport and sell, and it is the only crop against which farmers can borrow money.

Ironically, the US military intervention in October 2001 helped promote a resurgence in poppy production, not only through eliminating Taliban controls but also by arming and financially supporting unscrupulous commanders in return for collaboration. Some of these individuals proceeded to benefit from the lucrative drug trade, sometimes ridding themselves of potential competitors by fingering them as pro-Taliban or Al Qa'eda.

In some areas, particularly in Nangarhar province, farmers bitterly opposed government attempts to deny them such a highly lucrative cash crop and threatened to combat force with force. One of the many reasons forwarded for the assassination on July 6, 2002, of former guerrilla commander Hajji Abdul Qadir, ex-governor of Nangarhar and one of the country's three interim vice

presidents, was his own involvement in the drug trade, which had provided a principal source of revenue for his *mujahideen* during the Soviet-Afghan war of the 1980s. Qadir's death may have been the result of a local feud for control of the drug trade in eastern Afghanistan.

Despite the failure to make significant headway in poppy eradication, anti-narcotic officials say they are encouraged by Karzai's commitment to a 10-year drug control strategy, which includes establishing a national Counter-Narcotic Directorate and a new drug control law. But, as with so many negative aspects of Afghan society, whether involving warlords or traffickers, it is money that matters, not politics. The lawlessness that arose during the Soviet occupation and which continued in 2002 and 2003 in many parts of the country has enabled mainly Peshawar- and Middle East-based drug trafficking rings to turn Afghanistan into the world's major producer of illicit and speculative opium. Meanwhile, returning refugees in 2002 and 2003 brought back even more sophisticated equipment and agricultural support capable of producing an even bigger opium poppy crop.

Increasing amounts of raw opium are being converted into heroin inside Afghanistan, making the drug easier to conceal and transport, but harder to track. In 2000, the UN estimated that, out of a total production of 3,276 tonnes of raw opium, roughly one third was transformed into heroin, one third turned into base morphine and the remainder exported raw. It takes between 6-10 kilos of raw opium, plus four litres of the precursor chemical acetic anhydride, to produce one kilo of heroin.

Until the early 1990s, only a small proportion of the labs involved in heroin production operated out of Afghanistan. The poppy harvests were largely sold to the Peshawar-based trafficking groups (often operating in connivance with Pakistani military and government officials) with their own mobile production labs hidden among the tribal areas of the North West Frontier Province. Later, however, heroin processing labs were established in Afghanistan itself. In

2002, some production centres reportedly moved back into Pakistani tribal areas with the flight of pro-Taliban and Al Qa'eda operatives following the US and Coalition intervention. However, during 2003, reports were mounting of modern labs being established in many of the country's poppy-growing areas.

Tribal drug barons on both sides of the Pakistani/Afghan frontier are heavily involved, as are former Afghan warlords who developed their fiefdoms during the days of the Red Army occupation (1979-1989). Some worked closely with the Afghan resistance or the Soviet-backed regime in Kabul, or with both. The Soviets are often alleged to have encouraged the drug trade as a means of undermining Pakistan and the West. Members of the Afghan resistance parties in Peshawar, including some of its leaders, have been implicated in the trade. While publicly condemning drugs, some of the parties used poppy cultivation and opium production as a means of filling their coffers for the purchase of weapons and other supplies, as well as for personal enrichment. Peshawar's dramatic growth as a frontier city over the past two decades has been the result largely of international aid trickle down, overspill and corruption. But it has also benefited from the drug trade. Both in Pakistan and Afghanistan, there are lavish palatial compounds known to have been built by drug barons and often locally referred to as "the houses that drugs built."

A sizeable portion of domestically-produced heroin is consumed by a growing population of users in Pakistan, India and, increasingly, Afghanistan itself, mainly in the cities and particularly among young people. Heroin has been introduced largely by returnees from Pakistan. In August 2003, the UN estimated that at least 11,000 Afghans were using opium and 7,000 using heroin in Kabul alone.

Drug control efforts over the past decade in Afghanistan have been particularly hampered by civil strife and the lack of effective government. The Taliban first prohibited the production of opium in late 1996. This was coupled with a ban on hashish, which they considered un-Islamic. Enforcement, including severe punishment, significantly reduced the use of hash in many areas, but it was a different story with opium, which the Taliban perceived as a largely Western problem. The Taliban were reluctant to crack down on the opium trade for fear of losing support in rural areas. Many Afghans have not forgotten that efforts by the Kabul regime in 1978 to enforce agricultural reform in rural areas, particularly tribal zones, helped spark the anti-Communist revolt.

Only in October 1997 did the Taliban formally agree to a more decisive ban following considerable pressure from the UN, Pakistan, Western Europe and America. However, international aid representatives and journalists travelling in Afghanistan during the late 1990s reported not only Taliban tolerance of opium production but evidence that officials were taxing it for much-needed revenue. In July 2000, their Supreme Leader, Mullah Omar, issued a total ban. In return for taking firm action, the Taliban demanded appropriate international support and counter gestures such as the rehabilitation of the hydroelectric Kajakai Dam in the mountains northwest of Kandahar. However, most countries continued to keep the Taliban at a distance.

In Pakistan, the pressure to curb production hardly helped resolve the problem. Like trying to grapple with a bar of wet soap, it simply forced the trade to slip elsewhere. Destroyed labs were easily re-erected out of the country, but within the same region, notably inside Afghanistan. An estimated 100,000

Deadly drugs earn the poorest a living

Until 2000, hardly any aid agencies worked in Afghanistan's remote Ghor province. Then, as drought raised major concerns over harvest failure, the ICRC and Oxfam mounted a relief operation. In 2001, ICRC increased its programme to 68,000 beneficiaries; 11 September stopped work, but ICRC resumed in December, flying food into an area that would otherwise have been cut off by snow.

With a much-improved harvest in 2002, ICRC downsized its relief programme and began to look at projects of long-term benefit, such as improving irrigation systems. But in 2002, wheat wasn't Ghor's only crop. Opium traders from Helmand, in southern Afghanistan, had come with poppy seeds in one pocket and cash in the other. At the time of year when people are poorest, they offered farmers 50% cash upfront, the rest on harvest. It transformed the economy of the province, with the labour-intensive poppy crop providing work even for those living in areas too high to grow it themselves.

Ghor was not alone. When Oxfam started work in Uruzgan's remote Dai Kundi district in 1998, they were the first foreigners most villagers had ever seen. Dai Kundi's steep hillsides are badly eroded and landholdings are tiny. Now they too are growing poppy. As Shah Wali, Oxfam's programme manager, explains: "Every family has a small patch by their door, trying it out. The rewards have been good; last year it fetched ten times the price of wheat. In villages where people could only dream of owning a motorbike, now they have not one but several minibuses. Wait until next year, then you will see. This year people only grew small amounts. Next year it will be two, three times the amount."

Given that narcotics was one of the key issues for the international community in the time of the Taliban, the failure to curb poppy cultivation is a matter of major concern. Yet it is hard to see what can be done. The writ of the government does not extend to these areas. In many remote districts no one is in control – there are just commanders with guns and their own small patch of territory. Efforts at control risk driving up prices and pushing cultivation into more inaccessible highlands. Attempts during 2002 to pay landowners to tear up their crops backfired when farmers planted more poppy to qualify for more compensation. Crop substitution cannot match opium profits and much of the traditional work of NGOs (e.g. improving irrigation and reclaiming land) could benefit poppy as much as wheat. As most Afghans do not yet use the drug themselves, the problem appears not to be theirs. But, while growing poppy provides a livelihood for many desperately poor people, it directly supports the warlords who are the cause of what Afghans name as their greatest problem: insecurity.

A longer version of this box appeared in the World Disasters Report 2003

Pakistani soldiers and militiamen have been regularly deployed in the war against drugs. American, British, German and other anti-drug law enforcement officers based in Islamabad, Karachi, Peshawar and now Kabul are working closely with Pakistan.

Pakistani vigilance, however, appears directly linked to the amount of foreign aid made available. When the aid carrot is no longer dangled, their interest diminishes. Following the events of September 11, Pakistan's military-led government have proved keen to accommodate the Americans as much as possible in their 'war against terrorism,' which includes curbing the illicit drug trade, because of the potential funding it could provide for terrorists. Islamic fundamentalist Gulbuddin Hekmatyar, the most heavily Pakistani- and US-backed of the former resistance politicians, relied on significant drug revenue during the 1980s and 1990s to support his military operations against rival factions. Making a serious comeback in mid-2002 with his declared *jihad* against the United States, Gulbuddin is believed to be garnering support from among pro-Taliban Pashtuns – many of them living in the poppy-growing areas of eastern Afghanistan.

Capable of reacting quickly to international efforts to curb trafficking, the drug barons are constantly finding new smuggling routes. Criminal mafia in the Central Asian Republics of Tajikistan, Uzbekistan and Turkmenistan are increasingly dominating regional trafficking. With so many government officials implicated in the trade (reaching as high as the presidency in Turkmenistan), traffickers encounter few real restrictions and have been able to operate with virtual impunity. The signing in Islamabad in mid-2002 of a new oil and natural gas pipeline agreement between Pakistan, Afghanistan and Turkmenistan is expected to open new doors to international drug trafficking. New production labs have appeared in Tajikistan and Uzbekistan with smuggling routes heading northwards to take advantage of growing markets in Russia and Eastern Europe. Other trafficking routes include Iran and Turkey but also southwards through Baluchistan to the Indian Ocean along the Mekran coast, where speedboats transfer the merchandise to waiting ships.

Eradication of poppy fields alone is not enough to solve Afghanistan's drug problem. Experts argue that a long-term approach is required, which not only focuses on the physical destruction of the crop but also teaches farmers how to plant replacement staples and to market them. Eradication will never prove successful unless farmers are able to cultivate a crop that is just as lucrative as opium poppies (which can earn them five to ten times as much as wheat). In addition, buyers are willing to pay cash advances to help purchase poppy seeds and fertilizer. A smallholder, for example, can easily produce 45 kilos of raw opium a year, earning over US$ 15,000 at 2002 prices – an income that will prove hard to counter. Harvested in June and July, poppies provided Afghan farmers with an estimated US$ 1.2 billion of revenue in 2002. For a people who have suffered so long from war and devastation, poppy production offers many farmers the most realistic means of rebuilding their lives, their farms and the local economy.

Promoting alternative crops will be an enormous challenge. Poppies are easy to grow and serve as an insurance against the failure of other crops. Opium production requires almost no hired transport, such as donkeys. A saddlebag is sufficient to transport a farmer's annual production. Substitutes also need to be found for the poppy's other uses, including fodder for animals, oil for cooking and seed for baking. Another critical element is a credible mass information programme; there is no point in developing an elaborate eradication and crop replacement policy if it cannot be explained – simply and effectively – to the population it is intended to turn around.

An enormous amount is at stake, as drug trafficking permeates every aspect of Afghan life, from agriculture, health and the economy, to democracy, security and the rule of law. Speaking on 29 October 2003 about the US$ 2.3 billion income to Afghans generated by 2003's crop, the UNODC's executive director, Antonio Maria Costa, said: "Out of this drug chest, some provincial administrators and military commanders take a considerable share: the more they get used to this, the less likely it becomes that they will respect the law, be loyal to Kabul and support the legal economy". Honing his argument to focus on the issue of overriding concern to Western governments, Costa added: "Terrorists take a cut as well: the longer this happens, the greater the threat to security within the country and on its borders. There is a palpable risk that Afghanistan will again turn into a failed state, this time in the hands of drug cartels and narco-terrorists."

ESSENTIAL DATA

Opium production	Tonnes	Hectares (ha)	Income (US$)/ha
1978	200	n.a.	n.a.
1994	3,416	71,470	3,298
1995	2,335	53,759	2,823
1996	2,248	56,824	1,978
1997	2,804	58,416	3,408
1998	2,693	63,674	2,749
1999	4,565	90,983	2,760
2000	3,276	82,171	1,555
2001	185	7,606	7,321
2002	3,422	74,045	16,208
2003	3,600	80,000	13,000 approx.

Domestic income from opium production

	2002	*2003*
Farmers	US$ 1.2 billion	US$ 1 billion
Traffickers	US$ 1.3 billion	US$ 1.3 billion

Provinces producing illicit opium in 2003

28 out of 32 provinces, concentrated in six provinces (% change since 2002):

Nangarhar	18,904 ha	(-4%)
Helmand	15,371 ha	(-49%)
Badakhshan	12,756 ha	(+55%)
Uruzgan	7,143 ha	(+40%)
Ghor	3,782 ha	(+72%)
Kandahar	3,055 ha	(-23%)

Refined heroin production

	1996	2001
Global	220 tonnes	160 tonnes
Afghanistan	88 tonnes (40%)	18.5 tonnes

Refined heroin (average estimated street value in US$ per kilo)

	1997	2001
Pakistan (Karachi)	3,000	4,000
Iran	5,480	3,700 (4,325 in 2002)
European Union	89,000	59,000

Sources: UNODC , Western donor governments

ESSENTIAL AGENCIES

DEA, FAO, ORA, UNODC, UNOPS

ESSENTIAL READING

UNODC Afghanistan Opium Survey 2003, UN Office on Drugs and Crime (Vienna, October 2003)

Islamic State of Afghanistan: Rebuilding a Macroeconomic Framework for Reconstruction and Growth, Annex II.1. The Poppy Dimension in the Afghan Economy, International Monetary Fund (Washington DC, September 2003)

Economics

"Our problem is our geographical location and our resources. For this reason, Afghanistan has always been at war."

– Ahmed Shah Massoud, ex-mujahed commander and military head of the Northern Alliance, 1997

A quarter of a century of war, since the outbreak of fighting against the communist regime of the People's Democratic Party of Afghanistan (PDPA) in mid-1978, has had a shattering impact on the Afghan economy. Despite efforts at reconstruction, both during and after the Taliban era (1994-2001), much of the country remains destroyed or in a state of dereliction. As many as 1.5 million Afghans may have died from the consequences of war. The decade-long Red Army occupation (December 1979 to February 1989) resulted in the devastation of many rural areas and forced one third of the population, including most of its qualified people, to flee abroad. To the embarrassment and shame of many Afghans, however, it was not the Soviets but the civil war of the 1990s that inflicted the greatest damage on Kabul and other cities. Factional fighting amongst the *mujahideen* resulted in the systematic destruction and looting of numerous modern industrial production facilities. Additional devastation was caused in areas, such as the Shomali plain north of Kabul or in Bamiyan province, during the battles for supremacy between the Taliban and the United Front (also known as the Northern Alliance). This included deliberate 'scorched earth' destruction by the Taliban – the uprooting of vineyards, the mining of irrigation systems, and the razing of houses and bazaars. Heavy bombing and ground operations by US-led Coalition Forces against suspected Taliban and Al Qa'eda positions caused further damage, with civilian casualties similar to those killed during the September 11 attacks in the United States – an estimated 3,000-4,000 Afghans by mid-2003.

The challenges facing the Afghan economy are daunting: shattered industrial infrastructure, an agricultural sector afflicted by drought and landmines, a burgeoning illicit trade in drugs and smuggled goods, recalcitrant regional warlords pocketing huge tax revenues, and a deteriorating security situation hardly conducive to private sector investment.

Prior to the Soviet invasion of December 1979, agriculture and animal husbandry accounted for over half the nation's GDP. During the 1970s, modernization programmes under Presidents Mohammed Daoud and Nur Mohammed Taraki had begun to open up other economic areas. Financed largely through heavy borrowing and donor assistance, these initiatives sought to improve education and health services, at least in urban zones. They also established a large number of state-owned industries in sectors such as mining, energy, transport and communications. In turn, such initiatives helped create more small and medium-sized consumer goods or support enterprises, particularly in and around the towns.

In 1978, during the country's last days of peace, Afghanistan was largely self-sufficient in food and a major exporter of agricultural products. During the Red Army occupation, the Kabul regime – mainly with Soviet and Eastern bloc funding – tried to expand the country's administrative infrastructure. This went hand in hand with efforts to promote further industrial expansion, such as the establishment of textile and cement factories, as well as large-scale agricultural production. Increased *mujahed* resistance and general insecurity soon brought many of these projects to a halt. This prompted a major economic decline. Anxious to prove the benefits of their presence, the Soviets felt bound to prop up the PDPA government with heavily subsidised food imports. Ironically, this ensured that Afghans in the cities were probably better off than most Soviet citizens. Some of the crossborder international aid agencies seeking to assist civilian populations in resistance-held areas were quick to latch on to the availability of often ample stocks in the bazaars. They found it cheaper to support local populations at the height of the war by secretly buying wheat in nearby government-controlled towns rather than bring it in by costly horse caravans from Pakistan.

While numerous villagers in the 1990s had begun rebuilding their homes and re-cultivating their farms in areas where peace had returned, some have seen their holdings destroyed once, twice or even more with renewed outbreaks of fighting. Following the *mujahed* takeover in Kabul in 1992, Afghans who could afford it began repairing their houses and businesses, even constructing new buildings. This in turn encouraged new trade such as the import and sale of construction materials as well as jobs for craftsmen. Many of these edifices were damaged again in the rocketing and inter-factional conflict, particularly in January 1994, when some half a million people found themselves displaced by heavy fighting.

By the mid-1990s, most of the country's remaining modern infrastructure had been destroyed. Traditional irrigation systems were ruined by destruction and lack of maintenance, while the industrial sector was reported to be down to less than 20 percent of pre-war production. Only a small handful of manufacturing activities, such as handicrafts production, were earning foreign currency at the time of the 11 September events. Many formerly significant (or growing) sectors, notably commodity exports, mining, cement production and agro-processing, have been wiped out or severely damaged. However, a degree of recovery in Taliban and United Front areas free of conflict occurred

Thorkell Thorkelsson/International Federation

during the late 1990s, with projects such as 'food for work' road building programmes, irrigation rehabilitation and the establishment of horticultural nurseries. Agricultural production increased and substantial numbers of refugees returned home to certain parts of the country with international assistance.

The situation in the Afghan capital and other cities, however, worsened during the Taliban period. Roughly 80 percent of the population in Kabul was considered to be 'vulnerable', that is, not able to afford more than a basic diet of bread and tea. This included people from all walks of life: doctors, civil servants, teachers, casual labourers. During the Taliban era, the economy continued to function much as before. Prices tended to reflect costs with barter representing a significant portion of overall trade. Following rampant inflation during the 1990s, the Taliban sought to impose price regulations. But street currency trading remained one of the country's few thriving licit economic sectors. However, the value of Afghan currency was destroyed during the 1990s by the constant publishing of new notes by the United Front (whose members were recognized by most countries as the legal government) whenever cash was needed.

In 1999, Afghanistan was hit by a severe drought that dragged on into 2002. Given the wholesale breakdown of both the state and civil society, the drought led to famine in certain parts of the country, mainly in the north. Crop production in traditional rain-fed areas was halved and livestock herds were severely depleted, erasing the modest gains achieved earlier in the decade. Large numbers of people lost their means of livelihood and were forced to leave their homes, either as 'internally displaced persons' (IDPs) or as refugees in neighbouring countries. The international community was obliged to step in with stop-gap emergency food aid.

By early 2003, good rains with heavy snow in the mountains promised to break the drought, prompting organizations such as the World Food Programme to radically cut food rations in a bid to encourage IDPs in regions such as Herat province to return home. Many IDPs from the northern provinces, however, were reluctant to head back because of continued insecurity caused by clashes between rival political factions, but also because they had no more homes or animals left.

With the fall of the Taliban and the re-taking of Kabul in late 2001 by the Coalition-backed United Front forces, the international community was able to move forward with the reconstruction process. Even though parts of the Afghan capital had already been re-built during the Taliban period, much of the city remained gutted, particularly its southern and western sectors, with the haunting look of an Afghan Dresden at the end of World War II. Today, despite widespread rebuilding, whole swathes of shell-ravaged office buildings, apartment blocks and residential houses still look out onto rubble-lined streets, while cableless pylons and the torn remnants of trees pointedly remind one of the days when Kabul's urban population enjoyed leafy avenues, functioning trolley buses and regular electricity. In the countryside, where entire villages have been eradicated, all that remains are walls worn and crumbling with the rain and wind. Along many of the main roads, particularly outside the towns and villages, stand the ghostlike vestiges of schools, factories, industrial depots and former customs posts.

The Bonn Agreement of 5 December 2001, followed by the donor pledging conference a month later in Tokyo, brought new hope, coupled with high expectations for a complete recovery from Afghanistan's wars. A total of US$ 4.5 billion was pledged over five years. But this is now viewed as far too little. In mid-2003, the World Bank put the cost of reconstruction at US$ 20 billion over the next decade, while the Afghan government itself pegged the price at US$ 30 billion. With its collapsed economy, shattered infrastructure and formal institutions severely undermined or non-existent, all of Afghanistan's sectors – including agriculture, health, industry, tourism, administration and media – are in need of major investment.

By mid-2002, however, there was growing disappointment with the way the international community was handling the recovery process. Funding was slow to arrive – barely half of the pledged amounts had come in – and key projects, such as urgently-needed road improvements (an obvious initiative for demonstrating quick change) had not even begun. Most of the aid – roughly three-quarters – was being distributed via the United Nations system, rather than through government institutions, which in turn hampered the prospects of building local capacity to manage the recovery process. In addition, the level of aid provided for Afghanistan (US$ 75 per person in 2002) was relatively low when compared to other post-conflict countries. Bosnia-Herzegovina received

US$ 325 per person per year (1996-99), while nearly US$ 200 per capita went to East Timor (1999-2001) and Rwanda (1994).

One particularly contentious issue is the so-called "Kabul-Rural Divide." Despite recent efforts to spread the aid more equitably, much of it still appears to be focused on the Afghan capital rather than the countryside where the bulk of Afghanistan's 18-25 million people live. Parts of the capital, notably Wazir Akbar Khan and Shahr-e-Naw where most of the principal international agencies have congregated since the start of the recovery process, have quickly improved with the renovation of houses and offices, the stocking of shops with ample but expensive imported goods, and the re-opening of restaurants and guest lodges. But it remains a different story elsewhere.

Furthermore, at least during the first 12 months of the reconstruction process, the steering committee of the UN, the World Bank, Asia Development Bank and other donors failed to fully incorporate both local and international NGOs in their planning approaches. This is despite the fact that NGOs, particularly those who have been operating in Afghanistan since the early days of the Soviet war, command the most experience for dealing with this country. At a July 2002 meeting of the Afghan Support Group of donors in Geneva, the Norwegian chair did not even bother to invite the NGOs. Instead, Kabul witnessed the arrival of one costly international donor assessment team after another, some so short-term and out of touch that there was no way they could have honestly assessed the country's problems outside the capital. Many of these teams not only failed to coordinate with each other, prompting an extraordinary amount of duplication, but also within their own organizations. Once again, the lessons from past humanitarian and recovery operations were being thrown to the wind with only limited independent and effective public domain monitoring.

By early 2003, however, recovery approaches began to improve dramatically involving greater coordination by the donors with the central government, the NGOs and, more importantly, the private sector. For its part, the Kabul government elaborated a clear strategy for the country's reconstruction through its National Development Framework, consisting of 12 national programmes. The World Bank, which had not dealt with Afghanistan for 20 years, established the Afghanistan Reconstruction Trust Fund, a multi-donor initiative aimed at financing recurrent costs of the transitional government. Nevertheless, many of these developments remained largely limited to Kabul and other cities, such as Jalalabad, Herat and Mazar-e-Sharif, with numerous provinces complaining that they saw little or nothing of the pledged international aid.

A further challenge for Afghanistan's recovery process is the need to cope with the reintegration of two million refugees (five million fled the country since war first broke out in the summer of 1978) returning home from exile in Pakistan, Iran and elsewhere (SEE REFUGEES). Some seven million Afghans, many of them internally displaced refugees, were deemed by international aid agencies in 2002 to be experiencing extreme hardship with only limited resources to survive. Although 2003 witnessed the apparent breaking of the four-year drought in many parts of the country, numerous Afghans were still suffering from the effects of losing all their livestock and failing to bring in any harvests (SEE AGRICULTURE). The situation is perhaps even more desperate for those living in the cities as more and more people come back. There are few jobs available and breadwinners must often support painfully large extended families.

The fragile security situation and the ongoing power of regional warlords remain major factors behind the slow progress in recovery across many parts of the country. Neither the transitional administration of President Hamid Karzai nor international security forces have proved capable of curbing disaffected groups. By mid-2003, there were daily armed attacks by pro-Taliban and Islamic extremist elements, mainly in the eastern and southern parts of the country, against the Coalition and government forces coupled with a rise of assaults against international aid workers. This has obliged many agencies, such as Denmark's DACAAR and Médecins sans Frontières who seek to work in the poorer regions of the south, to reduce if not close down their field operations. Today, such belligerent activities continue to threaten the long-term stability of Afghanistan and the recovery process (SEE SECURITY).

While the 2001 international intervention may have proved positive for Kabul and other urban areas, many Afghans, particularly in the Pashtun-dominated eastern and southern Afghanistan where pro-Taliban sentiment remains strong, would beg to differ as to whether they were better off in 2003 than during the Taliban period when at least basic security was assured. The Afghan authorities and aid agencies have repeatedly called on the international community to broaden the mandate of the now NATO-led International Security Assistance Force (ISAF) to include the main towns outside of Kabul as the only way of protecting civilians against the corruption and abuses of the provincial warlords, plus to assure more open economic development directly involving the local population.

Many Afghans fear that unless ISAF expands its control to the provincial cities, the threat of renewed conflict will remain lurking in the wings. For some member countries, this would prove a risky and costly commitment given that a minimum of 30,000 troops would be needed to 'secure' the main population centres and communications links of the country. The decision by the UN Security Council on 13 October, 2003, to approve NATO expansion of ISAF from Kabul to other areas as a means of "extending the government's authority throughout the country and providing security for reconstruction" was considered promising. What remained to be seen, however, was to what extent NATO was actually prepared to increase significantly its presence on the ground and to which cities. Such commitment would in turn determine the effectiveness of reconstruction and economic expansion in the rest of Afghanistan.

Another major security problem is that of landmines and unexploded ordnance (UXO). Much progress has been made in their removal by local and international demining groups over the past decade or so, but landmines and UXO remain a curse capable of limiting development in many parts of the country for at least the next decade (SEE LANDMINES). Numerous rural areas, including densely populated locations, will have to contend with the threat of landmines on a daily basis, whether farming, grazing livestock or re-building homes.

While certain parts of the country have never been touched by the direct effects of war, Afghanistan's most crucial long-term challenge will be the total rebuilding of its basic infrastructure. Much will depend on whether Afghanistan and the international community will achieve the milestones set at Bonn, such as the implementation of a new constitution (agreed in January 2004) and the establishment of a representative government (SEE HUMAN RIGHTS). While

Gems and falcons

Precious and semi-precious stones such as lapis lazuli and emeralds have provided Afghans with an invaluable source of income, even during the height of the war with the Soviets. While weapons and other supplies were transported to the *mujahideen* across the mountains from Pakistan on the backs of mules and horses during the 1980s, the same caravans returned loaded with semi-precious stones from ancient mines in the Panjshair Valley and Badakhshan. The revenue from such exports helped finance the armed resistance of commanders such as Ahmed Shah Massoud.

Twenty-five years since the outbreak of fighting in mid-1978, the revenues produced by lapis lazuli extracted from the 6,000-year-old mines at Sar-e-Sang in the Hindu Kush – the world's only source of high grade lapis – are now being used to finance reconstruction efforts and personal requirements for local villagers involved in mining. For example, some villages in the Panjshair and neighbouring areas have been building bridges, refurbishing irrigation canals or installing small but efficient hydro-electric turbines along the edges of rivers and streams to provide electricity for nearby houses. But the revenue is also being used to launder profits from the heroin trade, as happened during the war. The deep blue lapis stones, often flecked with gold-like pyrite, are prized by American, Japanese and European jewellers as well as by Arabs in the Middle East. While local miners (who also pilfer what they find for private profit) earn barely two to three dollars per 12-hour shift, the best polished stones can sell for up to US$ 18,000 per kilo in Kabul and Peshawar. Many lapis merchants are also involved in drug trafficking and use the stones as cover.

During one trip to northern Afghanistan, a British journalist encountered a caravan carrying precious stones and six Siberian hawks destined for the Saudi Arabian falconry market. Even more highly-prized than the peregrine falcon is the endangered *saker* falcon – individual specimens can fetch over US$ 100,000.
EG

the *Loya Jirga* (Grand Assembly) was held with partial success in Kabul in June 2002, it remains doubtful that many of the country's (un-elected) warlords, particularly those benefiting financially from a weak central government, will agree to relinquish their power. This includes the likes of Herat's Ismail Khan who is thought to earn between US$ 7-10 million a month from import duties on goods brought in from Iran and Turkmenistan; precisely the sort of tax revenue that Kabul requires to achieve a degree of sustainability not reliant on international largesse. While he reportedly handed over US$ 20 million to the Kabul government during 2003, a durable administrative arrangement has yet to be worked out.

Already apparent in early 2002 was the need for the international community – and Afghans themselves – to move quickly to prevent the country from deteriorating once again into political instability and war. This includes a long-term commitment with concrete results to humanitarian, reconstruction and development assistance not only for the sake of Afghanistan, but for the region as a whole. As a strategic crossroads linking Iran, Central Asia, Pakistan, India and even the Gulf States, a stable and economically viable Afghanistan is possibly the best guarantor for peace. Dubai, which is seeking to develop itself as a principal service centre for the Middle East, Central and South Asia, has maintained that a peaceful Afghanistan is crucial for regional stability. At the same time, the international community's commitment to Afghanistan needs to be a realistic one. As experienced aid coordinators point out, concerned foreign governments must take heed of the underlying political and economic problems that could cause the country to unravel once again.

The lack of accurate information is a critical drawback in dealing effectively with Afghanistan's reconstruction. For years, little reliable data has existed regarding the state of Afghanistan's economy. While the World Bank, the Asian Development Bank, the UN and other organizations have carried out various needs assessments since December 2001, a comprehensive nationwide survey has yet to be completed. An otherwise excellent September 2003 International Monetary Fund report on reconstruction and growth in Afghanistan was distinctly lacking in post-2001 social indicators. With the last census taken in 1978, no-one, for example, is even certain of the size of Afghanistan's population; estimates range from 18 to 25 million. (A planned census is expected to take five years). What is certain is that Afghanistan remains in a severe state of dereliction. According to the *Agricultural Survey of Afghanistan* by the Swedish Committee (SCA), this landlocked nation remains, in the conventional sense, "one of the least developed countries in the world." Afghanistan did not even feature in the 2001 UN Human Development Index, although in 1986, Afghanistan ranked 169 out of 174 countries.

According to the IMF, World Bank and other financial institutions, Afghanistan's economic growth in 2002-2003 reached almost 30 percent with a somewhat smaller – but still impressive – growth of around 20 percent predicted for 2004. The IMF estimated Afghanistan's overall GDP for 2002-03 (excluding opium) at US$ 4.05 billion – which works out at a per capita GDP of US$ 180-190. If opium revenues are included, the GDP figure rises to US$ 6.59 billion. Agricultural production rose significantly with the end of the drought. Wheat and other forms of cereal production leapt from a paltry 1.76 million tonnes in 2000 to a staggering 5.37 million tonnes in 2003.

There was major growth in the construction and service industries, mainly fuelled by donor assistance. It is clear that much of Afghanistan would collapse without donor support. As before, Afghanistan's economy also remains highly dependent on illicit activities, mainly drug trafficking. The opium trade, severely affected in 2001 by the Taliban ban on poppy production, was estimated by the UN Office on Drugs and Crime in 2003 to be worth around US$ 2.5 billion to Afghanistan. This represents the country's most lucrative home-grown industry. If the opium trade were officially included in the economy, it would represent between 40-60 percent.

The sudden surge of aid agencies and companies seeking business following the international intervention of late 2001 brought a massive change to Kabul and other urban parts of Afghanistan, such as Jalalabad, Herat and Mazar-e-Sharif. The towns were suddenly filled with thousands of expatriate aid workers and peacekeepers, as well as returning Afghans, particularly after the June 2002 *Loya Jirga*. Many returnees, whether tailors, car dealers or video shopkeepers, have brought their businesses with them, or started up new ones. The once flourishing Afghan carpet industry in Peshawar disappeared almost overnight as refugees streamed back to their homeland taking their skills with them. The former centre for the Afghan carpet trade, Kabul is again re-asserting itself. The buying power of foreign aid workers and soldiers, however, caused carpet prices to rise, with Pakistan now the cheap place to buy.

Rents, too, have rocketed from US$ 100-150 a month for a house in Wazir Akbar Khan to US$ 6,000-10,000. This created enormous house shortages for returning Afghans, some of whom simply could not afford Kabul prices or who felt obliged to rent out their homes in order to ensure a steady hard currency income. Many returnees, too, began working on the renovation of their war-damaged homes prompting an enormous surge in the need for building materials and qualified workers. Nevertheless, much of this work can only be done piecemeal, because cash shortages oblige many families – and their relatives – to live crowded in the more habitable parts with poor water and sanitation (conditions that also prompt outbreaks of dysentery and other diseases). Meanwhile, from early 2002, thousands of legal disputes have arisen over ownership of plots of land or the houses that still stand. Numerous Afghans who were forced to flee have lost control over their homes with places being sold by tenants to new owners. People seeking to regain their properties have been threatened by armed men. Despite the setting up of a national commission, some of the disputes are so complicated that they may take years to resolve.

Salaries have risen for local employees as international aid agencies, journalists and military sought to hire the best people at inflationary rates. Qualified doctors were suddenly leaving their health-related jobs with the government and NGOs for positions as drivers or translators with the UN, World Bank and other richer organizations. One leading Western NGO lost 30 percent of its staff within a matter of weeks, unable to keep up with the higher salaries. The TV teams were among the worst, offering to pay US$ 200 or more a day for a good translator, four times more than a government doctor or teacher earns in an entire month. When queried as to why the European Commission delegation in Afghanistan was paying exorbitant rates to its own local staff, thereby undermining the capacity of local agencies and institutions trying to recover, an EC representative in Kabul admitted, somewhat in contradiction, that this was indeed "a problem." He argued that the EC could not afford to raise the salaries of the 200,000 government employees it supported, yet agreed that the international aid community should ensure they recruit the most qualified people for themselves. "There is no solution," he added.

Clearly, parts of Afghanistan's economy will only stagger back with help from the private sector. So far, however, outside investment has been limited. Members of Afghanistan's far-flung diaspora, whether in nearby Dubai and Abu Dhabi or Germany, the United States and Australia, are considered vital for supporting or investing in the reconstruction of their country. Some began filtering back during 2002 to take advantage of the enormous international presence for jobs and business opportunities, but also because many felt strongly about the need to help their country. Remittances from abroad have always played a significant role in the lives of Afghans and are now contributing heavily towards enabling those with no other means of support to survive, or to rebuild their homes and start new ventures, such as buying a taxi – one of the most viable forms of livelihood in the capital.

Many Afghan returnees continue to keep a 'foot in each camp'. A 1997 study by the British Agencies Afghanistan Group, for example, noted that even with the growing number of returnees to Farah province in western Afghanistan, employment opportunities in Iran still served as an important safety net for families. This approach has not changed, despite the continued risks of arrest, detention and deportation by the Iranian authorities. The same is the case for Afghan refugees returning from Pakistan. Many family members, including children, are involved in the small trading sector, selling anything from cigarettes to fresh fruit and medicines. Others seek to bring in supplies by bus or beast of burden, whether fuel from the countryside or basic essentials from Pakistan. Anything to keep the family going.

How can the Afghan economy recover? While there is a danger that Afghans will rely too heavily on donors, much of the country's economic recovery will depend on how committed the international community remains over the next few years. Short-, medium- and long-term approaches for turning Afghanistan's fortunes around have been proposed by the World Bank, among others. Short-term, transitional support initiatives – so-called 'quick wins' – would help promote stability and reduce the risks of renewed outbreaks of fighting. These would focus on agricultural and food security, generate livelihoods for returned refugees both locally displaced or from outside the country, support small-scale development and short-run income generation through public works programmes such as road construction. Medium-term development components would establish sound economic management institutions such as the Central Bank and the Ministry of Finance, and develop education and health systems that reach the bulk of the population. And finally, a long-term economic reconstruction strategy is needed to encourage sustainable private sector growth.

One major achievement has been to stabilize the currency, which was reissued in December 2002. Funding the Afghan administration's budget (US$ 460 million during its first year) remains an ongoing challenge. The government said it could only expect to cover US$ 83 million of its budget with revenue obtained from customs levies, based on the few goods legally entering the country and from taxes on the exports of lumber, carpets, and dried fruit. The rest would have to come from the donors – more than one million dollars a day. The US has been Afghanistan's most generous donor. On 23 October 2003, President George Bush asked Congress for an additional US$ 1.2 billion for Afghanistan, of which US$ 400 million would be available immediately and US$ 800 million as part of the 2004 allocation. This funding, it was stated, would be used specifically for the re-building of the Kandahar to Herat highway, the salaries of civil servants, the development of communications between Kabul and the provinces, backing for the electoral process, the funding of experts to Afghan government ministries and other areas in need of support.

In its September 2003 report, the IMF argued that sizeable international assistance would be required for several years in order to put the country back on its feet. It recommended that this should be done in the form of grants so as not to engender future debt servicing difficulties. At the same time, it warned that existing pledges in 2003 remained drastically short. There was a danger – as experienced in other post-conflict situations – of outside assistance dropping off within a few years, just at the time when the recipient country's capacity to absorb and use aid effectively is increasing. With Afghanistan, the IMF noted, such a drop off could happen even sooner. Along with numerous other organizations, including NGOs, the IMF reiterated the urgent need for proper security in the provinces to allow the implementation of reforms and projects, the resumption of private sector economic revival, and the provision of basic public services in all rural areas.

In terms of prospects for recovery, agriculture remains the country's principal economic sector with nearly four-fifths of the country's population living in rural areas (SEE AGRICULTURE). The proposed national census is expected to determine more effectively the extent of Afghanistan's population and whether the majority of refugees are indeed returning to their homes outside Kabul and other towns, and whether they will depend as heavily as before on agriculture for their existence. The government does not even know how many districts (360-400) actually exist in Afghanistan.

For the moment, the overwhelming majority of Afghans are still believed to rely on farming as their prime – if not only – source of revenue. For the moment, too, the illicit cultivation and production of opium (around 1.7 million Afghans depend on the drug trade for cash) represents the most lucrative form of agricultural production (SEE DRUGS). Normal agricultural production has far to go before it can move beyond providing mere subsistence for people living in the countryside. At the same time, many Afghans, particularly young men or former *mujahideen*, are reluctant to work in agriculture; many have known the 'bright lights' of the cities from their refugee days or experienced the power of 'have gun, no work', during their time with the resistance or armed militia groups.

Dealing with shattered infrastructure is another formidable problem. Where vital industrial machinery, fittings and vehicles were not wrecked in the fighting, equipment has been looted – often down to the last screw. This has contributed to a lively and highly profitable scrap metal and spare parts trade, mainly with Pakistan, leaving the country with little infrastructure. Most facilities, such as the industrial area on the Jalalabad road outside Kabul, will need to be completely recreated or overhauled.

Tourism, a growing industry before the war, could rapidly develop into a major hard currency earner. This will not only require new hotels and travel services, including airports (a US$ 37 million effort began in late 2002 to restore the country's devastated aviation system), but also basic support facilities with regulated yet open competition. A Panjshairi taxi cartel supported by the United Front-dominated Ministry of Aviation and Tourism sought 'officially' to corner the airport road traffic by refusing to allow other drivers access and by threatening visitors if they dared take another vehicle. Protests to ISAF and the international community finally obliged them to stand back, but the cartel was still alive and well in 2003, leaving a bad taste with visitors. Known mountaineering, trekking, fishing and wildlife areas will need to be cleared of landmines.

Another massive task requiring major international support will be the return of lost cultural treasures stolen during the fighting (SEE CULTURE).

By mid-2002, a small handful of tourist ventures were already beginning to explore the possibilities, such as rafting down the Panjshair and other rivers, while the first 'post-conflict' travellers with tourist visas were already beginning to turn up from Britain, Colombia and Japan. For its part, Ariana, the national airline, was moving fast to set up regional and international routes with Sharjah (UAE) as its service hub. In September 2002, Ariana launched its first twice-weekly Frankfurt-Istanbul-Kabul route, with talk of additional links planned over the next few years. While flight security concerns worry many internationals (the UN does not allow its personnel to travel with Ariana) the airline is also so short of money that technicians accompany each flight to save costs. Pilots are only paid US$ 100 a flight – yet numerous travellers, including expatriates, have reported relatively keen service and good flying. As it is, increasing numbers of aid workers are indulging in restricted forms of weekend tourism such as hiking. Already in early 2002, the Greek government expressed its interest in developing quality tourism support facilities, such as guest houses and tourism 'villages' whereby the income generated would benefit the local population.

By the time of the Taliban overthrow, most institutional facilities such as government offices and banks were barely functioning. This began to change by early 2002 as the ministries, such as foreign affairs and finance, were equipped by the World Bank with the latest computer technology. The government has begun looking at formal taxes, which had not been collected since the early 1990s. Many so-called regional or local governments continue to exact checkpoint 'taxes' from the movement of goods and people inside Afghanistan and at the borders. Little of this actually reaches Kabul, a serious loss of potential revenue which the transitional authorities hope to remedy. Prior to the arrival of the Taliban, merchants and farmers were often 'taxed' at will – normally 10 percent of produce, usually in kind – by local commanders. Under the Taliban, taxes were lower, with harsh *shari'a* punishment deterring a lot of impromptu revenue collection, but also providing fewer resources for social services.

With the country's heavy reliance on international aid and loans as its principal source of revenue, the bulk of Afghanistan's 'real' economy still consists of the large-scale illicit trafficking of drugs, lumber, art treasures and duty free goods from Pakistan and Dubai. On occasion, the looted gains from aid agency compounds have provided a ready source of income, and car thefts of up-market 4x4s remain a serious problem. Given the impact of high inflation, many Afghans have been reluctant to invest in projects that do not have quick, high rates of return. Hence the understandable need to rely on smuggling as a significant source of income. Some Afghan traders, a few closely linked with former warlords, have been making small fortunes out of smuggling. These smugglers have a strong vested interest in keeping Kabul's control of the provinces to a minimum, and may even be encouraging regional insecurity to prevent the central government from asserting itself.

Many donor governments and international organizations remain obsessed about the need for a firm, central administration if peace and political stability are to be assured. Only then, they feel, can any proper, long-term development be implemented. However, this has meant that much of the international effort in 2002 ignored the provinces, thereby bolstering the United Front's hold over Afghan affairs in the capital. Many on-the-ground observers and aid practitioners believe that Afghanistan's economic rehabilitation and development may be best guaranteed by working with all sides. Some warn of the dangers of alienating the Pashtun elements of Afghan society, who will never tolerate the domination of their country by northerners. But as long as there are interested communities with concerned local leaders or decision-making institutions, much can be achieved. While Kabul can provide direction, its permission should not be needed to rehabilitate irrigation schemes, construct clinics, open schools or establish agricultural extension services.

Afghans are a resilient people. For years, the country's chaotic private sector seemed to sprout up almost as soon as the echoes of mortar rounds and rockets recede in the distance. Transport services, *chaikhanas* (teashops) and shops selling the bare necessities suddenly appeared among the ruins, or wherever business could be made. This legendary resilience remains Afghanistan's most valuable resource for economic recovery.

ESSENTIAL READING

Islamic State of Afghanistan: Rebuilding a Macroeconomic Framework for Reconstruction and Growth, International Monetary Fund (Washington DC, September 2003)

Afghanistan Monthly Reviews, British Agencies Afghanistan Group/British Refugee Council, (London, monthly)

National Payments System for the Islamic Republic of Afghanistan, (Asia Development Bank, 2003)

Financial Development and Poverty Alleviation: Issues and Policy Implications for Developing and Transition Countries, Holden, Paul and Vassili Prokopenko, 2001 (Washington, DC, International Monetary Fund Working Paper)

Return and reconstruction: economic coping strategies among farmers in Farah Province, Afghanistan, British Agencies Afghanistan Group/ The Refugee Council (London, July 1997)

Understanding the Economy of Afghanistan, Kjell Öström, Swedish International Development Corporation (January, 1997)

Civilian Casualty Monitoring: Marc Herold, University of New Hampshire **www.cursor.org** and **http://pubpages.unh.edu/-mwherold**

Education

> *"Knowledge is a treasure which can never run dry, however much you take from it. The person who does not have knowledge is like a donkey that does not know what it is carrying."*
>
> – *Afghan girl, 2002*

Education in Afghanistan has been a hot international issue ever since 1994, when the Taliban movement forbade girls from going to school and women from teaching in schools. Yet, for many decades before the Taliban arrived, the idea of secular education was greeted with suspicion by much of Afghan society. That's changing now – partly as a result of millions of Afghan refugees coming into contact with education in exile. In March 2002, the start of the academic year, aid agencies helped engineer the return of around three million girls and boys back to school. But resources, from pens and books to teachers and buildings, are in desperately short supply, and will be for years. At least one generation of Afghan children have grown up with no education at all. Meanwhile, half of all adult men, and 94 percent of adult women, remain functionally illiterate at the dawn of the 21st Century.

In traditional Afghan society, a child's early development is the responsibility of the extended family – with grandparents passing on their wisdom through stories, poems and songs. When boys are around six years old, they are traditionally sent to the mosque to learn the *Qu'ran* by rote under the local mullah. Girls may also attend these classes, but by the time they are nine years old they will usually be required back home to help with household chores.

In the 1920s, secular education was introduced by the state – becoming both free and compulsory in 1935. For decades, however, the government lacked the resources to provide this education to all Afghan children, especially in rural areas. During the 1960s-70s this changed as more facilities and teachers became available. By 1975, the government reported that 780,000 children were in primary education – one in seven of them girls. By the outbreak of the Soviet war, 37 percent of boys and eight percent of girls were enrolled. Many conservative elements in Afghan society, however, regarded such education as a threat to Afghan culture and Islamic values.

And as Soviet influence permeated Afghan politics in the 1970s and 1980s, state-sponsored education became identified with communism and atheism.

Soon after the April 1978 communist coup, the *Khalq* faction of the Marxist People's Democratic Party of Afghanistan (PDPA) began a mass literacy campaign, which forced tribal and mainly veiled Afghan women into classrooms with male teachers. The women's male relatives were furious and reacted by boycotting lessons and even destroying schools. Following the Red Army invasion of 1979, Afghan traditions and culture were once again swept aside by Soviet teachers who imported their communist ideology and syllabus wholesale and imposed Russian as a compulsory language. Meanwhile, thousands of Afghan children were sent to the Soviet Union for education.

Nearly a quarter of a century of conflict has left Afghanistan's education system in ruins. During the Soviet war of the 1980s, around 2,000 schools were destroyed and over 15,000 teachers fled the country, many destined to become taxi drivers in Peshawar or New York. In 1990, the numbers enrolled in state primary schools were down by two-thirds from pre-war levels. During the 1990s, UNESCO reported an increase in the number of primary schools, despite fierce civil war in urban areas. But the quality of education deteriorated, as teachers fled the fighting and state support for schools dried up.

Meanwhile, from the 1980s onwards, numerous schools for Afghan refugee children were established in Pakistan's North West Frontier Province (NWFP) and Baluchistan. Supporters of the Afghan resistance were keen to bring up their children in the spirit of Islamic *jihad* and education once more became prey to political aspirations. Islamic schools, or *madrassas,* sprang up over the border in Pakistan, out of which the Taliban movement emerged in the early 1990s.

During the Taliban years (1994-2001), not only were all girls forbidden to attend school, but all women were banned from teaching. This had a major impact on the education of boys as well, since in Kabul, for example, nearly three-quarters of all teachers were women. Classroom sizes for boys soared to as much as 200, and the boys who did go to school often learnt virtually nothing. This provoked tremendous discontent among Kabulis, who have always valued the importance of education. Meanwhile, with only their education to sell, thousands of female teachers either fled the capital or were reduced to begging on the streets in *burqas*.

Yet although many Westerners were quick to condemn the Taliban, they reflected an attitude towards female education common in many rural, conservative parts of Afghanistan. The education situation in urban areas such as Kabul and Herat during the 1970s-80s was in many ways unique. These were cosmopolitan towns where students enjoyed mixed classes and a liberal dress code. But education in rural areas was less affected by Taliban strictures. In 1979, less than one in ten girls went to school – usually because many were never allowed by their rigidly patriarchal and conservative families to be formally educated. Under Taliban control, many schools became *madrassas,* and religious studies featured much more centrally in the syllabus. From 1997-99, the number of students studying in religious schools doubled.

One of the reasons the Taliban so mistrusted secular education was simply because many had not been well educated themselves, at least in the Western sense, having been brought up in the all-male *madrassas* of Pakistan and

Afghanistan where learning is limited to repeating the *Qu'ran* by rote and studying the *shari'a*. Furthermore their strict interpretation of the role of women in Islamic society is underpinned by the traditionalist Pashtun tribal code, the *Pashtunwali*, which emphasises the function of women as objects of male pride.

Nevertheless, during the Taliban years, NGOs became very creative in their attempts to educate girls. An underground network of 'home schools' sprang up to provide at least a basic education in a non-formal environment. One of the leading NGOs in education has been the Swedish Committee for Afghanistan (SCA), which supported 650 primary schools in 17 provinces under the Taliban. Independent surveys during 1998 revealed that 13 percent of SCA-supported students in rural Taliban areas were girls – many of them in home-schools. By early 2001, up to 60,000 children were being educated in this way in Kabul province alone. The Taliban closed home-schools down in some areas but tolerated them in others. By the end of the Taliban period, the US NGO CARE reported that 46 percent of students in their home schools were girls.

UNICEF, the lead UN agency for primary education, attracted much criticism for its policy during the late 1990s of refusing to support schools in Taliban areas. Critics claimed that not only did this policy of 'conditional' aid fail to change Taliban attitudes towards education for girls, it also undermined education for those boys in Taliban areas who were allowed to go to school. Nevertheless, UNICEF supported some home-schooling in rural areas and literacy and health training in camps for displaced Afghans.

The situation in non-Taliban areas was quite different, at least in attitude if not in practice. Girls were free to go to school throughout regions controlled by Northern Alliance and Hazara forces, but more often the problem was lack of school buildings, text books and teachers. The dropout rate was high, reflecting poor teaching, an irrelevant curriculum and continuing economic hardship which forced many boys to leave school and seek work. During the late 1990s, refugee camps in Pakistan's NWFP suffered serious cutbacks in educational funding. Many donors, including the US government, grew weary of supporting refugees who showed no sign of returning to Afghanistan.

The severe drought, which afflicted much of the country from 1997-2002, coupled with intense economic hardship, prevented many children from going to school. One elder in Zabul province, when asked by a UN field officer whether he would support a school in his village if it were to be constructed, replied: "Who will fetch water, firewood and look after our herd if we enlist our children in your school?"

By the end of the 20th Century, Afghanistan was near the bottom of world league tables for education. In 1999, UNESCO reported that only five percent of girls and 60 percent of boys were going to school. That meant 3.7 million – of the estimated 4.8 million children of primary school age – were out of school. A multiple indicator cluster survey carried out in 2000 found that less than one third of 5-12 year olds were attending any kind of school – whether primary, secondary or religious. Of this total, only one fifth were girls. By contrast, of the 150,000 children who were receiving primary education in refugee camps in Pakistan in 1999, one third were girls.

The collapse of the Taliban as a ruling power in late 2001 has provided a tremendous opportunity for Afghan girls and boys to receive a basic educa-

J. Hartley/UNICEF

tion for perhaps the first time in their lives. Meanwhile, the return of two million refugees – many of whose children went to school while in exile – has increased the demand for education.

But there are immense challenges. According to an assessment by the Afghan Interim Administration and the Asian Development Bank, carried out in early 2002, Afghanistan's education sector was "in a state of almost complete collapse". Over three quarters of Afghanistan's 4,000 school buildings had been damaged or destroyed. Many teachers and administrators had been killed or fled abroad. Those who remained had received no pay for six months. The assessment stated that rebuilding Afghanistan's education system would cost US$ 1.24 billion over the next decade – around US$ 125 million per year. That doesn't include recurrent costs such as teachers' salaries, which could add US$ 40-80 million per year. In 2002-03, teachers' salaries were around US$ 40 per month – not even enough to cover rent and transport costs.

During the Taliban years, the lack of school buildings, furniture and teaching materials, plus the poor or non-existent salaries for staff, resulted in a high dropout rate of both students and teachers. Replacing the educational infrastructure and attracting teachers back into the profession will prove an enormous challenge – especially considering that of the two million Afghans who returned home during 2002-03, many are children of schooling age. Teaching is one of Afghanistan's largest employers; currently international agencies pay most of their salaries, so transferring this responsibility to the new government is a long-term challenge. Meanwhile, the Ministry of Education plans to build 2,710 school buildings – but by mid-2003, there were only funds or pledges to build 450.

Educational policy and quality were devastated by two decades of war, and the support of NGOs and UN agencies was typically short-termist, based on annual funding cycles. Reforming the syllabus is a key issue. During the

1980s-90s, many schools used textbooks with a heavily anti-communist bias developed by the University of Nebraska in Omaha (UNO) and funded by USAID. As many as 12 million books were printed during the Soviet war and, despite adjustments to their content, have never been fully replaced. One mathematics textbook posed the following problem: "If you have two dead Communists, and kill three more, how many dead Communists do you have?" The Ministry of Education, with support from UNICEF, is working on reforming the syllabus.

The goal for NGOs is to integrate home-schools into the formal system. However, some argue that until the government is capable of providing universal education, home schools will remain relevant in rural areas. Many children – especially girls – have lost several years of education during the Taliban period. Some are receiving accelerated education, to try and cram three years of schooling into one year in order to catch up. Meanwhile an intensive series of refresher courses for female teachers is underway.

Another challenge is to help children, youths and adults with special needs, for example child soldiers. Following the fall of the Taliban, up to 30,000 ex-child soldiers were estimated to be living in Kandahar alone. Others who will prove difficult to integrate into a universal education system are the orphans and disabled, nomadic children and the 'lost generation' of Afghans, aged 12-30, whose education was interrupted or never started.

However, some early successes have been scored. In March 2002, UNICEF launched its 'back to school' campaign, which returned around three million children into education – out of a total of 4.8 million children believed to be of school age. Across Afghanistan during 2002, crocodiles of excited Afghan children could be seen rushing enthusiastically to school with their UNICEF knapsacks on their backs – even when 'school' may only have consisted of an unpaid teacher standing amid a pile of sun-baked rubble. Around 30 percent of those who went back to school were girls. This figure disguised regional variations – for example, in Kandahar about 10 percent of schoolchildren were girls, compared to 45 percent in Kabul. UNICEF also provided 6,000 tents as temporary classrooms and distributed millions of textbooks, in what it called its "largest logistical effort ever in support of education." Around 70,000 Afghan teachers rose to the challenge – a third of them women. Even so, the acute pressure on school facilities, materials and teachers during 2002 meant that teachers had to teach two or three shifts of children per day, clearly having a negative impact on the quality of education received. During 2003, around four million children were believed to be receiving some form of education.

During 2002-03, numerous attacks on schools and the staff of NGOs working in education were reported. Some schools were burned down in Wardak, Paktia, Logar and Nangarhar provinces, where conservative or Islamist elements remain opposed to the education of girls. Despite these security problems, more than 20,000 teachers are being formally trained – many for the first time in their lives – with a particular focus on improving literacy in Dari and Pashto. Educating children about the risks of landmines and unexploded ordnance (UXO) is another key priority.

Few Afghans are receiving secondary or tertiary education, since to date, most international assistance has focused on primary education. Some

Afghan provinces have no secondary schools at all. In 2002, among children of secondary school age, only 10 percent of boys and less than two percent of girls were thought to be enrolled.

From 1975-1990, the numbers of university students more than doubled to nearly 21,000 – despite the Soviet invasion. This figure slumped under the effects of civil war and the Taliban, but is now rising again. In Herat, an active engineering faculty was transferred from Peshawar during the late 1990s. In 2002, Balkh University in Mazar, set up in the late 1980s, boasted 4,000 students, making it the second largest of Afghanistan's eight universities. Kabul University, first founded as a medical faculty in 1932, was once home to 900 lecturers with links to other academic institutions around the world. After the fall of President Najibullah in 1992, however, it was virtually destroyed by inter-factional fighting among the *mujahideen*. A group of devoted professors started from scratch to rebuild the place, collecting a library of quarter of a million books and increasing the student body to 10,000 including 4,000 women. Then the Taliban arrived and it was once again closed down. In 2002, 16,000 students passed the university's entrance exams. But by November, poor hostel conditions drove thousands of students to demonstrate. The heavy-handed response by Afghan police which followed left at least two students dead and was widely criticised.

Books for higher education are in very short supply. Afghanistan's most significant collection, the Kabul Public Library, was systematically destroyed during the 1990s, first by *mujahideen* forces and then by the Taliban. Since 2002, New York University has been leading an effort to create the Afghanistan Digital Library – which aims to digitise, catalogue and upload all Dari and Pashto books published in Afghanistan between 1871 and 1930.

In a sign that Afghans place a high priority on education, local people of all kinds – including many expatriate Afghans – contributed over US$ 5 million towards paying for better education during 2002. The government was forced to appeal to the public for help when UN agencies and NGOs failed to provide enough funds. One Afghan working at the culture ministry gave US$ 12 – her entire weekly salary – and said: "After the collapse of the former Soviet Union the most important trigger of war in our country has been illiteracy and ignorance. As an Afghan woman, I want my children to study and in this way to understand their responsibilities." Meanwhile, President Karzai pledged that the Education ministry would receive the largest slice of his government's budget. In a flash of Afghan pride, he announced: "If we do not have a proper education system then this will be an illiterate country. An illiterate country will always have to rely on others and never be truly independent."

INFOBRIEFS

ESSENTIAL DATA

	Literacy: Male	Female	Primary school enrolment: Male	Female	Total
1970	13%	2%[1]			780,000
1975					
1979			37%	8%[2]	
1980			24%	13%[3]	
1990	44%	14%[4]			
1997	35% (urban)	10% (urban)[5]			
1997	26% (rural)	3% (rural)[6]			
1999			38-58%	3-6%[7]	c.1.1 million
2000	53%	6%[8]	47%	12%[9]	
2002					c. 3 million (of which 30% girls)[10]
2003					c. 4 million[11]

ESSENTIAL AGENCIES

CARE, Ministry of Education, SCA, SC-US, UNESCO, UNICEF, UNO

ESSENTIAL READING AND WEBLINKS

Comprehensive Needs Assessment in Education, Asian Development Bank (2002)
Lost Chances – the changing situation of children in Afghanistan, 1990-2000, Global Movement for Children in Afghanistan Working Group (2001)
Education in the Doldrums: Afghan tragedy, Dr S.B. Ekanayake, Al-Noor Publishers, (Islamabad, 2000)
EFA 2000, Afghanistan, UNESCO (Paris, 2000)
Initiatives in curriculum design and development, AG BAS-Ed & UNESCO (1997)
The State of the World's Children, UNICEF (New York, annually)

Afghanistan Higher Education Reconstruction: http://afghanhighered.lib.calpoly.edu
New York University's Afghanistan Digital Library: http://dlib.nyu.edu/divlib/bobst/adl

[1] Afghan Government figures
[2] Afghan Ministry of Education
[3] UNDP
[4] Afghan Government figures – widely questioned
[5] Multiple Indicator Cluster Survey (MICS) 1997, UNICEF/CIET International
[6] ibid.
[7] UNESCO, 2000
[8] MICS 2000, GTZ – conducted in Taliban areas
[9] ibid.
[10] UNICEF
[11] Afghan Ministry of Education

Environment & conservation

"The environment is man's first right"

– the late Ken Saro-Wiwa, Nigerian author and human rights activist

Afghanistan boasts one the most spectacular and ruggedly beautiful landscapes in the world. And with it, wild fauna and flora to match. As many a visitor can attest, there is a harsh, almost mystical beauty to this land. Even during the height of the war as refugees fled by foot across the high mountain passes of the Hindu Kush or rumbled through the shimmering steppelands of southern Afghanistan in overloaded trucks and tractors, it was hard not to be enthralled by a lone eagle soaring overhead or a light-footed gazelle sprinting along a dry river bed.

However, a quarter century of conflict has turned much of the country into a soulless terrain devoid of forests and wildlife. Four years of devastating drought from 1998-2002 left the land parched. Key wetlands for migrating and local waterfowl have been drained, causing many species to disappear – such as flamingos, which have not bred in Afghanistan since the late 1990s. The direct and indirect damage to this country's environment by the war may represent Afghanistan's second-most crucial loss, following that of its own people. Already during the early days of the war, when the Soviets launched deliberate security operations against civilians in rural areas and refugees fled in growing numbers, it was evident that the destruction of Afghanistan's ecology and natural resources would have a profound impact for generations to come.

Although Klaus Toepfer, the executive director of the United Nations Environment Programme (UNEP), warned in early 2003 that environmental restoration must play "a major part" in the country's reconstruction process, it is clear that this is still not happening. Environmental considerations remain largely neglected by the international aid community. As one major European aid representative in Kabul noted: "From the donor point of view, the environment is not exactly one of our priority concerns although there is no question that it should be."

As with numerous other current and former conflict zones worldwide – Angola, Cambodia, Mozambique, Somalia and the Gulf – the war has had a varying effect on the environment. Soviet bombing (often using phosphorous explosives to ensure burning), the relentless cutting of firewood by refugees and the *mujahideen*, and uncontrolled illicit lumbering by Afghans and Pakistanis alike have caused the devastation of thousands of hectares of forest since the early 1980s (SEE FORESTRY). This has caused severe erosion and destruction of habitat in many parts of the country, particularly in the eastern provinces. Huge landslides resulting from the felling of trees in Kunar and other provinces have already led to the wiping out of villages and fertile farmland over the past few years.

The proliferation of weapons has ensured the relentless hunting of wildlife in formerly remote regions, ever since the *mujahideen* took to the hills to launch their attacks or to run supply convoys along former caravan routes. Similarly, hundreds of thousands of refugees, obliged to avoid the main government-held roads and crossing points, travelled through remote mountain areas to cross one of the 300-odd passes that lead into Pakistan. Many brought with them cattle, camels and other livestock, causing abusive grazing of pasture lands. This has occurred around all the main farming centres and roads as civilians sought to flee the fighting, often accompanied by horses and donkeys.

Refugee influxes precipitated heavy pollution of water supplies as well as the progressive destruction of woodlands, in a desperate bid for fuel and shelter materials. Refugee returns from 2002 onwards are also having an impact. Despite UNEP's 2003 post-conflict environmental survey, and limited wildlife surveys, it is still not known what effect such additional pressures have had on the different species of fauna. Cheetah, lynx, otter and long-tailed marmot are all believed to be near extinction, or have sharply declined in the face of hunting and habitat degradation. Siberian cranes, whose cries used to echo across the early spring skies over Kabul as they migrated northwards, have not been seen since the mid-1980s. The fur trade, however, remains strong as pelts of the more common – but also endangered – species continue to reach the Kabul bazaars and the international market. This includes the rare snow leopard, which UNEP and other environmental surveys have shown still exists in small but significant numbers in the Wakhan Corridor, Badakhshan and Nuristan.

Yet the war has left other aspects of Afghanistan's natural heritage intact. The depopulation of farms and villages as well as the presence of landmines and other unexploded ordnance in fields, woodlands and riverbeds has enabled certain species of fauna and flora to proliferate in various former habitats, including along main roads. According to conservation groups such as the Swiss-based World Conservation Union (IUCN) and a local Afghan NGO, Save the Environment Afghanistan (SEA), many remote areas away from main towns and cities are believed to have retained their biodiversity. The abandonment of villages, particularly in the north-eastern mountain regions including the Wakhan Corridor, as well as the lack of hunting and other forms of human encroachment, have allowed some forms of fauna ranging from snow leopard and brown bear to ibex, Marco Polo sheep and *markhor* to exist without interference.

EFG editors visiting Nuristan and Kunar in November 2002 reported local sources, such as hunters and shepherds, describing regular sightings of bear,

Panjshair Valley *J. Walter*

wolf, fox and common leopard. The small rise in the number of snow leopard pelts reaching the market since the fall of the Taliban also seems to suggest a population growth in recent years. Similarly, wolf, bear and fox are regularly seen in the Hazarajat highlands. Some unsubstantiated reports even maintain that Caspian tigers continue to roam the more heavily forested, mountainous parts of eastern Afghanistan such as Paktia province, but this is largely refuted by environmental experts. "The last tiger to be shot in Afghanistan was sometime in the 1950s", argues agricultural specialist Anthony Fitzherbert, one of those participating in the 2003 UNEP survey. Nevertheless, both Nuristani and Kunari mountain people maintain they have seen traces of 'baber' (tiger) as opposed to 'palang' (leopard) with one shot near Kamdesh in Nuristan during the early 1990s.

Ironically, given the country's current devastation, the concept of biosphere reserves (protected habitats) reputedly originated in Afghanistan. The 5,000-year old city of Balkh, for example, boasted more than a million trees in the 17th Century. During this period, many other ancient Afghan cities made special efforts to ensure environmental protection. More recently, in 1973, Afghanistan became one of the first countries to become a party to the Man and Biosphere Reserves programme. As a result, a number of areas in Afghanistan were declared Biosphere Reserves. However, with any notion of conservation management or protection eliminated by the lack of government and war since the early 1980s, these spheres were quickly relegated to little more than theoretical notions. Seven so-called 'protected' conservation areas still exist, but there is currently no proper management to guarantee their survival. Unless protection measures are rapidly implemented as part of the country's overall recovery strategy, conservationists maintain, the situation could change drastically as more refugees return home, landmines are cleared, and farming areas are once again put to the plough.

It is clear that Afghanistan's current conservation problems could have a direct impact not only on its own natural resources but also on those of neighbouring countries. For example, illegal deforestation in Pakistan's North West Frontier Province and eastern Afghanistan often involves the same groups of traffickers, many of whom indulge in opium and wildlife smuggling. The Siberian cranes which breed in Siberia but winter in India must pass through Afghanistan as part of their migratory flyway, sheltering in major wetland areas such as the Ghazni Marshlands, also a home and migratory stopover for some 250 other species ranging from flamingos to ducks and pelicans. These and other wetlands, however, have been badly damaged if not destroyed by the four years of severe drought. Even if the drought appeared to have been partially broken in 2003, these wetlands could still take years to recuperate. The survival of endangered Marco Polo sheep in the Gojal area of Pakistan and in adjoining China is closely related to its protection in the Pamir-e-Buzarg district of the Wakhan Corridor. The proper functioning of Pakistan's Warsak dam near Peshawar is dependent on water catchments along the upper Kabul River from Sarobi dam west of Jalalabad to its entry point into Pakistan.

Organizations such as UNEP, the World Wide Fund for Nature (WWF), IUCN and SEA are now pushing for the development of a conservation strategy for Afghanistan as part of any overall long-term rehabilitation and development programme. In early 2003, Ahmed Yusuf Nuristani, Afghanistan's Minister for Irrigation, Water Resources and the Environment, was seeking a relatively modest eight million dollars to get the process moving. In the meantime, UNEP and other related organizations have been seeking to establish baselines of vulnerable and critically endangered species as well as assess the country's major ecosystems. Although some reports, including the UNEP survey, were published in 2002 and 2003, available and reliable data still remain limited and often only focus on certain parts of the country. Ongoing insecurity in some areas has also prevented teams from undertaking more detailed assessments.

Air quality

The quality of air in most Afghan towns was generally good before the war. As with many Third World towns, however, outdoor air conditions have deteriorated as a result of rising population, dust, excessive coal and wood burning, and exhaust fumes from growing numbers of trucks, cars and motor-scooters – especially since the start of reconstruction in early 2002. Rural areas are also becoming increasingly affected.

Kabul may have a way to go before it becomes as bad as Bangkok or Jakarta, but it is getting there. Partial peace and the post-Taliban international recovery effort have brought an influx of tens of thousands of vehicles both in Kabul and other towns such as Herat, Jalalabad and Mazar-e-Sharif. This has resulted in severe pollution. The fact that Kabul exists in a broad, crater-like valley does not help air circulation. Walking outside during the day and early evening is becoming intolerable, with the dust and smog during the dry season provoking what is known as the 'Kabul cough.'

Smoke from cooking and heating is the primary indoor air pollutant affecting health (respiratory and eye disorders), particularly that of women and children. Some aid agencies are seeking to help villagers construct larger windows as a means of improving air circulation, instead of the small openings covered with plastic that characterize traditional dwellings in poorer, more isolated areas such as Hazarajat, with its cold winters. And despite Islam frowning at tobacco, smoking is on the increase and is now considered a major indoor pollutant by health specialists. *EG*

Furthermore, Afghanistan's environmental degradation is not just a question of ensuring the renewal of the country's depleted water resources, forests and wildlife populations. It is also a matter of basic pollution, particularly of water, caused by sewage seeping into the aquifers of cities such as Kabul, contamination of surrounding water sources by oil refineries and the dumping of refuse which pollutes streams, rivers and irrigation canals. Barely 12 percent of urban Afghans have access to adequate sanitation. Nor are there any real waste management or sewage systems in Kabul and other cities. Sewage often simply runs off into the streets or nearby water channels, which are then used by children for swimming or women for washing. Medical refuse, such as syringes and used bandages, are also dumped without second thought behind hospitals or nearby garbage sites which are then picked through by human scavengers.

As part of its recovery efforts, Afghanistan needs to undertake:

- More effective protection of natural resources shared with other countries, such as water catchments from Jalalabad in Afghanistan to the

Warsak dam in Pakistan. With target areas to extend 10 kilometres on both sides of the Kabul river, such protection would seek to provide drinking and irrigation water to local communities and their agricultural lands as well as to harbour local biodiversity and large populations of migratory birds. It would also help assure the longevity of Warsak dam.

- Broader countrywide research to identify and quantify available resources and existing problems.
- Conservation of major flyways of cranes, falcons and *houbara* bustards in the trans-boundary zone of Ghazni province in Afghanistan and Baluchistan province in Pakistan. Easy access across Afghanistan's borders, particularly for wealthy hunters from Saudi Arabia and the Gulf region, has brought increased pressure on such species. Rare falcons protected by the Convention on the International Trade in Endangered Species (CITES) can command prices of US$ 50,000-100,000 – an absolute fortune for local Afghans and far more lucrative than drug trafficking.

Given ongoing insecurity concerns in eastern and southern Afghanistan, coupled with the government's lack of influence in many areas, it seems unlikely that any effective conservation strategy on a nationwide basis will be undertaken for some time to come. In the meantime, some conservationists point out that various local and regional conservation approaches should be included as part of the overall recovery process. Community-based public information campaigns coupled with financial and other incentives, for example, could make significant inroads in a short period of time by involving populations in areas where conditions for practical approaches exist.

Local initiatives were already being implemented in 2002 and 2003, such as an environmental programme near Qishem in Badakhshan, whereby hunting in one valley was banned and a nature reserve established with an eye to future tourism. Similarly, in Nuristan province, several local commanders claim to have introduced hunting bans and have approached aid agencies for assistance in developing ecotourism, such as trekking, trout fishing and bird watching.

ESSENTIAL DATA

- **Only one Afghan NGO – Save the Environment Afghanistan (SEA) – is dedicated solely to conservation**
- **In February 2003, UNEP published the first major post-conflict environment assessment of Afghanistan**
- **While nearly a quarter of a century of war has contributed heavily towards the environmental devastation of Afghanistan, it has resulted in modest population growths in certain areas of wild species, such as Marco Polo sheep, wolf and bear**
- **Satellite surveys indicate that over half of Afghanistan's forests have been destroyed by illegal or unmanaged logging in Nangarhar, Kunar and Nuristan since 1978. In other provinces, such as Paktia, it may be as much as 80 percent.**
- **Four years of drought from 1998-2002 have drained wetlands and other crucial waterfowl sites. Flamingos have not bred in Afghani-**

stan since the late 1990s, while the once-common Siberian Crane has not been seen since 1986

- **The endangered *saker* falcon can fetch up to US$ 100,000 per bird on the black market**
- **Endangered snow leopard pelts continue to be sold openly in Kabul for prices between US$ 400-1500**

ESSENTIAL AGENCIES

FAO, IUCN (including the TRAFFIC Network and The Wetlands Programme), SEA, UNEP, WWF-Pakistan
Ministry of Irrigation, Water Resources and the Environment

ESSENTIAL READING

Afghanistan: Post-Conflict Environmental Assessment, UN Environment Programme with the Afghanistan Transitional Authority (Nairobi, February 2003). Available online at http://postconflict.unep.ch
Fading Footprints: The Killing And Trade Of Snow Leopards, Stephanie Theile, Traffic International (Cambridge, UK, 2003)
Armed Conflicts and Humanitarian Concerns: how attention to environmental scarcity can prevent human tragedies, Jeffrey A. McNeely, Chief Scientist, IUCN (Gland, June 1997)
An overview and assessment of Afghanistan's environment, Tareq A. Formoli, M. Afzal Rashid and James P. Du Bruille, Afghanistan Horizon/ Afghan Development Association (September, 1994)
Nature Reserves of the Himalaya and the Mountains of Central Asia, World Conservation Monitoring Centre, IUCN (Gland, Switzerland, 1993)
Opportunities for improved environmental management in Afghanistan, Nancy MacPherson, IUCN/UNOCA (Gland, Switzerland, May 1991)

Ethnic & tribal summary

PASHTUN

- Largest ethnic group in Afghanistan
- Percentage of Afghanistan's settled population: 38% (Eighmy, 1990) to 63% (Wak Foundation, 1998)
- Dominant tribe from 1747 (Ahmed Shah Durrani) until the Soviet invasion in 1979
- *Key players:* Hamid Karzai, Hedayat Amin Arsala, Gulbuddin Hekmatyar
- *Location:* mainly eastern and southern Afghanistan, Kabul, Pakistan's North West Frontier Province
- *Language:* Pashto

TAJIK

- Second largest ethnic group in Afghanistan
- Percentage of Afghanistan's settled population: 12% (Wak Foundation, 1998) to 25% (Eighmy, 1990)
- *Key players:* Mohammad Qasim Fahim, Burhanuddin Rabbani, the late Ahmed Shah Massoud, Abdullah Abdullah
- *Location:* northeastern Afghanistan, Herat and Kabul
- *Language:* Dari (Persian)

HAZARA

- Largest *Shi'a* Muslim minority in Afghanistan
- Percentage of Afghanistan's settled population: 8% (USSR Academy of Sciences, 1981) to 19% (Eighmy, 1990)
- *Key players:* Karim Khalili, Sima Samar
- *Location:* Hazarajat (Bamiyan and surrounding provinces), Kabul, Mazar-e-Sharif, Quetta & Baluchistan (Pakistan)
- *Language:* Dari dialect

UZBEK

- One of the largest ethnic minorities in Afghanistan
- Percentage of Afghanistan's settled population: 6.3% (Eighmy, 1990) to 9% (USSR Academy of Sciences, 1981)
- *Key players:* Abdul Rashid Dostum
- *Location:* northern provinces of Jowzjan, Balkh, Baghlan and Kunduz between the Amu Darya (Oxus River) and the Hindu Kush mountains
- *Language:* Uzbeki (Turkic)

TURKMEN

- Semi-sedentary herders and farmers
- Percentage of Afghanistan's settled population: 2.5% (Eighmy, 1990) to 3% (USSR Academy of Sciences, 1981)
- *Location:* northern and northwestern provinces bordering Turkmenistan
- *Language:* Turkmeni – a Turkic language which is closely related to Uzbeki

AIMAQ

- Turkic nomads and herders – numbering around 800,000 (during early 1980s)
- *Location:* northwestern provinces
- *Language:* Dari

BALUCH AND BRAHUI

- Independent herders and traders – numbering around 300,000 (during early 1980s)
- *Location:* southwest of country on border with Iran and Baluchistan/Pakistan
- *Language:* Baluchi, Pashto

NURISTANI

- Independent mountain people – numbering around 100,000 (during early 1980s)
- Forcibly converted to Islam by Amir Abdur Rahman in 1896
- *Location:* Nuristan, eastern Afghanistan
- *Language:* Nuristani dialects

KUCHI

- Nomadic group, comprising mainly Pashtuns, with some Baluch and Kirghiz
- Estimated numbers range from 500,000 to three million
- *Location:* southwestern Afghanistan on borders with Iran and Pakistan

Forestry & deforestation

The destruction of Afghanistan's forests since the start of the war in 1978 may prove to be the country's greatest environmental disaster. Conservationists warn that the deforestation process has now reached the stage where a total loss of Afghanistan's once magnificent woodlands may be imminent unless urgent, decisive measures are taken to protect this fast dwindling natural resource. Not only are the country's trees vital as a timber and fuel supply for local populations, but forest cover also helps prevent erosion, replenish water and improve health by reducing dust and countering other forms of air pollution. Recent surveys of deforested parts in eastern and northern Afghanistan have shown a marked reduction over the past 25 years in arable land and grazing areas as well as water runoff from the mountains. While harsh drought conditions since the late 1990s have contributed much towards this deterioration, so has the cutting of trees.

As a primarily semi-arid and desert country, less than three percent (the so-called 'legal' figure) of total land in Afghanistan is covered by forest, much of it in the mountain zones of the north-eastern and eastern provinces. But more realistic 'guesstimates' suggest that remaining forest cover may be as little as 0.5 percent. According to a February 2003 United Nations Environment Programme (UNEP) Post-Conflict Environmental Assessment, satellite surveys show that many areas have lost over 50 percent of their forest cover since 1977-78, with more remote and less accessible parts such as Nuristan having undergone at least a 30 percent reduction, despite clearer land ownership and management. During the war years, many areas such as Paktia province were heavily plundered because forestry management had collapsed or local villagers had fled, leaving no-one to watch over the trees. EFG editors visiting north-eastern and northern Afghanistan in November 2002 and March 2003 reported considerable ongoing lumbering of cedar, pine and holly oak in the mountains overlooking the Kunar, Qerala and Pech rivers.

Historical evidence suggests that large portions of Afghanistan, such as the now treeless mountain slopes overlooking the Panjshair Valley, were once heavily wooded. Over the millennia, the cutting of forests by human beings for building materials and fuel, such as charcoal, but also grazing by domestic animals, helped create the present grassland steppes. A 1997 report by the World Wide Fund for Nature (WWF) estimated that Afghanistan's forests were being destroyed at the rate of 20,000 hectares a year. Similar rates of destruction were predicted for 2003, particularly given increased demands for lumber for construction materials by returning refugees. During both the *mujahed* (1978-1996) and Taliban (1994/96-2001) periods, there was also heavy trafficking of lumber (up to 200 truckloads a day according to UNEP) in Paktia and other eastern areas of Afghanistan. Most logs were destined for sale in neighbouring Pakistan, via the Terimangal and Chaman crossing points. In Badghis, Herat and Takhar, once resplendent stands of pistachio forests have been reduced by half. Trips by EFG editors in 2001 and 2003 revealed only single or scattered pistachio trees on previously wooded hillsides and mountains. The 2003 UNEP report confirms this. Current deforestation practices now threaten to destroy rapidly what little remains in the foothills and mountains.

Afghanistan boasts two main types of forests: broad-leaved and needle-leaved. The first consists of oak and nut trees (pistachio) growing in highland areas from 1,300 to 2,200 metres. Serving as firewood, charcoal, fodder for livestock and food, these trees are considered vital for soil and water conservation. The second consists of conifers (cedar, pine, fir, juniper, spruce) in mountainous zones from 2,000 to 3,000 metres. These provide good quality wood for construction and furniture, and are effective for erosion control.

Significant rapid deforestation of Afghanistan's forest in the early 1980s as government control over rural areas, particularly in the eastern provinces, deteriorated in the face of *mujahed* resistance. As villages emptied, existing forms of tree management dissipated. In Paktia province, for example, the West German government had established the beginnings of a successful forestry management programme. This collapsed with the Soviet-Afghan war. Elsewhere, shrubs growing in rangeland areas (70 percent of the country), and which play a vital role in soil and grassland conservation, have been increasingly uprooted and removed for fuel by refugees as well as by local and nomadic populations. Increased soil erosion in deforested or de-shrubbed areas in the mountains and lower rangelands is having an adverse effect on the land's ability to absorb water. So, wells are getting deeper and *karezes* (irrigation tunnels) are drying up.

During the height of the Soviet war, the Red Army regularly used phosphorous bombs in their efforts to curtail the *mujahideen* or to terrorise local villages. Such actions caused some large-scale burning of forests. The passage of hundreds of thousands of refugees every year to Pakistan caused further denuding of the trees. All state-controlled timber plantations, for example, were destroyed during the fighting. The most poignant form of destruction, however, has been that of deliberate cutting by Afghans and Pakistanis alike, mainly for commercial purposes during the 1980s and 1990s. While the Afghan resistance liked to blame the Soviets for this destruction, in many cases, it was they themselves together with militia groups and local warlords who turned to lumber as a source of revenue, fuel and building materials. Timber traders from both sides of the border have profited massively from this practice, often with the connivance of Pakistani government and military officials. One EFG journalist remembers trekking through the thick forests of Paktia and Kunar provinces during the early days of the war only to return less than a decade later to find huge tracts turned into scarred, moon-like wastelands of withered stumps and rocks.

Current limitations on timber cutting in Pakistan's North West Frontier Province (NWFP) encouraged the lumber *mafia* to turn its attention to Afghanistan as a source of timber as well as a transit route for illegally harvested logs taken from Pakistan's Dir District and Bajaur Agency. Major deforestation began encroaching on many of Afghanistan's remaining forested areas, including Nuristan – a region that had remained relatively unscathed during much of the Soviet war. Some observers maintained that wealthy Pakistani timber traders, among them ex-government ministers and military, were heavily involved in the stripping of entire mountainsides of natural forest in exchange for dollars paid in cash to local residents.

Until the late 1990s, logs were being transported from north-eastern Afghanistan to Kabul. From here, they were taken via Ghazni and Kandahar to the border post of Chaman and into Pakistan's Baluchistan province – observers counted between 50-100 trucks a day along these roads in mid-1997. Despite having officially banned timber smuggling, the Taliban in Kandahar routinely levied taxes on all traffic. For fear of undermining local support, the Taliban were reluctant – and unable – to crack down on trade in mountainous, tribal areas. Nevertheless, to avoid taxes and detection, some entrepreneurs took to floating log rafts down the Kunar and Kabul rivers back into Pakistan. The Pakistani border authorities were happy to believe that all timber transports originated from Afghanistan and not from the North West Frontier Province.

Trips by EFG writers since the fall of the Taliban to the eastern parts of Afghanistan have reported claims by local leaders that they no longer allow logs to cross over to Pakistan. However, many towns and villages in Kunar province all have heavily stocked lumber yards. One can also detect smoke from lumber camps in the mountains above the river valley with cut timber and recently opened land scars clearly visible through binoculars. Lumber trafficking evidently has not been halted. In fact, much of the insecurity in the region, while attributed officially to the Taliban and Al Qa'eda is said to be the result of armed clashes between rival groups of lumber traffickers, many of whom are also involved in the drug and wildlife trade. Only in Nuristan does there appear to be more limited – and managed – logging.

As in many rural areas badly affected by nearly a quarter of a century of war, Kabul and other urban areas have been depleted of trees and other greenery. Fighting and lack of irrigation have caused the destruction of countless trees, but so have fuel shortages. After food, energy represents the second most important requirement among local populations, particularly during harsh winters. Chopped stumps or withered trees and bushes are still a common sight in the city's parks, gardens and streets. This has contributed to dust storms, poor health and an increasingly dry atmosphere. Kabul now faces a massive reforestation challenge.

Reforestation

As Afghanistan suffers from a chronic wood deficit for building, furniture and other uses, and there is little or no effective control over timber trafficking, some observers believe that all natural forests could disappear by as early as 2005. A policy of protection and reforestation, they warn, needs to be implemented as soon as possible. However, given the country's lack of central authority beyond the capital and any form of forestry management, such approaches will need to be developed on a local and regional basis. Much of this

Thorkell Thorkelsson/International Federation

responsibility will lie with the United Nations and various NGOs involved in agricultural and forestry rehabilitation.

The most relevant forestry and agroforestry programmes that could be replicated in Afghanistan are located in neighbouring Pakistan, China and India, where similar climatic and topographical conditions exist. Some aid coordinators suggest that donors should promote linkages with these countries to help formulate a practical reforestation and conservation strategy for Afghanistan. So far, however, no real strategy exists. The FAO's 1997 *Agricultural Strategy for Afghanistan,* for example, sent an environmentalist on its first mission but did not consider it worthwhile including him on its second; apparently there were "other priorities."

The 2003 UNEP survey has emphasised the need for a comprehensive agroforestry strategy as soon as possible. Specialists strongly recommend that any such approach should seek to increase the profitability of Afghan tree-based industries as a means of promoting economic development and social equity, notably programmes aimed at both men and women. Such programmes should devised in a manner that contributes to the conservation of soil, water and biodiversity.

Various aid programmes have begun planting saplings as a first step toward reforesting parts of the country but this is only a drop in the desert.

MADERA, a French agency, has re-established a number of plantations to replace those destroyed in the fighting. In Nangarhar province, saplings have been distributed to schoolchildren for growing in schools and homes. Another nursery will begin providing saplings for the Darunta Watershed Management Scheme. In Kabul, the local Afghan conservation group, the Society for Afghanistan's Volunteer Environmentalists (SAVE), is planting saplings as part of a World Food Programme (WFP) project to re-green the city's parks and other degraded sites. It also distributes trees for replanting among private gardens and for reforestation in the hills around the Afghan capital to check landslides and soil erosion. In Herat, Ismail Khan's government has been replanting city trees and renovating public parks, while other cities such as Jalalabad, Mazar-e-Sharif and Faizabad are also witnessing various but still limited attempts at reforestation.

Both agriculture and horticulture in Afghanistan have been developed traditionally in an agroforestry landscape. Poplars and mulberry trees are often planted in blocks or along the edges of fields and irrigation canals where they serve as boundaries, shade or windbreaks. Fruit and nut orchards are used for so-called 'inter-cropping' with vegetables grown among the trees themselves. Some trees can dramatically improve crop yields, while others can serve as useful timber, animal fodder and fuel. As a result, farmers and returnees could play a significant role in afforestation approaches.

The cash-cropping of trees for fruit and timber, for example, could serve to reduce a farmer's dependency on poppy cultivation as an alternative source of lucrative income. As it is, aid groups and local authorities are already seeking to respond to this challenge. In the Janikhil areas of Khost province, where an estimated 30 percent of trees have been denuded by the war and commercial logging, some NGOs are seeking to make local populations aware of the need to protect their forests. With German assistance, tree nurseries are being established as a source for future large-scale afforestation. Local populations, however, need to be convinced that forest products will contribute towards their income. Similar efforts are being made in other provinces (Kunar, Nuristan, Nangarhar, Laghman and Paktia) where uncontrolled deforestation is continuing.

ESSENTIAL DATA

- **During the 1970s, up to 5% of total land in Afghanistan was considered forested. Today, a 'guesstimate' based on recent satellite photographs and field surveys points to nearer 0.5%**
- **Satellite surveys indicate that over half of Afghanistan's forests have been destroyed by illegal or unmanaged logging since 1978. In provinces such as Paktia and Paktika, it may be as high as 80%**
- **Given the rate of current illicit lumber trafficking, some observers believe Afghanistan may have no real forests left by 2005**

ESSENTIAL AGENCIES

ADA, FAO, IUCN (including the TRAFFIC Network and The Wetlands Programme), MADERA, SEA, UNEP, SAVE, WWF-Pakistan

ESSENTIAL READING

Afghanistan: Post-Conflict Environmental Survey, UNEP with the Afghanistan Transitional Authority (Nairobi, February 2003). Available online at http://postconflict.unep.ch

Armed Conflicts and Humanitarian Concerns: how attention to environmental scarcity can prevent human tragedies, Jeffrey A. McNeely, Chief Scientist, IUCN (Gland, June 1997)

Afghanistan Agricultural Strategy, FAO (Rome, January 1997)

An overview and assessment of Afghanistan's environment, Tareq A. Formoli, M. Afzal Rashid and James P. Du Bruille, Afghanistan Horizon/Afghan Development Association (September, 1994)

Nature Reserves of the Himalaya and the Mountains of Central Asia, World Conservation Monitoring Centre, IUCN (Gland, Switzerland, 1993)

Opportunities for improved environmental management in Afghanistan, Nancy MacPherson, IUCN/UNOCA (Gland, Switzerland, May 1991)

Glossary

Adat: custom, habit (plural: Ada't).

Afghani: Afghanistan's currency, reissued in October 2002 when three noughts were knocked off its face value.

Afghan Mellat: Afghan Social Democratic Party.

Alem (plural: **ulama**)**:** religious scholar; graduate in higher Islamic studies from a *madrassa.*

Amir: leader, lord, sometimes king.

ATA: Afghanistan Transitional Administration, led by Hamid Karzai since the June 2002 Loya Jirga.

Basmachi: Islamic and traditionalist fighters who resisted Soviet rule in Central Asia; literally 'bandits.' The Soviets often referred to the *mujahideen* as *basmachi.*

Buzkashi: violent sport played in northern Afghanistan by two teams of horsemen fighting to drop a decapitated goat inside a chalk circle.

Chador: garment worn by women in accordance with Islamic law or local custom to cover required parts of the body.

Durand Line: boundary imposed by the British in 1893 on Amir Abdur Rahman which separated Afghanistan from British India. The line still splits Pashto-speaking tribes between Afghanistan and Pakistan's NWFP.

Durrani: Pashtun tribe living in south-western Afghanistan, from which the Royal family came. Rivals of the Ghilzai.

Fundamentalist: "for fundamentalism it is of paramount importance to get back to the scriptures, clearing away the obfuscation of tradition. It always seeks to return to some former state; it is characterised by the practice of re-reading texts, and a search for origins. The enemy is not modernity but tradition... fundamentalism sits uneasily within the political spectrum, for the "return to first things" may take many different forms... in Afghanistan fundamentalism, defined as a desire to get back to *shari'at* as the sole authority, is the natural attitude of the educated clergy, the *ulama,* whereas the *mullah* of the villages, who have not mastered the whole corpus of the law, are traditionalists and not fundamentalists." (Olivier Roy) The Taliban movement is considered to be traditionalist not fundamentalist.

Gelim: woven rug from Turkic tribes of northern Afghanistan. General Dostum's men were nicknamed the *gelim jam* (literally "carpet-baggers") because of their reputation for looting and pillaging.

Hajj: Islamic pilgrimage to Mecca.

Ghilzai: Pashtun tribe in south-eastern Afghanistan. Rivals of the Durrani.

Hadith: Prophet Mohammed's sayings and doctrines, handed down through a line of authorities.

Harakat-e-Inqilab-e-Islami: Islamic Revolutionary Movement of Mohammed Nabi Mohammedi (died 2002). The largest *mujahideen* movement in the early 1980s. A traditionalist party based on *madrassa* and tribal Pashtun support, many of its members defected to the Taliban. (SEE KEY PLAYERS)

Harakat-e-Islami: moderate *Shi'a mujahideen* party, led by Mohammed Asef Muhseni. Not currently a member of the 'united' *Shi'a* Hezb-e-Wahdat. (SEE KEY PLAYERS)

Hezb-e-Islami (Hekmatyar): Party of Islam (*Sunni*) led by Gulbuddin Hekmatyar; mainly radical Pashtun Islamists. (SEE KEY PLAYERS)

Hezb-e-Islami (Khalis): Party of Islam (*Sunni*) led by Mawlawi Younis Khalis; a splinter group from Hekmatyar's party; mainly moderate Pashtun Islamists. (SEE KEY PLAYERS)

Hezb-e-Wahdat-e-Islami: Party of Islamic Unity (*Shi'a*/Hazara) led by Karim Khalili. (SEE KEY PLAYERS)

Hojra: guest room or house.

Imam: leader of any Islamic community; leader of a collective Islamic prayer.

ISI: Inter Services Intelligence (Pakistani military intelligence).

Islam: literally, 'submission' to the commands of Allah, the omniscient and omnipotent God. A monotheistic religion which completes the prophetic Judaeo-Christian tradition and recognises Mohammed as the last of the prophets. The Five Pillars of Islam are: 1) *Shahadat*, the profession of faith in Allah and Mohammed, made daily after waking up and before going to sleep; 2) *Salat,* ritual prayer five times a day facing Mecca, performed by all Muslims over the age of 10; 3) *Zakat*, compulsory gift of 2.5% of annual savings to the poor; 4) *Sawm* (*Ruza* in Dari), abstaining from all bodily pleasures (including food) between dawn and sunset during *Ramadan* or *ramzan* (literally, "the month during which the Koran was sent down") 5) *Hajj,* pilgrimage to Mecca (in Saudi Arabia), which all physically able Muslims should make at least once in a lifetime.

Islamist movement: originated in the late 1950s in reaction to the process of Westernization and liberal secularization in Afghanistan. Professor Burhanuddin Rabbani was pronounced Chairman in 1971 and it developed into the Jamiat-e-Islami. Puritanical reformists more than fundamentalists.

Isma'ilis: *Shi'a* Islamic sect led by the Aga Khan, numbering some 300,000 people living in north-eastern Afghanistan, Pakistan, India, Tajikistan, Iran, Syria and Africa. They are 'Sevener' *Shi'as* as opposed to the 'Twelver' Hazaras. (SEE ETHNIC & TRIBAL)

Ittihad-e-Islami: Islamic Alliance (*Sunni*/Pashtun); an Islamist group led by Abdul Rasul Sayyaf. (SEE KEY PLAYERS)

Izzat: honour (collective and individual)

Jamaat-e-Islami: Society of Islam (Pakistani *Sunni* party)

Jamiat-e-Islami: Society of Islam (Afghan *Sunni* party) led by ex-President Burhanuddin Rabbani. Mainly moderate Tajik Islamists, its military commander was Ahmed Shah Massoud, a Panjshairi Tajik. One of the major parties in the anti-Taliban "Northern Alliance." (SEE KEY PLAYERS)

Jihad: literally 'struggle' – interpreted either as inner spiritual struggle, or wider holy war to defend or propagate Islam.

Jirga: Pashtun tribal assembly for resolution of disputes and decision-making; literally, 'circle', denoting the equality of participants.

Jumbesh-e-Melli Islami: National Islamic Movement (*Sunni*/Uzbek) led by General Abdul Rashid Dostum. (SEE KEY PLAYERS)

Kafir: non-Muslim, unbeliever; literally, 'denier.' The inhabitants of Kafiristan remained pagans until they were converted to Islam by the sword in 1896, after which their land became known as Nuristan, "Land of Light."

Karez: underground gravity-fed irrigation canal.

KHAD: *Khademat-e-Ittela'at Dowlati*, State Information Services. The former Afghan communist government's East German-trained secret police. Once headed by Dr Najibullah.

Khalifa: caliph. Arabic word meaning successor. Following the Prophet Mohammed's death in 632 AD/CE, four of his companions competed to succeed him as Caliph: Abu Bakr, Omar, Uthman and Ali.

Khalq: one of the two main factions of the People's Democratic Party of Afghanistan (PDPA). Literally, "People" or "Masses," it was mainly Pashtun and military in its membership. Formed in 1967, it was led by Nur Mohammed Taraki (April 1978 to September 1979) and Hafizullah Amin (September to December 1979). (SEE KEY PLAYERS)

Khan: leader of a clan, ethnic group, professional caste; socially/locally appointed (unlike a *malik*).

Kuchi: nomad.

Loya Jirga: Great Council; highest representative institution in the Afghan state. Met in 1964, 2002 and 2003.

Madrassa: school for secondary or advanced Islamic studies, usually attached to a large mosque.

Malik: chief of a tribe or clan, usually one appointed by the state, as opposed to a *khan*; literally 'ruler.'

Masjid: mosque; **Masjid-e-Jami:** Friday Mosque.

Mawlawi: graduate from a *madrassa* (college of higher Islamic studies); similar to an *alem.*

Mazar: monument built over the tomb of an important figure; literally, "place of pilgrimage."

Melmastia: Pashtun hospitality, especially the feeding of guests.

Mir: lord or ruler, especially of Hazaras.

Mirab: someone elected and paid to ensure local water rights are respected.

Mujahideen: soldiers of Islam or holy warriors. A **mujahed** is one engaged in *jihad; mujahed* is also an adjective.

Mullah: a village-level religious leader and preacher.

Namus: Pashtun honour, law, principle; those things a man must defend to preserve his honour.

Nasr: Victory, a radical Islamist *Shi'a* Afghan group once supported by Iranian Hazaras.

Northern Alliance: anti-Taliban military alliance between the mainly Tajik Jamiat-e-Islami party of Rabbani and Massoud, the mainly Uzbek forces of General Dostum, centred on Mazar-e-Sharif and the predominantly Hazara Hezb-e-Wahdat-e-Islami. Replaced the earlier Shura-e-Hamahangi (Supreme Coordination Council, an alliance of the northern-based forces of General Dostum and Hezb-e-Islami-Hekmatyar) and Shura-e-Nezar Shomal (Supervisory Council of the North, an alliance led by Massoud). Allies of the US-led Coalition which toppled the Taliban in late 2001. Also known as the United Front.

NWFP: North West Frontier Province of Pakistan, largely Pashtun-inhabited. Part of Afghanistan since 1747 but assimilated under British control and divided up from Afghanistan by the Durand Line of 1893. Consisting of a number of tribal agencies it is today a semi-autonomous region not fully answerable to Islamabad.

PDPA: People's Democratic Party of Afghanistan. The Afghan Marxist party, founded in 1965 with the aim of turning the feudal society of Afghanistan into a socialist state. Rivalry led to a split in 1967, with Nur Mohammed Taraki creating the Khalq ('Masses') faction and Babrak Karmal forming the Parcham ('Flag') faction. Pressure from the Soviets caused the two factions to re-unite in 1977. The PDPA came to power after staging the April 1978 Saur Revolution which deposed (and killed) President Daoud. Taraki became President of the new Democratic Republic of Afghanistan, but was (murdered and) replaced first by Hafizullah Amin and then Karmal, on the eve of the Soviet invasion. Dr Najibullah replaced Karmal in 1986 and re-named the party Hezb-e-Watan ("Fatherland Party"), but it was ousted from power and dissolved when Najib's government fell to the *mujahideen* in 1992. The PDPA government is still referred to as the 'regime.' (SEE HISTORY)

Parcham: one of the two main factions of the People's Democratic Party of Afghanistan (PDPA). Literally, 'Flag' or 'Banner', its membership was mainly non-Pashtun intelligentsia and government officials. The party was formed in 1968 and led by Babrak Karmal, becoming dominant over the Khalq faction when Karmal was installed as the country's President by the Soviets in December 1979.

Pardah: seclusion or separation of women from men; literally, 'curtain.'

Pashto: the language spoken by Pashtuns.

Pashtun: also called *Pakhtun, Pukhtun* and *Pathan*. The largest ethnic/tribal group in Afghanistan. *Sunni* Muslim. (SEE ETHNIC & TRIBAL)

Pashtunwali: Pashtun tribal code.

Pir: religious leader of the Sufi order; literally "the old one."

Qabila: large and established tribe.

Qazi: Islamic judge.

Qizilbash: literally "red head"; Dari-speaking *Shi'a* Afghans descended from the 18th Century Turkic contingent left behind by Iran.

Qu'ran: the holy book of Islam.

Sardar: chief or military commander.

Sayyad: someone descended from the Prophet (through his daughter Fatima).

Shah: king (Persian).

Shari'a: Islamic law; literally, "the path to follow." The primary sources for Shari'a are the *Qu'ran* and the *Sunnah*, while its secondary sources are *Qiyas* (analogical reasoning by Islamic jurists) and *Ijma* (consensus of Islamic jurists). Rejected by the Communists in the 1980s but reintroduced as the basis of the Islamic State of

Afghanistan by both the *mujahideen* (1992-94) and the Taliban (1994-2001). According to Afghan expert Ali Wardak: "past experiences show that it is only that version of *shari'a* that is in harmony with Afghan cultural traditions, existing legal norms and fundamental principles of human rights that can make important contributions to a credible post-war justice system in Afghanistan."

Shi'a: Muslim sect which holds that leadership of the Islamic community should be by dynastic succession from Imam Ali (cousin and son-in-law of the Prophet Mohammed) and his descendants. Their view conflicts with the *Sunni* principle that Mohammed's successor or caliph should be elected. *Shi'as* divide into three main sects according to which of their *imams* is believed to be the "Expected One", who will return on judgement day: the 5th, 7th or 12th. In Afghanistan the Hazaras and Qizilbash are mostly 'twelvers', as in Iran; but the Isma'ilis are 'seveners.' *Shi'a* represent around 15% of Afghanistan's population. They are followers of the *Ja'afari* jurisprudential school.

Shura: council, assembly.

Sufism: Islamic mysticism; emerged in the 8th Century; seeks personal experience of union with God, rather than rational knowledge of God; long in conflict with more scholastic *Sunni* Islam. (Afghan contemporary *Sufi* orders include Qadiri and Naqshbandi).

Sunnah: the statements and deeds of the Prophet Mohammed.

Sunni: Muslim sect which holds that Mohammed's successor or caliph should be elected. Their view conflicts with the *Shi'a* principle that leadership of the Islamic community should be by dynastic succession from Imam Ali (cousin and son-in-law of the Prophet Mohammed) and his descendants. *Sunnis* constitute up to 85% of the population of Afghanistan, including most Pashtuns. They are followers of the *Hanafi* school.

Taliban (singular: **talib):** religious students (literally, 'seekers') from a *madrassa*; the Taliban are a Pashtun-based traditionalist armed political group which emerged as a powerful force in November 1994 and took Kabul in September 1996, before being toppled by the US-led Coalition and its Northern Alliance allies in late 2001. (SEE TALIBAN and Traditionalist below)

Traditionalist: "the desire to freeze society so that it conforms to the memory of what it once was: it is society as described by [our] grandfathers. In this vision history and tradition are merged; the historical development of society is effaced in favour of an imaginary timeless realm under attack from pernicious modernity. Traditionalism can never provide the basis for any coherent political programme; it is riddled with nostalgia and its politics naturally incline towards all that is conservative." (Olivier Roy) The Taliban movement is considered to be traditionalist not fundamentalist.

Ulama (singular: **alem**): academics specializing in Islamic learning and traditions.

Umma: pan-Islamic community, or Islamic nation.

United Front: alternative name for the Northern Alliance. Karzai's defence minister, the Panjshairi Tajik Mohammed Fahim, is one of the United Front's principal leaders (SEE KEY PLAYERS).

Wahabiism: puritanical Saudi Arabian Islamic sect.

Wali: governor of a province.

Watan: Literally means homeland; Fatherland Party (see PDPA).

Zakat: Islamic tax on capital, payable to the poor, clergy etc.

Health

In a remote village in the mountainous region of Ghor, a visiting Belgian doctor is puzzled by a stream of patients presenting blackened legs and bleeding gums. Some are feverish, raising fears of a highly infectious disease – perhaps transmitted by livestock. After an international team of health experts is helicoptered in from Kabul, the disease is identified as scurvy, a micronutrient deficiency that is rarely found anymore. This, however, is Afghanistan, where diseases that have long ago been brought under control in most countries continue to cause widespread death and disability.

With an average life expectancy of just 46 years, Afghanistan's human misery index competes for the last place on international lists – alongside the failed states of Sierra Leone and Liberia. A quarter of a century of widespread conflict, extreme poverty and relentless drought have so decimated the country's social services that an estimated two thirds of the population still have no access to health care whatsoever.

For the first time since fighting broke out in the summer of 1978, however, Afghanistan has a real chance of making inroads into the once seemingly impossible job of trying to provide basic health care for its people. A recent editorial in the widely respected British health journal, *Lancet*, claims Afghanistan is making good headway on tackling its health crisis. It has commended the Ministry of Health's staff for having identified the major health problems and working well with donors. Working hard too are many of the key NGOs, some of which have been in Afghanistan since the early days of the war, including the Swedish Committee for Afghanistan, Médecins sans Frontières, Médecins du Monde and Aide Medicale Internationale.

The problem, however, is that the donors have yet to commit the funds needed to really turn Afghanistan's disastrous health situation around. Furthermore, renewed insecurity in southern and eastern parts of the country may prevent many aid agencies and government services from setting up new operations, thus denying poor, largely Pashtun, populations access to health care.

The Afghan government says that equitable access to health services for all Afghans is its main priority. Its plan of action includes the development of a basic package of services defining the medical interventions to be made available throughout the country. The key areas are maternal and newborn health, child health and immunization, public nutrition, communicable diseases and mental health. The most crucial component of the plan is to extend health services to rural areas, where medical facilities are few and qualified health staff even fewer, if any.

Currently, there is a concentration of health facilities in urban areas. Kabul, for example, has 12 percent of the population but nearly half of all the hospital beds in the country. There is also a poor distribution of health workers throughout the country. In Kabul, there is one doctor per 1,000 people. In the central province of Bamiyan there is estimated to be just one doctor per 100,000 people.

At least 50 of Afghanistan's 330 districts have no health centres at all. Where centres do exist, patients living in remote or outlying areas often have to walk or ride for hours, even days, to reach treatment. The impact of the lack of health services in rural areas was tragically revealed in late autumn 2002 during an outbreak of the childhood killer whooping cough, in the northern part of Badakhshan. By the time international aid agencies and the Ministry of Health were able to organize an emergency vaccination response, weeks after the outbreak began, dozens of children had already choked to death.

The whooping cough outbreak is indicative of the country's poor immunization coverage (less than 40 percent) that contributes to the deaths of a quarter of all Afghan children before their fifth birthday. The main culprits are acute respiratory illnesses during the winter months and diarrhoeal diseases in the summer. In Afghanistan, many children are sentenced to early deaths simply because basic antibiotics and skilled health practitioners are not available to diagnose and cure them of routine diseases. In central Afghanistan's mountainous Hazarajat region and other isolated areas with long winters and poor road access, this situation is particularly acute.

Until President Najibullah, the last communist ruler of Afghanistan, was overthrown by the *mujahideen* in 1992, Kabul and the other main urban centres had relatively adequate health services. The capital and other cities had remained largely under government control throughout the decade-long Soviet-Afghan war and the remaining three years of PDPA administration following the Red Army pullout in February 1989. This enabled basic health services to continue operating. In select rural areas held by the guerrillas, basic but often extremely limited health care was provided by a small handful of humanitarian aid organizations.

After the fall of Najibullah, the Hezb-e-Wahdat resistance faction seized control of the area where Kabul University is located. Bitter fighting ensued, which kept the university's medical school closed for more than three years. Eventually, Ahmed Shah Massoud's Jamiat-e-Islami and other allied *mujahideen* took control of Kabul, and the medical faculty resumed teaching.

When the Taliban seized control of Kabul in 1996, many medical students, especially women, were thrown out or fled Afghanistan. Those who remained in university under the Taliban received poor and outdated medical training. A generation of Afghan medical staff subsequently lost the opportunity to pursue a decent education. Although there isn't a shortage of medical doctors, the overall quality of Afghan medical personnel is far below international standards.

Health care under the Taliban was severely segregated and strict rules dictated how male doctors could examine female patients. The Taliban regime's

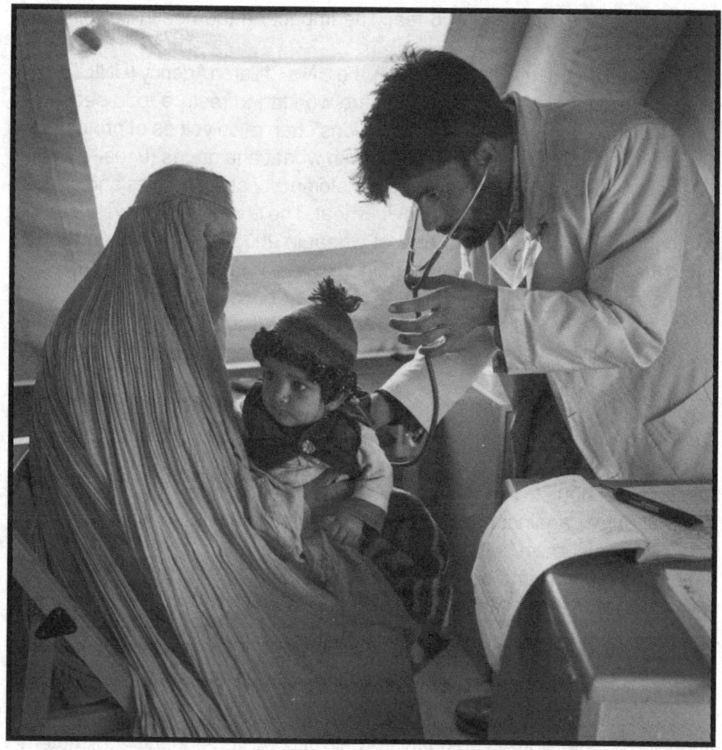

Thorkell Thorkelsson/International Federation

relations with NGOs, the traditional providers of medical services, deteriorated and eventually women were left without any real form of health care.

International efforts, strengthened following the collapse of the Taliban in late 2001, are now beginning to yield the first real benefits for Afghanistan's population. In 2002, 11 million children nationwide were immunized against measles. Prior to this campaign, measles accounted for up to 20 percent of all deaths among children under five in Afghanistan. In addition, polio – which used to be the primary cause of disability amongst Afghan children – has been nearly eradicated.

At the same time, large-scale vaccination programmes alone will not be enough to safeguard future generations of Afghans. About half of children under five years of age are stunted due to chronic malnutrition and up to 10 percent have acute malnutrition, making them far more susceptible to infectious diseases. Ensuring Afghan children have access to good nutrition is far more complex than simply placing health workers and medicines evenly around the country. In many areas, fighting and drought have caused impoverished families to lose their land. Families who had land have not been able to cultivate it because they have no seeds. Like the rivers that once wove their way through Afghanistan's rugged mountains, local economies have shrivelled and dried up. Without incomes, families are forced to live on subsistence levels of food –

often no more than bread and tea. The impact on the health of children is immeasurable.

The World Food Programme (WFP), the UN's Children Agency (UNICEF) and other international aid organizations are working to restore food security to endangered communities, but their actions often raise voices of protest. One argument is that by providing families with wheat and grains (usually fortified with essential micronutrients), they are distorting local economies and discouraging farmers from growing their own wheat. The end of the four-year drought in most areas produced a surplus of wheat in 2003, but numerous farmers found their expected markets undermined by free WFP distribution of cereals – albeit primarily directed at returning refugees and vulnerable populations (SEE AGRICULTURE). On the other hand, without food support, it is likely that the long-term health of yet another generation of Afghan children will be threatened.

Reproductive health in Afghanistan is atrocious. Although girls who survive to puberty in major urban centres now stand a greater chance of enjoying a healthy adulthood, little has changed in rural areas, where stalwart traditions continue to impose grave restrictions on female Afghans. The international outcry against the Taliban's repressive policies for women and the impact on their health helped galvanize subsequent donor support for improving gynaecological and obstetric care, particularly in Kabul. Training of midwives and renovation of the referral hospital Rabi'a Balkhi (the major maternity centre in Kabul) are all helping to improve women's health, but they do little to address to deeply embedded cultural and social conditions that impact so strongly on the health of Afghan women.

Early marriage, lack of family planning methods and widespread ignorance about the danger signs in pregnancies help account for Afghanistan's maternal mortality rate being the highest in the world, next to Sierra Leone. In Badakhshan, a recent maternal mortality assessment team recorded the highest ever death rate linked to pregnancy in the world – 6,500 out of 100,000. On average, 16 Afghan women per 1,000 will die from complications of pregnancy – one woman every 45 minutes. Afghan women have a one in seven chance of dying as a result of pregnancy (40 percent of all deaths of women of child-bearing age). In Africa, this rate is one in 12 whereas in Europe, the chance is less than one in 2,000. The knock-on effects of Afghanistan's distressing maternal mortality rate are significant: when a mother dies in childbirth, her child has only one chance in four of surviving until its first birthday.

Until antenatal care and deliveries by trained midwives and health workers become routine, the high level of maternal deaths will only continue. Less

Childhood killers

According to UNICEF (1999), each year 309,000 Afghan children under five years old die, mainly due to:

1. **Diarrhoea**
2. **Acute respiratory infections**
3. **Measles**

Soap opera cleans up

Effective health education programmes for the population in general, and for mothers and children in particular, can significantly reduce the incidence of medical conditions presented to clinics and hospitals. The BBC soap opera "New Home, New Life", to which as much as three-quarters of the population avidly listens, plays an important role in this respect. Issues such as the importance of young women receiving tetanus inoculations, personal health and hygiene, safe birthing practices and the rational use of pharmaceutical drugs have all been addressed through the characters of the drama.

One BBC listener from Rabat village remarked: "Our Paktia people are uneducated. When children are born they take dirty knives from the kitchen and cut the cord. After cutting the cord they put henna, ashes or powder on the cord. But now after listening to the drama most people have stopped this, including my family." *JW*

than 10 percent of deliveries are attended by trained health workers. Traditional birth attendants, with little or no training, are still the norm. Their lack of skills doesn't only affect mothers: it is not unusual to find traditional birth attendants in rural areas encouraging women to spread mud on the umbilical cords of newborn babies. Consequently, death rates of babies from neo-natal tetanus (brought on by dirt infection) remain staggeringly high in most provinces.

The greatest dangers for women are complications in pregnancy that require emergency obstetric care or other rapid intervention. Only 17 of the country's 124 hospitals are well-enough equipped to practice caesarean sections. It will take years before delivering a child in Afghanistan can be considered a routine and safe procedure. Rapid improvement of Afghanistan's emergency obstetric services continues to be a top priority for international organizations, and training programmes are under way across the country to strengthen the skills of midwives and obstetricians.

Given the dismal statistics related to women's reproductive health, a widespread family planning campaign would be another important component in saving women's lives. To date, however, the international community has been slow in funding the type of support required to have a real impact on birth rates. The UN Population Agency (UNFPA) says providing contraceptives and introducing them to rural areas is one of the main areas of focus for reproductive health. However, there has still been no large-scale family programming initiative (such as Iran's or Tunisia's) carried out in Afghanistan.

Partly, this is because of a reluctance among inter-governmental bodies to take on family planning as a health issue, on the grounds that limiting the number of births of a given population might run contrary to religious and social convictions. At the same time, however, many aid workers note that ordinary Afghan males often request "pills to stop their wives from having so many babies" and focus groups have revealed a keen interest among both men and women to practice birth control. The Ministry has named family planning as a priority component in the proposed basic health package, but such services are still far beyond the reach of most ordinary Afghans.

Sexuality remains a taboo subject in Afghanistan. Any medical intervention that requires a male doctor to have contact with a female is often refused by the woman and her family. Although most women prefer to be treated by a female doctor, 40 percent of all health facilities do not have a single woman on their staff. Therefore, an important priority for the new government has been to ensure that female health workers displaced during the Taliban regime return to the health sector and that new professionals are trained. An accelerated training programme for female midwives is being carried out by the Ministry of Health with NGOs. At present, however, far too few women regularly receive adequate health treatment – by either male or female health practitioners.

Women are further affected by Afghanistan's invisible but most prevalent health crisis. Experts estimate that up to 50 percent of the Afghan population suffers from some level of mental distress. Mental health problems that have been routinely treated in most countries have been left unattended in Afghanistan for decades. The full extent of Afghanistan's mental health crisis is not known because of the general lack of statistical health information. Although it is presumed that depression and anxiety disorders are extremely common in Afghanistan, there has yet to be a large-scale internationally-driven effort to address the problem.

Innovative NGO programmes in Herat and Nangarhar to sensitize medical staff to mental health issues and to maintain a regular supply of essential mental health drugs are providing much needed services. The World Health Organization (WHO) has been training general practitioners to recognize the symptoms of mental disorder and treat patients as part of primary health care services. However, as in so many parts of the Afghan health sector, these initiatives are too few to have a major impact on the overall population. In general, Afghanistan continues to limp along with an outdated and counterproductive hospitalized approach, rather than integrating mental health into primary health care services. Ensuring quality care for those Afghans with serious mental health diseases, such as schizophrenia, is a difficult challenge. Sadly, it is still possible to visit the dilapidated mental health hospital in Kabul and see patients chained to their beds.

Undoubtedly, the greatest problem facing Afghanistan's health sector is how to control endemic infectious diseases that stem from a destroyed infrastructure and continue to have enormous fatal consequences for the population. With only 23 percent of the population having access to safe water and some 12 percent with access to adequate sanitation, waterborne diseases – especially diarrhoea – are highly dangerous. Malaria has made a ferocious return to Afghanistan with some 3-4 million cases a year, of which around 20-30 percent are the deadly *falciparum* variety, according to the London School of Hygiene and Tropical Medicine. This is a country where malaria had been brought largely under control by the time war first broke out nearly 25 years ago.

The new Afghan government is faced with a massive task to rapidly expand health services to large numbers of people to treat killers such as tuberculosis

Malaria: novel solutions

Malaria is a disease of poverty and decay that flourishes in times of war. It has become a major health problem in Afghanistan owing to the breakdown of the country's public health system. Since the 1980s malaria has increased fivefold and *falciparum malaria* – the potentially lethal form more normally associated with Africa – has increased 100-fold due to the spread of drug resistant forms. Yet before the war, Afghanistan ran one of the more successful malaria control programmes in Asia.

The pre-war control strategy was to spray houses with insecticides such as DDT to kill mosquitoes and break the malaria transmission cycle. UNHCR adopted a similar strategy, using more modern insecticides, in Pakistan's refugee camps during the 1990s. This showed that spray campaigns can be very successful when properly managed. But the problem with house spraying is the expense, and the need to respray annually, so spray campaigns have been curtailed in the camps in recent years in line with cuts in aid to refugees. In Afghanistan house spraying is no longer a viable strategy as the scale of the problem is too large and the planning and organization required are impossible to achieve under current conditions.

An alternative strategy is needed: one that is cheap and simple to implement and gives long-lasting protection. Bednets are an old method of personal protection in South Asia but were rarely used by Afghans. Research has shown that when bednets are coated with *pyrethroid* insecticides, mosquitoes are deterred from biting through the mesh and protection is much improved. A study in an Afghan refugee camp showed that 'treated' nets give 80% protection against malaria and given the right promotion are readily adopted by Afghans. In 1992 several health sector NGOs, led by HealthNET International, launched a project to sell subsidized bednets in eastern Afghanistan. To date, 500,000 family-size nets have been sold through NGO clinics and by mobile teams, protecting an estimated 1.5 million Afghans. So far there is no sign of the market becoming saturated. Afghanistan is well on the way to becoming a bednet-using culture. Sales campaigns around Jalalabad have led to over 50% of families buying nets and the incidence of *falciparum* malaria has fallen by 70% in these districts. Stimulated by HealthNET's success, UNHCR has adopted a similar strategy in refugee camps in Pakistan

What started as a simple project to promote self protection has become Afghanistan's primary malaria control strategy (with the beneficiaries rather than the state bearing much of the cost). As government remains limited in its capacity to implement malaria control, the best strategy for the future is to ensure a steady supply of nets and insecticide through the private sector and local NGOs, and to make sure that those who are most impoverished have access to subsidized nets so they too can benefit from this novel solution.

Contributed and updated by Mark Rowland,
London School of Hygiene & Tropical Medicine

Malaria statistics

	1977	2003
Annual incidence:	80,000	3-4 million
Lethal P. Falciparum:	1%	20-30%
Chloroquine resistance:	none	over 80% in eastern Afghanistan

Sources: WHO 1997, London School of Hygiene and Tropical Medicine 2003

(TB). Unlike most other countries where young men make up the caseload, Afghanistan's young women are most susceptible to the killer lung disease. Of the 15,000 people who die each year of TB in Afghanistan, at least two thirds are women, many of whom are likely to have lived their lives in small, cramped airless homes – a natural haven for the spread of TB bacteria.

One of the most cost-effective interventions that could have a great impact, if it were carried out properly, is widespread health education. However, health promotion and education is mostly on an *ad hoc* NGO-led basis, with little coordination through the Ministry of Health. The result is that simple messages – such as basic hygiene – are only reaching target audiences in scattered regions of Afghanistan. Health officials familiar with remote areas, such as Nuristan, note that widespread ignorance of basic health concepts – clean latrines, washing hands, nutrition – is an overriding factor in high morbidity and mortality rates. The development of mass media as a means of transmitting health programming has yet to be properly exploited. There is tremendous scope for greatly expanding health education programmes in Afghanistan as a basic tool for combating deadly diseases such as TB. Additionally, effective health education is the greatest weapon in ensuring HIV/AIDS – still rare in Afghanistan – does not spread.

Although there is general agreement on the top priorities for recovery of the health care sector, the international community differs over the best approach to follow. A Joint Donor's Mission in 2002 recommended that Afghanistan build upon the fact that 80 percent of health care facilities are supported by NGOs, by adopting a controversial programme known as PPA (Performance-based Partnership Agreement). Under this scheme, Afghanistan would follow the example of Cambodia's post-conflict recovery, whereby the Ministry of Health contracts NGOs to provide health services to its provinces. The NGOs would be expected to deliver the ministry's basic package of health service to the local population in exchange for a fee. The World Bank has already provided US$ 60 million for the PPA programme, thereby jumpstarting Afghanistan's push to deliver health care to rural areas.

Nevertheless, US$ 60 million is still only a fraction of the funds required to repair a health care system that some would argue is simply beyond repair. Instead, Afghanistan has to start again from scratch – without anywhere near the funds required to ensure a satisfactory health status for the Afghan people. The sad reality is that – despite the tremendous efforts of NGOs, the rejuvenated Ministry of Health and UN agencies – Afghanistan is simply no longer at the forefront of donors' attention, and the health of the Afghan people is simply not a priority for what few international funds are available. Consequently, it is likely that Afghanistan will continue to share the bottom rungs of the human development ladder for decades to come.

Contributed by Loretta Hieber-Girardet, who works as a public information strategist with the World Health Organization in Geneva. She served as the WHO spokesperson in Kabul during 2002-03.

ESSENTIAL DATA

- **Average life expectancy: 46 years**
- **Percentage of population with no access to health care: estimated 70%**
- **25% of all Afghan children die before their 5th birthday – mainly from acute respiratory illnesses and diarrhoea**
- **In 2002, 11 million children were immunized against measles**
- **Half of all children under-5 are stunted due to chronic malnutrition; 10% have acute malnutrition**
- **On average, 16 out of every 1,000 Afghan women die from complications of pregnancy**
- **40% of all health facilities lack any female staff**
- **23% of Afghans have access to safe water; 12% to adequate sanitation**
- **3-4 million Afghans suffer from malaria each year**
- **15,000 Afghans die of TB each year**

ESSENTIAL AGENCIES

AMI, ARCS, Emergency, ICRC, IFRC, MDM, MSF, SCF, TDH, UNFPA, UNICEF, World Bank, WHO
Ministry of Health

ESSENTIAL READING

The public health system in Afghanistan, Ronald Waldman and Homaira Hanif, Afghanistan Research and Evaluation Unit (Kabul, June 2002)
Reconstruction of the Afghanistan Health Sector: a Preliminary Assessment of Needs and Opportunities, December 2001-January 2002, World Health Organization (Cairo, 2002)
Maternal and Child Health Home Visiting Programme, Kabul, Afghanistan, 1996-2001, Terre des Hommes (Kabul, 2001)

Key Players

The following potted biographies of key players in Afghanistan include both the quick and the dead. One feature of Afghan politics is that even when players disappear from the scene for a few months or years, they can never be ruled out from reappearing in force. When northern Uzbek warlord General Dostum was ousted by his one-time ally General Malik in 1997, he fled to 'exile' in Turkey. But he returned with a vengeance four months later to take over command of the United Front (also known as the Northern Alliance) in Mazar-e-Sharif and subsequently helped the US-led Coalition overthrow the Taliban in late 2001. Gulbuddin Hekmatyar, a Pashtun Islamic extremist heavily supported by the Pakistanis and Americans during the 1980s, was finally forced to leave Afghanistan for Iran as a 'spent force' during the 1990s. But he returned in 2002 and declared *jihad* against his former benefactors, the Americans, who promptly branded him a 'terrorist'. Other key players, notably assassinated northern leader Ahmed Shah Massoud, are possibly more influential today dead than alive.

ABDULLAH, Abdullah

Minister of Foreign Affairs. An eloquent and smartly dressed member of the so-called 'Panjshairi Mafia', Abdullah was a close associate of Ahmed Shah Massoud. Born in 1960 to a Pashtun father and an ethnic Tajik mother, Abdullah is a qualified doctor who speaks several languages, including fluent English and French. He sees his loyalties as principally pro-Tajik, although he has made efforts to stress his Afghan identity to diminish criticism of propping up the United Front's dominance in government.

Dr Abdullah joined Jamiat-e-Islami in the early 1980s as part of the anti-Soviet resistance. He spent several years in Pakistan with frequent trips abroad on behalf of the *mujahideen*. He became one of Massoud's principal spokesmen following the capture of Kabul in 1992 and was subsequently appointed deputy foreign minister for the United Front. In April 2001, he accompanied Massoud on his first European trip to Brussels and Paris, where he met with the French government to appeal for support against the Taliban and to warn of the activities of Al Qa'eda. Following Massoud's assassination on 9 September 2001, Abdullah became the United Front's official face for the international media during the US bombing of the Taliban, and foreign minister in the post-

Taliban interim administration. As with many Afghans, Abdullah had only one name, but when repeatedly quizzed by journalists for his full attribution, he kept telling them: "Abdullah…Abdullah". Hence his now double-barrelled identity. He lives partly in Kabul but seeks to return as often as possible to a lavish villa in the Panjshair Valley.

AKBARI, Mohammed

Shi'a leader of the smaller of the two Hezb-e-Wahdat groups.

ALI, Hazrat

Nangarhar warlord. Artificially built up by the Americans to help them in their battle against Al Qa'eda and the Taliban, Hazrat Ali is a tribal Pashai from north-eastern Afghanistan who now controls much of what goes on in Jalalabad and the surrounding region, primarily inhabited by Pashtuns. He and his men are resented by many locals who see him as an outsider imposed by US-led Coalition Forces. Although a powerful commander with very close ties to Defence Minister Fahim, Ali is becoming increasingly involved in 'import-export' activities, which some well-informed aid agencies believe include drug trafficking. During 2003, the UN reported that Nangarhar overtook Helmand as Afghanistan's top opium-producing province. Ali is said to be on "good but rivalrous terms" with Nangarhar governor Din Mohammed who, Ali has complained, may have helped Bin Laden, foreign militants and the Taliban escape the clutches of Coalition Forces.

ARSALA, Hedayat Amin

One of Afghanistan's four Vice Presidents. A former World Bank official with a long record of close involvement in Afghanistan's resistance struggle since the 1980s, Arsala joined the National Islamic Front to become a key Gaylani advisor. A Western-orientated Pashtun with a keen interest in education and reform, he was named Foreign Minister of the Islamic State of Afghanistan in 1992. However, he resigned when Rabbani took over as president. One of Afghanistan's few effective technocrats, Arsala was appointed Minister of Finance under Karzai's interim administration and then Vice President following the *Loya Jirga* in June 2002.

ATTA, Mohammed Usted

Northern, ethnic Tajik warlord. A former Jamiat-e-Islami commander of Ahmed Shah Massoud, Atta now operates as Defence Minister Fahim's principal man in the north. Since the fall of the Taliban, Atta – a robust commander in his forties – has been at constant loggerheads with Uzbek warlord Abdul Rashid Dostum. Repeated fighting between their two factions during 2002-03 led to scores of deaths and prompted many civilians to flee the region, as well as putting off many internally displaced Afghans from returning to the north. As ally of Marshal Fahim and supporter of the Kabul government, Atta is very much the 'boss' in Mazar. He runs a tight ship with a close interest in what goes on politically, economically, educationally and otherwise in the region. He commands his own highly respectful cabinet of advisors who are there at his beck and call to administer his affairs. Atta maintains close relations with the Americans and is definitely the man to see for getting anything done in Balkh province. As with certain other warlords, Atta now tends to appear in a formal suit rather than military uniform and has a peculiar penchant for woollen ski caps. He resents the title 'warlord', seeing himself more as a respected 'amir' with a political future in the new Afghanistan.

BARIYAN, Nasirullah

Head of the Abdul Haq Foundation. Younger brother of assassinated leaders Abdul Qadir and Abdul Haq, plus Nangarhar governor Din Mohammed, Nasirullah fought in the *jihad* and lived for years in Germany. As head of the Abdul Haq Foundation, he has developed an impressive strategic business plan for the development of Nangarhar province. Bariyan seeks to push through the family foundation with the constructive slogan: "Put out the guns, pick up the pens."

BIN LADEN, Osama

Saudi Islamic militant and declared terrorist. Described by the CIA as the financier and brains of Islamic terrorism, Bin Laden achieved global renown with his alleged involvement in the airplane assaults against New York's World Trade Center and other US targets on September 11, 2001. The US government has still to furnish hard evidence that he was directly implicated, although apparent statements by Bin Laden himself seem to suggest that he had prior knowledge of the incidents, carried out by his own Al Qa'eda organization. While some believe the Saudi militant is dead, following the US-led military intervention in Afghanistan, others say that he is currently operating – possibly suffering from kidney problems and injuries sustained during US attacks – from hideouts in the mountainous tribal areas of Pakistan along the Afghan border. Various audio recordings have emerged since the US intervention that are alleged to be the voice of Bin Laden.

A strikingly tall man, Bin Laden comes from a wealthy merchant family in Saudi Arabia. He is a long-time opponent of the Saudi government, particularly for allowing American troops to be stationed on Saudi soil – a situation which prompted him to declare *jihad* against the United States worldwide. During the 1980s, Bin Laden supported the *mujahideen* while pushing for a purist Islamic state that had little to do with Afghan culture. He lost around 500 of his men, some of them at the hands of the *mujahideen,* who often resented the arrogance of such outsider *Arabi* who were in effect part of an Islamic foreign legion. When the Soviets withdrew, Bin Laden became disillusioned with Afghan infighting and left for Sudan. Despite having enjoyed informal links with US intelligence officers during the Soviet-Afghan war, the Saudi militant was believed to have been responsible for a truck-bomb attack killing 19 American airmen in the Saudi city of Dhahran (there is still confusion as to what extent the Americans were involved with Bin Laden and whether they helped provide him with support against the Red Army). Arab and Western governments alike blame his supporters for fomenting insurrections in Egypt, Algeria and Saudi Arabia.

He returned to Afghanistan in the summer of 1994 on board an Ariana Afghan Airlines plane with the full knowledge and authorization of the *mujahed* government in Kabul. He stayed in Afghanistan, first as a guest of former resistance politician Younis Khalis and then, from May 1997 onwards, as an ally of Taliban leader Mullah Omar, based in Kandahar. In return for his assistance in financing the Taliban battle for control of Afghanistan, Bin Laden received protection – on the condition that he not speak out against the Saudi government. This resulted in recognition by Saudi Arabia in June 1997 of the Taliban movement. Bin Laden was suspected of having been involved in other terror attacks prior to the September 11, 2001 assaults. These included attacks against US soldiers in Saudi Arabia as well as the first bombing in 1993 of the World Trade Center, which killed seven people. Bin Laden now has a US$25 million price on his head, and is being sought by the Americans and the international community on numerous counts of terrorism.

BRAHIMI, Lakhdar

Special Representative of the United Nations Secretary General, 2001-2003. Considered the epitome of the dedicated UN official, former Algerian Foreign Minister Lakhdar Brahimi has been involved with Afghanistan since July 1997, when he was first sent as Kofi Annan's special envoy to seek an end to the long running conflict. However, the refined but tough diplomat resigned in disgust in October 1999 when it became clear that neighbouring countries such as Pakistan and Iran had little or no intention of reining in the warring factions they supported. Persuaded by Annan to return to Afghanistan in October 2001, Brahimi clearly voiced his concerns with regard to the limits to UN action and stressed the need for comprehensive action by Afghans themselves. He was closely involved in the December 2001 Bonn Agreement and the setting up of the Afghan Interim Administration.

While many Afghans, international aid workers and diplomats hold Brahimi in high esteem, he was heavily criticized for over-compromising with warlords at the June 2002 Emergency *Loya Jirga*. Much to the fury of experienced UN and other observers, Brahimi allowed non-elected warlords and factional operatives, who had originally been excluded, to participate. Their presence, including armed members of the United Front's secret police, intimidated numerous delegates, who felt the process had been hijacked. Brahimi was further criticized for having acquiesced too readily to US pressures to sideline former Afghan King Zahir Shah in favour of Karzai.

Overall, however, Brahimi has sought fervently to support Afghanistan's recovery, such as through the creation of a draft constitution and in keeping the peace process on track. He has warned of the dangers of growing insecurity in many parts of the country and of the need for the International Security Assistance Force (ISAF) to play a more assertive role outside the Afghan capital. Brahimi has pushed hard to persuade donors not to renege on their financial commitments and to ensure that more long-term recovery aid is directed outside Kabul to the provinces.

DAOUD, Mohammed (1909-1978)

Former President of Afghanistan and arch-manipulator of the two Cold War superpowers. President of the Republic of Afghanistan from July 1973 until his assassination in April 1978 as a result of the Saur (April) Revolution which brought the Marxist People's Democratic Party of Afghanistan (PDPA) to power in Kabul.

Born in 1909 in Kabul, he followed a military career, which saw him become Commander of the Central Forces (1939-47) and Minister of Defence in 1946. As Prime Minister from 1953-63 he built up the military as a power base, encouraged social reforms and in 1959 permitted women to abandon the veil. He received considerable military and economic aid from the USSR (and some from the US, prompting him to say "I light my American cigarettes with Russian matches"). However, by supporting the ambitions of Pakistan's NWFP to become an independent Pashtunistan he estranged both Pakistan and the US; this pro-Pashtun ambition and his disregard for the King eventually led to his resignation in 1963.

In July 1973, with the support of the Army, the PDPA and the USSR, he staged a coup against his cousin King Zahir Shah, and proclaimed himself President of the new Republic of Afghanistan. He employed left wing elements in suppressing the nascent Islamist movement. His establishment in 1975 of the National Revolution Party, however, was aimed at limiting the power of the left. In order to force centralization and the extension of his personal power he assumed direct control over the Armed Forces and tried to promote nationalism in place of traditional ethnic allegiances. He launched ambitious social and economic development projects (including a railway linking Afghanistan to Iran) and his first 5-year plan was considered as a major success. However Daoud's republic was plagued by economic inefficiencies and a lack of skilled personnel, which led to an increasing economic, military and political dependence on the USSR. He attempted to reverse this almost total reliance by approaching the West and Pakistan, and by using finance from Iran and the Arab Gulf States to help reduce Soviet influence, but it was too late and he was overthrown by the PDPA coup of 27 April 1978.

DIN MOHAMMED, Hajji

Governor of Nangarhar Province. Together with his brother Nasirullah Bariyan, one of two remaining male siblings from the family of assassinated former resistance leaders Abdul Haq and Abdul Qadir. Following Hajji Qadir's murder in July 2002, Din Mohammed replaced him as governor, and is now engaged in something of a power struggle with Hazrat Ali.

DOSTUM, Abdul Rashid

Northern, ethnic Uzbek warlord and former militia general under the Soviets. Leader of Jumbesh-e-Melli Islami (National Islamic Movement), Dostum remains one of the most powerful men in northern Afghanistan. Although a supporter of the United Front, Dostum remains at loggerheads with other United Front commanders, notably General Atta of Mazar-e-Sharif. One of the main reasons behind the reluctance of many refugees from these areas to return home is the continued fighting for control between these two commanders. Currently a member of Karzai's National Defense Commission, he seems keen to shrug off his warlord image, given his frequent appearances at official gatherings dressed in a respectable suit.

Born in 1954 in Jowzjan province of a peasant Uzbek family, Dostum received only a few years of formal schooling. He essentially taught himself to read and write. Dostum is a nickname he earned as a young man; *dost* means friend, and a *dostum* is everyone's friend. A product of the former Soviet Union, he received military training in the USSR in 1980 and rose through the ranks of President Najibullah's communist regime army. Under Najibullah, he was entrusted with guarding the northern provinces of Jowzjan, Faryab and Sar-e-Pol. He was awarded title of Hero of the Republic of Afghanistan and made a member of the central council of the Watan (formerly PDPA) Party. During the Soviet war, he emerged as a highly effective commander of both regular and militia pro-government forces.

By 1991, he was commander of the Jowzjani 'Dostum Militia' numbering some 20,000 troops, mostly ethnic Uzbek. However, he sensed the imminent downfall of Najibullah and in February 1992 switched sides to the *mujahideen*, thus precipitating the end of communist rule in Afghanistan. As he moved south through the Salang Pass towards Kabul with a column of armoured vehicles to claim his reward, his attempt to team up with Massoud against their mutual enemy Gulbuddin Hekmatyar backfired. Dostum's troops were involved in numerous incidents of murder, rape and pillage against non-Uzbek Afghans, earning themselves the nickname of *gelim jam*, meaning 'carpet-baggers'.

On New Year's Day 1994, Dostum switched sides again and joined Hekmatyar in a combined assault on Kabul, which destroyed large areas of the capital and nearly succeeded in dislodging Massoud. Dostum then concentrated on building his own fiefdom in the northern city of Mazar-e-Sharif, replete with its own army, flag, currency and airline, Balkh Air.

After the battle with the Taliban for Mazar-e-Sharif in May 1997, Dostum was ousted by his one-time ally Abdul Malik and retired to Turkey to plot his comeback. That September, he re-emerged – allegedly with American backing – to take control of Mazar and stave off further attacks by the Taliban. With the help of Hezb-e-Wahdat and Massoud's Jamiat-e-Islami forces, he beat back the Taliban – brutally massacring hundreds of their fighters in the process – and then directed his wrath against Malik whom he drove into exile. Dostum's brutality towards those who have dared cross him, ranging from beatings to tank-crushings, is renowned.

In charge of his own armed forces, Dostum very much considers the north his domain, particularly the region's access to oil and natural gas reserves. His forces are continually involved in armed conflict with those of Jamiat rival General Atta – despite numerous UN attempts to broker a ceasefire. As a whisky drinker, ex-Communist and political chameleon, Dostum has many enemies. He is hated and widely distrusted by numerous Afghans. Nonetheless, Dostum seeks to play the political game by cultivating good contacts with internationals and publicly supporting the Kabul government as long as it serves his own purposes.

FAHIM, Mohammed Qasim

Minister of Defence, Vice President and self-appointed Marshall of the Afghan Armed Forces. A highly ambitious Panjshairi, Fahim was virtually unknown to outsiders until the assassination of Ahmed Shah Massoud on September 9, 2001, two days prior to the World Trade Center assaults. The United Front's main intelligence officer, Fahim was appointed successor to the Massoud legacy and is now considered by the Americans to be the most effective man in charge of the Afghan military. Others, however, consider Fahim one of the principal obstacles to Afghan unity because of his alleged ruthlessness (including threats, beatings and other forms of thuggery against critics) and insistence on maintaining his own militia supported by ample stocks of weapons (including tanks and armoured vehicles in the Panjshair Valley).

Very much an advocate of the "winner takes all" school of thought, with little favour directed towards the Pashtuns, Fahim originally appointed his own close associates, primarily Panjshairis, to positions of power within the armed forces. Subsequently, he was forced to make concessions by replacing some of his generals with representatives from other ethnic groups. He is clearly intent on retaining control regardless of international efforts to encourage a more broad and ethnically balanced democratic base for Afghanistan. His grip over the country's defence ministry has stalled the country's vital disarmament, demobilization and reintegration (DDR) process, as many regional warlords are unwilling to surrender their forces to someone they consider a factional commander.

At the same time, as with many other lead figures with strong resistance credentials, Fahim seeks to push his 'respectable' side as a member of the post-Taliban government by wearing suits, giving press conferences and being seen at official receptions, such as the announcement of the draft constitution in late 2003. Fahim is said to have developed a keen interest in large scale 'import and export trade' (including the import of vehicles and luxury goods from Dubai) that is managed by his brothers in UAE and in Kabul.

GAYLANI, Pir Sayed Ahmed

Traditionalist leader of the National Islamic Front of Afghanistan. Born into a prominent Sufi family which claims descent from the Prophet, Gaylani read theology at Kabul University before fleeing the country after the Saur Revolution. He founded the National Islamic Front of Afghanistan (NIFA), the best known of the three 'traditionalist' *mujahideen* parties, and one of the seven parties to form the Afghan Interim Government (AIG) in Peshawar in 1989. His party was often called the Gucci Front by its detractors because of the veneer of urban sophistication associated with Pir's sons and nephews.

Ethnically Pashtun, Gaylani had a large religious following based mainly in Paktia, Kandahar and other eastern provinces, and by 1989 could claim to have around 20,000 supporters. He was never trusted by the fundamentalists because of his pro-monarchist tendencies. He has lost much of his influence, but has moved back to Kabul where he continues to play backroom politics and could still prove a pivotal figure pushing for a broader government that would include 'moderate' Taliban. Gaylani announced in July 2002 that he was disappointed with the failure of the interim government to assure a more professional and ethnically balanced cabinet. His daughter Fatima has played a significant role in asserting women's rights in the new Afghanistan.

GHANI, Ashraf

Minister of Finance. One of President Karzai's principal advisors, if not creators, Ghani remains one of the few professional technocrats in the Afghan government. A former professor of anthropology at Johns Hopkins University in the United States, Ghani served as a senior anthropologist with the World Bank before returning to Afghanistan following the fall of the Taliban. Under World Bank auspices, he became economic advisor to Karzai after the December 2001 Bonn Agreement and was in charge of reconstruction, particularly with regard to donor funding. He was appointed Minister of Finance in the new transitional government after the Emergency *Loya Jirga* in June 2002. A Pashtun of the Ahmadzai clan, Ghani focused in his studies on social theory and political economy in Afghanistan from 1747 to present. He also broadcast regularly for both the BBC and VOA. Ghani is widely regarded by the international community as a pivotal figure and partner in the long-term recovery of Afghanistan. His recent poor health, however, has given cause for concern.

HAQ, Abdul (1958-2001)

Leading ex-commander of the *mujahideen*. One of the most effective and autonomous guerrilla commanders during the 1980s alongside Ahmed Shah Massoud, Ismail Khan and others, Abdul Haq (formerly of the Hezb-e-Islami - Younis Khalis resistance faction) had sought to lay the groundwork for US intervention by slipping into Afghanistan in late 2001. He was betrayed to the Taliban, whom he despised. They captured and executed him prior to their collapse in October 2001. Many believe that Pakistan's Inter Services Intelligence (ISI) was behind his betrayal. Another theory is that Haq's death was the result of a personal settling of accounts by tribal enemies. A highly respected Pashtun, Haq once told an EFG editor that he could never expect to live in safety in a new Afghanistan because he had killed too many fellow countrymen involved with the Soviet-backed Kabul regime and whose families would almost certainly seek retribution.

Haq, who had already become involved in peace initiatives in Afghanistan as a UN mediator in 1998, saw his role as that of a facilitator among the Pashtuns and the northern United Front commanders. He also designed the Intra-Afghan dialogue process under the auspices of US congressman Don Ritter and his Afghanistan Foundation. Such efforts were tragically rewarded, however, by the assassination by unknown assailants of his wife and 11-year-old son in Peshawar in 1999. Haq, whose memorial portrait now adorns numerous government offices and shops in Nangarhar, Kunar and Logar provinces, was one of the few commanders whose integrity remained intact and who could have played a key role in a post-Taliban Afghanistan. One of the big mistakes of the current Tajik-dominated administration in Kabul is not to have built on Haq as a national hero alongside Massoud, as a means of promoting ethnic and tribal unity. The current impression is that commanders such as Haq never played a role in the ousting of the Soviets or establishing an independent Afghan identity. Only in Jalalabad have EFG editors seen Massoud's and Abdul Haq's portraits side by side.

Haq was born into an affluent Nangarhar family and joined the struggle against left-wing rule during the Daoud era in 1977, before becoming an active commander with the Soviet invasion in December 1979. After the overthrow of the communist Najibullah regime in April 1992, Haq was made Security Minister in the new *mujahed* interim "Islamic Council", but became disillusioned with the constant infighting. Specialized in hitting Soviet targets in and around Kabul during the Red Army occupation, Haq lost his foot in a landmine incident, an injury which severely curtailed his previous ability to act as a flying urban resistance commander.

A favourite of many foreign correspondents, Haq was described by one reporter as "the English-speaking acceptable face of Islamic fundamentalism." He later moved to the United Arab Emirates where he became involved in business, operating, amongst other things, an air cargo company from the Gulf to Afghanistan. Haq was brother of another leading *mujahed* and post-Taliban minister in the Karzai government, Abdul Qadir, who was assassinated in July 2002.

HEKMATYAR, Gulbuddin

Leader of the main faction of Hezb-e-Islami, one of seven former *mujahed* parties based in Peshawar. A typical example of the Afghan resistance politician who faded away only to blow back again, Hekmatyar now represents the new face of terrorism in Afghanistan. He is suspected of being involved (in possible collaboration with the Taliban and Al Qa'eda) in a number of attacks aimed at destabilizing the Karzai government and undermining the foreign presence in Afghanistan, both military and humanitarian. These include: the 5 September, 2002 car bombing outside the telecommunications office in Kabul which killed 26 civilians and wounded dozens more; the 3 January, 2003 explosion on a bridge near Kandahar killing eight civilians travelling in a bus; and rocket attacks in February 2003 against US and German positions in Khost and Kabul respectively. A former protégée of the Pakistanis and Americans, Hekmatyar has been seeking to assume the mantle of the Taliban as part of his *jihad* to oust the United States from Afghanistan. On 19 February 2003, the US government declared the man they had helped build up during the 1980s as a "Specially Designated Global Terrorist."

A 'transplanted' Ghilzai Pashtun, born in 1947 in Kunduz province, Hekmatyar was student of engineering at Kabul University but fled to Pakistan after the Daoud coup of 1973. In 1975 he became a leader of Afghan radical Islamists, and subsequently founded Hezb-e-Islami. He launched attacks into Afghanistan with the covert assistance of the Bhutto Government and participated with later arch rival, Ahmed Shah Massoud, in an abortive uprising in the Panjshair Valley. From December 1978, as leader of one of two Hezb factions, "Engineer Gulbuddin" gathered around him a group of mainly Pashtun *mujahed* commanders, some sharing his Islamic fervour, others his access to weapons, money and considerable resources. Hekmatyar enjoyed extensive support from the Pakistanis and the Americans, who ensured that his faction became the best-supported of the resistance parties.

An opportunistic man of few scruples, Hekmatyar has aroused violent antagonism over the years among many of his fellow compatriots. Moderate resistance leader Sibghatullah Mujaddedi once publicly accused Hekmatyar of killing more innocent Afghans than Soviet troops. He also described him as a monster created and sustained by Pakistan's Inter Services Intelligence (ISI). Hekmatyar's Hezb has been accused of killing numerous individuals and political opponents not to his liking, including at least two BBC journalists and a leading Afghan poet and intellectual, Dr Sayed Burhanuddin Madjruh. Hekmatyar endeavoured to weaken his fellow resistance rivals either through direct attack or by pulling out of anti-Soviet operations at the last minute in order to

Gulbuddin Hekmatyar *Nicola Jennings*

preserve his forces and ammunition. Hezb made repeated threats in the late 1980s against one EFG editor, then working as a foreign correspondent. This increasingly unsavoury reputation, coupled with assessments by experienced journalists and aid workers that Hezb's effectiveness as a guerrilla organization against the Soviets was highly questionable, did little to dampen the US Central Intelligence Agency's enthusiasm. The Americans also appeared to like Hekmatyar for the banal reason that he spoke good English, unlike Massoud (a Dari speaker with only passable French). By 1989, Hekmatyar's supporters were thought to number around 15,000, mainly Pashtuns, although Hekmatyar often claimed to have as many as 50,000 under his command.

Hezb-e-Islami was long considered as one of the most ideological and radical of the Islamist groups before the emergence of the Taliban. For his part, Hekmatyar has assiduously sought to establish himself as the leader of an Afghan Islamic Republic, which he claimed would be governed under strict Islamic law. His alliance with Shahnawaz Tanai (a general with the PDPA's Khalqi faction) to stage a coup – heavily backed by the Pakistani government – against the Kabul Government of Dr Najibullah was perhaps a typical example of the opportunism that has long coloured his career. Unfortunately for Hekmatyar, the assault proved an utter failure. For two months between April and June 1992, Hekmatyar's forces indiscriminately pounded the capital with artillery, mortar and rocket fire in a successful attempt to oust his enemy, the moderate Sibghatullah Mujaddedi, from power. From mid-1992 to late 1994, he served nominally as Prime Minister of the Islamic State of Afghanistan under President Rabbani. However, he avoided basing himself inside Kabul owing to fears (probably highly justified) for his own security, particularly from bitter rivals such as former resistance leader and defence minister, Ahmed Shah Massoud. During this period, Hekmatyar linked up with General Dostum's forces forming the Shura-e-Hamahangi alliance to fight against the Shura-e-Nezar alliance which included the Jamiat-e-Islami forces of Massoud. By mid-1995 Shura-e-Hamahangi, comprising Hekmatyar, Dostum and Hezb-e-Wahdat, controlled at least seven provinces in the north.

During the battle for Kabul between 1992-1996 it was Hekmatyar's troops, based in the southern parts of the city and on the slopes of Sher-e-Darwaza, who inflicted much of the damage on the capital. In June 1996, he formed an alliance with his old sworn enemy Rabbani to resist the Taliban, and once again became Prime Minister of Afghanistan. In an attempt to appear as zealous as the Taliban, he made himself highly unpopular by banning music, cinema and football in Kabul. The Pakistanis, however, eventually dropped their one-time stooge in favour of the more effective Taliban movement which first began sweeping into southern Afghanistan in 1994. Hekmatyar eventually fled to Iran, where he bided his time with various forays back onto the Afghan scene. In March 1998, he proposed a peace agreement between the Taliban and the United Front which failed to materialize. He returned full-time from Iran following the collapse of the Taliban, possibly in early 2002, and is believed to be operating along the Pakistan-Afghan frontier.

In April 2002, the CIA tried and failed to kill him with an unmanned drone. Since then, Hekmatyar has reportedly visited different parts of the country under the noses of the US-led Coalition Forces to recruit support. He is believed to have formed an alliance with the elusive head of the Taliban movement, Mullah Mohammed Omar. Reports indicate that the two men are now sharing fighters, material and intelligence in their common *jihad* against Western forces and their allies in Karzai's government. There are also strong indications that Hekmatyar is playing an increasingly powerful leadership role among former elements of the Taliban and Al Qa'eda in at least half a dozen Pashtun-dominated provinces, notably Khost, Paktia, Logar, Kandahar, Helmand and Uruzgan. Hekmatyar is further said to enjoy significant backing among pro-Taliban tribal groups, particularly in Waziristan and Bajaur, on the Pakistan side of the border.

Overall, Hekmatyar is considered unlikely to garner widespread popular support among ordinary Afghans because of war fatigue, tribal loyalties and still simmering hatred from the past. In addition, many tribal Pashtuns regard him as an outsider. Nevertheless, a quarter of a century of conflict and refugee flows have produced a new generation of Pashtuns who no longer feel constrained by traditional roots. Many harbour increasingly bitter anti-Western attitudes, coupled with deep resentment towards the northern Tajiks for their current domination of the Kabul government – once a stronghold of the Pashtun oligarchy. If Hekmatyar survives (there are many Afghans who have sworn to see him dead), and if he raises the funds to buy off the commanders and pay for the fighters he needs, this highly astute, shrewd – and it must be said, sometimes charming – fundamentalist can be expected to emerge as a growing threat fully capable of derailing Afghanistan's long-term recovery process.

KARMAL, Babrak (1929-1996)

Former President of Afghanistan under the Soviets from December 1979 to 1986. Born in 1929 in Kabul, the Persian-speaking son of an army general, Karmal became intoxicated by the left-wing ideas released into the liberal atmosphere of King Zahir Shah's rule of the 1950s. A founder member in 1965 of the Marxist-Leninist People's Democratic Party of Afghanistan (PDPA), he disputed leadership of the party with Nur Mohammed Taraki in 1965 and led the non-Pashtun Parcham ('Banner') faction until it reunited, through Soviet mediation, with Taraki's Pashtun Khalq ('Masses') faction in 1977.

On 27 April 1978 the PDPA with backing from the Army and massive Soviet support staged the violent coup known as the Saur Revolution, which killed President Daoud and established Taraki as the first PDPA President of the Democratic Republic of Afghanistan. Karmal was made Deputy Prime Minister but in July 1978 he fell foul of the Khalqi faction and was appointed as Afghanistan's ambassador in Prague. However, following the murders of both Taraki and his deputy Hafizullah Amin in late 1979, the Soviets decided to support the Parcham faction in order to avoid the new Communist government being overthrown by an Islamic government. As a result, Karmal was brought back from Prague and appointed the new President of Afghanistan with effect from 27 December 1979, the official date of the Soviet invasion.

Karmal's Kabul regime proved to be a puppet government, instigated and dictated to by the Soviets. It never formed any clear policies of its own, but instead became obsessed with internecine infighting which eventually led to the replacement of Karmal as President by Dr Najibullah in 1986.

Considered a KGB agent and traitor, Karmal is condemned by many Afghans as the man put in power at the point of a Russian bayonet. He left Afghanistan for Moscow at the height of his countrymen's war with the USSR and died there of liver cancer in December 1996.

KARZAI, Hamid

President of the Transitional Islamic State of Afghanistan. Perceived at the fall of the Taliban as one of the few potential Afghan leaders without blood on his hands, Hamid Karzai emerged at the UN-sponsored meeting in Bonn in December 2001 as the most acceptable compromise candidate to head the country during the interim period. A Kandahari Pashtun with exceptional charm and fluent English, Karzai was already relatively well-known among journalists and aid workers as a pro-monarch moderate based in Peshawar. Karzai was also promoted by former World Bank representative Ashraf Ghani and Washington's Zalmay Khalilzad as the best man for the job.

Born in 1957 in Kandahar, Karzai was educated in Kabul and in India. In 1982, he became operations director for the anti-Soviet National Liberation Front of Afghanistan. Subsequently, he supported the Taliban's rise to power, but by late 1994 his support for the movement waned as he suspected it had been infiltrated by foreigners. During October 2001, he is thought to have played a key role in negotiating the Taliban's withdrawal from Kandahar. Yet during 2003, he was talking of engaging 'moderate Taliban' in dialogue with his administration. Karzai has committed himself to the provisions of the Bonn Agreement, namely creating a broad-based, representative government, one national army loyal to the Kabul authorities, and the disarming of militia forces under regional warlords.

Now in his mid-forties, Karzai remains a weak president despite international efforts to promote him as firmly in charge of the country. Recalcitrant and pro-Taliban Pashtuns regard him as a stooge of the Americans, much as Babrak Karmal was considered a lackey of the Soviets. Some have criticized him for giving in to American pressure to sideline the King during the Emergency *Loya Jirga* in June 2002. Others simply regard Karzai as a southern Pashtun controlled by the dominant 'Panjshairi mafia.' Although Karzai's authority appears to be growing now that international aid is finally reaching the provinces, his control barely reaches beyond the environs of Kabul and other areas held by pro-government commanders. Most regions are run by local warlords who, even if considered pro-government, are reluctant to hand over more authority – or taxes – than they have to. In May 2003, Karzai threatened to resign if regional governors did not do more to hand over tax revenues to the centre. He has sought to dilute the power of the warlords – for example, through partial reform of the Defence Ministry – but only with limited success. His Defence Minister, Marshall Fahim, continues to maintain a private army with access to heavy weapons – within range of Kabul's presidential palace and in defiance of the Bonn Agreement.

As a national leader, however, Karzai probably remains one of Afghanistan's best assets for representing it abroad. He has promoted the Afghan cause well and makes a particular effort to be seen as 'multi-ethnic' in the way he comports himself, such as his clothing. One of his problems, however, is that he still needs to impose more competent Afghan technocrats without any particular ethnic or political affiliation on the various ministries in an effort to encourage professionalism rather than ethnic or tribal favouritism. At the same time, Karzai's apparent political feebleness may be precisely why so many Afghans accept him. Traditionally, Afghans have always preferred weak leaders in Kabul with much of the real power lying in the provinces. Karzai needs to assert his authority (for example over Afghanistan's customs entry points), but will need the help of the international community in providing more robust security support, especially the expansion of ISAF, and more effective aid programmes to rural areas. If not, Karzai will continue to remain the president of Kabul as opposed to Afghanistan.

KHALILI, Karim

Hazara Shi'a leader and one of the country's four Vice Presidents, Khalili has led the former *Shi'a* resistance party Hezb-e-Wahdat Islami (The Party of Islamic Unity) since March 1995, when the previous Hazara chief, Abdul Ali Mazar, died in Taliban custody. Hezb-e-Wahdat was formed with Iranian backing in June 1990 in order to consolidate power among the eight previous Iran-backed *Shi'a mujahed* groups. Hezb-e-Wahdat, however, has split into two groups, the larger of which is controlled by Khalili. Based in Bamiyan, which Wahdat forces re-captured from the Taliban in November 2001, Khalili maintains a high profile among the Hazara majority there. He also retains a major influence in Mazar-e-Sharif alongside northern United Front leader, General Atta. While Khalili supports the Karzai government and the US-backed military coalition, this allegiance is dependent on the Hazaras obtaining not only a fair say in the running of Afghanistan but also a share of international donor support.

KHALILI, Massoud

Afghan Ambassador to India. A close associate of Ahmed Shah Massoud since the late 1970s, Khalili was severely injured in the assassination attack in September 2001 that killed Massoud. Son of the renowned 20th Century Afghan poet, Khalilullah Khalili, he first started out as a highly popular teenage heart-throb on Afghan radio. He then joined Massoud in his resistance against the communist PDPA regime in Kabul and then against the Soviet occupation of Afghanistan. A fluent English-speaker well-known amongst journalists and aid workers, Khalili acted as Massoud's front to the outside world both in the United States, Pakistan and then India during the 1980s and 1990s. He is highly respected by Afghans, including Pashtuns, particularly because of his family's enormous stature in Afghan culture, and is often mentioned as a possible president for Afghanistan.

KHALILZAD, Zalmay

US Ambassador to Afghanistan. An Afghan-born American brought up in Kabul, Zalmay Khalilzad returned to Afghanistan in late 2001 for the first time in 30 years as US special envoy under President George W. Bush. A Columbia University political science professor, who consulted with the American oil consortium Unocal in 1997, Khalilzad was appointed to the National Security Council in Washington in June 2001. With the events of 11 September, Khalilzad rapidly emerged as one of the key proponents for military action in Afghanistan.

It is Khalilzad's involvement with Unocal, however, that has persuaded some analysts to conclude that oil interests were among the principal reasons behind the US intervention. During the late 1990s, Unocal had vied with the Argentinean oil company, Bridas, for pipeline rights from the Taliban and the United Front for transporting Turkmen oil and natural gas from the Caspian Sea to the Indian Ocean. This was seen as a means of reducing Russia's grip on Central Asian petroleum supplies (through her 70 percent control of Caspian Sea reserves). At the time, Khalilzad advocated engagement of the Taliban as part of US policy, but Unocal's pipedreams eventually evaporated. Caspian Sea reserves are not considered vital to the United States, but the Americans are evidently seeking to diversify their sources and broaden their influence among oil producing countries, particularly in the former Soviet Union. To what extent oil proved to be instrumental in persuading the Bush administration to act remains unclear. Since the overthrow of the Taliban, Unocal has shown no interest in becoming re-involved with Afghanistan. (The pipeline project was re-instigated following the fall of the Taliban, resulting in 2003 in a tripartite deal involving the governments of Turkmenistan, Afghanistan and Pakistan.) Others regard Khalilzad's advocacy for intervention as more linked to the need to instil greater security in the region.

As a pro-resistance advocate during the 1980s, Khalilzad was closely involved with the Friends of Afghanistan Organization, which included anti-Soviet hardliners such as Brzezinski. He also supported Washington's efforts, as an advisor to the Reagan administration, to use Afghanistan as a means of undermining the Soviet Union. His expertise as a foreign policy strategist on the region, including the Muslim world, made him a likely figure for the Bush administration to appoint as special envoy in 2001. The same thinking ensured a broadening of his role to include Iraq prior to the US intervention there in early 2003. Khalilzad, who has manoeuvred himself through Afghan politics with both intrigue and exceptional political arm-twisting, such as the sidelining of former King Zahir Shah at the *Loya Jirga*, remains a key player in the development of the new Afghanistan. In summer 2003, he was appointed US ambassador to Afghanistan

Khalilzad has denied that the US was aware of supporting Islamic fundamentalists, including foreign operatives such as Osama Bin Laden, during the 1980s and early 1990s. He maintains that no one realized what they were really up to. However, some critics argue that individuals such as Khalilzad knew perfectly well that the United States was in the process of creating monsters. According to Pakistan-British writer Ahmed Rashid, the US, advised by the likes of Khalilzad, used taxpayers' money to support the Taliban against the United Front with weapons and funding during the 1990s, covering the salaries of Taliban civil servants right up till 1999. Since the US intervention against the Taliban, Washington has once again been involved – at the behest of Khalilzad and others – in establishing and propping up local and regional warlords, some of whom can now no longer be controlled and are involved in political or commercial actions of their own, notably drug trafficking.

KHALIS, Mohammed Younis

Pashtun leader of his own Hezb-e-Islami faction. Born in 1919 in Gandamak, and educated in Islamic law and theology, Khalis is a radical Islamist and anti-Communist. Forced to flee Afghanistan after the Soviet-backed Daoud coup of 1973, he joined Hezb-e-Islami with Hekmatyar, then seceded to form his own faction to fight the Soviets, launching attacks from Pakistan. His commanders included Abdul Haq in the Kabul area, Amin Wardak in Wardak and Hajji Qadir (Abdul Haq's brother and later governor of Nangarhar province). One of the few political leaders to have taken an active part in military operations, Khalis was known as the "Fighting Mullah." He is opposed to universal suffrage and the emancipation of women. In May 1991, while serving as interior minister in the Afghan Interim Government (AIG) in Peshawar, he resigned because of his opposition to *Shi'a* participation. Khalis is notorious for taking a teenage wife in his later years. Khalis also provided Osama Bin Laden with refuge in 1994 when he fled Sudan.

KHAN, Ismail

Leading Afghan warlord and self-styled "Amir of Herat". Born in 1947 into a modest Dari-speaking family in Shindand, 100 km south of Herat, Ismail Khan remains one of Afghanistan's most rich and powerful post-Taliban warlords. Khan made his name by leading the anti-communist mutiny of March 1979 when, as a captain in the PDPA army, he disobeyed orders to fire on a mob in the Herat bazaar. Instead, his troops massacred 350 of Herat's Soviet advisors and their families. Moscow retaliated by carpet-bombing Herat, shattering historic mosques and mausolea and killing anywhere between 5,000 and 25,000 people. The mutiny sparked open rebellion against the communists throughout the province, but Khan left Herat to join Rabbani's party Jamiat-e-Islami.

The mid-1980s saw him constantly on the move as one of Jamiat's key commanders. He established his reputation as a staunch nationalist and die-hard Islamist with a healthy disrespect for Iranian and Arabian interference. In 1993 he was quoted as saying "Nobody, not even the Iranians, can impose their will on us." He has been highly critical of *mujahed* infighting and foreign interference which have conspired to deny Afghanistan the peace for which he fought for so long.

By the early 1990s, Ismail Khan had promoted himself as the self-styled Amir of Herat, building himself a palace on a hill overlooking the city (this was later used as a base following the collapse of the Taliban by US Special Forces and Central Intelligence Agency operatives). As Governor of Herat, Khan exercised power over five provinces in south-western Afghanistan; but he failed to hold back the Taliban advance on his fiefdom in September 1995, and consequently fled to Iran. About two years later, with financial and military support from Iran, Khan returned to Afghanistan again in order to fight the Taliban. But in May 1997 on a trip to Faryab, he was captured by Uzbek warlord General Abdul Malik and handed over to the Taliban who flew him to Kandahar. Reportedly denied access to radio and newspapers, and not even granted pen or paper with which to write his memoirs, Khan spent three years in Taliban custody where he was badly beaten before managing to escape to Iran once again.

During the autumn of 2001, Khan returned to Afghanistan and joined the US-led military coalition to fight the Taliban and regain control of Herat, where he re-appointed himself governor. Khan claims to support the Karzai government but has been reluctant to water down his own authority in favour of Kabul's. He controls an armed force estimated at 30,000 soldiers, police and militiamen and, despite vague promises, has so far refused to downsize or integrate it as part of the national army. Khan relies for his income largely on highly lucrative import duties (US$ 7-9 million dollars a month) on goods ranging from Japanese vehicles to Russian air conditioners brought in via Iran and Turkmenistan. In 2003, he agreed to channel some of this tax revenue towards Kabul, but this has yet to prove a fixed feature of his administration.

While both the Coalition Forces and certain international aid agencies regard Khan as the sort of warlord currently undermining Kabul's authority, they also consider him one of the most effective governors in Afghanistan. Herat city appears well-run and clean and Khan likes to portray himself as a benefactor of the people. Human rights activists, however, including Herati women's groups, believe that he has become even more fundamentalist and repressive than the Taliban, particularly against political opponents and the Pashtun minority. Dissident opponents have been beaten and jailed, while women have been threatened in the streets by Khan's men. Many critics believe that it is now high time for the so-called *Jihadists* (former *mujahideen* who resisted during the Soviet war and now consider it their right to be in charge) to make way for democratic government and professional technocrats to run state affairs, rather than illiterate or incompetent *mujahideen* benefiting from political favours. While Khan has always been regarded as a religious conservative, he was known to be open and reformist prior to the Taliban period. Some believe that the beatings he suffered during his incarceration by the Taliban may have damaged him psychologically, with the effects now emerging in the former of an intolerant dictator.

MALIK, Abdul

Uzbek warlord. One of the Uzbek Pahlawan brothers of Badghis province, Malik rose to become a general in Abdul Rashid Dostum's Jumbesh-e-Melli party in northern Afghanistan. In May 1997 he allowed Taliban forces into Mazar in what appeared to be an attempt to switch sides and oust General Dostum. Two days later Malik turned against the Taliban and joined Hezb-e-Wahdat forces in massacring several hundred Taliban soldiers. Dostum, who had left Afghanistan to plot his return from the safety of Turkey, reappeared in Mazar in September 1997 and shortly afterwards defeated Malik, forcing him into exile.

MASSOUD, Ahmed Shah (1956-2001)

Leading Tajik commander. Often referred to during the Soviet war as the "Lion of Panjshair", but also the Che Guevara and even Tito of Afghanistan, Massoud was the military head of Jamiat-e-Islami and the leading figure of the anti-Taliban United Front, also known as the Northern Alliance. He was assassinated in Khodja Bahauddin in northern Takhar province on 9 September, 2001, two days prior to the World Trade Center and other terror assaults in the United States. The two Arab killers, posing as journalists, are believed to have been Al Qa'eda operatives seeking to rid Afghanistan of the only opposition leader capable of galvanizing Afghans in the wake of the planned events of 11 September. Ironically, Massoud had repeatedly warned the West of the dangers of Bin Laden and other foreign Islamic militants using Afghanistan as a launching pad for terrorist activities. On his first trip to Europe in April 2001, he again warned the international community about Al Qa'eda – noting that terrorist attacks were being prepared against the United States – but to little avail.

Born an ethnic Tajik, Ahmed Shah Massoud was one of the most successful and publicised *mujahed* commanders, based initially in the Panjshair (the valley of "five tigers" or "five lions", but also, depending on how you pronounce it, "five milks") northeast of Kabul. Renowned for instilling discipline into his troops and teaching modern tactical warfare techniques, Massoud fought off numerous Red Army attacks aimed at dislodging him from the Panjshair. In 1983, he reached a temporary truce with the Soviets, giving safe passage to the Red Army (through the Salang tunnel) to supply its forces that were engaged in fierce battles against the *mujahideen* in various other parts of Afghanistan. Despite his success as one of the country's most prominent 'commanders of the interior' during the Soviet war, Massoud was largely ignored by the Americans, who preferred to support the likes of Islamic fundamentalist Gulbuddin Hekmatyar.

Following the departure of the Soviets in 1989, Massoud engaged in a bloody internecine war against Hekmatyar's Hezb-e--Islami. In October 1990 the two factions appeared to reach a truce, but from 1992-94 Massoud's Shura-e-Nezar Shomal (Supervisory Council of the North) continued to clash with Dostum's and Hekmatyar's Shura-e-Hamahangi alliance. Despite Massoud's popularity among many Afghans during the Soviet war (he was a charismatic

Ahmed Shah Massoud (left) *E. Girardet*

favourite of the French media), his reputation suffered badly when he moved to Kabul following the overthrow of the Najibullah regime in 1992. Some accused Massoud of human rights abuses by allowing certain victorious *mujahideen* to 'terrorise' the Afghan capital. According to Amnesty International, during 1993-94 some of the most serious human rights abuses of the war were committed in Kabul – including the aerial bombing of an entire Hazara neighbourhood, killing scores of innocent civilians and destroying their houses.

As defence minister in the Rabbani government in the mid-1990s, Massoud was surrounded mainly by his Panjshairi clique, some of whom indulged in severe abuses of power and corruption. Massoud later maintained that this was one of his biggest mistakes, and he would seek to make amends in any future government. However, such dominance has persisted under the so-called 'Panjshairi Mafia', who have occupied many positions of power in Kabul following the fall of the Taliban in late 2001.

On being ousted from Kabul by the Taliban in 1996, Massoud began once again to demonstrate the courage and leadership qualities for which he was so long known. While a number of his commanders crossed over to the Taliban, largely in return for bribes, Massoud announced to his fighters that they could leave, or stay with him to help oust the Taliban in what would probably be a long and arduous struggle. Most chose to stay. Massoud was one of the few commanders who persisted in battling the Taliban despite having seen his area of control reduced to between 10-20 percent of the country.

Considered a devout Muslim but also a pragmatic modernist, Massoud was always aware of the plight of civilians. On several occasions during the Soviet war, he ordered the Panjshair to be temporarily abandoned by its population so that he could undertake military operations against the Soviets unhindered by humanitarian concerns. One of the reasons why Massoud reportedly hesitated from launching any direct attacks against the Taliban in Kabul during the late 1990s and early 2000s was for fear of causing even greater civilian suffering and destruction of the city. At the time, Massoud made it clear that any return to Kabul by his forces would include a rescinding of all Taliban decrees. "People hate the Taliban," he claimed in a 1997 interview; "Once our government returns to Kabul, we will restore rights for women 100 percent."

Buried in a 'martyr's grave' on a hill overlooking the Panjshair Valley, Massoud today probably asserts more influence in Afghanistan dead than when he was alive. His heroic-style portraits dominate numerous Afghan streets, *chaikhane* and offices in government-controlled areas far more than any other figure. However, his name appears to be taken increasingly in vain by former United Front commanders who are now in positions of dominance in the post-Taliban government and who insist on maintaining Tajik control to the detriment of other ethnic groups, particularly Pashtuns. One of the principal lessons learned by Massoud prior to his death was that a new Afghanistan could only exist if it fully involved all Afghans. During the 1990s and early 2000s, Massoud had pushed hard among the Pashtuns for establishing a government of national unity. In fact, just before his death, he was actively seeking a compromise with moderate Taliban for ending the war.

MAZARI, Abdul Ali (d. 1995)

Former leader of the Iran-backed *Shi'a* group Hezb-e-Wahdat (Unity Party), Mazari was killed while being held by the Taliban in March 1995.

MOHAMMEDI, Mohammed Nabi (1921-2003)

Traditionalist Pashtun leader of Harakat-e-Inqilab-e-Islami. Mohammedi was born in Logar and educated at the local *madrassa*, from which he graduated as a *Mawlawi*. In the 1950s he was one of the first religious leaders to campaign against communist influences in the Afghan educational system. Elected to parliament in 1964 during King Zahir Shah's experiment with democracy, he fled to Pakistan after the Saur Revolution and organized armed resistance to the Kabul regime through a network of other *Mawlawis*. In the 1980s he was leader of the so-called Islamic moderates and concentrated more on liberating his country than personal advancement. Early on in the war, his party, Harakat-e-Inqilab-e-Islami (Movement for Islamic Revolution) was one of the more effective of the seven resistance forces based in Peshawar during the Soviet War, and enjoyed widespread support from Paktia in the east of Afghanistan to Farah province bordering Iran. Harakat was more of a clerical association than a political party, and stood between fundamentalists seeking an Islamic state and the more secular-minded royalists. However, as the war ground on, Mohammedi lost many supporters to the more radical Islamist parties of Sayyaf and Rabbani. Mohammedi died in 2003.

MOHSENI, Mohammed Asif

Hazara leader of the Shi'a *mujahed* faction Harakat-e-Islami. Born in Kandahar in 1935 and educated in the *Shi'a* universities of Iraq, Mohseni is called Ayatollah by his supporters. On returning to Afghanistan he founded the rural-based *mujahed* group Harakat-e-Islami (Islamic Movement of Afghanistan), and in 1980 was elected chairman of the "Afghan *Shi'a* Alliance," a *mujahed* umbrella group headquartered in Iran. In the 1980s, Harakat-e-Islami was the largest and most important of the eight Iran-backed *Shi'a* groups. In June 1990 the *Shi'a* groups announced the formation a new organization called Hezb-e-Wahdat (Unity Party) in an attempt to consolidate *Shi'a* power. As a non-radical *Shi'a* leader, Mohseni did not receive the extent of military and financial support from Iran that the radical pro-Iranian Hezb-e-Wahdat received. Since political influence is closely associated with guns and money in Afghanistan today, Mohseni now appears to have little power.

MUJADDEDI, Professor Sibghatullah

Afghanistan's interim President, April to June 1992. Born in 1925 in Kabul, Mujaddedi comes from an aristocratic Ghilzai Pashtun family in southern Afghanistan. Leaders of a prominent Sufi mystical order, the Mujaddedis have been fierce nationalists ever since one of the family led the Shor Bazaar uprising against the British in Kabul in the 19th Century. After studying at Cairo's prestigious al-Azhar Islamic University, he became teacher of Islamic studies at a Kabul high school. A radical anti-communist, he was jailed from 1959-1964 for involvement in a purported plot to assassinate the Soviet premier Nikita Khrushchev. His protests against growing Soviet influence in the early 1970s forced him into exile, and at the time of the Saur Revolution he was head of the Islamic Centre in Copenhagen. When over 70 members of his clan were picked out by the communists and murdered, he returned to Pakistan to found and lead the armed resistance of the traditionalist and moderate National Liberation Front of Afghanistan, always the smallest of the seven Peshawar-based resistance parties.

Throughout the 1980s, his largely Pashtun guerrilla force was considered ineffective by Western arms suppliers, although he believes the ISI, Pakistan's military intelligence service, fabricated this myth to funnel more weapons to their stooge Gulbuddin Hekmatyar. In March 1989, Mujaddedi was named President of the so-called Afghan Interim Government (AIG), a Peshawar-based rebel administration-in-exile. Many believed he was given the role precisely because he was the weakest of the seven *mujahed* leaders operating from Pakistan.

In April 1992, he re-appeared in Kabul as the unlikely head of the new *mujahed* interim "Islamic Council", ending 14 years of communist rule in Afghanistan. "We are all Muslims", he said, "It is now time for us to join hands in unity and work for the reconstruction of our homeland." However, in a country filled with armed radicals, the tolerant Mujaddedi, who had even extended the olive branch to former collaborators of the communist regime, could not last. After two months of shelling from his hated enemy, the radical Islamist Gulbuddin Hekmatyar, he was ousted as President by Burhanuddin Rabbani, and departed Kabul an embittered man. As an Islamic moderate and an aristocrat,

Mujaddedi makes no secret of his monarchist tendencies; he continues to play a role in peacemaking efforts, and acted as chairman of the Constitutional Loya Jirga in December 2003.

NAJIBULLAH, Mohammed (1947-1996)

Communist President of the Republic of Afghanistan from 1986 to 1992, executed by the Taliban in September 1996. Born in 1947 in Kabul to Ghilzai Pashtun parents, Najibullah graduated from the Faculty of Medicine at Kabul University in 1975. In 1965 he joined the Parcham faction of the PDPA, and was purged from government by Taraki along with other Parchamis in 1978. He remained abroad, but returned to Kabul with Babrak Karmal after the Soviet invasion in December 1979. Known as the 'ox,' he was president of KHAD, the secret police or State Information Service, from 1980-1986. In May 1986, Najib (another nickname) replaced Karmal as President of Afghanistan and Secretary-General of the PDPA.

Continuing friction between Parcham and Khalq factions led to further fragmentation of the PDPA into half a dozen or more splinter groups, encouraged by the Soviets who adopted this policy of divide and rule to ensure no one faction became too powerful or potentially anti-Soviet. Najib successfully headed off a Khalqi coup in March 1990, organized by his own defence minister Shahnawaz Tanai, although the Army was still very pro-Khalq. Under Najibullah the Army and all government ministries were dictated to by the USSR. Priority was given to education and the social services, modelled on Soviet examples, and the media and all cultural institutions such as theatres and music were controlled by the Soviets.

Najibullah presided over the withdrawal of Soviet troops in February 1989, and called for reconciliation with the *mujahideen* and power sharing with them. As the *mujahideen* rejected Najib's repeated calls, he accepted a UN plan that envisaged the establishment of a neutral transitional administration made up of Afghan technocrats and his resignation as president. But with the assistance of General Dostum, the *mujahideen* foiled the UN plan, forcing Najibullah to take refuge in the UN compound in Kabul. This resulted in the collapse of Najibullah's regime in April 1992, when a four-member council of the ruling Watan party (lit. 'Fatherland' party – previously the PDPA), transferred 'power' to Mujaddedi as the first president of the *mujahideen* government.

When the Taliban took Kabul in September 1996, Najibullah welcomed their arrival, but not for long. They dragged him from his UN refuge (thus contravening international law), beat him and then shot him dead. They hanged his body by the neck from a lamp-post in the middle of Kabul, the symbolism of which did little to endear the Taliban movement to the West.

OMAR, Mullah Mohammed

Leader of the Taliban. Also known as Amir ul-Momineen (Leader of All Believers). Ousted by the US-led military intervention in late 2001, Mullah Omar was Supreme Leader of the Taliban movement which swept to power through southern Afghanistan in 1994. He led a reclusive life in Kandahar and refused to meet foreign diplomats, journalists, aid agencies or UN officials. A former *mujahed*, Omar was wounded fighting the Russians, and had one eye removed at the Red Cross hospital in Quetta in neighbouring Pakistan. Alongside Osama Bin Laden, his killing or capture were originally cited by the Americans as the two main objectives for intervening in Afghanistan. The US failed in both. The Americans reportedly narrowly missed killing Omar in an aerial attack outside the village of Singesar in Kandahar province on 12 October 2001. His 10-year-old son, however, died instantly. To date, neither Bin Laden (whom many believe is still alive) nor Mullah Omar has been apprehended. Omar is believed to be hiding in southern Afghanistan and still actively involved in the organization of insurgency operations against the Western-backed Kabul government.

Now in his early 40s, Omar was born into a poor family in Maiwand district near Kandahar. In the early 1990s he launched a movement from his local *madrassa* to combat the moral degradation to which he felt the *mujahideen* had succumbed. The main goal of the movement, whose membership was limited to *Taliban* (Islamic students) only, was to rid Afghanistan of "corrupt Western-oriented timeservers," and re-establish the rule of *shari'a*. Ironically for the leader of one of the most repressive Islamic regimes in the world, he had, in the Governor of Kandahar's words, "not too much religious knowledge." Nevertheless his authority in all military operations and over the Taliban six-man ruling *shura* remained absolute. Mullah Omar claimed to support the possibility of peace negotiations, even with ex-communists such as General Dostum, and had this to say to the Pakistani newspaper *The News on Sunday* about female Afghans:

"As for women's rights, we are willing to talk about it and we feel Islam has given the most rights to women. We aren't opposed to girls' education but we have to decide about our priorities keeping in view our meagre resources. Islam supports education for both men and women and we have every intention of following Islamic teachings."

Despite the Taliban re-emerging as an armed terrorist force, Mullah Omar appears to have ceded part of his military authority to fellow fundamentalist Gulbuddin Hekmatyar. This is reportedly the result of a loose alliance established in Quetta in early 2003 among radical members of Pakistan's military Inter Services Intelligence, Al Qa'eda, Hezb-e-Islami and other anti-Western Islamic military groups, aiming to undermine the recovery process in Afghanistan. These fighters have been deliberately targeting Afghans working with Western aid agencies, international aid workers, Afghan government representatives and foreign soldiers. Ironically, one of the first foreign aid workers to be deliberately murdered in March 2003 as part of this strategy was a delegate with the International Committee of the Red Cross, the very organization which had helped care for Mullah Omar when he was wounded during the *jihad*.

QADIR, Hajji Abdul

Assassinated Vice President and Minister of Public Works in the interim government. Brother of former guerrilla commander Abdul Haq, who was executed by the Taliban, Hajji Abdul Qadir was a congenial merchant with business links to (West) Germany, who operated as a leading guerrilla commander in Nangarhar province during the Afghan-Soviet war. On the fall of the communists and the takeover of Jalalabad by the *mujahideen*, he assumed the governorship of Nangarhar province. After the arrival of the Taliban, Qadir pulled back from the governorship but began operating in support of Massoud's United Front, one of the few Pashtuns to hold a senior position in the northern-dominated opposition. With the collapse of the Taliban, he became governor of Nangarhar once again but was then appointed Minister of Public Works and eventually one of Karzai's Vice Presidents.

He was killed in broad daylight on July 6, 2002, in front of his ministry by unknown assassins. The government and the Americans were quick to accuse the Taliban and Al Qa'eda for being responsible. Others, however, believe that the killing may have been the result of a settling of accounts by business rivals, or of political rivalry within the government. Qadir was known to have been involved in opium trafficking during the *jihad* as a means of raising funds to fight the Soviets. Some sources believe that he was still involved in the process but was beginning to crack down on this highly lucrative trade in support of the government. One of Qadir's main rivals was Hazrat Ali, a leading Pashai warlord supported by the Americans. Official government investigations regarding Qadir's assassination – as well as the death of former Minister of Aviation Dr Abdur Rahman – have yet to yield any results.

QANOONI, Younis

Minister of Education. Qanooni, who is a graduate of Kabul University in Islamic studies, was the Northern Alliance's head of delegation at the Bonn Conference in December 2001, which resulted in the first post-Taliban administration in Afghanistan. A former senior Massoud stalwart, Qanooni became Interior Minister under the first Northern Alliance/United Front-dominated government after the fall of the Taliban. This meant that the so-called 'Panjshairi Mafia' controlled three key ministries: Interior, Defence and Foreign Affairs – a situation deemed unacceptable by many Afghans and the international community alike. Qanooni was obliged to relinquish his post under international pressure and to become Minister of Education. A savvy, affable individual, he has proven an extremely adept politician by energetically seeking to improve not only the educational situation in Afghanistan, but also his own standing.

RABBANI, Burhanuddin

President of the Islamic State of Afghanistan from June 1992 to September 1996. Born an ethnic Tajik in 1940 in Faizabad, Badakhshan province, and educated at Kabul and al-Azhar Universities in Islamic Studies, Rabbani was a founding father of the anti-communist Islamist movement from the late 1950s onwards. An inspirational Kabul campus leader in the mid-1960s, shortly after Afghanistan's Communist Party was founded, he attacked the relatively liberal regime of the King for its secular modernization and communist sympathies. In 1971 he was selected as leader of Jamiat-e-Islami (Islamic Society of Afghanistan) and in 1974 he fled from Daoud's regime into Pakistan, seeking government support there against left-wing influences in Afghanistan. In 1975 failed Jamiat raids into Afghanistan revealed policy differences between Rabbani and Hekmatyar, which led to the latter forming his own Hezb-e-Islami party in 1976. Rabbani continued to lead Jamiat after the Saur Revolution. Throughout the Soviet-Afghan war, Rabbani remained based in Peshawar before moving to Kabul in 1992.

Jamiat became one of the largest and best organized of the resistance groups during the Soviet War with an array of highly effective guerrilla "fronts of the interior" affiliated with the party in return for outside support, weapons and other supplies. By 1989 it had an estimated 20,000 followers, mainly Tajiks from northern and western Afghanistan, but including some Pashtuns. Rabbani's legendary senior military commander was Ahmed Shah Massoud.

In June 1992, Rabbani took over power of the new *mujahed* interim "Islamic Council" from Sibghatullah Mujaddedi and declared the Islamic State of Afghanistan. In contrast to the moderate Mujaddedi, Rabbani called for the radical transformation of Afghan society on the basis of Islamic law and Qu'ranic principles. He was elected President in December 1992 and Hekmatyar was appointed his Prime Minister. However, this fragile interim government was not destined to last. Vicious fighting over Kabul erupted in the first half of 1994 with President Rabbani's and Defence Minister Massoud's Shura-e-Nezar forces pitted against those of Dostum's and Hekmatyar's Shura-e-Hamahangi forces.

The emergence of the Taliban in late 1994 and their capture of Kabul in September 1996 spelt the end of Rabbani's term of leadership. However, he remained President of the Afghan government even when its territory had diminished to less than 20 percent of the country by 2001. On the fall of the Taliban, Rabbani continued to act as self-proclaimed President by insisting on living in the presidential palace in Kabul. Even after the ushering in of the Karzai government in December, it took two months for the UN to persuade the former resistance politician to leave the compound.

Rabbani, who still has numerous armed men at his disposal in the Afghan capital, is reportedly seeking a leadership role, including presidential aspirations, in the new Afghanistan. Although some consider him sidelined, he is a figure not to be ignored. Like most *mujahed* leaders, Rabbani is said to be one of the wealthiest people in Afghanistan today, with property and businesses in Europe, UAE and Kabul – often registered in the names of family members and close associates.

SAMAR, Sima

Former Minister of Women's Affairs, now Human Rights Commissioner for Afghanistan.

SAYYAF, Abdul Rasul

Leader of the radical, fundamentalist Ittehad-e-Islami. After theological training at Kabul University and al-Azhar in Cairo, Sayyaf joined the Islamist movement under Rabbani. In 1980 he became the spokesman for the *mujahideen* alliance in Peshawar, and two years later formed his own group, Ittehad-e-Islami (Islamic Union for the Liberation of Afghanistan), which was the smallest of the *Sunni* fundamentalist factions. Now in his 60s, Sayyaf is an eloquent Arabic speaker and has secured considerable financial support from Arabic Gulf states, especially the Saudi royal family. Ideologically close to Hekmatyar and Khalis, he has however been accused of allying himself with Arab *Wahabi* groups.

Sayyaf supported the anti-Taliban Kunar uprising and then the Western-backed battle against the Taliban following Massoud's death. However, Sayyaf remains a conservative fundamentalist who is now seeking to influence the new Afghanistan, possibly in conjunction with Rabbani.

SHAHRANI, Ne'amatullah

One of Afghanistan's four Vice Presidents, and head of the independent commission set up to draft the country's new constitution.

SHINWARI, Fazul Hadi

Chief Justice of the Supreme Court. Shinwari's appointment following the June 2002 *Loya Jirga* raised serious human rights concerns, given his hardline approach similar to that of the Taliban. While supporting *shari'a* punishments such as stoning and amputation, Shinwari has stressed nevertheless that there should be stricter guarantees of legal due process. Close to the religious thinking of Sayyaf, Rabbani and Hekmatyar, Shinwari pushed his fundamentalist position during the drafting in 2003 of the country's proposed new constitution, much to the dismay of more moderate Afghan constitutionalists.

SHIRZAI, Gul Agha

Former governor of Kandahar. Powerful pro-government warlord with up to 20,000 armed men at his disposal. Ousted as governor of Kandahar by the Taliban in 1994, Gul Agha was quick to return accompanied by 3,000 guerrillas on 7 December 2001, with the collapse of the Islamic movement. During 2002-03, he benefited financially from customs duties at Spinboldak on the Quetta-Kandahar highway and enjoyed support from the Americans based at Kandahar airport. However, the Kabul government put him on a shortlist of warlords to rein in, and he was sacked as governor of Kandahar in August 2003.

TANIWAL, Hakim

Governor of Khost. Trained as a sociologist and lived in Australia. Appointed Governor of Khost by President Karzai, in an attempt to curtail the power of local strong-man, Badshah Khan Zadran.

ZADRAN, Badshah Khan

Rebel warlord of Khost. Built-up by US-led Coalition Forces as a military commander to counter Taliban and Al Qa'eda influence, Zadran shows little inclination of bowing to efforts by the Karzai government to appoint Hakim Taniwal as its own governor of Khost. Zadran is reputedly involved in drugs and timber trafficking as well as other forms of 'import-export' business.

ZAHIR SHAH, Mohammed

King of Afghanistan from 1933 to 1973. Zahir Shah was proclaimed monarch, aged 19, within hours of the assassination of his father, Nadir Shah. His cousin Mohammed Daoud was Prime Minister from 1953-1963, until Zahir Shah forced his resignation. In 1964 he introduced a new constitution, which limited the role of the royal family in government and provided for free elections, a free press and the formation of political parties.

While Kabul grew considerably during this period, through the flow of economic aid from both the East and the West, many sectors of Afghan society did not benefit. In 1973 while on a trip abroad, the King was ousted in a coup by Mohammed Daoud who proclaimed Afghanistan a republic with himself as President. Zahir Shah abdicated shortly afterwards and went to live in exile near Rome.

During the late 1980s both the US and the Soviet Union were promoting the idea of Zahir Shah returning to Afghanistan not as King but as State President of a 'neutral' and coalition government. This administration could have held a *Loya Jirga* or National Council of tribal, resistance and religious leaders to form a consensus on the possibility of future elections. Unlike their often misguided support of extremist Muslim fundamentalist factions, the Americans viewed the King as a moderate who could work to avert a bloody civil war for power among patriotic and extreme religious rivals in the wake of a Soviet withdrawal.

The monarchist cause was popular among other moderate leaders, such as Sibghatullah Mujaddedi who believed that the King was the only real symbol of national unity. This notion, however, was anathema to radical Islamists such as Gulbuddin Hekmatyar, who blamed the origin of Afghanistan's troubles on the King and his acquiescence to communist ambitions.

Zahir himself declined US proposals for a government-in-exile and later dismissed President Najibullah's offer to share power. "I have no ambition to restore the monarchy," he has repeated over and over again. "All I want is to restore the unity and prosperity of my country." Many Afghans saw the return of the King in the summer of 2002 as crucial to the success of the *Loya Jirga*. However, despite the King's readiness to play a role, American politicking assured his ousting from the political scene, a move that may prove seriously detrimental in the long run. Due to his advanced age and fragile health, Zahir Shah's role in Afghan politics is now largely symbolic. In December 2003, the new constitution named him "Father of the nation". However, some of Zahir Shah's family members are active in Afghan politics and have high political aspirations.

Landmines and UXO summary

ESSENTIAL DATA

- 200,000 Afghans have been killed or wounded by mines since 1979 (ICRC)
- 150-300 Afghan civilians are killed or wounded by mines and UXO each month (UN)
- In July 2002, Afghanistan signed the Ottawa Landmine Convention
- Area still contaminated by mines and UXO by end-2002: 850 sq.km (126 sq.km more than in 2001)
- High-priority contaminated area remaining by end-2002: 324 sq.km
- From 1989-2002, the UN and partner NGOs cleared or declared safe 754 sq.km of minefields and battlefields, and taught 2.4 million people about mine awareness
- 12 years of war from 1989-2000 inflicted economic losses on Afghanistan totalling an estimated US$ 550 million
- Benefits from clearing irrigated cropland: US$ 1.5 million annually per sq. km
- Cost of clearing one square metre of contaminated land: US$ 0.60
- US dropped around 125,000 cluster bomblets in at least 234 locations across Afghanistan during 2001
- Each bomblet can puncture 125mm of armoured steel and is deadly to any human within a 50 metre radius – around 10 per cent fail to explode
- UN's demining budget was US$ 66 million in 2002, up from US$ 26 million in 2001
- 7,200 Afghans work in the mine action programme – up from 5,000 in 2001
- Around 100 deminers have been killed and 500 more injured during the past 13 years of mine clearing
- Estimates that there are 10 million mines in Afghanistan are not considered credible

ESSENTIAL CONTACTS

ACBL, AMAA, ARCS, AREA, ARI, ATC, BBC AEP, DAFA, HALO Trust, HI, MAG, MCPA, MDC, META, OMAR, SC-US, DDG, UNMAPA

ESSENTIAL READING AND WEBLINKS

Mine Action Programme for Afghanistan Annual Report, UNMAPA (Kabul, September 2003)

Afghanistan, Landmine Monitor Report 2002, Human Rights Watch/ICBL, August 2002

Landmine Use in Afghanistan, Human Rights Watch Backgrounder, October 2001

Landmine Monitor Research, 2000, Afghanistan, Afghan Campaign to Ban Landmines (2000)

Landmine and UXO Safety Handbook, United Nations and CARE International (2000)

MAPA Study of the Socio-economic Impact of Mine Action in Afghanistan, United Nations (2000)

Afghanistan – the 1997 National Mine Awareness Evaluation, CIET International (1998)

Living in a minefield: A report on the mine problem in Afghanistan, Médecins Sans Frontières (May 1997)

www.halousa.org
www.hrw.org/arms
www.icbl.org/lm
www.mineaction.org
www.un.org/Depts/Landmineswww.un.org/Depts/Landmines

For practical advice on mine awareness and how to avoid mines while in Afghanistan SEE SECURITY TIPS

Language & poetry

The two main languages of Afghanistan are Dari (Afghan Persian/Farsi) and Pashto, both from the Iranian branch of the Indo-European family. Dari literally means "language of the court" and was the court language in Moghul India. Both languages use the Arabic script, written horizontally from right to left, but they are no more mutually intelligible than English is to German. Pashto is itself often divided into the softer 'Pushtu' of the Kandahar area, and the harder 'Pukhtu' of the North West Frontier Province.

The late American writer and archaeologist Louis Dupree makes the point that Afghanistan has a literate culture, but a non-literate society: "Most literate or non-literate Afghans, be they Persian-, Pashto-, or Turkic-speakers, consider themselves poets. Poetry, essentially a spoken, not a written, art, gives non-literates the same general opportunities for expression as the literates in a society. Afghanistan, therefore is fundamentally a nation of poets." (*Afghanistan, 1973*)

Poetry in Afghanistan flowered from the 9th to the 17th Centuries, climaxing in the cultural oasis of the court of Mahmud of Ghazni in the early 11th Century. In his court lived 900 scholars and 400 poets, probably the greatest of which was Firdausi, whose *Shah-Namah, Book of the Kings of Persia* had 60,000 couplets. Abdullah Ansari, the Pir of Herat (1005-1088 AD), was a Sufi leader who composed poetry to express his journey from orthodox religion to mysticism. Perhaps the greatest of the Pashto poets are the 17th Century Khushal Khan Khattak (1613-1690) and Rahman Baba. Khushal is the epitome of the Pashtun warrior-poet, the ideal Afghan character-type, who revelled as much in the beauty of man and nature as in waging war on neighbouring Moghuls or hostile Pashtuns. Rahman Baba, a contemporary of Khushal, was inspired by Sufism to turn more towards religious mysticism than to war. One of Afghanistan's greatest 20th Century poets was Khalilullah Khalili (SEE BOX).

The following is a selection of Afghan poetry, both Persian and Pashtun:

"A solitary orphan – pain-ridden and voiceless –
Suddenly, somehow, cries from the heart of the desert.
If someday you want to reach an oasis,
Don't let the candle of hope slip from your palm."

– Khalilullah Khalili (1908-1987)

"The Lasses of the Adam Khel,
As every lover knows,
Are delicately coloured – like
The petals of a rose;
My Love a snowy partridge is,
Who chooses winter time
To seek among the stony fells
A cloak of silver rime.
My Love, my Bird, remember that
A hawk, when he grows old,
Becomes more subtle in the chase,
His stoop becomes more bold:
Surrender then to me, for though
I seem no longer young,
The fervour of my love will taste
Like honey on your tongue."

– Khushal Khan Khattak, 17th Century
(trans. Bowen)

"From among all the good and bad things of the world,
Daqiqi has chosen four:
Ruby-red lips, the wail of the flute,
Blood-coloured wine, and the Zoroastrian religion."

– Daqiqi of Balkh, 10th Century
(trans. S. Shpoon)

"If leadership rests inside the lion's jaw,
So be it. Go, snatch it from his jaw.
Your lot shall be greatness, prestige, honour and glory.
If all fails, face death like a man."

– Hanzala of Badghis, 9th Century AD
(trans. S. Shpoon)

"My beauty, I cannot exchange you for the cash of my life.
You are priceless. I will not sell you so cheap.
I hold your skirt with both my hands.
I may loosen my hold on my life, but not my hold on your skirt."

– Mahmud Warraq, 9th Century
(trans. S. Shpoon)

"Your face is a rose and your eyes are candles:
Faith! I am lost. Should I become a butterfly or a moth?"

"My beloved returned unsuccessful from battle;
I regret the kiss I gave him last night."

"If you don't wield a sword, what else will you do?
You, who have suckled at the breast of an Afghan mother!"

– Traditional 'landay' or Pashto couplets

A Pathan Warrior's Farewell

"Beloved, on a parchment white
With my heart's blood to thee I write;
My pen a dagger, sharp and clean,
Inlaid with golden damascene,
Which I have used, and not in vain,
To keep my honour free from stain.
Now, when our house its mourning wears,
Do not thyself give way to tears:
Instruct our eldest son that I
Was ever anxious thus to die,
For when Death comes the brave are free –
So in thy dreams remember me."

– anon

Khalilullah Khalili (1908-1987)

Khalili's extraordinary life epitomizes the Afghan observation that great pressure can occasionally transform coal into diamonds. Most coal – like most people – responds negatively and remains undeveloped. Only the rare pieces are transformed.

Born in Kabul, Khalili's life at first entailed little pressure. His family roots were Saafi Pashtun, but his parents formed part of the capital's Persian-speaking establishment. His father was King Habibullah's finance minister and closest advisor.

Until age 11, young Khalil enjoyed a privileged childhood: fine houses, vineyards and one of Afghanistan's three automobiles. The boy showed special gifts in Persian classical poetry and mathematics. Then disaster struck: his mother died in 1915 and, in 1919, his father was executed by Amanullah – the new king. Suddenly orphaned, Khalili was then banned by the king from ever attending school.

Khalili was now responsible for himself and three younger siblings. Penniless and with no roof in Kabul, they walked north at night across the Shomali Plain. Local people, aware of the king's wrath, feared to help these orphans openly. A period of enormous pressure had begun.

Interestingly – so the story goes – Khalili never cursed the king. Rather he gave thanks to God that he and his siblings were spared. Here his character was revealed: what happens in life is less important than how one reacts to it. Khalili found odd jobs by day and studied secretly by night with sympathetic elders. He made use of scant resources, collecting scraps of discarded writing from the ground and imagining the text as a whole. Imagination was to become his genius.

Regime change in 1929 provided opportunities. Khalili's uncle became governor of Herat and took Khalili, then 21, with him. Khalili loved this intellectual city. Hobnobbing with artists, writers and sufi sheikhs, he came into his own. "It was there that I became a poet," he said. Indeed he became locally known as *Malik-u-shuaraa*, the King of Poets.

Yet the pressure continued. Khalili was alternately debased (prison in the 1940s) and exalted (minister and ambassador in the 1950s-70s). The Soviet invasion of 1979 made him an exile. His 1987 funeral in Pakistan was attended by 10,000 displaced Afghans.

His works include three large volumes of poetry, numerous short stories, and 35 books of history, biography and literary criticism. *From Balkh to Konya*, his work on 13th Century mystic poet Jalalludin Rumi, is prized everywhere in the Persian-speaking world.

A model of tolerance, moderation and national unity, Khalili is remembered as Afghanistan's greatest writer of the last hundred years. A selection of his work – *An Assembly of Moths* – is newly available in English translation.

Contributed by: Whitney Azoy

Refugees summary

1978: First refugees begin fleeing from midsummer onwards as fighting erupts in the wake of the Saur (April) Revolution.

1979: 600,000 refugees by the end of the year, fleeing to Pakistan (400,000) and Iran (200,000).

1980-83: Refugee exodus increases dramatically to 3.9 million as Soviet-Afghan military strikes against the resistance, including deliberate attacks on the civilian population in what some observers describe as "migratory genocide."

1987: Refugee populations in Pakistan, Iran and elsewhere reach 5.9 million.

1989: Red Army troops withdraw in February. Fighting in Afghanistan reverts to that of a civil war as *mujahideen* continue their battle against the communist PDPA Kabul regime. Refugee numbers continue to rise to 6.1 million despite some refugee returns.

1990: The Afghan exile population reaches a record 6.2 million, nearly half the world's total refugee population. An estimated 350,000 have returned to Afghanistan since 1988.

1992: Najibullah's communist government falls to the *mujahideen* in April. An estimated 1.6 million refugees return home. Fighting in Kabul displaces 1 million Afghans.

1993-94: Factional fighting devastates much of Kabul with fighters often showing complete disregard for civilians. Up to 1 million 'internally displaced persons' (IDPs) believed to have fled to other parts of the country. Another 1.3 million refugees return to peaceful areas. 3.4 million refugees still outside the country at the end of the year.

1994: Taliban forces capture Kandahar. Refugee numbers continue to fall slowly with returns.

1995: Taliban capture Herat in September. Repatriation of refugees from Iran comes to a halt. The Taliban reach the outskirts of Kabul. Refugee numbers stabilize at 2.7 million.

1996: Taliban capture Kabul in September. Fighting continues in northern and central Afghanistan.

1997: Refugee population in exile stands at 2.6 million.

1998: Two huge earthquakes leave thousands homeless in N Afghanistan.

1999: Taliban scorched earth policy in Shomali plain and Parwan displaces up to 100,000 Afghans. Concerns over forced repatriations of Afghans from Iran.

2000: Drought displaces at least 500,000 during 2000-01. Pakistan refuses aid for 'environmental refugees'. Thousands flee to Iran. An estimated 1 million Afghans remain internally displaced. Taliban conquer Takhar in September forcing 170,000 to flee to Pakistan.

2001: US bombing campaign from October-December – UN agencies evacuated to Pakistan. 300,000 flee US bombing around Kandahar. Approx. 1.2 million internally displaced. All neighbouring countries close borders to refugees. Afghan refugees total 3.4 million in Pakistan and 2.3 million in Iran, according to host governments.

2002: Nearly 1.8 million refugees return to Afghanistan, mainly from Pakistan – the world's largest repatriation for 30 years. Around 400,000 IDPs return home while 800,000 more remain displaced. Over 50% of refugees return to Kabul and Jalalabad. Around 100,000 Pashtuns flee persecution in the north and west.

2003: Pakistan and Iran home to an estimated 4 million refugees even though nearly 2 million had returned by July 2003. Some returnees also heading back to Pakistan or Iran where conditions are less difficult. Britain begins forcible repatriation of refugees. Over 400,000 people remain displaced within Afghanistan, including persecuted Pashtuns from northern regions, where intermittent conflict continues, and *kuchis*, whose nomadic life has been shattered by drought and landmines.

Sources: AFP, BAAG, UNHCR

ESSENTIAL CONTACTS

BAAG, ICRC, IOM, MSF, UNHCR, UNICEF, WFP

ESSENTIAL READING

Taking refugees for a ride? The politics of refugee return to Afghanistan, David Turton and Peter Marsden, Afghanistan Research and Evaluation Unit (Kabul, December 2002)

UNHCR Global Report 2002, UNHCR (Geneva, 2002)

Living in Exile: Report on a study of economic coping strategies among Afghan refugees in Pakistan, British Agencies Afghanistan Group (London, December 1996)

Exile and Return: Report on a study on coping strategies among Afghan refugees in Iran and returnees to Afghanistan, British Agencies Afghanistan Group (London, June 1996)

Tradition and Dynamism Among Afghan Refugees, International Labour Organisation

Left out in the Cold: The Perilous Homecoming of Afghan Refugees, Hiram A Ruiz, US Committee for Refugees

Long Years of Exile: Central Asian Refugees in Afghanistan and Pakistan, Dr Shalinsky, University Press of America

The State of the World's Refugees, UNHCR (annually)

TRAVEL

Restored Timurid tilework in Herat *J.Walter*

Travel overland

In the days of the "Great Game" – that vast strategic game of chess played across Central Asia between the foreign ministries of Britain and Russia throughout the 19th and early 20th Centuries – you would travel to Afghanistan in disguise. Slipping away from your regiment or colonial office on the pretext of "shooting leave," you would head for the frontier clad in the garb of a Muslim holy man or Baluch carpet dealer, with nothing but your wits and a few gold sovereigns between you and an anonymous death in a dark dungeon or dank defile.

Today, travelling into Afghanistan is more prosaic and less risky than a hundred years ago or during the Soviet war. But it is not without its share of danger. Crossborder infiltration is still possible, although there is not much point now that you can drive into most of Afghanistan's major towns. Travelling overland is an excellent way to see the country. You get more of a feel for what's happening than if you simply jet in and out of Kabul International Airport. But before heading in, find out as much as you can about the security situation from other travellers or aid workers. For details on visa regulations, SEE VISAS.

From Pakistan

The route from Peshawar over the Khyber Pass towards Jalalabad and Kabul remains one of the most exciting and romantic ways to enter Afghanistan. This rocky cleft in the Hindu Kush has been breached in both directions by invaders for most of recorded history – from columns of Alexander the Great's army to Moghuls, Persians and British imperialists.

Before leaving, you must get a special tribal agencies permit and an armed guard in advance from the office of the Political Agent of the Khyber Agency in Peshawar (SEE PESHAWAR). If you do not have access to your own vehicle, ask around in Peshawar – aid agencies are often happy to carry an extra passenger, but you may need to break the journey in Jalalabad. Pakistani taxis run to the border at Torkham, where you can change to an Afghan taxi which will take you to Kabul (around US$ 50 for the car or US$ 10 per seat). Foreigners are not allowed to take a bus. World Food Programme (WFP) food convoys sometimes offer lifts to freelancers, but take two days to reach Kabul from Peshawar. Check with the logistics department of WFP in Islamabad.

Heading west from Peshawar, the road takes you through the semi-autonomous tribal agencies of the North West Frontier Province, which for centuries has been home to smugglers, arms dealers, drug barons and, more recently, Al Qa'eda. The route then winds up into the Khyber Pass before reaching the border crossing at Torkham – about one and a half hours by car. The frontier closes between 1200 hrs and 1300 hrs and Pakistan time is ahead of Afghanistan (half an hour in winter, one and a half hours in summer) so time your arrival at the border appropriately if you are driving back to Peshawar. The Pakistanis close their side of the border at 1700 hrs but may still be persuaded to let you through later.

From the forts and picket posts of the Khyber you descend into the Nangarhar valley. Before the war, this area boasted several hundred thousand acres of irrigated citrus fruit and olive farms created under a joint Afghan-Soviet scheme to reclaim the desert. Tall poplars planted as windbreaks still sway elegantly in the breeze, but most of the cash-crops have been ripped up during two decades of fighting. The *mujahideen* gave the farms their *coup de grace* by completely trashing and looting them, hard on the heels of the government forces in 1989. The odd fir and cypress tree herald your arrival in Jalalabad (one and a half hours from Torkham), a town founded by the Moghuls who were among the first to make this route via the Khyber popular. The military garrison at Jalalabad was the distant sanctuary towards which a British column of 4,500 soldiers and 12,000 camp-followers was desperately retreating after an ignominious departure from Kabul in January 1842. Apart from a few prisoners who strayed back months later, only one Englishman, Dr Brydon, completed the retreat; the remainder were cut to pieces in the passes which lie between here and Kabul.

West of Jalalabad the road joins the Kabul River – the most westerly tributary of the Indus. On the other side are Buddhist caves carved into the cliff-face. Over one thousand Buddhist sites and *stupas* are scattered across the Jalalabad valley, the most famous of which is Hadda, which once housed the Buddha's skull bone. Some *stupas* date back as far as 200 AD but many have now been badly looted (SEE CULTURE). The road continues past the turquoise Darunta Reservoir, built in the 1960s and once home to four types of Chinese carp, and across a flat plain punctuated with typical fortified *qala* (Pashtun houses) and *chaikhane* (teahouses). With the Taliban gone, the strains of MTV and Hindi movies emanate from these *chaikhane.* Women in the fields or by the road seldom wear the all-encompassing *burqa*, but still cover their heads at the sight of strangers.

The next part of the journey from Darunta dam to Sarobi – scenes of heavy fighting during the Soviet war – used to be a potholed dirt track. But in late 2002 it was graded, cutting the driving time from Jalalabad to Kabul down to around three and a half hours. Before Sarobi you pass through Tangi Abreshom, the Silk Gorge, which was the scene of one of the most spectacular *mujahed* ambushes of the war: several hundred Soviet soldiers are believed to have perished when their armoured column was fired on. Some of their vehicles remain, as still as headstones, in mute testimony to a misguided war. This gorge

Thorkell Thorkelsson/International Federation

was where four foreign journalists were murdered by Al Qa'eda in November 2001.

From Sarobi the route passes high to the south of the Naglu Reservoir before plunging between the sheer rock faces of the Tangi Gharu gorge, considerably more impressive than the Khyber Pass. Once spat out onto the Kabul Plateau, the capital is within sight. Almost immediately on your left is the massive edifice of Pul-e-Charkhi, the notorious East German-built prison used by the communist government for detaining thousands of political and military opponents during the 1980s. The whole journey from Peshawar to Kabul can be done in a day, if you start early. The Torkham-Kabul leg takes about four and a half hours, without stops.

An alternative overland route from Pakistan involves travelling from Quetta, via the border crossing at Spinboldak, to Kandahar. But this region was dangerous for Westerners during much of 2003, so check the security situation before setting out.

From Iran and Central Asia

More intrepid overlanders can enter Afghanistan from the west and north, as restrictions on border crossings have gradually eased following the fall of the Taliban. From Mashad in Iran, the journey to Herat is now fairly straightforward. The Afghan consulate in Mashad will sell you a tourist visa for US$ 30. A three hour bus service takes you to Taybad, from where you can get a taxi or minibus to the border post at Dogharun. From Islam Qala (the Afghan side of the border), it's another four or five hours by truck or bus to Herat. Iran is paying to reconstruct this route, which will shorten journey times in due course. Iran maintains very close links with Ismail Khan, the self-styled Amir of Herat – who earns a fortune from the transit taxes he levies at Islam Qala.

To the north, Afghanistan borders Turkmenistan, Uzbekistan and Tajikistan. During the Taliban years, these border crossings were resolutely shut and heavily guarded by Russian troops, as Moscow was determined to prevent radical Islam from percolating into its sphere of influence. The 'Friendship

Bridge', which joins Afghanistan to Uzbekistan across the Amu Darya (Oxus River), was blocked by concrete and barbed wire. Since 2002, accredited aid workers and journalists have been able to cross here, but freelance travellers have encountered difficulties. One alternative is to head to Tajikistan, where Afghan visas can be obtained in Dushanbe as long as you have a letter of introduction from your embassy or agency. Then head south to Nizhny Pyanj, across the Pyanj river by boat and on to Kunduz.

Once inside

Road travel within Afghanistan is always exhilarating, but never without its risks – the past few years have seen frequent shootings, car-jackings (especially of conspicuous white aid vehicles) and accidents involving landmines. Some regions are safer than others – it's best to check with the UN security office in Kabul before heading out. During 2003, security deteriorated sharply – especially along the roads from Kabul to Khost, Ghazni and Kandahar. Illegal checkpoints – outlawed under the Taliban – have also made a comeback, forcing drivers to pay dollar bribes. From Kabul, the principal arteries are east towards Jalalabad and over the Khyber Pass to Peshawar; north through the Salang Tunnel to Mazar and Central Asia; and south-west to Kandahar, then up to Herat and Iran. But there are innumerable exciting detours – for example up the Panjshair Valley or into Bamiyan.

During 2002, many commentators, including Afghanistan's Finance Minister, Ashraf Ghani, argued that too much international aid had gone on humanitarian needs and not enough had gone on reconstruction – especially of roads. Eighteen months after the US bombing campaign began in October 2001, barely a kilometre of road had been paved outside of Kabul. Not only would new roads provide badly needed lines of communication for Afghanistan's budding private sector, their construction could employ thousands of ex-combatants and returnees, kick-starting the local economy and attracting young men away from two decades of gun-culture.

Some roads remain lethal – for different reasons. In February 2002, half a dozen died in blizzards in the Salang Tunnel. The tunnel, Afghanistan's main artery linking Kabul to the markets of Central Asia, remained unlit, unpaved, heavily polluted and choked with snow for much of the year. In 2003, the tunnel was closed altogether for repairs. Portions of the highway from Pul-e-Khumri to Kunduz and Badakhshan are good, but many stretches are still joltingly bad. The road to Mazar, however, is tarred most of the way and relatively comfortable. The Jalalabad to Kabul road was finally graded in late summer 2002, reducing the travel time from seven to about four hours.

In December 2003, the new Kabul-Kandahar road was finally opened after considerable delays in reconstruction. Once a desperate 2-day journey of dust and potholes, the tarmac surface has cut driving times to just six hours. But throughout 2003, foreigners, Afghan aid workers and road construction teams alike fell victim to targeted attacks by pro-Taliban and anti-government forces along this route. Meanwhile, cars and buses which divert off main roads to avoid potholes and blown bridges frequently hit anti-personnel and anti-tank mines – with fatal results.

Many donors have expressed interest in rebuilding roads, but progress has been painfully slow. In May 2002, Iran began to repair the road between their border and Herat, and showed some interest in extending this road through to Bamiyan. In March 2003, the World Bank finally approved a US$ 108 million credit to improve the vital Kabul-Pul-e-Khumri-Kunduz highway, including the Salang Tunnel. Germany undertook repairs to Kabul's road system. The Asian Development Bank announced investments to repair the connection between Kandahar and Spinboldak. The European Union has donated money for the Kabul-Jalalabad route. Italy has promised to fund the road from Kabul-Maidan-Bamiyan. And the US, Japanese and Saudi governments have pledged funds to rebuild the shattered road from Kandahar to Herat. But reconstruction has been seriously held up by the deteriorating security situation.

For more details on road travel within Afghanistan, refer to the regional Travel sections which follow. For the latest, detailed information on the conditions of roads and reconstruction, check with UNAMA in Kabul.

ESSENTIAL READING AND WEBLINKS

The Survival Guide to Kabul, Dominic Medley & Jude Barrand, Bradt Travel Guides Ltd (England, 2003)
http://www.kabulcaravan.com (online travel guide to Afghanistan)
http://thorntree.lonelyplanet.com (online chat room – see Asia/Central Asia section)

Travel by air

Since the fall of the Taliban, international and domestic air connections have improved considerably. There are numerous charter and commercial services into the region, principally via Dubai and Pakistan. For aid workers, one of the most popular routings is to fly to Dubai and take the **United Nations'** connecting flight direct to Kabul. Alternatively fly to Islamabad and take the UN's flight to Kabul. Emirates is a popular carrier for the Dubai-Islamabad routing. If you find yourself in Peshawar, the **International Committee of the Red Cross** may fly you from there into Kabul. Another possible routing is via Dushanbe, from where the UN flies to Kabul. **PACTEC/Air Serv International** operate two light aircraft out of Kabul for aid workers. See below for more details.

Commercial operators flying into Kabul include the national carrier, **Ariana Afghan Airlines** (from Dubai or Islamabad), plus **Azerbaijan Airlines** (from Baku) and **Pakistan International Airlines** (from Islamabad). In June 2003, **Swiss Skies AG** teamed up with World Airways to announce they would start flying a 233-seater MD-11 aircraft from Washington to Kabul via Geneva twice a week. However, at the time of writing, the service had not started, owing to security concerns (for more details, visit www.swissskies.com). In August 2003, the German operator **LTU** announced it would start direct flights to Kabul. Some journalists have, unofficially, reported 'hitching' a ride back to Europe with military peacekeeping aircraft. For details on visa regulations, SEE VISAS.

United Nations Humanitarian Air Service (UNHAS)

The World Food Programme (WFP) operates a humanitarian air service (UNHAS) for the benefit of UN agencies, eligible NGOs and donor representatives. Their aircraft include three Beechcraft and a 55-seater jet, based in Kabul. International destinations out of Kabul include: Dubai, Dushanbe and Islamabad. Domestic flights operate to Bamiyan, Faizabad, Herat, Jalalabad, Kandahar, Kunduz, Maimana and Mazar. UNHAS does not usually fly on Fridays. Flights for accredited agencies used to be free, but are now charged at around US$ 100 for domestic routes (US$ 50 for Jalalabad and Bamiyan) and US$ 400 for the one-way fare to or from Dubai. Journalists, unaccredited NGOs and dependents may use UNHAS flights, but have to pay the full fare (see table below).

Eligible NGOs are those which have been running programmes in Afghanistan for two years and which are UN implementing partners or are funded through the Consolidated Appeal process. Flight reservations must be made at least 48 hours in advance (in person or by email) and confirmed 24 hours before departure. Prospective passengers must provide an agency identity card or request letter on an official letterhead. A maximum of two persons per agency is allowed per flight. "No shows" are taken seriously and may lead to a ban. All passengers should hold valid passports and visas. For more details, contact:

UNHAS Kabul Office,
WFP Compound,
Opposite the French Embassy,
Wazir Akbar Khan, Kabul
Tel: +93 (0)70 281 7826, 282559, 070 282560
Fax: +873 762904936
Email: kabul.unhas@wfp.org

UNHAS Islamabad Office,
House 4, Street 5, F/8-3,
Islamabad, Pakistan
Tel: +92 51 2264077, 2264101
Fax +92 51 2264054
Email: islamabad.unhas@wfp.org

UNHAS flight schedule

A flight schedule is issued during the last week of each month for the following month. Copies are available from all UN agencies or at the UNHAS Flight Operations Office in Kabul. The flight schedule for June 2003 was as follows, leaving Kabul and returning the same day:

Destination	Day	Fare o/w US$ (ex-Kabul) for non-accredited travellers
Dubai	Tue, Sat (rtn next day)	400 (all travellers)
Dushanbe	Mon, Thu	
Islamabad	Mon, Tue, Wed, Thu, Sat, Sun	600
Bamiyan	Tue, Thu, Sun	125
Faizabad	Sun, Mon, Tue, Wed, Thu	335
Herat	Mon, Wed, Thu, Sat	600
Jalalabad	Mon, Thu, Sat	120
Kandahar	Mon, Wed, Thu, Sat	440
Kunduz	Sun, Mon, Tue, Wed, Thu,	230

United Nations Assistance Mission to Afghanistan (UNAMA) AirOps

UNAMA operates separate air services within the country for UNAMA's political missions. Other UN agencies, diplomatic missions and selected NGOs (but no journalists) may use the service according to availability. The provisional flight schedule is: Mazar & Kunduz (Mon); Kandahar (Tue); Jalalabad (Wed); Herat (Thu); Bamiyan (Sun). UNAMA flights may also go to Delhi, Dubai, Tehran, Dushanbe and Islamabad on demand. For more information, go to: UNAMA Compound A, Jalalabad Road, Kabul.

International Committee of the Red Cross (ICRC)

The ICRC operates two light aircraft out of Kabul, providing daily flights to most regional centres, plus Peshawar. A short list of relief NGOs is authorized for free flights, but journalists are not normally permitted onboard. As well as flying to most domestic destinations several times per week, ICRC flies from Kabul-Peshawar-Kabul daily except Fridays. To register your agency, contact ICRC's sub delegation in Peshawar. Bookings must be made at least three days in advance. Passengers require a valid passport and Pakistani visa, even for internal flights – in case, for any reason, the plane needs to divert to Pakistan. For more details, contact:

ICRC Air Operations
Charah-e-Hajji Yaqub,
Shahr-e-Naw,
Kabul
Tel: +93 (0)70 279078,
020 220 0326

40 Sayed Jamalud-Din Afghani Road,
University Town, PO Box 418,
Peshawar.
Tel: +92 (91) 840146, 43723, 41371
Fax: +92 (91) 840413
Email: peshawar.pesh@icrc.org

PACTEC/Air Serv International

PACTEC (Partners in Aviation and Communications Technology) and Air Serv International are two non-profit NGOs which have combined to provide two light aircraft flying out of Kabul to most regional centres, plus Islamabad. Services are daily, except for Fridays, and are available for UN agencies, eligible NGOs and donor representatives. For more details, contact:

PACTEC Kabul
2nd house on the left,
Street 11, Wazir Akbar Khan,
Kabul
Tel: +93 (0)70 282679
E-mail: bookingkbl@pactec.net
www.pactec.net
www.airserv.org

PACTEC Islamabad
House 494-A, Street 9,
F-10/2, Islamabad
Tel: +92 (0)51 210 5261-4
Fax: + 92 (0)51 210 5265
Email: pakbooking@airserv.org

"One lump or two?"

As I peered through the window, eight US-made Pakistani F-16 fighter aircraft landed, refuelled and took off again, their wings weighed heavy with weapons of war. Once the last of the jets had vanished in a haze of airfuel, our slim white aircraft, emblazoned with the protective red crosses of the ICRC, taxied to the end of the runway. We were flying into Kabul from Peshawar Airport – the Pakistan Air Force's closest airfield to the frontline.

It was 1997: my first time into Afghanistan. I was expecting to rough it – tossed in the back of a Hercules military transport plane perhaps, surrounded by sacks of food-aid or boxes of medicine. I had some US Army boots on, khaki trousers and a rather mangy beard (which an old Afghan hand had advised me to grow). But on boarding the plane I found all the male passengers were clean-shaven, sporting neatly-pressed chinos and shiny loafers. The women wore elegant long summer dresses and shawls. Inside, the aircraft was cleaner than a dentist's waiting room. The deep-upholstered seats even had white "anti-macassars" folded over the headrests (originally introduced by 19th Century English hostesses to protect their antique furniture from the exotic gentlemen's hair oil which it was fashionable to import from the Celebes at that time). And we were flying into a war-zone?

As we waited for clearance from air-traffic control, the pilot gave us a security briefing. Here we go, I thought, heart racing: Action in the event of mid-air interception? Tactics to avoid anti-aircraft fire? A calm, clipped South African accent crackled over the intercom. "Good morning ladies and gentlemen, this is your captain speaking. Our flight time to Kabul will be approximately one hour. Coffee is in the flasks at the front of the cabin, but take care to use two cups – it's very hot." Was this the hottest it got?

Flying over the mountains flanking the Khyber Pass, ridge after ridge of rock thrust skywards like shark's teeth. To the north lay the snowcapped mountains of the Hindu Kush. Westwards the land became drier and more parched, with only the thin emerald ribbon of the Kabul river for relief. As we dipped and landed, the airport was littered with wrecked Soviet aircraft and pockmarked with the potholes of past rocket attacks. Despite the smashed windows and scarred walls of the terminal building, there was an Afghan official checking everyone's visas. As we waited in the queue, one of the passengers whispered to me: "You'd better shave that goatee off. It makes you look like a Tajik – they're the enemy around here!" *JW*

Ariana Afghan Airlines

Ariana, the national carrier, lost six of its eight aircraft during the US bombing of late 2001. Nevertheless by 2002, it had resumed international services out of Kabul, helped by India's donation of three Airbus A300 jets. Ariana also has four Boeing 727-200s and one Antonov 24. Its weekly flight from Frankfurt via Istanbul to Kabul is the first scheduled service with the West for nearly three decades. In mid-2003, the return flight from Frankfurt to Kabul was competitively priced at Euros 722. Other flight prices include: Dubai-Kabul (US$ 185 one-way, US$ 370 return) and Islamabad-Kabul (US$ 200 return).

Ariana also offers regular domestic flights from Kabul to Herat and Mazar – a much cheaper service than the UN alternatives. Ariana's timetable as at 12 October 2003 was:

Destination	Day
Amritsar-Kabul	Sun
Kabul-Amritsar	Sat
Delhi-Kabul	Mon, Thu
Kabul-Delhi	Wed, Sun
Dubai-Kabul	Wed, Sun
Kabul-Dubai	Tue, Sat
Frankfurt-Kabul (via Istanbul)	Wed
Kabul-Frankfurt (via Baku)	Wed
Islamabad-Kabul	Mon
Kabul-Islamabad	Mon
Istanbul-Kabul (via Baku)	Sat
Kabul-Istanbul (via Baku)	Fri
Moscow-Kabul	Tue
Kabul-Moscow (via Baku)	Mon
Sharjah-Kabul	Mon, Thu
Kabul-Sharjah	Wed, Sun
Tehran-Kabul	Fri
Kabul-Tehran	Fri
Kabul-**Herat**-Kabul	Daily (Afs. 2,000 o/w)
Kabul-**Mazar**-Kabul	Tue, Fri (Afs. 1,200 o/w)

J. Walter

For the latest timetables and online booking, go to: www.flyariana.com. Their website also has details of Ariana agents in Canada, Germany, India, Iran, Pakistan, Russia, Saudi Arabia, Turkey, United Kingdom, UAE and the United States. In Afghanistan, contact:

Ariana Afghan Main Office
Kabul Hotel, Kabul.
Reservation Number: +93 (0)20 210 0351
Reservation Fax: +873 762 523 846

Azerbaijan Airlines (AZAL)

Azerbaijan Airlines operates a Boeing 727 passenger service three times a week between Baku and Kabul (Wed, Fri, Sun). The Baku-Kabul return flight costs around US$ 340. They also provide international connections to Baku from Ankara, Dubai, Frankfurt, Istanbul, London, Moscow, Paris, Tehran and numerous other cities in Europe and North America. For connections in Baku of more than six hours, the airline offers transfer and hotel accommodation. For more details, contact:

AZAL
May 28 str., 66/68
Baku 370000,
Azerbaijan
Tel: +994 12 934004, 937121
Fax: +994 12 981545
Email: azal@azal.baku.az
Web: www.icd-azal.com

Pakistan International Airlines (PIA)

PIA operates a regular service from Islamabad-Kabul-Islamabad every Monday, Thursday and Saturday (US$ 200 one-way). For more details, contact:

PIA
Quaid-e-Azam International Airport
Karachi 75200
Tel: +92 (0)21 457 2011, 457 6881
Email: info@piac.com.pk
Web: www.piac.com.pk

Central region

Central Afghanistan may be said to comprise the provinces of Kabul, Kapisa, Parwan and Wardak, with the city of Kabul as its strategic crossroads. To the north lies the snowcapped Hindu Kush mountain range, soaring to over 5,000 metres and through which the Salang Tunnel blasts its way towards Mazar and Central Asia. To the east the main artery to Jalalabad and the subcontinent follows the course of the Kabul River, plunging through the spectacular Tangi Gharu and Silk Gorges before climbing through the Khyber Pass into Pakistan. The road towards Ghazni and Persia – for millennia the route of choice for successive conquerors of Kabul, Kandahar and beyond – escapes south-west through a cleft in the mountains. To the west and northwest lie difficult mountain passes into Hazarajat and central Afghanistan proper.

Kabul

The capital of Afghanistan – and its largest city – is situated at around 1,800 metres above sea-level. Its population has fluctuated wildly according to the military situation. In 1978 the city had some 500,000 inhabitants; by 2003, Afghans returning from exile had swelled this figure to around 2-3 million.

Kabul's strategic location, in a fertile valley surrounded by high mountains and straddling major trade routes to the four corners of the compass, has made it the natural choice for a settlement since antiquity. It was known as Kubha in the Rig Veda of c.1500 BC and as Kabura by Ptolemy (2nd Century AD). In the mid-7th Century AD Muslim Arabs captured the city, but its Hindu rulers were not ousted for another 200 years when the Saffarids finally established Islam in Kabul. As part of the Ghaznavid empire Kabul was attacked by Genghis Khan's hordes in the 13th Century and became the capital of a province of the Moghul empire, whose founder, Babur Shah (1483-1530), is buried on the eastern slope of the Sher Darwaza mountain. The Moghuls held Kabul until the mid-18th Century, when the Pashtun Ahmed Shah Durrani established the first Afghan Empire based on Kandahar in 1747.

From 1776 onwards Timur Shah, son of Ahmed Shah, made Kabul his capital, and for the next 40 years bitter infighting between Timur Shah's Sadozai brothers destabilized the capital. From 1819 right through to 1973 a rival Pashtun clan, the Mohammedzais, held sway, both as Amirs and as Kings. The "Great

Amir" Dost Mohammed emerges as the key figure in mid-19th Century Kabuli politics, ruling the city from 1826-39 and again, after a brief and bloody British interlude, from 1843 until his death in 1863. Dost had provoked the British by making overtures to Russia and Persia, permitting a Russian agent, Vitkevich, to come to Kabul, and casting acquisitive eyes on Punjab territory captured by Ranjit Singh. The British backed Singh, invaded Afghanistan and sacked Kabul in July 1839. Thus began the First Afghan War.

The British installed a puppet ruler of Kabul, Shah Shuja, but he was so weak and unpopular that the British invading force became an army of occupation, complete with polo matches, ladies with parasols and thousands of Indian camp-followers. However, Afghan resentment was fired up and in November 1841 a mob attacked the British delegation, hacking to death the head of mission Sir Alexander Burnes in the process. During the subsequent and infamous retreat from Kabul the following January only a handful of the 16,000 British troops, wives and camp-followers survived, cut down in the passes between Kabul and Jalalabad by tribesmen who had treacherously offered them safe passage. Exacting vengeance, the British invaded a second time in 1842 torching the covered bazaar and plundering much of the city bare. Dost Mohammed returned to Kabul for 20 years during which time he brought Herat, Kandahar and the north under the sway of his capital. Meanwhile the British withdrew to lick their wounds and watch – a policy known in the diplomatic language of the day as "masterly inactivity."

However, Dost Mohammed's son Sher Ali, who became Amir on his father's death, provoked Britain into the Second Afghan War by inviting a Russian General into Kabul in 1878 to sign a treaty. Britain invaded and established a new mission in Kabul the following year, but after only six weeks mutinous troops murdered the hapless envoy and his staff. In 1880 Amir Abdur Rahman consolidated rule in Kabul and established the present day boundaries of Afghanistan. From his time onwards, the history of Kabul and that of Afghanistan as a nation become inseparable (SEE HISTORY).

A series of Pashtun kings ruled from Kabul until the ousting of Zahir Shah in 1973. Kabul creaked slowly into the 20th Century, but the provinces never followed. The radical reforms of King Amanullah, who ruled in the 1920s, backfired. The first school appeared in Kabul in the early 1900s, and Kabul University was founded in 1932 with the establishment of the school of medicine. A new campus was built in 1964. As Soviet influence infiltrated Afghanistan's ruling elite from the 1960s-70s, the gulf between the modernizing capital and the traditional hinterland rapidly widened. Afghan women wandered the streets of Kabul in mini-skirts, and the capital became a stopping off point along the hippie trail to Kathmandu. However, when Kabul's pro-Moscow ruling party seized power in the 1978 coup, their attempts to impose communist ideology on rural Afghans led to open revolt. When the Soviets invaded the following year to bolster the communist regime, rural revolt rapidly became *jihad.*

In the 1980s, Kabul became the power base for Soviet forces and their Afghan allies, known as the 'Regime'. Life in Kabul became increasingly westernised, as Soviet-style factories and offices spread. Women studied and went to work, and the number of university students doubled. But beneath the surface, the hated KHAD agents – the East German-trained secret police – were everywhere to ensure pro-Soviet sentiment. At least this meant the city escaped much of the carnage inflicted on rural areas during the Soviet war,

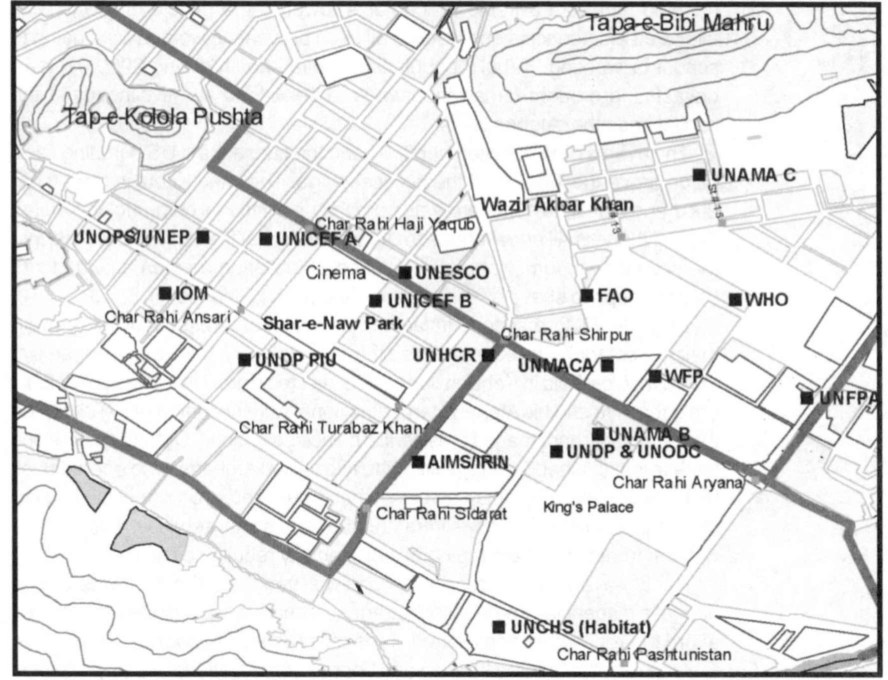

Central Kabul: UN offices *Crosslines and AIMS*

which killed over a million Afghans and forced six million more into exile. As the war wrecked the country's economy and the value of the *Afghani* plummeted, urban dwellers were sheltered by government subsidies on food. However, when the Russians finally retreated in 1989, and when their favourite, President Najibullah, resigned in the face of invading *mujahideen* in 1992, Afghanistan descended into civil war.

During the devastating battle for power between rival *mujahed* factions from 1992-1996, at least two-thirds of the capital's buildings were reduced to rubble. Four opposing factions slugged it out, with Kabul as their battleground: the Tajik-dominated forces of Jamiat-e-Islami, under Ahmed Shah Massoud and Burhanuddin Rabbani; the Uzbek-dominated Jumbesh-e-Melli, under Abdul Rashid Dostum; the Pashtun-dominated Hezb-e-Islami under Gulbuddin Hekmatyar; and the Hazara-dominated Hezb-e-Wahdat. Soldiers on every side committed atrocities. Kabul's professional classes fled, and the government machinery ground to a halt. The fighting killed over 20,000 Kabulis, and forced a million to flee towards Pakistan.

Then, in September 1996, the Taliban arrived in Kabul and disarmed factional fighters. Security returned, but with a heavy price-tag. They smashed televisions and dangled audio and video tape from their checkpoints. They enforced untrimmed beards on men and the all-encompassing *burqa* veil on women. They provoked international outrage by dragging the communist Najibullah from his sanctuary in a United Nations compound, executing him and hanging him from a traffic policeman's tower in the middle of town. They alienated aid agencies and Kabulis alike by preventing women from going to school or working. Kabul's population swelled again during 2000-01, as a devastating drought forced thousands to seek food and livelihoods in the capital and other Afghan cities.

The events of 11th September 2001 and the subsequent US bombing campaign drove the Taliban off the political stage. They fled Kabul in November 2001 and – despite some protests from the international community – United Front (Northern Alliance) troops (mainly Tajik Jamiat forces) were sucked into the security vacuum. Kabul saw scenes of jubilation as men crowded into barber-shops to shave off their beards and music filled the air.

By early 2002, a second invasion – this time of foreign aid workers with their trademark white 4x4s – flooded the capital. Over a thousand delegates at the *Loya Jirga*, held in Kabul in June 2002, elected Hamid Karzai as provisional president. He and his Afghanistan Transitional Administration (ATA) occupied the remarkably undamaged presidential palace compound. Diplomatic missions were re-established. Around half of the two million Afghans, who poured back home from exile in Pakistan and elsewhere, descended on Kabul, putting immense pressure on the city's infrastructure and social services. The air filled with car fumes and the banging of a broken city rebuilding itself.

Rents have rocketed ten-fold – forced sky-high by the presence of big-budget aid agencies and wealthy returnees. Small Afghan NGOs who couldn't afford the rent have been evicted. Tens of thousands of poorer Kabulis have to sleep rough, in ruins still mined and booby-trapped, offering scant protection against the elements. Squatter settlements comprise half the city's housing stock, only 20 percent of the city has access to clean water and electricity is scarce.

Security in the city is maintained by the presence of foreign peacekeeping troops, the UN-mandated International Security Assistance Force (ISAF). Nevertheless throughout 2002, Kabul was rocked by the assassinations of two cabinet ministers, occasional rocket attacks and several fatal car bombs. In June 2003, a chill ran down the capital's collective spine, when four German peacekeeping troops were killed by a suicide bomb.

Getting there

By air

Kabul's international airport is slowly being rehabilitated after two decades of war. The shell holes on the runway have been filled in. But the airfield is still littered with the wrecks of old Soviet MiG fighters, helicopters and transport aircraft. As far as the terminal goes, your passports and visas will be checked (exit visa no longer necessary) but Kabul International is not the place for duty-free shopping. Smuggling alcohol in by air is not recommended.

You can now fly direct to Kabul from Baku, Delhi, Dubai, Dushanbe, Frankfurt, Geneva, Islamabad, Istanbul, Peshawar, Sharjah and Tehran. For details of these flights, SEE TRAVEL BY AIR.

Slowly but Surely Culture Re-appears in Poor Old Kabul

Overland

Short of trekking in by foot disguised as a *mullah* or lurching in on a camel, the most interesting and atmospheric way to reach Kabul is by road. The eastern approach from Pakistan takes between five to six hours by car from Peshawar to Kabul – not including border stops. The trip is quicker and less bone-shattering than in the past, now that the road has been graded. On a good day the views are fantastic, ranging from spectacular rocky passes and snowcapped mountains to turquoise lakes and emerald green pastures fringing the Kabul River. During the Soviet war the road was thick with Russian tanks, APCs and troop columns, so most journalists and adventurers entering or leaving Afghanistan from the east had to trek in by foot through the mountains to the north or south. In the "bad old days" from '92-'96 you could be stopped at over 60 different checkpoints along this road, all manned by local commanders loaded with similar weapons but varying allegiances. Numerous aid workers and journalists have been held up at gunpoint and had their possessions or vehicles stolen from in front of them. During the Taliban era, the road was pretty safe. But in November 2001, four journalists were killed along it, and for much of 2002-03 the route was considered high risk by UN security advisors. Dozens of yellow Kabuli cabs now make the trip to the border and back each day – expect to pay around US$ 50 to hire the whole car, depending on your bargaining skills. For more details on this journey, SEE TRAVEL OVERLAND.

To the north, the road from Mazar across the Hindu Kush and through the Salang tunnel is magnificent but takes at least a day in a 4x4. The tunnel and its approaches are derelict, unlit and often snow-blocked – although major repairs got underway in late-2003. For more details of this route, SEE NORTHERN. A central route from Herat to Kabul taking at least four days via Chakhcharan and Bamiyan is also possible. Donors have promised to repair

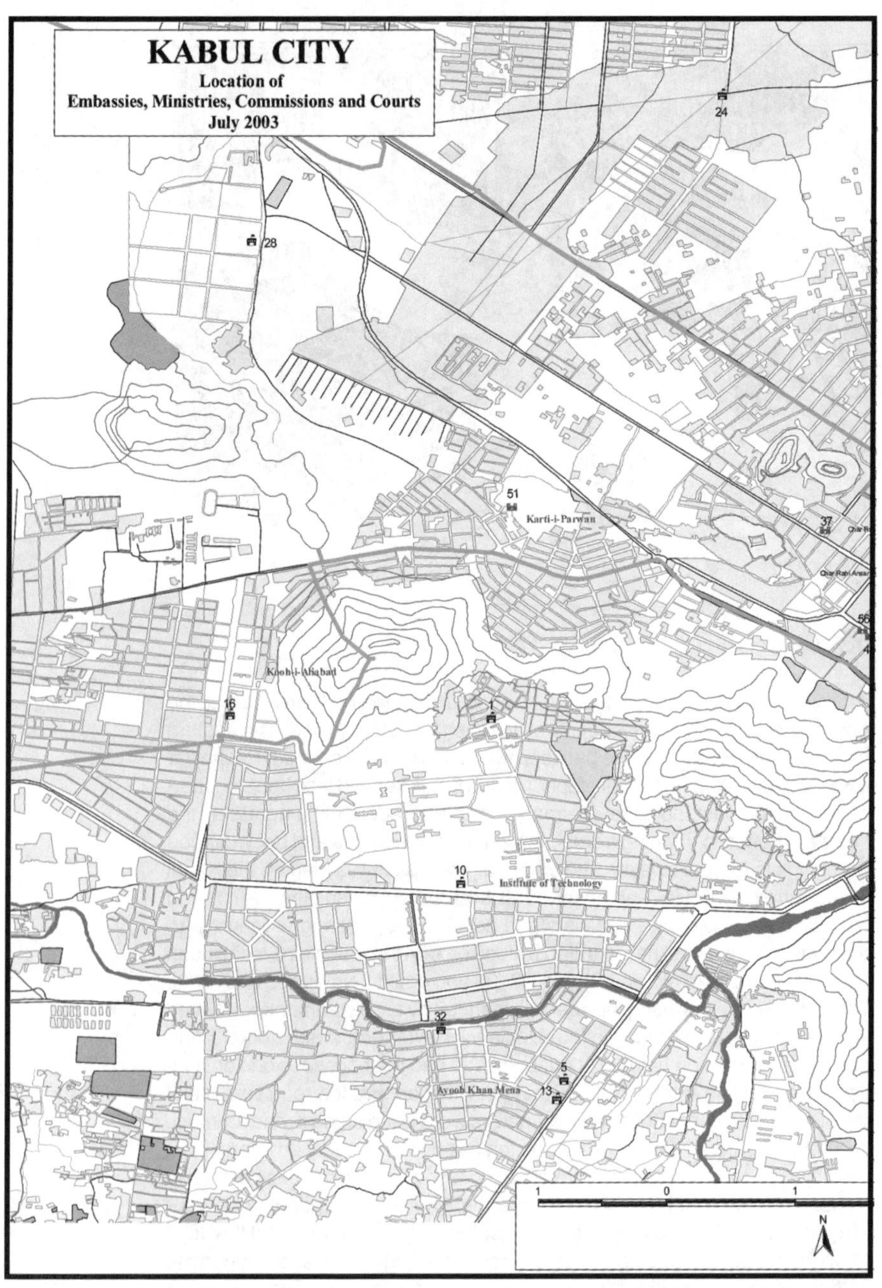

KABUL CITY
Location of
Embassies, Ministries, Commissions and Courts
July 2003
24
28
51
Karti-i-Parwan
37
56
Kooh-i-Aliabad
16
1
10
Institute of Technology
32
5
Ayoob Khan Mena
13
1
0
1
N

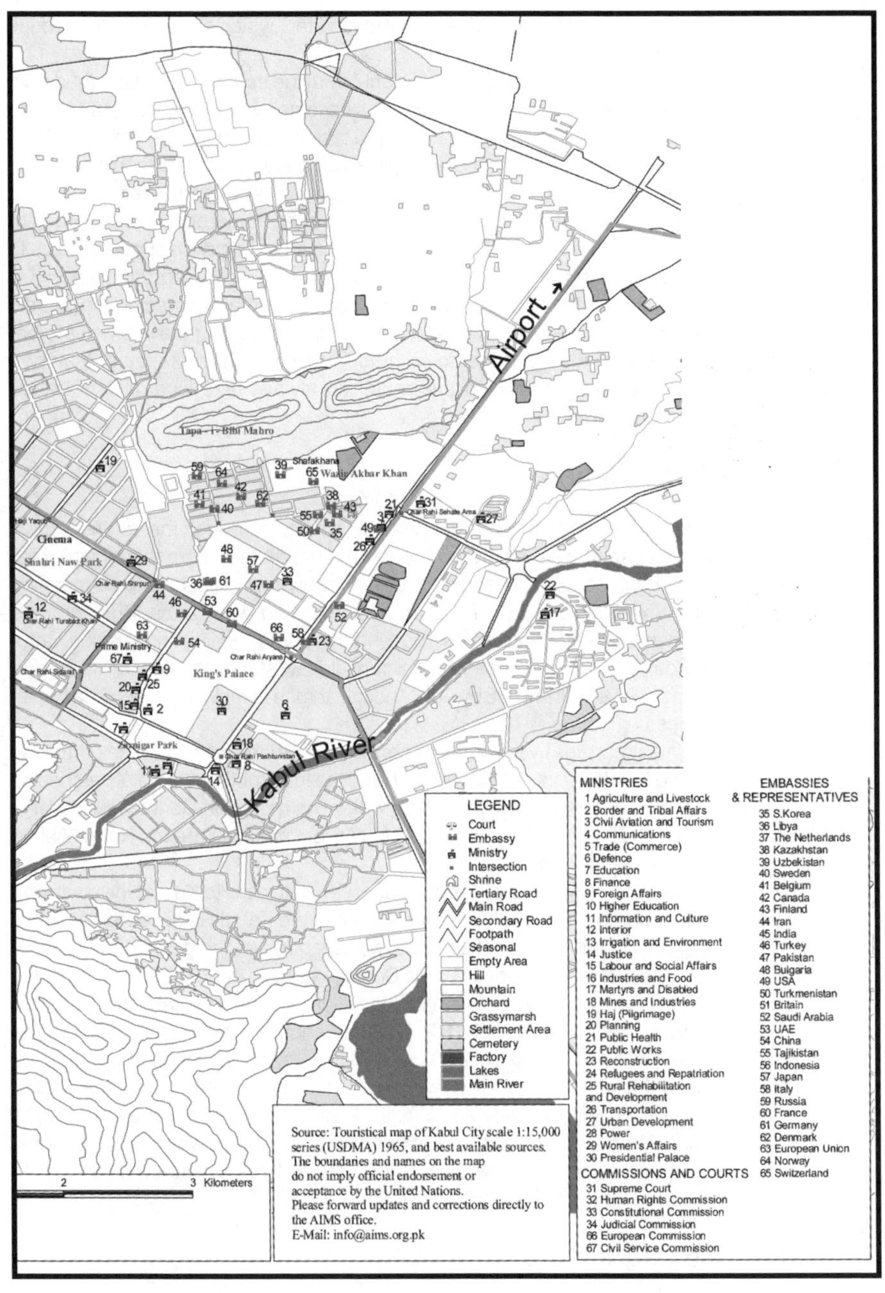

Airport
Tapa - i - Bibi Mahro
Shafakhana
Wazir Akbar Khan
Cinema
Shahri Naw Park
Prime Ministry
King's Palace
Char Rahi Aryana
Char Rahi Pashtunistan
Kabul River
LEGEND
Court
Embassy
Ministry
Intersection
Shrine
Tertiary Road
Main Road
Secondary Road
Footpath
Seasonal
Empty Area
Hill
Mountain
Orchard
Grassymarsh
Settlement Area
Cemetery
Factory
Lakes
Main River
MINISTRIES
1 Agriculture and Livestock
2 Border and Tribal Affairs
3 Civil Aviation and Tourism
4 Communications
5 Trade (Commerce)
6 Defence
7 Education
8 Finance
9 Foreign Affairs
10 Higher Education
11 Information and Culture
12 Interior
13 Irrigation and Environment
14 Justice
15 Labour and Social Affairs
16 Industries and Food
17 Martyrs and Disabled
18 Mines and Industries
19 Haj (Pilgrimage)
20 Planning
21 Public Health
22 Public Works
23 Reconstruction
24 Refugees and Repatriation
25 Rural Rehabilitation and Development
26 Transportation
27 Urban Development
28 Power
29 Women's Affairs
30 Presidential Palace
COMMISSIONS AND COURTS
31 Supreme Court
32 Human Rights Commission
33 Constitutional Commission
34 Judicial Commission
66 European Commission
67 Civil Service Commission
EMBASSIES & REPRESENTATIVES
35 S.Korea
36 Libya
37 The Netherlands
38 Kazakhstan
39 Uzbekistan
40 Sweden
41 Belgium
42 Canada
43 Finland
44 Iran
45 India
46 Turkey
47 Pakistan
48 Bulgaria
49 USA
50 Turkmenistan
51 Britain
52 Saudi Arabia
53 UAE
54 China
55 Tajikistan
56 Indonesia
57 Japan
58 Italy
59 Russia
60 France
61 Germany
62 Denmark
63 European Union
64 Norway
65 Switzerland
2
3 Kilometers
Source: Touristical map of Kabul City scale 1:15,000 series (USDMA) 1965, and best available sources.
The boundaries and names on the map do not imply official endorsement or acceptance by the United Nations.
Please forward updates and corrections directly to the AIMS office.
E-Mail: info@aims.org.pk

these and many other roads within Afghanistan, which may eventually reduce travel times.

Alexander the Great arrived in Kabul from the southwest, but the road from Kandahar, via Ghazni, to the capital has become increasingly dangerous since the fall of the Taliban. During 2003, the task of rebuilding this vital trunk road rocketed in priority when President Bush promised it would be a 'black-top' by the end of the year. Pro-Taliban and anti-government fighters – often mounted on small motorbikes – have killed and wounded numerous aid staff and construction workers in hit-and-run attacks in the area. Their aim appeared to be to hold up reconstruction and thereby discredit the US-backed authorities in Kabul. By December 2003, under the protection of several hundred armed guards, the route had finally been graded and tarmaced, cutting the driving time between Kabul and Kandahar to six hours. However, potshots rather than potholes are the new risk on this route, so always take local advice before travelling on it.

Orientation

Kabul is bisected by the Kabul River, which flows through the centre of town from the southwest to the northeast. Almost all the international agencies operating in Kabul are based north of the Kabul River in Shahr-e-Naw (meaning "new town" and begun in 1935) and the adjoining Wazir Akbar Khan (named after Amir Dost Mohammed's son who murdered the British Garrison Commander in 1842). In the centre of Shahr-e-Naw stands the Arg, a citadel and walled palace built in 1888 by Amir Abdur Rahman to replace the old Bala Hissar fortress.

The airport lies five kilometres northeast of Shahr-e-Naw. To the northwest lies the Kolola Pushta or Round Fort, and the Intercontinental Hotel perches on a spur of rock four kilometres to the west. The mountains to the southwest of Shahr-e-Naw through which the Kabul River squeezes are the Koh-e-Asmai and Koh-e-Sher Darwaza.

The road running west through this rocky cleft leads to Kabul University and the shattered quarter of Karte Seh. South of the Kabul River lies the old town and, nestling at the foot of Sher Darwaza mountain, the original Bala Hissar fortress which was destroyed by the British in 1878. In the 1920s King Amanullah built his own capital at Darulaman, nine kilometres southwest from the centre of town beyond Karte Seh. His palace, various government buildings, the Kabul Museum and most of the surrounding area, which remained largely intact during the Soviet occupation, were devastated by the civil war of the 1990s.

Maps of Shahr-e-Naw and Wazir Akbar Khan are produced by the UN's Afghanistan Information Management Service (AIMS), while one of the best city maps of Kabul is still to be found at the back of Nancy Dupree's *An Historical Guide to Kabul* (2nd Edition 1972).

Getting around

Kabul is awash with 4x4s, ranging from the latest shiny UN white and blue Toyota Land Cruisers complete with snorkels and air-conditioning, to the rather more battered and understated Mark II Land Rover of the BBC World Service. The greatest barriers to getting around in Kabul now are not roadblocks or shellfire, but traffic jams. The German-trained traffic police valiantly try to control the flow with their whistles but are routinely ignored. Occasionally you'll see them beating drivers with truncheons for infringing the rules at roundabouts.

If you are not working for, or sponsored by, a humanitarian agency, the alternative as a newcomer is to hire a yellow taxi, but negotiate the rate before you get in and check the driver isn't drunk. There have been reports of foreigners being robbed by taxi drivers, so make sure you travel two to a taxi. And get home before the evening curfew – if it is in force (SEE SECURITY TIPS).

Some experienced aid workers like to get around by bicycle or on foot. If you have the time this can be extremely rewarding, although it helps if you speak the local language. Always bear in mind the threat of mines and never walk or cycle "off the beaten track." The simplest rule of thumb is: check with local Afghans, and if they avoid somewhere then so do you. Travel in pairs or take a guide and you should not go wrong.

Public transport in Kabul is still rudimentary. The director of Kabul's bus department estimates that 2,500 buses would be needed to provide the city with a decent service. Various governments have promised buses, but by early 2003, there were just 200 buses in the city.

Agencies

Aid agencies have flooded into Kabul since the events of autumn 2001. The number of international NGOs registered with the Ministry of Planning shot up from 46 in 1999 to 350 by November 2002. Virtually every UN agency has an office in town – staffed by a total of over 600 expatriates. Most agencies – including the UN – transferred their headquarters from Pakistan to Kabul after the departure of the Taliban, leaving support offices in Peshawar and Islamabad. For an overview of agency activities in Kabul and the latest humanitarian situation try calling on the Kabul offices of the:

- Afghanistan Information Management Service (AIMS) – housed in the Prime Minister's compound in Shahr-e-Naw
- Agency Coordinating Body for Afghan Relief (ACBAR) – House 12, Jami Watt, Shahr-e-Naw, Kabul
- Afghan Assistance Coordination Authority (AACA) – Prime Minister's compound, Flower House Palace (Qasr-e-Gulkhana, Sadarat)

Kabul A-Z

Accommodation & Food

Accommodation in Kabul has become very expensive since the departure of the Taliban and the arrival of hundreds of well paid expatriates. One of the best places to start is the **Mustafa Hotel**, on Chahrahi Sadarat near Chicken and Flower Streets in Shahr-e-Naw. It's popular with journalists and travellers for its roof terrace and pizzas. Its windows are pasted with notices of upcoming events and it has a small gift shop with trinkets and books for sale. Wais Faizi, the manager, is very helpful. Prices start at around US$ 35/room. Facilities include: satellite TV, internet café, pool, darts, DVD room, bar and basketball. Contact: mustafa_hotel@hotmail.com.

The biggest hotel in town is the **Intercontinental Hotel** (Satphone: +873 761 469690; Local Tel: 020 220 1320/1321), although it's half an hour from Shahr-e-Naw and it's seen better days. It's slowly being renovated. Rooms start at US$ 74/night. Facilities include an internet café (broadband), printing and scanning, restaurant, new fitness centre, tennis court, swimming pool, billiards, sauna, barbershop, giftshop, Ariana Airlines office and an excellent bookstore. In late 1996 the arriving Taliban discovered several thousand bottles of beer concealed in the cellar and crushed the lot beneath the tracks of a Soviet tank, while a group of parched correspondents looked on longingly.

Numerous private guesthouses have sprung up in the area, started by adventurous foreign and Afghan entrepreneurs. Prices can normally be negotiated down if you're staying for a week or more. Passport Lane, near the Indian Embassy to the west of Shahr-e-Naw park, has three: **Chez Ana/ Media Action International** (Tel: 070 282699) – US$ 35-50/room incl. breakfast); the **Gandamack Lodge** (Tel: 070 276937) – a very comfortable guesthouse, formerly home to one of Osama Bin Laden's wives, now popular with well-heeled journalists and aid workers (US$ 45-65/room). It has free internet access in each room and a nice walled garden. For fans of Flashman, there is a fine collection of antique Lee Enfields; and, **Ariana Guesthouse** – opposite Gandamack Lodge and run by very efficient and friendly Afghans (US$ 30-40/ room). **Global Guesthouse** (Tel: 070 281907), run by Global Risk Strategies, is situated just off Flower Street/Cinema Street (US$ 50/night including meals). Facilities include: volleyball, weights, large TV, internet, DVD and café. **Bs Place** (Tel: 070 276416) – located in Qala-e-Fatullah in Wazir Akbar Khan – is expensive, but has a great garden for eating outdoors, plus a gym (US$ 65-75 incl. breakfast).

The UNICA Guesthouse is where most visiting UN and World Bank missions stay. Located at the north-western end of Kolola Pushta road in Shahr-e-Naw and known locally as the "UN Club", it has been a guesthouse since 1945. Unfortunately Afghans are not allowed to enter the Club at any time. NGO workers and journalists are not permitted to stay, but can visit the shop. Thursday night is open night, when non-UN types are allowed in for a stiff drink between 6.30-9pm, but you need a letter of introduction from your head of agency. Don't hang around at the entrance – a bomb went off outside in July 2002. Facilities include: restaurant, swimming pool, two pool tables, table tennis, badminton, a weights room and a beautiful garden. Rates are US$ 45/room, but there are only eight guestrooms. **The German Club**, located near the foot of the Kolola Pushta fort in Shahr-e-Naw, has two guestrooms with *en suite* bathrooms (US$ 100/room). Previously the International Club, one waiter who worked here for 40 years remembered hundreds of guests before 1992 and a thriving amateur dramatic scene. Now its bar is dry and its swimming pool empty – although tennis and indoor bowls are available. Guests of all nationalities are welcome to stay or use the facilities. Food can be provided but order early – they need half a day's warning. Expect changes now it's under new management.

Eating out in Kabul has come a long way since the sheep curry and kebabs available under the Taliban. But as more Westerners flood into Kabul, there is always the risk of terrorism to bear in mind – take advice about where to go when you arrive. Here's a flavour of what's on offer:

Darulaman Palace, damaged by mujahed infighting from 1992-1996
J. Walter

Afghan: The **Herat restaurant** serves excellent local food. A lunch of *qabuli, maast & chai sabz* (rice & mutton, yogurt and green tea) will cost little more than a dollar. *Afghanis*, dollars and Pakistani rupees are all accepted. For more upmarket, atmospheric Afghan dining (with a view), try **Karwansara** (117 Interior Ministry Road, next to Malalai High School; Tel: 070 291794). The **Khyber Restaurant,** (Pashtunistan Watt, opposite the fountain) offers a good Afghan, Chinese or Italian buffet lunch or dinner (US$ 6). The **Marco Polo** restaurant, on Kolola Pushta road west of the park, serves outstanding Afghan dishes. Its menu boasts: "Meat Kabab, Chicken Soap, Kabuli, Lintels, Custard, Tea and Cold Drinks". Opposite the 'Titanic Bazaar' is the first floor **Pashtunistan restaurant**, where you can sample local cuisine on an outdoor balcony with a view of Timur Shah's mausoleum.

Chinese: The **Golden Lotos** restaurant, opposite the UN demining office, advertises that it is "ready again to serve you each kind of internal and external delicious foods". Its speciality is Chinese food and it's popular with expatriates. **Chinese Restaurant** (Ansari Square; Tel: 020 220 1618) – a range of Chinese dishes (US$ 6) plus alcohol available.

International: **Bs Place** (see above) serves a good pepper steak in the garden, as well as pizzas, Thai curry, alcohol and takeaway. **Gandamack Lodge** (see above) is open to non-residents craving an English breakfast or delicious 3-course dinner (US$ 20). The **German Restaurant** has a buffet on Thursday nights. The **Hotel Intercontinental** offers a buffet brunch on Fridays, Saturdays and Sundays in the Bamiyan Room, as well as the new à la carte Bukhara Restaurant. The **Irish Club** (Qala-e-Fatullah, near Bibi Mahro

Hill in Wazir Akbar Khan; Tel: 070 296698) serves a slap-up breakfast, buffet lunch and à la carte dinner – washed down by draught Guinness or a pint of Stella. Being a club, it charges entrance and membership fees. In October 2003, a new Croatian restaurant opened – the **Zadar Restaurant**, near the International Organisation for Migration.

Iranian: **Shandiz** restaurant (Street 10, Wazir Akbar Khan; Tel: 070 284026) is a new addition to the Kabul scene and serves Iranian kebabs with rice for US$ 9.

Italian: **Mustafa Hotel** (see above) claims to sell the best pizzas in town and offers rooftop eating. It also has a ground floor café for milkshakes and fruit juices. **Popo Lano** restaurant (Insaf Hotel, Ansari Square, Shahr-e-Naw) is good for pizzas and takeaways.

Thai: **Anaar** restaurant (behind the UNICA guesthouse in Kolola Pushta, Tel: 070 284315) serves a delicious green and red Thai curry for US$ 10. Indian and Chinese dishes are also available. The decor is authentic Afghan – low tables, cushions, carpets and beautiful carved Nuristani woodwork. The **Lal Thai** (Street 15, Wazir Akbar Khan; Tel: 070 297557) boasts probably Kabul's only genuinely Thai chef, with main courses starting at US$ 7.

For more information on sleeping, eating and drinking in Kabul, check out the excellent *Survival Guide to Kabul*, published in 2003 by Bradt Travel Guides.

Books

Kabul is surprisingly well-served by bookshops, considering over half the city has been reduced to rubble. There are several good ones down Chicken Street (e.g. Habibi Book Centre) where you can still pick up 1970s guidebooks, maps and tourist brochures. The Shah M. Book Co, one of the country's best booksellers, has two shops in Kabul – one at the Hotel Intercontinental, one downtown in Chahrai Saddarat. Both stock the latest titles on Afghanistan and the region, plus a range of interesting titles now out of print. There are libraries of books in English and European languages at the UNICA Guesthouse and the German Club. For more reading on Kabul, try:

The Survival Guide to Kabul, Dominic Medley & Jude Barrand, Bradt Travel Guides Ltd (England, 2003) – ISBN 1 84162 085 8. Small but perfectly formed pocket guide, essential for anyone visiting Kabul. Some copies are sold by street children, who keep the profits.
An Historical Guide to Afghanistan, Nancy Hatch Dupree (Kabul, 2nd Edition, 1977) – required reading
An Historical Guide to Kabul, Nancy Hatch Dupree (Kabul, 2nd Edition, 1972)
Cabool in 1836-37 and 8, Being the Personal Narrative of a Journey to, and Residence in, that City, Sir Alexander Burnes, (London, 1842; reprinted by Ferozsons, Lahore, 1964 and by Akade-mische Druk-u. Verlagsanstalt, Graz, 1973). Despite the author's knowledge of the city, he was hacked to death by a frenzied mob in 1841.

WARNING

KABUL IS ONE OF THE MOST HEAVILY MINED CITIES IN THE WORLD — STICK TO THE TRODDEN PATH OR TRAVEL WITH A GUIDE !

An Account of the Kingdom of Caubul, Mountstuart Elphinstone, John Murray (London, 1815; reprinted by Akademische Druk-u. Verlagsanstalt, Graz, 1969 and by Oxford University Press, Karachi, 1972)
Signal Catastrophe; The Retreat from Kabul, 1842, Patrick Macrory, Hodder and Stoughton (London, 1966).

Embassies & Visas

During 2002 many diplomatic missions, which had abandoned Kabul during the 1980s-90s, re-established heavily guarded embassies in the city – by the end of the year 25 countries were represented. But the fighting had taken its toll on the buildings themselves. The Russian embassy lies in ruins; and the magnificent British mission – home to the "best housed man in Asia" and guarded until 1994 by a team of Gurkhas armed with little more than *kukris* – was handed back to Pakistan and promptly shelled. Make sure you register with your own embassy on arrival. Afghan visas may be renewed at the Ministry of Foreign Affairs (MFA), but "exit visas" to leave the country are no longer necessary. For getting visas to visit Afghanistan SEE VISAS.

Emergencies

If you find yourself in Kabul when the city comes under attack, the only thing to do is lie low and wait for an opportunity to leave if things get too hot for your liking. (So bring along a good book and your short-wave radio). There is a 16-man bunker under the UNICA club in Shahr-e-Naw if you are desperate, otherwise take shelter in the cellar of your house or under the stairs. It may sound obvious, but try and resist the temptation to go outside if there is shooting: what goes up must come down and many people have been killed or injured by falling bullets and shrapnel. In an emergency both the ICRC and the UN will try to evacuate their own staff and everyone else (in that order) either by vehicle or by air, so keep in touch with them (SEE SECURITY TIPS).

Information

First stop should be for a security briefing – call on ACBAR, ICRC or the UN for details. For more information about United Nations activities, contact AIMS, whose staff can brief you on the latest security and humanitarian situation.

Make sure you receive some kind of landmine awareness briefing, preferably from the UN's Mine Action Programme in Kabul (MAPA) before travelling widely in Afghanistan. For more details on NGO activities contact ACBAR in Shahr-e-Naw. The best way to connect to the humanitarian grapevine is to turn up for a drink at the UNICA Guesthouse on a Thursday night between 6.30-9pm – or else visit one of the newer watering holes like the Irish Club.

For internet updates, check out:

http://www.aims.org.af (website for the UN's Afghanistan Information Management Service/AIMS)

http://www.kabulcaravan.com (online travel guide to Afghanistan)

http://www.kabulguide.net (website for *The Survival Guide to Kabul*)

http://thorntree.lonelyplanet.com (online chat room – see Asia/Central Asia section)

Local Rules

Kabul is in many ways a unique city, and quite different from the rest of Afghanistan. Although the Taliban have vanished, security is still a concern. Many Kabuli women still wear the *burqa*, fearing for their safety on the streets. Avoid travelling alone and dress in respectable Western clothes. This is especially the case for women, who must ensure their arms and legs are fully covered. *Chadors* (head veils) for western women are optional in Kabul now. Shorts worn by either sex are considered offensive, so leave them at home. Check whether there is a curfew or not – it was lifted for the first time in a decade in November 2002. Never leave valuables unattended in taxis or unlocked rooms. Be very discreet in your consumption of alcohol. Always ask permission before taking photos of people – especially Afghan women.

Begging and *baksheesh* are a constant issue – and ultimately one on which you must make a personal decision. State salaries are so low that it's good to tip any Afghan who helps you out. As for begging, giving to the poor is one of the central tenets of Islam. EFG editors found the best solution was to carry a quantity of small denomination *Afghanis* to give to women who ask. Giving to children runs the risk of encouraging families to take children out of school to beg.

Medical

Access to health care in Kabul may well be better than in many Western towns. There are dozens of agencies specializing in the medical sector and over 20 hospitals in the capital. If you are suffering it is probably best to arrange to see a health NGO through ACBAR – most agencies are more than willing to help out. The Italian NGO, Emergency, runs a highly efficient hospital on Cinema Zainab road in Shahr-e-Naw, full of friendly staff. The ICRC runs surgical units at Karte Seh and Wazir Akbar Khan hospitals and will operate on all emergency cases. The ISAF base on the Jalalabad Road also has a field hospital which will treat you (SEE PERSONAL HEALTH).

Money

There are no international banks in Kabul (although in September 2003, Standard Chartered Bank announced they would be opening a Kabul branch) and no-one takes credit cards, so make sure you bring enough cash; US dollars or Pakistani rupees are the best. Ask around for the current exchange rate and the best place to change money. Some dealers (if they trust you) take personal cheques drawn on European and North American banks. The market is open rather than black. In order to avoid carrying vast wads of cash around, the Transitional Administration reissued the *Afghani* currency in late 2002, knocking three zeros off the face-value of bank notes. The rate by early 2003 was around 50 *Afghanis* to the dollar. You can open a dollar account at Da Afghanistan Bank, minimum deposit US$ 1,000 (SEE MONEY).

Post & Telecommunications

Kabul is better connected now than it has been for at least 25 years. You can buy a SIM card (US$ 130) for your GSM **mobile phone** from the state-affiliated Afghan Wireless Communication Company (AWCC), which enables you to make international calls from within the city. Handsets and top-up cards can be bought at the airport, post office, Intercontinental Hotel and AWCC building at the Ministry of Communications. The more expensive *Thuraya* handheld satphone became something of a fashion accessory for well-heeled aid workers during 2002-03 – its main advantage is that it works in both urban and rural areas.

While UN agencies set up their own internet and email access in early 2002, NGOs and journalists had to rely on expensive satellite downloads until the first internet cafés began opening in late 2002. In early 2003, Neda Telecommunications set up Kabul's first dial-up internet access – as long as you have access to a digital phone. Otherwise, you can now get online via the **internet cafés** at: Afghan Media and Culture Centre (AINA) (next to the Ministry of Planning), CHA's arts and crafts gallery (Cinema Zainab Road), Intercontinental Hotel, Mustafa Hotel (Shahr-e-Naw), PACTEC (Wazir Akbar Khan), plus various guest-houses (SEE TELECOMS).

Recreation

Roller-blading around Kabul hasn't caught on yet, but a surprising amount of recreational possibilities do exist. For UN and World Bank staff, the **UNICA Guesthouse** is the best place to start. The club boasts a badminton court (the squash court was cracked by a bomb in 2002), a grass volleyball court, table tennis, weights room and even two pool tables for diehard fitness freaks. Couch-potatoes can sunbathe by the swimming pool (closed October-April), or watch satellite TV. The **Intercontinental Hotel** has a swimming pool, fitness room (US$ 80/month) and has hosted the local Hash House Harriers. If you can't find anyone to run with, try scaling **Bibi Mahro** hill behind Wazir Akbar Khan – popular with expat joggers. **Gold Gym** at Macrorayon 2 (an old Soviet estate) has new weights machines and is much cheaper than the Intercontinental.

The **German Club** has three clay tennis courts in good condition, and a swimming pool (often empty). Tennis racquets and balls are available, as well as changing and washing facilities. Volleyball, bowling, billiards and bingo are all on offer, as is a theatre fully equipped with stage curtain and lighting.

Despite the departure of the Taliban, bear in mind Islamic restrictions on dress before taking exercise in Kabul. Always change at the club and never wander around Kabul in shorts. Joggers can stretch their legs running around the garden of the **Turkish Embassy**, but do not try running around suburban Kabul because you will most likely either get arrested or tread on a mine. If you must undress, do it beside a swimming pool, not on the roof of your guest-house. The local extreme sport is ***buzkashi***, currently making a comeback in Kabul Stadium most Fridays. If you're looking for rough and tumble but don't have a horse, try rugby at **ISAF** (opposite the US embassy) on Fridays.

For film lovers, AINA (next to the Ministry of Planning) provides an **open-air cinema** in its grassy courtyard – 8pm every Tuesday. Turkish baths and massage parlours are also popping up around town.

Shopping

Shopping in Kabul took a turn for the worse after the British Army torched the famous covered bazaar 120 years ago. The Afghans however, never ones to miss out on a quick buck, have bounced back and now import numerous Western goods from Dubai. If *qabuli, maast & chai sabz* are not your style, then 'Chelsi Shop' on Chicken Street will sell you everything from Pringles to Pampers nappies, Marmite to Milk Tray – at a price. Its promotional literature boasts: "Selling of All Groceries, food in Addition, Exchang Dollar Check and Ropes". There's a good bakery at Popo Lano restaurant, at Insaf Hotel.

Chicken Street still attracts the rookie trophy hunters, but for bargains you need to look elsewhere. Turcoman carpets, lapis jewellery, *Kuchi* bedspreads, and fake Lee Enfield pistols are all on sale – but the men in black flak jackets and shades have pushed up prices. Be prepared to drink lots of green tea and haggle hard.

A local NGO called CHA has opened a gallery selling good quality Afghan crafts – carpets, miniatures, jewellery, calligraphy, clothes, pottery, embroidery and glass – at reasonable, haggle-free prices. CHA provides the craftspeople – mainly Afghan women – with the raw materials and charges a small admin fee. In return the women receive half of the profits. Carpets are all woven to traditional 14th and 15th Century designs. The gallery is located on Cinema Zainab road, near Shahr-e-Naw park.

Whatever you do, please don't buy animal skins – especially snow leopard pelts – as many of Afghanistan's fauna are now seriously endangered.

Sights in Kabul

Sightseeing may not be the first thing which comes to mind on a visit to Kabul, but there are still a number of places well worth visiting if you have the time. For great **panoramic views** of the city and the mountains, drive up one the hills to the south west of Shahr-e-Naw (e.g. **Koh-e-Asmai**) early or late in the day. Alternatively, climb **Bibi Mahro** hill behind Wazir Akbar Khan. The best sources of information on sightseeing remain the two guidebooks written in the 1970s by Nancy Dupree. What follows is a modest update.

Babur's Garden. The 16th Century founder of the Moghul dynasty, Babur, so loved Kabul that he asked to be buried here. The gardens climb the sides of Sher-e-Darwaza mountain. At the top are the finely carved marble tombs of Babur and his wife, plus a beautiful little mosque built by Shah Jehan (more famous for creating the Taj Mahal). There are great views from the top, where a restaurant is under construction. Not much of the greenery survived the war, but UNESCO and the Aga Khan Foundation are coordinating a major restoration of this remarkable spot (SEE CULTURE).

Bala Hissar. Afghanistan's historic citadel, located in Karte Naw, was finally destroyed by the British in the 19th Century. But the ruins and old city walls are worth looking at. Don't wander off the road as the place is littered with mines and UXO.

Christian Cemetery. Located at Char-e-Shahid in Shahr-e-Naw, this walled graveyard contains over a century-worth of Christian remains – including those of the intrepid scholar-explorer Sir Aurel Stein.

Kabul Museum. Before the war this was one of the most important collections of archaeology and ethnography in Central Asia. The Hellenistic, Greco-Buddhist, Ghaznavid and subsequent periods were all represented. Its neo-classical home, constructed by King Amanullah in Darulaman, 10 km from the centre of town, was shattered by factional fighting between 1992-1996, and much of the collection has since been looted or destroyed. Some of the collection was moved in 1996 to the Kabul Hotel for safekeeping. Progress to rebuild the museum on its current site has been very slow (SEE CULTURE). The shell-shattered remains of Amanullah's early 20th Century **Darulaman Palace** are nearby. Again – be very careful of mines in this part of town: stick to the roads.

Kabul Zoo. Despite taking a direct rocket hit during the 1990s, the zoo is a popular destination for Kabulis during their time off. Founded in the 1960s, many of the original animals were killed or stolen during the fighting. Its most famous inmate, Marjan the Lion, survived decades of war and a Taliban grenade attack, only to die in 2002. Various sorry-looking inmates remain, including: a jackal, four wolves, some baboons, a small wild cat, a fox, hundreds of rabbits, two monkeys, a deer, a few vultures, some owls and a sore-nosed Asiatic black bear called Donatella. Their pitiful living conditions are slowly being improved. China recently donated some lions.

Mausoleum of Amir Abdur Rahman. Located in the centre of town, just north of the river, the mausoleum stands in Zarnegar (lit. "adorned with gold") Park, although neither gold nor park is much in evidence today. Originally built by the Amir (1880-1901) as a private pleasure pavilion, his son Amir Habibullah laid him to rest here. Nowadays the mausoleum is popular with graffiti artists and drop outs. The nearby tomb of King Amanullah's brother Hayatullah is used for drying laundry.

Mausoleum of Timur Shah. Dedicated not to the great Tamerlane, but to one of Ahmed Shah Durrani's sons, this impressive early 19th Century monument was saved during the war by freight containers stacked around it. Sited near the Kabul river, by the 'Titanic Market', the octagonal brick mausoleum and the garden which once surrounded it are now being restored.

Letter from Kabul, July 15 2003

Mobile phone ringtones are the new sound on the streets of Kabul. The Lambada tone is particularly popular, annoyingly so. The James Bond theme tune is moving up the Top Ten ladder.

Afghans are relishing new freedoms like other post war countries: everyone wants communications. But the Afghans are too polite and friendly for mobile phones. Their extensive greetings to each other when they meet go on for minutes. They'll need to adapt. Otherwise they'll keep greeting each other over and over again, getting cut off after 30 seconds each time.

Everyone wants to travel. The streets are as clogged as the mobile phone network. There might be as many as 40,000 taxis in Kabul. New cars keep appearing – the yellow Mazda MX5, the stretched Mercedes limo, the flashy Land Cruisers. Toyota Corolla drivers have to be the worst. Every car crash usually involves a Corolla. It's worth learning a few choice words in Dari to shout at them.

Internet cafés are springing up. Hourly charges are beyond the reach of most Afghans. But the cafés are still full of youngsters surfing for photos of their favourite Bollywood film stars.

Radio Arman on 98.1FM is pumping out Western, Indian, Iranian and Afghan music across the city. The radio station sometimes gets 400 letters and 1,500 phone calls a day. Radio TV Afghanistan has criticised the station for lowering standards. But the whole city is listening to Arman, which means 'Hope'. The letters people write to the DJs are usually accompanied by a postcard of an Indian star with a message such as "I don't know who she is but please play a song by her".

In February last year the Faisal Guesthouse in Wazir Akbar Khan had a steady diet of soup, chicken, chips and rice, seven days a week. The houseboy Najibullah was always proud to announce "dinner tonight: soup, chicken, chips and rice." But now it's possible to eat anything you want in the city. In June 2002 the curfew was still at 10pm, and the Golden Lotus restaurant had just reopened. Foreign agency cars were always outside the Herat and Marco Polo restaurants. Now they're never seen there. The Lai Thai and German restaurants have stolen the market.

Shahr-e-Naw is buzzing. Thursday night is like a Friday night west of Suez. Pizzeria Milano and Chief Burger are packed. Parties rage across the city. The Afghans are the busiest partygoers. Weddings and birthdays are celebrated enthusiastically, complete with dancing and alcohol. And of course, the Lambada.

Even last October, TV Afghanistan was showing music videos after the news. At the same time the debate raged over women appearing on television and whether Indian films should be broadcast. But everybody has seen the blockbuster film *Titanic* several times, though the Cinema Park didn't screen it last year for being too erotic. Leonardo di Caprio hairstyles are popular, the market in the Kabul River is known as the Titanic market (for being flooded, when it rains), buses are called Titanic. A

Mullah once told his Friday gathering that they would all end up like the passengers on the Titanic if they didn't behave properly.

All this was impossible under Taliban rule. The changes, the music, the cars, the Lambaba, show you something about the ability of the Afghans to change, and fast. Some people tell you to take things a step at a time, "this is Afghanistan". But ordinary people seem to be voting with their feet and moving their city forward themselves.

That speed can be embarrassing. The road outside the old UN headquarters was only repaired when they vacated the compound. Reconstruction has been slow, except in Wazir Akbar Khan, where private houses were quickly spruced up in time for US$10,000 a month rents. But the roads in WAK are just as bad.

Kabul may yet regain its cosmopolitan past. The Hotel Kabul is being renovated into a five star hotel, with plans for a pedestrian area from Pashtunistan Square, past Da Afghanistan Bank up to the hotel. Café culture might just return.

Security is always a concern, but perhaps too hyped up. There are so many security gurus. Most seem to think it's better to be locked down in guesthouse, land cruiser and office rather than venture out. Yes, there have been serious attacks. Thirty people were killed outside the Hotel Spinzar in September 2002; four Germans with ISAF were killed in June 2003. There are always reports of bombs coming into the city. Perhaps it is still too early for international staff to venture out *en masse*, but there have never been reports of drive-by shootings of internationals. One criticism of internationals in Kabul from the Afghans is that we don't engage enough with the local population.

Outside Kabul, life is very different. People are starving and fighting is still continuing near Herat, Mazar, Kandahar and Khost. So perhaps it is too much to expect massive reconstruction in the capital when so many people are still struggling to survive. The struggle has come into the city. There are more and more beggars. People with appalling disabilities and destitute women needing *baksheesh* frequent traffic jams and international hangouts. City services are struggling to cope with the number of people who have returned.

Tourists have been spotted. Not in planeloads but in small numbers from Japan, Australia, the UK and elsewhere. Some are remembering the happy days of the coach trip from Dusseldorf. Others are coming to get a look at this famous city for this first time.

Kabul is changing. The political change may be slow and tense. The international aid may be slow. But even without this, the Kabulis have started moving their city forward again. They've had enough of 23 years of wreckage.

By Dominic Medley, co-author of The Survival Guide to Kabul (www.kabulguide.net).
A longer version of this article was first published in the Crosslines Afghan Monitor

Minaret of Maiwand. Only the stump of this unremarkable monument remains; but it signified a remarkable Afghan victory over the British near Kandahar in 1880. The Afghans were about to give up when out rushed a young Pashtun bride named Malalai, ripped off her veil and raised it over her head as a battle standard with the cry, "My love, if you do not fall today in the battle of Maiwand, by Allah you will be saved as a symbol of shame!" What would the Taliban have made of her?

Pul-e-Khisti Mosque. A large blue dome rising above the markets just across the river from Zarnegar is that of Kabul's largest mosque, originally built at the end of the 18th Century. It stands next to the Pul-e-Khisti (lit. "Bridge of Bricks") in what was the centre of Kabul from the 17th-19th Centuries. Damaged during recent fighting, it is now being restored.

Shah-Do Shamshira Mosque. This yellow two-storey mosque is probably the best preserved in Kabul and sits picturesquely beside the Kabul River in the centre of town. Built in the reign of King Amanullah, its name means the Mosque of the King of Two Swords.

Sights outside Kabul

Kargha Lake, a reservoir built in the 1950s, provides some good swimming and picnicking (but not much shade) – 10 km to the west of the city.

Koh-e-Daman. An hour's drive north of Kabul brings you into this beautiful plain – literally the 'skirt of the mountains' – once famous for its orchards and vineyards. The village of **Istalif** is well worth exploring. The ruins are a stark reminder of the years when this was a fiercely fought-over frontline between the Taliban and the Northern Alliance. But a handful of local craftsmen have set up shop to recreate the village's famous blue pottery and the views are marvellous.

Minar-e-Chakari. This Buddhist column, dating from the Kushan dynasty (3rd-4th Century AD) stands on a mountain saddle overlooking Kabul. It once stood at least 85 feet high, although bits have fallen off over the years. Leaving Kabul, aim for the villages of Beni Hissar and Shewaki. The column is reached after an hour or more's strenuous hike from the roadhead at Yakhdara. The views are said to be fantastic. For more details, see Nancy Dupree's 1970s guide to Afghanistan. Take local advice on the security situation before leaving.

Paghman. The famous gardens and villas of Paghman were created by the royal family in the 1920s. Largely shattered by war, all that remains are some ruins and an arch commemorating Afghans who fell in the 1919 war of independence. There is a grass amphitheatre where parliament met in 1928. It's a peaceful spot with great views of the mountains surrounding Kabul. Allow 45 minutes to drive here from town.

Weather

At an altitude of 1,800 metres, Kabul is the highest of Afghanistan's main cities, so pack warm clothes for all times of year. Average temperatures for the capital are: January, minus 2.8°C; July, 24.4°C.

Northern region

Northern Afghanistan may be defined as the region of the country lying to the north of the Hindu Kush mountains. Both geographically and culturally it is an area more closely related to Central Asia than to Persia or the Indian subcontinent. Its ethnic mix of Tajik, Uzbek and Turkmen reflects the nationalities of those living over the border of the Amu Darya (Oxus River) to the north.

For nearly three millennia, the region was dominated by the city of Balkh. Zoroaster preached fire-worship here around 1000-600 BC. Alexander the Great based his army here for two years in 329 BC. And in the first centuries after Christ, Buddhist pilgrims flocked to temples which thrived under the Kushan dynasty. In 663 the Chinese adventurer Hsuan-tsang remarked that Balkh had three of the most beautiful buildings in the world. With the advent of Islam in the 8th to 9th Centuries, Balkh became known as the "Mother of Cities", so numerous were its mosques and so rich its intellectual, poetical and spiritual culture. However, the destructive habits of Genghis Khan put an end to this glorious city in 1220, and even 100 years later the famous traveller Ibn Battuta found the entire area "in ruins."

With Balkh and northern Afghanistan straddling the important trade routes to Central Asia, the city made a brief recovery in the 15th Century under the patronage of the Timurid ruler of Herat, Shah Rukh. Then for several centuries Kabul and Bokhara competed for influence over the northern territories, until Ahmed Shah Durrani, "Father of Afghanistan", finally established the frontier of his kingdom along the line of the Amu Darya in 1768. Balkh was then made the capital of Afghan Turkestan, but for health reasons the city was abandoned in 1866 in favour of a small village by the name of Mazar-e-Sharif. From the lengthy perspective of Afghan history, therefore, Mazar is rather a gatecrasher to the party. For many centuries famous only for its shrine to the cousin of the Prophet Mohammed, it has prospered over the last century at Balkh's expense.

The significance of northern Afghanistan did not escape the Russians either. In the words of the French Central Asian specialist, Olivier Roy, "that part of Afghanistan which is of strategic importance is shaped somewhat like an hourglass in which the Salang Pass is the neck." To the north are the plains from Shibarghan to Kunduz and the land route to Termez and Central Asia. To the south lies the strategically crucial crossing of the Hindu Kush range through the Salang tunnel, and the route via Kabul and Jalalabad to India. The area encompassed is rich and well-populated, with the added attraction of the country's main natural resources: the gas and oil fields of Shibarghan, and the copper mines at Any in Logar. This of course was also the route of the Soviet invasion in 1979, mounted from Termez and mobilized through the Salang Pass to Kabul.

Parts of the north are among the most heavily mined in Afghanistan – especially along the old Taliban/Northern Alliance frontline between Kunduz and Taloqan. During the US 'war on terrorism', Kunduz was heavily affected by 'cluster bombs', which have proved lethal to civilians and mine clearance experts alike (SEE LANDMINES). Apart from over two decades of conflict, the northern region has been one of the hardest hit by the devastating drought of 1997-2002. Tens of thousands of families were displaced across the region, with the province of Badghis particularly affected.

Mazar-e-Sharif

Before the Soviet war Mazar had become a centre of militant Muslim youth, along with Panjshair, Baghlan and Badakhshan. In the early 1980s, the influence of Rabbani's party Jamiat-e-Islami spread throughout the north of Afghanistan, closely linked to the local reputation of three commanders. Mazar was the base for Zabiullah, who was killed in 1984, while Ismail Khan held sway in Herat to the west, and Ahmed Shah Massoud operated throughout the northeast. Jamiat took root in the north partly because of the political and military astuteness of its leaders, but also because this area of Afghanistan was far less tribal than the Pashtun south, and hence more amenable to military organization across a whole region.

From February 1992, when General Dostum mutinied against the communist regime of President Najibullah, until May 1997, when the Taliban launched their first, ill-fated assault on the city, Mazar-e-Sharif was an island of peace. For five years Dostum controlled an independent militia force – Jumbesh-e-Melli – numbering at least 20,000 soldiers. On the strength of this private army, he created a personal fiefdom in Mazar, complete with its own flag, currency and airline – Balkh Air. Many educated Afghans fled the factional fighting which rocked Kabul from 1992-1996 and settled in Mazar. More joined them when the ultra-conservative Taliban overran Kabul. Thus Mazar became an alternative capital, with a more liberal environment where women and children had greater access to education and work than in Taliban-controlled areas.

General Dostum enjoyed the financial and military support of Uzbekistan and Russia who saw him as the one man capable of preventing Taliban-inspired Islamic fundamentalism from spreading north into their territories. Two months after the Taliban took Kabul in 1996, Dostum's Jumbesh party and ousted President Rabbani's Jamiat party – previously enemies – joined forces to create the anti-Taliban Northern Alliance, based in Mazar. Towards the end of the year, both Hazara parties – Hezb-e-Wahdat and Harakat-e-Islami – also joined the Northern Alliance. During 1997, Mazar became a battlefield, variously in the hands of the Taliban, Dostum and a local warlord, Abdul Malik, who allegedly killed 3,000 Taliban in one 24 hour spree of revenge. The Taliban regrouped and conquered Faryab, Jowzjan and Mazar in 1998. Residents described a "killing frenzy" on the August day when the Taliban occupied Mazar and took swift revenge on hundreds of Hazara and Uzbek civilians.

Jamiat was pushed back to its heartland in Takhar and Badakhshan. Dostum retreated to Turkey to lick his wounds.

From 1999-2001, eyewitness reports tell of large numbers of Arabs, Chechens and Pakistanis arriving in the north to support the Taliban, who were fighting off periodic assaults by the Northern Alliance. Hazaras and Uzbeks were routinely terrorized on the streets of Mazar and, occasionally, shot by Taliban troops. With the arrival of the Taliban, Uzbekistan and Turkmenistan closed their borders, restricting trade and cramping the economy of the north. Meanwhile, food security in Mazar plummeted as the drought took hold.

Following the events of 11th September 2001, the Northern Alliance – supported by US airpower and special forces – attacked the Taliban in Mazar and took the city. The last of the Taliban's forces were besieged in Kunduz. A ceasefire was negotiated and thousands were taken captive and sent to Dostum's prisons in Shibarghan and Qala-e-Jangi, outside Mazar. Reports later emerged of hundreds of prisoners dying of suffocation after being transported in sealed freight containers. Thousands more were incarcerated in Shibarghan prison, where many would have starved to death but for the intervention of the ICRC. Meanwhile, the inmates at Qala-e-Jangi – mainly foreign Taliban sympathizers – attacked their guards, prompting the US to launch an airstrike which killed over 300 prisoners. Some died with their hands still tied behind their backs. It was one of the most notorious actions of the Coalition campaign in Afghanistan.

During 2002-03, the north has been characterized by ongoing clashes between Dostum's Jumbesh forces and the Jamiat troops of another regional commander, Mohammed Usted Atta. The latter is an ethnic Tajik with close ties to Defence Minister Fahim. Dostum, meanwhile, has been made Karzai's special representative in the north. The eventual aim is to merge both men's troops into one force under a single, neutral commander. Meanwhile, poor security throughout the region, aggravated by the lack of an international peacekeeping force, has seriously hampered aid operations. There have been a number of violent assaults on ethnic minorities and on both expatriate and Afghan aid workers.

In 2003, Britain sent a small Provisional Reconstruction Team of troops and civilian advisors in a bid to improve security and begin disarming the militias. Meanwhile, in October 2003, Karzai negotiated for 300 Kabul policemen to enter the city and appointed a new governor.

As a gateway to the Central Asian Republics, and with largely untapped oil and natural gas fields nearby, Mazar could potentially become very prosperous. For that reason, no doubt, it will continue to be fought over.

Getting there

By air

Mazar airport escaped the years of fighting relatively unscathed. The flight from Kabul offers stunning views of the crumpled snowy crests of the Hindu Kush collapsing into the baked northern plains bordering the Oxus.

The UN flies five times a week between Kabul and Mazar (no flights on Fridays and Saturdays). Flights cost US$ 100 for UN staff and accredited

NGOs and US$ 290 for everyone else. The UN also flies twice a week from Mazar to Islamabad, and twice a week to Kunduz, Faizabad, Maimana and Bamiyan through Mazar.

ICRC flies up to three times per week between Mazar, Kabul and Peshawar. Accredited NGO staff are permitted to use this service. As long as you book at least three days in advance, you won't be "bumped off". PACTEC/Air Serv International flies once a week between Mazar and Islamabad (Sundays). Ariana Afghan Airlines flies a Boeing 737 between Mazar and Kabul twice a week (Tuesdays and Fridays), costing US$ 47 for international staff and *Afghanis* 1,200 for locals.

Overland

The Uzbek border lies about 60km north of Mazar at Hairaton on the Amu Darya (Oxus River). The journey takes about one hour by car, mainly through semi-arid desert and scrub. Sand dunes often drift across the road, so a 4x4 is advisable. If you see children or old people trying to clear the road for you, the tradition is to toss a few *Afghanis* out of the window for them. The border remained closed while the Taliban controlled Mazar and opened again for the first time in four years in late 2001. Check with the UNAMA office in Mazar for the latest situation.

Leave plenty of time to cross the border as the Uzbeks are notoriously slow with formalities and both border posts close at different times for lunch breaks. You are unlikely to get into Afghanistan from Uzbekistan unless you have a letter of accreditation from an aid agency or media organization. The crossing of the 'Friendship Bridge' is quite long, so if you are on foot keep the luggage as light as possible. When the Scottish adventurer Fitzroy Maclean crossed here by boat in the 1930s, he reported riding through "jungle" a mile wide on the Afghan bank. No sign of it now.

If you are travelling from Mazar to Termez in Uzbekistan, make sure before you leave that your name is on the bridge or else prepare to get very frustrated. You can contact the UN office in Termez to organize this and to provide transport from the Uzbek side of the bridge to Termez (US$ 10, 15 minute drive). Otherwise, the walk from the border to the taxi rank is 3km.

The journey from Bamiyan to Mazar takes about one and a half days by four-wheel drive jeep. The route from Kabul via the Salang Pass takes a full day but is a magnificent drive (see below). Between June and October it is possible to drive from Kabul, via the Panjshair Valley, to Faizabad and from Chitral in Pakistan to Faizabad – but you need plenty of time and an off road vehicle.

You can catch a bus near the Bharat Hotel from Mazar to Kabul for around US$ 5 (10-13 hours); minibuses are quicker but a little more expensive. Jeeps will take you on the 2-day journey via Maimana to Herat for around US$ 18.

Before travelling into or out of Mazar, check on the security situation prior to departure, since there have been continual skirmishes between the various ethnic groups and commanders controlling surrounding areas. Travel in two-car convoys off the beaten track and, if you have a radio, communicate with base every three hours. The UNAMA office in Mazar provides excellent security reports.

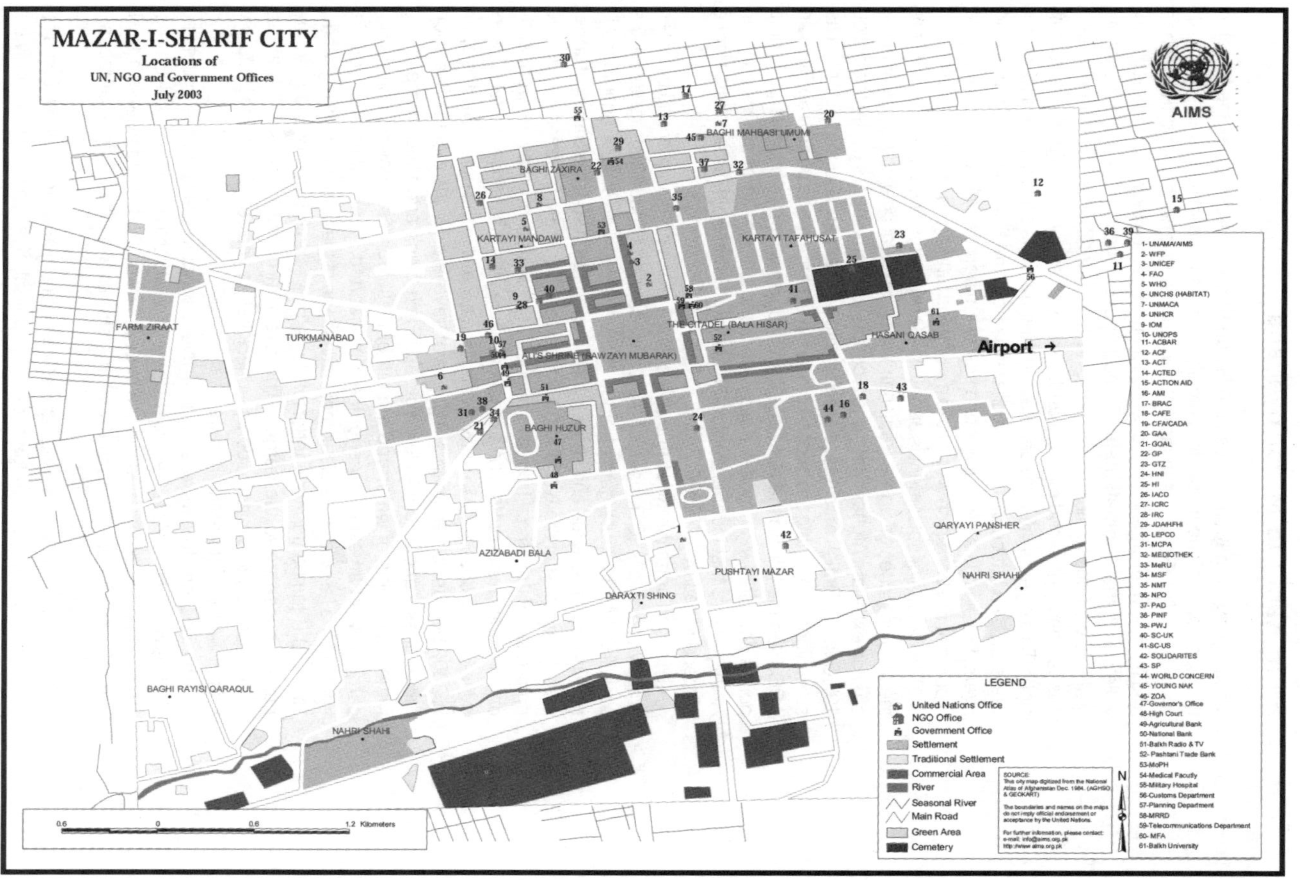
MAZAR-I-SHARIF CITY
Locations of
UN, NGO and Government Offices
July 2003
AIMS
FARMI ZIRAAT
TURKMANABAD
BAGHI ZAXIRA
KARTAYI MANDAWI
ALI'S SHRINE (RAWZAYI MUBARAK)
BAGHI HUZUR
THE CITADEL (BALA HISAR)
KARTAYI TAFAHUSAT
BAGHI MAHBASI UMUMI
HASANI QASAB
Airport →
QARYAYI PANSHER
NAHRI SHAHI
PUSHTAYI MAZAR
DARAXTI SHING
AZIZABADI BALA
BAGHI RAYISI QARAQUL
0.6 0 0.6 1.2 Kilometers
LEGEND
United Nations Office
NGO Office
Government Office
Settlement
Traditional Settlement
Commercial Area
River
Seasonal River
Main Road
Green Area
Cemetery
SOURCE:
This city map digitized from the National Atlas of Afghanistan Dec. 1984. (AGHSO & GEOKART)
The boundaries and names on the maps do not imply official endorsement or acceptance by the United Nations.
For further information, please contact:
e-mail: info@aims.org.pk
http://www.aims.org.pk
N
1- UNAMA/AIMS
2- WFP
3- UNICEF
4- FAO
5- WHO
6- UNCHS (HABITAT)
7- UNMACA
8- UNHCR
9- IOM
10- UNOPS
11- ACBAR
12- ACF
13- ACT
14- ACTED
15- ACTION AID
16- AMI
17- BRAC
18- CAFE
19- CFA/CADA
20- GAA
21- GOAL
22- GP
23- GTZ
24- HNI
25- HI
26- IACD
27- ICRC
28- IRC
29- JDA/HFHI
30- LEPCO
31- MCPA
32- MEDIOTHEK
33- MeRU
34- MSF
35- NMT
36- NPO
37- PAD
38- PINF
39- PWJ
40- SC-UK
41- SC-US
42- SOLIDARITES
43- SP
44- WORLD CONCERN
45- YOUNG NAK
46- ZOA
47-Governor's Office
48-High Court
49-Agricultural Bank
50-National Bank
51-Balkh Radio & TV
52- Pashtani Trade Bank
53-MoPH
54-Medical Faculty
55-Military Hospital
56-Customs Department
57-Planning Department
58-MRRD
59-Telecommunications Department
60- MFA
61-Balkh University

From Kabul to Mazar overland

The journey from Kabul across the Hindu Kush to Mazar takes the traveller through some of the most strategically important – and scenic – parts of Afghanistan. The Russians invaded down this road, and for years the Taliban and Northern Alliance fought over it. The road climbs slowly out of the Kabul valley, onto the **Shomali plain**. Ruined houses and burned out tanks testify that this was once a fiercely fought-over frontline. Then in 1999, the Taliban pushed back Massoud's troops and destroyed every village and vineyard in sight. Three years later the people and their gardens are beginning to return. Watered by a lattice of irrigation channels from the Panjshair and Ghorband rivers, the plain is a like an emerald sea of mulberries, willows and wild vines lapping at the barren shores of the mountains fringing its northern flank.

The first major settlement is **Jebel-us-Saraj** – a thriving bazaar town where the road branches off up the Panjshair Valley. Several *chaikhane* (tea houses) provide excellent Afghan food, and a couple of shopkeepers will try to sell you 19th Century British muskets, stamped with *VR* denoting Queen Victoria. The stanchions supporting the bridge across the river are made of piled up Russian APCs. On the hill are the remains of an impressive fort and two large fishing ponds complete with model 'decoy' ducks to attract live game for hunters. Afghanistan's first independent radio station, Radio Solh, broadcasts from a compound nearby (SEE MEDIA).

The road north threads through a brilliant green gorge squeezed between craggy rock walls. Glimpses of the snow-capped Hindu Kush tantalize the traveller. As the route gains height, the vegetation dies back until there is nothing but rock, scree and snow. When it opened in 1964, the **Salang Tunnel** was the highest in the world at 3,360 metres. Concrete galleries protect the entrances of the tunnel from avalanches and rockfall, but they are frequently choked with snow drifts. The tunnel entrance was blocked for several years by Massoud, desperate to deny the Taliban access to the north. Blasted open in 2002 by Russian engineers, it gapes at travellers like the mouth of an enormous snake about to swallow you up. Pitch black and filled with exhaust fumes, icy pools of water and the din of diesel lorries groaning under their cargo, it's not an experience for the faint-hearted. Nearly 3km later, you are spat out the far end into a bleak mountainscape of glaciers and howling winds. Resist the temptation to wander off for a pee – both sides of the road are heavily mined up to the verges. The direction of traffic through the tunnel alternates daily to avoid accidents – check before you set out. During 2003, the tunnel was shut for major repairs.

The descent follows a series of rivers winding between the crumpled foothills of the Hindu Kush. At **Doshi** there is an attractive looking hotel. Emerging from the mountains, you reach a large plain and the town of **Pul-e-Khumri**. For the traveller only used to Kabul, the streets are full of unfamiliar faces – Uzbeks, Tajiks and Hazaras.

The Zadran Hotel has a vast and efficient dining area and grubby rooms for the night. Just past the bridge over the Andherab river on the left is a holy hot spring, the Chasma-e-Shafar. Invalids come here to treat skin problems and infections. Others come just for a free hot bath. Back on the road, the route passes through fields of wheat and brilliant green paddy. The flatness of the plain is relieved by stands of poplar growing ramrod straight. Travellers share

Surkh Kotal

North of the Hindu Kush, near Pul-e-Khumri, lies Surkh Kotal, the once-magnificent acropolis of the Kushan King Kanishka. Five great terraces, carved 1,900 years ago into a spur of camel-coloured rock, overlook the fertile valley of the Andherab river. Well into the 1970s, a vast marble staircase 20 metres wide swept steeply up its lower slopes. But the stairs fell foul of factional fighting and no longer exist. Only the earth ramps connecting each terrace remain. Half a dozen massive stone pillar bases still litter the terraces. But everything smaller has gone.

Kanishka's rule, which embraced a range of religions, from Buddhism to fire-worshipping Zoroastrians, was one of the most tolerant in Afghan history. His dynasty followed that of the Bactrian Greeks, and the temple complex he created at Surkh Kotal sported Hellenistic fluted columns, pediments and an agora for displaying colossal statues. When Surkh Kotal was excavated in the 1950s, the lower half of a huge statue, thought to be of Kanishka himself, was discovered. Famously depicting the king in a pair of baggy trousers gathered at the ankle, it was the centrepiece of the Kabul Museum until 2001, when Taliban soldiers sledge-hammered it to pieces. Also smashed was a tablet of stone bearing an inscription in Greek letters – one of two known examples of the Kushan script.

We met a young guard on the summit, a Hazara soldier from the Hezb-e-Wahdat faction based in Bamiyan. Supposedly there to protect the historic site from further looting, he told us how he had sold fragments of engraved stone to a couple of Westerners who visited the site in 1999. "I dug out these pieces of stone with writing on," he said, "but I couldn't understand what they said." We showed him a photograph of the now-smashed Kushan inscription from Kabul Museum. "Yes the letters were like that," he said. "I found 32 fragments, each the size of my hand," he added. "I sold them for 12 lakh *Afghanis* each." That adds up to more than US$ 1,000 for the entire haul – equivalent to three years' earnings for the average Afghan. Little wonder that the treasures of Afghanistan are being looted mercilessly. *JW*

the road with brightly-coloured nomads driving their flocks of goats, or boys riding donkeys sidesaddle.

About 13km north of Pul-e-Khumri is a small track leading left towards the foot of some low mountains – the site of **Surkh Kotal**, the 1st Century AD acropolis of Kanishka, King of the Kushans. Although most of the site has been looted or destroyed, the view from the summit is well worth the detour (SEE BOX above and photo, p.177). On north, the road sweeps across bare brown plains, past an old battlefield littered with military debris and skirts the attractive

Lala Gul

Lala Gul looked like a rogue – the kind of man who'd been in too many fights. The right side of his dark, tanned face was heavily scarred. A chequered turban hung down the back of his neck. He grinned like a cartoon pirate with teeth stained brown by years of chewing *naswar* tobacco. He hunched over his steering wheel possessively, staring at the road with steady, expressionless eyes. But at least he had a four-wheel drive van and a few spare days to drive us to Panjshair and Mazar. And he had a great ear for music. For every town we drove through, Lala Gul had a song which sang of its charms – the heavy-boughed orchards of Tashkurgan, the fearless *buzkashi* players of Shibarghan.

After a few days on the road, Lala Gul told us his story. "I was driving from Bamiyan to Kabul with six passengers. The Americans had just started bombing. There were three other cars on the road too. My passengers were a bride, her new husband and members of her family. They had just got married and were on their way to Paktia." He swerved to avoid several large potholes. We were making the switchback, snowdrifted descent from the Salang tunnel. On either verge were lines of stones painted red – minefields.

"Suddenly, I saw a jetfighter in the sky", continued Gul. "I thought it was going to bomb Bamiyan, which was still held by the Taliban. I saw a bright flash. The next thing I remember was opening my eyes in the Red Cross hospital in Kabul. I realised I was seriously injured." Lala Gul gestured to the scars on his face, arms and feet. "I heard that all the other people in my car were killed. I was the only one alive. I heard my car was completely smashed to pieces. The people following were amazed anyone survived. I spent four months in hospital recovering. I wrap my head in this turban to cover the scars."

Was he angry with the Americans, I asked. "Because the Taliban are overturned, I am happy – even though I was injured. Of course I am sad my passengers died. But no, I am not angry. I just want America to pay for my new car."*JW*

oasis town of **Aybak** (also known as Samangan). Tongas drawn by horses decked in multicoloured tassels stand ready to take travellers into town from the main road. The town is full of men with Central Asian features wearing turbans wrapped around embroidered pill box hats with a tail of silk hanging over one shoulder. The women flit about like phantoms in the all-encompassing white or blue *burqa*. A massive invasion of locusts destroyed a third of this area's crops in 2002. There is an ancient Buddhist site hidden in the hills nearby, but you'll need a local guide.

Further on, the road weaves through the deeply fissured, rust-red gorges of the Koh-e-Baba mountains. On their far flank lies the oasis town of **Tashkurgan**, also known as Khulm – the last stop before Mazar. The Khulm river irrigates the valley, filled with mulberry, almond, apple and peach trees. King Amanullah was so taken with the place that he built a small palace on the hill. The fortress here commands a magnificent view. To the south, a wall of mountains cuts off all memory of Kabul. To the north, the vast plains of Central Asia melt into the horizon. In the 1820s, the intrepid British traveller, William Moorcroft, and his companions were incarcerated here for six months by the dreaded Chief of Kunduz, Murad Beg. They later escaped, only to be poisoned while prospecting for Central Asia's finest ponies.

For a more detailed, pre-war account of this journey and sights along the way, read The Road to Balkh, *by Nancy Dupree (Kabul, 1967)*

Orientation & getting around

Mazar is named after the large turquoise-tiled Shrine of Hazrat Ali, which dominates the central square of the city, and is a useful reference point for getting around. The main road leading off the north side of the square contains a cluster of UN offices. The curfew in Mazar (2100-0430 hrs) is rigorously respected by foreigners and locals alike. There are no mines in the immediate vicinity, but check with UNAMA if you are planning to visit areas further afield. Taxis are a reasonable way to get around, if you don't have access to your own vehicle – but travel in pairs.

Agencies

The fighting of 1997-98 and again in late 2001 seriously affected the work of international organizations in Mazar. Compounds and warehouses were looted of vehicles, electronics and food supplies several times over. Expatriate personnel became used to sheltering in underground bunkers before being airlifted to safety. But for most Afghan staff and inhabitants, evacuation is not an option. In 2003, ACBAR listed about 16 NGOs present in Mazar – a far cry from the hundreds in Kabul. For a briefing on UN activities, visit the UNAMA office, about 1.5km down the road leading off the south side of Hazrat Ali square.

Mazar A-Z

Accommodation and Food

Accommodation possibilities in Mazar are fairly limited. The **UNICA guest-house** is located some distance from the centre of town, but has the twin attractions of a large garden and a cash bar. However, only UN and World Bank staff are permitted to stay (US$ 65/night). For journalists and itinerant travellers, the best bet is the **Bharat Hotel**, a 7-storey modern red building on the northeast corner of Hazrat Ali square. Rooms cost US$ 25-60 per night, and some come with a balcony overlooking the shrine. Their large dining room serves up decent food and non-stop Hindi movies. Two cheaper (and grubbier) options near the Hazrat Ali shrine are the **Aria Hotel** and **Aamo Hotel** – rooms start from US$ 10. Alternatively call on one of the international NGOs, which may have a spare bed for the night.

Eating out in Mazar is limited to several *kebab-khanas* on the west side of Hazrat Ali square, or at the expensive UNICA guesthouse. One excellent local eatery goes by the name of the **'Titanic Restaurant'** – its décor features a large painting of the passenger liner perfectly afloat on a calm sea. You can fill up three people for a dollar here. Cuisine is distinctly Central Asian. Try the *mantu* (meaning 'me you' – pasta stuffed with minced meat), *burani* (fried eggplant), *bollogne* (potato/leek fried in batter) or the usual *pilaw* (rice/mutton). In the streets to the south of the shrine are some markets selling succulent melons in summer and apples or oranges in winter. Avoid salads and unpeeled fruits, and only drink bottled or filtered water.

Embassies & Visas

A number of foreign consulates are located in Mazar, including the missions of Iran, Turkey, and Turkmenistan. You can renew your Afghan visa here in one day, but for Pakistani visas you need to go to Kabul. A 3-month Afghan or Turkmen visa will cost around US$ 100-150.

Emergencies

During 2002, the UN and NGOs came very close to evacuating expatriate staff due to security problems. Check with coordinating bodies before abandoning the city during times of unrest. Leaving Mazar at such times is both difficult and – since UN/NGO departures can be seen as a signal of loss of control – may be opposed by the local authorities. If you're here for any length of time, it's worth registering with the UN.

Overland evacuation into Uzbekistan may be possible, depending on whether the border bridge over the Amu Darya remains open. Otherwise, both the UN and ICRC have organized airlifts in the past to evacuate key personnel, but this is dependent on negotiating a ceasefire with local commanders to enable the planes to land. If you decide to try your luck with the UN or ICRC in an emergency situation, make sure you obey orders, because UN evacuation convoys in the past have been kept waiting by journalists keen to get one last shot. Any large collection of expatriates and expensive jeeps is a conspicuous target, so it is best not to hang around or force other people to (SEE SECURITY TIPS).

Information

Call in at UNAMA or ICRC for the latest security information. The Department of Foreign Affairs is the first stop for information on work permits. Their staff can be very helpful on security issues and in organizing ministerial meetings and introductions to other government departments.

For internet updates, check out:

http://www.kabulcaravan.com (online travel guide to Afghanistan)

http://thorntree.lonelyplanet.com (online chat room – see Asia/Central Asia section)

Local Rules

Despite the departure of the Taliban, the dress code is still conservative, especially for foreign women. Loose clothing covering most of the body is recommended. Foreign women are given more concessions than local women when it comes to dress and behaviour, but dressing appropriately goes a long way towards avoiding problems. Do not try and stare down the men staring at you – it only makes them more interested; and do not walk around alone at night. It is inappropriate to touch the opposite sex in public, so only shake hands if they are offered. However, women embracing women is as normal as men embracing men. On Wednesday mornings ladies can visit the precincts of the Hazrat Ali shrine, but you won't be allowed into the inner rooms unless you are a Muslim. As a foreign man in northern Afghanistan, there are less restrictions, but remember not to wear shorts or look at local women (SEE CLOTHING & KIT).

Medical

The main health risk is from dehydration or water-borne bugs leading to diarrhoea, hepatitis and typhoid. Take precautions against malaria and leishmaniasis-carrying sandflies. There are numerous local pharmacies and medical NGOs provide backup for most problems. However, any serious treatment should be carried out in Pakistan. The dusty environment may be irritable to contact lens wearers, so bring plenty of cleaning solution – none is available in Mazar. The Jordanian Hospital at Mazar airport offers medical care to foreigners and has a fully supplied pharmacy. The hospital run by Samaritan's Purse in Khulm, 30 minutes from Mazar, is also recommended (SEE PERSONAL HEALTH).

Money

A huge three-story money market, known as the Kefayat, is located on the west side of the Hazrat Ali shrine in the centre of Mazar. The old currency, known as the Dostum Dollar, was replaced in late 2002 by the new national *Afghani.* The rate has fluctuated between 45-65 *Afghanis* to the dollar (SEE MONEY & BARGAINING).

Post & Telecommunications

Mail is sent by UN and ICRC flights to and from Pakistan. Since the departure of the Taliban, telecommunications have developed rapidly. Several companies around the main square offer IDD calls. The Afghan Wireless Communication Company (AWCC) has activated a mobile GSM network – you can buy a SIM card for your existing handset to make international calls. Thuraya satphones are widely used in the field as the local mobile phone network has no coverage outside Mazar (SEE TELECOMS).

Recreation

Assuming you wish to give *buzkashi* a miss, there are a number of other organised sports – usually on a Friday. Try volleyball and tennis at the UNICA

Bullet to ballot

"The Taliban executed people here every week", said Mohammed Shah quietly. "Once they stoned a woman to death, because they believed she was spying for the Northern Alliance. They rounded us up in the bazaar and forced us to watch." He spoke without emotion, as though years of brutality had flattened his feelings. His moustache and hair were grey with dust; his face deeply tanned. He was a teacher, but it didn't look like he'd spent much time indoors recently.

It was 29 May 2002. We were sitting on the terraces of Mazar's sports stadium. The black, red and green national flag fluttered over the five Olympic rings painted on the stadium's wall. Local people used to play football here, and stage wrestling and gymnastics competitions. Then the Taliban made it a killing field. They executed educated people, especially Dari-speakers, said Mohammed. They used machine guns, stones or a rope suspended from a crane. Up to 20,000 people at a time were made to watch.

Now the stadium was the scene of Mazar's first vote for nearly 40 years. Fifty UN tents were lined up on the dusty pitch, each lined with Turkoman carpets and filled with candidates elected by their districts from across northern Afghanistan. Some men sported beards and turbans trailing long white tails. Uzbeks in embroidered skullcaps mingled with Tajiks in their trademark *pakools*, worn Massoud-style at a jaunty angle. Hazaras and Pashtuns came in smaller numbers. There were even some women – huddled in the corner of the stadium in *burqas*.

The vote had been going on for several weeks in the provinces, to elect the 800 candidates to go to Mazar. Now, the candidates from Mazar city were selecting 12 representatives to go to Kabul for the national *Loya Jirga*. Of those 12, four would be women.

The late afternoon sun slanted across the dusty lilac crags of the Koh-e-Baba mountains to the south. A warm wind blew in from the northeast, across the baking plains of the Oxus river. Meaty-smelling steam rose from a dozen vast cauldrons as local chefs laid on by the UN prepared *al fresco* meals for a thousand mouths.

The candidates mounted the gallery where local dignitaries had once viewed the day's sport. Speeches dragged on into dusk. "Don't vote for the man who has power or money. Vote for the freedom of Afghanistan", announced one candidate over the tannoy. A large red fire truck creaked into view firing jets of water from its cannon. Dust control, not crowd control.

"Is this a chance for peace in Afghanistan?" I asked. "Maybe" replied Mohammed guardedly. "Who's being elected?" I added. "Not commanders – the people don't vote for them", he said. "To be a representative of the *Loya Jirga*, you should be educated, you shouldn't be a drugs trafficker or a smuggler. You shouldn't belong to any faction – you should be someone helpful to the people. "

But the truth is less simple. The previous day, General Dostum – the brutal and much feared leader of the Jumbesh-e-Melli faction – had swept into town on his own election campaign. He surprised UN staff by marching straight into the stadium with his supporters and a small group of armed Turkish bodyguards and went from tent to tent explaining the virtues of voting for him. Not surprisingly, his "constituency" of Shibarghan, three hours' drive west of Mazar, returned a full house of Jumbesh candidates.

Groups of men unrolled their prayer mats and knelt in a line towards the dying sun. A three quarter moon shone overhead. Finally the time came to vote. The women were invited to cast their ballots first. A dozen blue and white *burqas* flitted through the half-light like phantoms, about to make a small piece of history.

Afterwards, we approached them. One confident lady with fine, Oriental features introduced herself as Homayra. She wore a long, powder green two-piece suit and headscarf – no *burqa*. "Today is the day that wisdom will replace the gun in the decision-making of Afghanistan", she announced. "I feel delighted, because this event will finish off the warlords and make Afghanistan united. Brothers will not kill brothers anymore." Homayra was a poet and showed us her latest book. "For 23 years," she continued, "men have been martyred on the frontlines. But we women have been martyred four times – we have lost husbands and sons, fathers and brothers." What message did Homayra have for the outside world? "I ask the international community to use all their efforts to educate Afghan women. If a man is educated he can teach one person, but if a woman is educated she can teach the entire country. The first school for our children is their mother."

The other women – all in *burqas* – were more timid. I asked one how she felt. She lifted back her veil and said quietly: "I am very happy that after a long time women have got the right to vote." It was the first time in her life that she had voted. Her face – worn down by fatigue and anxiety – revealed no joy. Her eyebrows were dark and brooding. The fear had not yet left her deep brown eyes. A kindergarten teacher, she'd been elected by her district to come to the *jirga* in Mazar. "I am a widow with two daughters. After the death of my husband, I don't want my children to suffer. This event can bring prosperity and peace for my children." How had her husband died? "The Taliban looted my home and martyred him", she said. "He was a reciter of the Holy Qu'ran – but he was not one of them." Was she angry with the Taliban, I asked. She replied simply: "My vote is my revenge."

By Jonathan Walter

guesthouse, volleyball at the NGO Solidarités, soccer at the Turkish consulate, or basketball at UNHCR. Some people jog in the WFP compound or around the airport – but wear long sleeves and trousers. Walking through the bazaar or possibly through the desert to the north of the city are more sedate options. The desert and hill area to the south of the city is unsafe. Aid workers often get together for a drink on a Thursday night – usually in one of the agency guesthouses. But don't expect a late night as long as the curfew kicks in at 9pm.

Shopping

You can find carpets and handicrafts on the west side of the Hazrat Ali shrine, but they are usually overpriced so bargain hard. As well as traditional Turcoman and Baluch carpets, you should be able to find Uzbek *gelim* which are woven rugs rather than knotted carpets. Stop by the *mandawi* (vegetable market) and see how the vast majority of locals pick over vegetables that foreigners would probably not even consider edible. The cost of living has soared recently, so remember that bargaining for non-luxury items may be denying locals the few cents benefit they desperately need. The local second-hand bazaar is full of very cheap clothes in various sizes. The traditional long-sleeved coat worn by the men of Mazar is known as the *chapan* and comes in both single-weight summer and quilted winter variants. There are some good antique shops around the city selling traditional carpet bags and jewellery.

Sights

Shrine of Hazrat Ali. This magnificent shrine, which gave rise to the name Mazar-e-Sharif – "Tomb of the Exalted" – still stands in the central square, relatively unscathed after 24 years of war. The faithful believe that Hazrat Ali – cousin and son-in-law of the Prophet Mohammed, and the fourth orthodox Caliph of Islam – lies buried here. Thousands of worshippers converge on the shrine during the elaborate festival of Nawroz in March to celebrate the coming of spring and a new year of hoped-for prosperity.

Although Hazrat Ali was murdered in 661 AD and buried near Baghdad, local tradition relates that his followers feared the body would be desecrated by his enemies. So they mounted the Caliph's mortal remains on a white female camel. After many weeks of wandering she collapsed exhausted and the body was buried here, where she fell. Genghis Khan destroyed the original shrine, and the present building dates from the 15th Century, including some modern restoration.

The shrine is the city's natural focal point. The air is filled with doves which roost among the minarets. Allegedly, they arrive as pigeons but the holy atmosphere turns them white within 40 days. The peace is punctuated five times a day by the piercing call to prayer from the *muezzin*. The most atmospheric time to visit the shrine is at dawn or dusk, when the faithful hurry barefoot across the spotless marble courtyard for prayers and the sun casts long shadows across the shrine's turquoise domes (SEE COVER).

Balkh, "Mother of Cities". Balkh, which lies half an hour's drive west of Mazar, has several buildings well worth visiting. The city has never quite recovered from the time Genghis Khan paid a visit in the early 13th Century.

Shrine of Khwaja Parsa, Balkh *J. Walter*

But the broad tree-lined streets are a welcome oasis from the hustle of Mazar. Set in a park of soaring sycamore and pine trees, the 15th Century Timurid **Shrine of Khwaja Parsa** still sports an impressive tiled façade flanked by a pair of corkscrew columns. Its dome is reminiscent of Gawhar Shad's mausoleum in Herat. Nearby are some well-kept public conveniences and the tomb of the ill-fated 9th Century poetess Rabi'a Balkhi, who slit her wrists after her love-affair with a servant was uncovered. At the far end of the park is the massive gateway of a 17th Century ***madrassa***. Beware the fake antiquities being sold at its feet.

On the edge of town are the impressive **Bala Hissar and city walls** of ancient Balkh. The Masjid-e-No Gumbad (meaning "nine domes" but more correctly known as **Hajji Piyada Mosque**) stands in a ploughed field under a large corrugated iron roof to protect it from the elements. The mosque dates from the early 9th Century, making it the earliest Islamic monument yet identified in Afghanistan. A number of massive, but beautifully decorated brick and earth arches remain. Hajji Piyada (meaning "the feet that went to Mecca") is something of a local hero, having walked from here to Mecca and back seven times.

Weather

From December to March, Mazar is very cold (toothpaste freezes in the tube), and the only heating is by 'bukhari' – simple diesel stoves which make everyone in the vicinity smell the same after a few days. Little snow falls in the city, but the mountains to the south are snowcapped most of the winter. Spring brings rain and mud, but summer is very hot and dusty, with temperatures reaching 40 degrees Celsius in July and August.

Eastern region

The eastern region of Afghanistan consists of the area neighbouring the North West Frontier Province and tribal agencies of Pakistan, namely the provinces of Kunar, Nangarhar, Nuristan, Paktia and Khost. It is a mountainous region traditionally dominated by various competing Pashtun tribes. The largest town in the area, and the capital of Nangarhar province, is Jalalabad which sits astride the strategically significant route from Kabul via the Khyber Pass to the Indian subcontinent.

During the 1990s Nangarhar province competed with Helmand province in the far west as the country's prime producer of the opium poppy. One journalist reported in May 1992: "For miles around Jalalabad, 80 percent of the arable land produces nothing but poppies, UN officials say. And the farmers like it that way. Today opium brings the farmer 10 times more money than wheat – and there is plenty of cheap bread for sale in town, thanks to the flow of free flour [from USAID]."

Opium remains an emotive issue in this part of Afghanistan. When officials from Karzai's administration attempted to persuade Nangarhar's farmers to stop growing poppy in spring 2002, they were shot dead on the spot. The farmers claimed they could earn US$ 3,500 per acre of opium – far more than the compensation on offer for not growing it. Meanwhile, the assassination later that year of Nangarhar's governor, Hajji Qadir, may well have been drug-related.

In 2003, Nangarhar overtook Helmand as Afghanistan's number one poppy province. A total of 19,000 hectares were under cultivation, mainly in the south of the province, producing 964 tonnes of raw opium – over one quarter of the country's entire production.

The east of Afghanistan has suffered from widespread illegal logging in recent years. During 2003, timber smuggling reportedly shot up, due to demand in Pakistan for the high quality timber found in Kunar's forests.

Security across the region deteriorated during 2002-03, as remnants of the Taliban and Al Qa'eda launched crossborder raids from Pakistan's neighbouring provinces. Several rocket, grenade and gun attacks have targeted the offices and staff of UN agencies and international organizations in Jalalabad. In July 2003, a diplomatic row blew up when Afghan forces traded fire with Pakistani soldiers who had allegedly dug in positions on the Kunar side of Mohmand Agency, along the disputed Durand Line which forms Afghanistan's eastern border.

Jalalabad

Situated at an altitude of 569 metres in a fertile plain irrigated by the Kabul and Kunar rivers, and flanked by the mountains of the Hindu Kush to the north and the Spinghar (or Safed Koh) to the south, Jalalabad is an oasis compared to most Afghan towns. Traditionally a warm winter retreat for royalty and wealthy urbanites, it is famous for its springtime orange-blooms, which still blossom in the centre of town. Before the war Jalalabad thrived on its orchards of citrus fruit, watered and powered by the hydroelectric dam at Darunta to the north-west of the city. However, most of these mechanized farms built by the Soviets were looted and destroyed by *mujahed* factions in 1989 and are only now beginning to be replanted. During the 1990s, the city became a foothold for many aid agencies keen to expand their operations crossborder into Afghanistan from nearby Peshawar.

In 329 BC Alexander the Great passed this way with 30,000 troops *en route* to his conquest of India. From the 2nd to 7th Centuries AD over a thousand Buddhist *stupas* in nearby Hadda and Basawal echoed to the chants and incantations of meditating monks, and Nangarhar was one of the most important pilgrimage sites in the Buddhist world. The region was also at the centre of the remarkable Gandhara school of sculpture which represented the Buddha for the first time in human form, complete with Greco-Roman robes (SEE CULTURE). Indeed the Buddha himself is said to have visited the valley in order to slay the demon dragon Gopala, and Chinese pilgrims have written of the sacred relics once housed in Hadda's shrines: a fragment of the Buddha's skull entirely covered in gold-leaf, a tooth, some hair – there was even a *stupa* erected where he had clipped his fingernails. The city resisted the spread of Islam until the 10th Century, when Sultan Mahmud of Ghazni swept through the region on his way to Delhi.

The name Jalalabad means Abode of Splendour, and is said to descend from Jalaluddin Akbar, Moghul Emperor of India, who founded the city in 1570. It was the Moghuls who established the Khyber Pass as the main route through to India. For many years the town was in the margins of history, but reappears in the drama of the retreat from Kabul of the 16,000 strong column of British troops and camp followers in January 1842. They were desperately seeking sanctuary in the British garrison at Jalalabad, but only the legendary Dr Brydon made it, while the remainder were hacked to death and a lucky few taken prisoner. In 1919, the British bombed Jalalabad from the air, before losing heart and negotiating independence for Afghanistan. The same year, Amir Habibullah was murdered while hunting near Jalalabad and is commemorated by a neo-classical mausoleum.

For most of the Soviet war Jalalabad was a bastion of the communist government regime supported by Red Army forces. The airport was used for numerous Soviet offensives against guerrilla positions in the nearby Safed Koh region to the south and the Hindu Kush to the north.

Throughout the 1980s, the *mujahideen* made repeated – but not particularly effective – attacks against government positions deliberately located on the outskirts of the city to draw fire. In March 1989, in the aftermath of the Soviet withdrawal, Jalalabad became the focus of an ill-conceived guerrilla assault, but government forces held off the rebels. The plan was thrust upon the

SOURCE:
Atlas of Afghanistan Dec. 1984. (AGCHO, & GEOKART)

Date: December 2002

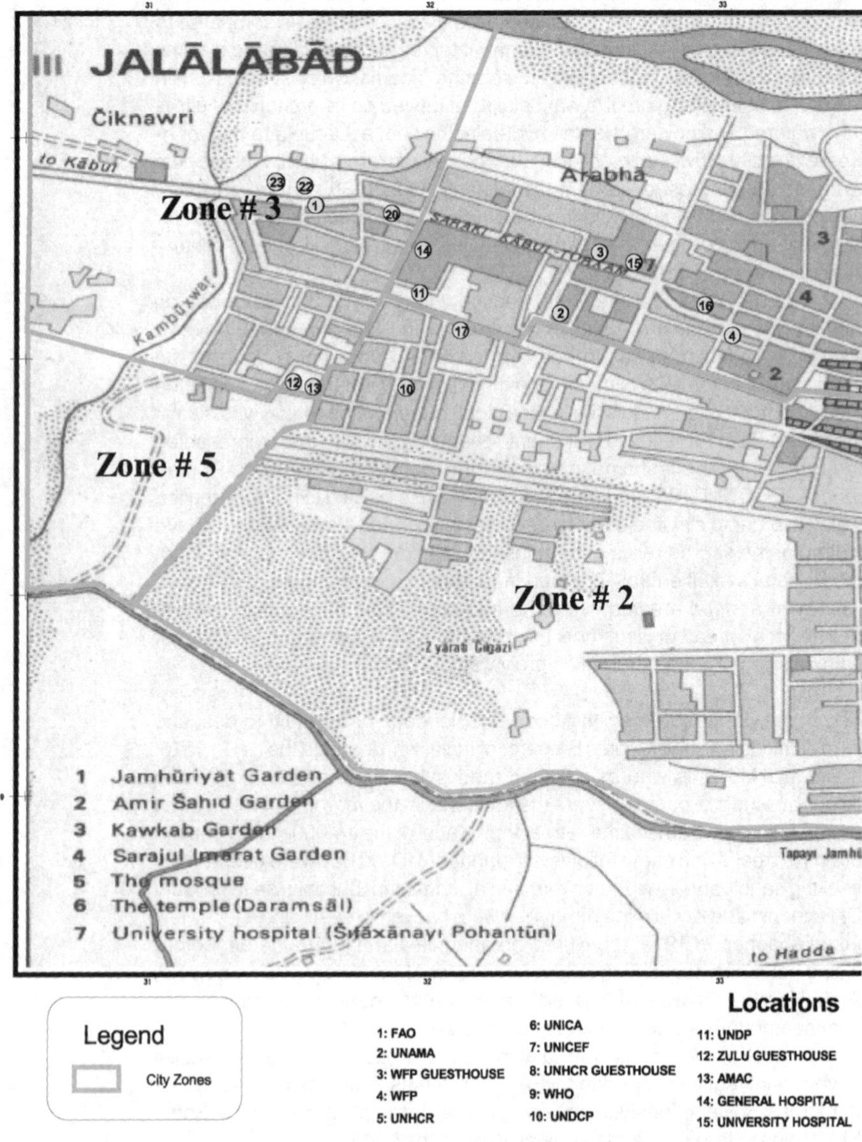

Legend

City Zones

Locations

1: FAO
2: UNAMA
3: WFP GUESTHOUSE
4: WFP
5: UNHCR
6: UNICA
7: UNICEF
8: UNHCR GUESTHOUSE
9: WHO
10: UNDCP
11: UNDP
12: ZULU GUESTHOUSE
13: AMAC
14: GENERAL HOSPITAL
15: UNIVERSITY HOSPITAL

AIMS

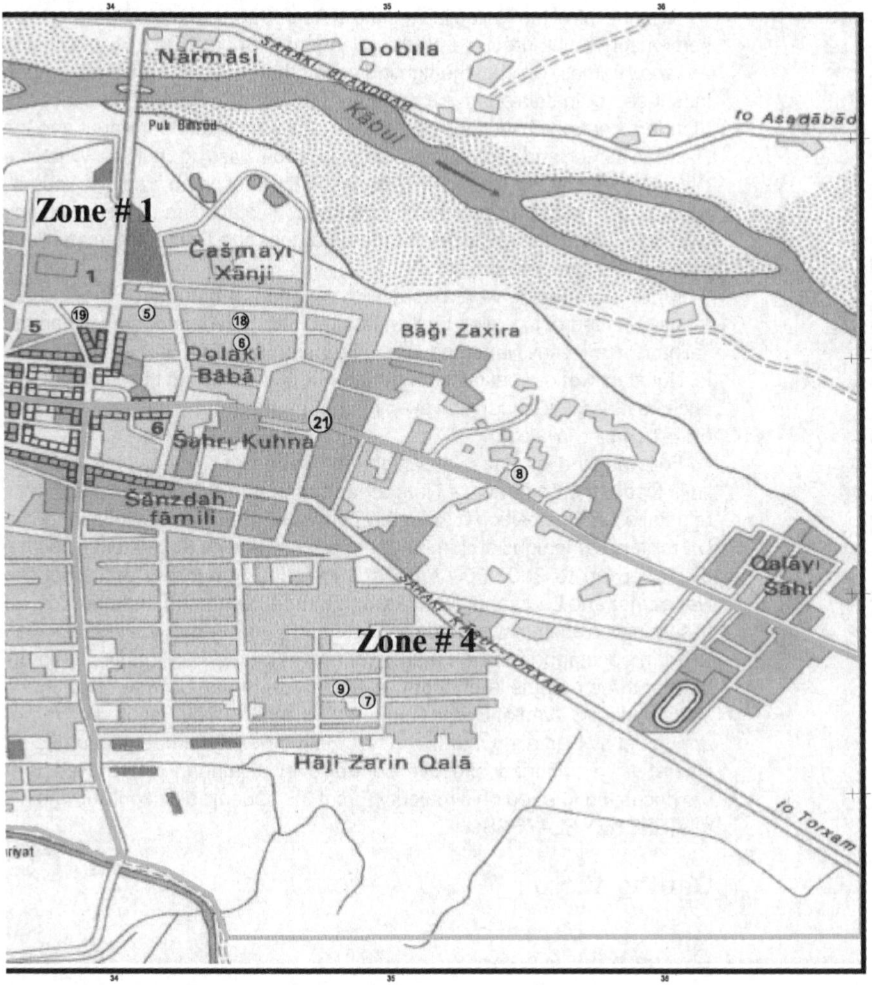

34 35 36

Nārmāsi
Dobıla
SARAKI BLANDGAR
Kābul
to Asadābād
Puk Bāsod
Zone # 1
Čašmayı Xānji
1
5
19
5
18
6
Bāğı Zaxira
Dolaki Bābā
21
6
Šahrı Kuhna
8
Šānzdah fāmili
Qalāyı Šāhi
SARAKI KABUL TORXAM
Zone # 4
9
7
Hāji Zarin Qalā
to Torxam
riyat

34 35 36

16: SPEEN GHAR HOTEL
17: PAKISTAN CONSULATE
18: GOVERNOR HOUSE
19: WHITE MOSQUE
20: UNAMA GH
21: Globe Traffic Center
22: FAO SO #2
23: Security HQ

N
W E
S

resistance alliance of Peshawar-based parties by the Americans and Pakistan's Inter Services Intelligence agency (ISI) in an attempt to force a swift *mujahed* victory over the communists in Kabul. But the attack failed due to a lack of broad-based resistance support.

After the fall of the Najibullah regime in April 1992, Jalalabad was ruled as a semi-autonomous province by the "Nangarhar Shura." Representatives of *mujahed* parties, which were fighting each other in Kabul, would hold meetings together in Jalalabad. From 1992-1996 dozens of different local commanders controlled sections of the road between Jalalabad, Kabul and the Pakistan border, and each extorted tax or loot from passing vehicles. When the city was taken by the Taliban in 1996, without a shot being fired, the security situation both in and around the city improved. Jalalabad and the surrounding area are predominately Pashtun so there was less anti-Taliban resentment and tension here than in Kabul or Herat.

While local people were happy with the security brought by the Taliban, many resented being ruled by Kandaharis. This resentment grew when the Taliban forced many Nangarharis to fight against their will. Hazrat Ali, a powerful Nuristani warlord based in Laghman with military ties to the Northern Alliance, resisted the Taliban and eventually threw them out of Jalalabad in wake of US bombing in late 2001.

Following the fall of the Taliban, the region became increasingly unstable. Hajji Qadir, the governor of Nangarhar during the *mujahideen* years, was reinstalled in the position by a locally convened *shura*. Meanwhile, ongoing US military campaigns during 2002 – especially around Khost, to the south – displaced up to 200,000 Afghans who found temporary settlement in Nangarhar and Laghman. Robbery and murder increased. In April 2002 an assassination attempt was made on Defence Minister Fahim, visiting Jalalabad to drum up support for the *Loya Jirga*. And following Hajji Qadir's untimely murder three months later, a power struggle emerged between Hazrat Ali, Jalalabad's pro-Jamiat Corps Commander, and the new Pashtun governor appointed by Karzai – Qadir's brother, Hajji Din Mohammed. During 2003, Hazrat Ali maintained effective control over Jalalabad and the eastern provinces; but the region's majority Pashtuns appeared discontent with his rule (SEE KEY PLAYERS).

Getting there

By air

Jalalabad airport is situated three or four kilometres east of town. It is served by regular UN flights from Kabul (Mon, Thu, Sat) and Islamabad. You may also be able to fly here with ICRC or PACTEC/Air Serv International (SEE TRAVEL BY AIR).

Overland

Jalalabad is the first major Afghan town over the border from Pakistan. As such, it is an important logistical staging post for convoys of food and supplies. If you are travelling independently you may be able to hitch a lift on a WFP

Nuristan – land of light

Nuristan is a remote – and in parts, still heavily forested – mountainous area of the Hindu Kush northeast of Jalalabad, whose people are famous for their spirit of independence. Alexander the Great and his men donned ivy-wreaths in the mountains there, drank the local homebrew and "lost their wits in true Bacchic frenzy." Tamerlane had a tougher time and had to be lowered down a cliff face in a basket, although history does not relate whether this was due to the moonshine or poor map-reading. Throughout the centuries the Nuristanis resisted all conquest and conversion. They became known as *Kafirs*, or Infidels, because they worshipped numerous nature and ancestor spirits. They left the bodies of their dead exposed to the elements for a year in wooden coffins, and then placed over the graves carved wooden effigies which the deceased spirits were believed to inhabit. A number of large carved wooden figures depicting fertility goddesses and ancestors were kept in the Kabul Museum. It was not until 1896 that Amir Abdur Rahman succeeded in subduing the *Kafirs* and converting them by the sword to Islam; from then on he renamed their land Nuristan, "Land of Light." Among the first pre-Soviet, anti-communist revolts occurred in Nuristan in 1978 resulting in severe bombing of the region's main town, Kamdesh. *JW*

food convoy. They take a day to reach Jalalabad from Peshawar. In a car the drive from Peshawar to the border is about one and a half hours, and the same again on to Jalalabad, along a sealed road. Remember that the border at Torkham is shut between 1200-1300 hrs and Pakistani time is ahead of Afghan time (half an hour in winter, one and a half hours in summer) so make sure you arrive at the border in good time to cross into Pakistan. The Pakistanis close their side at 1700 hrs. A tribal areas permit is needed if you are driving from Peshawar to Jalalabad, but it is not required for travel in the other direction. From the west, Jalalabad is about 3-4 hours' car or jeep ride from Kabul, through the spectacular Tangi Gharu gorge. This road, once desperately potholed, has now been graded and major repairs were due to start in late 2003. For more details of the journey from Peshawar to Kabul, SEE TRAVEL OVERLAND.

In August 2003, the UN suspended all road missions between Jalalabad and Kunar on the Asadabad road because of security concerns – so check the latest situation before heading off in that direction.

Orientation & getting around

Jalalabad is laid out on a grid plan, with the Kabul river and the Hindu Kush to the north, the Spinghar mountains to the south, and the main Kabul-Torkham road which runs east-west. Three-wheeled rickshaws are available if you do not have access to a jeep. The UN's Afghanistan Information Management Service (AIMS) produces street maps of Jalalabad showing the locations of most agencies and key offices.

Agencies

In February 2003, ACBAR listed the presence of over 35 international NGOS, 62 national NGOS and eight UN agencies based in Jalalabad. The International Committee of the Red Cross (ICRC) supports the public hospital, which is the main health facility for the whole of eastern Afghanistan. For more information on UN activities visit the UNAMA office in Arzaq Road, two blocks west of the Spinghar Hotel.

Jalalabad A-Z

Accommodation and Food

UN guesthouses are only available for UN and World Bank staff. Otherwise, the **Afghan Hotel and Restaurant** is a friendly guesthouse, situated opposite the TV Centre in the middle of town. Rooms are small and hot, but the food is good and they have satellite TV. Otherwise the **Spinghar Hotel** (TEL: 2367) is a plusher alternative, but take care not to get ripped off. Located opposite the WFP office, its luxuriant gardens are a relief from the dusty road. The restaurant serves adequate Afghan food for both residents and non-residents.

Embassies & Visas

By mid-2003, India, Iran and Pakistan all had diplomatic missions present in Jalalabad. The Pakistan Consulate (Satphone: +882 168 980 1266) issues transit, single, double and multiple entry visas; it is situated in Zone 3 in the west of the city.

Information

Call in at the local UN office. For internet updates, check out:

http://www.aims.org.af (website for the UN's Afghanistan Information Management Service/AIMS)
http://www.kabulcaravan.com (online travel guide to Afghanistan)
http://thorntree.lonelyplanet.com (online chat room – see Asia/Central Asia section)

Medical

The ICRC surgical unit at the Jalalabad Public Hospital will treat any emergency surgical cases. The city is full of malaria-bearing mosquitoes so make sure you cover up at dawn and dusk, and sleep either under a treated bednet or with the windows shut (SEE PERSONAL HEALTH).

Security

In December 2002, a curfew from 10pm-4am was re-imposed on Jalalabad after what the police chief called a 'dramatic increase' in criminal activity. During 2003, international aid agencies were the target of sporadic attacks blamed on the Taliban or Gulbuddin Hekmatyar. The city itself remains relatively safe, but outlying areas less so. Check the latest situation with UNAMA.

Post & Telecommunications

At the time of writing, radio remained the main tool for agency communications, although the Afghan Wireless Communication Company (AWCC) had established mobile GSM coverage in the city. For more information, try calling AWCC on 060 600 000. Some international NGOs and UN agencies have set up their own satellite email and internet access (SEE TELECOMS).

Sights

Jalalabad's greatest attractions are its gardens. The Buddhist stupas at **Hadda** provided an underground haven for the *mujahideen*, but were largely destroyed by Soviet bombing during the 1980s. Whatever was left was completely looted by the end of 2001. The **Seraj-ul Emorat** is a palace built by Amir Habibullah around 1910. Set in pleasant gardens, just to the east of the Spinghar Hotel, the building was sacked during tribal revolts in 1928 and remains an impressive ruin. During 2002-03, a public swimming pool was being built beside the palace. The **Mausoleum of Amir Habibullah,** down a lane opposite the Seraj-ul Emorat, is a rather gaudy-coloured neoclassical creation complete with dome and porticos. The Amir ruled from 1901 until 1919 when an unknown assassin killed him near Jalalabad, probably because his political stance was not sufficiently pro-Islamic/anti-British. His two sons and successors, Amanullah (*ruled* 1919-1929) and Enayatullah (*ruled* 14-17 January 1929) are also buried here. The mausoleum is set in a garden of orange trees. The beautiful **Kawkab gardens** are filled with roses, fountains (dry) and Afghans practising taekwondo. The view of the broad **Kabul river** is worth catching at sunset, from the Pul-e-Behsud.

The Moghul garden at **Nimla** lies about 40 km west of Jalalabad towards Kabul. Said to have been laid out by the beautiful wife of Emperor Jahangir (1605-1627), it is the only remaining Moghul garden in Afghanistan, and has recently been restored by FAO. The foundations of an old British fort may be seen at **Gandamak**, 11 km from Nimla, where, in January 1842, British infantry soldiers made one desperate last stand against the marauding Afghans – they were killed to a man.

Weather

Jalalabad is 1100 metres lower in elevation than Kabul and enjoys a much milder climate in winter. Palm trees grow beside the Kabul River and some geographers have referred to the Jalalabad valley as sub-tropical. Spring (March-April) is an excellent time to visit, but summers are very hot and dusty with temperatures reaching over 40 degrees Celsius.

Southern region

Southern Afghanistan stretches from the foothills of the Hindu Kush down to the deserts of Seistan and the Baluch border. Geographically it is a region dominated by the Helmand River which rises in Hazarajat and flows southwest for 1,300 km through Uruzgan, Helmand and Nimruz provinces before vanishing into the marshes that stretch across into Iran. Ethnically, the south is heavily Pashtun, with pockets of Baluch and Brahui in the sparsely inhabited deserts on the borders of Iran and Pakistan. As Baluch are also found in Iran and Pakistan, there is a strong sense of a single (albeit not unified) Baluch identity in all three countries.

The main city of the south is Kandahar, which was the centre of the Pashtun kingdom formed in the mid-18th Century by the so-called "Father of Afghanistan" Ahmed Shah Durrani. Kandahar however has not always been the pre-eminent city in this region. From the 9th to 12th Centuries the cities of Zaranj in Seistan (modern-day Nimruz) and Bost (modern-day Lashkar Gah) were thriving, such that "once there were so many fine buildings and palaces that one could easily walk from Bost to Zaranj on the rooftops without once touching the ground" (N. Dupree), and medieval historians referred to the area as the "garden of Asia" and the "granary of the East." But today these ancient cities are all but consumed by the shifting sands of the Dasht-e-Margo (Desert of Death) and the Dasht-e-Jehanum (Desert of Hell), and the riverside pleasure palaces of Bost lie in ruins.

The devastating drought, which began in 1998 and is still continuing in some southern provinces, has wrecked the livelihoods of many farmers and kuchi nomads, whose livestock herds have been decimated. Opium poppy, however, which needs less water than wheat or cotton, is thriving, especially in Helmand, one of Afghanistan's most productive poppy provinces.

Since the fall of the Taliban in late 2001, the region has seen drug production surge, while US-led Coalition Forces have conducted intensive – and often heavy-handed – operations to root out pro-Taliban and Al Qa'eda fighters. However, security has deteriorated across the region, as anti-government fighters continue to launch attacks against aid workers, moderate clerics and state employees. In September 2002, President Karzai narrowly avoided being assassinated while visiting Kandahar. In March 2003, a delegate with the International Committee of the Red Cross was executed in cold blood, while on the way to a water project in neighbouring Uruzgan. The Taliban have openly regrouped over the Pakistan border in Quetta, just a couple of hours' drive from Kandahar, and have launched many hit-and-run attacks on motorbikes, killing as many as 400 people during August-October 2003. Funded by a combination of drugs trafficking and Al Qa'eda, their aim appears to be to discredit the US-backed Karzai administration by attacking projects and people associated with the Kabul authorities. Reconstruction of the Kabul-Kandahar trunk road was dogged by numerous attacks on engineering teams, but was finally completed in December 2003. Increasing numbers of aid agencies are now cutting back or halting their operations. Sadly, much of this poor southern region is home to many who desperately need some form of international development assistance.

Kandahar

For many centuries Kandahar has been of great historical and strategic significance. Located at the intersection of three key roads to Herat, Kabul and Quetta over the border in Pakistan, it has found itself astride the main route of adventurers and empire-builders from Alexander the Great to the Taliban. Situated at around 1,000 metres, Kandahar has been settled since antiquity. Alexander rebuilt the city in 329 BC and the name Kandahar may derive from his Eastern name 'Sikander' or 'Iskandar.' From the 7th Century onwards it was absorbed into various Islamic kingdoms; and during the 11th and 12th Centuries it was very much eclipsed in significance by the Ghaznavid winter capital of Bost. In the 1150s Bost was destroyed by the Ghorid ruler Alauddin the "World Burner", and in the 1380s Timur razed Zaranj to the ground, after which Kandahar rose in prominence. From the 16th to 18th Centuries Persian Safavids and Indian Moghuls argued over it; and the famous *Chihlzina*, a rock chamber at the top of "Forty Steps" hewn out of a rock face outside the city, contains a Persian inscription recording the conquests of the Moghul emperor Babur.

Safavid influence however gained the upper hand in Kandahar, until in the early 1700s Mir Wais Hotak, the Ghilzai Pashtun chief of the city, rebelled against the decadent Persians by murdering one of their envoys during a picnic. Mir Wais died in 1715, but as Afghanistan's first great nationalist he had set in train the process which resulted in Ahmed Shah Durrani forming the last great Afghan empire in 1747. Ahmed Shah Baba – "Father of Afghanistan" as he is popularly known – made Kandahar his capital until his death in 1772, extending his influence as far as Kashmir and Delhi. Internecine struggles forced his second son and successor Timur Shah to move his capital to Kabul in 1776.

In the 19th Century, British forces occupied Kandahar in the first two Afghan Wars and suffered one of their heavier defeats nearby at Maiwand in 1880, when the famous bride Malalai ripped off her veil and, waving it aloft as a battle standard, fired up the Afghans to claim victory. General Roberts was sent from Kabul immediately to avenge the defeat, marching his force of 10,000 men on foot for 324 miles to Kandahar in the searing heat of August, covering the distance in just 23 days. While this appears an astonishing feat to a modern reader, it was no big deal for the average Victorian soldier; as Major Ashe writes: "...our march up to the present time has been a veritable picnic, not unaccompanied by a rubber of whist in the afternoon, and not divested of that little duck and quail slaughter which in measure consoles our youngsters for their banishment from Hurlingham..." (quoted by N. Dupree). The British defeated

Kandhari boys playing near mined ruins. *J. Walter*

the Afghans the day after arriving in Kandahar, but departed after eight months and left Amir Abdur Rahman to fight his cousins for control of the city.

Apart from Red Army occupation during the 1980s, Kandahar has been controlled by Pashtuns ever since the British departed. Owing to its strategically significant situation, the city became one of the key points of the Soviet "Security Ring" after the 1979 invasion. The American-built airport, which was supposed to serve as a fuelling stop for long distance aircraft from Europe to India but lost out with the arrival of the Jumbo 747, was transformed into a major base for anti-resistance operations. The Soviets launched regular MiG and helicopter gunship assaults against *mujahed* positions throughout the region. (The airport now serves as the regional operations base for American-led Coalition Forces). While the Soviets occupied the centre of the city, the *mujahideen* controlled the surrounding area right up to the district of Dand on the southern fringe of Kandahar. This district was heavily defended and bombed, and as a result remains largely ruins and minefields today.

Following the Red Army withdrawal, Afghan infighting only added to the destruction. From 1989-1992 the mujahideen fought the Communist regime troops of President Najibullah; and from 1992-1994 five different mujahideen factions all competed with each other for control. When the Taliban took Kandahar (without a shot fired) in September 1994, they found the city virtually deserted, heavily mined and with most of its citizens living as refugees in Pakistan. Through disarming the mujahideen and skilful negotiations with local commanders they managed to bring peace and security to the area for the first time since 1980.

Kandahar is the most conservative and Pashtun of Afghanistan's major cities. As a result the Taliban movement preferred to base itself here rather than in the more ethnically mixed and cosmopolitan Kabul. Many of the Taliban's strict interpretations of *shari'a* law, such as untrimmed beards for men and *pardah* for women (which prevented them from working away from home or even leaving the house unattended by a male relative), derived from the traditional southern Pashtun customs of this region. Huge numbers of refugees returned after the Taliban brought stability to the city. One of the more notorious was the Saudi terrorist Osama Bin Laden, who built a smart new villa in the city. When the Taliban took Herat in September 1995, the opening of the main road from Central Asia to Pakistan via Kandahar boosted the city's economic trade in both legal and smuggled goods. Taxes on this trade kept the Taliban war chest topped-up, while international agencies were left to look after the city's rehabilitation.

In October 2001, Hamid Karzai – then hardly known on the world stage – was instrumental in negotiating the withdrawal of the Taliban from the city. However, the city's infrastructure has been devastated by war, and the damage caused by mines and the shelling of irrigation systems has badly affected local agricultural capacity. With a population estimated at 500,000 inhabitants, Kandahar is the second largest city in Afghanistan.

Getting there

By air

The UN Humanitarian Air Service operates flights to Kandahar four times per week from Kabul (Mon, Wed, Thu, Sat) – often flying via Herat. The cost for a one-way ticket is around US$ 100 for accredited agency staff and US$ 440 for the rest. Maximum luggage allowance is 20 kg, with high charges for going overweight. On Wednesdays, the UN flies from Islamabad-Kabul-Kandahar and back. For more details, call mobile number: 070 301552.

PACTEC/Air Serv International operates return flights between Kabul and Kandahar twice a week. The cost per one-way ticket is US$ 100 for all passengers. PACTEC has no office in Kandahar, so passengers need to contact the Kabul office for bookings on mobile number: 070 282679.

In late 2003, Ariana Afghan Airlines began operating a weekly rotation between Kabul and Kandahar every Wednesday. The cost per one-way ticket is 1,400 Afghanis. This is the cheapest flight available and therefore the most booked up.

ICRC flights are reserved for NGO representatives with an accreditation letter and valid Pakistani and Afghan visas (in case the plane has to land in Peshawar due to weather conditions). ICRC has two flights a week to Kandahar on Mondays and Thursdays. For bookings, you need to apply four days in advance.

Cargo flights to Kandahar are operated by AWCC and DHL. For more details on domestic passenger flights, SEE TRAVEL BY AIR.

Overland

TRAVELLERS BEWARE! Given the growing insecurity due to insurgents in the region, there is no safe way to reach Kandahar by road. The southern region of Afghanistan is also the most heavily mined in the country, with numerous unmarked anti-tank minefields near main roads. When driving always remember to avoid verges or short cuts – stick to the beaten track if you want to stay alive!

The road from Kabul to Kandahar used to be 490 km of bone-shattering potholes and corrugations, taking two days by car. But at present, the route – particularly between Ghazni and Kandahar – is very dangerous (despite being resurfaced). Both Afghans and foreigners have been assaulted and killed along this road. In November 2003, a French national working for the UN High Commissioner for Refugees was shot dead in central Ghazni in the middle of the day, sending shock waves through the aid community. At present, people travelling from Kabul to Kandahar are strongly recommended to avoid using this road, even in convoy.

Driving to Kandahar from Herat, the Delaram section is dangerous at present. Both thieves and insurgents are known to be very active in this area. The journey from Herat, however, is beautiful, skirting some fascinating scenery between the last remnants of the Hindu Kush mountains and the deserts to the southwest. Allow 13-14 hours to drive the 565 km from Herat to Kandahar in a sturdy car or jeep, or two days by bus.

The road to Kandahar from Pakistan, via Quetta and the border at Chaman, is currently considered unsafe for foreigners. In 'normal' circumstances, the journey should take between six and seven hours by car. From Quetta to the border at Chaman is around 120 km, while Kandahar lies a further 110 km to the northwest.

The road from Zaranj, on the Iranian frontier, is also considered unsafe. The best advice is to check up on the latest security situation with UN or NGO sources before making the journey overland to Kandahar.

Orientation & getting around

The original town laid out by Ahmed Shah Durrani in the 1760s still exists in the form of the *Charsuq* and its various bazaars laid out in a quartered rectangular plan. To the east of this Old Town lies the airport and the road to Kabul; to the west lies the New Town (Shahr-e-Naw), the road to Herat, and the jagged crests of some low mountains.

Most of the international agencies that remain operational (given current security concerns) are located in the New Town, while to the south much of

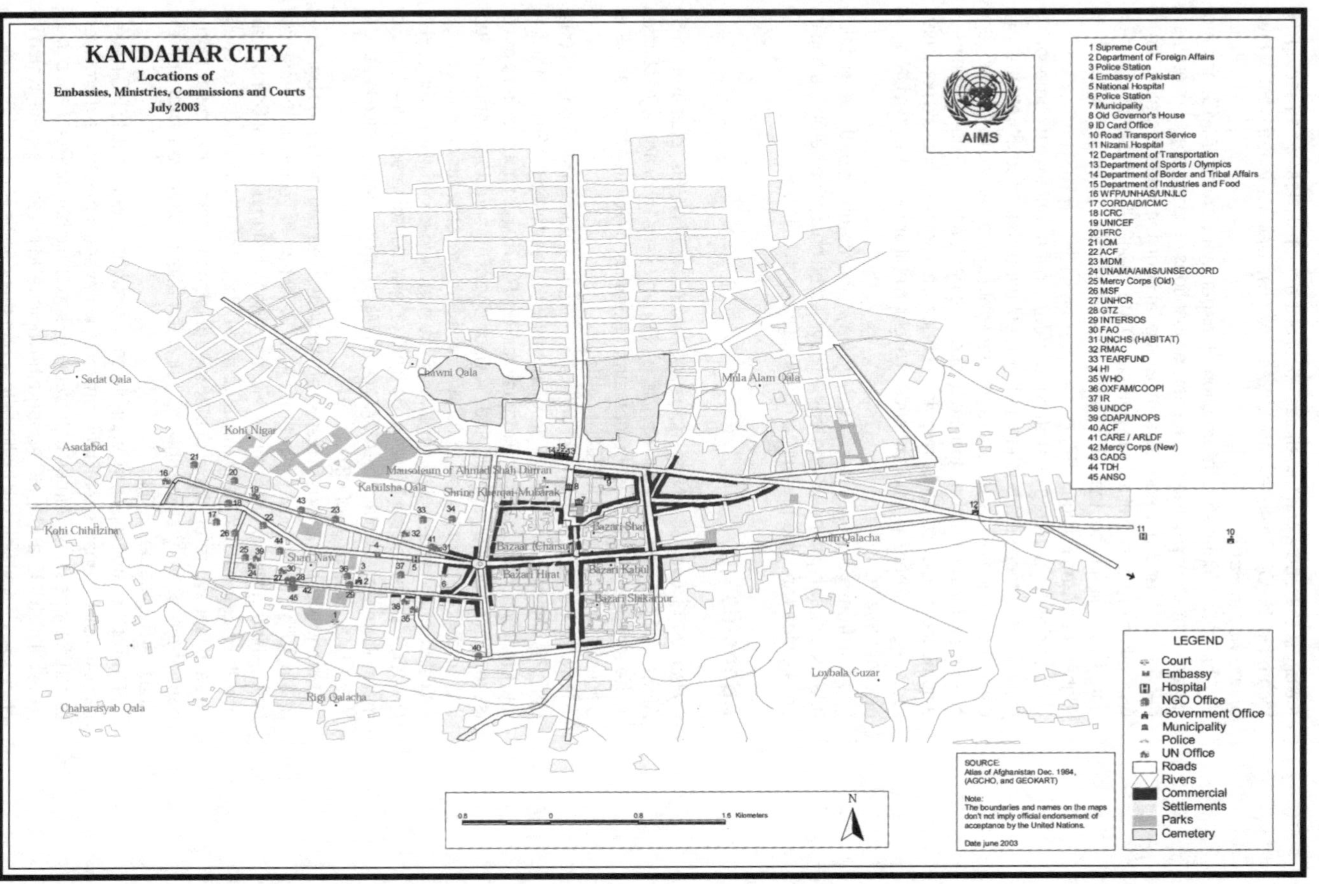
KANDAHAR CITY
Locations of
Embassies, Ministries, Commissions and Courts
July 2003
AIMS
1 Supreme Court
2 Department of Foreign Affairs
3 Police Station
4 Embassy of Pakistan
5 National Hospital
6 Police Station
7 Municipality
8 Old Governor's House
9 ID Card Office
10 Road Transport Service
11 Nizami Hospital
12 Department of Transportation
13 Department of Sports / Olympics
14 Department of Border and Tribal Affairs
15 Department of Industries and Food
16 WFP/UNHAS/UNJLC
17 CORDAID/ICMC
18 ICRC
19 UNICEF
20 IFRC
21 IOM
22 ACF
23 MDM
24 UNAMA/AIMS/UNSECOORD
25 Mercy Corps (Old)
26 MSF
27 UNHCR
28 GTZ
29 INTERSOS
30 FAO
31 UNCHS (HABITAT)
32 RMAC
33 TEARFUND
34 HI
35 WHO
36 OXFAM/COOPI
37 IR
38 UNDCP
39 CDAP/UNOPS
40 ACF
41 CARE / ARLDF
42 Mercy Corps (New)
43 CADG
44 TDH
45 ANSO
Sadat Qala
Chawni Qala
Mula Alam Qala
Kohi Nigar
Asadabad
Mausoleum of Ahmad Shah Durran
Kabulsha Qala
Shrine Kherqai-Mubarak
Kohi Chihilzina
Bazari Shal
Bazaar (Charsu)
Amin Qalacha
Shari Naw
Bazari Hirat
Bazari Kabul
Bazari Shikarpur
Loybala Guzar
Rigi Qalacha
Chaharasyab Qala
LEGEND
Court
Embassy
Hospital
NGO Office
Government Office
Municipality
Police
UN Office
Roads
Rivers
Commercial
Settlements
Parks
Cemetery
SOURCE:
Atlas of Afghanistan Dec. 1984,
(AGCHO, and GEOKART)
Note:
The boundaries and names on the maps don't not imply official endorsement of acceptance by the United Nations.
Date june 2003
0.8
0
0.8
1.6 Kilometers
N

the city is still rubble and minefields. Most of the "tourist sites" worth seeing are located in the Old Town, except for the *Chihlzina* which is to the west of town on the way to Herat.

The UN's Afghanistan Information Management Service (AIMS) has produced a street map of Kandahar showing locations of consulates, government departments and aid agencies (see above). For the latest version, go to www.aims.org.af or call mobile number: 070 304042. A very clear but out-of-date street plan is contained in Nancy Dupree's book An Historical Guide to Afghanistan (2nd Edition, 1977).

Call in at the UN's regional office (UNAMA) in the south-west corner of the New Town to receive a briefing on the latest mine clearance situation. Avoid using the verges of roads, where anti-tank mines are sometimes found, and never wander into uninhabited areas or off the beaten track. There have been a number of tragic accidents involving both local and international aid personnel in the region. There may be a chance of hitching a lift around town in a UN or aid agency vehicle.

Apart from aid agency jeeps the best way to get around is by three-wheeled tuk-tuk, or taxi if you have long legs. Always agree on a price before getting in. Local guides and interpreters can be hired through UNAMA.

Agencies

By late 2003, over 35 UN agencies and international NGOs, plus around 50 Afghan NGOs, had offices in Kandahar. For an overview of agency activities in the region and the latest humanitarian situation, check in at the Kandahar offices of UNAMA or the ICRC.

UNAMA is aiming to register voters in the region, prior to elections in 2004. UNDP is implementing a major development initiative entitled the Reconstruction and Employment Afghanistan Programme (REAP). Drug control remains a major issue, with neighbouring Helmand province one of Afghanistan's most productive areas for opium poppy. Local warlords and crossborder operatives from Pakistan (and increasingly Central Asia) are heavily involved in trafficking (SEE DRUGS). Demining continues to be a major task, coordinated by the UN. For more information, contact the AMAC (Area Mine Action Centre) office located in Kabul Shah (Tel: 070 302037).

Meanwhile, thousands of displaced Afghans, who fled the US-led bombing of the Taliban and tried to find refuge in Pakistan, have found themselves languishing in temporary camps – either on the Pakistan border at Spinboldak, or in the desert west of Kandahar at Zhar-e-Dasht. The UN has had to cut back its assistance to refugees and internally-displaced persons in the south and east of the country since one of their international staff was shot dead in Ghazni in November 2003.

One of the largest jails in Afghanistan is located in Kandahar. ICRC makes regular visits to ensure that sufficient food, water and sanitation are provided, to check for possible human rights abuse, and to exchange Red Cross messages. The ICRC and WHO support the regional Mir Wais Hospital, which includes a surgical unit and facilities to fit prosthetic limbs.

Education is making a slow comeback. Before the war there was coeducation in towns like Lashkar Gah, known as "Little America" in the 1950s because of the vast amounts of State Department money poured into the Helmand Valley

WARNING

THERE ARE STILL OVER 100 UNCLEARED MINEFIELDS WITHIN THE CITY OF KANDAHAR — NEVER GO ANYWHERE WITHOUT A GUIDE!

reclamation project. Some girls' schools were established in Kandahar under the communist regime, but these were all shut when the Taliban arrived in 1994. With the collapse of the Taliban in late 2001, schools re-opened, although levels of enrolment for girls (around 10 percent) are much lower than elsewhere in the country. The NGO Islamic Relief (UK) has rebuilt the Dar-ul-Malimeen Teacher Training Institute, while the government of Japan is contributing new buildings to Kandahar University, first established in 1993. Support for local media initiatives has come from the NGO AINA.

Kandahar A-Z

Accommodation and Food

The **UNICA Guesthouse** is only available for UN or World Bank guests, at the time of writing. Facilities include satellite television and satphone, air-conditioned rooms and a wide selection of drinks available most nights of the week. Non-residents may be allowed to visit UNICA for a drink on a Thursday or Friday evening.

There are a number of private guesthouses in the city. **Continental Guest House** provides rooms from US$ 60 (1 bed) to US$ 80 (3 beds) per night. The guesthouse has 24-hour internet and cable TV. It is located in Herat Darwaza, opposite Clinic Kandahar (Tel: +93 (0)30 300 1924, Mobile: 070 302613). **Yasin International** is close to Continental Guesthouse and similarly priced (Mobile: 070 301042). Many journalists stay at the **Noor Jahan Hotale**. Rooms range from US$ 30-50, the more expensive rooms featuring cable TV and fridge. Both the Yasin and Noor Jahan have good restaurants.

The **MK Afghan Hotel** is a newly established hotel with good food and accommodation, located in Kabul Darwaza. Many international NGO staff stay here. The prices are: 120 *Afghanis* for a single bed, 200 Afs for two beds and 300 Afs for three beds – including cable TV cable and fridge. Alternatively you can find local accommodation and food at the **Khiber Hotel** located opposite the Id Gah gateway at the northern end of the Old Town.

Embassies and Visas

You can extend your Afghan visa via the Department of Foreign Affairs, who will introduce you to the police headquarters responsible for issuing visa extensions. Visas are free for Pakistani, Turkish and Indian citizens. Otherwise, single-entry visas cost US$ 10 while multiple entry visas are US$ 30. For more information SEE VISAS. During 2003, the following consulates were operating in Kandahar:

Pakistan Consulate
Shahr-e-Naw, opposite Kandahar Hotel
Mobile: 070 300622
Open every day except national holidays and Fridays for visas. You'll need the appropriate form, plus three photos and a photocopy of your passport.

Iran Consulate
Dand district, near ICRC office
Mobile: 070 301952
The visa section is open two days per week (Mon, Sat).

India Consulate
Shahr-e-Naw, District 6
Tel: +93 (0)30 300 1856; +87 376 30 95 995
The visa section is open every day (0900-1200) except Fridays and Saturdays.

Emergencies

The Mir Wais hospital has a surgical unit supported by ICRC. Otherwise, medical emergencies are best evacuated to Kabul or Islamabad by ICRC or UN aircraft. Alternatively, UNAMA may be able to put you in contact with medical facilities at the US air base. Call mobile number: 070 302583. For more on personal safety, SEE SECURITY TIPS.

Information

For more information about aid agency activities, and for a security briefing, contact the regional office of UNAMA in Shahr-e-Naw. Make sure you receive some kind of landmine awareness briefing before going off the beaten track.

For local information, try visiting the Department of Culture and Information (near Shahidano Chowk, Mobile: 070 300024) or the Department of Foreign Affairs (Shahr-e-Naw, Mobile: 070 300006).

Local Rules

Under the Taliban, photography, cinema and TV were strictly banned. Rules have relaxed somewhat since 2001, but remember that this remains one of the most conservative corners of Afghanistan. Always ask before taking pictures of people (SEE PHOTOGRAPHY). There are plenty of photography studios in Shahidano Chowk if you need to renew a visa. You can even rent videos now.

It is still difficult for Western women to go into the bazaar. However, the situation changes constantly, so ask around. Be careful while travelling through tribal agency areas if going by road between Kandahar and Quetta in Pakistan. Take a local Afghan guide or colleague who speaks Pashto, Dari and Urdu to smooth the way.

Medical

Take precautions against mosquitoes and sandflies: they carry malaria and leishmaniasis. The latter is a particularly unpleasant disfiguring disease which causes open lesions on the face and body. Hepatitis, cholera and typhoid vaccines are also recommended. At least two Western journalists and aid workers known to the EFG editors have died from hepatitis while working in the region. Diarrhoea is a major problem in Kandahar, so boil your drinking water for 10 minutes or use a good-quality filter. For medical emergencies there is always the Mir Wais hospital at the western end of the New Town which has an ICRC surgical unit. Al-Hadi Farhad is a private hospital located in Shahidano Chowk, offering 24 hour service (SEE PERSONAL HEALTH).

Money

Bring US dollars for guesthouse bills. You can change dollars into *Afghanis* at the money changing market in the middle of the Old Town (SEE MONEY & BARGAINING).

Post & Telecommunications

You can reportedly mail letters internationally via the Afghan postal system in Kandahar. The post office is located in Id Gah Darwaza. Alternatively, DHL and FedEx have regular flights to Kandahar airport.

The AWCC (Afghan Wireless Communication Company) is active in the city, with an office in the Department of Telecommunications. Local, national and international mobile phone calls can be made using an AWCC sim card (costing around US$ 50). For more details, contact AWCC in Kandahar on Tel: 030 300 1011; Mobile: 030 210011. A digital telephone system is also operational in Kandahar.

Recreation

There are around 11 cultural associations and 10 libraries in Kandahar. For more information, contact AINA in Shahr-e-Naw, behind Zarghoona Ana secondary school (Mobile: 070 303054, 070 202137).

Shopping

Baluch handicrafts are available in the bazaars of the Old Town. For embroidery and handicrafts from Kandahar and southwest Afghanistan, try Bana Hindu Sraie in Charsuq bazaar. For electronic goods, try Nikai near the Kandahar hotel. For stationery, go to Herat Darwaza. There are new markets in Kiptan Madad Chowk and in Charsuq, close to Rangraizan Dana.

Kandahar is also famous for its fabulous pomegranates, peaches, figs, grapes and extremely juicy melons.

Sights in Kandahar

The most comprehensive guidebook available on the historical sights of Kandahar remains Nancy Dupree's *An Historical Guide to Afghanistan* (2nd Edition, 1977) available through ACBAR or at various bookshops in Peshawar and Kabul. Many of the sights worth seeing are located in the Old Town. Laid out by Ahmed Shah Durrani in the 1760s this rectangular city was once

The Shrine of the Cloak of the Prophet Mohammed J. Walter

surrounded by walls up to 30 feet thick, punctuated by six huge gateways. These fortifications were largely demolished in the 1940s.

Mausoleum of Ahmed Shah Durrani. This colourful octagonal building is dedicated to the memory of Ahmed Shah Baba, the "Father of Afghanistan", who inaugurated and ruled over the first great Pashtun Afghan dynasty from 1747-1772. It is located in the northwest quarter of the Old Town near the Id Gah gateway.

The Shrine of the Cloak of the Prophet Mohammed. Known locally as Da Kherqa Sherif Ziarat, the shrine is located next to Ahmed Shah's mausoleum and is one of the most holy shrines in Afghanistan. The exterior decoration of the shrine is magnificent: foundations of green Lashkar Gah marble, sparkling tilework over every surface and gilded archways make the nearby mausoleum of the city's founder look somewhat pedestrian. The cloak itself cannot be seen. It was handed over to Ahmed Shah by the Amir of Bokhara in 1768 to consolidate a treaty over territories to the north. Traditionally the cloak is only brought out during times of national crisis. It had not been seen in public since the 1930s, when in 1994 when Mullah Omar, the Supreme Leader of the Taliban, removed the cloak from its shrine and held it before a crowd of several thousand clerics and Kandaharis, claiming it as a visible symbol of his role as Mullah Al-Momineen, Leader of All Pious Muslims.

The Mosque of the Hair of the Prophet. Known locally as the Jame Mui Mobarak, you will find the entrance to this mosque off the covered bazaar just to the east of the *Charsuq*, where the four bazaars of the Old Town converge. The Hair came from the Amir of Bokhara at the same time as the cloak, and is kept in a golden sheath in a casket under mountains of holy blankets and banners. The local mullah or caretaker will let you into the side chapel where the Hair is enshrined. The mosque itself was built in the 19th Century and a water canal flows through the spacious shady courtyard, attracting travellers and the destitute.

Sights outside Kandahar

Chihlzina ("Forty Steps"). About four km west of Kandahar, high above the plains on a rocky outcrop, is a cave carved out of the mountain. Known as the *Chihlzina*, forty steps lead to this chamber, inside which is an inscription relating the conquests of the Moghul emperor Babur and his son Humayun. After Babur's death in 1530, the struggle for succession drove his son into temporary exile in Persia. Humayun staged his return to Delhi by first occupying Kandahar in 1545 with the help of the Persians. After his own death in 1556 the city fell within the Persian sphere of influence. One of the most important battles in Afghanistan's history was fought at the foot of the *Chihlzina*. Here in 1881 Amir Abdur Rahman conquered the forces of his rebellious cousin Ayub Khan, making way for him to establish not just Kabul as his kingdom, but the whole nation of Afghanistan.

Zor Shahr ("Old City"). Check with the UNAMA office and local Afghans about possible minefields before exploring this site. The original "Old City" of Kandahar – destroyed by Nadir Shah of Persia in 1738 – lies at the foot of the cliffs into which the *Chihlzina* is cut. Earlier this century archaeologists found Buddhist, Greek and Islamic treasures here, including two edicts of the Emperor Ashoka carved into blocks of stone in Greek and Aramaic. Dating from the 3rd Century BC, the familiar themes of piety and humility are ones which modern-day players on the Afghan stage would do well to note:

> *"Those who praise themselves and denigrate their neighbours are self-seekers, wishing to shine in comparison with the others but in fact hurting themselves. It behoves to respect one another and to accept one another's lessons."*
> *(trans. Wheeler)*

One of the most popular picnic spots for Kandahari families on Fridays is **Babawally**, to the north of Kandahar. You can swim in the river and a shrine is under construction. To get there from Shahr-e-Naw, a taxi will cost around 150 *Afghanis*.

To the west of Kandahar lies the **Shrine of Mirwais Nika** ("Grandfather") – founder of modern Afghanistan. Local people come here to worship. Families often bring picnics or cook food under the trees. Along the road, about 2-3 km after the Shrine of Mirwais Nika, is **Bagh-e-Pol,** a popular spot by the side of the river, with a small park and public swimming pool.

Weather

Temperatures range from around freezing point in winter (December to February) up to 35-40 degrees Celsius in summer (June to August). Spring (March to May) and Autumn (September to November) are the most pleasant times to visit.

EFG editors would like to acknowledge the invaluable help of Firoten Ghausuddin in updating this chapter.

Western region

Western Afghanistan is a land which looks more towards Persia than the Indian subcontinent for its inspiration and its history. Lying at the eastern fringe of the great Iranian plateau, its parched earth is baked for months on end by fifty degrees of sun and blasted by a wind which blows nonstop for one hundred and twenty days. This land is a world away from the glacial mountains of the Hindu Kush, whose remnants barely penetrate the west of the country, trailing away into low, craggy ridgelines like the tip of a crocodile's tail. The wide plains which characterize this region make it difficult to defend, and for much of its history Herat and western Afghanistan have been invaded and liberated by competing Russian, Persian, British and Afghan forces keen to maintain a buffer between their spheres of influence and hostile neighbours.

Herat

"Here at last is Asia without an inferiority complex"

– Robert Byron, on arrival in Herat in 1933

Of all the cities of Central Asia, Herat must rank as one of the richest not only in terms of its history and strategic importance, but in the whole cultural spectrum of architecture, painting, poetry and music. Capital of the province of Herat and the largest city in western Afghanistan, Herat borders both Iran and Turkmenistan, and the city's prominent merchants make the most of border-trade and smuggling opportunities. Situated at an altitude of 950 metres, Herat used to be famous for grapes, fruit and cotton crops grown with the aid of extensive irrigation. Before the Soviet war its population was around 160,000, comprising mainly Persian-speaking, non-Pashtun *Sunni* Muslims, with a large minority of *Shi'as*. With Kabul over a thousand kilometres away by road, Herat established a reputation for being independent, both strategically and culturally.

Cultural Herat reached its height in the Timurid Renaissance of the 15th Century, under the rule of a dynasty of Uzbek princes who have been described as the Oriental Medici. While the artistic climax of the Timurid Empire may have been in the delicate tile-mosaics and painted miniatures for which Herat is justly famous, the Empire was conceived in more violent circumstances.

In the 13th Century Herat was governed by a local Persian dynasty known as the Karts – the bronze cauldron in the Friday Mosque is all that remains of their stay here. However an Uzbek adventurer by the name of Timur rallied the northern tribes to his cause, took control of Balkh and then destroyed Herat in 1381. An old war wound in his right leg caused him to limp and gave rise to his nickname Timur-e-Lang, otherwise known to Western historians as "Timur the Lame" or Tamerlane. Timur's death in 1405 precipitated a series of bloody intrigues out of which his youngest son Shah Rukh emerged victorious to rule an empire stretching from Mesopotamia to the borders of China. His generous patronage of the arts, and that of his remarkable Queen, Gawhar Shad, led to a cultural renaissance which saw the flourishing of Bihzad the miniaturist and Jami the poet, not to mention countless other court artists, architects and philosophers. From the portraits of these Timurid princes of pleasure we can, in Byron's words, detect:

> *"a personal idiosyncrasy about them which tells of that rare phenomenon in Mohammedan history, an age of humanism. Judged by European standards, it was humanism within limits. The Timurid Renascence, like ours, took place in the fifteenth century, owed its course to the patronage of princes, and preceded the emergence of nationalist states. But in one respect the two movements differed. While the European was largely a reaction against faith in favour of reason, the Timurid coincided with a new consolidation of the power of faith. The Turks of Central Asia had already lost contact with Chinese materialism; and it was Timur who led them to the acceptance of Islam, not merely as a religion, for that was already accomplished, but as a basis of social institutions."*

Despite Shah Rukh's death in 1447 and his Queen's murder a decade later, Herat continued to blossom in a golden age under the rule of their successor Sultan Husain Baiqara (1468-1506). However, decadence and personal ambition conspired to bring about the end of the Timurid Renaissance. In 1507 Herat fell to another Uzbek invader, Babur, who went on to found the Moghul Empire in India. But Herat must have made an impact on him for he did not destroy the city. Quite the opposite in fact. The towering *iwan* portals of the Friday Mosque and the Shrine of Ansari near Herat – surmounted by arcaded galleries and twin lantern-turrets – are architectural motifs which reappear again and again in the now world-famous mosques and mausolea which Babur and his successors created in Delhi and Agra.

Babur died in 1530. Herat soon fell under the sway of the Persian Safavid empire for two centuries. During most of the 18th and 19th Centuries Herat was a semi-autonomous state occupied by a succession of Pashtun princes who alternately fought off Persian advances on their city and attempted to advance their control over Kabul. In 1828 the Russians defeated Persia and began to entertain ambitions eastwards towards India. Their support for the Persian siege on Herat from November 1837 to September 1838, along with Amir Dost Mohammed's Russophile leanings, were to provoke the ill-fated British invasion of Afghanistan in 1839. Herat survived the siege, was spared either Russian or British occupation, and remained independent until Amir Dost Mohammed completed his unification of Afghanistan by seizing the city in 1863. He died a month after taking Herat and lies buried at Gazargah, five kilometres to the east of the city. Turbulent years of succession followed, with Amir Abdur Rahman struggling to wrest Herat from a rebellious cousin in 1881 and making himself unpopular by resettling Pashtun southerners up in Badghis.

From 1887-1888 the northern and western boundaries of Afghanistan were formally established by a joint Russian-British Boundary Commission, but Britain remained exceptionally touchy about western Afghanistan in general, and Herat in particular, because of its highly strategic role as a buffer between British India and Persian and Russian ambitions. The so-called "Panjdeh Incident" in 1885, when Russian troops seized the Afghan fort of Panjdeh north of Herat, led to British officers advising on the defence of Herat – advice which led to the destruction of the fabulous Timurid *musalla* complex in order to deny an army advancing on the citadel any cover from fire.

Herat has maintained its independent reputation for much of the 20th Century. In the 1960s the city was a stronghold for the new Islamist movement. The communist reforms of 1978-1979 sparked off widespread rebellion across the country, and the first organized revolt against the People's Democratic Party of Afghanistan (PDPA) was in Herat in March 1979. The Herat revolt was unique in being a carefully planned cooperation of militant Islamists from the Jamiat party, local *mawlawi* clergy and a mutinous army garrison led by Captain Ismail Khan. Hundreds of communist officers, teachers, Russian advisors and their families were killed in Herat and the surrounding villages. A week later government troops with air support from the USSR retook the town and killed between 5,000 and 25,000 of Herat's population in the process. This was the first instance of direct Soviet military intervention into Afghanistan prior to the invasion of December 1979.

For most of the 1980s Ismail Khan extended his influence over Herat and northwest Afghanistan as far as Maimana, and the region became predominately supporters of Rabbani's *Sunni* party Jamiat-e-Islami. Along the border between Afghanistan and Iran pockets of *Shi'a* resistance fighters appeared but to little military effect. The Soviets stationed a large number of troops 150 kilometres south of Herat at Shindand where a major airbase directly threatened the Persian Gulf. Three divisions of Russian military and airborne troops were based between Herat and Kandahar throughout the early 1980s, but their role was as much to contain Iranian territorial ambitions as to dislodge the Afghan resistance. Thus western Afghanistan once again became a strategic buffer zone.

Following the withdrawal of Soviet troops in 1989, Ismail Khan established himself as the *de facto* 'Amir of Herat', ruling over a semi-autonomous region of the country. He captured tanks, fighter aircraft, helicopters and transport planes from the retreating Soviets. He played host to delegations from Pakistan and Saudi Arabia who were afraid that Iran might take Herat in the absence of a strong government in Kabul. Apart from the fact that they considered the

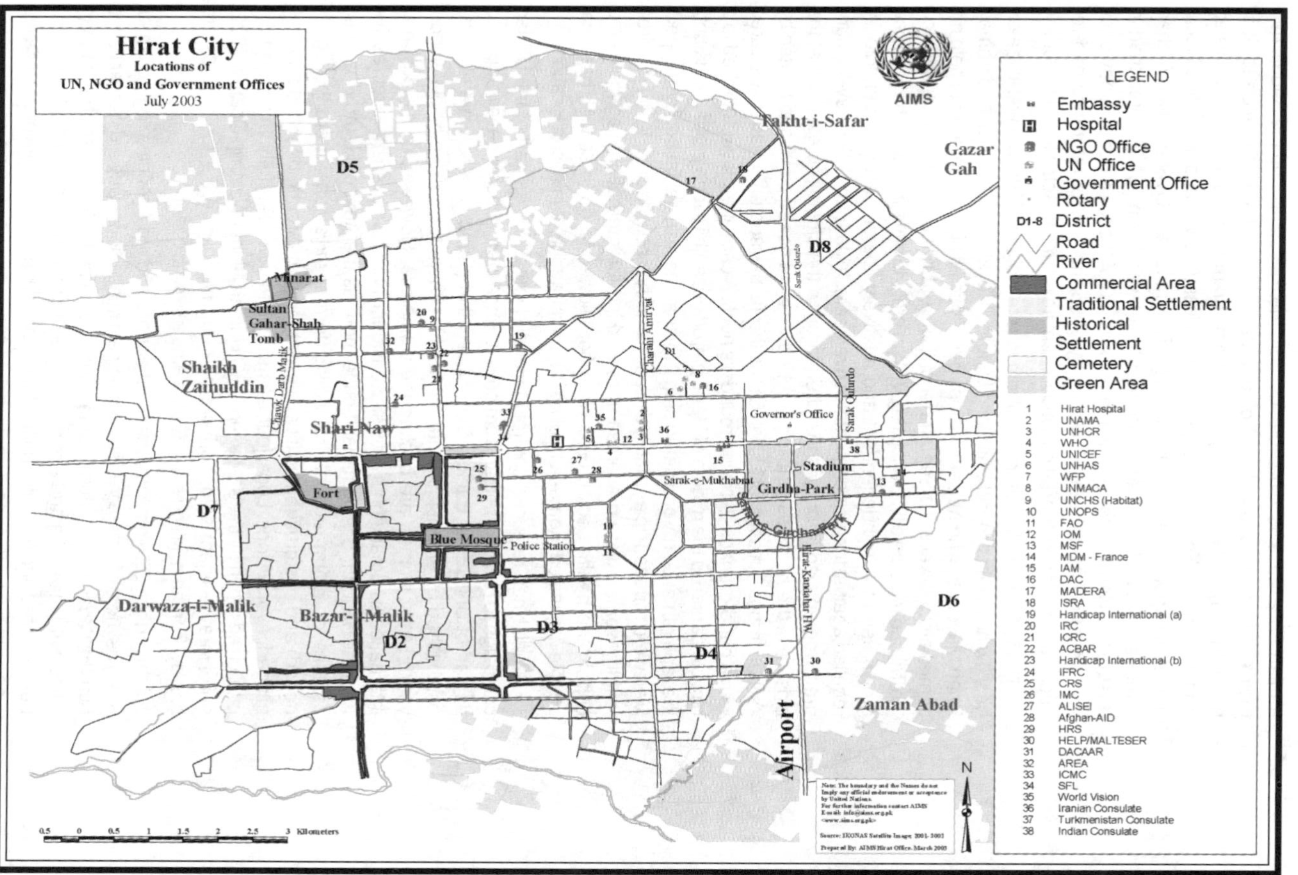

Hirat City
Locations of
UN, NGO and Government Offices
July 2003
AIMS
LEGEND
Embassy
Hospital
NGO Office
UN Office
Government Office
Rotary
D1-8 District
Road
River
Commercial Area
Traditional Settlement
Historical Settlement
Cemetery
Green Area
1 Hirat Hospital
2 UNAMA
3 UNHCR
4 WHO
5 UNICEF
6 UNHAS
7 WFP
8 UNMACA
9 UNCHS (Habitat)
10 UNOPS
11 FAO
12 IOM
13 MSF
14 MDM - France
15 IAM
16 DAC
17 MADERA
18 ISRA
19 Handicap International (a)
20 IRC
21 ICRC
22 ACBAR
23 Handicap International (b)
24 IFRC
25 CRS
26 IMC
27 ALISEI
28 Afghan-AID
29 HRS
30 HELP/MALTESER
31 DACAAR
32 AREA
33 ICMC
34 SFL
35 World Vision
36 Iranian Consulate
37 Turkmenistan Consulate
38 Indian Consulate
Takht-i-Safar
Gazar Gah
D5
D8
D7
D6
D2
D3
D4
Minarat
Sultan Gahar-Shah Tomb
Shaikh Zainuddin
Shari Naw
Chawk Darb Malik
Charahi Amiryat
Sarak Qulurdo
Governor's Office
Stadium
Girdha-Park
Sarak-e-Mukhabrat
Sarak-e-Girdha-Park
Fort
Blue Mosque
Police Station
Darwaza-i-Malik
Bazar-i-Malik
Hirat-Kandahar HW
Airport
Zaman Abad
N
0.5 0 0.5 1 1.5 2 2.5 3 Kilometers

Iranian *Shi'a* Muslims to be heretics, both the Pakistanis and the Saudis had their eyes on the possibility of oil and gas – either the exploration for it in northern Afghanistan, or the piping of it from Turkmenistan via Herat to Pakistan and the Arabian Sea. Iran stepped up the pressure by imposing a trade blockade, and supplies had to come through Turkmenistan. Over a million Afghan refugees had fled into Iran during the Soviet war. From 1993-94 Iran tried to destabilize Herat by forcing as many as 1,500 of these refugees a day back into western Afghanistan. However, by 1995 the flow of returnees had reduced to a trickle as the Taliban movement flexed its muscles in the region.

The Taliban made several attempts to take Herat in 1995, but were beaten back twice at Girishk and Shindand by forces loyal to Ismail Khan and Ahmed Shah Massoud, who had sent troops over specially from Panjshair to help his Jamiat ally. However, in September of that year Khan's forces collapsed and the Taliban took the city. During the Taliban era, the city's inhabitants – who had grown used to an independent and relatively liberal lifestyle – periodically rebelled against their fundamentalist overseers. In January 1997, several hundred women clad in *burqas* marched through the city to protest against the closure of the *hamams* (public baths) – they were hosed down and beaten by Taliban troops. An effigy of Mullah Omar, the Taliban supreme leader, appeared with a hand-grenade dangling round his neck. A cassette-player attached to a bicycle parked in the middle of Herat blared out anti-Taliban propaganda until the tape ran out – no-one dared stop it for fear that it might be booby-trapped. Men were rounded up and locked in cells until their beards grew to the required length; women were prevented from working for international agencies except in the health sector. Girls were not allowed to go to school, but local people organized "home-schooling" for their daughters in secret locations.

Ismail Khan regained control of Herat in late 2001, as part of the US-led campaign to oust the Taliban from power. Since then, schools have re-opened as part of UNICEF's 'Back to School' initiative (some classes were even re-established by enthusiastic parents and teachers prior to the official school year). Many women are back in the workplace. However, some local and international human rights activists consider Khan to be even more repressive than the Taliban. Styling himself once more as the Amir of Herat, Khan has established a firm regime of *Jihadists* (former *mujahideen* from the Soviet period) and has crushed political dissent through threats, beatings and, it is alleged, even killings. Local journalists have to tread carefully. In one widely-publicized report by the US-based NGO Human Rights Watch in October 2002, one Herat resident said: "Ismail Khan and his followers – their hands are bloody. For them, killing a bird is the same as killing a man".

Nevertheless, some international donors and aid agencies regard Ismail Khan as more of a benign dictator who gets things done. One aid worker called him the Mussolini of Afghanistan. Herat remains the cleanest of all Afghan cities, with the parks and streets well-maintained. Countless new trees have been planted and free telephones for calling within the city have been installed along the main avenues. The university, too, is fast developing into one of the most innovative and open in the country, although it still lacks resources as most international aid has been supporting seats of learning in Kabul.

Getting there

By air

The most convenient and least exciting way into Herat is by air. The wrecks of half a dozen Soviet MiG fighters that used to lie on the airstrip to greet your arrival have been shifted and the airport has been spruced up by Ismail Khan's authorities. If you are travelling independently, arrange beforehand for someone to meet you at the airport. There are taxis but they only wait if they have already brought people to catch the outgoing flight. The best way is to catch a lift with an aid agency.

The UN's Humanitarian Air Service (UNHAS) flies between Kabul and Herat four times per week (Mon, Wed, Thu, Sat). One-way tickets cost accredited agencies around US$ 100, while everyone else must pay US$ 600. The ICRC flies here on Saturdays and Tuesdays. PACTEC/Airserv International flies light aircraft between Kabul and Herat. There are now regular flights here with Ariana Afghan Airlines, costing 2,000 *Afghanis* one-way from Kabul, although most NGOs do not use this service. It is also possible to fly commercially into Mary (Turkmenistan) or Mashad (Iran) and then take public transport to Herat. The UN flies into Farah on Sundays (on demand). For more details, SEE TRAVEL BY AIR.

Overland

Four overland routes converge on Herat from each point of the compass. The roads from Mashad in Iran and Mary in Turkmenistan arrive from the west and the north respectively. These routes are major arteries for licit and smuggled goods, as well as entry points into Afghanistan for the more intrepid overland traveller. Ismail Khan now receives millions of dollars in revenue from duties on imported goods at these border posts. You can also approach Herat from the south, via Kandahar, or from the east, via Hazarajat.

The overland route from Iran is a useful alternative to flying during winter, when ICRC and UN flights from Kabul are regularly cancelled due to poor weather conditions. Asseman Air has daily flight connections between Tehran and Mashad and twice weekly services direct from Dubai to Mashad (one-way: US$ 125). Tourist visas are reportedly available at the Afghan consulate in Mashad. From Mashad to the Afghan border at Islam Kala (Zero-Point) takes around four hours by taxi; followed by a further three hours to Herat. You can also make the journey from Mashad more cheaply and slowly by bus or truck. Going the other way, there are taxi drivers (mafia!) waiting on the Iranian side of the border who will take you to Mashad for around US$ 20.

Getting to and from Herat from the north, via Ashkhabad in Turkmenistan (with direct flights to Frankfurt and the Gulf states) is another alternative – although longer and more expensive. If leaving Afghanistan, you will need to have ordered a taxi from Ashkhabad (expensive) to meet you on the Turkmen side of the border, as it is about five miles from the nearest town. From Ashkhabad to the Afghan border at Tourghondy takes around seven hours by car, then another three hours on to Herat.

The journey to Herat from the south arrives from Kandahar via Shindand, and has reverberated to the sounds of countless conquerors through history, from the marching step of Alexander's army to the mechanical roar of Taliban tanks. The road threads a delicate path between the mountains of the Hindu Kush and the shifting sands of *Dasht-e-Margo* – the Desert of Death. Its arrival in Herat is heralded by thirty-two thousand jack-pines planted in the 1940s on either side of the road by one of the city's more enlightened governors (although many have now been cut down). Allow 13-14 hours to drive from Kandahar to Herat in a jeep, or two days by bus. The Americans began rebuilding this road in mid-2003 as part of their international aid contribution, but progress has been hampered by security problems as well as delays in funding.

An exciting eastern approach to Herat is possible from Kabul via Bamiyan, Chakhcharan and Chisht-e-Sharif. During the Taliban period the route used to cross a frontline between Taliban and Hazara forces. Although the route was once mined, it is now open and is being slowly repaired by an Afghan NGO. According to lorry drivers in Bamiyan, vehicles regularly ply this route – although much depends on whether the roads can be kept clear of snow during the winter (November-March) or landslides during the summer. One intrepid Scottish traveller, Rory Stewart, walked from Herat to Kabul through Hazarajat in February 2002 with his dog and encountered few problems along the way. The attraction of driving this central route for those with a few days to spare is that it passes through magnificent mountain scenery, visiting the Minaret of Jam (now a World Heritage Site) and the turquoise lakes of Band-e-Amir *en route*. This "central route" is described in some detail in Nancy Dupree's guide to Afghanistan. The journey takes up to five days to complete by jeep.

Orientation & getting around

Herat lies in a long fertile plain which spreads east and west between the Paropamisus mountains five kilometres to the north, and the Hari river (*Harirud*) as far again to the south. The Harirud, which rises in the highlands of Bamiyan and flows west into Iran, is Herat's lifeline; you cross it while driving into the city from the airport. The Old City is divided into four quarters containing the Citadel, Friday Mosque (*Masjid-e-Jami*) and covered bazaar. To the north and east of the Citadel lies the New Town (*Shahr-e-Naw*) where most of the UN and NGO offices are located. To the northwest lies the *musalla* complex.

Street maps of Herat, showing locations of government offices and aid agencies, are available from the UN's Afghanistan Information Management Service (AIMS) in Kabul (see above). For the latest online copy, go to www.aims.org.af. Call in at the regional offices of UNAMA (the UN Assistance Mission to Afghanistan) and UNMACA (the UN's mine clearance agency) to the north-west of the Governor's Office for briefings on the latest security and landmine situation. There may be a chance of hitching a lift around town in a UN or aid agency vehicle. Otherwise, the best way to get around is by taxi (US$ 5-10 for a morning's work).

Agencies

In mid-2003, around 35 UN agencies and NGOs had offices based in Herat. For an overview of agency activities in the region and the latest humanitarian situation it is best to visit UNAMA or the Agency Coordinating Body for Afghan Relief (ACBAR).

WARNING

THERE ARE STILL MINEFIELDS IN THE VICINITY OF HERAT — NEVER GO ANYWHERE WITHOUT A GUIDE !

Agriculture is crucial for Herat's economy, and the construction of irrigation canals, seed multiplication, soil conservation and animal husbandry are all supported by DACAAR which has been in the area since 1993. Water shortages throughout much of the year are aggravated by flash floods in February and March which destroy irrigation channels and take away topsoil. Wheat and rice have replaced cotton and fruit as the main crops, although some opium poppy has appeared in Farah province.

ICRC supports the Herat military hospital plus provincial hospitals in Badghis and Ghor, along with a 40-bed orthopaedic centre for Afghans disabled by disease or war. UNICEF and partner NGOs organise immunization campaigns for preventable diseases. Key health problems in western Afghanistan are diarrhoea during summer months, cholera from June to September, and acute respiratory infections during winter. And in a region as dry as this, drinking water and sanitation are major problems. In terms of mine clearance, Herat city is largely cleared, but parts of the countryside are still heavily mined.

Herat has seen the ebb and flow of thousands of refugees and displaced Afghans in recent years. In 1993 the number of Afghan refugees returning from Iran peaked at over 600,000 persons, many of whom settled in Herat province. But by 1997 this had reduced to a mere 834, largely because of the Taliban presence in western Afghanistan. Many would-be returnees were put off by reports of 'ethnic-cleansing' on the border, where Taliban troops seized Tajik, Hazara and *Shi'a* men they suspected of being hostile and locked them up. Following the fall of the Taliban in late 2001, Iran became increasingly eager to repatriate its refugee caseload back over the Afghan border.

Meanwhile, tens of thousands of Afghans in the region have been 'internally displaced', first by the fighting in Badghis, Faryab and Jowzjan provinces between the Taliban and Dostum's Jumbesh forces – then more recently by four years of catastrophic drought from 1998/99-2003. During 2003, the UN (especially WFP) began to pressure the estimated 60,000 IDPs who remained in camps around Herat to return home by reducing food rations – despite security concerns voiced by MSF and other NGOs. Many fear to return to their homes, as clashes between Generals Dostum and Atta to the north-east have continued throughout 2002-03. Another reason for the current reluctance to return home is the lack of jobs and the means to survive in their villages. Many no longer have livestock because of the drought. Lastly, given the high proportion of Pashtuns among these IDPs, there is a well-founded fear of persecution at the hands ethnic Tajiks and Uzbeks in the north.

Herat A-Z

Accommodation and Food

Agonising over where to stay in Herat is a predicament unlikely to confront any visitors to this city at present. The ideal choice would be the **UNICA Guesthouse**, located in a walled compound just to the northeast of the Old Town, but places are normally reserved for UN or World Bank staff only. Guesthouse facilities include a pool, tennis and volleyball. Alternatively, many NGO workers and travellers find sleeping space in the **guesthouses of aid agencies** based in Herat, but this is very much on an *ad hoc* basis. Most agencies have rooms for travellers – often for free if you're friends, or otherwise for a fee (around US$ 20 per night). Much depends on what you are doing. Ask around in Kabul before arriving, or else go to the UN Club for a drink on a Thursday or Friday night and check out the lie of the land.

Several hotels now operate in Herat. The **Moafaq Hotel,** overlooking the main roundabout downtown, offers rooms at US$ 20 per night, and their restaurant on the first floor offers excellent chicken dishes. As for dining out, most expatriates tend to eat in their own houses or at the UN Club (US$ 6 for lunch or dinner). Some occasionally go down to the bazaar in the Old Town for kebabs. There is good food at the **Bahar Restaurant** situated one block east of the Moafaq Hotel on the road heading south to the Friday Mosque. Its menu comes in English, and their *mantu* and *ashak* specialities are worth trying.

Books

Good bookshops with foreign reading are pretty nonexistent in Herat so bring all your reading with you. There is a small library at the UNICA Guesthouse. For more local information read the following:

All Our Hopes Are Crushed: Violence and Repression in Western Afghanistan, Human Rights Watch (Washington DC, November 2002)

Les Nouvelles d'Afghanistan (No. 41-42, Mars 1989) – contains numerous articles on Herat plus a bibliography of books, newspaper articles and video films.

Three Women of Herat, Veronica Doubleday, Jonathan Cape (London, 1988)

Music of Afghanistan: Professional musicians in the city of Herat, John Baily, Cambridge University Press (1988 – incls. Audio-cassette)

A Catalogue of the Toponyms and Monuments of Timurid Herat, Terry Allen, Massachusetts Institute of Technology (1981)

The Road to Oxiana, Robert Byron, Macmillan (London, 1937; reprinted by Picador, 1981)

An Historical Guide to Afghanistan, Nancy Hatch Dupree, (2nd Edition, Kabul, 1977)

Embassies & Visas

Iranian and Turkmen visas, as well as extensions for your Afghan visa, can be obtained in Herat. To date, there are no Pakistani visa services in Herat, so sort out your Pakistan visa in Kabul or Kandahar. The Iran and Turkmenistan consulates are situated across the road from each other, one hundred metres east from the ICRC orthopaedic hospital. For visas, you will need to get permission from Tehran and Ashkhabad respectively, so apply at least two weeks before your departure. As of December 2002, transit visas have been easily available (around US$ 50) for travel through Iran to Mashad and onwards to the Gulf states and Europe – even for nationals of "less desired" countries such as the US, UK and Australia. The US has diplomatic, aid and other forms of representation in Herat but no consular services. US Special Forces live up by Ismail Khan's palace overlooking town.

Emergencies

There is a UN bunker underneath the UNICA Guesthouse which doubles up as a bar and disco when the city is not under siege. For a medical emergency, the best course is evacuation to Pakistan. Going to Mashad in a hurry is difficult from a visa point of view, and there are very few expatriate doctors in Herat. If you cannot get out to Pakistan, try contacting ICRC or MSF. The advantage of being evacuated by the Red Cross is that they may provide medical staff to accompany you in the air. The International Medical Corps (IMC) is also present in Herat and will attend to medical emergencies. For more details SEE SECURITY TIPS.

Information

For more information about UN activities, contact their regional representative at the UNAMA office for a briefing on the latest security situation. Make sure you receive some kind of landmine awareness briefing, preferably from UNMACA in Kabul before you go, or from Handicap International in Herat. The UNAMA office in Herat should be able to find you an interpreter. For more details on NGO activities in Herat contact ACBAR. The best way to meet aid agency workers and resident journalists is to turn up for a drink at the UNICA Guesthouse on a Thursday or Friday night between six and eight-thirty in the evening.

Medical

Apart from the odd cholera epidemic, Herat is reasonably safe from nasty diseases; although preventive measures for malaria and hepatitis are recommended. Well-water is safe to drink, but boil and/or treat anything coming out of a tap (SEE PERSONAL HEALTH).

Money

There are no banks in Herat – all money-changing is done on the open market. Bring US dollars, Pakistani rupees or Iranian rials (SEE MONEY & BARGAINING).

Post & Telecommunications

Many NGOs send their post with the ICRC aeroplane to Peshawar. Herat does have a functioning local telephone service, but for international calls you need a satphone or CTOR radio. There is now a functioning prepay cell phone network available, hosted by the Afghan Wireless Communications Company (AWCC), but you need to buy an AWCC sim card (US$ 50). While the system does not allow roaming access for non-AWCC GSM chips, AWCC provides probably the cheapest form of international communication (both for incoming and outgoing calls).

Recreation

The UNICA Guesthouse has a volleyball pitch, a hard tennis court and a swimming pool. Go down on a Friday or Saturday and you are bound to find a game of some sort going on. There are two satellite TVs as well – remember international news comes on at half past the hour in Afghanistan. For liquid recreation, "international night" for non residents is on a Thursday from six or seven in the evening onwards. ICRC opens their bar on Friday nights – supplies permitting. There is a swimming pool in the ICRC compound, as well as a public pool right next to the Moafaq Hotel.

Shopping

Herat is most famous for its blue glass which is still made locally. It comes in three colours – green, turquoise and royal blue – and any number of shapes, from wine goblets and decanters to candlesticks and tumblers. During the Taliban years, one local entrepreneur called "Hajji Dollar" developed a line in blue glass champagne flutes, which seemed a little ambitious under the circumstances. The quality is rather poor, although the odd pieces of straw or dung which find their way into the glass lend it a certain rustic authenticity.

There is a line of shops opposite the north-eastern corner of the Friday Mosque crammed full of blue glass and numerous other *objets d'art* of dubious provenance. The going rate for a glass goblet is no more than a dollar. Lapis jewellery, Greek coins and Buddhist earthenware will all be proffered in your direction as well – but look out for fakes. There is an increasingly good selection of Baluch rugs and Turcoman carpets in the rug bazaar located at the south-western corner of the *Charsuq* in the Old Town. One local workshop, supported by CHA, trains local people in vocational skills – they will sell you hand-knotted carpets which have been made to old Turcoman patterns and coloured with natural dyes.

There are also many Iranian and, to a lesser extent, Pakistani goods and products throughout the bazaars of Herat.

Sights in Herat

Herat is one of the most rewarding cities in Afghanistan for sightseeing. Despite the ravages of over 100 years of modern explosives, a great deal remains which is worth seeing. Some sights, like the Friday Mosque, are actually more spectacular now after restoration than they were a century ago.

Citadel *(Qala-e-Ikhtiyaruddin).* The Citadel perches atop a rocky bluff at the northern end of the Old Town and dominates the bazaar and the low plain to the north. Built in 1305 by a Kart governor, it was attacked by both Genghis Khan and Timur before becoming the centre of the Timurid Empire for the whole of the 15th Century. Timur's son Shah Rukh repaired the fortress and decorated some of its towers with blue tiles, but once the sun had set on the Timurid Renaissance in 1507 Herat and its citadel were subjected to waves of Persian and Uzbek attacks. In 1838 a British Army officer, Lieutenant Eldred Pottinger, occupied the citadel and organized its defences against the siege of a Russian-backed Persian army. In the 1980s UNESCO restored some of the citadel's walls and Timurid decoration. Today, the citadel is occupied by the military, although permission to visit may be obtained from the Department of Culture. Unfortunately no photographing of the fantastic view from the top is allowed.

Friday Mosque *(Masjid-e-Jami).* The Friday Mosque in Herat is undoubtedly one of the finest examples of Islamic art and architecture to be found anywhere in Afghanistan, even in all Central Asia. Yet as recently as the 1930s it was described as having "no colour; only whitewash, bad brick, and broken bits of mosaic" (Byron). Almost all of the magnificent tilework which can still be seen today was recreated according to original Timurid designs under a remarkable restoration programme which started in 1943. This work has continued, despite the conflict across the country in recent years. WFP provides boys with food in return for learning how to make the tiles and working to complete the restoration.

The mosque was laid out in 1200 by the Ghorid Sultan Ghiyas-ud-Din who established his capital at Herat after the collapse of the Ghaznavid Empire. All that remains of the Ghorid decoration is one portal to the south of the main entrance carved with floral motifs, geometric patterns and bright turquoise-blue Kufic script in high relief. Entrance to the mosque is permitted for men only, through a passageway in the eastern portal. Inside is a splendidly shining marble courtyard nearly 100 metres long, surrounded on four sides by arcaded walls in the centres of which are four *iwans,* or vaulted open-fronted halls, all covered with exuberant Timurid-style tilework. A large bronze cauldron dating from the 14th Century sits in the courtyard; once it contained *sherbat,* a sweet drink supplied to the faithful on feast-days, but now it acts as a large donation box. The best time to visit the mosque is in the early morning, before crowds of curious Afghans appear and the intense sun bleaches the walls of colour. But try to avoid visiting during Friday morning prayers between 12 and two o'clock.

During the late-90s if you wanted to take photographs, you had to make sure no-one was in the picture and do it quickly before black-turbaned Taliban zealots caught you with a camera dangling round your neck. Nowadays, you can photograph freely here. The Ministry of Culture has an office inside the Friday Mosque and will provide you with a guide to show you around. You can also visit the on-site restoration workshop, where artisans hammer away on intricate mosaics.

The Musalla Complex. Were you to look north from the ramparts of the Citadel of Herat at dusk you would catch sight of five strange towers rising from the gloom like the chimneys of a brick factory or the legs of an upturned table. These minarets and a badly damaged mausoleum are all that remain of

Musalla complex, Herat *J. Walter*

Queen Gawhar Shad's *musalla* (place of worship), which once comprised "the most glorious productions of Mohammedan architecture in the fifteenth century" (Byron). The complex survived the collapse of the Timurid Empire and successive assaults by Uzbeks and Persians, but was largely destroyed in 1885 on the advice of British Army officers who were keen to help Amir Abdur Rahman defend the westernmost outpost of Afghanistan against Russian advances from the north. Two earthquakes and the Soviet War inflicted more damage and today only five of the original thirty minarets survive, lurching at dangerous angles and pockmarked with rocket and small-arms fire. The *musalla* represented the climax of Timurid decorative art – tile-mosaics of ever more intense colour and intricate design which had developed from the coloured brick patterns of the 12th Century Seljuks and the geometric terracotta mouldings of the Ghorids. Today only tantalizing traces remain.

The complex originally comprised of a mosque to the north and a *madrassa* or theological college to the south. Queen Gawhar Shad, wife of Shah Rukh and daughter-in-law of Timur, commissioned the madrassa in 1417 and, after being murdered 40 years later, she was buried in a mausoleum within its walls. She was a remarkable woman, not only on account of her inspired artistic taste and patronage, but also because of her religious tolerance: as a *Sunni* queen she was responsible for the construction of the *Shi'a* Imam Reza mosque of Mashad in modern-day Iran, then under her sway.

The Queen's mausoleum still stands today. Look for the caretaker who will open it up, show you around inside and ask you to sign the guestbook. By climbing up to the base of its Persian-blue ribbed dome you can look out over the whole of Herat – from the Citadel in the south towards Gazargah in the east, and from the Paropamisus mountains in the north towards the setting sun. The lone leaning minaret to the east of the mausoleum was one of a pair marking the entrance to the *madrassa,* and by all accounts its decoration was plainer than that of the college itself. The surface of the shaft is adorned with robust diamonds of royal blue tile-mosaic filled with flowers. Within the tower local boys dare each other to scramble up the spiral staircase and wave from the top balcony where the muezzin used to cry the call to prayer for the faithful 120 feet below.

To the north of the mausoleum stand four minarets dating from the reign of Sultan Husain Baiqara (1468-1506), last of Herat's Timurid rulers. Originally marking the four corners of another *madrassa,* their delicate lacy decoration speaks eloquently of the decadence of empire. In 1507 Herat fell to the Uzbek adventurer Babur, the founder of the Moghul Empire. Of Baiqara's reign he writes: "what happened with his sons, the soldiers and the town was that everyone pursued vice and pleasure to excess."

Sights outside Herat

Gazargah. "Everyone goes to Gazar Gah," wrote Byron in the 1930s, "Babur went. Humayun went." Today it is hardly crowded with tourists, but it is still a popular retreat for *Heratis* on holiday. Situated under a stand of umbrella-pines on a low hill five kilometres east of Herat, Gazargah is the Shrine of Khwaja Abdullah Ansari, a famous Sufi poet and mystic philosopher who lived in Herat during the 11th Century. His shrine was rebuilt by Shah Rukh in 1428 and consists of a large rectangular walled courtyard filled with graves, a sacred well and a royal picnic pavilion. Of Ansari himself Byron had this to say:

> *"Khoja Abdullah Ansari died in the year 1088 at the age of eighty-four, because some boys threw stones at him while he was at penance. One sympathises with those boys: even among saints he was a prodigious bore. He spoke in the cradle; he began to preach at fourteen; during his life he held intercourse with 1,000 sheikhs, learnt 100,000 verses by heart (some say 1,200,000) and composed as many more. He doted on cats."*

Within the main courtyard is a splendid 30 metre high *iwan* whose Timurid decoration reveals Chinese influence, testimony perhaps to the diplomatic and cultural missions which Shah Rukh exchanged with the Chinese Emperor during the first half of the 15th Century. The tomb of the saint is enclosed in a blue cage and beside it are a superbly carved marble pillar five metres high and a holy ilex tree. Rather like Roman Catholic saints in rural Europe it seems that Ansari is believed to possess magical powers, and specifically power to cure barrenness. Women who cannot conceive choose a stone from near the saint's tomb to represent the child for which they long; they then wrap it in its cradle of linen, dangle it from a branch of the sacred ilex tree and say a prayer for their baby to Ansari.

The courtyard is full of tombs. Amir Dost Mohammed, the bane of the British for much of the 19th Century, is buried here in a white marble tomb behind a balustrade. Inside a small chamber set into the north wall of the courtyard is the *Haft Kalam* ("seven pens"), a stunningly carved late 15th Century sarcophagus of black marble. You may need to ask the caretaker to unlock the chamber.

To the south of the main shrine is the *Khana Zarnegar* ("Pavilion adorned with Gold") whose interior used to be painted in gold and lapis lazuli; it is currently locked. Just to the north of the shrine is the early 15th Century *Hauz-*

e-Zamzam, a small covered reservoir whose crystal clear contents were said to have been purified by several goatskins of water from the sacred well of *Zamzam* in Mecca. Beneath the pine trees is the 17th Century picnic pavilion known as the *Namakdan* or 'Saltcellar' because of its many-sided shape. From here you can enjoy a good view of Herat, its distant minarets and the Paropamisus mountains.

Pul-e-Malan. About 12 kilometres south of the city is the Pul-e-Malan ("Bridge of Riches") which was a tourist attraction 500 years ago when the Moghul Emperor Babur paid it a special visit.

Obey. The road east along the Harirud valley from Herat to Obey and Chisht-e-Sharif is meant to be delightful. Obey (107 km from Herat) used to be famous for its hot springs and wooded gorge; Chisht (173 km from Herat) was well-known for its two 12th Century *gumbad* or domes, and for being the home of the Chishtiya Sufi brotherhood.

Minaret of Jam. Continuing along the Obey road you will reach the 800 year-old Minaret of Jam (313 km from Herat), a spectacular tower 65 metres high, tottering on the banks of the Hari river in a remote mountain valley. Reportedly not 'discovered' by Western archaeologists until 1957, it is the second highest minaret in the world after the Qutb Minar in Delhi. As the only surviving architectural monument from the Ghorid period, it is of enormous cultural and historic significance. Unfortunately, the Minaret and the surrounding area – although gaining endangered "World Heritage Site" status in June 2002 – are still being pillaged. Half-dug trenches are everywhere, littered with bits of broken pottery and ceramics not considered valuable enough to sell to the antique dealers of Herat (SEE CULTURE). The latest reports suggest that driving to Jam (in summer) takes around 14 hours. From Jam to Chakhcharan (capital of Ghor) is another five hours. Continuing east along this road, Kabul is a further 575 km away via Bamiyan.

Weather

The weather in Herat is dry and hot in summer, with temperatures reaching over 30 degrees Celsius and 120 days of ripping winds from May to August. In January the thermometer can drop to freezing, and from February to April the rains often cause flash flooding. Best times to visit are from September to October and April to May.

Hazarajat

Hazarajat is a remote and mountainous region in central Afghanistan which covers the three provinces of Bamiyan, Uruzgan and Ghor, plus parts of neighbouring provinces. It is one of the poorest areas of the country, and for much of the 20th Century was oppressed by hostile Pashtun rulers. This oppression has conspired with harsh geography and (until recently) a lack of donor interest to make Hazarajat one of the least developed corners of Afghanistan.

Dominated by the snowcapped Hindu Kush range, known here as the Koh-e-Baba, which soars to over 5,000 metres, it is a region of striking natural beauty. Emerald-green valleys thread thin as ribbons through barren rocky gorges, and at harvest time the blazing autumn tints compete with brightly-clad farmers and their families in a festival of colour. The Hazaras who traditionally inhabit this region are the third largest ethnic group in Afghanistan, yet one of the least known. They are distinguishable from other Afghans both by their faces, which appear Mongolian, and their religion, which is largely *Shi'a* Muslim. Although many Hazara men sought work in Afghanistan's towns as casual labourers, the majority still live in Hazarajat.

Traditionally Hazarajat has resisted any attempt at rule from a central Afghan power. But in the 1890s, the Hazaras clashed with an invasion force of Pashtun troops sent in by Amir Abdur Rahman, and many Hazaras were scattered as far afield as Iran and Pakistan. The traditional tribal system of those who remained was seriously undermined by Pashtun immigrant settlers. In the 20th Century, the Hazaras openly rebelled against the communists in late 1978 and 1979, and from the start of the Soviet war Hazarajat was independent of communist influence, largely remaining so for the duration of the war. This was mainly because of the region's geography, which made it both inaccessible and strategically irrelevant. The only communist government post in the whole of Hazarajat was at Bamiyan, and the Soviets stopped their military operations in the region in 1981. Resistance to the Soviets centred around two competing factions, the *shura* of Sayed Beheshti, and the Nasr, a party formed by followers of Iran's Ayatollah Khomeiny. But in the 1980s, despite internal divisions, the Hazaras succeeded – with Iranian support – in winning autonomy for their region from the Pashtun-dominated centre for the first time in a century.

In June 1990 Iran put pressure on the eight separate Hazara *mujahed* groups to form a single Party of Islamic Unity, the Hezb-e-Wahdat Islami, in order to consolidate the power of Iran-backed *Shi'as* in Afghanistan. It was led by Abdul Ali Mazari until March 1995, when he was killed while in Taliban custody. Hezb-e-Wahdat later split into two groups, the smaller led by Mohammed Akbari, and the larger controlled by Karim Khalili. Based in Bamiyan, Khalili's Hezb-e-Wahdat party held the balance of power in Mazar-e-Sharif until early 1998. Although Khalili denied Iranian military support for his faction, large amounts of food aid, engineering supplies and technical expertise were flown in by air from Tehran to his Bamiyan stronghold in central Afghanistan. However, resentment in Hazarajat against Tehran grew in 1995 after thousands of Hazara refugees were forcibly repatriated from Iran.

The Taliban, being *Sunni* Muslims, considered the *Shi'a* Hazaras to be infidels and targeted them ruthlessly. In August 1998, during the battle for control of Mazar-e-Sharif, the Taliban killed at least 2,000 civilians, of whom most were Hazaras. (The massacre was allegedly in retaliation for the killing of 2,000 Taliban prisoners by Uzbek and Hazara forces in the city in May 1997). Those Hazaras in Mazar who survived were threatened with execution if they did not convert to the *Sunni* faith. Many Hazara civilians, along with Khalili's Hezb-e-Wahdat forces, fled south to seek refuge in Hazarajat. However, during 1997, the Taliban had been quietly strangling Hazarajat with an air and land blockade, to starve its people into submission. When the UN tried to fly in much-needed food aid, Taliban forces bombed both the airport and the market at Bamiyan.

Eventually, in September 1998, most of Hazarajat fell to the Talibs, who controlled the area through a mixture of direct rule in Bamiyan and Yakaolang, while cutting deals with compliant *Shi'a* leaders elsewhere. However, Khalili managed to maintain control over several outposts, in alliance with another *Shi'a* party, Harakat-e-Islami. Both Wahdat and Harakat were members of the United Front (also known as the Northern Alliance), which attempted to fuse Tajik, Uzbek and Hazara parties into one anti-Taliban force. During 1999-2000, the Taliban bombed these outposts of Khalili's, triggering more flows of refugees into Iran. In return, Khalili and his supporters continued to fight the Taliban for control of Bamiyan and Yakaolang. *Shi'a* forces succeeded in dislodging the Taliban from Yakaolang for a couple of weeks. But in January 2001, the Taliban returned with a vengeance and, in a particularly horrific massacre, publicly executed at least 170 civilian men – including local aid workers – by firing squad. Shortly afterwards, the Taliban were once again forced out of Yakaolang.

Meanwhile, during early 2001, the regional capital, Bamiyan, changed hands several times between Taliban and United Front forces. In March, the Taliban – with help from Al Qa'eda – blew up the two colossal Buddhas, despite pleas from the international community to spare the 1,700-year old masterpieces. During the year, there were grim reports of the Taliban pursuing a scorched earth policy of massacring civilians and burning entire villages. According to the *BBC,* well over 1,000 Hazaras were killed in the 100-km long valley and four mass graves have been found in the town of Bamiyan alone.

Finally, things seem to be looking up – at least in the Bamiyan valley. With the toppling of the Taliban by United Front forces and their powerful US allies in November 2001, reconstruction has slowly started. The bazaar, which was razed to the ground by the Taliban, has been completely rebuilt. The UN and a handful of NGOs are trying to improve health and education facilities. And in

2003, New Zealand sent 120 troops to Bamiyan as a provincial reconstruction team (PRT), whose aim is to improve security and promote development projects supported by the Kabul government. Other plans – such as building a new road to the capital – have not yet materialized. Karim Khalili, meanwhile, is once again the leading figure in Hazarajat. He has been made one of the country's four vice presidents, and supports the government in Kabul – as long as its policies are to his benefit.

Bamiyan

Most famous for the 1,700-year-old colossal Buddha statues, demolished in early 2001 by the Taliban, and for the turquoise waters of Band-e-Amir, Bamiyan was a popular watering hole along the hippie trail in the 1970s. Situated in a deep valley 100 km long and surrounded by barren, snowcapped mountains, Bamiyan feels cut off from the outside world. For many years, it was neglected by Peshawar-based aid organizations.

In 2001, the Taliban, along with numerous Pakistani and Arab fighters, burned down the bazaar in punishment for local support of the United Front, and destroyed pretty much everything except the mosque. But now the town is back on its way to recovery, with the help of the UN and a handful of dedicated international aid agencies. Unlike other Afghan towns, such as Herat and Mazar, however, Bamiyan cannot raise revenue through taxing imports, so it is likely to remain dependent on national and international assistance for some time.

Getting there

By air

The **UN's Humanitarian Air Service** (UNHAS) flies between Kabul and Bamiyan three times per week (Tue, Thu, Sun). One-way tickets cost accredited agencies around US$ 50, while others must pay US$ 125. The **ICRC** and **PACTEC/Airserv International** operate flights (on demand) into Bamiyan. There are also flights to Yakaolang. The Bamiyan airstrip, which lies on a plateau overlooking the town, is controlled by international and pro-government forces. An aeroplane crash here on 21 August 1997 killed Abdul Rahim Ghaforzai, an ethnic Pashtun who had been Afghanistan's ambassador to the UN and a leading light in the anti-Taliban United Front. For more details, SEE TRAVEL BY AIR.

Overland

Bamiyan is a days' journey by four-wheel drive from Kabul and up to two days from Mazar depending on road conditions. The route from Mazar is via Pul-e-Khumri and Doshi leading through a never-ending series of gorges. From Kabul, there are two routes: a southern route via the Hajigak Pass (177 km) and a northern route via the Shibar Pass (237 km). The northern route passes through Charikar and the Ghorband Valley, which looks like a broader but equally verdant version of the Panjshair Valley with its irrigated wheat fields and fruit orchards, including almond trees – an absolute spectacle of pink and

Hazara girls, Bamiyan *J. Walter*

white when flowering during early spring. The southern route leads northwest off the main Kabul-Ghazni road at Maidan Shar. From November until May the roads may be impassable due to snow and flooding from rain and snowmelt. Yakaolang and Band-e-Amir are both about four to five hours drive west of Bamiyan.

Orientation & getting around

Bamiyan lies in the valley of the Bamiyan river which flows here from west to east. To the north of the river rises the rocky ridge into which the niches of the destroyed Buddhas and monks' caves are carved; to the south on a raised plateau lie Khalili's headquarters and farmland stretching up into the Koh-e-Baba mountains.

Check with locally-based agencies about the mine-clearance situation; most of Bamiyan is not affected, but the hilltop fort of Shahr-e-Gholghola is thought to be mined still. Getting around in Bamiyan can be difficult. You may be able to hitch a ride in an aid agency jeep. There are private cars for hire. The best thing is to bring your own vehicle. Roads throughout the region are very poor however, and for half the year may be unusable due to snow or flooding.

Agencies

Although Hazarajat did not suffer as badly as other parts of Afghanistan from the military assaults of the Soviets or *mujahideen,* the Taliban destroyed numerous farms and villages. And its isolation from the rest of the country has reduced economic activity to very low levels. Previously Hazaras earned money through unskilled labour in Kabul and other towns, but the urban warfare and ethnic tension of the 1990s forced many of them to return home or to flee to Iran. This placed greater pressure on already overstretched agricultural resources, leading to erosion and food shortages. Access to markets was restricted by Taliban blockades of Hazarajat, limiting farmers' ability to generate income through selling livestock or potatoes. Hence, tens of thousands of Hazaras risked starvation, while agencies' attempts to solve the problem were only partially successful. With the fall of the Taliban, food aid poured into the valley in early 2002, feeding an estimated 60,000 of Bamiyan's 85,000 inhabitants.

Standards of healthcare and education, which were extremely low during the 1990s, are slowly improving thanks to the work of international agencies such as Save the Children, ICRC, MSF and the UN. The end of the Taliban era has opened up the region to increasing trade with Mazar-e-Sharif and Kabul. Efforts by NGOs such as Madera and Caritas to keep the roads open in winter with food-for-work programmes have brought about dramatic changes. Lorry drivers can now travel from Kabul to Herat using the Central Highland route and local bazaars now offer most basic goods from Singer sewing machines to Pakistani cloth.

The only health facilities in the region are those run by NGOs such as the Iranian Red Crescent hospital in Yakaolang, the MSF clinic in Panjao, and the Lepco leprosy and TB clinic in Lal (Ghor province). The French agency, Solidarité has been improving infrastructure, such as roads and other public works projects. Oxfam has been working in Lal, Panjao and Yakaolang to improve agriculture, health and education. UNCHS (Habitat) has been involved in urban rehabilitation, including improved water and sanitation, new schools and latrines for the migrants and local workers living in the caves situated around the Buddha niches. In 2003, New Zealand forces deployed a provincial reconstruction team, which patrolled the valley by horse and supported Kabul-sponsored development projects.

Bamiyan A-Z

Accommodation and Food

If you can arrange an introduction to Karim Khalili then he has a very comfortable guesthouse perched above the Bamiyan river with an excellent view of what remains of the Buddhas. The Afghan Red Crescent Society runs a guesthouse with four bedrooms. The French NGO Solidarité also has rooms for rent, but be prepared to pay up to US$ 40 per night. There are several very basic *chaikhane* in the bazaar with places to sleep.

Books

The Hazaras of Afghanistan – An Historical, Cultural, Economic and Political Study, Dr Sayed Askar Mousavi, Curzon Press Ltd. (London, 1997)
The Valley of Bamiyan, Nancy Hatch Dupree, Afghan Tourist Association (2nd Edition, Kabul, 1967)

Embassies & Visas

There are no consulates in Hazarajat.

Local Rules

In terms of working and living in Bamiyan, access to both women and men is easier. The Hazaras are a very friendly, hospitable and approachable people. Dress for women should be modest and loose-fitting, but a *chador* is not necessary. Nevertheless, local women often wear *burqas* when away from their homes or fields.

Medical

There are no proper government medical facilities in the region, so if you get ill try to contact one of the international medical aid agencies or fly out to Pakistan.

Post & Telecommunications

There are no telephones or GSM facilities in the region. Satphones are best. A few organizations have radios.

Sights in Bamiyan

Before visiting any of the following sights, pay a visit to the Office of the Director of Culture for Bamiyan Province, situated just to the southwest of the vestiges of the Large Buddha. You may need to pay for permits or receive letters of introduction from the Director.

The Large and Small Buddhas. The crumbled ruins of the once colossal Buddhas of Bamiyan are all that remain of one of Afghanistan's most impressive cultural sites. Some say that, on a full moon, you can still see the Buddhas' ghostly outline in the enormous rock niches which remain.

The Buddhas were deliberately destroyed in March 2001 by the Taliban (including Pakistani and Arab fighters), commanded by a Kandahar chief. They first sought to wreck the statues by firing at them with rockets and other artillery. Then they forced the local cave dwellers to climb up the statues – at considerable personal risk – to hack out holes and plant explosives. They blasted the statues, which used to tower 38 and 55 metres respectively, to smithereens – leaving nothing save for piles of crumbled stones and masonry covered with blue plastic UNHCR tarpaulins. Some Afghan and international cultural groups have proposed rebuilding the statues, but others argue that this would be a waste of money and cheapen the overall setting. UNESCO has stated that Bamiyan would lose its recently acquired World Heritage status if it did so. Far better, say many experts, would be to use precious resources to save other cultural sites – in Bamiyan and elsewhere – from further plundering and destruction (SEE CULTURE).

The Bamiyan statues were among the largest images of the Buddha ever created. Carved out of a sheer rockface overlooking the Bamiyan river, their empty niches continue to dominate a valley which has been Muslim for over a thousand years. Many Afghans, including conservative Muslims, were furious at the wrecking of their country's Buddhist heritage by the Taliban. They saw it as an assault not only on Afghanistan's rich cultural diversity but also as destroying a potentially lucrative tourist attraction.

Dating from the 3rd to 4th Centuries AD, the statues represented the culmination of a Buddhist culture inspired by the religious vision and business acumen of the Kushan King Kanishka, who ruled the Afghan area in around 130 AD. Bamiyan was a staging post for the Silk Route whose luxurious caravans linked the fabulous jewel and spice markets of China and India with the wealth and avarice of Imperial Rome.

A council of Buddhist leaders, which met in Kashmir at Kanishka's behest, were the catalyst for a new interpretation of Buddhism, known as Mahayana or the "Great Vehicle". This sees the Buddha as a compassionate demigod surrounded by cohorts of *boddhisattvas*, rather like the saints of the Roman Catholic tradition. Unlike the earlier Theravada/Hinayana tradition which concentrates on meditation as the route to *nirvana*, Mahayana Buddhists pray to their lord and saints for assistance in their spiritual quest.

As part of this personalizing of their religion, the Buddha came to be represented for the first time in human form. The colossal statues of Bamiyan are thus cousins of the first human images of the Buddha created from the 2nd Century onwards by the Gandhara school of art centred around what is now Peshawar. As Nancy Dupree, author of a guide to the valley in 1962, wrote:

> *"Here, as the embodiment of cosmic man, the Buddha stands not so much as a god but as an extraordinary man, one who participates in human experiences but exists above them because of his oneness with moral precepts."*

The statues occupied large niches cut into the cliff-face about quarter of a mile apart. They were roughly hewn out of the sandstone cliffs and their features then modelled in an applied mixture of mud and wheat straw. This was covered in a fine plaster which was painted: the Large Buddha was clothed in a red cloak, the smaller one in blue. Both their faces were gilded. The niches above the statues' heads were filled with wall-paintings which you could examine at close quarters by climbing onto the heads of the statues (via a sandstone staircase carved out of the cliff). Archaeologists are still assessing the damage to see what remains. Until its destruction, one could decipher above the head of the Small Buddha the figure of a Sun-God riding his chariot through a dark blue sky. This links the Bamiyan Buddhas with the sun-god traditions of Greece (Helios and Apollo), Sasanian Persia (Mithra) and India (Surya). The wall-paintings above the Large Buddha's head were in better condition (until March 2001): the Buddha was seated with his *boddhisattvas* and surrounded rather incongruously by scantily-clad ladies playing musical instruments. These latter figures are thought to have been inspired by the sensual Indian Gupta tradition of the 7th Century AD.

The two colossal Buddhas of Bamiyan did not, however, impress the eccentric English traveller Robert Byron when he visited them in 1934. He had this to say:

> *"Neither has any artistic value. But one could bear that; it is their negation of sense, the lack of any pride in their monstrous flaccid bulk, that sickens."*

The Large Buddha, prior to its destruction in 2001 *J. Walter*

And yet the "negation of sense" is a central tenet of Buddhism, which teaches its disciples that through releasing themselves from the suffering caused by clinging to the senses, they may reach *nirvana*. But what about the bare-breasted girls dancing above the head of the Large Buddha's "flaccid bulk"? Or the 7th Century account of the Chinese traveller Hsuan-tsang, who wrote of the Large Buddha: "The golden hues sparkle on every side, and its

WARNING

THE AREA OF SHAHR-E-GHOLGHOLA IS STILL MINED. DO NOT TRY TO CLIMB THE HILL WITHOUT A GUIDE !

precious ornaments dazzle the eye by their brightness." The Buddhist complex of Bamiyan – in its celebration of both sheer physical bulk and sparkling superficial beauty – embodied the central paradox of the Mahayanan tradition. The Buddha rejected the metaphysics of Hindu gods and human souls in favour of a physician's philosophy to cure the ills of the world. He preached a doctrine of detachment from the pain of a transient, physical existence. Yet he was represented here, vast and resplendent in the (once) glittering robes of a demigod.

Even prior to their final destruction, the statues were showing their age: the Persian Nadir Shah chopped off the legs of the Large Buddha about 250 years ago, and Muslim iconoclasts sawed off both the Buddhas' faces. During the 1990s, *mujahed* fighters took pot shots at the 1,700 year-old wall paintings with their kalashnikovs and sold off the fragments. In April 1997 a Talib commander caused an international outcry when he threatened to blow up the statues if he ever made it into the Bamiyan valley.

Hundreds of monks' cells pepper the cliff-face between the two niches and once featured wall-paintings, grottoes and statues donated by worshippers. Most have been damaged by graffiti or woodsmoke. Dozens of troglodyte families and workers, many of whom were here well before the outbreak of war in the late 1970s, still live here.

In 2002, an Afghan archaeologist began excavations in the valley, convinced that there was a third giant Buddha, measuring 300 metres in length. The so-called Sleeping Buddha is thought to be reclining in a pose representing the last moments of the Buddha's earthly life before entering *nirvana.*

Kakrak Buddha. A third statue of the Buddha, standing 6.5 metres high, was carved out of a cave in the Kakrak valley to the east of Bamiyan town. Wall-paintings, which were removed from the site before the war, depicted a central Buddha surrounded by concentric rings of smaller seated Buddhas. These diagrams are thought to be the first examples of the cosmic *mandalas* which subsequently gained great popularity in the art and worship of Nepalese and Tibetan Buddhism. The paintings probably date from the 8th to 9th Centuries AD, the end of the Buddhist period in Bamiyan. The Kakrak valley lies 20-30 minutes drive east of town; 4x4 transport is recommended as the route crosses a small river.

Shahr-e-Gholghola ("City of Screams"). This rocky hilltop citadel towers above the south bank of the river about two kilometres east of Bamiyan. Once the centre of the 12th Century Islamic Shansabani dynasty, the citadel now lies deserted, its ghostly stones bleached as white as bone.

For two centuries the Buddhist culture of Bamiyan was subjected to the proselytising efforts of Abbasids and Saffarids, until the late 10th Century when the valley finally succumbed to the rule of Islam. Two centuries later, the brother of Ghorid King Alauddin the "World Burner" (so-called for razing Ghazni to the ground in 1151) presided over his magnificent capital from this rocky stronghold.

Then in 1221 Genghis Khan arrived, looking for trouble. According to a local legend, related by Nancy Dupree in her 1970s guide to Afghanistan, the citadel was betrayed by the daughter of Bamiyan's ruler, Jalaluddin, who took offence when her father married a young princess from Ghazni. In a fit of rage, she fired an arrow into the tent of Genghis Khan, who was camped nearby. Attached to the arrow was a note advising Khan to block up a crucial underground spring on which the citadel's people depended. The plan worked, the citadel fell, and Genghis Khan's utter destruction of every living thing in the valley gave rise to the name *Shahr-e-Gholghola* which means, literally, "City of Screams." Meanwhile, Jalaluddin's daughter put on her best dress, expecting a visit from the grateful conqueror. Instead, he ordered her to be stoned to death. ***BEWARE – THIS HILLTOP IS BELIEVED TO BE MINED!***

Sights outside Bamiyan

Shahr-e-Zohak ("The Red City"). This magnificent pile of ruins occupies a highly strategic mountain spur 17 km east of Bamiyan, at the confluence of the Bamiyan and Kalu rivers. For two millennia the fertile valleys to the west have been defended by fortresses built atop this crimson-coloured cliff. The present fortifications date from the reign of the Shansabani kings during the 12th to 13th Centuries, and it was here that Genghis Khan's favourite grandson was mortally wounded while leading an attack in 1221. His grandfather's revenge on the valley of Bamiyan and its inhabitants was murderous and merciless.

The entrance to the fortress is via a ramp on the east side of the spur which zig-zags up the cliff-face between decorated defensive towers. If you look up you will notice that every step is covered by firing positions from at least two of these towers. Furthermore the towers had no doors, so to reach the parapets the defenders clambered up ladders, pulling them up afterwards so as to make the fortress even more impregnable. The view from the summit of the "Red City" is well-worth the climb: snowcapped mountains and jagged pinnacles of rock rise all around, looking especially fantastic at sunset.

You may need a permit from the Director of Culture in Bamiyan to visit Shahr-e-Zohak, as well as a letter from him to the local commander on the ground to authorize your passage. The drive to Shahr-e-Zohak takes about one hour, but allow at least four hours for a round trip from Bamiyan, to leave time for exploring the site and having tea with local commanders *en route.*

Band-e-Amir. These fabled turquoise lakes lie deep in the arid ochre mountains of the Koh-e-Baba range, 75 km west of Bamiyan town. The name means "Dam of the King", and refers to the sulphurous mineral deposits which have created natural dams, some up to 12 metres high, behind which five lakes have formed. The miraculous presence of these glittering lakes in such a desolate land is attributed to the superhuman powers of Hazrat Ali, who not only made the dams but also killed the dragon of Bamiyan, all in one day.

The four to five hour drive to Band-e-Amir, via the village of Shahidan, is magnificent but only to be attempted in summer months by four-wheel drive vehicle. The lakes are situated at an altitude of over 2,900 metres, so swimming is a bracing experience. There is no accommodation at the lakes and precious little vegetation, so take a tent, warm clothing and cooking fuel with you.

Weather

Bamiyan town is situated at an altitude of 2,500 metres so pack some warm clothes whatever time of year you are visiting. Winters are harsh and the entire region is often snowbound for months at a time from November onwards. Spring brings flooding caused by snowmelt and rains, making road travel difficult. Summer and autumn are when most of the agricultural work is done. In October the valleys are a blaze of colour with autumnal tints firing the hillsides gold and brightly-clad families out in the fields for the harvest.

Islamabad

From the outbreak of war in Afghanistan in 1978, and the start of large-scale humanitarian aid for fleeing refugees, until the fall of the Taliban in late 2001, the Pakistani capital of Islamabad served as the principal headquarters for international humanitarian assistance. While the North West Frontier city of Peshawar, and to a lesser extent the Baluchistan provincial capital of Quetta, functioned more as an operational base for the majority of NGOs and UN agencies, Islamabad was where all the embassies and UN agencies for the region were located.

With the fall of the Taliban and the launching of a massive international recovery programme for Afghanistan, many UN agencies and NGOs have moved their headquarters to Kabul. By mid-2003, 30 countries had opened diplomatic missions in the Afghan capital, although Islamabad remains a convenient place to go for visas or passport renewals. And while many Afghans have now set up supply enterprises in Kabul, Islamabad and Rawalpindi remain good (and cheaper) shopping centres, particularly for technical support and materials, but also for items such as DVDs, furniture, cloth and kitchen gear.

During 2002, security for Westerners in Pakistan deteriorated, with armed Islamic groups killing 11 French technicians in Karachi and murdering the US-based journalist Danny Pearl. The US embassy in Islamabad cut back its activities drastically, closing the American Centre and warning its nationals to stay away from the country. In May 2002, Britain evacuated all non-essential diplomatic staff from Islamabad and closed the British school.

If you take a taxi up to the viewpoint of Daman-e-Koh in the Margalla Hills just to the north of Islamabad, you will see that the city has been laid out with the imagination of an accountant. In 1958 the President decided that Karachi was too hot and crowded to be the country's capital, so a new, somewhat cooler, more hospitable and open site was selected near the former British garrison town of Rawalpindi in northern Pakistan.

Three years later, the spacious and leafy Islamabad began to emerge. It conforms to a gridded masterplan devised by Greek architects, with separate enclaves designated for administrative, diplomatic, recreational, educational, industrial and residential purposes. Rather than name these districts, they are referred to simply by a letter (referring to North-South position) and a number (East-West position); the district F-16 always amuses Pakistani plane-spotters.

Getting there

By air

The events of September 11, 2001, caused British Airways to suspend its direct flights to Islamabad. Other international carriers include Pakistan International Airways (PIA), Royal Saudi Airlines, Emirates and Gulf Air (the last two via Dubai). If flights are full, check with PIA for routing via Lahore or Peshawar. Beware, however, that many European travel agencies refuse to deal with PIA so you may have to purchase tickets at PIA counters in London, Paris or Dubai.

PIA operate domestic flights from Islamabad to Peshawar and Quetta at least twice a day. There are also direct flights from Islamabad to Kabul with PIA (Mon, Thu, Sat), Ariana Afghan Airlines (Mon), the UN's Humanitarian Air Service (every day except Fri) and PACTEC/Airserv International. For more information on flights in and out of Islamabad and Afghanistan, SEE TRAVEL BY AIR. Contact numbers in Islamabad are as follows:

Emirates:
2-C Mohammadi Plaza, Blue Area, Jinnah Avenue, Islamabad
Agent's Tel: +92 (21) 227 9999
Airport Ticket Office Tel: +92 (51) 590 542

Pakistan International Airways:
PIA Building, 49 Blue Area, Islamabad
Tel: +92 (51) 920 9911 Fax: +92 (51) 920 9966

UN Humanitarian Air Service:
House 4, Street 5, F/8-3, Islamabad
Tel: +92 51 2264077, 2264101 Fax +92 51 2264054
Email: islamabad.unhas@wfp.org

PACTEC/Airserv:
House 494-A, Street 9, F-10/2, Islamabad
Tel: +92 (0)51 210 5261-4 Fax: + 92 (0)51 210 5265
Email: pakbooking@airserv.org

Overland

The Grand Trunk (GT) road, which runs between Lahore and Peshawar, passes 14 km to the southwest of Islamabad. This is the Pakistani equivalent of the Nairobi-Mombasa highway, and just as dangerous despite the fact that major road construction has been carried out over the past few years. Part of the GT now passes as 'highway', but the road improvements have done nothing to improve driving. Careering trucks and buses are determined to dominate and show little mercy to cautious drivers. While the GT road was a relatively pleasant drive during the early 1980s, it is now a definite health hazard as traffic, casualty rates and pollution increase by the year.

The best time to do the journey is at the weekend (Friday). Avoid travelling at night (beware of roaming camels and donkeys, but also stoned Pakistanis) and drive defensively by day. Most hotel drivers drive relatively well; hold on to a good one if you find one. The trip to Peshawar now takes about two hours. Taxis are as quick as flying, but more expensive than a one-way air ticket. Plenty of buses make the journey day and night. Along the route lie the Margalla Pass (defined by the historian Sir Olaf Caroe as the real boundary between the

Indian subcontinent and Central Asia) and Taxila, once a centre of the Buddhist Gandhara Kingdom. For more information on driving into Afghanistan from Islamabad/Peshawar, SEE TRAVEL OVERLAND.

Orientation & getting around

Islamabad is sandwiched between the wooded Margalla Hills (still alive with jackals, mongooses and the occasional leopard), which rise from the city's northern edge, and the noisy – and rapidly expanding – bazaar town and cantonment of Rawalpindi, 15 km to the south. The international airport is on the way to Rawalpindi. There are good views of the city from both the Margalla range and from Shakarparian Park to the south. To the east lie the Presidential Palace and Diplomatic Enclave, to the west lies the Grand Trunk road to Peshawar. The centre of town is dominated by the dual-carriageway of the so-called "Blue Area" which contains most of the modern shops and office blocks. 'F' districts lie to the north of the Blue Area, and 'G' districts to the south. See maps in guidebooks listed below.

If you cannot get a lift in an aid agency vehicle, taxis can be hired by the day. You can arrange one through your guesthouse/hotel or flag one down in the street. Daily rates are around PakRupees 800, but agree on the price before getting in. Motorscooter rickshaws and some horse-drawn *tongas* are also available in Rawalpindi.

Agencies

Most of the UN agencies (UNICEF, UNDP, WHO, FAO, WFP, etc.) have offices in Islamabad – although these are primarily for Pakistan-based activities. Nevertheless, they can put you in touch with their Afghan-related offices in Peshawar, Quetta and Kabul. For more information on UN agencies, contact:

UN Information Centre (UNIC), Islamabad
Tel: +92 (51) 227 0610, 282 1012
Email: unic@isb.comsats.net.pk
Web: http://www.un.org.pk/unic

Most of the international NGOs dealing with Afghanistan have left for Kabul, although some retain regional offices and guest houses in Peshawar and Quetta. For more details, call on the **Agency Coordinating Body for Afghan Relief (ACBAR)** in Kabul, or SEE CONTACTS. Alternatively, check online with the UN's ReliefWeb and Reuters' AlertNet.

Islamabad A-Z:

Accommodation and Food

Islamabad has a wide range of international standard hotels and excellent guesthouses. Most establishments accept credit cards and provide *en suite* 'Western' bathrooms, satellite TV in your room and international phone/fax facilities at reception. Here is a small selection within Islamabad:

Marriott Hotel (formerly the Holiday Inn), Aga Khan Road, Shalimar 5, PO Box 1251. Tel: +92 (51) 282 6121 Fax: +92 (51) 282 0648

Double rooms from US$ 123 upwards. Centrally-located luxury five-star hotel at the north-eastern end of the Blue Area. Facilities include swimming pool, tennis courts, health club, international direct dialling (IDD) from your room, and business centre with computer, fax and e-mail.

Serena Hotel Islamabad, Khayaban-e-Suhrawardy.
Tel: +92 (51) 111 133 133, 287 4000
Fax: +92 (51) 287 1092, 287 1001, 287 1100
E-mail: dsish@serena.com.pk
Double rooms from US$ 220 upwards. Luxury hotel only 500 metres from the French Embassy and the diplomatic enclave. Pool, spa & gym facilities, shops, restaurants. Computer modem outlets in rooms plus business centre. It opened ahead of schedule in autumn 2001 to accommodate the journalist hordes covering the US intervention in Afghanistan.

Holiday Inn (former Islamabad Hotel), Municipal Road.
Tel: +92 (51) 282 7311
E-mail: holiday@isb.comsats.net.pk
Single rooms from US$ 60 upwards. Modern downtown hotel located near administrative enclave. Facilities include IDD from your room and e-mail. UN and NGO agency personnel, and accredited journalists get a 30% discount on room rates.

Continental Guest House, 94, Nazimuddin Road, F-8/4.
Tel: +92 (51) 225 6670-1
Luxury guesthouse with international phone and fax facilities, satellite TV and "round the clock coffee bar."

Chez Soi, 6 Kohsar Road, F-7/3.
Tel: +92 (51) 227 6921

Jacaranda Inn, 17 College Road, F-7/3.
Tel: +92 (51) 273 1834

International Guesthouse, House 12, 7th Avenue.
Tel: +92 (51) 282 7098-9

For politically incorrect MacDonald-Fraser enthusiasts, there is also **Flashman's Hotel** in downtown Rawalpindi, but it does not quite live up to its name.

Books

Welcome to Pakistan: Islamabad, Rawalpindi (United Nations Women's Association). This excellent 100-page guidebook contains the most up-to-date and comprehensive information available on Islamabad, and is aimed mainly at those moving out here to live. Chapters contain details on geography & history, language, customs, religion, health, housing, schooling, cars & driving, pets, leisure & charitable activities, gardening, sightseeing, and a practical guide to everything from carpet cleaning and Christmas trees to hairdressers and handymen. It also contains useful maps of the markets and bazaars of both cities. The book costs PakRupees 200 (sales support a home for retarded children) and is available from: **UN Community Liaison Officer,** 2nd Floor, Saudi Pak Tower, 61-A Jinnah Avenue (Tel: +92 (51) 279165 Fax: +92 (51) 279080-83)

Insight Guide to Pakistan, Tony Holliday (2000)

Lonely Planet Guide to Pakistan, David St Vincent, Bradley Mayhew, John King (1998)

Pakistan Handbook, Isobel Shaw, Moon Travel Handbooks (1997); includes walks and maps of Peshawar and the North West Frontier Province.

Good bookshops include **Book Fair** (Jinnah Market, F-7), **London Book Co.** (Khosar Market, F-6/3), **Mr Books** (Super Market, F-6), and **Vanguard Books** (Super Market, F-6). There are also bookshops in Rawalpindi.

Good **libraries** include the following:
The British Council Library, 14 Civic Centre, Melody Market, G-6/3
Tel: +92 (51) 111 424 424 Fax: +92 (51) 111 425 425
Email: info@britishcouncil.org.pk
This English-language library stocks some titles on Afghanistan, along with international newspapers, periodicals and videos.

French Cultural Centre
House 15, Street 18. F-7/2

Embassies & Visas

For Pakistan. Three types of visa are available for Pakistan: single and double entry for tourists and multiple entry for foreigners working in the country. In order to get a multiple entry visa, you need a letter from a company or agency in Pakistan to vouch for you. For a list of Pakistan embassies worldwide and foreign missions based in Islamabad, SEE CONTACTS.

For the Khyber Pass. SEE PESHAWAR

For Afghanistan. Try to arrange an Afghan visa in your home country if possible. (If you are really persuasive and have good local contacts in Kabul, immigration at Kabul airport can issue a two-week visa for US$ 30, sometimes more.) Otherwise the Afghan Embassy in Islamabad issues visas, but the procedure for 'newcomers' can take up to a week even for accredited journalists and aid workers. Start your application process early in the week and remember that Friday afternoon, Saturday and Sunday are holidays. Visas cost US$ 30 and you will need two passport-size photos (there are studios in Super Market). If you are a regular visitor to Afghanistan and sponsored by the UN or a major aid agency you may be able to get a visa in as little as one day. While visa procedures were slow under the Taliban, do not expect major improvements with the current authorities. You are still dealing with bureaucracy, but the embassy officials do try hard, particularly if you show yourself to be patient, pleasant and sympathetic to their problems. For more information, SEE VISAS, JOURNALISM or contact:

Embassy of Afghanistan in Islamabad

House No. 8, Street 90, G-6/3
Tel: +92 (51) 282 4505-6 Fax: +92 (51) 282 4504
Consular Section: +92 (51) 227 8213

Information

There is a comprehensive online listing of everything in Islamabad from bakers and barbers to video rental and veterinarians on: http://flm.com.pk/guide_islamabad.html. For general information, contact:

UN Information Centre (UNIC), Islamabad
Tel: +92 (51) 227 0610, 282 1012
Email: unic@isb.comsats.net.pk
Web: http://www.un.org.pk/unic

Medical

Make sure your vaccinations are up to date for polio, typhoid, tetanus, rabies and hepatitis A and B, as vaccine quality in Pakistan cannot be guaranteed. Islamabad is not considered to be a malarial zone, but take precautions to be safe. If you get sick, consult your embassy for advice. Otherwise the Shifa Hospital, H-8, is one of the best in town. There are also some good dentists registered with various embassies (SEE PERSONAL HEALTH).

Money

If you are bringing cash, US dollars – and increasingly Euros – are widely accepted. The newer and crisper the notes the better. You will get a better rate for big denomination bills. American Express Bank has a branch in the Blue Area (the service is not that great if you are having funds sent from abroad), as does Bank of America; Standard Chartered Bank in the Diplomatic Enclave is probably the best bank to deal with as this is where most of the aid agencies have their accounts and they are used to dealing with complicated transfers. Credit cards are also used in certain shops and even in the bazaars. So are personal cheques from European and American banks if the shopkeepers know you or have solid introductions.

Post & Telecommunications

The General Post Office is located on Post Office Road, G-6/2, and the Telegraph and Telephone Office is situated behind the Marriott Hotel on Ataturk Avenue, F-5. Long-distance telephone, fax and telex facilities are available but you may have to wait. Email is available from the major international hotels as well as with some of the guesthouses. There are also growing numbers of good Internet cafes available. Mobile telephones can be rented or bought from a number of companies based in Islamabad. While local calls cost more, international calls by mobile phone are up to three times cheaper than calling from a hotel.

Recreation

UNISRAP (United Nations International Staff Recreation Association in Pakistan). Known more simply as the UN Club, it sports a bar and restaurant, table tennis, satellite TV and a grassy garden containing a swimming pool. International (open) nights are on Fridays from 1930-0030 hrs, and Saturday brunch (which can keep you going all weekend) is also open to visitors from 1200-1530 hrs.

The **Marriott Hotel** has probably the best sports facilities in town, including a 50 metre swimming pool, health club with sauna, weights room and jogging machines. You can also arrange to play squash, tennis and golf at the Islamabad Club through the Marriott.

The **Islamabad Club** is on Murree Road – horse-riding is one of the sports on offer. Most of the foreign diplomatic missions also have clubs which may be open to visitors, depending on the security situation.

For less clubby types, there are some wonderful walks in the **Margalla Hills** just to the north of Islamabad, with particularly good bird-watching for ornithologists. For more details read *Hiking in the Margallas* published by the **Asian Study Group** (ASG). The ASG is located in the Malik Complex, 80W. Jinnah Ave., Blue Area and holds lectures and film evenings on Pakistani culture etc. An arboretum on top of **Shakaparian Hill** to the south of the city affords good views. It is filled with trees planted by visiting politicians: a magnolia from Kurt Waldheim nestles near chir pines from Nicolae Ceaucescu and Burhanuddin Rabbani…Mullah Omar next?

Shopping

There are now various bazaars worth visiting in Islamabad. The Sunday Market (previously the Friday market) is held all day every Sunday between Municipal Road and Garden Road, south of the Holiday Inn Hotel. There is also an excellent market, including Afghan produce, out by Peshawar Mall in G-10. A lot of the good Afghan tailors have left for Kabul, Jalalabad and other Afghan towns, but you can find excellent Pakistan ones at reasonable prices. Behind the Holiday Inn, you can find quite a few but the cheaper ones (just as good) are out by F-10. If you are serious about your tailoring, you may also wish to bring in your own materials from Europe or the Far East, as the best Pakistani cotton and wool is exported, and what remains is expensive. Prices are often better than Peshawar.

The bazaars of Rawalpindi are also very colourful places to shop – and cheaper than Islamabad, particularly for items such as China dining sets, lamps and furniture. Bara Bazaar is good for imported Japanese and English electrical goods, kitchen things and Chinese silks; Moti Bazaar specializes in women's clothing and jewellery; Raja Bazaar is in the old part of Rawalpindi where you will find everything from vegetables to false teeth; Saddar Bazaar specializes in handicrafts, car parts and fish; and Sarafa Bazaar is the place to find silver and gold.

Weather

Islamabad is situated 518 metres above sea-level (higher than Peshawar) and enjoys cool weather from October to March (lowest temperature around 3 degrees Celsius). May and June can be very hot (up to 48 degrees), prior to the monsoon rains which sweep through from July to September. The Margalla Hills rise up to 2,500 metres so there is always somewhere to escape to if things get sticky.

Peshawar

Ever since the first refugees began trickling into the North West Frontier Province of Pakistan in mid-1978, until well into 2002, Peshawar served as an operations base for numerous aid agencies. It also functioned as an exile headquarters for guerrilla factions, Afghan advocacy groups and media, including at least 20 Pashtun or Dari language publications focusing on subjects such as politics and poetry. As the war developed, this dusty provincial capital of drug smugglers and arms traffickers 35 km from the Khyber Pass began to establish itself as a principal humanitarian centre and launching pad for journalists seeking to cover the Afghan story. With its crowded bazaars and smoke-filled teashops, Peshawar still retained, during the late 1970s and early 1980s, some of the exhilarating frontier flavour of Kipling's India.

By March 1980, well over 20 resistance groups had set up shop in Peshawar, many with sub-offices in Quetta in Baluchistan province to the southwest. The international press corps had descended *en masse,* while hundreds of thousands of refugees were flocking to the camps on the outskirts of town or up and down the frontier. Peshawar exuded the atmosphere of a den of spies. Diplomats, reporters, intelligence agents, war junkies, smugglers, drug enforcement officials and various travellers were constantly drifting through this romantic Casablanca of the East to check on the Afghans, the opium trafficking scene and whatever plots one cared to unearth. Everyone seemed to have an agenda. Sadly, the gardened colonial-style Dean's Hotel, the traditional haunt of journalists and diplomats as well as an array of savoury and unsavoury characters, was bulldozed in 2002 to make way for a tasteless commercial centre.

During the early years of the war, Peshawar remained a modest town with relatively little traffic and pollution. It was easy to travel from the Cantonment (where most of the visiting foreign correspondents stayed) out to University Town (where the aid agencies began to establish themselves) or to the Old Town bazaar area by *tuk-tuk* (motor scooter rickshaw) or even *tonga,* a horse-drawn trap.

For numerous reporters and aid workers, Peshawar represented one of the most exciting towns in the world. Apart from the hundreds (later several thousand) expat relief workers operating in the region, the city emerged as a crucial transit centre for countless reporters, camera teams and crossborder relief workers seeking to "go inside." The nights were often rocked by gunshots (usually bravado firing into the air) but occasionally rockets or bombs that killed and injured people. There was definite frontline atmosphere that appealed to the romantic notions of many. Today, Peshawar is still the most interesting way of entering Afghanistan by travelling via the Khyber Pass (SEE TRAVEL OVERLAND).

But as massive international aid poured in, Pakistani government and Afghan resistance leaders became even more corrupt, and the drug and weapons trafficking industry grew, this once alluring provincial capital on the razor's edge of conflict developed into a veritable nightmare. The war, refugees, aid and drugs completely changed the city. By the late 1980s, some 200 international agencies and NGOs had established operations bases in the town. The Pakistani and Afghan population more than tripled, while the streets became clogged with brand-new vehicles and whole new residential areas sprang up with shops, villas, garages and satellite-dishes. Even worse, a pall of dust, filth and fumes hung perpetually over the city. The frontier romanticism had gone.

With the transfer of most aid agencies to Afghanistan following the fall of the Taliban in late 2001, plus the return of hundreds of thousands of refugees, Peshawar has become a more quiet, even manageable town. The war, drugs and aid have definitely helped develop various new industries that would not have existed otherwise. It is now the residence of quite a few traffickers who benefited sumptuously from international aid and drug rake-offs.

In many respects, Peshawar will remain a Pakistani-Afghan commercial centre, whether for licit or illicit trade. Many Afghans with jobs are reluctant to return home, and may never do so. Others have settled in Kabul and other cities, but retain business interests in Pakistan with Peshawar serving as a commercial jumping off point to exploit the commercial markets of the Indian subcontinent. Only two hours away, Jalalabad has simply become an extension of Peshawar with heavy daily traffic between the two cities. For journalists, but also aid coordinators, the town remains a useful stopping-off point for contacts, research, background briefings and interviews before heading off into Afghanistan.

You need to go to the Khyber Political Agency to pick up a travel permit (it now takes only ten minutes) if you wish to go by road via the Khyber Pass to Afghanistan. In addition, there are now a number of comfortable and well-equipped guesthouses with international phone lines and fax machines that did not exist before. But as many old hands will tell you, Peshawar just ain't the same when compared to the more tense but scintillating heyday of humanitarian relief and crossborder journalism during the early and mid-1980s.

Getting there

By air

You can fly here directly from Dubai, Islamabad and Tashkent on Pakistan International Airways. Other airlines, such as Aero Asia, also operate to Peshawar as part of their regional services.

Overland

The Grand Trunk (GT) road runs between Lahore and Peshawar, passing within 14 km of Islamabad. To reach Peshawar from Islamabad, head west from Zero Point and turn right when you meet the GT road. The trip takes two to three hours. Taxis are as quick as flying, but more expensive than a single air ticket. Plenty of buses make the journey day and night. Along the route lie the Margalla Pass (defined by the historian Sir Olaf Caroe as the real boundary between the Indian subcontinent and Central Asia) and Taxila, once a centre of the Gandhara Kingdom.

For more information on driving into Afghanistan from Peshawar SEE TRAVEL OVERLAND.

Orientation & getting around

The few aid agencies that remain are based in University Town, which lies a couple of kilometres west of the airport, down Jamrud Road. The Cantonment, Saddar Bazaar and the Old City lie to the east of the airport. Getting around

Even up to the mid-1980s, the best form of travel around Peshawar was the *tonga* – a horse-drawn trap. Some people still use them, but Peshawar is now awash with minibuses and that scourge of third-world cities, *tuk-tuk* motor-rickshaws. Taxis can be hired by the day – flag one down in the street or arrange one through your guesthouse. Agree on the price before getting in.

Peshawar A-Z:

Accommodation and Food

There is no shortage of places to eat and sleep in Peshawar. Here are some ideas:

Pearl-Continental Hotel, PO Box 197, Khyber Road. Tel: +92 (91) 276361
If you need to off-load some excess dollars then this is the place for you. The most luxurious hotel in Peshawar, it is situated several kilometres east of University Town near the Old Fort. Facilities include a good restaurant for body-building breakfasts, the 'gulbar' for imported drinks, swimming pool, health club and access to an 18-hole golf course. You can make international direct-dial telephone calls from your room, and a business centre provides fax, telex and photocopying services.

Khan Klub, No. 225, K, New Rampura Gate, Nevay Darwaza, Old Town. Tel: +92 (91) 214802, 2567156
For an authentic 'frontier' feel the Khan Klub is hard to beat. The 200 year-old traditional *haveli* has been beautifully restored to create a restaurant and eight luxurious suites. Both excellent local and international food is served to the strains of classical eastern music while diners sit cross-legged on cushions.

Green's Hotel, Saddar Road, Cantonment. Tel: +92 (91) 276035-7

The Khyber Club (formerly American Club), 24-D Circular Road, University Town. Tel: +92 (91) 41321
Still one of the best places to stay or hang out, but now all very quiet. Liquid refreshment in the form of a swimming pool and a bar make this a particularly

popular venue for expats at weekends and on Friday and Saturday nights. Other facilities include tennis courts, a pool table, restaurant and satellite TV. Four or five double rooms provide accommodation. Officially known as the United States Government Employees' Association (USGEA), membership must be arranged through the US Consulate (Tel: +92 (91) 279801-3, Fax: +92 (91) 276712). Full members may sign in guests but temporary membership is available free of charge if you provide the Consulate with a letter of introduction from your office or sponsoring agency.

University Town guesthouses: there are a good dozen or more guesthouses from which to choose with prices starting at US$ 30 a night. Most provide *en suite* 'Western' bathrooms, satellite TV in your room and international phone/fax facilities at reception.

For traditional "frontier food" and musical accompaniment, the **Khan Klub** (see above) is one of the best places to eat out, although it is about 20-30 minutes drive from University Town. If mad-cow disease appeals to you, then try **Khyber Bazaar** in the Old Town where you can sit outside on *charpoys* and tuck into hunks of dead meat and slabs of *naan* the size of snowshoes.

For western-style and Chinese food the **Pearl-Continental** restaurants are very good – they also do an open-air barbecue with live music. A number of Pakistani-run "fast food" outlets have opened up just across Jamrud Road from University Town. For something oriental try the **Hong Kong Chinese Restaurant** (Tel: 274504) on The Mall in the Cantonment. Other local favourites include **Shiraz** and **Usmania** restaurants on Jamrud Road near the airport.

Books & Information

The **ACBAR Resource and Information Centre (ARIC)** provides probably the best reference library on Afghanistan in the region. Located at 2 Rehman Baba Road, University Town, it is open from 0800-1630 hrs on Mondays to Thursdays, and from 0800-1230 hrs on Fridays. It is closed on Saturdays and Sundays. It contains nearly 4,000 books, agency reports, maps, journals and videos on every conceivable sector of interest in Afghanistan. Photocopying for documents and maps is available for a small fee. A number of Nancy Hatch Dupree's books are for sale at ARIC. The *CROSSLINES Essential Field Guide to Afghanistan* is also available here.

Saddar Bazaar in the Cantonment has two of the best bookshops in Pakistan: the **London Book Co.** on Arbab Road (Tel: 272722) and **Saheed Bookbank**. They sell a good selection of titles on Afghanistan as well as Persian and Pashto dictionaries.

Embassies & Visas

For Pakistan. SEE ISLAMABAD and VISAS

For the Khyber Pass. All expats travelling from Peshawar by road up to Landi Kotal, the border at Torkham and on through the Khyber Pass into Afghanistan need to get a Tribal Areas Permit from the Khyber Political Agency. This can now be procured in about ten minutes. The application should be accompanied by photocopies of your passport and relevant Pakistani and Afghan visas. The Political Agent's office is on Bara Road near Qayum Stadium in Saddar Bazaar. Coming back from Afghanistan by road through the Khyber Pass, you do not need a Tribal Areas permit – the local militia will give you an armed escort but will expect tips (US$ 1-2) for their 'protection'.

For Afghanistan. Try to arrange an Afghan visa in your home country if possible (SEE VISAS). Otherwise the Afghan Consulate in Peshawar issues visas, but the procedure for 'newcomers' can take up to a week even for accredited journalists and aid workers. Start your application process early in the week and remember that Friday afternoon, Saturday and Sunday are holidays. Visas cost US$ 30 and you will need two passport-size photos (there are studios in Saddar Bazaar). If you are a regular visitor to Afghanistan and sponsored by the UN or a major aid agency you may be able to get a visa in as little as one day.

Consulate General of the Islamic State of Afghanistan
Gul Mohar Lane, University Town
(GPO Box 119), Peshawar.
Tel: +92 (91) 842486 Mobile: +92 (351) 290133

Local Rules

Peshawar is a Muslim town and you should respect the local dress code. The NWFP became strongly fundamentalist during elections in 2002 and Taliban-style restrictions have been introduced, such as the removal of 'offensive' cinema billboards depicting women. There is also much more aggression and resentment towards Westerners since the US-led intervention in Afghanistan, given that so many Pakistani frontier tribesmen support the Taliban. Both expatriate men and women should cover their legs and wear reasonably loose-fitting clothes, but there is no need to wear *shalwar kameez* around town. If you must take your kit off, the pools at the Khyber Club and Pearl Continental Hotel are the best place to do it.

If as a woman you are touched-up in the bazaar, do not keep quiet otherwise the offender may think you quite like it! Make a scene, shout, even scream. By reacting strongly you will probably shame him into stopping or running off. An EFG editor sent one assailant of a female colleague into the gutter to the hearty congratulations of numerous bazaar-goers.

Medical

Make sure your vaccinations are up to date for polio, typhoid, tetanus, rabies and hepatitis A and B as vaccine quality in Pakistan cannot be guaranteed. Take precautions against malaria and diarrhoea. If you get sick, consult a medical NGO or call the Khyber Club for a list of doctors who could refer you to the Combined Military Hospital (SEE PERSONAL HEALTH).

Money

If you are bringing cash, US dollars and euros are widely accepted. The newer and crisper the notes the better. You will get a better rate for big denomination bills. Most of the money-changers are down at Khyber Bazaar in the Old Town or at Saddar Bazaar in the Cantonment. Check what the official bank rate is before street-dealing on the "open market". Travellers' cheques are only accepted at the major banks. Personal cheques on US and UK banks are also accepted if the dealer knows you.

Post & Telecommunications

There are some reports of mail being opened at the GPO in University Town, so it may be better to send your letters from the post office in Saddar Bazaar. For important documents or cash, try to find someone flying out of the country who can post it for you. A courier service operates between Peshawar and Kabul.

Mobile telephones can be rented or bought from a number of companies based in Islamabad. While local calls cost more, international calls by mobile phone are up to three times cheaper than calling from a hotel. There are numerous Internet cafes operating, some speedier than others, particularly along the GT Road in University Town.

Recreation

For couch-potatoes and sun-worshippers the **Khyber Club** is the best place to relax: swimming with poolside waiter service is laid on, plus satellite TV and a video library. A pool table is upstairs and tennis is over the road. There is a **squash and tennis club on Park Road**, University Town, which costs PakRupees 200 per month to join.

The **Pearl-Continental Hotel** has a swimming pool, badminton, health club and golf course. There is also squash and tennis available on temporary membership basis at the rather sleepy **Peshawar Club**, a throwback from the British Raj. It used to be one of the most imperious clubs in India, but went virtually broke when Pakistan introduced prohibition for Muslims and the establishment lost one of its best sources of revenue.

For the more adventurous, there is **trekking** up in the Swat, Chitral and Gilgit valleys to the north. Call Green Tours at Green's Hotel for more details. The **Khyber Steam Safari** is a novel way to visit the Afghan border. The British built the railway from Peshawar up to Landi Kotal on the Khyber Pass in the 1920s. A must for train-spotters, the route takes in 34 tunnels, crosses 92 bridges and culverts and the 42 km journey takes about four and a half hours up and three hours back. By road the trip to the border takes about an hour.

For more details of steam railway tours call the Railway or a local travel agency such as Sehrai Travels and Tours.

Shopping

Peshawar is a shopper's paradise – you can buy anything from rubber bands to rocket-propelled grenades if you know where to look. The Old City is full of bazaars (including **Khyber Bazaar**) crammed full of carpets, clothes stalls, teashops, brassware, jewellers, leather goods, fruit, vegetables and pyramids of spices bright as powder-paint.

Saddar Bazaar in the Cantonment is the place for off-the-peg clothes, books and other modern kit. Peshawar is a good place to have clothes tailor-made, and there are outfitters on The Mall and down the Jamrud Road.

For contraband and electrical goods, **Smugglers' Bazaar** is where things fall off the backs of lorries. Known locally as the Karkhanai Bazaar, it lies near the Kachagari refugee camp on Jamrud Road. For counterfeit British guns, drive to **Darra Adam Khel**, 40 minutes south of Peshawar on the road to Kohat. The Pathan tribes have made arms here since 1897, when the British tolerated the trade in return for unmolested travel along frontier roads. Check locally to find out if foreigners are still allowed to visit.

Weather

Weather in Peshawar is hot and sticky most of the year, although relatively pleasant from October to February, and hotter and stickier from June to August. Bring loose-fitting cotton clothes, a sunhat and plenty of patience.

ESSENTIAL A-Z

E. Girardet

Clothing & kit

During the Soviet-Afghan war, most reporters and aid workers operating on a crossborder basis would dress up in *shalwar kameez* with a *patou* (brown woollen shawl/blanket) slung over their shoulders while wearing a turban (mainly in Pashtun areas) or *pakool* (brown woollen hat, Massoud-style) for the northern regions. Often such garb was simply the best way to slip by the Pakistani control posts and to avoid informers inside Afghanistan, but was not necessarily needed inside resistance-held areas.

By the mid and late 1980s, US and European army surplus gear made its appearance among many *mujahideen* – and foreigners. Once inside the country, it was often easier to wear a pair of jeans or trousers, particularly if trekking through the Hindu Kush. There is nothing worse than trying to negotiate rocky terrain with a pair of loose flowing *shalwars.*

Nevertheless, for many foreigners during the 1980s, it became *de rigeur* to sport the Afghan 'clandestine' look. Some did it very well too, particularly the French photographers and visiting Paris intellectuals with their *causes celebres.* They managed to make their Afghan garb look thoroughly *romantique* and *Rimbaudesque* (the poet, not the macho hunk) with a silk scarf flung haphazardly – but carefully – around their necks. It looked good in *Paris Match.* The Brits, some of whom were ex-military, tended to be more down-to-earth by combining the best of SAS equipment (night-sights, bivvy bags and survival belts) with solid trekking gear from mountaineering outfitters. The Americans often arrived with the latest but not necessarily most practical gear (computers, water filters and ABC airline guides); but they made sure they picked up the best-looking Afghan costumes for their rugged 'reporters-at-the-front' on-camera presentations. One blond-haired Dutch journalist insisted on wearing the 'Soviet look,' a khaki *shalwar kameez* topped by a khaki Red Army hat, which did not exactly endear him with his colleagues, particularly when travelling in resistance-held areas.

Perhaps the most popular – and useful – import, quickly copied by the bazaar tailors and increasingly worn by image-conscious *mujahideen*, was the Banana Republic photo-vest with all its pockets. But what mattered most of all then – and now – if working in the field was a solid pair of boots.

Dress for non-combatant Afghans has always been traditional, except prewar in some of the larger cities. The mini-skirts and sleeveless tops which some Afghan women wore in Kabul in the 1970s were very much the exception, not the rule. The all-covering tent-like *burqa* has been worn by mainly rural women since long before the Taliban arrived. Until the war and their exposure to crowded refugee camps, however, rural women remained unveiled in their villages or while working in fields. Only when strange males were present or when visiting towns did they cover up. The Taliban made it an across-the-board rule to wear the *burqa,* but since the end of 2001 many female returnees from Pakistan still wear them whenever in public, particularly if they have simply exchanged their Peshawar abodes for crowded conditions on the outskirts of Kabul or other towns.

Most visitors to Afghanistan nowadays do not try, or need, to disguise themselves as native Afghans. In Kabul and cities like Herat and Mazar-e-Sharif, growing numbers of Afghans working in official positions are wearing pin-striped suits, and are proud of them. For many, suits signify a return to normalcy. Even General Atta, the military boss of Mazar, is more likely to be encountered in a stylish city suit than battle fatigues. He also has a penchant for wearing furry or colourful woollen caps, as if fresh from the ski slopes.

However, since the US-led intervention in October 2001, insecurity has drastically accelerated in eastern and southern frontier areas, where Westerners are now being specifically targeted. From the point of view of personal security, it would be best to dress in a low-key way and avoid carrying conspicuous valuables. But don't fool yourself that everyone will think you're a Pashtun tribesman. While some concessions have to be made to Muslim customs – especially by Western women – it is important to "be who you are" and remain straightforward about your work so as not to arouse suspicion.

The following are some general suggestions for suitable clothing for Western visitors. See the relevant travel chapters for advice on local rules and climate at different times of year.

Women

In general, ordinary loose-fitting Western dresses and below-the-knee skirts can be worn, with loose trousers on underneath to cover the legs, calves and ankles. Wear blouses with long sleeves and avoid low bust-lines or figure-hugging outfits. Even though the Taliban are gone (at least in most areas), conservatism remains. When you are in public, cover your head with a shoulder-length scarf or *chador*. In more traditional parts, *shalwar kameez* may be more appropriate. In more liberal areas you may not need to wear a *chador* at all. Be careful when sitting on the floor in the presence of Afghan men to cover your knees and feet.

Men

Long trousers and long-sleeved shirts are fine. Shorts should not be worn in public except when playing sports within NGO or UN compounds. Jeans or khaki trousers with bush jackets or other forms of 'rugged' dress are fine if travelling or operating in the field. When visiting government officials or educated people, jackets and ties are appropriate, if the weather is not too hot. Clean, presentable clothes are a sign of respect for your Afghan hosts or colleagues. There is no need for Western men to grow beards or wear headdress.

Thorkell Thorkelsson/International Federation

Clothing for the frontline

If your work takes you into the line of fire, you must wear the right kit to protect yourself. Flak jackets are essential to safeguard you against the threat of flying shrapnel and stray bullets. Make sure the jacket has removable ceramic plates front and rear to protect your heart. Each plate should weigh around five kilos to be at all effective, and should be fitted when there is a threat of gunfire. Practise wearing the jacket with plates fitted to get used to the weight before going to the frontline. Combat helmets are also essential and have saved the lives of a number of journalists working in Afghanistan. Good walking boots – already worn in – are essential. Wear a survival belt containing a first aid kit, shell dressing, Swiss army knife, string, space blanket, poncho, pen, notebook and your personal documents. If you lose everything else, you have at least got this. An essential item for all travel in Afghanistan is a portable shortwave radio to catch the latest on the *BBC, VOA* or *Deutsche Welle*, particularly in times of crisis.

ESSENTIAL READING

SAS Survival Handbook: How to Survive in the Wild, in Any Climate, on Land or at Sea, John 'Lofty' Wiseman, Collins (London, 2003). A useful book if travelling in difficult terrain or war zones.

Medicine for Mountaineering and Other Wilderness Activities, Ed. James A. Wilkerson, MD, Mountaineers Books (Seattle, 1996). For backcountry and mountain trekking.

Festivals & holidays

Festivities in Afghanistan have made a resurgence since the departure of the Taliban. Music and kite flying, once banned by the Religious Police, are back. Roadside hotels and *chaikhane* ring with the songs of Hindi movies and MTV – something unimaginable during the Taliban era. Friday remains the weekly holiday, unlike Pakistan which observes a Western-style weekend. This can make liaison between agencies in both countries difficult from Thursday afternoon to Monday morning. The following official holidays are observed:

15 February: National Survival Day. Celebrating defeat of the Soviet Union.

21 March: New Year's Day (*Now-Roz*), also known as Farmers' Day. Agricultural fairs and *buzkashi,* the Afghan version of polo.

1 May: Labour Day

19 August: Independence Day. Celebrating freedom from the British in 1919.

31 August: Pashtunistan Day.

9 September: National Assembly Day.

15 October: Deliverance Day. Commemorated the victory of King Nadir Shah over Bacha Saqao in 1929.

24 October: United Nations Day

Islamic religious holidays are set according to the lunar calendar and hence, from a Western point of view, vary in timing from year to year. The main festivals are as follows:

Ashura: 10th day of *Moharram,* otherwise known as Martyrs' Day, anniversary of the death of Husain, cousin and son-in-law of the Prophet.

Mawlud-e-Sharif: The Prophet's Birthday

Ramazan: (also *Ram'zan* or *Ramadan*) the month of fasting

Id ul-Fitr: Three day feast at the end of *Ramazan*

Id-e-Qurban (Azha): Day of sacrifice during the month of the *Hajj* (pilgrimage to Mecca)

Shepherd boy in Paghman J. Walter

Health tips

"When you're wounded
and left on Afghanistan's plains,
An' the women come out to cut up what remains,
Jest roll to your rifle an' blow out your brains,
An' go to your Gawd like a soldier."

Rudyard Kipling, Barrack-room Ballads (1892)

The main threats to personal health in Afghanistan – other than landmines and unexploded ordnance – are malaria and infections caused by dirty food and drink. None of these can be prevented by injections, so be aware of the dangers at all times, take the necessary precautions and you should be able to avoid the Kipling option. Carry a basic first aid kit on you to cope with malaria, diarrhoea, headaches, animal bites, small cuts etc., plus sterilized needles and syringes for emergencies. Ticks and bedbugs can also be a problem, particularly when staying in rural areas with cattle in the vicinity. Try to bring all the drugs you need with you, although the quality of Pakistani-manufactured drugs has greatly improved in recent years.

Immunization

Make sure you visit your doctor or a specialist travel clinic as soon as you know you are travelling to the region, as vaccination regimes can take several months to be administered. The London-based organization, MASTA (see below) will send you a health brief tailored to visiting Afghanistan, with details of which diseases to avoid and how. What follows is based on their health brief for rural Afghanistan, dated December 2003. The following immunizations are strongly recommended:

Polio: a viral disease usually transmitted via contaminated food and water. The live vaccine lasts 10 years and is given as drops on the tongue, although an injectable vaccine is available.
Hepatitis A: a virus, usually transmitted via contaminated food and water, which attacks the liver and may cause jaundice and a prolonged illness. Mod-

ern vaccines are very effective and, if boosted at 6-12 months, provide at least 10 years of protection.
Typhoid fever: bacteria which enter through the mouth, causing high fever and even coma. An injected vaccine is available, boosted every three years, although this is less important for short-term visitors staying in clean accommodation.
Tetanus: a serious bacterial disease caused by contamination of wounds. The vaccine provides 10 years of protection and can be combined with a diphtheria vaccine.
Diphtheria: usually transmitted by close contact with infected people. A booster vaccine lasts 10 years. In mid-2003 an outbreak was reported in a refugee camp in Kandahar province.

The following immunizations should be considered, in consultation with your doctor:

Hepatitis B: a virus, transmitted sexually or by puncturing the skin with contaminated instruments (e.g. needles), which can cause liver damage and eventual liver failure. The vaccine is usually a 3-dose course over six months, but can be accelerated.
Rabies: invariably fatal once symptoms begin, rabies is transmitted by the saliva of infected animals (a scratch or lick may be sufficient). However, modern vaccines are very effective.
Tuberculosis (TB): transmitted through close contact with infected people. The BCG vaccine is more effective in children than adults, and a booster provides no benefit.

Take advice from your doctor on coverage against Japanese encephalitis and meningitis, but at present these are not considered necessary.

Malaria and leishmaniasis

Malaria can be a killer, and exists all year round in regions of Afghanistan below 2,000 metres. Spread by mosquitoes that bite from dusk till dawn, it is present in both rural and urban areas (especially Jalalabad, Kandahar, Pul-e-Khumri and Faizabad).

There is no vaccination available to prevent it, so the best way to avoid getting malaria is to avoid getting bitten by mosquitoes in the first place. Wear long-sleeved shirts, socks and long trousers, especially from early evening onwards when the mosquitoes come out. Use insect repellent (containing 35% or more of the active agent DEET) on all exposed skin and apply it regularly. If your skin reacts to DEET-based repellent, try a natural lemon-eucalyptus alternative. At night, try using smoke coils (outside) and plug-in "King Mat" vaporizers (inside). Spray inside rooms to kill any rogue mosquitoes and use a fan or air conditioning in your bedroom – especially in summer. Finally, buy an insecticide-treated bednet before you go, obtainable from major airports and travel equipment shops, and make sure you sleep under it every night. If you follow this advice, your chances of getting malaria become much lower.

Two types of malaria are found in Afghanistan and Pakistan: 75 percent is due to *vivax* malaria, the non-lethal type, while 25 percent is due to *falciparum* malaria, which causes more severe symptoms and even death if left undiagnosed or untreated. *Falciparum* malaria is resistant to chloroquine in Afghanistan and must be treated with effective alternative drugs.

Prophylaxis with malarone or mefloquine (Larium) will give protection against both forms of malaria. Malarone has few side effects but is expensive and has to be taken daily. Mefloquine needs only to be taken weekly but the side effects can be distressing and in extreme cases may include anxiety, depression and other psychiatric disturbances. Prophylaxis with weekly chloroquine (two tablets) and daily proguanil (two tablets) will protect against *vivax* malaria but cannot be guaranteed to protect against resistant *falciparum* malaria, which is why malarone or mefloquine are favoured. These courses of drugs must be started one week prior to arrival in the malarial region, taken without a break while there, and continued until one month after departure from the malarial area.

However, no prophylaxis is perfect, so if you develop a fever (38 degrees Celsius or higher, starting at least one week after first potential exposure to malaria) visit a competent laboratory or health NGO and have a blood smear examined for malarial parasites. Other symptoms of malaria include periodic shivering, headache, body ache and possible bouts of diarrhoea. Vomiting can be a symptom of the potentially deadly *falciparum* malaria. For adults, curative treatment of *falciparum* malaria requires a single dose of three Fansidar tablets, that of *vivax* malaria requires 10 tablets of chloroquine taken over three days. Follow dosage instructions exactly.

Visitors should take particular precautions against malaria if intending to stay overnight in rural areas during the main transmission season from May to November. While it is mainly a rural disease in Pakistan and Afghanistan, you may be troubled by 'nuisance' mosquitoes in urban environments. Malaria is rare in Herat and Mazar-e-Sharif but is common in rice-growing areas in the northern provinces of Kunduz and Baghlan, in the eastern provinces of Nangarhar, Kunar, Laghman and Khost, and in the southern provinces of Kandahar and Helmand.

Kabul lies at too high an altitude for malaria transmission; the risk in that city is from cutaneous leishmaniasis, a disease transmitted by biting sandflies, in which ulcerous lesions occur on the face and limbs around the site of the bite and persist for up to one year unless treated. At the peak of the epidemic, in 1996, 12 percent of the Kabul population had active leishmaniasis. In mid-2003, there were an estimated 200,000 cases of leishmaniasis in Kabul alone. The current prevalence is around three percent.

The five Fs of dysentery

Dysentery (bloody diarrhoea) is usually caused by infections picked up from one or more of the following 'carriers':

FOOD – FINGERS – FAECES – FLIES – FOAMITES (ANTS)

You can reduce the chances of getting diarrhoea by one third simply by washing your hands before eating!

Thorkell Thorkelsson/International Federation

Diarrhoea and cholera

Diarrhoea is caused by careless eating and drinking. Most visitors to this region suffer from it sometime during their stay. Chances of getting diarrhoea can be reduced by one third simply by washing your hands with soap and water before handling and eating food.

Never drink tap water – always boil it (for 20 minutes), add chlorine or use an iodine-resin water purifier. Use purified water or green tea (it will have been boiled) for brushing your teeth. Activated charcoal filters are OK as long as you clean them regularly. Check bottles of "mineral water" for intact seals. Avoid ice in drinks, ice-cream, unpasteurised milk, salads, raw vegetables and seafood (unlikely in Afghanistan!). Yoghurt (*maast*) is a popular side dish with many Afghan meals and should be fine to eat, but make sure that it is fresh and has not been watered down. Avoid cold meats and sauces and make sure any meat you eat has been well-cooked. Stick to food which is piping hot. Drink tea rather than Pepsi (often locally bottled) or blended fruit juice. A good general rule is: ***Cook it, Peel it, or Leave it.***

If you get diarrhoea you must rehydrate with large amounts of purified water and oral rehydration salts (ORS). ORS can taste pretty grim so try and buy flavoured ones and drink with cold water. Don't stop eating, but stick to simple, dry, non-fatty food. Drugs such as Imodium (one dose after each loose stool, up to a maximum of eight a day) can help relieve the symptoms. Most cases of travellers' diarrhoea end within 3-4 days. A single dose of 500mg of the antibiotic ciprofloxacin (on prescription) can often reduce this to one day.

Cholera is a food/water-borne illness causing acute watery diarrhoea, vomiting and dehydration. A large outbreak was reported in Kabul during 2002, affecting over 6,500 people. However, the vaccine for cholera is ineffective and the condition can be easily treated.

HIV/AIDS

HIV/AIDS is increasing more rapidly in Central Asia than anywhere else in the world – from 1999 to 2002, the number of people infected almost tripled. It is believed to be driven mainly by intravenous drug use among young men and is becoming a growing problem in the countries bordering Afghanistan. Stigma and denial are helping the disease spread. Apart from the usual advice to practice safe sex, make sure you avoid contaminated needles. If travelling to remote areas, carry a set of sterilized needles and syringes to guard against possible infection. The most common circumstances for blood transfusions are following road traffic accidents, so make sure you drive carefully and wear seatbelts at all times.

Emergencies

In a medical emergency the best course of action is to go to the office of the nearest international NGO specializing in health, or find a hospital supported by the International Committee for the Red Cross (ICRC). The ICRC will operate on all emergency cases and can arrange emergency air evacuations if necessary. But don't pester health NGOs with requests for pills you forgot to bring out. Make sure your travel insurance covers you for emergency medical repatriation, as well as protecting you in the event of "war and kindred risks" (SEE INSURANCE).

Kit list

- First aid kit: plasters, bandages, antiseptic cream/spray, scissors, tweezers, thermometer
- Consider sterilized needle & syringe kit, emergency dental kit
- Medicine: painkillers, anti-malarial drugs (including curative Fansidar dose), oral rehydration salts, Imodium or Loperamide for diarrhoea, antibiotics (e.g. ciprofloxacin)
- Record of your blood group, vaccination history/certificates, travel insurance policy and emergency contact numbers
- Insect repellent, impregnated bednet, plug-in insecticide vaporizer
- Iodine resin water purifier, water purification tablets
- Sun block

This health information was correct as at December 2003. However, disease profiles and drugs change, so always check with your doctor for the latest health advice before going to Afghanistan. We would like to thank Dr Mark Rowland of the London School of Hygiene and Tropical Medicine for updating the information on malaria. Immunization advice is based on the latest MASTA health brief for a long-term visit to rural Afghanistan. We are also grateful to Dr Antony van der Bunt and Dr Tim Winch for general health advice.

ESSENTIAL CONTACTS

The London Hospital for Tropical Diseases
The Hospital has a Travel Clinic which provides advice, up-to-date information on all anti-malarials and prophylactic drugs, consultant-led clinics, screening, 24-hour healthline, fax-back service and range of travel products.
Tel:
+44 (20) 7388 9600 (appointments)
+44 (20) 7387 9300 Ext. 5967 (clinical research)
+44 (0) 9061 33 77 33 (travellers healthline advisory service)
www.uclh.org/services/htd/travelclinic

Medical Advisory Services for Travellers Abroad (MASTA)
UK-based 24-hour travel healthline and website, which provides latest health news, general health advice for travellers, 'healthbriefs' tailored to particular locations and health supplies by post.
52 Margaret Street, London W1W 8SQ
Tel: +44 (0) 9068 224100
www.masta.org

International Traveler's Hotline
US-based healthline, Monday-Friday 0800-1630 (EST)
Tel: +1 (404) 332 4559
US Centers for Disease Control
www.cdc.gov

Travellers' and Migration Medical Unit
Policlinique de Médecine (Asia Dept.)
Hôpital Cantonal Universitaire
25, rue Micheli-du-Crest
1211 Geneva 14
Switzerland.
Tel: +41 (22) 372 9603

ESSENTIAL READING

Where There is No Doctor, David Werner, Hesperian Foundation (revised edition, 1992)
Staying Healthy in Asia, Africa and Latin America, Moon Publications, 722 Wall St, Chico, CA 95928 USA
Wilderness Medicine, Beyond First Aid, William Forgey, Globe Pequot Publishers (5th edition, 1999)

Insurance

As Afghanistan is still considered a conflict zone, most of the insurance companies we contacted said they would not cover groups and individuals operating in the region. One large Swiss company proudly declared that it did not take "risks with risks." The security situation during 2003, particularly in the southern and eastern parts of the country where aid workers have been deliberately targeted, has not helped matters. The vast majority of travel insurance policies will not provide cover for "war and kindred risks".

The United Nations and other organizations have their own coverage but often forbid their employees to remain in a conflict area if the security situation deteriorates. The International Committee of the Red Cross, which operates in war zones throughout the world, has special arrangements with Lloyds which are not available to NGOs and journalists. A number of travel companies, such as Cooks, have their own insurance deals but not for war zones. This poses a serious problem for NGO aid workers, particularly volunteers, and freelance journalists (often the only ones doing the real reporting on a long-term basis) who have to fork out considerable funding every month to provide coverage. Several initiatives have been proposed to major donors, such as the European Union, to develop group cover for those required to work in conflict zones rather than oblige aid groups, which can ill afford it, to spend thousands in hard-won donations on insurance. So far, this has not happened.

There are a few specialist brokers around, plus companies prepared to do deals – but beware: cover does not come cheap! Prices vary widely, so it is worth shopping around. After much research, EFG editors have come up with the options below.

ESSENTIAL CONTACTS

ACE Insurance (Brokers: SARL MBA)
Cover and Risk Management for Expatriates
Administrative Offices: BP 714 – 58007 NEVERS CEDEX, France
Tel: +33 (3) 8659 9572 Fax: +33 (3) 8659 9571
Email: geodesk@wanadoo.fr
ACE is an extremely helpful and not too expensive group which covers journalists, aid workers and others in war zones. Provides variable cover, including negotiable life insurance. They insure the French NGO Réporters sans Frontières.

AKE Group
Mortimer House, Holmer Road, Hereford, HR4 9TA, UK
Tel: +44 (0) 1432 267111 Fax: +44 (0) 1432 350227
Email: services@akegroup.com
Web: www.akegroup.com
Gallery 4, Lloyd's Building, 12 Leadenhall Street, London, EC3V 1LP, UK
Tel: +44 (0) 20 7816 5454 Fax: +44 (0) 20 7816 5455
Email: services@akegroup.com

AKE LLC, 1825 I Street NW, Suite 400, Washington DC 20006, USA
Tel: +1 202 429 2026/2016
Email: services@akellc.com

AKE Asia-Pacific Pty Ltd, Level 4, 201 Miller Street, North Sydney, NSW 2060, Australia
Tel: +61 (0)2 9025 3525 Mobile: +61 412 552 888
Email: australia@akegroup.com

AKE can organise insurance for war zones as well as offering a 5-day course entitled 'Surviving Hostile Regions' – those who successfully pass the course qualify for one year's free hostile environments insurance cover (SEE SECURITY TIPS).

Greenshields, Cowie & Co Ltd
St Nicholas House, St Nicholas Road, Sutton, Surrey, SM1 1EL, UK.
Tel: +44 (0)20 8643 3533
Email: rai.bramdaw@crownagents.co.uk

HMT Insurance Brokers Ltd
Old Bank House, 26 Station Approach, Esher, Surrey, KT10 0SR, UK.
Tel: +44 (0)20 8398 2362 Fax: +44 (0)20 8398 4568
Email: hmt@hmitb.co.uk

Marsh Private Client Services
Garden House, 42 Bancroft, Hitchen, Herts, SG5 1DD, UK.
Tel: +44 (0)1462 42800 Fax: +44 (0)1462 42008

West Midland Brokers Ltd.
4A St Nicholas St, Hereford HR4 0BG, UK.
Tel: +44 (0) 1432 268301 Fax: +44 (0) 1432 355235
Email: brianjbarnard@hotmail.com

West Midland provides tailor-made insurance cover for people operating in hostile environments or in dangerous jobs. Premiums reflect the current level of risk and vary according to where you go and what you do. If your journey is limited to Kabul, for example, cover would be cheaper than if you go to more dangerous parts of Afghanistan. Costs for cover may come down if you complete a hostile environments training course.

Other contacts for general medical coverage in Afghanistan but not specific war risks:

International Health Insurance – Denmark a/s
Palaengade 8, DK-12881, Copenhagen K, Denmark
Tel: +45 (33) 15 3099 Fax: +45 (33) 32 2560
Email. Ihdk@ibm.net
Web: www.ihi.dk

Medibroker – Independent Health Insurance Broker
Medibroker House, 17 Seatonville Road, Whitley Bay, Tyne & Wear, NE25 9DA, UK
Tel: +44 (0) 191 297 2411 Fax: +44 (0) 191 251 6424
Email: advice@medibroker.com
Medibroker works with key insurance companies specialised in expatriate coverage.

Private Patient Plan Healthcare
Phillips House, Crescent Road, Tunbridge Wells, Kent, TN1 2PL, UK
Tel: +44 (0) 1892 503856 Fax: +44 (0) 1892 503189
Web: www.ppphealthcare.co.uk
PPP provides good value annual cover, including £5 million for medical emergencies or repatriation. Will cover medical expenses arising from landmine injuries in Afghanistan, as long as you can prove you've taken 'reasonable care' to avoid injuring yourself. However, make sure you get some confirmation of this in writing. Does not cover risks arising in conflict situations.

REGA
GAC, PO Box 1414, 8058 Zurich Airport, Switzerland
Tel: +41 (1) 654 3222 Fax: +41 (1) 654 3590
Web: www.rega.ch
REGA is a member-supported medical air service which can fly you out of war zones and back to Europe if injured or sick.

Journalism & reporting in the field

During the Soviet-Afghan war, it was in many respects far easier to report the situation in Afghanistan than during the Taliban period or, ironically, following the American-led intervention of October 2001. This is despite the fact that journalists in the 1980s were often required to travel by foot with the *mujahideen* for days or weeks at a time prior to filing their reports. The portable satphone or TV satdish were still too impractical for journalists to carry with them and it was difficult to obtain a balanced and accurate view of the situation in the country as a whole. Travelling 'inside' often meant relying on the access provided by a single guerrilla faction which sought to project its own very partisan view of the war. Journalists, however, usually had choice over "how, where and what" they sought to cover. There was a degree of healthy competition among the various *mujahed* parties to attract those reporters with the most influential access to the outside world (e.g. US television networks) as a means of raising their own profiles. Some guerrilla groups operated more effectively than others, and journalists tended to focus on those with proven track records. The 'when,' however, was always unpredictable as planning in Afghanistan had to be implemented on an *ad hoc* basis. Even the simplest arrangements or itineraries tended to change on a daily basis (SEE MEDIA).

Following the Soviet withdrawal in 1989 and the takeover of Kabul by the *mujahideen* in 1992, media attention was limited generally to human interest stories. These focused primarily on the hardships of the people of Kabul who lived under an almost constant barrage of rockets and artillery. Much of the coverage remained limited, with Afghanistan well off the map of global attention. Nevertheless, the *mujahideen's* new Minister of Defence, former guerrilla commander Ahmed Shah Massoud, continued with his tradition of media openness to foreign journalists. There was little interference. (This very openness led to his assassination by Al Qa'eda assailants in September 2001, as no appropriate check-up was made of his two Tunisian Arab killers, who posed as journalists for a Middle East television network). His aides were usually on hand to explain the party line and to protect reporters from the excesses of less disciplined fighters (such as confiscating camera equipment). On the other hand, Massoud's arch rival Gulbuddin Hekmatyar did little to encourage good press relations. The killing in 1994 by his men of a BBC radio correspondent did little for his media charm. Nor did his indiscriminate shelling of the Afghan capital, which destroyed much of the city and inflicted an estimated 50,000 deaths amongst the civilian population.

The Taliban takeover in September 1996 sparked renewed media interest. The International Committee of the Red Cross (ICRC) alone flew 120 journalists into the city in a matter of weeks. Many reports gave the impression that Kabul had changed overnight to a version of Phnom Penh at Year Zero. During the Taliban period, the dominant themes focused on the movement's treatment of women and some of the more extreme edicts promulgated in their drive to establish the world's purist Islamic state (SEE TALIBAN). The Taliban placed various restrictions on reporters, some ideological, others stemming from practical concerns, severely reducing overall coverage. For many observers, such policies turned Afghanistan into a 'closed' conflict more than ever before, at least in Taliban-controlled areas.

The Taliban banned photography and filming of living animals, including humans, on the grounds that the depiction of living creatures is prohibited under Islam (SEE PHOTOGRAPHY). They further prohibited reporters from talking to Afghan women, who were ordered not to have any contacts with males outside their own immediate families. It remained unclear, however, if this ban extended to female journalists. In fact, the Taliban seemed uncertain how to deal with Western female journalists entering Afghanistan (SEE WOMEN). In the United Front areas, mainly Badakhshan province prior to September 11, 2001, it remained relatively easy for journalists to travel. In many respects, it was no different from operating in Afghan civilian areas during the Soviet war.

By 2003, the situation had changed dramatically. Journalistically, one was still dealing with many of the same problems, notably the challenge of establishing reliable facts and figures on what was going, whether in the military or recovery sectors. With the start of US bombing of Taliban and Al Qa'eda forces, the Pentagon went out of its way to control information. There was, and still is, significant disinformation unloaded on journalists albeit sometimes not intentionally. Particularly during the early stages of the intervention, US military intelligence on-the-ground was considered by experienced aid workers and journalists to be generally poor. Even British military counterparts of the Americans privately expressed dismay at the way US forces conducted their operations based on flimsy local intelligence. This later raised questions among journalists covering the Middle East as to the veracity of US assertions regarding Iraq prior to the March 2003 US invasion.

As during the 1980s, when the US Central Intelligence Agency relied heavily on the Pakistanis for guidance (usually unabashedly biased toward Islamabad's own political agenda), the Americans in Afghanistan were once again relying heavily on compromised intelligence sources – this time provided by pro-United Front (Northern Alliance) warlords, commanders and other informants who often fingered political rivals as 'Taliban' or 'Al Qa'eda' to suit their own purposes. The Pentagon also made it difficult for journalists to operate on their own in security zones during the final days of the Taliban by persuading the United Front to limit media access. During the Soviet War, the *mujahideen* would have gone out of their way to help journalists reach the frontlines. Some Western journalists who attempted to penetrate security zones where Coalition Forces were operating were detained by US, Australian and other foreign troops and sent back.

During the first few months of the military intervention, the risks were far higher than during the Soviet war. Four journalists, for example, were executed by suspected Al Qa'eda or Taliban operatives along the Jalalabad to Kabul road in November 2001. Even experienced journalists with good local contacts hesitated to travel in former *mujahed*-controlled areas of eastern Afghanistan for fear of being betrayed by villagers or attacked by roaming pro-Taliban groups or simply bandits. No longer could a journalist rely on the hospitality of local commanders while travelling in many rural areas, a situation that has grown worse in much of eastern and southern Afghanistan from early 2003 onwards. Even in provinces such as Kunar or Nuristan where pro-government militia ensure relatively good security, it is best to stay in close touch with local commanders and aid groups.

For journalists working in Afghanistan now, it is vital to cultivate one's own mix of reliable sources. It is critical to report as much as possible from different parts of the country in order to obtain a relatively credible picture of the overall situation. Neither Kabul nor any other single region is representative of the country as a whole. As before, the Afghan capital remains the centre of media attention. News agencies, newspapers and broadcasters – many of whom came in force to cover the war against the Taliban and then the subsequent recovery process – still maintain offices, guest houses and other forms of representation. The security situation notwithstanding, it is now far easier to travel around the country, whether by road or by plane, than during the 1990s. This means that there is no reason why any serious journalist should not be able to put together a relatively comprehensive picture of what is going on.

Today, many aid workers and journalists tend to restrict their trips to Kabul with only the odd side-trip into the countryside, such as the Panjshair Valley or

"New home, new life"

The BBC World Service first began broadcasting educational dramas in Persian and Pashto in the late 1980s. The success of these led to the formation of the BBC Afghan Education Drama Project (AED) and the launching in 1994 of its radio soap opera "New Home, New Life", which now enjoys an enormous listenership believed to be between 70-80% of the Afghan population.

Up to 80 themes ranging from landmine awareness, cultural heritage and drug production to personal hygiene, safe birthing practices and environmental issues are addressed through the medium of an entertaining radio drama. Topics are discussed at monthly consultations with aid agency representatives. Three episodes are broadcast a week, repeated three times, including an omnibus edition specially aimed at women and timed to coincide with Friday prayers when their husbands are at the mosque. The broadcasts are reinforced by a monthly cartoon magazine which includes a section entitled "Where there is no school", aimed at teaching basic reading and writing skills.

Field-based partnerships with local NGOs reinforce the messages of the radio drama by compiling topical individual storylines and producing educational songs. A listener from Khost wrote in to say: "We have learnt lessons from the drama. For example, if someone is killed, then giving a girl away to atone for the deed is wrong. Before, when we saw a mine we diffused it ourselves, but now we inform the demining office. If sometimes there is a dispute now we settle conflicts by discussion [*jirga*]." Throughout much of Afghanistan "New Home, New Life" has become compulsory listening, and provokes considerable village discussion and uncannily realistic reactions. When one of its most popular characters, Khair Mohammed, was killed by a stray bullet, people in Chaman held condolence meetings to mourn his death. *JW*

the Plains of Shomali, if time permits. Kabul, however, is not Afghanistan. Over 70 percent of the country's population live in rural areas, which present a far different picture of conditions (little or no proper health care, fewer jobs and only limited access to facilities such as electric power). The urban-rural divide remains almost as pronounced today as it did at the beginning of the war. The educated urban elite, with whom Westerners have contact, tend to live in the Afghan capital and other cities and work for international aid agencies, within government ministries or, increasingly, for private enterprise. As a result, it is crucial to get out on the road, particularly to traditionally remote areas such as the Hazarajat, if one is to obtain a more accurate assessment of the country.

This is where many of the international aid agencies, whether UN organizations such as UNHCR or UNICEF or NGOs ranging from the Swedish Committee to Afghanistan, Médecins sans Frontières and Save the Children can prove exceptionally useful. Depending on one's story perspective (e.g. women's health in rural areas or environmental devastation), there are over 800 aid agencies operating inside Afghanistan today. Not all are credible, but there are many both capable and willing to assist serious journalists, particularly if their reporting relates to the organization's own particular activities.

Good publicity is good for funding. Aid agencies also have a responsibility to be transparent to their donors and the public-at-large, including Afghans themselves, with regard to what they are doing, so this is where a journalist can play a role. Certain organizations, however, have developed extremely arrogant 'holier-than-thou' attitudes, arguing that they have no responsibility via the media to their funding constituents (e.g. taxpayers and private contributors). At the same time, many organizations simply have not got the means to help because they are overstretched or lack the resources. Many, too, fail to grasp the importance of developing effective media or public information strategies and are at a loss with how to deal with journalists. Some, too, have been abused in the past (e.g. reporters who treat aid organizations as a means for free travel, lodging and food, or who have shown little sensitivity when dealing with patients in clinics or photographing women) and this has left a bad taste with regard to the media. So there needs to be a degree of understanding and give-and-take from both sides.

Communications & information

International communications have improved dramatically since the start of reconstruction in 2002. If you have not got a satphone, then you can buy or rent a mobile telephone from the AWCC in Kabul with a local sim card. By summer 2003, you could use such mobile phones in Kabul and other major towns such as Herat, Jalalabad and Mazar, but not in the countryside. Internet cafes have also been mushrooming in Kabul with facilities available at the Intercontinental Hotel, the Aina Media and Cultural Centre, the departure lounge of Kabul international airport and elsewhere (SEE TELECOMMUNICATIONS & RADIO).

Before travelling to Afghanistan, journalists can call or email the United Nations Assistance Mission to Afghanistan (UNAMA) to arrange a briefing by the Public Affairs Officer, who can also put you in touch with other Public Affairs Officers from UN agencies working in Afghanistan, and can help plan itineraries.

Helpful points for working with aid agencies:

- **Contact aid agencies in advance:** If possible, get in touch with relevant aid agencies (either their headquarters or their Afghan offices) prior to leaving on assignment (SEE CONTACTS). Let them know when you plan to pass through, which stories you hope to explore and what sort of assistance you are looking for. A good UN or NGO communications officer may have useful ideas on how to develop a story and may be able to provide relevant background materials in advance. Some may also suggest other key sources. Serious aid agencies tend to recognize the need to promote issues (e.g. mother-child health education or human rights) rather than their own activities and are more than willing to help coordinate coverage with other groups.

- **Don't abuse your privileges as a journalist:** If an aid organization is willing to help organize a trip by providing transport or offering to put you up at one of its field operations, make it clear that you are willing to participate in the costs or make a donation. Most of the aid agencies will probably refuse, but the gesture will be well appreciated. It demonstrates your own seriousness. Sometimes a small gift, such as chocolate or a bottle or two, can make all the difference to field workers with few luxuries other than a tin of Nescafé or the occasional Mars bar. If the aid agency provides you with a driver and/or a translator, check to see whether you should cover their fees (particularly if someone is hired in) or at least offer a tip.

- **In-kind collaboration:** For photographers and camera teams, particularly freelance, some aid agencies are willing to provide free on-the-ground logistics in return for courtesy photographs or file footage that they can use for their own public information or promotional purposes.

- **Do not take aid workers for granted:** They have their own jobs to do. Make sure that your reporting activities (particularly television) do not undermine their work in the field. In the end, it is your personal relationship with aid workers that will determine how effectively you can collaborate with each other.

- **What you can expect inside Afghanistan:** UN officials in Afghanistan are happy to help journalists – within reason. They will readily demonstrate the work they are doing and talk about it. Many of them have considerable experience in Afghanistan and are very knowledgeable, but will not talk on record about other issues. They can advise you on how to get the permits you need, but will not be able to do this for you.

- **Respect security and other concerns:** As a journalist, you can come and go, but the aid agencies need to continue working. Sometimes, it may prove compromising if not dangerous to quote an aid worker, whether an international or a local. There have been incidents whereby aid workers have spoken out against local warlords and have suffered repercussions. Either double-check or use your common sense.

Rules & regulations

From the government point of view, journalists are meant to register with the Ministry of Foreign Affairs as soon as they arrive, or at least within several days. Many journalists, particularly those coming in on short trips, never bother with this. But government permits and letters-of-introduction often help for passing checkpoints or setting up meetings with commanders in the field. In Kabul, journalists should go to the Press Department of the Ministry of Foreign

Affairs with two photographs and a letter of introduction from your organization or a press card for registration.

Travelling to Afghanistan and getting around

Most journalists travel into Afghanistan via Dubai on regular commercial flights and then to Kabul on United Nations flights or Ariana Afghan Airways. Another route is via Islamabad and Peshawar, where you can fly with Ariana, PIA, UN, ICRC and PACTEC/Airserv International. Other routes have also opened up such as Azerbaijan Airways from Paris via Baku to Kabul and Swiss Skies from Washington and Geneva directly to Kabul (not operational at time of writing). The UN will fly journalists (US$ 400 one way) into Kabul, but insist on a letter of commission/employment from a recognised news organization and a valid visa. The UN does not give precedence to journalists. The ICRC will not usually fly journalists unless previously arranged. PACTEC/Airserv flies to many of the more isolated parts of Afghanistan either on a regular or charter basis There is a relatively trouble-free road from Peshawar to Jalalabad and Kabul. Travellers will need to get permits from the Khyber Tribal Agency office in Peshawar Cantonment to transit the tribal areas *en route* to the border.

Taxis are generally safe and good value. Be careful, however, of the Panjshairi Mafia cartel working with the Ministry of Tourism and Aviation who seek to charge you anywhere from US$ 20 to US$ 50 to drive you into town with an "officially approved" vehicle. Some are no more than thugs who have even threatened potential passengers (or other drivers) with violence unless their vehicles are used. Either arrange to be picked up or catch a ride with one of the aid agencies. Or simply walk out of the airport and pick up a regular cab at the gate for a couple of dollars. Curfews in Kabul and other towns come and go according to the security situation, and take special care when travelling in the countryside. Check with the UN on the latest security reports. The southern and eastern parts of Afghanistan have become extremely volatile with the upsurge of attacks against foreigners. Taxis are available for long trips, as are buses. In many cases, you can also fly between Afghan cities (SEE TRAVEL BY AIR, TRAVEL OVERLAND and SECURITY TIPS).

Visas

Most major Afghan embassies (Paris, London, Washington, UAE, Islamabad) can provide visas for journalists. You can also pick up a temporary visa on arrival at Kabul airport if you don't tell anyone and your powers of persuasion are good (SEE VISAS).

Maps

Since September 11th 2001, a handful of new, detailed maps of Afghanistan and the region have become available. It wasn't always this way... One EFG editor used a combination of tactical air pilotage charts, a CIA satellite map and a British 1893 map torn out of a book to travel through northeastern Afghanistan during the early 1980s. The aerial maps covered topography with a few select locations – some completely wrong – while the old map of the British Raj had more accurate names of villages and rivers albeit with curious spellings. Commercially available maps are detailed below.

For aid workers or those with a specific interest in humanitarian, development or security issues, the first port of call is the **Afghanistan Information Management Service** (www.aims.org.af). AIMS is part of the UN system, based in Kabul. Its map products are available in pdf format and include detailed city plans (see below for more map details). You can request maps by emailing: request@aims.org.af. AIMS works with the Afghan government's Central Statistics Office and Geodesy and Cartography Office to create computerized maps. This enables a number of different layers to be built up, each with its accompanying database of information sitting 'behind' the visual image. The process is known as GIS (Geographic Information Systems), whereby existing maps are scanned into a computer in a digitized format and then linked to a database of information, ultimately enabling the map to be 'questioned.' The first layer is the baseline map detailing topography, roads and buildings; subsequent layers could cover anything from minefield locations to water resources. Layers are created by a combination of remote-sensed satellite imagery and ground reconnaissance. To view GIS data, you can download ArcExplorer from the AIMS website or from www.esri.com. The UN's online information resource – **ReliefWeb** (www.reliefweb.int) – also has an extensive list of maps on Afghanistan which includes maps from governmental aid departments and other UN agencies.

The **Afghan Resource and Information Centre (ARIC)** – based in Peshawar, Pakistan – currently holds around 500 different sorts of maps – going right down to a scale of 1:50,000. A full bibliography of ARIC's materials is available on CD-ROM or as an online searchable database. For more information, visit: www.afghanresources.org.

Probably the only available source for maps of smaller Afghan towns and cultural sites is Nancy Hatch Dupree's *An Historical Guide to Afghanistan* (2nd

Edition, 1977) which can be found in bookshops in Peshawar and Kabul, or through ARIC Peshawar. In a wallet at the back of the book is a very clear but rather out of date street map of Kabul which is still useful for general orientation.

US military maps, produced from remote satellite imaging, of the entire region can be tracked down at Stanford's in London and the ARIC Library in Peshawar. Tactical Air Pilotage Charts (1:500,000) and Operational Navigational Charts (1:1,000,000) give detailed if somewhat out-of-date coverage of the whole country.

One of the largest private map collections in the world is held at the Royal Geographical Society in London. It contains one million sheets of maps and charts, 2,600 atlases, 40 globes and 700 gazetteers. It has numerous maps of Afghanistan, and those out of copyright may be photocopied. The Map Room is normally open for consultation by any "serious enquirer" – however, it was closed during 2003 for renovation. For more details visit: www.rgs.org.

Currently available maps of Afghanistan are listed below under the following headings: Region, Country, City, United Nations. The most recently published maps are listed first. Actual map titles are in bold. Those maps dated before 1984 do not contain the 'new' provinces of Kunar and Paktika.

REGION

AFGHANISTAN, PAKISTAN AND THE MIDDLE EAST – National Geographic Society
1:6 million
2001
77x60cm
This map includes Afghanistan and countries surrounding the Persian Gulf and Red Sea. Detail includes: coloured political borders, relief shading, different types of terrain, roads, railways, oilfields and pipelines.
Available from:
Edward Stanford, UK (£8.95)
National Geographic Society, US: www.nationalgeographic.com (US$7.99)

AFGHANISTAN AND SURROUNDING TERRITORY – GiziMap
1:3 million
2001
66x71cm
This map covers all Afghanistan, Pakistan and Tajikistan. Detail includes: relief shading, provinces, towns, roads, driving distances, railways, rivers, deserts, airports. The map is also available as a 'political' version, without relief shading but with countries in different colours.
Available from: Edward Stanford, UK (Physical – £6.99, Political – £7.95)

AFGHANISTAN, CENTRAL ASIA AND MIDDLE EAST – Jimapco
1:3 million
2001
Basic double-sided map. One side covers the region from Turkey to India and Uzbekistan to Yemen at 1:10 million. The other side shows Afghanistan at 1:3 million. Detail includes: spot heights, provinces, main towns, roads, rivers, railways, airports. Countries shown in different colours.
Available from:
Edward Stanford, UK (£5.95)
Jimapco: www.jimapco.com (US$5.95)

CASPIAN REGION/AFGHANISTAN/PAKISTAN – National Geographic Society
May 1999
31x20in
Double-sided map showing Afghanistan and countries bordering the Caspian and Black Seas. Other side details physical geography, major ethnolinguistic groups, pipelines, oil and gas export routes, oil fields and ports.
Available from:
National Geographic Society, US: www.nationalgeographic.com (US$8.99)

AFGHANISTAN PAKISTAN – RV Verlag
1:2 million
49x98cm
ISBN: 3575332169
Clear and informative map of both countries. Detail includes: relief shading, provinces, main and minor towns, roads, rivers, airports. It is a reprint, so not fully updated.
Available from:
Edward Stanford, UK (£8.95)

COUNTRY: AFGHANISTAN

AFGHANISTAN – ITMB Publishing
1:1 million
2002
98x68cm
A new first edition double-sided map (east on one side, west on other). Detail includes: basic relief shading, provinces, main towns, many villages, roads and tracks, rivers, airports, ruins and points of interest, index of place names.
Available from:
Edward Stanford, UK (£8.95)
www.itmb.com (Can$13.95)

AFGHANISTAN WALLMAP – Ayazi Publishing
1:1.5 million
2001
102x71cm
Probably the most detailed country map available, showing over 2,500 place names. Put together single-handedly by Abdullah Ayazi, a US-based Afghan who devoted three years to the task. Detail includes: towns, villages, major and minor roads, airports, pipelines, rivers, climate, historical sites and provincial boundaries; but no relief shading – only spot heights. Inset map (1:15 million) locates Afghanistan within the region.
Available from: Edward Stanford, UK (£17.95)

AFGHANISTAN LAND IN CRISIS – National Geographic Society
1:3.3 million
December 2001
31x20in
Excellent double-sided wall map. One side shows political map of Afghanistan, Pakistan and bordering countries. Detail includes: relief shading, provinces, main towns, roads, rivers, airports, historical sites, land area, population, GDP, troops. Other side shows satellite image of Afghanistan, plus colour photos, historical timeline, mini-maps of ethnic groups, natural disasters and refugee camps.
Available from:
National Geographic Society, US: www.nationalgeographic.com (US$8.99)

AFGHANISTAN – Reise Know-How Verlag
1:1 million
2001
70x92cm
ISBN: 383177031X
Double-sided map (west on one side, east on other) on waterproof paper. Detail includes: relief shading, provinces, main towns, roads, rivers, airports, tourist sites, index of place names
Available from:
Edward Stanford, UK (£7.95)
www.reise-know-how.de (Euro7.90)

AFGHANISTAN – Nelles Verlag
1:1.5 million
80x50cm
ISBN: 3886186652
Double-sided map (north on one side, south on other). Detail includes: relief shading, provinces, main towns, roads, rivers, airports, tourist sites, street plan of central Kabul
Available from:
Edward Stanford, UK (£5.95)
www.nelles-verlag.de (Euro7.90, CHF14.20)
Bookshops in Islamabad and Peshawar

NATIONAL ATLAS OF THE DEMOCRATIC REPUBLIC OF AFGHANISTAN – Geokart
Various scales
1984
27x37cm hardback
This atlas represents a joint Afghan-Polish mapping effort, started in 1977. It is the first original collection of thematic maps of the country and includes: 63 colour maps on 36 pages, showing Afghanistan's physical, social and economic geography. Data is from the period 1975-1981.
English and Dari
Available from:
Edward Stanford, UK (£98)
Some Kabul bookshops

CITY

The Afghanistan Information Management Service (www.aims.org.af), a UN-backed agency, provides a wide range of maps in hard copy or as online pdf documents. You can request maps by emailing: request@aims.org.af. The following list was correct as at December 2003. Map size is listed both physically (A1/A2 etc.) and electronically (KB).

- Hirat City Map (A3/A4, 40KB)
- Jalalabad City Map (A3/A4, 750KB)
- Kabul City Map (A1, 907KB)
- Kandahar City Map (A3/A4, 40KB)
- Kunduz City Map (A3, 86KB)
- Mazari Sharif City Map (A3/A4, 262KB)
- Location of Embassies, Ministries, Commissions and Courts in Kabul (A3, 275KB)
- Location of UN Offices in Kabul (A3, 306KB)

UNITED NATIONS

The Afghanistan Information Management Service (www.aims.org.af), a UN-backed agency, provides a wide range of maps in hard copy or as online pdf documents. You can request maps by emailing: request@aims.org.af. The following list was correct as at December 2003. Map size is listed both physically (A1/A2 etc.) and electronically (KB).

- Afghanistan Administrative Divisions in Dari (32 Province) (A1, 220KB)
- Afghanistan Administrative Divisions in English (32 Province) (A2, 225KB)
- Afghanistan Administrative Geo Codes (32 Province Divisions) (A2, 221KB)
- Afghanistan District Vulnerability Mapping – Accessibility (A3/A4, 832KB)
- Afghanistan District Vulnerability Mapping – Combined (A3/A4, 823KB)
- Afghanistan District Vulnerability Mapping – Food (A3/A4, 831KB)
- Afghanistan District Vulnerability Mapping – Health (A3/A4, 833KB)
- Afghanistan District Vulnerability Mapping – Landmines/UXO (A3/A4, 822KB)

- Afghanistan IDP Camps & IDP Concentrations (A2, 161KB)
- Afghanistan IDPs Aggregated to District (A2, 149KB)
- Afghanistan Land Cover Maps (A1)
- Afghanistan Physical Map (A1/A2, 1.15MB)
- Afghanistan Physical Map – North East (A1, 1.42MB)
- Afghanistan Physical Map – North West (A1, 902KB)
- Afghanistan Physical Map – South East (A1, 470KB)
- Afghanistan Physical Map – South West (A1, 778KB)
- Afghanistan Population Density 2002 (A1, 738KB)
- Afghanistan Provincial Health Maps in Dari (A4)
- Afghanistan Provincial Health Maps in English (A4)
- Afghanistan Provincial Maps (A1)
- Afghanistan Route Map (A1/A2, 549KB)
- Afghanistan Road Reconstruction Donors (A1, 459KB)
- Afghanistan Road Reconstruction Status (A1, 332KB)
- Afghanistan Rivers (A1, 674KB)
- Afghanistan Watersheds Map (A1, 780KB)
- Areas Potentially Blocked by Snow (A3, 404KB)
- Estimated Population Map 1998 (Central Statistics Office) (A2, 146KB)
- Estimated Population Map 2000 (Satellite) (A2, 142KB)
- Military Sectoral Activities (Custom Metric, 1.18MB)
- International NGOs Sectoral Activities in Afghanistan (Custom Metric, 1.92MB)
- Local NGOs Sectoral Activities in Afghanistan (Custom Metric, 1.51MB)
- United Nations Sectoral Activities in Afghanistan (Custom Metric, 1.87MB)
- 65 Sheet Topographical Maps of Afghanistan Showing Detail Down to Village Level (With Background) (A2, Average 800KB)

ESSENTIAL SUPPLIERS

- **Afghanistan Information Management Service (AIMS)**
  Wazir Akbar Khan, Kabul, Afghanistan
  Tel: +93 (0) 7028 5389 Email: request@aims.org.af
  Web: www.aims.org.af

- **Afghan Resource and Information Centre (ARIC)**
  2 Rehman Baba Road (UPO Box 1084),
  University Town, Peshawar, Pakistan
  Tel: +92 (0) 91 570 4392; 850 839; 570 2531; 570 2962
  Fax: +92 (0) 91 840 471
  Email: aric@brain.net.pk, info@afghanresources.org
  Web: www.afghanresources.org

- **Edward Stanford Ltd. (UK)**
  12-14 Long Acre, Covent Garden
  London WC2E 9LP, UK.
  Tel: +44 (171) 836 1321 Fax: +44 (171) 836 0189
  Web: www.stanfords.co.uk

- **International Map Trade Association**
  2629 Manhattan Avenue, PMB 281, Hermosa Beach, CA 90254-2447, U.S.A.
  Tel: +1 310 376 7731 Fax:+1 310 376 7287 Email: imta@maptrade.org
  Web: www.maptrade.org

- **National Geographic Society (US)**
  1145 17th Street N.W.
  Washington, D.C. 20036-4688, USA
  Tel: +1 813 979 6845 Web: www.nationalgeographic.com

- **Map Room, Royal Geographical Society**
  (with The Institute of British Geographers)
  1 Kensington Gore, London SW7 2AR, UK.
  Tel: +44 (0) 20 7591 3000 Fax: +44 (0) 20 7591 3001
  Email: info@rgs.org Web: www.rgs.org

Money & bargaining

Afghanistan is only just beginning to have a functioning banking system. In September 2003, President Karzai approved a law permitting foreign banks to operate in Afghanistan. Expatriate Afghans, particularly wealthy businessmen in Russia and the Gulf states, are thought to hold up to US$ 5 billion in savings – money the Afghan government would like to see repatriated. Initially, three banks were offered operating licenses: Standard Chartered of Britain, the National Bank of Pakistan and a microcredit bank supported by the Aga Khan Foundation. Standard Chartered announced they were intending to open a Kabul branch, enabling aid agencies and individuals to maintain US dollar or euro accounts as well as to transfer funds from abroad.

Although credit cards, mainly VISA, are accepted increasingly by some hotels and guest houses as well as Afghan entrepreneurs, many of whom have transferred their operations from Pakistan or have come from abroad, make sure that you bring enough cash. US dollars, euros and Pakistani rupees are the best. Go for new rather than old or creased notes to avoid fakes or being summarily rejected by the dealer. Larger denomination notes will fetch better rates of exchange. The market in Afghanistan is open rather than black, and currency trading is one of the few 'industries' thriving in the country (SEE ECONOMICS).

Changing money

Ask around for the current exchange rate and the best places to change money. Some dealers (if they trust you) take personal cheques from European and North American banks. The local currency is the *Afghani.* Prior to the December 2002 currency reform, there were three versions of the *Afghani* in operation. At early 1998 rates of exchange, you could buy 20,000-25,000 *Afghanis* for a dollar. By mid-2003, the new currency changed hands for between 50-60 *Afghanis* per dollar. If you are travelling via Pakistan, there are international banks in Peshawar and Islamabad which can give you Pak rupees in exchange for travellers' cheques or credit card cash advances. Bear in mind that if you intend to stay in UN guesthouses while in Afghanistan, they will only accept cash payments in dollars.

Select money dealers also function as 'banks' for currency transfers to and from abroad, much like Western Union; but they are costly, often demanding

10-15 percent. Known as the *hawala* system, transfers can be made immediately and in most major currencies. Your contact must pay US dollars, pounds sterling or euros to an Afghan currency representative abroad (a recent example was an Afghan fish 'n' chip shop in Islington), and the same amount, minus the commission, is made available to you in Kabul or Jalalabad.

Bargaining

As a foreigner, it is worth bargaining over luxury items such as carpets, glass or jewellery. Try the usual tricks – initial enthusiasm, mock horror at the exorbitant price, feigned disinterest, walkout and reluctant return, large amounts of green tea and good humour – and you should be able to knock between a third and two thirds off the asking price, depending how ruthless you are feeling. Blue glass sellers in Herat will demand two dollars per glass or vase but will come down to one dollar or 50 cents if pushed.

Even with the 2002 currency reform, most entrepreneurs, particularly those dealing with artefacts, still prefer to be paid in dollars or euros. Most ordinary Afghans shopkeepers, however, will accept local currency. Overall, the cost of living in Kabul and other cities is high and many support large families, often as the sole money earner. So when it comes to buying non-luxury goods, be generous and pay the asking price rather than arguing over a few cents which local traders need far more than you do. If you feel it is a matter of pride to bargain hard, pay the price agreed and but then, graciously with a knowing wink, offer a small *baksheesh* or tip for their good services. It is all part of cultivating good local relations.

Begging

The giving of alms to beggars is an acceptable and necessary facet of the Muslim faith. However, the combination of urban drift, unemployment, disability and poverty which arose from 25 years of war has given rise to many more beggars on the streets. This is aggravated in cities such as Kabul and Herat where numerous returnees have now migrated. Many widows, too, are dependent on their own meagre resources for survival, resulting in women begging for money in *burqas.* Lack of work and poor schooling force mothers to send their children out onto the streets to beg, especially in the NGO and UN quarters of town, such as Wazir Akbar Khan in Kabul. Some children will make an effort to sell you something or perform a service, such as shoe-cleaning or guarding your vehicle, in return for a few *Afghanis.* Prostitution is reportedly on the rise (SEE CHILDREN). Numerous children, too, sell newspapers and magazines, but many tend to be orphans operating in a coordinated manner with the Terre des Hommes orphanage in Kabul, so they are receiving a monetary return as well as food, shelter and education provided by the NGO.

Whether you should or should not give money to beggars is a desperately difficult question, for which each visitor must make a personal decision. Some feel that to give money only encourages dependency on handouts – precisely the situation that most aid agencies are trying to get away from in their programmes. They say that Westerners who hand out cash only encourage more and more aggressive begging. Others argue that a handful of *Afghanis* mean nothing to an expatriate but a great deal to an Afghan, although this itself

Thorkell Thorkelsson/International Federation

sounds patronizing. One solution is to give money to women or handicapped individuals but not to children. Some experienced aid workers, however, have suggested that time and attention are more important than money. If the coast is clear, speak to the women who beg and let them know that you understand their plight. Remind them why you are there and what you are doing to help. Banter and joke with the children who beg, and they will often forget about asking you for money. Or donate some funds to the NGOs dealing with street children and widows. You can probably help these people more by helping aid agencies provide appropriate assistance to children, widows and handicapped. Job-creation and food-for-work programmes can help alleviate begging and aid dependency.

Baksheesh

As in many developing countries, *baksheesh* can be regarded as a tip to a hotel porter or a taxi driver. But in Afghanistan, *baksheesh* is also the word for bribery (or extortion) to people in positions of influence such as a government official, policeman or a fighter cradling a kalashnikov. It is not advisable to palm government officials although many are certainly not averse to receiving some *Afghanis* or dollars in return for 'services' rendered. Many have to survive on less than 30-50 US dollars a month. *Baksheesh*, however, is definitely current in many areas. The taxis outside Kabul airport, for example, are run by a thuggish cartel of Panjshairis operating with the blessing of the Ministry of Aviation and Tourism. They have been reprimanded on various occasions by the UN and ISAF, but they still persist, often pushing or thumping Afghan interlopers seeking to assist foreign visitors. Clearly, they rely on newcomers not knowing the name of the game. The cartel charges US$ 20-50 per taxi to take you into town, a trip that normally costs 2-3 dollars with an ordinary taxi. The drivers maintain that the 'extra charge' or '*baksheesh*' is to cover the costs of providing security, but it is little more than a protection racket. The sooner these *mafiosi* are removed from the airport, allowing more open competition, the better.

Overall, *baksheesh* is up to you. As a form of bribery, however, it is not necessary. It can even be insulting to people with a deep tradition of hospitality – even given that so many people are without jobs. You may be able to get round a stubborn or obstructive official by reminding him that you are a *guest* in their country! Patience, banter and studied ignorance of what is being suggested are often the best ways of getting things done. Numerous experienced journalists and aid workers who have worked in Afghanistan since the early days of the war have never been obliged to pay bribes, despite often determined demands by various corrupt individuals. More often than not, the matter was turned into a joke (amid slight embarrassment) when it was realized that no bribes would be forthcoming.

Of course, there are always bad eggs, usually the higher up the ladder you go. The Peshawar-based resistance parties during the Soviet-Afghan war were notoriously corrupt as were many commanders, Pakistani government officials and others benefiting from the aid bandwagon. Even the humanitarian agencies were sometimes forced to pay for the honour of dispatching relief caravans into Afghanistan. Prior to the Taliban, numerous *ad hoc* checkpoints demanding 'tolls' (normally not from foreigners) used to abound along the main roads leading to Kabul and other main towns. These came to an end under the Taliban in their zones of control. Today, corruption is rife once again in the government with some ministers and their cohorts deeply involved in using their positions to aid and abet their own business activities.

Since the end of the Taliban era, however, local and regional warlords in the provinces, as well as police in the Afghan capital, are once again imposing roadblocks and checkpoints as a means of obtaining quick cash. This resurgence of unofficial road tolls is one reason why increasing numbers of Afghans are openly voicing a longing for the security imposed by the Taliban where such thieving was not permitted at risk of dire punishment.

Having said all this…the fatal mistake the British made, prior to their disastrous retreat from Kabul in January 1842, was to stop paying off the local tribal commanders between the capital and the British garrison at Jalalabad. Is there a difference between a payment for loyalty and a bribe? Best bear in mind the old adage: "You can always rent an Afghan but you can never buy one."

Photography & filming

Taking photographs or filming in Afghanistan has never proved the easiest of tasks, but that is no reason to be put off. The arrival of the Taliban made matters far more difficult but not impossible. Since their departure in the autumn of 2001, things have become a lot easier. Most Afghan men and children seem quite happy to have their photographs taken. During one recent tea stop at a *chaikhana* at Sarobi along the road from Kabul to Jalalabad, where Talib influences remain strong, patrons enthusiastically asked for their photographs to be taken. Photoshops have sprung up left and right (particularly near Passport Lane in Kabul) and the photographing and videoing of weddings and other occasions have now become the norm again. Nevertheless, as before, working with a camera requires a combination of persistence, wit, imagination and inordinate amounts of patience (SEE JOURNALISM, MEDIA).

An extraordinary array of photo-essays and television documentaries have emerged over the past quarter of a century about Afghanistan, many of them produced under extremely hazardous conditions, and not just in frontline war zones. Afghan males enjoy their vanity and we have encountered few, particularly among the fighters (including the Taliban), who dislike having their photographs taken. "Ax, ax" ("picture, picture") is often the most common request when a camera is produced, particularly if there is a gun to show off, or beautiful flower or park settings at hand. For many Afghans, there is nothing like a portrait of friends with flowers or at a picnic.

When the Taliban first came onto the scene in 1994, they immediately began banning films and television. They also forbade the photographing of living creatures including humans. Film teams encountered similar obstacles during the 1980s and early 1990s in areas where fundamentalist groups operated, such as those backed by Gulbuddin Hekmatyar's Hezb-e-Islami or Arab *Wahabi.* Journalists have been threatened, shot at and, in at least once instance, murdered because of their efforts to film. Photographers have also encountered problems in Hazara areas in the central highlands, where Iranian *Shi'a* influences are strong. However, if you travel with one of their people, such as Hazara guide, they can be extremely friendly and hospitable. Arriving with an aid vehicle accompanied by a Tajik or Pashtun guide may cause suspicion. During the Taliban era, news organizations, such as the BBC, were still able to film in heavily Talib areas.

E. Girardet

Most photographers and cameramen we interviewed say filming is only a problem in certain areas where local people are suspicious or conservative, such as the eastern border regions including Nuristan. Even Afghan cameramen have had boys throwing stones or men threatening to get their guns if they felt that their women are being filmed. As one leading journalist noted, while the Taliban may have been difficult, they were not invariably hostile. Nor were their rules always hard and fast; out of the capital, one could always find some reasonable individuals among their ranks. In Kandahar during the late 1990s, one EFG editor received a photo permit specifically granting him permission to photograph anything but living creatures. But when he tried to photograph a local shrine, Taliban troops still prevented him from shooting, despite the official document. In another encounter with a British journalist, a Talib official explained that the notion of creating an idolatrous graven image related only to the face. If one pictured him down to the waist, this would not constitute a "graven image" (SEE BOX).

Today, many Pashtuns from the south, where the Taliban had their principal support, are still very sensitive to the intrusion of the camera, but experiences vary widely. It helps to have local contacts, such as respected aid agencies, to break the ice. Many organizations have established their own friendly relations with local people who are ready to help or who realize the importance of some good television footage over the international airwaves. But even then, it doesn't always quite work that way.

As one veteran cameraman, who has filmed in most parts of the country, notes: "You just play it by ear. If they look hostile, then you talk with them and explain what you're doing. Usually they're quite sympathetic. But then the problem is that they all want to be filmed." It also helps to address rural Pashtuns in Pashto rather than Dari. The latter may suggest affiliation with the northern-dominated government. One possible rule of thumb is that it is often easier to film in the non-Pashtun areas, such as among Tajiks and Uzbeks in the north, than in the eastern border zones with Pakistan, where Pashtun tribesmen dominate.

Photographing agricultural projects or clinics in rural areas may prove relatively easy given that many Afghans are proud of what they have achieved. They are all the more delighted to show it off. And if a zealous Islamist appears on the scene, as they inevitably do, wait till he leaves or get someone to distract him. Nevertheless, even in Mazar it is not necessarily that easy. There is still a strong legacy of the Soviet period. The local government there requires all journalists to report to the Department of Foreign Affairs on arrival.

Perhaps one of the biggest frustrations is filming where children are present, such as in refugee camps or villages. Hordes of shouting, squealing youngsters will suddenly appear out of nowhere jostling for position in front of the camera lens. More often than not, it becomes impossible to work. Good luck to anyone trying to hold them back. Usually the best approach is simply to photograph as quickly and as surreptitiously as you can. One camera team filming in Kabul during the fighting in 1994 had armed soldiers keep the children back so that the cameraman could film normal "life under siege" in the bazaar. Unfortunately, when the shopkeepers saw armed men chasing the children, they thought a new attack was in the offing and immediately closed their shops producing instantly abandoned streets.

Women and photography

It is a different situation among Afghan women. It is best to avoid openly photographing women as this may be considered highly offensive and un-Islamic, particularly in the more conservative Pashtun areas. Usually, it is the men who object the most. If you fail to ask their consent and try filming women working in the fields or gliding through the bazaars in their *chadors*, they will immediately berate you and an ugly situation could ensue. Filming women is particularly difficult at close quarters for male cameramen. In 1994 one EFG editor had little problem, as a male journalist, in photographing widows in Kabul and Pakistani refugee camps, once permission had been obtained. In 2003, foreign journalists visiting central Hazarajat – a normally conservative *Shi'a* area – were surprised by one particular woman washing dishes by the Helmand River calling out to them to join her family for tea and then quite happily having her picture taken while her husband looked on.

Over the years, a number of foreign women photographers and filmmakers have managed to produce some excellent footage of Afghan women and their surroundings. To do so, they infiltrated circles of Afghan women and obtained their trust. Female aid workers, too, have succeeded in photographing women while working with them out of the direct glare of Afghan men. It is often easier to film women in 'humanitarian' surroundings such as clinics or food distribution centres, where they become part of the overall story and are not considered principal subjects. Some camera teams have also relied on hidden cameras although usually with the connivance of the Afghan women with whom they are working.

Nevertheless, discretion is crucial and asking permission helps. One CNN crew visiting Kabul in September 1997 barged into a female hospital ward and began filming without permission. This was sheer stupidity and caused an entire delegation of visiting journalists and aid representatives, including the

Photography – Taliban logic

"Photography is impossible in this city", assured the Kandahar field director of Médecins Sans Frontières. It was 1997 and, with the roads awash with black-turbaned Taliban, I could understand his point. But why should it matter if I just stuck to inanimate objects like mosques and mausoleums? My local Afghan guide recommended that we visit the Department of Foreign Affairs to get a permit. I needed to renew my visa anyway so I agreed to go along. We were ushered into a small office where a delicate young Taliban official sat behind a desk, beside a much older, burlier man. The former dealt with photo permits, the latter with visas. The Taliban wore a shimmering white shalwar kameez with gold trimming and an embroidered waistcoat. Beneath a neat little cap peeped a carefully coiffured bob-style haircut, and he was sporting both wispy beard and black eyeliner. He looked more like an haute couture fashion model than a fundamentalist fighter. But his indoctrination shone through as he signed and stamped the permit: "Make sure you do not snap any living creatures," he said vacantly. Meanwhile the burly Afghan – obviously an official who had worked in the office long before the Taliban movement was ever heard of – looked on with a mixture of disdain and disbelief. "For your visa renewal," he barked, "we require two passport size photographs." I looked astonished, but couldn't resist a quick smirk in the direction of the talib. He grinned back at me the grin of a man on whom logic has only the most tenuous hold. "You may have your photo taken here in Kandahar," added the burly one, "there are plenty of studios in the bazaar." *JW*

European Union's Commissioner for Humanitarian Affairs, Emma Bonino, to be detained at gunpoint for three hours. A more experienced crew might have got away with it by being somewhat less obtrusive. At the same time, however, even discretion may achieve little or nothing, so it's your call. But remember that heavy-handed behaviour often results in the Afghans accompanying you being more severely treated (and even beaten) than the Westerners. It also makes life for the resident correspondents and aid workers much more difficult after the offending journalists have gone home.

Advice for photographers in Afghanistan:

- Use common sense and discretion when photographing. Try and gauge what the mood is.

- If you can't be discreet (or surreptitious as the case may be), ask the permission of people you would like to photograph. Get them into conversation first and explain what you are doing. Then see if it is alright to take photographs.

- Avoid photographing military installations and potential targets (airports, bridges, government buildings etc.) unless you are accompanied by Afghans who know the area and are aware of what is or is not acceptable. In Pakistan, for example, it is strictly forbidden to photograph anything strategic, be it a hydroelectric dam or an historic Moghul fort. Ancient fortresses may be documented in full detail in the museums, but they still seem to be considered military secrets.

- Learn to shoot from the hip if you can't point your camera directly at what you want. Or pretend to be doing something else. Small digital or video cameras are being used increasingly by professionals because they are discreet and produce good quality coverage. Many people do not take such cameras seriously, so you can be discreet and film to your heart's content.

- Cover your red recording light if filming clandestinely. Many Afghans, particularly in towns, are aware of how video-cams work.

- If you are with a fellow journalist or companion, have one of you do all the talking while the other quietly gets on with filming or taking photographs.

- Carry a polaroid camera to give away instant photographs. Or show your digital screen to those you are photographing. This is the best way of breaking down barriers. Even the most hardened, anti-camera fundamentalist or conservative farmer may soften if he can see his portrait instantly.

Security tips

Following the fall of the Taliban, Afghanistan has become even more dangerous to visit than before. During 2002-03, security across many parts of the country deteriorated as US forces continued to hunt down Taliban or Al Qa'eda 'remnants', and local warlords competed for control. US soldiers are no longer the only targets. In spring 2003, the Islamic extremist Gulbuddin Hekmatyar and a former Taliban commander both declared a *jihad* against US forces, foreigners and their Afghan collaborators. By June 2003, one third of the country – mainly in the south and east – was considered too dangerous for UN aid and political personnel. In contrast, under the Taliban, aid agencies were able to operate in around 80 percent of the country.

Despite repeated requests from President Karzai and the UN's special representative, the International Security Assistance Force (ISAF) – which has brought a measure of security to Kabul – has not been extended beyond the capital (although in late 2003 NATO, which has taken control of peacekeeping, pledged to extend the force outside Kabul). Afghanistan's own police force and national army will take years to train. Meanwhile, the atmosphere of lawlessness and the huge amounts of money aid workers are sometimes forced to carry around – in the absence of any functioning banking system – make a dangerous combination. Personal security, therefore, will continue to depend largely on your own alertness and behaviour.

The south and east of the country remain the most dangerous – since these provinces are vulnerable to hit-and-run attacks from Taliban militants hiding in tribal areas astride the Pakistani/Afghan border. The road from Kandahar to Ghazni and the provinces of Paktia, Paktika and Khost are notoriously dangerous. Numerous attacks and hijacks have been made on both international and Afghan aid workers in the south – especially mine action teams. In August 2002, Karzai himself narrowly escaped assassination while visiting Kandahar. In spring 2003, an expatriate Red Cross delegate and an Italian tourist were executed in separate incidents near Kandahar – reportedly by the Taliban. Then, in November 2003, an expatriate working for UNHCR was shot at point blank range in broad daylight in Ghazni bazaar – the Taliban later claimed responsibility. The murder sent shock waves through the aid community, with ACBAR – an umbrella organization representing over 90 national and international NGOs – citing the killing as "a critical indicator of the unacceptably dangerous security situation faced by the assistance community in the south-east

and south of Afghanistan". According to the director of a leading Danish NGO, the attack "indicates a change in tactics by those seeking to force us out". Combined with bomb attacks on aid offices in Kabul and Kandahar, the aim of the Taliban appears to be to force aid agencies to abandon the region, leaving the stage clear for cultivating opium and a return to hardline Islamic rule.

The north has seen sporadic fighting during 2002-03 between Tajik and Uzbek commanders, which brought aid agencies close to evacuating. Security concerns for expatriates around Mazar heightened after the gang-rape of a female aid worker in 2002. In the west, the areas around Farah and Shindand have seen armed conflict. Across the country, robbery, murder and persecution of Afghan ethnic minorities are commonplace.

Even the security blanket brought to Kabul by ISAF's 5,000 foreign troops has been ripped apart by increasingly audacious attacks. In 2002, two cabinet ministers were assassinated in broad daylight, while 26 people were killed by an enormous car bomb outside a Kabul hotel popular with Westerners. In June 2003, four German ISAF peacekeepers were killed by a suicide bomber.

Aid agency staff are concerned that the boundaries between impartial humanitarian workers and military belligerents are becoming dangerously blurred. Controversially, US warplanes dropped 'humanitarian rations' as well as bombs during late 2001. Since then, armed Coalition Forces have engaged in relief and reconstruction activities – either as part of a campaign to win local 'hearts and minds', or as a cover for intelligence-gathering. This trend continued in 2003, when civil-military Provincial Reconstruction Teams (PRTs) were established in key regional cities, with a mixed mandate for security and reconstruction. The result, argue experienced observers, has been to undermine the neutrality and independence of humanitarian workers and to associate them, in the minds of Afghans, with Coalition Forces making war on the Taliban and Al Qa'eda. This fear would appear to be borne out by a recent statement from a Taliban spokesman in Spinboldak: "Most of the foreigners working in our country are American agents and have no sympathy for Afghanistan. We will not spare them" (reported in *The Times,* London, 19 November 2003).

Another deadly legacy of the war is the presence in Afghan soil of millions of landmines and large quantities of unexploded ordnance (UXO) – left behind from 24 years of war. These show no respect for faction, nationality or religious denomination. Twice, while on assignment in Afghanistan, EFG editor Edward Girardet travelled with groups where one individual inadvertently left the path only to step on a mine. What may look like an idyllic pastoral scene with gurgling irrigation canals, green pastures, and fruit-laden orchards may in fact be a minefield.

Nevertheless, the great importance Afghans attach to hospitality and the protection of guests can enhance the personal security of travellers and visitors – as long as you are friends with the right side! If you can learn a few words and greetings in Dari and Pashto, and pick up some of the local gestures and ways of behaving, you will feel much more secure around Afghans (SEE DARI & PASHTO PHRASEBOOK and TRADITIONS & CUSTOMS).

The following security tips are based on the personal experience of EFG editors, interviews with journalists and NGO staff, and advice provided by UN security manuals.

Before entering Afghanistan:

- Make sure you receive the correct **immunizations** prior to visiting Afghanistan. Maintain any antimalarial regime, and always carry oral rehydration salts (ORS) in your bag.
- Make up a **survival belt** containing a basic first aid kit, shell dressing, penknife, string, space blanket, poncho, biro, notebook and your personal documents. If you lose everything else, you have at least got this.
- Ensure you are sufficiently **insured** before travelling out to Afghanistan. Check with insurers that the threat of "war and kindred risks" does not invalidate your policy. Make sure you are covered for possible loss of limb or life through landmine damage (SEE INSURANCE).
- Consider going on a personal **security course**, for example the 'Surviving Hostile Regions' course offered by ex-SAS soldiers through UK-based company AKE (SEE INSURANCE).

On arrival in-country

- Attend one of the daily security briefings held by UNSECOORD officers at the UNDP's headquarters in Kabul.
- Attend a landmine and UXO awareness briefing (through the UN's Mine Action Centre for Afghanistan or Handicap International). Become familiar with different types of mines, what 'cluster bombs' and minefields look like, and what to do in a mine-casualty situation.
- Stay constantly alert to the threat of landmines and UXO. Do not step off main roads onto verges or into fields, either in towns or rural areas. Do not take "short-cuts" when travelling by road. Stones painted red denote mined areas.

REMEMBER: SECURITY IS A STATE OF MIND

Keep well informed of events and raise your level of security awareness accordingly. Over 50% of security incidents occur during travel and most occur after dark. So prepare and plan your work accordingly.

- Do not walk off the road into the bushes for a leak!
- Never walk alone through unknown city/village streets. Find a local guide or driver.
- Minimize your time spent in bazaars and crowded areas.
- Be aware of the curfew time in each destination you visit and stick to it.
- Dress and behave in a way sensitive to the local culture and religion (SEE CLOTHING & KIT and TRADITIONS & CUSTOMS).
- Avoid asking indiscreet questions or discussing religion and politics in public.
- Avoid wearing or carrying valuable items in public, e.g. gold chains, cameras etc.
- Always carry a torch (flashlight), personal identification and a minimal amount of money on you at all times.
- If an incident occurs while you are away from your office or residence, radio your headquarters and move immediately to the nearest international agency building. Where possible, inform the UN Area Security Coordinator (ASC) of the situation (SEE TELECOMMUNICATIONS & RADIO).
- If you are hijacked or robbed, do not resist. Stay calm, act confidently and cooperate (within reason).
- Remain constantly alert to any changes in the situation where you are working.
- Do not take alcohol on any mission at any time.
- Do not promise local people anything you cannot deliver.
- Do not handle or fire weapons of any sort.
- Do not use or carry illicit drugs.

- Do not buy any obviously looted historical items which may be offered to you.
- Ensure you travel with your passport and necessary visas on you at all times.
- Be aware of the location of the nearest hospitals and medical posts.
- Always stay well-informed. Accurate information can enhance your safety, as long as you increase your security awareness accordingly.
- Be very careful where you speak to Afghan women, and take the advice of experienced agency workers.

Road travel

Check for the latest security information on travel around Afghanistan with UNSECOORD. The UN's Afghanistan Information Management Service (AIMS) publishes maps of high risk areas. If you are stopped at a checkpoint, it is important to defuse any tension in the situation as soon as possible. Do not be arrogant or insistent about your "rights of passage," and do not force the guard to lose face. Listen before speaking. Try to find common ground. Bring in some humour – practise your Dari or Pashto. Although you should generally stay inside your vehicle, smile and, if you have to get out, shake hands or touch the guard gently on the shoulder – Afghan men are very tactile, especially in Kandahar!

When travelling by car there are some basic rules to remember:

- Never drive off-road onto verges or along short-cuts – they may be mined.
- Never drive alone. Use a local driver.
- When travelling by road, take two vehicles, especially at night.
- Take an HF or VHF radio to inform your headquarters of your departure, proposed route and arrival.
- Keep cameras, cassettes and other valuable items hidden from view at checkpoints.
- Keep the windows wound up and the doors locked, especially after dark.
- Never jump a checkpoint: slow down, turn on the cabin lights (if you are travelling at night), chat to the guard, and always be patient and cooperative if searched.
- Never raise your voice or get into an argument at a checkpoint.
- Let your Afghan colleagues or driver talk with checkpoint guards first.
- Do not get out of your vehicle at checkpoints and keep the doors locked.
- Never stay out after curfew (2100 hrs or 2200 hrs depending on the situation – check).

WARNING

MINES ARE LAID TO BE INVISIBLE...

- Avoid driving after dark in rural areas.
- Log in any long journeys with the local UN/ACBAR office.
- Vary your routes to and from the office/residence as much as possible.
- Do not leave vehicles unattended.
- Keep your fuel tanks full at all times.
- Carry basic spare parts, tools, tyres, torches, fire extinguishers, water and first-aid kit in your vehicle at all times.
- Reverse your vehicle into your compound at night in case you need to make a quick exit.
- Take advice on where you may need armed escorts or unarmed guides.
- If you are being hijacked, try to radio your base station without the hijackers noticing.
- Do not attempt to rescue vehicles or goods from bandits.
- If driving from Peshawar to the Afghan border at Torkham remember to get a tribal agencies permit. On the return journey pick up an armed escort at the Pakistani border post.
- Be careful of what you say in front of any Afghan drivers or passengers.
- Divide large amounts of money up between yourself and your colleagues.
- Consider using public transport if aid vehicles are too prominent – a solution some NGO workers in southern Afghanistan adopted in 2003.

Walking and cycling

Some experienced aid workers like to get around by bicycle or on foot. If you have the time this can be extremely rewarding, although it helps if you speak the local language. Always bear in mind the threat of mines and adhere to the following basic rules:

- Never walk or cycle “off the beaten track.”
- Check with the local Afghans, and if they avoid somewhere then so should you.

- Travel in pairs and/or take a local guide.
- If as a women you are "touched-up", or worse still beaten, in the bazaar or on the street, then make a scene by shouting or screaming. Often the offending persons will take fright if other passers-by start noticing.

Emergencies

There have been a number of emergencies involving international aid agency personnel, most notoriously the evacuations from Mazar-e-Sharif during the fighting in May and September 1997. In the May situation, a BBC team of journalists and cameramen came under heavy criticism from the UN for keeping an evacuation convoy waiting while they were out getting last-minute footage for their report. The UN in turn was criticized for assembling such a large and obvious convoy of expensive white vehicles and international staff together in a public place, while armed factions were on the loose. In the September evacuation, many NGO personnel decided to entrust themselves to the International Committee of the Red Cross (ICRC) instead of the UN. Some journalists argue that the best course of action in an emergency is to seek out the local Afghan commander who – if he takes you in as his guest – will offer you protection as a matter of honour. The point is that whatever course of action you decide on, you should make your decision early and stick by it. The UN and ICRC have different phases of emergency, involving increasingly drastic action such as the evacuation of all non-essential personnel. If you want UN or ICRC protection then you must inform them in good time and play by their rules. Do not expect to be able to jump on the evacuation bandwagon at the last minute.

Some basic rules for emergency situations:

- In a potential emergency, check your information is accurate and do not overreact.
- Consult with both the ICRC Delegate and UN Regional Representative for evacuation plans in an emergency. Once you have committed yourself to the care of the UN or ICRC, obey orders.
- The UN has protective bunkers at Kabul, Herat, Jalalabad and Kandahar, designed to provide protection against rockets and artillery shelling. Non-UN personnel may use them in time of emergency, subject to space. Contact the local UN Area Security Coordinator for details.
- If your location is being shelled or rocketed and you cannot reach a UN bunker, take shelter under the staircase or in the basement of your house, and stay away from windows.
- If in an active war zone, sleep with your boots on and keep a small emergency pack by your side at all times with extra clothes, a space blanket, some rations, a first aid kit, and if possible, a shortwave transistor radio. You need to be able to leave on the spur of the moment.
- Do not go outside while there is shooting – what goes up must come down. Many people have been injured or killed by stray bullets and flying shrapnel.

- In a medical emergency, go straight to the nearest ICRC, medical NGO or UN office. There are ICRC-supported hospitals with surgical units in Kabul (Karte Seh and Wazir Akbar Khan hospitals), Jalalabad, Ghazni and Kandahar (Mirwais hospital). The ICRC treats all medical emergency cases regardless of nationality.

Loss of personal possessions

- If moving to Afghanistan to live, ensure that you provide your main office with a detailed inventory of personal possessions to facilitate reimbursement in case of loss or destruction.
- If you are robbed of your passport or any possessions, report the incident immediately to the UN or ACBAR.

Kidnapping

Kidnapping has been widespread throughout many areas of Afghanistan over the past few years, although these incidents have rarely involved international staff. To minimize the threat of kidnapping:

- Make sure that your presence in-country is known by the regional UN office, ACBAR, an NGO office or media organization, so that if you go missing someone will notice.
- Keep a low profile, especially after normal working hours.
- When entering and leaving your house and office, keep an eye out for suspicious vehicles or individuals. Potential kidnappers will often watch a house for several days to check up on your movements. If in doubt, stay at home or drive past the house, and report anything suspicious to the UN office.
- Alternate your routes between home and office when possible.
- Watch out for any vehicles which may be following you. If you think you are being followed drive to the nearest UN/NGO office, checkpost or village (if on mission). Do not let the other vehicle overtake you.
- Avoid driving or walking alone. Lone people are the easiest targets. Travel in pairs or take a guide, and always carry a hand-held radio with you.
- Take advice on what sort of dress is appropriate for the location. Do not try to disguise yourself as an Afghan, but try not to be too distinctive either.
- When answering the door or gate to your house, check who the caller is *before you open the door.* Look from an upstairs room if no windows are near the door/gate.
- If in the worst case kidnappers try to abduct you at gunpoint, do not resist – they may shoot you!

Suggestions if you are abducted:

- Cooperate with your captors (to the minimum extent), but do not volunteer money, information or other assistance.
- Avoid staring directly at your captors, but try to get a good mental picture of their faces and other physical attributes.
- Do not try to escape unless you are certain of success. If recaptured, your situation will be much worse.
- Observe your kidnap location and routes to it, if possible.
- Talk to your captors, if appropriate. Human contact sometimes reduces the risk of violence, but do not be too friendly or submissive as this may only provoke them.
- Try to appear strong and impassive, even if you are feeling terrified. Do not display your emotions or react to your captors' provocations.
- Eat and drink as much as possible, even if stress takes away your appetite. You need to maintain strength in these situations.
- Stay mentally alert by getting as much sleep as permitted, and use "mental exercises" to take your mind off the immediate situation.

Remember: *Kidnappers are often ruthless and desperate people, but they have usually planned the abduction well. In the majority of cases they will try for 'soft' or easy targets first. Your personal awareness and habits can reduce the likelihood of your being considered a 'soft' target for kidnapping.*

Landmine and UXO awareness

This section is adapted from advice contained in the UN Summary of Security Procedures in Afghanistan (SSP)

Afghanistan is one of the most heavily mined countries in the world. Millions of landmines and unexploded ammunition lie concealed in fields, road verges, water canals and the rubble of ruined buildings. The best personal defence against this threat is to be able to recognize which areas are likely to be mined, and to avoid taking unnecessary risks.

Types of exploding devices

Landmines come in two types: anti-personnel and anti-tank mines. Anti-personnel mines are designed to maim rather than to kill. Typical injuries are the loss of one or more limbs either below or above the knee/elbow. Anti-tank mines are designed to destroy a fully-armoured battle tank and are therefore enormously dangerous: there are numerous stories of trucks and minibuses which have been blown up by these mines while driving 'off-road,' with all occupants on board being killed.

Unexploded ordnance (UXO) comprises any explosive devices which have not detonated, such as rockets, grenades, bombs and booby-traps. UXO is found all over Afghanistan in rural and urban areas and can be even more dangerous than mines. The cluster munitions dropped by Coalition Forces in late 2001 are particularly deadly – most have been cleared, but keep an eye out for their telltale yellow metal casings.

Mines and UXO come in all shapes and sizes, some are metal and some are plastic, some lie buried while others sit on the surface. Previously, mine awareness briefings concentrated on what these weapons looked like and what their technical specifications were. But since mines are designed and laid not to be seen, this approach is impractical – far better identify areas where mines are likely to be laid and avoid them.

Mines and UXO can be found almost anywhere – if in any doubt, take local advice. Mines are normally used to defend a specific area, deny access to a position, or are randomly placed as a deadly form of harassment. UXO can land anywhere – even in your back yard! Steer clear of the following areas:

- Unused footpaths, tracks and short-cuts.
- Verges of vehicle tracks and roads.
- Vehicle turnaround points.
- In and around culverts and bridge abutments.
- Alongside walls, especially those of damaged buildings.
- In the doorways and room corners of deserted houses.
- In and around wells and water access points.
- In irrigation and drainage canals.
- Around abandoned military posts and destroyed vehicles.
- In low-lying or hidden areas of cover where an enemy could hide from view.

Telltale signs

The UN's Mine Action Programme paints rocks with RED paint to signify dangerous areas and known minefields. After an area is cleared the rocks are repainted white. In unmarked areas you can look for these telltale signs:

- Skeletons and dead animals (e.g. donkeys, cows, goats or dogs).
- Small, round but regularly spaced potholes (mine detonation points).
- Uncultivated ground in otherwise cultivated areas.
- Ammunition cases or containers (fighting and mines go together).
- Tin cans (food cans from soldiers or tin from bounding mines).
- Deserted buildings in a populated area.
- Pieces of wire and small wooden stakes (POMZ mines).
- 'Bypasses' lying on the ground (they can look like pens).

- Small piles of rocks, crossed sticks, or rocks across a track, may be used to indicate that mines or UXOs are nearby.
- Yellow metal casings denoting presence of cluster munitions.

DOs and DON'Ts

- DO NOT touch or move interesting or unknown objects.
- DO NOT pull or cut unknown wires.
- DO NOT leave well-worn paths or tracks – even for calls of nature!
- DO NOT throw rocks at unknown devices.
- DO NOT think it is safe to jump from rock to rock in mined areas.
- DO NOT let drivers leave the main road or track for overtaking.
- DO NOT rush to an accident victim unless the track to them is cleared of mines.
- DO NOT walk or drive in unknown areas without a local guide.
- DO seek information on local mine problems before starting work in an area.
- DO ask local people about mine problems and take a local guide when you travel.
- DO retrace your steps out of suspect areas whenever possible.
- DO send drivers and new staff on a mine awareness course.
- DO mark, photograph (from a distance) and report suspicious devices.
- DO always stay alert to the telltale signs for mines and UXO.
- DO trust your own judgement and don't follow others blindly.

What do you do if you see a mine or UXO?

- STOP, STAY CALM, THINK!
- Shout a warning to anyone with you.
- Turn around and retrace your steps slowly and *exactly.*
- Once on safe ground, mark the danger area with a line of rocks.
- Report it to the nearest UN representative or demining NGO office immediately.

ESSENTIAL READING AND WEBLINKS

AKE (Surviving Hostile Regions): www.akegroup.com

Articles on security: www.developmentgateway.org/afghanistan

British Agencies Afghanistan Group (BAAG), Monthly Review: www.baag.org.uk

British Foreign and Commonwealth Office, Country Travel Advice: www.fco.gov.uk

Maps and security updates: www.aims.org.af

SAS Survival Handbook: How to Survive in the Wild, in Any Climate, on Land or at Sea, John 'Lofty' Wiseman, Collins (London, 2003).

Security Awareness – an aide memoire, UNHCR (Geneva)

Security Guidelines for Women, UN Security Coordination Office (New York)

UN Summary of Security Procedures in Afghanistan (SSP) – available from UN Field Security Officer, UNDP, Kabul

Telecommunications & radio

Telecommunications have developed at a rapid rate since the departure of the Taliban, under whom any non-governmental use of email or websites was punishable by death. Domestic landlines and international mobile phone connections are being developed to serve the major cities, although satphones may remain the best form of communication in remoter areas. In the early 1990s satphones were the size of suitcases; by 2002, handheld Thurayas were *de rigeur*. Most Afghan commanders have their own satphone numbers as well. Resident journalists in Afghanistan guard their satphones jealously so if you are a freelancer do not assume you can make use of their facilities – best bring your own.

The Afghan Wireless Communication Company (AWCC) started business in 1999. By 2003, it had activated both mobile GSM and IDD lines in Kabul, Jalalabad, Herat, Mazar and Kandahar. You can buy a SIM card (US$ 130) for your mobile phone from AWCC which enables you to make international calls from within several Afghan cities. Handsets and top-up cards can be bought in Kabul at the airport, post office, Intercontinental Hotel and AWCC building at the Ministry of Communications. To reach a mobile from outside the country dial +93 (Afghanistan's country code) and (0)70 for the mobile code, then the six digit mobile number. To reach an IDD line from outside the country, dial the country code followed by the relevant city code, then the six digit landline number. City codes are as follows:

020 for Kabul

030 for Kandahar

040 for Herat

050 for Mazar

060 for Jalalabad

While UN agencies set up their own internet and email access in early 2002, NGOs and journalists had to rely on expensive satellite downloads until the first internet cafés or *chaikhane* began opening in Kabul in late 2002.

If you have an IDD line or mobile phone provided by the AWCC, you can connect to your ISP server. During 2002, AWCC tested a wireless LAN system for organizations' data requirements. Users will be able to choose connection

speeds from 64k to 256k. There will be no limit on the amount of data downloaded, only a monthly fixed cost for the leased line. Potential users will need to have clear line of sight to the roof of the Ministry of Communications in Kabul.

In early 2003, Neda Telecommunications set up Kabul's first dial-up internet access – as long as you have access to a digital phone. Otherwise, you can now get online (in Kabul) via the internet cafés at: Afghan Media and Culture Centre (AINA) (next to the Ministry of Planning), CHA's arts and crafts gallery (Cinema Zainab Road), Intercontinental Hotel, Mustafa Hotel (Shahr-e-Naw), PACTEC (Wazir Akbar Khan), plus various guesthouses. AWCC's internet *chaikhana* in the basement of the Intercontinental Hotel in Kabul is equipped with Pentium computers with wireless broadband internet access. Opening hours are from 0800 to 2000 daily. The cost for this service is US$ 5 per hour. Travellers during late 2003 reported that you can even get online in the departure lounge of Kabul international airport.

In March 2003, Afghanistan inaugurated its .af domain name for websites and email addresses.

Afghan Wireless Communication Company (AWCC)

Afghan Wireless Communication Company (AWCC)
Ministry of Communications Building
Mohammad Jan Khan Watt, Kabul
Tel: +93 (0) 20 200 000; Fax: +93 (0) 20 200 200
Email: info@afghanwireless.com
Web: www.afghanwireless.com

Kandahar Tel. +93 (0) 30 300 000

Herat Tel. +93 (0) 40 400 000

Mazar-e-Sharif Tel. +93 (0) 50 500 000

Jalalabad Tel. +93 (0) 60 600 000

PACTEC email centre

PACTEC office,
Ist left on Street 13,
Wazir Akbar Khan, Kabul

PACTEC (Partners in Aviation and Communications Technology) is a non-profit humanitarian agency operating in a range of developing countries. Its Kabul office is open to all approved NGOs and their staff. Services include:

- Web mail and PACTEC email on PC terminals ($4 per hour)
- Laptop hook-ups for connecting to Internet and downloading POP3 email
- Secure email accounts set up for local POP3 access ($35 month)
- Computer repair, software & networks installed
- Open Sat-Wed: 0800-1600; Thu: 0800-1200

Ministry of Communications

Ministry of Communications
Mohammad Jan Khan Watt, Kabul
Tel: +93-20-2102655
Fax: +93-20-290022
Web: www.moc.gov.af

Radio

The United Nations operates a system of radio communications in all the principal towns of Afghanistan for the benefit of both UN and NGO agencies. In areas where there is no local telephone network (most rural parts of the country), radio provides not only a lifeline in emergencies but the only means of day-to-day routine communication.

Long-distance communication is usually by High Frequency (HF) radios. The range of these radios is hundreds, sometimes thousands, of kilometres. Short-distance communication is usually by Very High Frequency (VHF) radios, typically in the form of hand-held walkie-talkies. Their range is very short unless used with a frequency 'repeater' which extends the range to 40-50 km. Radios are not like telephones. There are a limited number of channels available which have to be shared between everyone. Hence radio traffic and conversations should be kept to a minimum.

Rules for radio use

- Keep your radio switched on and in the battery charger at night to enable emergency contact.
- Before calling anyone else, listen first to check that the channel is free.
- Most duty stations have a VHF stand-by channel to make initial contact, and another channel to which you switch to continue talking.

- Press the 'call' switch firmly and hold down for half a second before speaking, to ensure that all of your message is transmitted.
- For security reasons, refer to each other by call-sign not by name, and where possible refer to "your location" or "my location" rather than specifying place names.
- Never mention UN or ICRC flight times over the radio.
- Never mention the movement or payment of money over the radio.
- Keep your conversations brief. Radios are not telephones.
- Where possible always travel with some form of radio: VHF walkie-talkie for short distances, or HF radio for longer distances.
- Report all your general movements to your base station.

Radio security

If you are in an emergency, use the phrase "BREAK, BREAK, BREAK, THIS IS…" in order to alert users that you wish to send an urgent message. If you hear this phrase it means that someone is in trouble! Stop your call, listen to the emergency message, and then respond as appropriate. Radio communication is not secure. Anyone with a radio can listen in, so never mention confidential information while "on air."

Phonetic Alphabet

The phonetic alphabet is an international system used by civil, military, marine, aviation and ground organizations. It is a standard system which allows for clear communications, and should be used on all UN radio nets.

A–ALPHA	J–JULIET	S–SIERRA
B–BRAVO	K–KILO	T–TANGO
C–CHARLIE	L–LIMA	U–UNIFORM
D–DELTA	M–MIKE	V–VICTOR
E–ECHO	N–NOVEMBER	W–WHISKEY
F–FOXTROT	O–OSCAR	X–X-RAY
G–GOLF	P–PAPA	Y–YANKEE
H–HOTEL	Q–QUEBEC	Z–ZULU
I–INDIA	R–ROMEO	

Radio broadcasters

The number of radio broadcasters in Afghanistan mushroomed during 2002. The main international broadcasters, which transmit programmes in English, Dari and Pashto languages, remain: *BBC, VOA, Deutsche Welle.* Local and regional broadcasters include: *Radio Kabul, Radio Free Afghanistan, Radio Iran.* In addition, most of Afghanistan's main towns now have radio stations.

British Broadcasting Corporation (BBC)

BBC World Service, Bush House, Strand, London WC2B 4PH, UK
Tel: +44 (20) 7240 3456 Fax: +44 (20) 7257 8258
Email: worldservice.letters@bbc.co.uk
Web: www.bbc.co.uk/worldservice

English language service. News is broadcast every hour on the half hour in Afghanistan. BBC World Service short wave frequencies in Khz and local times for Afghanistan are as follows:

Frequency (kHz)	Time (GMT)
9410	0100-0200 (South Asia schedule); 0200-0300
9740	1800-2000
11760	0700-1400
12095	0200-0500; 1700-1900
15565	1500-1800
15575	0300-0730 (0900 Sat & Sun); 0900-1500
17640	0700-1500
17790	0100-0700 (0300-0700 South Asia schedule)

Medium-wave frequencies for Iran and western Afghanistan:

1413 kHz	0200-0230; 0300-0400; 1745-1830; 1900-2100 GMT
1314 kHz	2200-0100; 1300-1400

Local time in Afghanistan is GMT +4.5 hours.

Suggestions for improved reception

Shortwave reception conditions change from day-to-day and sometimes from hour-to-hour, so try all available frequencies to get the best reception. Short wave signals travel thousands of kilometres, and a simple external aerial can help improve reception. This can be a few metres of any wire (insulated or un-insulated) clamped to or coiled round your radio's whip antenna. Extend the wire aerial near to or outside a window. Be careful not to dangle the aerial above or below electric power lines, and disconnect it from your radio during electric storms. You can also improve frequency by holding your transistor at different angles or stepping outside into the open away from any engine or other interference. *Sources: BBC, VOA*

Voice of America (VOA)

300 Independence Ave. SW, Washington DC 20547, USA.
Fax: +1 (202)619 0211 Email: letters@voa.gov

English language service. English language news is broadcast daily on the following Khz frequencies (local Afghan time):
0530 and 0630: 7115, 7205, 9740, 9850 Khz
1830, 1930, 2030 and 2130: 6110, 7125, 7215, 9575/9645 Khz

Deutsche Welle radio

50588 Cologne, North Rhein Westphalia (NRW), Germany
Tel: +49 (221) 389 2500 Fax: +49 (221) 389 2510
Email: online@dwelle.de Web: www.dwelle.de

German language service. German language news is broadcast daily on the following Khz frequencies (local Afghan time):
0630-0720: 1548, 6035, 7160, 7285, 7355, 9515, 9615 Khz
2030-2115: 1548, 6170, 7225, 7305, 9585 Khz

Traditions & customs

Success in your work and travels in Afghanistan will depend to a large extent on how well you get on with Afghans, to what extent you respect their traditions and customs, and how well you adapt your way of behaving to be in tune with your environment. From dealing with bored guards at roadblocks to stubborn government officials to tribal elders or women's groups, your understanding of the different aspects of the Afghan character will be critically important, and possibly life-saving (SEE SECURITY TIPS). It is crucial to remember that drinking tea is not just a means of quenching one's thirst, but also a sign of respect, hospitality and, in some cases, political astuteness. Even if you are not thirsty, or cannot bear the thought of yet another cup of tea, it may be best not to refuse too often.

Nancy Dupree summarizes the importance to Afghans of correct behaviour as follows:

> *"By disregarding social niceties, a person brings discredit upon himself and thereby diminishes the reputation of both his immediate family as well as his extended family or group. Conversely, individuals gain respect, maintain status and enhance their standing in the community through polite behaviour. Much of etiquette, therefore, is designed to preserve* zat, *honour. As a consequence, Afghan society places much emphasis on correct behaviour."*

Traditionally the elder women of the Afghan household are responsible for teaching etiquette, while the male elders ensure its enforcement. However increased migration into urban areas in the 1960s, coupled with the concurrent rise of Communism in the 1960s and 1970s undermined traditional social values. Nevertheless, the disrespect which young Afghan intellectuals – fired with Marxist zeal – showed towards village elders and their wives and daughters during the attempted land and education reforms of 1978 led to widespread revolt across the entire country. Much of Afghanistan's history in the 20th Century was characterized by this conflict between the more Westernised intellectuals of the urban centres and the more traditional rural inhabitants. King Amanullah was forced out of office because his reforms of the 1920s – including abolishing the veil for women – were considered too radical. The

E. Girardet

backlash against 'modernizing' Afghan communists in 1978-1979 led to the invasion of the country by the Soviet Union.

Even the Taliban movement can be seen as a traditionalist response to the perceived moral corruption and lawlessness of Western-backed *mujahed* factions. The conservative customs of rural Afghanistan should not be underestimated. On the vexed issue of girls' education, for example, in many agricultural communities – long before the Taliban was ever heard of – girls were never permitted to go to school by their parents. It simply was not the tradition. One of the most contentious questions facing Western assistance efforts has been the extent to which these traditions should be respected, especially when they come into conflict with principles passionately-held by the so-called 'developed world'. The BBC soap opera *New Home, New Life* has pioneered programmes aimed at gently changing social attitudes and traditions, such as the time-honoured Afghan treatment for the wound left after cutting a child's umbilical cord: rubbing in cow-dung. But where do you draw the line between traditions and bad habits?

During 2002-03, however, the two million refugees who returned home from Pakistan, Iran and further afield have brought with them new sets of values learned in exile. Many had, for the first time, come into contact with secular primary education, modern healthcare, even satellite TV. Some Afghans who had fled as rural children returned as sophisticated, computer-literate urbanites. Their experience, skills and expectations challenge long-held traditional customs and create tensions with fellow Afghans who have never fled their homeland. At the same time, many members of President Karzai's Transitional Authority are former *mujahideen,* and adhere to strict Islamic principles. Meanwhile, the insecurity which has pervaded much of the country since the fall of the Taliban means that most Afghan women continue to wear the *burqa* out of choice in order to afford themselves a degree of protection.

Foreigners beware!

Rural Afghan society may be traditionally hospitable. But it also has a long tradition of suspicion towards any new-fangled ideas, especially if those introducing them come from the city or from a foreign land. Traditionalist resentment and rebellion at Kabul-led communist reforms in 1978-1979 precipitated the Soviet invasion. Taliban mistrust of Western values has led to the incarceration of thousands of Afghan women. For anyone from overseas attempting to employ alien means to achieve Western ends, it may be worth remembering what Olivier Roy has to say in his book *Islam and Resistance in Afghanistan* about such attempts:

"the proverbial hospitality of the Afghans is also a form of defensive screen. The guest, assigned to a precise place (the *hujra*) which he dares not leave without offending his host, is enmeshed in a formalism in which the ceremony of greetings and the ritual of the meal leaves little place for the exercise of authority or even simple investigation... The foreigner finds himself confronted by an endless series of evasions, procrastinations and side-stepping of the issue. The person who is responsible is always somewhere else, the horses are in the mountains and the truth is in the depths of the well."

Day-to-day manners

In terms of manners, Westerners often appear crude and unpolished compared to Afghans. The Western way of business is brisk, no-nonsense, and 'up-front.' But for Afghans it is extremely rude to launch straight into business without proper greetings and a good banter over a glass or two of tea. The advantage of the Afghan way is its civility and relaxing effect; the disadvantage is that meetings can drag on for hours and hours without reaching a definite conclusion. Efforts to shortcut traditional greetings with a quick 'hello' will be considered rude or indifferent. Most Westerners find a balance, but just remember to *observe* how your hosts and colleagues behave before launching in yourself.

"It is a matter of gauging the situation and not offending your hosts," noted one veteran journalist. "Newcomers who are in a hurry often don't understand this. For Afghans, hospitality is part of their dignity. Even if they are very poor and have almost nothing to offer, it allows them to retain their own self-respect." At the same time, however, one must know when to decline. If someone in the bazaar or in a *chaikhana* offers you their food, gratefully decline, several times if necessary. They are simply being polite. If they still insist on sharing their meal, then sit down and eat a little with them lest they become offended. (Be careful, however, not to take the choice bits of the food.) Don't forget, they also wish to know who you are and it is their country. When you feel that you have done your bit for decorum, then place your right hand against your heart to indicate that you have had your fill and thank them.

On one occasion early during the Soviet war, an EFG editor had to indulge in at least half a dozen lunches in the Baluch region of the Chagai Hills in Helmand province as each village or camp on the way back to Pakistan was waiting with a specially prepared meal for a group of journalists who were passing through the area that morning. The situation nearly erupted into a *crise d'état*, when two reporters in the group – anxious to get back to Quetta to file their stories – refused to stop. Only when it was made clear to them that insult might very quickly develop into injury did they agree to ceremoniously accept a few bites from each meal. Overall, the best advice is to play it by ear and to be sensitive to your hosts.

As regards Afghan women, it is best for Western men not to stare at them in the street or in rural areas, let alone touch them. This is for the women's own protection. In private, however, it is acceptable for Western men to acknowledge Afghan women with a smile, and if they are Westernized or you know them, then you can shake hands and talk with them where appropriate. In mid-2002, US soldiers manning a checkpoint in Uruzgan stopped and physically searched eight Afghan women, causing near-revolt among local residents. Subsequently the US military command had to apologise to the governor and dismantle the checkpoints. In general, Western women enjoy better access to Afghan women than do Western men.

Here are some basic rules:

First meeting:

- Stand up when any Afghan – and especially an elder – enters the room.
- Exchange greetings whenever meeting friends or strangers. For men this involves crossing your heart with your right hand, shaking hands and sometimes even a 'bear-hug', if you are good friends. Afghans go through this whole procedure many times a day, often with the same people.
- Never interrupt Afghans while they are praying or deep in conversation.
- The most common verbal greeting is *A-salaam a-laykum* ("Peace be upon you"), to which the reply is *w-laykum o a-salaam* ("And upon you be peace"). (SEE DARI & PASHTO PHRASEBOOK)
- Show respect for elders and superiors by referring to them by their title rather than first name. The word for 'father' is *baba*, 'mother' is *madar*, and someone who has been on pilgrimage to Mecca is *hajji.*
- Before embarking on any business talk, you should ask after your host's/visitor's health, life, family etc. However, men should not inquire about Afghans' wives or daughters unless you are very close friends.

Buzkashi

Buzkashi (Persian for "goat grabbing") may be the wildest game in the world. Massive stallions rear and lurch. Their riders, buffeted from all sides, lean from the saddle and try to grasp a 40 kg animal carcass. Then it's up and across the Central Asian steppes at full gallop in an unparalleled show of equestrian skill and daring.

Buzkashi originated with nomadic forebears of the same Turkic peoples (Uzbek, Turkomen, Kazakh, Kirghiz) who are its core players today. The game quite likely developed, in much the same way as American rodeo, as a recreational variant of everyday herding or raiding activity. Stemming almost certainly from the time of Genghis Khan, it remains a vivid and potentially violent pastime in formerly Soviet Central Asia, China's Xinjiang Province, and – most authentically – northern Afghanistan.

Other Afghan ethnic groups have recently joined buzkashi culture: Tajiks, Hazaras, and even Pashtun migrants from south of the Hindu Kush. Beginning in the early 1950s the Kabul-based central government promoted buzkashi as the national game by hosting tournaments, first on the birthday of King Mohammed Zahir and then on anniversaries advantageous to subsequent regimes. As central authority collapsed during the Afghan-Soviet War (1979-1989), so did the tournament.

Buzkashi has two main forms: the traditional, grassroots game (*tudabarai*) and a modern, governmental sport (*qarajai*). Both feature powerful horses and riders who struggle for control of a goat or calf carcass. While regarded primarily as playful fun, both forms of buzkashi also exist as an implicitly political arena in which patron/sponsors seek to demonstrate and thus enhance their capacity for controlling volatile events.

Sponsors own champion horses, hire specialized riders (*chapandazan*), and host ceremonial gatherings (*toois*) in which buzkashi is played. In northern Afghanistan, sponsorship has traditionally been exercised by khans, elite members of the informal, ever-shifting power structure. A *tooi's* centrepiece is a day or several days of buzkashi: a status-oriented initiative in which the social, economic, and political resources of the khan sponsor (*tooi-wala*) are publicly tested. If those resources prove sufficient and the *tooi* is a success, its sponsor's "name will rise." If not, the *tooi-wala's* reputation can be ruined.

Some traditional games (*tudabarai*) involve hundreds of riders with no formal teams or spatial boundaries. The expert *chapandazan* (the equivalent to professional riders) dominate the play but "everyone has the right" to participate. The *tudabarai* objective is to gain sole control of the carcass and ride it free and clear of all other riders. "Free and clear," however, is difficult to adjudicate, and disputes are frequent. Tumultuous play can then shift to real violence and serious injury. Such shifts discredit the *tooi* sponsor.

Since the onset of war in 1978, sponsorship of traditional buzkashi has shifted from old-style khans to newer, younger military commanders (*commandaan*). Their backgrounds may be more modern, but their attention to buzkashi – and political status – is as pronounced as ever.

Government-sponsored buzkashi (*qarajai*) is more standardized and thus easier to control. Two teams, totalling no more than two dozen riders, compete on a bounded field with specified scoring flags and circles. The Kabul tournament referees were typically military officers, and quarrelsome riders were threatened with prison. Government control over previously volatile buzkashi was total by the last pre-Marxist era tournament (1977).

Then things fell apart. The increasing failure of Marxist leaders to bring the game to Kabul and stage it successfully compromised the prestige of their regimes. This effort was abandoned after 1982 and by mid-2003 had not been resumed on a tournament basis. Rural buzkashis, however, continued in the North despite Soviet linkage with anti-regime "banditry" and subsequent Taliban accusations of "wasteful frivolity."

The buzkashi season in northern Afghanistan runs from October to March. *Toois* are still held in the countryside. While the central government as yet lacks sponsorship capacity, local leaders often provide a game on Friday afternoons. The country's foremost buzkashi is currently held as part of *Now Roz* (New Year) celebrations beginning March 21 on a field called Dasht-e-Shadian in the southern outskirts of Mazar-e-Sharif.

Buzkashi is not native to Kabul, but you may be lucky. Check two venues: Ghazi Stadium near the Id Gah mosque and a new field near the ISAF compound, directly facing the US embassy.

Contributed by: Whitney Azoy, author of Buzkashi: Game and Power in Afghanistan (2nd edition); Waveland Press, 2003)

- Western men should not look at, point at or shake hands with Afghan women in the streets or in rural areas.
- As a Western woman it is best not to offer your hand to an Afghan man to shake. Wait for him to offer you his hand first.
- Men and women, even married couples, should not touch each other in public.
- Never use the left hand for passing or touching anything or anyone.

As a guest in an Afghan home or at a meal:

Afghans across the country are renowned for their generous hospitality, and Pashtuns in particular regard the comfort and security of their guests as a matter of great honour. Even unexpected guests must be welcomed, regardless of how inconvenient their arrival may be. As a journalist covering the Soviet war, EFG editor Edward Girardet was almost always offered the most congenial hospitality in numerous villages and refugee camps. Only on two or three occasions did villagers refuse to offer tea or provide a place in the mosque or a house to sleep. When this happened, they tended to be Afghans associated with Arab or other foreign Islamic groups. Afghans travelling with Girardet sought to explain this embarrassment by saying that such people did not understand what Islam and Afghan traditions were about.

On greeting a guest to his house or tent, the host will usually offer tea and then wait for the visitor to explain why he is there. Guests are never turned away, nor asked how long they may be staying. Some basic rules to observe in this situation are as follows:

- Do not visit someone's house without getting prior permission from the head of the household.
- Afghans will often ask you to share a meal with them when they cannot afford it, so let them ask you several times to make sure they really mean it.
- A gift for your hosts, such as a small bag of sweets, is appropriate.
- Never enter a room or home without knocking or coughing to announce your presence. On entering, greet everyone with "*A-salaam a-laykum*" or "*salaam alek*," even if you have only been absent from the room for a few moments.
- Remove your shoes before entering the guest room. (A good tip is to wear a pair of shoes you can slip on and off easily – laced-up boots are bad news! Or keep a pair of sandals in your pack).
- Never walk on prayer mats.

- Men and women are often entertained separately. It is best to go along with this custom unless you are confident of behaving otherwise.
- If you are guest of honour you will be seated at the top of the room (although still on the floor) away from the entrance. Seating is usually by precedence, with those of lowest status seated nearest the door.
- Sit cross-legged – never stretch your legs out towards others or stick your feet up on tables or desks.
- Only serve, touch and eat food with the right hand.
- Afghans take pride in offering large amounts of food to their guests. Take less than you can eat at first so that you have room for the second and third helpings which will be offered to you.
- Eat slowly; when you finish eating then your hosts will too.
- Do not shout, laugh too loudly or sing during meal times.
- Do not interrupt others in conversation.
- Never blow your nose in public – go outside or into a bathroom.
- Always ask before lighting up a cigarette

For more information on beggars and baksheesh SEE MONEY; for more on dress SEE CLOTHING & KIT.

Visas

During the heady days of the Soviet War, many freelance journalists entered Afghanistan clandestinely, trudging over some remote frontier mountain pass at the dead of night, accompanied by armed *mujahideen*. Nowadays, however, it is essential to obtain a visa before going into the country. Foreigners attract a great deal of attention, not least because of their access to money and international media. You will be noticed, and if you do not have a visa, you will probably end up in jail, or at least detained at some police or militia post. This in turn will make you a burden to overstretched Red Cross, UN or NGO workers who will be involved in extricating you. You have two choices: get a visa in your country of origin (preferable), or wait until you arrive in Pakistan or Iran and sort it out on the spot.

Officially, the following documents will be needed when you apply for a visa at any Afghan mission abroad:

- One visa application form
- Two passport-sized photos
- Passport, valid for at least six months beyond end date of your trip
- A letter of introduction on headed paper from your organization, embassy or sponsor, stating the purpose of your trip
- Visa application fee (money order, postal order, cheque or cash in person)
- If you are a U.S. Alien Resident, a copy of your Green Card
- If applying by mail, include a pre-paid, self-addressed envelope (Certified Mail, Registered, Federal Express or UPS)

Visas available include: single entry (valid for three months for a 15-day stay), tourist (valid for three months for a 30-day stay), and multiple entry (either three or six month stay). As at December 2003, prices charged at the Afghan Embassy in London range from £30-115. In Australia, prices range from Aus$ 60-360. Visas take 2-5 days to issue in London and the consulate's opening hours are 0930-1330, Mon-Fri. At the Afghan Embassy in the US, you can get a visa the same day by paying US$ 100.

An official letter of introduction is essential if you want to get a multiple-entry Afghan visa, or if you're entering from Central Asia. However, several Afghan Embassies contacted by EFG editors in December 2003 confirmed that single entry tourist visas are available (valid for three months for a 30-day stay) as long as you provide a letter detailing the nature of your tour and the places you intend to visit. To get a tourist visa from the Afghan Embassy in London, you must provide a letter from your employer which confirms your identity and that you work for them.

Informal reports during 2003 suggest that freelance travellers may be able to obtain short-stay Afghan visas in Pakistan (Peshawar) and Iran (Mashad) for US$ 30 without a letter of introduction. While some embassies provide same day processing, it's best to count on two to three days. If you are applying for an Afghan visa in Pakistan, remember that not much work is done from Thursday afternoon through to Monday morning, so start your application early in the week. In Pakistan and Iran, visas are readily available from the Afghan missions in Islamabad, Peshawar, Quetta, Tehran and Mashad. Renewing visas within Afghanistan can normally be done while you wait. Bank on US$10 per month of extension plus two passport photos.

All expats travelling from Peshawar by road up to Landi Kotal, the border at Torkham and on through the Khyber Pass into Afghanistan need to get a Tribal Areas Permit from the Khyber Political Agency. This can now be procured in about ten minutes. The application should be accompanied by photocopies of your passport and relevant Pakistani and Afghan visas. The Political Agent's office is on Bara Road near Qayum Stadium in Saddar Bazaar. Coming back from Afghanistan by road through the Khyber Pass, you do not need a Tribal Areas permit – the local militia will give you an armed escort but will expect tips (US$ 1-2) for their 'protection'.

Afghan embassies and consulates abroad:

AUSTRALIA

PO Box 155
Deakin West ACT 2600, Canberra
Tel: (+61 2) 62827311
Fax: (+61 2) 62827322
Email: admin@afghanembassy.net
Web: www.afghanembassy.net

AUSTRIA

Lackierergasse 8, Top 9, 1090, Vienna
Tel: (+43 1) 5247806
Fax: (+43 1) 5247807
Email: afg.emb.vie@chello.at

BANGLADESH

House No. CWN (C) 2A
Road No. 24, Culshan, Dhaka
Tel: (+880 2) 9884767
Fax: (+880 2) 9884764

BELGIUM

281 Rue Francoise Gay
B-1150 Brussels
Tel: (+32 2) 7613166
Fax: (+32 2) 7613167
Email: ambassade.afghanistan@brutele.be

BULGARIA

61 "Boryana" Street
Bl. 216-A App. 15,
Ovcha Kupel 1618, Sofia
Tel: (+359 2) 8708394
Fax: (+359 2) 9559976

CANADA

246 Queen Street
Suite 400
Ottawa, Ontario KIP 5E4
Tel: (+1 613) 563 4223/65
Fax: (+1 613) 563 4962
Email: afghanembott@hotmail.com
Web: www.afghanistanembassy.ca/

CHINA

8 Tung Chih Men Wia
Chao Yang District, Beijing
Tel: (+86 10) 65320240
Fax: (+86 10) 65322269

CZECH REPUBLIC

Nakazance 634/7 17100
Praha 7, Troja, Prague
Tel: (+420 2) 33566228
Fax: (+420 2) 7650732

EGYPT

59 El-Orouba Street,
Heliopolis, Cairo
Tel: (+20 2) 4177236;
Fax: (+20 2) 4177238

FRANCE

32 Avenue Raphael, 75016, Paris
Tel: (+33 1) 4568 2771
Fax: (+33 1) 4568 2772
Email: ambafghane@wanadoo.fr
Web: www.ambafghane.web.com

GERMANY

Wilhelmstrasse 65, D 10117, Berlin
Tel: (+49 30) 2292612
Fax: (+49 30) 2291510
Email: afghanische-botschaft@t-online.de

Consulate
Liebfrauenweg 1A, 53125, Bonn
Tel: (+49 228) 256797
Fax: (+49 228) 255310

INDIA

Plat No. 5, Block 50F, Shantipath,
Chanakyapuri, New Delhi 110021
Tel: (+91 11) 410 3331
Fax: (+ 91 11) 6875439
Email: afghanspirit@yahoo.com

INDONESIA

15 Jalan DR Kuskmas Atmaja, Jakarta
Tel: (+62 21) 335390
Fax: (+62 21) 316 3169

IRAN

Dr. Beheshti Avenue,
4th Street, Tehran
Tel (+98 21) 8737050, 8737531
Fax (+98 21) 8735600

Consulate

Imam Khomeini Avenue,
Doshahid Street, Sevom Isfand Sq., Mashad
Tel +98 511 8544829 and 8597552
Fax +98 511 8544404
Email:
Afghanistan_Ge_con_mashad@samanir.net

IRAQ

Shareh Al-Maghreb Aldifaeih
Waziria 27/1/12, Baghdad
Tel: (+964 1) 5569508
Fax: (+964 1) 5560331

ITALY

Via Nomentana 120, 00161, Rome
Tel: (+39 06) 86216111, 8611009
Fax: (+39 06) 86322939

JAPAN

Matsumoto International House (MIH)
37-8 Nishihara 3 Chome
Shibuya Ku, Tokyo 151-0066
Tel: (+81 03) 5465 1219
Fax: (+81 03) 5465 1229
Email: akbary6373@hotmail.com

KAZAKHSTAN

Mir 12 Alma-Ata
Tel: (+7 327) 247660, 338711
Fax: (+7 327) 2738711

KUWAIT

Surra, Block 6,
Surra Street Across
Surra Co-op Society House
No. 16 P.O. Box 33186, Rawdah, 73452
Tel: (+965) 5329461 or 5328156
Fax: (+965) 5326274
Email: afg_emb_kuw@hotmail.com

KYRGYZSTAN

Embassy of Afghanistan in Beshkek
Tel: (+996 312) 4263726
Fax: (+996 312) 543428

MALAYSIA

Suite 6.06 North Block, The Amp Walk, 218 Jln Ampang,
50450 Kuala Lumpur
Tel: (+60 3) 21628897
Fax: (+60 3) 21628924
Email: afghanem@tm.net.my
Web: www.afghanembassy.com

NETHERLANDS

Wellemsparkweg 114 1070 HN, Amsterdam
Tel: (+31 20) 6721311
Fax: (+31 20) 6722672
Email:
afghanconsulholland@hotmail.com

PAKISTAN

House No. 8, Street 90,
G-6/3 Islamabad
Tel: (+92 51) 2824505, 2278213
Fax: (+92 51) 2824504

Consulates

33/2 Off. Khayaban-e-Shamsi 9th Street,
Phase V., D.H.S., Karachi 75500
Tel: (+92 21) 5821264 or 582126
Fax: (+92 21) 5842263 or 5841257

45 Price Road, Quetta
Tel: (+92 81) 843364
Fax: (+92 81) 9202549

Gul Mohar Lane, University Town, Peshawar
Tel: (+92 91) 285963
Fax: (+92 91) 285961

POLAND

Ul. Zakopianska 8-03-934 Warsaw
Tel: (+48 22) 6163006/7
Fax: (+48 22) 6163008
Email:
consul@afghanambasada.cjb.net
Web: afghanambasada.cjb.net

QATAR

Embassy of Afghanistan in Doha
Tel: (+974) 5237177

RUSSIA

Sverchkov Per 3/2, Moscow
Tel: (+ 7 095) 9287581 or 9217094 or 9285044
Fax: (+7 095) 9240478 or 9219563
Email: afghanem@online.ru

SAUDI ARABIA

P.O.Box 93337, Riyadh 11673
Tel: (+966 1) 4803459
Fax: (+966 1) 4803451

Consulate
P.O. Box 6349
Tariq Al-Madina Kilo No. 3, Jeddah 21442
Tel: (+966 2) 6547579
Fax: (+966 2) 6549977

SUDAN

Madinatol Riyadh Shareol Moshtal, Square 10, House No. 81, Khartoum
Tel: (+249 11) 221852 or 221827
Fax: (+249 11) 222059

SWITZERLAND/UN

63 Rue de Lausanne,
5e etage, CH-1202 Geneva
Tel: (+41 22) 7311449
Fax: (+41 22) 7314510
Email: afghanistan@itu.com
Web: www.afghan.gov.af

SYRIA

Mozzo, West Villas Juber Ben Hayan Bus Station, Damascus
Tel: (+963 11) 6112910
Fax: (+963 11) 6133595

TAJIKISTAN

Ul. Pushkina, House 34, Dushanbe
Tel: (+992 372) 216735
Fax: (+992 372) 510096

TURKEY

Cinnah Caddesi, No. 88 Cankaya, Ankara
Tel: (+90 312) 4381121
Fax: (+90 312) 4426256

TURKMENISTAN

14 Gerogli Street, Ashkhabad 744000
Tel: (+993 12) 395821
Fax: (+993 12) 395820

UKRAINE

Chervonozoryany Ave.42 UA-252037, Kiev
Tel: (+380 44) 2458104
Fax: (+380 44) 2458104
Email: afghanem@afghanem.kiev.ua

UNITED ARAB EMIRATES

P.O. Box 5687, Abu Dhabi
Tel: (+971 2) 6661244
Fax: (+971 2) 6655310

UNITED KINGDOM

31 Prince's Gate, London SW7 1QQ
Tel: (+44 20) 7589 8891/2
Fax: (+44 20) 7584 4801, 7581 3452
Email: info@afghanembassy.co.uk
Web: www.afghanembassy.co.uk

UNITED STATES OF AMERICA

2341 Wyoming Avenue, NW, Washington, DC 20036
Tel: (+1 202) 483 6410
Fax: (+1 202) 483 6488
Email: info@embassyofafghanistan.org
Web: www.embassyofafghanistan.org

Consulate
360 Lexington Avenue,
11th Floor, New York, NY 10017
Tel: (+1 212) 972 2276 or 972 2277
Fax: (+1 212) 972 9046
Email: afghancons@aol.com

UZBEKISTAN

Ul. Gogol, House 73, Tashkent 700047
Tel:(+998 71) 2354112
Fax:(+998 71) 2348458
Email: afgemuz@mail.tps.uz

Permanent Mission to United Nations

360 Lexington Avenue,
11th Floor, New York, NY 10017
Tel: (+212) 9721212 or 9721213 or 9721221
Fax: (+212) 9721216
Email: afgwatan@aol.com

Permanent Delegation to UNESCO

1, Rue Miollis, 75015 Paris
Tel: (+33 01) 45682771
Fax: +33 01) 45682772
Email: dl.afghanistan@unesco.org

Weather

Afghanistan has an extreme, but mainly dry continental climate. Hot, dry summers – reaching over 50 degrees Celsius in the deserts of the southwest – are complemented by bitter winters – with temperatures plunging to minus 40 or 50 degrees in the mountains of the Hindu Kush.

Nevertheless, between these extremes, Afghanistan, like Europe, has four distinct seasons. From November to March, the snow-line creeps down to around 1,800 metres and snow blankets Kabul most winters. The rains last from January into spring, but increase the higher up you go. Average annual rainfall across the country is 13 inches/338mm. From March to May the warmer weather encourages fruit blossoms, wild flowers, carpets of grass and rivers full of rainfall and snowmelt. The summer months from June to August are extremely hot and dusty, unless you are in the mountains. From September to November, the fresh mornings, warm days and spectacular autumnal tints make these among the best months to travel in Afghanistan.

There is great regional variation in weather across Afghanistan. Out of the five main cities, Kabul (situated at 1,800 metres) is the highest in elevation, so pack warm clothes for all times of year. Average temperatures for the capital are: January, minus 2.8°C; July, 24.4°C. However, the thermometer can drop to freezing in Mazar, Kandahar and Herat as well during winter. In summer, temperatures in these cities can reach 35-40 degrees Celsius. In Herat the heat is relieved by 120 days of tearing winds from May to August.

The baking heat in many arid or semi-arid regions also makes overland travel difficult for ill-equipped travellers, so always take water. Breakdowns are no fun. Jalalabad (elevation 700 metres) enjoys a subtropical climate and is much milder in winter than Kabul, but extremely hot in summer. The Jalalabad plains are frost-free all year, enabling the cultivation of orange and olive groves within view of the snow-covered Safed Koh and Hindu Kush ranges. Bamiyan, situated at 2,500 metres, is often blocked by snow for several months of the year.

During the 1980s, numerous refugees, particularly children and the aged (as well as their animals) died from exposure, bitterly cold blizzards and flash-floods as they sought to cross the Hindu Kush into Pakistan. Heavy snows and mud from spring thaws seriously hampered humanitarian relief operations in northern Afghanistan, following the earthquake near Rustaq in February 1998.

Spring floods take a heavy toll on both people and agricultural land every year, often devastating the plains of the southwest.

From 1997-2002, the worst drought for over a century afflicted the entire region. Around half a million rural Afghans were forced from their homes, desperate to find food in nearby cities or temporary camps. Widespread loss of crops and livestock, combined with a drop in ground water levels, added to the hardships of a country riven by 24 years of war.

Advice for women

Afghanistan may sound like a nightmare for any Western woman to visit, let alone to work in. Things may have improved with the fall of the Taliban but everything is relative. Herat may be worse off now under warlord Ismail Khan than his Talib predecessors. One European UN aid representative was forced to cover herself with a plastic sheeting in mid-2002 in order to meet with the slickly dressed (Western-suited) head of Herat Radio and Television, a known fundamentalist. Western women have also complained of being accosted or insulted in the streets of Kabul for walking either alone or without 'appropriate' clothing. In general, most Afghans, particularly in rural areas, must be considered to be 'conservative' in outlook with regard to women.

A lot of it, however, has to do with attitude. With the post-Taliban recovery effort, foreign and Afghan women are able to operate openly – and uncovered – in most government ministries and international aid offices. A late summer 2002 straw-poll in the main Kabul bazaars indicated that as many as one in five Afghan women were doing their shopping unveiled, albeit almost all with some sort of discreet head cover. Six months earlier, one would have been hard-pushed to find more than a handful of Afghan women, primarily educated or working with aid agencies, daring to walk the streets of Kabul without proper cover.

On the whole, female aid workers and journalists generally enjoy better access to ordinary Afghans than do Western men. This is for the simple reason that foreign men cannot meet Afghan women as easily as foreign women can meet both Afghan men and women. This aspect of 'gender privilege' is something often overlooked by people who assume that being female in Afghanistan is automatically bad news. In addition, as many female medical aid workers found while working inside Afghanistan during the Soviet war, women were often made 'honorary' men (or 'neutered' as one French doctor preferred to describe it) by the Afghans. This meant that they could sit, eat, drink tea and even sleep (that is, in the same room) with Afghan men without any problem. Only strict fundamentalists, often influenced by Arab *Wahabi,* would refuse to acknowledge foreign women or even shake hands with them.

Dress is one of the most obviously limiting factors for women working in Afghanistan. Even in today's post-Taliban period the dress code is conservative, particularly in Pashtun areas where little has changed. Many northerners, too, are rigidly conservative. One of our contributors had this to add: "Foreign women are given more concessions than local women when it comes to dress and behaviour, but dressing appropriately goes a long way towards avoiding problems." Some Western women have gone out of their way to dress 'conservatively' by covering themselves even more than urban Afghan women, yet such conformism angers many educated women who believe that Westerners should set a standard if they are ever to get out from underneath the *burqa*. Probably the best approach is to simply be respectful (both of men and women) but assertive of your own identity. Some basic guidelines are as follows:

- Do not try to look too 'Afghan' or you may be treated accordingly. Dress conservatively but look recognisably 'Western.'
- Avoid wearing figure-hugging or revealing clothes.
- Ordinary loose-fitting Western dresses and below-the-knee skirts can be worn, with loose trousers on underneath to cover the legs, calves and ankles.
- Do not walk off the road to find a bush to spring a leak behind – you may walk into a minefield. Long, baggy dresses/skirts provide good cover for answering calls of nature while on the road.
- Wear blouses with long sleeves and avoid low bust-lines.
- In more conservative areas, *shalwar kameez* may be more appropriate.
- In public, cover your head and chest discreetly with a long shawl or *chador*, but there is no need to overdo it.
- In more liberal areas you may not need to wear a *chador* at all, but check first. This now includes 'international' space in Kabul and other towns.
- In general, dress more conservatively and discreet in rural areas, including refugee camps. There is no point in 'making a statement' which will only be interpreted as an insult. What you do in the privacy of an international aid office or guest house is up to you, but also bear in mind the house personnel who may not be as 'aware' as their urban counterparts (SEE CLOTHING & KIT).

Security is something to be aware of but not paranoid about. It is very rare for Western women to be threatened by Afghans; in fact, many women working or travelling in Afghanistan say that sexual harassment is far worse in Pakistan. If you are harassed in a public place, it is best to make as much of a scene as possible so as to shame whoever the culprit is. In 1997 a foreign woman working for an international aid agency was beaten by Taliban soldiers in Herat, despite wearing a *chador*. Reportedly it was not until she started screaming that the soldiers ran off. However, this type of incident is very much the exception, and Taliban authorities later apologised for the mistake. Unless recognized as foreigners, Western women wearing *chadors* have been roughed up by Pakistani frontier scouts at the border on the assumption that they are 'only' Afghan women. In 2002, a female aid worker was gang-raped and robbed near Mazar. However, some observers argue this was in part because of her decision to ignore security advice by travelling at night, in a single car, with large sums of money.

J. Hartley/UNICEF

Many experienced female expatriates continue life nearly as normal in Afghanistan: they drive vehicles, walk or cycle through the bazaar and play very much an equal role with their male colleagues. In Kabul particularly, there is a strong community of female aid workers to give you support. However, some towns – such as Kandahar – are more conservative than others. So if you are a new arrival, check out the situation with someone experienced before wandering around on your own.

In order not to attract unwanted attention, bear in mind some basic ground rules:

- As a Western woman it is best not to offer your hand to an Afghan man to shake – wait for him to offer you his hand first.
- Avoid sitting near Afghan men (choose your own small chair)
- Keep your conversations off the streets and behind closed doors.
- Women and men (even married couples) should not touch each other in public.
- Be careful, when sitting on the floor in the presence of Afghan men, to cover your knees and feet.
- Do not try and stare down the men staring at you – it only makes them more interested.
- Do not walk alone at night.

ESSENTIAL READING

Security Guidelines for Women, UN Security Coordination Office

For more essential data and advice SEE WOMEN, SECURITY TIPS and TRADITIONS & CUSTOMS

CONTACTS

J. Hartley/UNICEF

Coordinating agencies

AFGHAN ASSISTANCE COORDINATION AUTHORITY (AACA)

Established by the Afghanistan Interim Administration on 1 April 2002, AACA is a transitional mechanism designed to ensure a coherent, Afghan-led vision for development supported by accountable and efficient mechanisms for the use of aid.
ADDRESS: Prime Minister's Compound, Flower House Palace, (Qasr-e-Gulkhana, Sadarat), Kabul
Tel: + 93 (0)70 279 720 Email: afghanistanaca@afghanistangov.org
Web: www.afghanistangov.org/aaca

AGENCY COORDINATING BODY FOR AFGHAN RELIEF (ACBAR)

Established in 1988, ACBAR is an umbrella organIZATION for over 90 NGOs, both international and Afghan. Their aim is to provide a framework for members to exchange information to promote more coordinated, efficient and effective use of aid resources.
ADDRESSES:
Kabul: House 12, Jami Watt, Shahr-e-Naw, Kabul. Tel: + 93 (0)20 220 02 08
Mobile: + 93 (0)702 820 90 (Executive Coordinator), +93 (0)70 282 229 (Area Manager) Email: acbarkbl@atge.automail.com Web: www.acbar.org
Mazar: Darwaza-e-Jamhuriat, Kuch-e-Aka Yaseen, Mazar-e-Sharif, Tel: 40261
Herat: Jad-e-Bank Khoon, Chahar Rahee Haji Ayoob, Herat, Tel: 223 390
Jalalabad: Chahar Rahi-e-Mukhaberat, Had-e-Kama, First Street on the Right, Jalalabad

AFGHANISTAN INFORMATION MANAGEMENT SERVICE (AIMS)

SEE UN AGENCIES

AFGHAN NGOs COORDINATION BUREAU (ANCB)

Established in 1991 to coordinate the activities of Afghan NGOs. Their aim is to improve the quality of life of Afghans and to encourage their voluntary return to their home country.
ADDRESSES:
Kabul: 1st House, 3rd Street, Qalai Fatullah, Shahr-e-Naw,
"Mobile: +93 (0) 70 278221 Email: ancb@ancb.org
Peshawar: 1st House, 1st Street, 25 Chinar Road, University Town, Peshawar. Tel: +92 (91) 853849 Fax: +92 (91) 853804
Web: www.ancb.org

BRITISH AGENCIES AFGHANISTAN GROUP (BAAG)

Coordinating body for British NGOs working in Afghanistan, which produces an excellent monthly news update.
ADDRESS: BAAG, c/o British Refugee Council, 240/250 Ferndale Road, London SW9 8BB, UK. Tel: +44 (0)20 7820 3000 Fax: +44 (0)20 7840-4388 Email: Peter.Marsden@refugeecouncil.org.uk Web: www.baag.org.uk

ISLAMIC COORDINATION COUNCIL (ICC)

ICC coordinates 16 Muslim humanitarian organizations working to help refugees and internally displaced. It provides a forum in which member organizations can discuss aid policy guidelines, resource management and other operational issues.
ADDRESS: 409, 4th Floor, Gul Haji Plaza, Peshawar, Pakistan Tel: +92 (91) 45342 3 Email: iccpsh@brain.net.pk Web: www.pcpafg.org/Organizations/icc

SOUTHERN/WESTERN AFGHANISTAN AND BALUCHISTAN ASSOCIATION FOR COORDINATION (SWABAC)

Formed in Quetta in August 1988 by NGOs undertaking relief and rehabilitation assistance in the south-west. It provides a forum in which members can discuss their concerns, policies and other operational issues.
ADDRESSES:
Pakistan: House 119 E, Block No.4, Satellite Town, Quetta Tel/Fax: +92 (0) 81 442 525, Email: swabac@swb.qta.sdnpkundp.org, swabac@qta.inforlink.net.pk
Afghanistan: House No. 12 Shahr-e-Naw, Behind the Kandahar Hotel, Near Pataw Canal , Kandahar Tel: +93 (0) 3 210-080

UNITED NATIONS ASSISTANCE MISSION IN AFGHANISTAN (UNAMA)

SEE UN AGENCIES

NGOs active in the region[1]

AFGHANAID (A-AID)

British NGO founded in 1991. Sectors: economic and social development of impoverished rural Afghan communities (especially marginalized), women's organIZATIONs, community infrastructure, watershed management and road rehabilitation.
ADDRESSES:
Afghanistan: Premises of ISRA office, Wazir Akbar Khan, Street No. 15. Avenue 5th, Kabul. Tel: 62704 Satphone: + 873 762 155 450
Pakistan: 5B Gul Mohar Road, University Town, Peshawar. Tel: +92 (91) 5702030, 5702021 Fax: +92 (91) 840322 Email: hoaaid@brain.net.pk
International: 2nd Floor, 16 Mortimer Street, London W1N 7RD, UK
Tel: +44 020 7255 3355 Fax: +44 020 7255 3344 Email: info@afghanaid.org.uk Web: www.afghanaid.org.uk

AFGHAN AMPUTEE BICYCLISTS FOR REHABILITATION AND RECREATION (AABRAR)

Founded in 1992. Sectors: rehabilitation and physical therapy for disabled Afghans.
ADDRESSES:
Afghanistan: Tel: +92 (91) 84407, Jalalabad 2024.
Satphone: +8821650265570
Pakistan: AABRAR, C/O KJRC, Jamrud Road, University Town, Peshawar +92 (91) 844078 Fax: +92 (91) 840521 Email: aabrarps@psh.pak.net.pk

[1] *This is only a selected list. Please contact UNAMA, ACBAR, AIMS and other coordinating groups for a full list of agencies operating in Afghanistan and the region.*

AFGHAN COMMUNITY DEVELOPMENT ORGANIZATION (ACDO)

Founded in 1991. Sectors: sustainable rehabilitation of engineering, agricultural, health, income generation, infrastructure and relief projects.
ADDRESS: 10th Street, Taimani Watt, Taimani, Kabul. Mobile + 93 (0) 70 281991 Tel: 31952 Email: acdo1232003@yahoo.com

ACTION CONTRE LA FAIM (ACF)

Founded in 1979. Sectors: to fight famine and hunger around the world. Since 1995 ACF Afghanistan has been involved in nutrition, health, water and sanitation, food security and other programmes.
ADDRESSES:
Afghanistan: ACF Afghanistan Coordination office: Wazir Akbar Khan, Street No.13, Line 3, House No.1 Mobile +93 (0)7 02 77 33 7
Email: acfafgha@kbl.pactec.net
ACF Kabul office: Charahi Microrayan 3, Kabul. Satphone: +873 763 439 198
Fax: +873 763 439 210 Email: acfafgha@kbl.pactec.net
International: 4 rue Niepce, 75014 Paris Tel: +33 (0)1 43 35 88 88
Fax: +33 (0)1 43 35 88 00 Email: acf@acf.imaginet.fr
Web: www.acf-fr.org

ACTED

Agence d'Aide a la Cooperation Technique Et au Developpement (Agency For Technical Cooperation and Development). Sectors: bakeries; coalmining to supply hospitals, clinics and orphanages with power and heat; urban rehabilitation; mapping.
ADDRESSES:
Afghanistan: Malikyar Watt House, 30 Shahr-e-Naw, Kabul.
Tel: +93 70-20 2201 266 Email: kabul@acted.org
International: 33 rue Godot de Mauroy, 75009 Paris, France.
tel: +33 (1) 42 65 33 33 Fax: +33 (1) 42 65 33 46 Email: paris@acted.org
Web: www.acted.org

AFGHAN DEVELOPMENT ASSOCIATION (ADA)

Created in 1990. Sectors: rehabilitation and development, integrated agricultural and environmental training.
ADDRESSES:
Afghanistan: Frokhi Watt House No. 8, Street No. 6, Opposite Park Shahr-e-Naw, Kabul. Tel: +93 (0)20 2200660
Pakistan: House 17-F/A-1, Khushal Khan Khattak Road, UPO Box 922, University Town. Tel: +92 91 845212, 845312 Fax: +92 91 5700096 Email: Afgdevas@brain.net.pk Web: www.Afgdevas.org
International: P.O. Box 660351, Sacramento, CA 95866, USA.
Tel: +1 482 1019 Tel/Fax: +1 916 446 0806

ANATOLIAN DEVELOPMENT FOUNDATION (ADF)

Operating with other agencies in Pakistan and Afghanistan since October 2001. Sectors: agriculture, construction, education, relief.
ADDRESSES:
Afghanistan: H No 87, Charayi Haji Moh. Dad, Kabul. Tel: +93 (0)20 2200119
Fax: +93 (0) 2031875 Email: adf-afghanistan@hotmail.com;
Pakistan: House No. 1/A, Street 63, F-7/3, Islamabad
Mobile: +92 300 8579789 Fax: +92 (0) 51 2826432
Email: adf-pakistan@hotmail.com
International: Ataturk Bulvari, No. 121/818, 06640, Bakanliklar, Ankara, Turkey. Tel: +90 312 4257804 Fax: +90 312 4176728 Email: akv@marketweb.net.tr Web www.akv.org.tr

ASIA FOUNDATION (AF)

A US foundation committed to the development of a peaceful, prosperous and open Asia-Pacific region. Sectors: governance and law, economic reform and development, women's participation, international relations.
ADDRESSES:
Afghanistan: House No. 252 Street 2, Ashraf Watt, Shahr-e-Naw, Kabul. Tel: +93 (0) 70 276509, (0)70 277284
International: 465 California Street. San Francisco, CA 94194, USA. Tel: +1 415 982 4640 Fax: +1 415 392 8863 Email: info@asiafound.org www.asiafoundation.org

AMITIE FRANCO-AFGHANE AIDE HUMANITARIE ET INFORMATION (AFRANE)

From its foundation in 1980 until 1986, AFRANE concentrated on humanitarian aid and information, through a quarterly review called *Les Nouvelles d'Afghanistan* in collaboration with the Center de Recherches et d'Etudes Documentaires sur l'Afghanistan (CEREDAF). From 1986 onwards the agency has focused on rural development and education.
ADDRESSES:
Charahi Ansari, Street 2, Shahr-e-Naw, Kabul. Tel: +93 (0) 20 2201154
CEREDAF: 16 passage de la Main d'Or, 75011 Paris, France.
Tel: +33 (1) 43 55 63 50 Web: www.afrane.org

AFGHAN GERMAN BASIC EDUCATION (AG BAS-Ed)

Created in 1996 as a follow-up agency for the GTZ-funded Basic Education for Afghan Refugees project (BEFARe). Sectors: formal and non-formal education.
ADDRESS:
House 685, Street 6, Parwan 3, Kabul. Mobile: +93 (0)70 280666
Email: najeebnur@hotmail.com

AFGHAN HEALTH AND DEVELOPMENT SERVICES (AHDS)

Founded by Afghans in 1990. Sectors: rehabilitation of health infrastructure, primary healthcare.
ADDRESS: House 38, Street 4, Zarghoona Maiden, close to Filling Station, Shahr-e-Naw, Central P.O. Box 1712, Kabul. Tel: +93 (0)20 2102716 Mobile: +93 (0)70 284275 Email: ahdskabul@hotmail.com Web www.ahds.org

AFGHAN INSTITUTE OF LEARNING (AIL)

Founded in 1995 to assist Afghan women and children, AIL is run entirely by Afghan women and is one of the largest employers of Afghan women in the country. Sectors: empowering Afghan women by expanding their educational and health opportunities and by fostering self-reliance and community participation.
ADDRESS: House 387, Masomi Street, Rd 3, Behind Cinema Baharistan, Kart-e-Parwan, Kabul. Tel: 30582 Satphone: +882 1650265266
Or contact through: Women's Learning Partnership (WLP), 4343 Montgomery Avenue, Suite 201, Bethesda, MD 20814, USA. Tel: +1 301 654 2774
Fax: +1 301 654 2775 Email: wlp@learningpartnership.org
Web: www.learningpartnership.org

AIDE MEDICALE INTERNATIONAL (AMI)

One of the oldest aid agencies operating in Afghanistan, founded in 1979. Sectors: basic healthcare, healthcare training.
ADDRESSES:
Afghanistan: House No. 914, Farokhi Road, East of Shahr-e-Naw Park, Kabul. Satphone: +873 762 602 018 Email: amiafghan@iinmarsat.francetelecom.fr
Mazar: Kalandar Shah Street, Behind Mazar Hotel, Mazar-e-Sharif. Satphone: +873 762 053 566 Email: amifam@inmarsat.francetelecom.fr
International: 119, rue des Amandiers, 75020 Paris, France.
Tel: +33 (1) 46 36 04 04 Fax: +33 (1) 46 36 66 10 Email: info@amifrance.org
Web: www.amifrance.org

AGENCY FOR REHABILITATION ENERGY CONSERVATION IN AFGHANISTAN (AREA)

An extension of the GTZ Domestic Energy Saving Project (DESP) established in 1984. Sectors: agriculture, construction, community development, environment, income generation, relief, mines, alternative technology and vocational training.
ADDRESSES:
Afghanistan: Darul Aman main street, Shura Road, opposite Rukhshana High School, Kabul. Tel: +93 (0) 20 2501193, 2500268 Email: mayel@brain.net.pk
Web: www.area-afg.org or www.area-afg.cc.
Pakistan: 39-D/3, S.J.A, Lane, University Town, Peshawar.
Tel: +92 (91) 5702803 Fax: +92 (91) 844647 Email: area@comsats.net.pl

AFGHANISTAN RECONSTRUCTION AND ENGINEERING COMMITTEE (AREC)

Afghan NGO focusing on agriculture, construction and education, refugee rehabilitation.
ADDRESSES:
Afghanistan: Room No. 201m, Salangwat Cinema, Kabul.
Pakistan: 405, Gul Haji plaza, 4th floor, University Road, GPO.Box 467, Peshawar. Mobile: +92 0333 9108871, 0300 9591862 Email: arec2000@hotmail.com Web: www.arec2000.tripol.com

AFGHAN TECHNICAL CONSULTANTS (ATC)

Created in 1989 to deal with mine clearance, now an implementing partner of the Mine Action Programme for Afghanistan (MAPA).
ADDRESSES:
Afghanistan: House No. 23 & 24 Road No. 13, Behind Wazir Akbar Khan Mosque, Kabul. Tel: + 882 1689800329 Fax: +882 1689800324 Email: atckabul@apollo.net.pk.
Pakistan: 45 D-4, Old Jamrud Road, University Town, Peshawar.
Tel: +92 (91) 840122, 40412 Fax: +92 (91) 44780

AFGHAN-TURK CAG EDUCATIONAL (ATCE)

Established in 1995. Sectors: secondary education for rural children in English, Biology, Chemistry, Physics, Maths and Computer studies.
ADDRESSES:
Afghanistan: 14 Storey Building, Cinema Pamir 9th Floor, Kabul.
Mobile: +93 (0)20 210 0722, +93 (0)70 28 5511 Email: fkarakoc@hotmail.com
International: Erasmusstr. 14, 40322 Dusselldorf, Germany.
Tel: +49 211 933 76125 Email: yudigerew@yahoo.de

BBC AFGHAN EDUCATION DRAMA (BBC AED)

The BBC World Service first began broadcasting educational dramas in Persian and Pashto in the late 1980s. The success of these shows led to the formation of BBC AED and the launching in 1994 of its radio soap opera "New Home, New Life". Towards the end of the 1990s, AED also launched the Media Action International-initiated programme, Radio Education for Afghan Children (REACH).
ADDRESS: Kabul: BBC/AEP H No. 271, 1st Street, Qala-e-Najara, Next to New Zarif Pharmacy, Khair Khana, Kabul.
Mobile: +93 (0)70 282226, (0)70 278093

CORD AID (CA)

Dutch member of the Caritas Confederation. Sectors: construction, agriculture, education, emergency, health, income generation, water & sanitarian, veterinary programmes and gender issues.
ADDRESSES:
Afghanistan: Charahi Shahid, Shahr-e-Naw, District 10, Kabul. Email: caritas.kabul@caritas.org Web: www.caritas-network-for.afghanistan.org
Pakistan: House No.7, Gul Mohar Road, University Town, Peshawar.
Tel: +92 (91) 852030 Fax: +92 (91) 843467
Email: cordaid@psh.comsats.net.pk.

CARITAS Germany

Working in Afghanistan since 1994. Sectors: handicapped people, education (rehabilitation of girls' winter programmes/schools), workshop training for war orphans, and construction of roads, bridges and schools.
ADDRESS: House No. 649, Charye Shaid, District 10, Shahr-e-Naw, Kabul.
Tel: +93 (0)70-280291 Email: office.kabul@caritas.de.

COOPERATION CENTRE FOR AFGHANISTAN (CCA)

Operational in Afghanistan since 1990, CCA specializes in the promotion of human rights and sustainable development. It produces three periodicals, CCA Newsletter (English), Taawoon (Dari/Pashto), and Sadaf, mainly for women.
ADDRESSES:
Afghanistan: Shah Bubu Jan street, Shahr-e-Naw, Kabul. Tel: 2200451, 33722 Mobile: +93 (0)70 274985 Email: hussaini@pes.comsats.net.pk Web: www.ccamata.com
Mazar: Karte Bukhdi, Close to FRCS. Tel: +93 (0)70 500373
Bamiyan: Moalem Ikram House, Charasia, Bamiyan City
Pakistan: House No.4, Sector P/1, Opposite to PDA , Phase 4, Hayatabad, Peshawar. Tel: +92 (91) 816386, 815647

CARE INTERNATIONAL (CI)

Founded at the end of World War II as the Committee for Aid and Relief in Europe, CARE is now one of the world's largest international humanitarian agencies. CARE established its first mission in Afghanistan in 1961 with a focus on medical training and improving healthcare services. Sectors now include: fighting poverty in south-eastern Afghanistan, agriculture, construction, education, health, income generation, relief, and water supply.
ADDRESSES:
Afghanistan: Haji Yaqoob, Square, Park Road, Shahr-e-Naw, Kabul.
Tel: +93 (0)20 290064 Fax: +873 7762212631 Email: carekbl@care.automail.com Web: www.care.org
Pakistan: 6 Park Lane, Park Road, University Town, Peshawar.
Tel: +92 (91) 850614 Fax: +92 (91) 8418226 Email: afghan@care.org.

International: CARE USA, 151 Ellis Street NE, Atlanta, GA 30303-2439, USA. Tel: +1 (404) 681 2552 Fax: +1 (404) 589 2651
Email: (name)@care.org Web: www.care.org
CARE International UK, 10-13 Rushworth Street, London SE1 0RB. Tel: +44 (0)20 7934 9334 Fax: +44 (0)20 7934 9335 Email: info@uk.care.org

CENTER FOR HUMANITARIAN PSYCHOLOGY (CHP)

International: Center for Humanitarian Psychology, 15 rue des Savoises, 1205 Geneva, Switzerland. Tel: +41 22 800 21 15 Fax: +41 22 800 21 16 Web: www.humanitarian-psy.org Email: info@humanitarian-psy.org

CHILDREN IN CRISIS (CIC)

Founded in UK by the Duchess of York, it began work in Afghanistan in 1997 through support to the India Ghandi Hospital, home-based schools and Tahia Masuan and Allauddin Orphanages. Sectors: teacher training education for vulnerable groups (IDPs and street working children).
ADDRESS: House No. 281, 1st street, Wazir Akbar Khan, Kabul.
Tel: +93 (0)70 281401 Email: caicic@aol.com.

CIET INTERNATIONAL

New York-based survey and research organization, Community Information and Epidemiological Technologies (CIET) specializes in researching data for emergency situations, using a Multiple Indicators Cluster Survey method (MICS).
ADDRESSES:
Pakistan: PO Box 13018, Karachi, 75350. Tel: +92 320 450 4648 Email: cietpakistan@ciet.org
International: 847A 2nd Avenue, Suite 387, New York 10017, USA.
Tel: +1 212 242 3428 Fax: +1 212 242 5453 Email: cietinter@ciet.org Web: www.ciet.org

COORDINATION OF AFGHAN RELIEF (CoAR)

Created by Afghans in December 1989 to contribute towards rehabilitation. Implementing programmes for donor agencies such as Norwegian Church Aid or World Food Programme, CoAR focuses on: sustainable development, agriculture, water provision, environment, livestock, rural engineering, health, women's programmes and education.
ADDRESSES:
House No. 1, Bunbast Street, in front of German Embassy, Wazir Akbar Khan, Kabul. Tel: +93 (0)70 280725-27 Fax: +882 1689800756 Email: coarkbl@brain.net.pk.
Herat: Public Park, Charahi Mustufiat, near to UNAMA. Tel: +020 223141.
Pakistan: 19 Chinar Road, University Town, Peshawar. Tel: +92 (91) 851789 Fax: +92 (91) 852789 Email: coarnet@brain.net.pk.

DANISH AFGHAN COMMITTEE (DAC)

Danish NGO created in 1984. Sectors: humanitarian assistance, basic healthcare, nursing training, emergency medical assistance.
ADDRESSES:
Afghanistan: DAC-House, Jadah Mahbas, Herat. Tel: +873 762496625 Fax: +873 762496626 Email: dac.herat@mail.dk
International: Chairman Viggo Fischer, Gammel Køgelandevej 117/1, 2650 Valby, Denmark. Tel: +45 36169038 Fax: +45 36450205
Email: dac@afghan.dk Web: www.afghan.dk

DANISH COMMITTEE FOR AID TO AFGHAN REFUGEES (DACAAR)

Founded in 1984 to provide humanitarian support to Afghan refugees. Its members are Danish People's Aid, Danish Refugee Council and MS-Danish Association for International Co-operation. Sectors: agriculture, construction, emergency, health and water supply, particularly in support of returnees and IDPs.
ADDRESSES:
Pakistan: 10-Gul Mohar Lane, UPO Box 885, University Town, Peshawar. Tel: +92 (91) 850732/ 853856 Fax: +92 (91) 840516, Email: dacaar@pes.comsats.net.pk Web: www.dacaar.org.
Kabul: House 403, Street No. 2, Qala-e-Fatullah, Kabul.
Tel: +93 (0) 70 276443 Email: dacaar1@get2net.dk.
International: c/o Danish Refugee Council, PO Box 53, Borgergade 10, DK-1002, Copenhagen, Denmark. Tel: +45 3373 5000
Fax: +45 3332 8448 Email: drc@drc.dk Web: www.dacaar.org

DEMINING AGENCY FOR AFGHANISTAN (DAFA)

Established by UNOCHA (now UNAMA) in 1990. Sectors: mine clearance in south and west of country.
ADDRESS: 139/F Block 4, Satellite Town, PO Box 548, Quetta, Pakistan.
Tel: +92 (81) 442056, 448309 Fax: +92 (81) 447206

DUTCH COMMITTEE FOR AFGHANISTAN VETERINARY PROGRAMMES (DCA-VET)

Began crossborder operations to the Panjshair Valley in 1985. It established the Veterinary Training and Support Centre (VTSC) in 1988 which trains around 45 'para-vets' a year.
ADDRESSES:
Pakistan: PO Box 792, Peshawar. Tel: +92 (91) 852 191, 852 192
Fax: +92 (91) 840 258 Email: dcapak@psh.paknet.com.pk
International: PO Box 65, Lelystad, The Netherlands. Tel: +31 320 238 385
Fax: +31 320 238 050 Web: www.dca-vet.nl

GERMAN AGRO ACTION (GAA)

Sectors: urban reconstruction, sanitation, agriculture and food for work programmes.
ADDRESS: 31 C Circular Road, University Town, Peshawar, Pakistan.
Tel: +92 (91) 851815 Fax: +92 (91) Email: coordgaa-afg@les-raisting.de

GOAL

Founded in Ireland 25 years ago. Sectors: food security for IDPs in north, construction and engineering, agriculture and food distribution.
ADDRESSES:
Afghanistan: House 2172, Street 4, Qala-e-Fatullah, Kabul. Tel: +882 1650612121 Email: august@inmarsat.francetelecom.fr Web: www.goal.ie.
Saleh House, Bank Mili Street, Mazar-e-Sharif. Tel: +873 763020678
Email: digital@inmarsats.francetelecom.fr.
Pakistan: House 12, Street 39, F6/1, Islamabad. Tel: +92 (51) 28284429
Email: goal@comsats.net.pk

HELP THE AFGHANS FOUNDATION (HAF)

Established 1984 in The Netherlands. Sectors: relief, medical assistance for refugees, particularly women, children and the disabled.
ADDRESS: Binckhorstlaan 309, 2516 BC, The Hague, Holland.
Tel: +31 (70) 383 6641

HILFE ZUR SELBSTHLIFE e.V. (HELP Germany)

Founded in 1981 as a fund raising agency to help Afghan refugees. Sectors: infrastructure, rehabilitation, construction, education, demining, water, sanitation.
ADDRESSES:
Afghanistan: Checkpost 1 Shah Mohd Khan Street, Qala-e-Naw, Badghis. Tel: +873 76 3032580
International: Reuterstrasse. 39, D-53113 Bonn, Germany. Tel: +49-22891529-0 Fax: +49-22891529-99 Email: info@help-ev.de Web: www.help-ev.de

HANDICAP INTERNATIONAL-FRANCE (HI)

Founded in 1982 in France. Sectors: rehabilitation of people with disabilities (orthopaedics, fitting of prostheses, physiotherapy, occupational therapy, etc), landmine clearance, health, including psychology and HIV/AIDS, social development and education, emergency aid, water and sanitation, micro-credit and economic development.
ADDRESSES:
Afghanistan: Street 10, Wazir Akbar Khan, Kabul. Mobile: + 93 (0)70 2745540 Satphone: + 870 76 14 72 715 Email: hisat2@inmarsat.francetelecom.fr
International: 14, avenue Berthelot, 69361 Lyon Cedex 07, France. Tel: +33 (4) 78 69 79 79 Fax: +33 (4) 78 69 79 94 Email: handicap-international@infonie.fr Web: www.handicap-international.org

HANDICAP INTERNATIONAL – BELGIUM & UK

ADDRESSES:
Rue de Spa 67, B-1000, Brussels, Belgium. Tel: + 32 2 280 16 01 Fax: + 32 2 230 60 30 Email: headoffice@handicap.be
Handicap International UK, 5 Station Hill, Farnham, Surrey, United Kingdom. Tel: + 44 (0)1252 821429 Fax: + 44 (0)1252 821428 Email: hi-uk@hi-uk.org

HEALTHNET INTERNATIONAL (HNI)

Initiated under the umbrella of MSF-Holland, but in 1993 was formed into a separate organization. Sectors: malaria and leishmaniasis control, research and implementation, technical lab support to other agencies.
ADDRESSES:
Afghanistan: House No. 810, Street No. 7, Nahia 10, Taimani-Kabul.
Pakistan: 1-A, Circular Lane, University Town, P.O. Box 889, Peshawar. Tel: +92 (91) 844474, 5702551, 852567 Fax: +92 (91) 840379 Email: hni@pes.comsats.net.pk, or: hnipesh@pes.comsats.net.pk

HALO TRUST (HT)

Established in Kabul in 1988. Sectors: mine clearance, medical dispensaries in Kabul, Jabul-us Seraj and Pul-e-Khumri, and clinics in Kabul treating malnourished children and pregnant women.
ADDRESSES:
Afghanistan: Charahi Ansari. PO Box. 3036, Kabul. Tel: 2201483 Satphone: +873 761931817 Fax: +873 761931818 Email: haloafg@yahoo.com Web: www.halotrust.org
International: PO Box 7905, Thornhill, DG3 5WA, UK. Fax: +44 (0)1848 331122 Email: mail@halotrust.org

INTERNATIONAL ASSISTANCE MISSION (IAM)

Founded in 1966, IAM has worked continuously in Afghanistan since then. All expatriate personnel are unpaid volunteers who attend a four-month Dari language course on arrival. IAM offers Dari and English language courses to non-IAM personnel by prior arrangement. Sectors: operations in Kabul, Herat and Mazar-e-Sharif, focusing on health and eye care (Noor Eye Hospital in Kabul), ophthalmic centres, mobile eye clinics, secondment of expatriate surgeons and nurses to train/assist government doctors, education, rehabilitation and economic development, notably the Renewable Energy Sources in Afghanistan Programme (RESAP).
ADDRESSES:
Afghanistan: Wazir Akbar Khan, Lane 1, Street 15, PO Box 625, Kabul. Satphone: + 873 762 841 460 / 461 Mobile: +93 (0)70 276417
Pakistan: PO Box 1167, Peshawar. Tel: +92 (91) 842 634
International: Partnership House, 157 Waterloo Road, London, SE1 UU, UK. Tel: +44 (20) 7928 8681 Fax: +44 (20) 7401 3215

IBNSINA

Operates extensive primary healthcare programme in 13 provinces through both fixed and mobile clinics. Sectors: mother and child healthcare, treatment of common diseases, provision of essential drugs, TBA programmes, laboratory facilities, reproductive health and family planning, expanded immunization, and other forms of medical assistance and training.
ADDRESSES:
Afghanistan: House No. 7, Street 10, Wazir Akbar Khan, Kabul. Tel: +93 (0)70 282122, (0)20 2 100 734 Email: ibnsina_kabul@hotmail.com Web: www.ibnsina.net
Pakistan: House No. 81, Street 6, G2 Phase 2, Hayatabad, Peshawar. Tel: +92 (91) 825442, 825489, 816380 Fax: +92 (91) 825516 Email: ibnsina@brain.net.pk, or: ibph@brain.net.pk

INTERNATIONAL FOUNDATION OF HOPE (IF HOPE)

Based in Colorado, USA. Sectors: healthcare, education, construction, relief, agriculture and income generation.
ADDRESSES:
Afghanistan: House No. 11, Street No. 10, Wazir Akbar Khan, Kabul. Tel+93 (0)20 290093 Fax: +93 (0)20 290093 Email: Wazir Akbar KhanIL@IFHope.org.
Jadah-e-Gullistan, House No. 119, Herat. Tel+020 225840.
Pakistan: House No. 186, Street 9, Phase 4, Hayatabad, Peshawar. Tel: +92 (91) 814316 Fax: +92 (91) 824288 Email: awzada@brain.net.pk

INTERNATIONAL ISLAMIC RELIEF ORGANIZATION (IIRO)

Based in Saudi Arabia. Sectors: health and education, hospitals in Pakistan and Afghanistan, orphan support.
ADDRESS: F-10/4, 13 Nazimuddin Road, GPO Box 1850, Islamabad, Pakistan. Tel: +92 (51) 281594, 290581 Fax: +92 (51) 282138

INTERNATIONAL MEDICAL CORPS (IMC)

Sectors: agriculture, emergency, health, income generation.
ADDRESSES:
Afghanistan: Wazir Akbar Khan, Across from Pakistan Embassy, Kabul. Tel: +93 (0)70 278678 Email: imckbl@imcworldwide.org Web: www.imcworldwide.org
Pakistan: House 6, F/11-3, Islamabad Email: shanson@imcworldwide.org

INTERNATIONAL RESCUE COMMITTEE (IRC)

Founded in the US in 1933 at the request of Albert Einstein to assist opponents of the Nazi regime in Germany. IRC began crossborder rehabilitation in 1988. Sectors: rural assistance, education, agriculture, health, infrastructure rehabilitation, protection and advocacy.
ADDRESSES:
Afghanistan: House 61, Kocha Afghana, Shash Darak, Kabul. Mobile: +93 (0) 70 285245 Tel: +93 (0)20 290208 Fax: + 873 761 351 927
Pakistan: 5C-II Abdra Road, University Town, Peshawar. Tel: +92 (91) 5703574, 850645 Fax: +92 (91) 850973 Email: ircpa@irc-pk.org
International: 122 East 42nd Street, 12th Floor, New York, NY 10168, USA. Tel: +1 (212) 551 3000 Fax: +1 (212) 551 3185 Web: www.theirc.org

ISLAMIC RELIEF-AGENCY (ISRA)

Began working with Afghan refugees in 1984. Sectors: health, agriculture, education, social welfare, rural development, environment, gender issues, human rights, relief & protection.
ADDRESSES:
Afghanistan: Kolola Pushta, Street 8, House No. 207, Kabul.
Pakistan: House 68-D/2, S.J. Afghani, University Town, Peshawar.
Tel: +92 (91) 840365, 844961 Fax: +92 (91) 840429
Email: isra@pes.comsats.net.pk

JAPAN AFGHAN MEDICAL SERVICE (JAMS)

Founded in 1986 as an Afghan Leprosy Service for refugees in Pakistan. Sectors: common diseases, minor and reconstructive surgery, hospitals and clinics, tropical disease training for Afghan doctors.
ADDRESS: 3-C II, Circular Road, University Town, Peshawar, Pakistan. Tel: +92 (91) 44350 Fax: +92 (91) 841167

MADERA

Mission d'Aide au Developpement des Economies Rurales en Afghanistan has operated in Afghanistan since the early 1980s. MADERA works through 26 permanent centres in eastern and central Afghanistan, and aims to link present rehabilitation concerns with a long-term development perspective. Sectors: integrated refugee return, rural rehabilitation – notably reforestation and agricultural support.
ADDRESSES:
Afghanistan: Qala-e-Fatullah, Sarak 4, House No. 471, Kabul.
Tel: +93 (0)70 281869 Email: kabul@inmarsats.francetelecom.fr.
Sahat-e-Ama Crossroads, Opposite to Sahat-e-Ama Hospital, Jalalabad. Tel: +2825 2565 3421 Email: madjalal@inmarsats.francetelecom.fr.
Pakistan: 4 D, Park Avenue, University Town, Peshawar. Tel: +92 91 842 237 Fax: +92 91 840 234 Email: Office@madera.psw.erum.com.pk
International: 3 Rue Roubo, 75011 Paris, France. Tel: +33 (1) 43 70 60 07 Fax: +33 (1) 43 70 60 07 Email: madera@globenet.org

MERCY CORPS INTERNATIONAL (MCI)

Began medical work for war-wounded and refugees in Quetta in 1986. Sectors: drought mitigation, cash-for-work projects, agricultural development, health, education, landmine rehabilitation and NGO capacity building.
ADDRESSES:
Afghanistan: House No. 558. Street 5, Herat Bus Transportation Street, Qala-e-Fatullah, Kabul. Mobile +93 (0)70 278379, (0)70 282145 Tel: +93 (0)20 290161 Email: msmatnev@yahoo.com
Pakistan: 10, Arbab Karam Khan Road, GPO Box 314, Quetta. Tel: +92 (81) 442863 Fax: +92 (81) 449473 Email: mail@mci-qat.sdnpk.undp.org

International: 3030 SW First Avenue, Portland, Oregon, 97201, USA.
Tel: +1 (503) 796 6800 Fax: +1 (503) 796 6844 Email: info@mercycorps.org
Web: www.mercycorps.org

MINE CLEARANCE PLANNING AGENCY (MCPA)

Afghan NGO established in 1997. Sectors: minefield surveys and mine clearance, maintaining the Mine Action Programme information system.
ADDRESSES:
Afghanistan: House No. 140, Street 10, Near Pakistan Embassy, Wazir Akbar Khan, Kabul. Tel: 24262
Pakistan: House 58, Street 4, H-2, Phase 2, Hayatabad, Peshwar.
Tel: +92 (91) 810 803, 810 194, 812 541 Email: mcpa@psh.paknet.com.pk

MINE DETECTION DOG CENTER (MDC)

Established in 1989 by the US Agency for International Development (USAID), MDC has started its own Mine Dog Groups and successful dog-breeding programme.
ADDRESSES:
Afghanistan: House No. 271, Street No. 14, Wazir Akbar Khan, Kabul.
Tel: + 93 (0)20 2301201 Email: mdc@brain.net.pk.
Tape Malang Jan, Chaman Hozori, Kabul. Tel: + 93 (0)20 210182
Pakistan: House No. 1, Main Abdara Road, University Town, Peshawar.
Tel: +92 (91) 510007 Fax: +92 (91) 842684 Email: mdc@brain.net.pk

MÉDECINS DU MONDE (MDM)

First began with crossborder assistance in early 1980. Sectors: support for Herat regional hospital, camp dispensaries, mother-child healthcare, rehabilitation of provincial hospitals in western Afghanistan, and protection of internally displaced refugees.
ADDRESSES:
Afghanistan: Kolola Pushta Main Street, in front of Kolola Pushta Blocks, Near Estagah-e-Barq, Kabul. Tel: +93 (0)20 282412 Fax: +873 762094174
Email: mdm59@inmarsat.francetelecom
International: 62, Rue Marcadet, 75018 Paris, France.
Tel: +33 (1) 44 92 15 15 Email: medmonde@medecinsdumonde.org
Web: www.medecinsdumonde.org

MEDAIR

Swiss-based NGO working in Afghanistan since 1996. Sectors: relief and rehabilitation, TB treatment, winter distribution of non-food items to widows in Kabul, shelter, sanitation, and M-Link (to facilitate contact between international and Afghan NGOs).
ADDRESSES:
Afghanistan: House 499, Street 4, Qala-e-Fatullah, Kabul. Tel: + 93 (0)70 274501 Fax: +873 762945645 Email: Kabul-lag@medair.automail.com
Pakistan: 28 Khushal Khan Khattak Road, University Town, Peshawar.
Tel: +92 (91) 841336 Email: medairp@drain.net.pk
International: Chemin de Croset 9, CH-1024 Ecublens, Switzerland.
Tel: +41 21 694 35 35 Fax: +41 21 694 35 40 Email: info@medair.org Web: www.medair.org

MEDICAL EMERGENCY RELIEF INTERNATIONAL (MERLIN)

Began working in Afghanistan in 1995. Sectors: emergency healthcare.
ADDRESSES:
Afghanistan: House No. 32, Street 4, Shahr-e-Naw, Kabul. Tel: +93 (0)70 280252 Email: kabul@merlin.uk Web: www.merlin.org.uk
House 1, Street 1, Taloqan City. Tel: +873 762 139352
Email: taloqan@merlin.org.uk
International: 5-13 Trinity Street, Borough, London SE1 1DB, UK.
Tel: +44 (0)20 7378 4888 Fax: +44 (0)20 7378 4899
Email: hq@merlin.org.uk Web: www.merlin.org.uk

MÉDECINS SANS FRONTIÈRES (MSF)

Established in 1971 and operational inside Afghanistan since the early 1980s, MSF has various national sections (Switzerland, France, Holland and Belgium) operating in different parts of Afghanistan. Sectors: primary healthcare, mother-child healthcare, water and sanitation, emergency preparedness.
ADDRESSES:
Afghanistan: Behind Cinema Zinah, Shahr-e-Naw, Kabul.
Tel: Kabul 30511 Satphone: +873 382 040112 Satfax: +873 382 040117
Kandahar: +873 762 880 340
Pakistan: 25 SJ Afghani Road, GPO Box 889, University Town, Peshawar.
Tel: +92 (91) 42400 Fax: +92 (91) 843154
International:
MSF Belgium: Rue Dupréstraat 94, 1090 Brussels, Belgium.
Tel: +34 (02) 474 74 74 Email: info@azg.be
MSF France: 8, rue Street Sabine, 75011 Paris, France.
Tel: +33 (1) 40 21 29 29 Fax: +33 (1) 48 06 68 68
Email: Office@paris.msf.org
MSF Holland: Max Euweplein 40, PO Box 10014, 1001 EA Amsterdam, The Netherlands. Tel: +31 (20) 52 08 705 Fax: +31 (20) 62 05 170 Email: (name)@amsterdam.msf.org

MANAGEMENT SCIENCE FOR HEALTH (MSH)

Sectors: surveying health facilities, workers and other potential healthcare providers, such as shops and pharmacies. MSH is working with the Ministry of Public Health to help coordinate donor support and NGOs.
ADDRESSES:
House No. 22, Tarabaz Khan Road, Shabobo Street, Shahr-e-Naw, Kabul.
Tel: +93 (0)20 2200339 Email: afghan@msh.org Web: www.msh.org.

NORWEGIAN AFGHANISTAN COMMITTEE (NAC)

Founded in 1979 in response to the Soviet invasion. Sectors: education, health, environment and infrastructure (engineering/construction).
ADDRESSES:
Afghanistan: House No.137, Forokhi Wat, Shahr-e-Naw, Kabul. Tel: 33684
Other offices in Ghazni, Faizabad and Keshem.
Pakistan: 68-Sahibzada Abdul Qayyum Road, University Town, P.O. Box. 993, Peshawar. Tel: +92 (91) 41346, 45268, 43717 Fax: +92 (91) 840517
Email: norac@brain.net.pk
International: Solidaritetshuset, Osterhausgate 27, 0183 Oslo, Norway. Tel: +47 22 98 93 15 Fax: +47 22 98 93 01 Email: afghanistankomiteen@c2i.net
Web: www.solidaritetshuset.org/ain

NORWEGIAN PROJECT OFFICE/RURAL REHABILITATION ASSOCIATION FOR AFGHANISTAN (NPO/RRAA)

Established in Peshawar in 1990, now an independent Afghan NGO with offices in Jalalabad, Gardez, Mazar and Herat. Sectors: income generation and skills training, construction, agriculture, education.
ADDRESS: 15-B Old Jamrud Road, University Town, Peshawar. Tel: 92 (91) 41129/ 45210 Fax: 92 (91) 840107 Email: nporraa@pes.comsats.net.pk

OCKENDEN INTERNATIONAL (OI)

Founded in England in 1960, Ockenden has been working with Afghan refugees since 1984. Sectors: returnees and IDPs, community development, returnee reintegration.
ADDRESSES:
Afghanistan: House No. 531, Jami Watt, Next to Charahi Shaheed, Shahr-e-Naw, Kabul. Tel: +93 (0)20 2200602 Fax: +93 (0)20 290143 Email: kabul@ockenden.org.uk
Herat: House No. 250, Jade-e-Mahtab, District No 5, Herat. Tel: 040 224059, 222205 Fax: + 870 761375176 Email: ocken4@inmarsat.francetelecom.fr
Kandahar: Haji Mohammad Omer's House, Chinese Hospital Street, Kandahar. Tel: +93 (0)70 286485 Satphone: +882 16898104
Email: oikandahar@brain.net.pk
International: Constitution Hill, Woking, Surrey GU22 7UU, UK.
Tel: +44 (0)1483 772012 Fax: +44 (0)1483 750774
Email: oi@ockenden.org.uk Web: www.ockenden.org.uk

ORGANIZATION FOR MINE CLEARANCE AND AFGHAN REHABILITATION (OMAR)

Afghan NGO established in 1990. Sectors: mine awareness courses, training aids and publications on mine awareness, manual mine clearance, primary education, healthcare, rehabilitation.
ADDRESSES:
Afghanistan: House 20, Street 10, Wazar Akbar Khan, Kabul.
Mobile: +93 (0)70 275793 Tel: +93 (0)20 2100833 Fax: +93 (0)20 2102152
Email: omarinti@liwal.com
Pakistan: House 19, Street 2, K.1, Phase 3, Hayatabad, Peshawar.
Tel: +92 (91) 812084 Email: omarintl@psh.paknet.com.pk

ORPHANS, REFUGEES & AID (ORA INTERNATIONAL)

German-based organization founded in 1981, ORA began assisting Afghan refugees in 1983. Sectors: drug addiction, rehabilitation and awareness, and HIV/AIDS
ADDRESSES:
Pakistan: F-27, Khushal Khan Khattak Road, University Town, Peshawar GPO Box 594. Tel: +92 (91) 841280 Fax: +92 (91) 5701089
Email: ora.peshawar@altavista.net
International: Am Rothbusch 26, D-34497 Korbach, Germany.
Tel: +49 (5631) 63011/4 Fax: +49 (5631) 63015

OXFAM

British NGO established in 1942, Oxfam has worked in Afghanistan since 1989. Sectors: education and health in rural areas, livelihoods, emergency & drought relief in Hazarajat, Badakhshan, Kandahar, Herat.
ADDRESSES:
Afghanistan: House No 319/322, Main Darulaman Road, Ayob Khan Mina, Kabul. Mobile: + 93 (0)70 278657 Satphone: +873 762 945672 Satfax: +873 672 155989 Email: agnprog@oxfam.org.uk, oxfam-kabul@oxfam.org.uk
Pakistan: House 44, Street 59, F1-8/3, Islamabad. Tel: +92 (51) 4449791, 4449445 Fax: +92 (51) 4449790 Email: oxfampak@oxfam.org.uk
International: 266 Banbury Road, Oxford, OX2 7DL, UK. Tel: +44 (0)1865 311311 Fax: 44 (0)1865 312600 Email: oxfam@oxfam.org.uk Web: www.oxfaminternational.org

PAMIR DEVELOPMENT AUTHORITY (PDA)

Afghan NGO established in 1993. Sectors: relief & protection, water supply, irrigation, shelter, road rehabilitation.
ADDRESS: Taimani Street No. 3, Across from IOMG, House No. 306, beside RAFA, Kabul. Tel: +93 (0)70 278048

PAMIR RECONSTRUCTION BUREAU (PRB)

Afghan NGO founded in 1990. Sectors: relief, reconstruction, civil engineering & construction, animal health & livestock production, agriculture, skills training, income generation, community development.
ADDRESSES:
Afghanistan: House 1, Chahar Rahi Sedarat, opp. Sadarat Main Gate, Kabul. Tel: +93 (20) 200012, 33262 Email: prbkabul@hotmail.com
Pakistan: 8-A, Rehman Baba Rd, University Town, Peshawar.
Tel+92 (91) 5701641 Fax: +92 (91) 841474 Email: prb@brain.net.pk

PHARMACIENS SANS FRONTIÈRES (PSF)

French medical NGO which began work in Afghanistan in 1995. Sectors: drug procurement, distribution of essential drugs and medical material.
ADDRESSES:
Afghanistan: Karte Wali Noshi, 9 Main Street, Chasshdarak, Kabul. Satphone: +873 763 22 22 30 Mobile: +93 (0)70 281 009 Email: psfafgh1@inmarsat.francetelecom.fr
International: 4 voie Militaire des Gravanches, 63100 Clermand Ferrand, France. Tel: +33 (4) 73 98 24 98 Fax: + 33 (0)4 73 98 24 90
Email: psf@psf-ci.org Web: www.psfci.org

RECONSTRUCTION AUTHORITY FOR AFGHNISTAN (RAFA)

Afghan NGO founded in 1988 to assist repatriation of refugees. Sectors: water supply, sanitation, emergency relief, shelter and construction, protection for refugees.
ADDRESSES:
Afghanistan: House No. 305, Street No. 1, Opposite IOM Office, Near Haji M. Dad Masque, Taimani Watt, Kabul. Tel: +93 (0)70 277124
Email: rafa_org@yahoo.com
Pakistan: Flat No. 402, Gul Haji Plaza, Peshawar. Tel: +92 (91) 850593
Fax: +92 (91) 850593 Email: rafa@brain.net.pk

RÄDDA BARNEN (RBS)

Swedish Save the Children, founded in 1919 as a child rights organization. Sectors: disabled Afghans, mine awareness, refugee & IDP rehabilitation, health.
ADDRESSES:
Pakistan: 228, Gulhaji Plaza, UPO Box 1424, Peshawar.
Tel: +92 (91) 44784, 840987 Fax: +92 (91) 840349
International: Grensesvingen 7, 0661, Oslo 6, Norway.
Tel: +47 (22) 570080 Fax: +47 (22) 688547

SOLIDARITE AFGHANISTAN BELGIUM (SAB)

Began assistance to Afghan refugees in 1985. Sectors: education and income generation.
ADDRESS: House No. 311, Street No. 3, Chahrahi Haji Yaqub, Shahr-e-Naw, Kabul. Tel: 33671 Mobile: +93 (0)70 278263 Email: sabpew@brain.net.pk

SAVE THE FOREST ANIMALS ORGANIZATION (SAFO)

Afghan NGO focusing on agriculture, construction, education, water supply and irrigation.
ADDRESS: Wellayat Street, Opposite General Hospital, Herat.
Tel: 020 220223

SOCIETY OF AFGHANISTAN'S VOLUNTEER ENVIRONMENTALISTS (SAVE)

Founded in 1993. Sectors: environment, forestry, education, income generation, resource centre.
ADDRESS: House 514, Street 15, E2 Phase 1, Hayatabad, Peshawar.
Tel: +92 (91) 813838

SWEDISH COMMITTEE FOR AFGHANISTAN (SCA)

Founded in 1980, SCA is one of the oldest NGOs operating in Afghanistan. Sectors: primary healthcare, education and agriculture in 18 provinces.
ADDRESSES:
Afghanistan: Sarak-e Kuala-e Pushta, near Parwan-e Sewom Square, Kabul. Mobile: +93 (0)70 284740 Email: scaero@eikmail.com
Pakistan: 24D/E Chinar Rd, University Town, Peshawar, GPO Box 689.
Tel: + 92 (91) 111 114 114 Fax: + 92 (92) 84 05 19 Email: scapsh@brain.net.pk
International: Trekantsvagen 1, S-117 43 Stockholm, Sweden.
Tel: +46 (8) 545 818 40 Email: info@sak.a.se Web: www.sak.a.se

SAVE THE CHILDREN UK (SCF-UK)

Began working in Afghanistan in 1994. Sectors: primary education, child-to-child health education, children's rights.
ADDRESSES:
Afghanistan: House No 2127, Street A (Alpha), District 6, Karte Seh, Kabul. Mobile: +93 (0)70 276371 Satphone: +873 762 944989 Email: scukkbl@pes.paknet.com.pk, scfafghan@aol.com
Kartemamoreen, Mazar-e-Sharif. Satphone: +998 762 229246
Fax: +873 762 944830
Pakistan: 34-B, Railway Road, University Town, Peshawar.
Tel: +92 (91) 5701510 Fax: 92 (91) 841367
Email: qanwar@scuk-peshawar.org.pk
International: 17 Grove Lane, London SE5 8RD, UK (moving in Spring 2004).
Tel: +44 (0)20 7703 5400 Web: www.savethechildren.org.uk

SAVE THE CHILDREN-US (SC-US)

Began working in Afghanistan in 1988. Sectors: education, economic opportunities, health, food and livelihoods.
ADDRESSES:
Kabul: Main Darulaman Road, near Ministry of Commerce, District 7, Kabul. Tel: +93 (0)70 276578, (0)70 276451 Email: staff@kabul.isb.sdnpk.org.
Mazar-e-Sharif: Tel: +873 762 269861 Email: firshad@scfmaza.isb.sdnpk.org
Pakistan: House 7A, Street 58, F7/4 Islamabad. Tel: +92 (51) 111 107 108 Email: pafo@savechildren.org;pk
International: 54 Wilton Road, Westport, Connecticut, 06880, USA. Tel: +1 (203) 221 4000 Fax: +1 (203) 221 4210
Web: www.savethechildren.org

SERVING EMERGENCY RELIEF AND VOCATIONAL ENTERPRISES (SERVE)

Began operations in 1980 in Peshawar. Sectors: disability, health, agriculture, forestry, literacy and community development.
ADDRESSES:
Afghanistan: Near Karte Seh Park, Kabul. Tel: +93 (0)20 2500919, +93 (0)70 280506 Email: serve@atge.automail.com
Pakistan: P.O. Box 477, Peshawar. Tel: +92 91 840292
Fax: +92 (91) 840422 Email: adminp@serve.psh.brain.net.pk

SANDY GALLS'S AFGHANISTAN APPEAL (SGAA)

British NGO set up in 1986. Sectors: orthopaedic workshops and physiotherapy departments for disabled Afghans. Based in Kabul and Jalalabad, SGAA is part of the Comprehensive Disabled Afghans Project (CDAP). ADDRESS: 5A Circular Lane, University Town, Peshawar. Tel: +92 (91) 843028 Fax: +92 (91) 843028

SHELTER NOW INTERNATIONAL PAKISTAN/AFGHANISTAN (SNI-P/A)

Established in 1979 as an international volunteer relief organization. Sectors: reconstruction of clinics, hospitals, schools, roads and canals.
ADDRESSES:
Afghanistan: Kabul Street No. 4, Qala-e-Fatullah. Tel: +881 6314267 Email: gerogt@gmx.net.
Pakistan: 60E Canal Road, University Town, Peshawar. Tel: +92 (91) 851130 Fax: +92 (91) 840522 Email: sni@pes.comsats.net.pk
International: Shelter Germany, Am Aleten Bannhof 15, 38122 Bravschweig, Germany. Tel: +49(0) 531 88 53 957 Fax: +49(0) 531 88 53 959
Email: info@shelter.de Web: www.shelternow.org
1780 EB denhelder, Nethercawa, Holland. Tel: +31 223632279
Email: info@shelterholland.nl

SOLIDARITÉS (SOLID)

Sectors: food and shelter to drought victims, reconstruction and rehabilitation, agricultural support.
ADDRESSES:
Afghanistan: North East of Haji Yaqub Square, Opposite to Lucky Five Hotel, Kabul. Mobile: + 93 (0)70 282704 Satphone: +873 763221948 Fax: +873 763221950 Email: solkabul@inmarsat.francetelecom.fr
Pakistan: 32/F KKK Road, University Town, Peshawar. Tel: +92 (91) 5703978 Fax: +92 (91) 844745 Email: solpesh@brain.net.pk
International: Villa Souchet, 105, avenue Gambetta, 75020 Paris, France. Tel: +33 (0)1 43 15 13 13 Fax: +33 (0)1 43 15 08 09
Email: info@solidarites.org Web: www.solidarites.org

SOCIETY FOR THE PRESERVATION OF AFGHANISTAN'S CULTURAL HERITAGE (SPACH)

Established in 1994 in response to a growing awareness of the vulnerability of the cultural heritage of Afghanistan, SPACH aims primarily to share information about the state of collections, historic monuments and archaeological sites among local and international cultural institutions and individuals.
ADDRESSES:
Pakistan: SPACH, c/o ARIC, PO Box 1084, University Town, Peshawar.
Tel: +92 (91) 840387, 40839 Fax: +92 (91) 840471
Email: spach@undpafg.org.pk

TEARFUND DRT

Sectors: support to refugees, IDPs and disaster affected communities, water and sanitation, school reconstruction, public health education.
ADDRESSES:
Afghanistan: Tearfund (Disaster Response Team), Kabul Shah Baba, District 6, Kandahar.
International: Tearfund, 100 Church Road, Teddington, Middlesex TW11 8QE, UK. Tel: +44 (20) 8977 9144

TERRE DES HOMMES (TdH)

Swiss-based NGO which began work in Afghanistan in 1995. Sectors: street children in Kabul, child day-care, mother and child home-visiting teams, post-earthquake rehabilitation.
ADDRESSES:
Afghanistan: Street 5, Ghiasuddinwat, Shahr-e-Naw, Kabul. Tel: +93 (20) 22 90 152 Mobile: +93 (70) 277 202 Satphone: +873 761 638 760
Email: tdhafghanistan@kbl.pactec.net Web: www.tdhafghanistan.org
Pakistan: Administration Office for Afghanistan & Pakistan, 3-C Abdara Road, PO Box 729, Peshawar. Tel: +92 (91) 570 3814 Mobile: +92 300 859 0658 Fax: +92 (91) 852 062 Email: tdhkabul@brain.net.pk
International: En Budron C8, 1052 Le Mont-sur-Lausanne, Vaud, Switzerland. Tel: +41 (0)21 654 66 66 Fax: +41 (0)21 654 66 77
Email: terredeshommes@tdh.ch Web: www.tdh.ch

TROCAIRE

Sectors: emergency relief, human rights, income generation, peace building.
ADDRESS: 649 Chahra-e-Shaid, Shahr-e-Naw, District 10, Kabul.
Tel: +93 (0)70 279742, Web: www.trocaire.org

UNITED METHODIST COMMITTEE FOR RELIEF (UMCOR)

Sectors: agriculture, construction, education, environment, income generation, water & irrigation.
ADDRESS: House No. 507, Street 13, Wazir Akbar Khan, Kabul.
Tel: +93 (0)70 224498 Email: henry@uncor-afg.org
Web: www.uncor-ngo.org

UNIVERSITY OF NEBRASKA AT OMAHA (UNO)

Throughout the Soviet War, UNO produced more than 12 million textbooks (notoriously anti-communist) for Afghan primary schools, and provided literacy training to 48,000 *mujahideen* in their winter camps. UNO seeks to respond to educational needs by revising textbooks, printing instructional materials and conducting teacher training.
ADDRESSES:
Afghanistan: Shahr-e-Naw, Haji Yaqub Cross, Street 3, Kabul. Tel: +93 (0)20 2200731 Fax: +93 (0)20 2200731 Email: unoarrena_kab@yahoo.com.
Pakistan: 56-C Old Bara Road, University Town, U.P.O. Box 967, Peshawar. Fax: +92 (91) 840492 Email: unoatep-pes@yahoo.com

WOMEN'S UNITY FOR REHABILITATION (WUR)

Afghan NGO focusing on vulnerable Afghan women. Sectors: agriculture, education, health, income generation, relief & protection.
ADDRESSES:
Afghanistan: Charhi-e-Ansari, Kolola Pushta Road 2nd H/165, Shahr-e-Naw, Kabul. Tel: 34048
Pakistan: Gul Haji Plaza, Flat No. 311, University Road, Peshawar.

WORLD VISION AFGHANISTAN (WVA)

Part of World Vision International. Sectors: agriculture, infrastructure, education, emergency, health, relief & protection.
ADDRESS: House 1b, Street H, Taimani, Kabul. Tel: +732 762419466 Email: cart-uxe-5@wvi.org

WORLD WIDE FUND FOR NATURE (WWF-PAKISTAN)

WWF-Pakistan, which has established links with the Afghan Ministry of Environment and Planning, believes in linking the environmental problems of Afghanistan into a region-wide approach to conservation, particularly with regard to deforestation and the protection of wildlife.
ADDRESS: 34-D-2, Sahibzada Abdul Qayyum Road, UPO Box 1439, University Town, Peshawar. Tel: +92 (91) 841593, 842096
Fax: +92 (91) 841594 Email: wwfpsh@brain.net.pk

ZOA Refugee Care/CORD

Operating in Afghanistan as an alliance since September 2000. Sectors: assisting rural communities affected by large-scale displacement, nutrition, food assistance and community development.
ADDRESSES:
Afghanistan: House No 307, Street 10, Wazir Akbar Khan, Kabul.
Tel: +93 (0)70 282809, +93 (0)20 2300 553 Satphone: +873 761 477 552
Email: Afghanistan@zoaweb.org
International: PO Box 4130, 7320 AC Apeldoorn, The Netherlands. Tel: +31 (0) 55 366 33 39 Fax: +31 (0) 55 366 87 99 Email: a.luijer@ZOAweb.org
1 New Street, Leamington Spa, Warwickshire, CV31 1HP, UK. Tel: +44 (0)1926 315 301 Fax: +44 (0)1926 885 786 Email: shucklesby@cord.org.uk

ZUFLUCHT

Supports the Leprosy Control Program. Sectors: construction, health, relief and social programmes.
ADDRESSES:
Afghanistan: Niak, Yakaolang District, Bamiyan Province.
Pakistan: G 7/2-4, 149 Chenab Road, Islamabad. Tel: +92 (51) 2204375

United Nations agencies

AFGHANISTAN INFORMATION MANAGEMENT SERVICE (AIMS)

AIMS primary role is to support coordination through information management. It provides map products (incl. GIS), database development and maintenance, technical support and capacity-building for the Afghanistan Transitional Administration.
ADDRESSES:
Prime Ministry Compound (Western Door), Kabul. Email: info@aims.org.af
Web: www.aims.org.af
Field Offices in Herat, Mazar, Kunduz, Jalalabad, Kabul and Kandahar.

FOOD AND AGRICULTURE ORGANIZATION (FAO)

FAO has a mandate to raise levels of nutrition and standards of living as well as to improve agricultural productivity. FAO is the leading UN agency for the rehabilitation of Afghanistan's agricultural sector and seeks to operate as much as possible through NGOs. FAO has four principal objectives: to create national food security, to increase economic and social development, to raise the levels of skills and knowledge and to protect scarce natural resources.
ADDRESSES:
Afghanistan: PO Box 5, UNDP Compound, Kabul. Tel: +93 (0)20 2101722 Email: FAO-AF@fao.org
Pakistan: 19A-C, 3 Gul Mohar Lane, University Town, Peshawar.
International: Division of Information, Viale delle Terme do Caracalla, 00100 Rome, Italy. Tel: +39 (6) 57051 Fax: +39 (6) 57052-3
Web: www.fao.org, www.faoafg.org

INTERNATIONAL LABOUR ORGANISATION (ILO)

ILO promotes decent work and social safety nets by setting and supervising international labour standards in the form of conventions and recommendations. ILO has set up computer training and English language centres in the Ministries of Labour & Social Affairs and Women's Affairs.
ADDRESS: ILO Office in the UNDP compound, Kabul. Mobile: +93 (0)70 275811 Email: baheer@ilo.org

UN ASSISTANCE MISSION IN AFGHANISTAN (UNAMA)

UNAMA was established in an effort to integrate all UN activities in Afghanistan. There are some 16 UN agencies in the country working together with their Afghan government counterparts and with national and international NGO partners. The Special Representative of the Secretary-General for Afghanistan (SRSG), who leads UNAMA, has overall responsibility for all UN activities (political and humanitarian) in the country. UNAMA has a core mandate which entails: promoting national reconciliation, human rights, the rule of law and gender issues (as detailed in the Bonn Agreement); and managing all UN humanitarian, relief, recovery and reconstruction activities in coordination with the Afghan Administration. In addition to its Kabul headquarters, the Mission has regional offices in Bamiyan, Gardez, Herat, Jalalabad, Kabul, Kandahar, Kunduz and Mazar-e-Sharif. There are two liaison offices in Islamabad, Pakistan, and Teheran, Iran.
ADDRESSES:
Afghanistan: Compound "A", Street 10, House No. 310, Wazir Akbar Khan, Kabul. Tel: +39 0831 24 6000 Fax: +39 0831 24 6069 Email: spokesman-unama@un.org Web: www.unama-afg.org
Pakistan: UNAMA, P. O. BOX 1428, Islamabad.
International: P. O. Box 5858, Grand Central Station, New York, NY, 10163-5858, USA. Tel: +1 212 963 2668 Fax: +1 212 963 2669

UN DEVELOPMENT PROGRAMME (UNDP)

UNDP is focusing on providing support to the Afghan Government in its recovery and reconstruction efforts and developing its capacity to deliver basic services to the people, with the long term objective of alleviating poverty. The UNDP Country Programme rests on three fundamental pillars: *Recovery and Reconstruction* – focusing on programmes and projects designed to yield quick results; *Governance* – which includes Public Administration, Justice, Security, Gender; *Policy Support and Advice* – to generate data for decision-makers and provide analytical perspectives to make informed policy choices. *(continued)*

ADDRESSES:
Afghanistan: Shah Mahmood Ghazi Watt, Kabul. Tel: +93 (0)20 2102085, 2101685
Pakistan: House 292, Street 55, Sector F-10/4, (PO Box 1051) Islamabad. Tel: +92 (51) 2211451-5 Fax: +92 (51) 2211450
Email: (name)@undpafg.org.pk
International: One UN Plaza, New York, NY 10017, USA. Tel: +1 (212) 906 5558 Fax: +1 (212) 906 6365 Email: (name)@undp.org Web: www.undp.org

UN EDUCATION, SCIENTIFIC AND CULTURAL ORGANIZATION (UNESCO)

UNESCO has been working in Afghanistan since 1948. It re-established a full office in Kabul in December 2001. Activities include:
Education: Capacity-building at the Ministry of Education and Ministry of Higher Education, teacher training, basic education, curriculum development, literacy, English language teaching; *Science:* Water resource management, environmental issues; *Culture and communication:* capacity-building at the Ministry of Information and Culture, conservation of the physical heritage, preservation of intangible heritage, development of free press, media training, support for radio, television and news agencies.
ADDRESSES:
Afghanistan: UN Compound, Kabul. Tel: +93 (0) 70 283008
Email: martin.hadlow@undpafg.org.pk
International: 7 place de Fontenoy, 75352, Paris, France. Tel: +33 (1) 45 68 10 00 Fax: +33 (1) 45 67 16 90 Web: www.unesco.org

UN POPULATION FUND (UNFPA)

UNFPA assists in providing population assistance through improving reproductive health and contraception services and formulating population policies. A key principle is the focus on individual male and female choice, not on achieving demographic targets. Half of UNFPA assistance is targeted at reproductive health including maternal and child healthcare and family planning. A further 15% of UNFPA assistance goes into projects carried out by NGOs.
ADDRESSES:
Afghanistan: Radio TV Road, Ansari Watt, Beside Italian Embassy, Kabul. Mobile: +93 (0)70 275358 Email: huff-rouselle@unfpa.org
International: 220 East 42nd Street, New York, NY 10017, USA. Tel: +1 (212) 297 5020, 297 5087 Fax: +1 (212) 557 6416 Email: (name)@unfpa.org

UN-HABITAT

The mission of UN-HABITAT is to promote socially and environmentally sustainable human settlements. It has worked in Afghanistan since the early 1990s, addressing the rehabilitation of urban areas in Kabul, Kandahar, Mazar-e-Sharif, Herat, Farah and Bamiyan. Their focus is not only on restoring citywide infrastructure, but also on rebuilding communities through a community development & support strategy – working closely with local municipalities.
ADDRESSES:
Afghanistan: Gulestan Sarai, Park Zernegar, Behind Kabul Muncipality Building, Kabul. Tel: +93 (0)20 210 1651/1652 Email: unhabitat@web-sat.com Web: www.pcpafg.org/organizations/unchs, www.fukuoka.unhabitat.org, www.unhabitat.org
Regional Office: UN-HABITAT Regional Office for Asia and the Pacific, ACROS Fukuoka Building, 8th Floor, 1-1-1 Tenjin, Chuo-ku Fukuoka 810, Japan. Tel: +81 (92) 724 7121 Fax: +81 (92) 724 7124
International: UN-HABITAT Headquarters, P.O. Box 30030, Nairobi, Kenya. Tel: +254 (2) 621234 Fax: +254 (2) 624266, 624267

UN HIGH COMMISSIONER FOR REFUGEES (UNHCR)

The UN Refugee Agency's main objectives are to provide protection to refugees who flee their country due to persecution or conflict and to find durable solutions to their plight through repatriation, integration or resettlement to third countries. By mid-2003, over 2 million refugees had returned to Afghanistan. With 30 offices and 600 staff members throughout Afghanistan, UNHCR's assistance programs include: *Return assistance:* provides drinking water, shelter material and seeds to returnee communities in rural areas; *Community services:* supports extremely vulnerable individuals and provides vocational training for women; *Mass Information:* provides refugees and internally displaced people with information on the conditions in the areas of return through the local media; *Protection:* monitors the situation of returnee communities, paying particular attention to ethnic minorities; *Government capacity building:* provides expert advice, skills training, human resources and administrative support to ministries responsible for the return and reintegration of refugees.
ADDRESSES:
Afghanistan: 41 Jadai Solh, Shahr-e-Naw, District 4, Kabul.
Tel: +93 (0)20 200 3812 Email: afgamr@unhcr.ch
Pakistan: House 24, Street 89, G-6/3, PO Box 1263, Islamabad.
Tel: +92 (51) 820877, 821683, 827663
International: PO Box 2500, CH-1211, Geneva 2, Switzerland.
Tel: +41 (22) 739 8502 Fax: +41 (22) 739 7314
Email: hqpi00@unhcr.ch Web: www.unhcr.ch

UN CHILDREN'S FUND (UNICEF)

UNICEF's primary goal is to realize the rights of all children and women, enabling even the most disadvantaged to fulfil their basic needs, to receive protection form harm and abuse and to develop their full potential as human beings. These rights to protection, survival and development lie at the heart of the Convention on the Rights of the Child. Through its offices in Kabul, Herat, Jalalabad, Kandahar, Kunduz and Mazar-e-Sharif, UNICEF implements the following programmes: *Humanitarian relief:* life-saving humanitarian assistance including winterized non-food items, essential emergency medical supplies, therapeutic foods and equipment for provision of safe drinking water; *Education:* assisting the ministries of Education in the restoration of learning opportunities of all children at the primary level; deployment and training of teachers, provision of essential learning supplies; provision of safer learning spaces and increase of access to secondary education, particularly for girls; *Health & Nutrition:* immunization (mass measles campaigns and polio National Immunization Days); treatment and prevention of protein energy and micronutrient malnutrition' and safe motherhood initiative as a component of maternal and child health programs; *Water & Environmental Sanitation:* increased access to safe drinking water and sanitation facilities for the underserved rural areas and IDP camps, improved knowledge of hygiene practices and involvement of women in their promotion; rights-based community schemes; development of a water resources management plan; and training of national partners in systems maintenance, including on drought mitigation; *Child Protection:* juvenile justice; legal protection of children and women; mine/unexploded ordnance awareness; protection and integration of child soldiers and other war-affected young people; psycho-social support for children and families; and social protection of vulnerable children and women.
ADDRESSES:
Afghanistan: House 83, Street P, Part 2, District 4, Shahr-e-Naw, Kabul.
Satphone: +873 762 925 533 Tel: +93 (0)20 2200439 Fax: +873 761 924 996
Email: aco@unicef.org, kabul@unicef.org
International: 3 United Nations Plaza, H-9F, New York, NY10017, USA. Email: pubdoc@unicef.org Web: www.unicef.org

UN MINE ACTION CENTRE FOR AFGHANISTAN (UNMACA)

UNMACA is the secretariat for the Mine Action Programme in Afghanistan (MAPA) and has been operating since 1989. It is responsible for the strategic planning, operations management, coordination, and fund-raising of MAPA activities. MAPA consists of eight UN Area Mine Action Centres (AMACs) and 14 NGOs who implement the activities associated with mine action including awareness, technical training, survey, clearance, and monitoring. UNMACA provides technical support for MAPA agencies and ensures the proper integration of mine action into wider humanitarian assistance programmes.
ADDRESS: House 95, Street Jeem, Wazir Akbar Khan, Kabul.
Mobile: +93 (0)70 276645 Fax: +873 761660769
Email: demining@unmaca.org Web: www.mineaction.org

UN OFFICE ON DRUGS AND CRIME (UNODC)

UNODC activities for Afghanistan in countering illicit drugs production, processing, consumption, trafficking and crime prevention are centred on assisting the government in the sectors of Alternative Development, Drug Demand Reduction, Law Enforcement and Institutional building/Judicial reforms. The agency has been assisting the Afghan authorities in strengthening their capacity in dealing with the issues and mainstreaming of the drug control element in development assistance. It has also been supporting the authorities in the rehabilitation of drug addicts, formulation of narcotic drugs law, legal reform and combating organized crime.
ADDRESSES:
Afghanistan: Shah Mohmood Ghazi Wat, Shahr-e-Naw, Kabul.
Tel: +93 (0)20 2101994 Mobile: +93 (0)70 279698 Email: amirkhizi@undp.org
Web: www.unodc.org/afg
International: UNODC, Vienna International Centre, PO Box 500, A-1400 Vienna, Austria. Tel: +43 1 26060 0 Fax: +43 1 26060 5866 Email: unodc@unodc.org

UN FUND FOR WOMEN'S DEVELOPMENT (UNIFEM)

UNIFEM's primary objective is to build Afghan women's capacity and leadership for their effective participation in the social, economic and political reconstruction process. UNIFEM seeks to promote female Afghan leadership at all levels, from local communities to national governments. Key elements of the strategy include: building capacity of the Ministry of Women's Affairs, supporting women's leadership at the community level, strengthening Afghan women's NGOs and networks, promoting Afghan women's economic security, promoting Afghan women's rights and their participation in the governance process.
ADDRESS: UNDP Compound, Kabul. Mobile: +93 (0)70 282721 Tel: +93 (0)20 2101682 (Ext. 210) Fax: +873 761660769

WORLD FOOD PROGRAMME (WFP)

The largest international food aid organization in the world, WFP first began operating in Afghanistan in 1964. Seeking to counter the effects of Afghanistan's four-year-long drought plus the overall economic degradation of the country from war, WFP started to implement a US$ 285 million emergency operation from 1 April 2002 onwards aimed at providing food relief for more than nine million vulnerable Afghans.
ADDRESSES:
Afghanistan: Opposite French Embassy, Wazir Akbar Khan, Kabul.
Tel: +873 763 044 995, +882 1621 110 189 Fax: +873 763 044 996
Email: WFP.Kabul@wfp.org
Area Offices: Kabul, Faizabad, Herat, Jalalabad, Kandahar, Mazar-e-Sharif.
Sub-Offices: Bamiyan, Chakhcharan, Maimana, Qala-e-Naw, Kunduz

International: Via Cesare Giulio Viola 68/70, Parco de'Medici, 00148 Rome, Italy. Tel: +39 06-65131 Fax: +39 06-6590632/6590637
Email: firstname.lastname@wfp.org Web: www.wfp.org

WORLD HEALTH ORGANIZATION (WHO)

WHO is one of the leading UN agencies working in the field of health. With a main office in Kabul, WHO also has sub-offices in Herat, Mazar, Kandahar, Faizabad, Kunduz, Ghazni, Bamiyan, Jalalabad and Islamabad. Activities include: *Disease prevention control:* TB, malaria, leishmaniasis, vaccine preventable diseases, CDD, ARI, meningitis, typhoid, tetanus, measles and rabies; *Supplies:* provision of medical/surgical supplies to Ministry of Public Health, hospitals and clinics; *Training:* of doctors, nurses, public heath workers, TBAs; *Water supply:* provision of safe drinking water supplies, rehabilitation of networks in Kandahar, Ghazni, Jalalabad, Kunduz and Badakhshan; *Rehabilitation* of hospital and medical facilities.
ADDRESSES:
Afghanistan: WHO main office, Kabul. Mobile: +93 (0)70 279010-2 Tel: +93 (0)20 2300181-2 Email: registry@afg.emro.who.int
Pakistan: WHO support office, PO Box 1936, Islamabad.
Tel: +92 (51) 2104770-4 Fax: +92 (51) 2280830
International: Ave Appia 20, CH-1211 Geneva, Switzerland.
Tel: +41(22) 791 2111 Fax: +41(22) 791 4844

Red Cross & Red Crescent

AFGHAN RED CRESCENT SOCIETY (ARCS)

Founded in 1934, ARCS operates in four main areas: health, relief, *Marastoons* (homes for the homeless) and voluntary self-help. ARCS is a member of the International Federation of Red Cross and Red Crescent Societies (see below) and has re-established active branches in 31 of Afghanistan's 32 provinces.
ADDRESS: Shafa Khana Qwai Markaz, Kabul. Tel: Kabul 32853

INTERNATIONAL COMMITTEE OF THE RED CROSS (ICRC)

The ICRC's permanent presence in Afghanistan dates from 1986. Afghanistan is currently the ICRC's biggest operation in the world. Its principal activities include *Emergency Relief:* focusing on the drought and conflict-affected areas of Bamiyan, Ghor, Balkh and Samangan; *Protection:* visits to security detainees and prisoners in 65 places of detection, including Guantanamo Bay; *Red Cross Messages network:* exchange of Red Cross messages to restore contact between families and detainees separated by conflict; *Water and Habitat:* emergency interventions on water networks, hand pump repair, wider scale projects on well field sites; *Environmental sanitation:* building or rehabilitating latrines, giving health education, repairing sewage collectors and pumps; *Health:* focus on facilities providing surgical care and regular assistance to six main hospitals in Kabul, Kandahar, Ghazni, Gulbahar and Jalalabad; *Physical Rehabilitation:* six rehabilitation centres in Afghanistan (since opening in 1989, they have served over 50,000 disabled persons); *Mine Action:* collection of data from victims of mines / UXO for recording in a database shared with other organizations involved in mine action, improvement of mine awareness in selected central and eastern provinces; *Promotion of International Humanitarian Law:* instruction in IHL to the Afghan National Army as well as to other groups and arms carriers. Currently there are over 150 expatriates and over 1,000 local staff in Afghanistan, with the main delegation in Kabul and sub-delegations in Kandahar, Herat, Jalalabad, Mazar-e-Sharif, Kunduz and sub-offices in Bamiyan and Chakhcharan. The ICRC has a specific humanitarian mandate based on neutrality and impartiality, and enshrined in the Geneva Conventions.

ADDRESSES:
Afghanistan: Charrahi Haji Yaqub, Shahr-e-Naw, Kabul. Tel: +93 (0)20 290067 Fax: + 93 (0)20 290130 Satphone: +873 762 730 940 or 43 Satfax: +873 762 730 941 Email: kaboul.kab@icrc.org
Pakistan: 40 Jamalud-Din Afghani Road, University Town, GPO Box 418, Peshawar. Tel: +92 (91) 42071, 41673, 41371 Fax: +92 (91) 840413
International: 19, Avenue de la Paix, CH-1202, Geneva, Switzerland. Tel: +41 (22) 734 6001 Fax: +41 (22) 733 2057
Email: asia.gva@gwn.icrc.org Web: www.icrc.org

INTERNATIONAL FEDERATION OF RED CROSS AND RED CRESCENT SOCIETIES (INTERNATIONAL FEDERATION)

The International Federation is the umbrella organIZATION for all national Red Cross/Crescent societies worldwide. It aims to prevent and alleviate human suffering by coordinating disaster relief, disaster preparedness and primary healthcare. Since 1989, the International Federation has supported the Afghan Red Crescent Society (ARCS) in its health and relief programmes, and has reinforced ARCS's organizational structure nationwide. This support enables the ARCS to assist vulnerable people in 31 provinces in the following fields: *Basic Health Care:* through outpatient clinics providing curative services, preventive healthcare and health education; *Community-based First Aid:* through a network of 12,000 trained volunteers who carry out first-aid, community health and referral services; *Emergency mobile units:* immediate mobilization of personnel, equipment, medicines and vehicles in an emergency; *Water and Sanitation:* construction of wells and latrines in drought-affected areas; *Disaster management:* comprehensive disaster preparedness and response programme at national and provincial levels – including training volunteers and stockpiling essential relief materials. The International Federation delegation has 18-20 expatriates and around 140 local employees, with offices in Kabul, Herat, Kandahar, Jalalabad and Mazar-e-Sharif.
ADDRESSES:
Afghanistan: 61, Dawakhana Street, Shash Darak Han, PO Box 3039, Kabul. Tel: +873 382 280 530 Fax: +873 382 280 534 Email: hod.kabuldel@wireless.ifrc.org or kabuldel@wireless.ifrc.org
Pakistan: c/o Pakistan Red Crescent Society national headquarters, H-8, Islamabad. Tel: +92 (51) 925 7122 Fax: +92 (51) 443 0745 Email: ifrcpk1@ifrc.org or ifrcpk08@ifrc.org
International: 17 Chemin des Crets, Case Postale 372, Petit-Saconnex, CH-1211, Geneva, Switzerland. Tel: +41 (22) 730 4222 Fax: +41 (22) 733 0395 Email: (name.name)@ifrc.org Web: www.ifrc.org

Governmental & inter-governmental agencies

EUROPEAN COMMISSION (EC)

The European Union hosted the Bonn Conference which provided the blue-print for Afghanistan's future and has participated in security, humanitarian and development sectors. Its programmes include: *Support for public administration:* funding for technical assistance, equipment and salaries for Afghan ministries and public sector workers; *Rural recovery:* to support recovery of rural livelihoods by creating employment through an injection of capital into the local economy, providing an alternative to poppy cultivation; *Mine action:* mine clearance, impact survey, mine awareness, victims' rehabilitation; *Basic urban infrastructure:* water and sanitation, waste disposal, housing, power supply, public amenities, improved public buildings and the re-launch of urban planning; *Information and co-ordination:* to

ensure a consistent and improving flow of data, focusing on information standards, processing of information at regional level, and the relay of data to implementing partners and decision makers; *Food security:* re-starting agricultural activities and rural production systems), aid to uprooted people; *Special initiatives:* including human rights, asylum and migration, rapid reaction mechanism, humanitarian assistance through the European Commission Humanitarian Aid Office (ECHO).
ADDRESSES:
Afghanistan: House 2, Street 1, Behind Amani High School, East Wazir Akbar Khan, Kabul. Mobile: + 93 (0)70 224947 Satphone: +882 216 89801582 Fax: + 873 762 364 065 Email: DELEGATION-AFGHANISTAN@cec.eu.int
International: c/o ECHO, 200 rue de la Loi, B-1049, Brussels, Belgium (see below).

EUROPEAN COMMISSION HUMANITARIAN AID OFFICE (ECHO)

ECHO is the humanitarian arm of the European Union and has funded short-term humanitarian activities in all parts of Afghanistan since 1995. ECHO supports former refugees returning to Afghanistan from neighbouring countries, internally displaced people (IDPs) and other vulnerable and drought-affected populations. Sectors include: food security, medical, water supply, shelter and protection. ECHO also finances logistical and coordination activities to support the work of its NGO partners.
ADDRESSES:
Afghanistan: House 103, Abu Hanifa Lane, Kolola Pushta, Kabul.
Mobile: +93 (0)70 280148 Email: echoafghan@oceanpost.net
International: ECHO, 200 rue de la Loi, B-1049, Brussels, Belgium.
Tel: +32 2 295 4400 Fax: +32 2 295 4572 Email: echo-info@cec.eu.int
Web: http://europa.eu.int/comm/echo/index_en.htm

GERMAN AGENCY FOR TECHNICAL COOPERATION (GTZ)

GTZ is the main implementing agency for technical assistance from the German government. After an emergency programme in early 2002, GTZ initiated programmes of structural reconstruction, development-oriented emergency aid and measures to promote democracy. GTZ shares an office in Kabul with the Kreditanstalt für Wiederaufbau (KfW). KfW finances programmes in the areas of drinking water, energy, road repair, education and health.
ADDRESS: House 386, Street No. 15 Wazir Akbar Khan, Kabul.
Tel: +93 (020 2300389/90 Satphone: + 870 761 618 388 Email: GTZ-Afghanistan@gtz.de; kfwkabul@t-online.de

INTERNATIONAL ORGANIZATION FOR MIGRATION (IOM)

IOM is a non-UN intergovernmental body with 93 member states and 37 observer states. IOM programming focuses on the return and reintegration of qualified Afghan nationals. Other sectors include: camp management, emergency assistance and quick impact programmes to provide shelter and non-food assistance to Afghans displaced across the country.
ADDRESSES:
Afghanistan:
Kabul: Ansari Wat, House 1093, behind UNICA Guest House, Kabul.
Satphone: +873 762 869 855 Fax: +873 762 869 856 Email:
iom.kabul@iomkabul.net ; IOMKabul-Reporting@iomkabul.net
Mazar: House No 8, Street no 2, Darwazi Balkh, Mazar. Satphone: +870 762 925 765 Fax: 00 870 763 057 486 Email: iommazar@mazar.iomkabul.net
Herat: Welayat Street, House No.129, District No.1, Herat. Satphone: + 871 762 881 852 Tel: +93 4 400073 Email: iomherat@herat.iomkabul.net
More offices in Bamiyan, Kunduz, Maimana and Kandahar
(continued)

International: 17 route des Morillons, CH-1211, Geneva 19, Switzerland. Tel: +41 (22) 717 9111 Fax: +41 (22) 798 6150 Email: hq@iom.int Web: www.iom.int

SWEDISH INTERNATIONAL DEVELOPMENT CO-OPERATION AGENCY (SIDA)

Swedish government-funded development assistance programmes. Sectors include: education and infrastructure.
ADDRESS: Street 13, Wazir Akbar Khan, Kabul. Mobile: +93 (0)70 280555, +93 (0)70 284210 Email: sida.kabul@mail.com Web: www.sida.se

SWISS AGENCY FOR DEVELOPMENT AND COOPERATION (SDC)

Part of Switzerland's foreign ministry, SDC provides emergency relief and reconstruction aid to Afghanistan. Sectors include: public healthcare, food aid, agriculture. Contributions are partly channelled through multilateral agencies (ICRC, UN). SDC also seconds engineers, logistics experts and doctors from the Swiss Disaster Relief Unit.
ADDRESS: Street 13, Side-street 3, House 486, Wazir Akbar Khan, Kabul. Tel: +93 (0)70 274 902 Satphone: +873 762 71 80 80, +882 16 506 01 629 Email: kabul@sdc.net Web: www.sdc.admin.ch

UNITED KINGDOM'S DEPARTMENT FOR INTERNATIONAL DEVELOPMENT (DFID)

Funding projects in the sectors of humanitarian aid, recovery, economic management, peace process, sustainable livelihoods. DFID also supports the Afghanistan Reconstruction Trust Fund.
ADDRESS: Shahr-e-Naw, German Club Road, in front of German Club, Kabul. Tel: +93 (0)70 277652, +93 (0)70 275425

UNITED STATES AGENCY FOR INTERNATIONAL DEVELOPMENT (USAID)

USAID aims to meet Afghans' relief and reconstruction needs. As well as emergency food aid, sectors include: *Infrastructure*: primary and secondary roads (including the Kabul-Kandahar road), government buildings, power, electricity, irrigation and drinking water; *Health:* maternal healthcare, clinic construction; *Education:* books, accelerated learning for girls who missed out on primary education, school construction, teacher training; *Economic governance:* providing advisors to strengthen the ministry of finance; *Democracy and governance:* working with various commissions to strengthen their capacity; *Media:* journalist training, setting up community radio stations, production of radio programmes.
ADDRESSES:
Afghanistan: 3B, Jami Street. Shar-e-Naw, Kabul. Tel: +93 (0)20 2200511/ 31165 Mobile: +93 (0)70 275 910 / (0)70 276049 Email: mreabold@usaid.gov Web: www.usaid.gov/index.html
International: Ronald Reagan Building, Washington D.C. 20523-1000, USA. Tel: +1 202 712 4810 Fax: +1 202 216 3524 Web: www.usaid.gov

WORLD BANK (WB)

The World Bank has the following four projects currently under implementation: emergency infrastructure rehabilitation, emergency public administration, emergency education rehabilitation and development, and emergency community empowerment and public works. Other activities include projects in health, transport and micro-finance and providing technical assistance and policy advice in areas such as civil service reform, oil and gas, and financial sector reform.
ADDRESSES:
Afghanistan: House No. 19, Street No. 15, Wazir Akbar Khan, Kabul. Tel: +93 (0)70 276002 , +93 (0)70 279239
International: 1818 H Street N. W., Washington D.C. 20433, USA. Tel: +1 202 477 1234, 473 1000 Fax: +1 202 477 6391

CONTACTS

Diplomatic missions[2]

Diplomatic missions in Afghanistan

Bulgaria

Next to Palace No.8, Kabul
Tel: +93 (0)20 210 1089

China

Shah Mahmood Ghazi Watt, Kabul
Tel: +93 (0)20 230 0109, 230 0490

Denmark

House 36, Street 13, Lane 2, Wazir Akbar Khan, Kabul
Tel: +93 (0)70 280275, 280284 Email: kabul@umweb.dk

European Commission

House 2, Street 1, Behind Amani High School, East Wazir Akbar Khan, Kabul.
Tel: +873 762 337 570 Fax: +873 762 364 065 Email: ecpesh@oceanpost.net

France

Opposite Alms and Tithes Dept., Kabul
Tel: +93 (0)70 284033 Satphone: +873 763 036 212 Fax: + 873 682 086 817
Email: afkabul@inmarsat.francetelecom.fr

Germany

Zanbaq Square, opposite WFP office, Wazir Akbar Khan, Kabul
Tel: +93 (0)20 210 1512

India

Qua-e-Markaz, near Passport Dept., Kabul
Tel: +93 (0)20 220 0181-4

Indonesia

Interior Ministry Road, near Passport Dept., Kabul
Tel: +93 (0)20 220 1066

Iran

Shirpoor Sq, Shahr-e-Naw, Kabul
Tel: +93 (0)20 22803

Italy

Khwaja Abdullah Ansari Rd, Kabul
Tel: + 873 763 068 371, +873 761 280 634

Japan

House No. 422, Street 13, Wazir Akbar Khan, Kabul
Tel: +873 761 218 271 Fax: +873 762 853 778 Email: ejkabul@vc.kcom.ne.jp

[2] *For Afghan embassies and consulates worldwide: SEE VISAS*

Netherlands

House No. 70, Lane No. 1, Street No. 15, Wazir Akbar Khan, Kabul

Norway

Opposite German Club, Kabul
Mobile: +93 (0)70 274 529, (0)70 274 532 Fax: +873 6000 61156
Email: emb.kabul@mfa.no

Pakistan

Najat Watt, Wazir Akbar Khan, opposite WHO Office, Kabul
Tel: +93 (0)20 230 0913

Russia

Street 15, Wazir Akbar Khan, Kabul
Tel: 628 90

Saudi Arabia

Shash Darak, Kabul
Tel: +93 (0)20 210 0167

South Korea

House No. 34, Street 10, Wazir Akbar Khan, Kabul
Mobile: +93 (0)70 276743 Fax: +873 762 272 8481

Sweden

c/o Swedish Committee for Afghanistan
Mobile: +93 (0)70 278 111 Email: scaero@eikmail.com

Tajikistan

House No. 122, Street No. 15, Wazir Akbar Khan, Kabul
Tel: +93 (0)20 210 108

Turkey

Shah Moh'd, Ghazi Watt, Opposite UNDP Office, Kabul
Tel: +93 (0)20 210 1579, 220 1518

United Arab Emirates

Golden Lotus Intersection, Wazir Akbar Khan, Kabul
Tel: +93 (0)20 210 1578

United Kingdom

Kart-e-Parwan, PO Box 344, Kabul
Tel: +93 (0)20 220 0147/8

United States of America

Ariana Watt, near Radio Kabul, Kabul
Tel: +93 (0)20 290 0005, 290 0002 Mobile: +93 (0)70 201 910

Diplomatic missions in Islamabad and Peshawar

Afghanistan

Embassy, House No. 8, Street 90, G-6/3, Islamabad.
Tel: +92 (0)51 282 4505-6 Fax: +92 (0)51 282 4504
Consulate, Gul Mohar Lane, University Town, GPO Box 119, Peshawar.
Tel: +92 (0)91 842486

Australia

Diplomatic Enclave No.1, P.O. Box 1046, Islamabad.
Tel: +92 (0)51 282 4345 Fax: +92 (0)51 282 0112

Canada

Diplomatic Enclave, P.O. Box 1042, Islamabad.
Tel: +92 (0)51 2271938-40 Fax: +92 (0)51 2279137

China

Diplomatic Enclave, Ramna 4, Islamabad.
Tel: +92 (0)51 2822540 Fax: +92 (0)51 2821116

Denmark

House 9, Street 90, Ramna G-6/3, Islamabad.
Tel: +92 (0)51 282 4722-24 Fax: +92 (0)51 282 3483

France

G-5 Diplomatic Enclave, P.O. Box 1068, Islamabad.
Tel: +92 (0)51 227 8730-32 Fax: +92 (0)51 282 5389

Germany

Diplomatic Enclave, Ramna 5 Ispahani Road, Islamabad.
Tel: +92 (0)51 227 9430-35

India

G-5, Diplomatic Enclave, Islamabad.
Tel: +92 (0)51 282 1134 Fax: +92 (0)51 285 3102

Iran

Plot No.222-238, Street No.2, G-5/1, Diplomatic Enclave, Islamabad.
Tel: +92 (51) 227 6270-2 Fax: +92 (51) 282 4839

Italy

54 Margalla Road, F-6/3, Islamabad.
Tel: +92 (51) 282 9106/08/09, 282 8982, 282 9229
Fax: +92 (51) 282 9026, 227 5956 Email: segreter@embassy.italy.org.pk

Netherlands

2nd Floor, PIA Building, Blue Area, PO Box 1065, Islamabad.
Tel: +92 (51) 227 9510, 279 511, 227 9513 Fax: +92 (51) 227 9512, 227 5702

Norway

House No. 25, Street 19, F 6/2, P.O. Box 1336, Islamabad
Tel: +92 (51) 227 9720/21/22/23/24 Fax: +92 (51) 227 9726/29
Email: emb.islamabad@mfa.no

Sweden

House No. 4, Street 5, F-6/3, P.O. Box 1100, Islamabad.
Tel: +92 (51) 282 8712-3 Fax: +92 (51) 282 5284
Email: ambassaden.islamabad@foreign.ministry.se

United Kingdom

Diplomatic Enclave, PO Box 1122, Ramna 5, Islamabad.
Tel: + 92 (51) 220 6071-75, 282 2131-5 Fax: +92 (51) 227 9356
Email: bhcmedia@isb.comsats.net.pk

United States of America

Ramna 5, Diplomatic Enclave, Islamabad.
Tel: +92 (51) 2080 0000 Fax: +92 (51) 227 6427
Consulate, 11 Hospital Road, Peshawar, NWFP.
Tel: +92 (91) 279 801-3 Fax: +92 (91) 276 712

Media organizations

International:

Agence France-Presse (AFP)

Afghanistan: House 5, Wazir Akbar Khan Road
Satphone: +873 761 795 963
Pakistan: G-6/3 Ataturk Avenue, House 90, P.O Box 1276, Islamabad.
Tel: +92 (51) 282 2485 Fax: +92 (51) 282 2203 Email: Islamabad@afp.com

AÏNA (Afghan Media and Culture Centre)

Afghanistan: Next to the Ministry of Planning, Kabul
Mobile: +93 (0)70 276019 Satphone: +873 763 080 776

AlertNet

International: c/o Reuters Foundation, 85 Fleet Street, London EC4P 4AJ, UK.
Tel: +44 (0)20 7542 3334 Fax: + 44 (0)20 7278 9345 Email: alertnet@rtrlondon.co.uk

Associated Press (AP)

Afghanistan: House No 95, Street 11, Wazir Akbar Khan, Kabul
Tel: +93 (0)20 230 0335 Mobile +93 (0)70 278 2290 Satphone: +873 761 375 775 Email: (name)@ap.org
Pakistan: House 6A, Street 25, F-8/2, Islamabad.
Tel: +92 (51) 2260957, 2252566 Fax: + 92 (51) 2256176, 2251640
Email: (name)@ap.org
International: 50 Rockefeller Plaza, New York, N.Y. 10020, USA.
Tel: +1 212 621 1500

API

Afghanistan: Pul-e-Artal, Opposite Education Printing Press, Kabul
Tel: 21112, 26932

Associated Press Television News (APTN)

Afghanistan: House 34-10th Street, Wazir Akbar Khan, Kabul
Mobile: +93 (0)70 275701-4 Satphone: +873 762 945 826

British Broadcasting Corporation (BBC)

Afghanistan: House No. 5 Right, Lane No. 5 Left, Street 15, Wazir Akbar Khan, Kabul
Tel: +93 (0)20 230 0088 Satphone: + 873 762 222 2545/6
Email: Kabul@zoom.co.uk
Pakistan: House 12, Street 66, F-7/3, Islamabad.
Tel: +92 (51) 2820717 826026, 826076 Fax: + 92 (51) 270420
Mobile: +92 (351) 265109
Peshawar: Tel: +92 (91) 842320, 42767 Fax: + 92 (91) 842319

BBC Afghan Education Drama (AED):

Afghanistan: House No. 271, 1st Street, Qala-e- Najara, Next to New Zarif Pharmacy, Khair Khana, Kabul.
Mobile: +93 (0)70 282226/ (0)70 278093
Pakistan: 8 Abdara Road, PO Box 946, University Town, Peshawar.
Tel: +92 (91) 842320, 42765-7 Fax: + 92 (91) 842319

BBC Persian and Pashto Service:

International: Bush House, Strand, London WC2B 4PH, UK
Tel: +44 (0)20 7240 3456 Fax: + 44 (0)20 7379 6785 Email: (name)@bbc.co.uk
English Service: Bush House, Strand, London WC2B 4PH, UK
Tel: +44 (0)20 7485 8063

CNN

Afghanistan: Qala-e-Fatullah, Kabul

Deutsche Welle

Pakistan: House 8, Street 32/1, F-8/1, Islamabad
Tel: +92 (51) 280213 Fax: + 92 (51) 256506

DPA (German Press Agency)

Pakistan: Block 18, 2nd Floor, Supermarket, F-6 Markaz, Islamabad.
Tel: +92 (51) 2820863 Fax: + 92 (51) 821997

European Community Humanitarian Office (ECHO)

International: Press and Information, Rue de la Loi 200, B-1049 Brussels, Belgium.
Tel: +32 (2) 295 2627 Fax: + 32 (2) 295 4572 Email: (name)@echo.cec.be

Far Eastern Economic Review

Pakistan: 108/10 Tufail Road, Lahore Cantt
Tel: +92 (42) 372072 Fax: + 92 (42) 666 2895

Financial Times

Pakistan: 222 Khadim Hussain Road, Rawalpindi
Tel: +92 (51) 581005 Fax: + 92 (51) 586421 Mobile: +92 (351) 370970

Frankfurter Rundschau

India: D-433 Defence Colony, New Delhi 110 003
Tel: +33 (11) 464 9367 Fax: + 91 (11) 464 9367

German Radio (ARD) South Asia

India: 148 Golf Links, New Delhi 110 003
Tel: +91 (11) 462 3022 Fax: + 91 (11) 460 2771

The Guardian

India: 2 Nizamuddin East, New Delhi 110 013, India.
Tel: +91 (11) 469 7985 Fax: + 91 (11) 464 7613

Kyodo (Japanese Press Agency)

Pakistan: House 31, Street 28, F-10/1, Islamabad.
Tel: +92 (51) 291577 Fax: + 92 (51) 297031

NBS

Afghanistan: Street 15, Lane No. 5, Wazir Akbar Khan, Kabul

NCB News

Afghanistan: Road 5, Street 15, Wazir Akbar Khan, Kabul
Satphone: +873 762 417 128

Newsweek

Afghanistan: Street 10, House No.7, Wazir Akbar Khan, Kabul
Tel: 23488

New York Times

India: 56 Janpath, New Delhi 110 001
Tel: +91 (11) 332 1965, 332 2853 Fax: + 91 (11) 371 2237

Reuters

Afghanistan: House No. 125, Street 15, Wazir Akbar Khan, Kabul
Tel: +93(0) 20 229 0027 Satphone: +873 171 6412
Email: syed@reuters.isb-com.net
Pakistan: House 4, Street 2, F-6/3, PO Box 1069, Islamabad
Tel: +92 (51) 2274750 Fax: + 92 (51) 274759 Mobile: +92 (351) 375144
International: 85 Fleet Street, London EC4P 4AJ, UK.
Tel: +44 (0)20 7250 1122 Email: (name)@reuters.com

Time

Pakistan: House 5B, Street 18, F-8/2, Islamabad.
Tel: +92 (51) 261440 Fax: + 92 (51) 260331

The Times

India: Fax: + 91 (11) 643 1527

United Nations Assistance Mission in Afghanistan (UNAMA)

Afghanistan: Compound "A", Street 10, House No. 310, Wazir Akbar Khan, Kabul
Tel: +1 (212) 963 2668 Fax: +1 (212) 963 2669
Pakistan: UNAMA, PO Box 1428, Islamabad

United Nations Children's Fund (UNICEF)

Pakistan:
House 60 A/78, Street 6, Defence Officers Colony, Near Defence Park, Khyber Road, Peshawar Cantt.
Tel: +92 (91) 278 524, 279 284 Fax: + 92 (91) 276 952
Email: psh@unicef.org.pk
6-7 Floors, Saudi-Pak Tower, 61-A, Jinnah Avenue, Blue Area, Islamabad, Pakistan.
Tel: +92 (51) 2800133 to 2800142 Fax: +92 (51) 2800132
Email: islamabad@unicef.org
Afghanistan:
Kabul: House No. 81, Nawhi Watt, Shar-e-Nau, Kabul, Afghanistan.
Tel: +93 (0)20 220 0439 Fax: +873 761 924 996 Email: kabulfo@unicef.org
Herat: Walayat Road, Opposite Agricultural Department, Herat City
Mazar: House No. 99, Hospital Road District 3, Mazar-e-Shari Email: mazar@unicef.org
Kandahar: Kotti 188 Dand Road, District 6, Kandahar Email: kandahar@unicef.org
Jalalabad: Raig Shah Mard Khan Road, Zone 4, Manzili Said Abass, Jalalabad-4

Voice of America (VOA)

Afghanistan: House No. 525, Street 10, Wazir Akbar Khan, Kabul Tel: 61831
Pakistan: House No 1. Street 89, G-6/3, Islamabad Tel: +92 (51) 2209069 278784, 277344 Fax: + 92 (51) 277349
Mobile: +92 (351) 370273
Dari Service, Washington: Tel: +1 (202) 619 0340 Fax: + 1 (202) 619 2400

The Washington Post

Afghanistan: House 7, Street 10, Wazir Akbar Khan, Kabul
Tel: + 93 (0)20 230 1199 Satphone: +873 762 598 677
India: B-56 Paschim Marg, Vasant Vihar, New Delhi 110057
Tel: +91 (11) 611 1368 Fax: + 91 (11) 611 1368

ZDF (Zweites Deutsches Frensehen – German TV)

Afghanistan: Kart-e-Parwan, Dahan-e-Nal, near the Car Wash, Kabul
Tel: +93 (0)20 220 0332 Satphone: +873 762 005 634
Email: zdf-kabul@les-raisting.de

Afghan/Regional:

Afghan Media Resource Centre (AMRC)

Afghanistan: The Street Opposite Rastagar Medical, Parwan Meena, Near Cinema Baharistan, Kabul Mobile: +93 (0)70 224787
Pakistan: 2 Canal Bank Road, UPO Box 909, University Town, Peshawar. Tel: +92 (91) 41691, 45256

Asia Times

Pakistan: House 7B, Street 43, F-8/1, Islamabad.
Tel: +92 (51) 263185 Fax: + 92 (51) 263215

APP (Associated Press of Pakistan)

Associated Press of Pakistan
Room No. 408, Poonch House Adamji Rd, Rawalpindi
Tel: +92 (0)51 5562637Fax: +92 (0)51 5517520

Dawn

Pakistan: Plot No.12, Sector G-7/1, Mauve Area, Near Zero Point, Islamabad
Tel: +92 (51) 220 2705, 220 2701, 220 2704, 220 2702 Fax: + 92 (51) 220 2707 Email: gmndawn@isb.paknet.com.pk

The Economic Daily, China

Pakistan: The Economic Daily, China House No. 1, Street 16, F-6/3, Islamabad
Tel: +92 (0)51 2279699

The Frontier Post

Pakistan: 62,Bazar Road,G-6/4 Islamabad
Tel: +92 (51) 281 9841, 281 9840, 282 1395 Fax: +92 (51) 2275641
Email: info@fpost.ibrain.brain.net.pk
32,Stadium Road, Peshawar Cantt.
Tel: +92 (91) 270504-270501, 270502 Fax: + 92 (91) 270505
Email: info@fpost.brain.net.pk

Financial Post

Pakistan: 107, G/6-7, West Fazle Haq Road, Blue Area, Islamabad
Tel: +92 (51) 2275594, 2275591 Fax: +92 (51) 2206294 Email: ilcl@ilcl.isb.sdnpk.undp.org

Kabul Weekly

Afghanistan: Aina Compound, Next to Ministry of Planning, Kabul
Tel: +93 (0)20 210 1589 Mobile: +93 (0)70 27 274526

Iran Radio/TV

Pakistan: Fax: + 92 (51) 255536

IRNA (Iranian Press Agency)

Pakistan: Tel: +92 (51) 827954 Fax: + 92 (51) 282778

Daily Jang

Pakistan: Tel: +92 (0)51 5555202, 5556223

Middle East Broadcasting

Pakistan: House 301, Street 49, G-10/3, Islamabad
Tel: +92 (51) 252151 Fax: + 92 (51) 282778

The Muslim

Pakistan: 9-Hameed Chambers, Aabpara, Islamabad
Tel: +92 (51) 2277482, 2277479 Fax: +92 (51) 2277485
Flat No.19, NWR Plaza, Khyber Super Market, Bara Road, Peshawar
Tel: +92 (91) 276301 Fax: +92 (91 275537

The Nation Daily

Pakistan: Nawa-i-Waqt House, Zero Point, Islamabad
Tel: +92 (51) 220 2641-4 Fax: +92 (51) 220 2645-6

The News

Islamabad: Tel: +92 (51) 555 6228 Fax: + 92 (51) 555 5371
Peshawar: Tel: +92 (91) 271612 Fax: + 92 (91) 555371

The Pakistan Observer

Pakistan: Ali Akbar House, Markaz G-8, Islamabad
Tel: +92 (51) 2852029, 2852027 Fax: +92 (51) 2262258 Email: observer@comsats.net.pk Web: www.pakobserver.net
Opposite Technical Training Centre, Gul Bahar Road, Peshawar
Tel: +92 (91) 264215

The Pakistan Times

Pakistan: PT House, 1-A Civil Lines, Pakistan Times Avenue, Mayo Road, Rawalpindi-46000
Tel: +92 (51) 44 33/51 41 000 Fax: + 92 (51) 5501779 Web: www.pakistantimes.net

Daily Pakistan

Pakistan: Haroon Chamber, Civic Centre, Islamabad
Tel: +92 (51) 2272730, 2272727 Fax: +92 (51) 2272731

Pakistan TV

Islamabad: Tel: +92 (51) 920 2194 Fax: + 92 (51) 920 8655

PPI (Pakistan Press Institute)

Karachi: Press Centre, Shahrah Kamal Ataturk, Karachi, 74200
Islamabad: Tel: +92 (51) 816747 Fax: + 92 (51) 810435

Russian Press Agency

Pakistan: Fax: + 92 (51) 278023
Wadat 20,Islamia Club Building, Khyber Bazaar, Peshawar
Tel: +92 (91) 214154, 414034, 43154 Fax: + 92 (91) 214321

Wafa

Pakistan: Street No.7, Gulbahar Colony No.2, Peshawar
Tel: +92 (91) 216544, 264635 Fax: + 92 (91) 264635 Email: watan@pes.comsats.net.pk

Xinhua News Agency

Pakistan: House No. 12-A Street 31, F-8/1, Islamabad
Tel: +92 (51) 2252779, 2250816

Humanitarian photography

Editors' Note: the following agencies have active photographic departments or are interested in approaches from freelance photographers. Where no specific address is indicated, apply to the Press and Public Information department at the agency's headquarters.

Canadian International Development Agency (CIDA)

CIDA is a provider of international development assistance to developing and emerging countries.
ADDRESS:
Media Relations Office, 200 Promenade de Portage Hull, Quebec, K1A OG4 Canada.
Tel: +1 (819) 953 6534 Fax: + 1 (819) 997 7397 Email: Christine_Skaladany@acdi-cida.gc.ca Web: www.acdi-cida.gc.ca

CARE International

CARE International is a confederation of ten CARE agencies which deliver relief assistance to people in need and long-term solutions to global poverty.
ADDRESSES:
International Secretariat, Boulevard du Regent 58/10, B-1000, Brussels, Belgium.
Tel: +32 (2) 502 4333 Fax: + 32 (2) 502 8202
Email: info@care-international.org Web: www.care.org
Afghanistan: Chahar Rahi Haji Yaqoob, Park Road, Shahr-e-Naw, Kabul
Mobile: +93 (0)70 276 716 Satphone: +873 762 212 633

The International Red Cross and Red Crescent Movement

Combines the 176 National Red Cross and Red Crescent Societies, the ICRC and the International Federation. Most National Societies have publications and are usually in need of photographers, volunteer or otherwise.
ADDRESSES:
International Federation of Red Cross and Red Crescent Societies, 17 chemin des Crêts, Petit Saconnex , PO Box 372, CH-1211 Geneva 19, Switzerland.
Tel: +41 (22) 730 42 22 Fax: + 41 (22) 733 03 95 Web: www.ifrc.org
ICRC Kabul: Charrahi Haji Yaqub, Shahr-e-Naw, Kabul.
Tel: +93 (0)20 290067 Fax: + 93 (0)20 290130 Satphone: +873 762 730 940 or 43 Satfax: + 873 762 730 941
Email: kaboul.kab@icrc.org

Magnum Photos

A cooperative of photojournalists and documentary photographers founded in 1947 with a unique selection of humanitarian and conflict coverage worldwide. Offices in Paris, London, New York and Tokyo.
ADDRESS: Magnum Photos Paris, 19 Rue Hegesippe Moreau, 75018 Paris, France.
Tel: + 33 (1) 53 42 50 00 Fax: + 33 (1) 53 42 50 01
Email: magnum@magnumphotos.fr Web: www.magnumarchive.com

PANOS Institute

PANOS promotes development which is socially, environmentally and economically sustainable. It has offices in London, Paris and Washington DC.
ADDRESS: 9, White Lion Street, London N1 9PD, UK. Tel: +44 (0)20 7278 1111 Fax: + 44 (0)20 7278 0345
Email: info@panoslondon.org.uk Web: www.panos.org.uk

United Nations (UN)

Subjects mainly on United Nations issues, such as international conferences, peacekeeping initiatives, etc.
ADDRESS: Photothèque, Palais des Nations, CH-1211 Geneva, Switzerland.
Tel: +41 (22) 917 33 17 Fax: + 41 (22) 917 00 73 Web: www.un.org

United Nations High Commissioner for Refugees (UNHCR)

Subjects: Refugee issues worldwide with excellent coverage of Somalia, Rwanda, Afghanistan, South East Asia and other regions.
ADDRESSES:
Photo Archives, Palais des Nations, Case Postale 2500, CH-1211, Geneva, Switzerland.
Tel: +41 (22) 739 8513 Fax: + 41 (22) 739 7314 Email: hollmann@unhcr.ch
Web: www.unhcr.ch
Afghanistan: 41 Jadai Solh, Shahr-e-Naw, District 4, Kabul. Tel: +93 (0)20 200 3812 Email: afgamr@unhcr.ch

United Nations Children's Fund (UNICEF)

Subjects extremely varied, including coverage of children's issues in war and humanitarian situations.
ADDRESSES:
International: Press & Information, Photo Library, Palais des Nations, CH-1211 Geneva 10, Switzerland.
Tel: +41 (22) 909 5519 Fax: + 41 (22) 909 5907 Web: www.unicef.org
Afghanistan: House 83, Street P, Part 2, District 4, Shahr-e-Naw, Kabul. Satphone: +873 762 925 533 Tel: +93 (0)20 2200439 Fax: + 873 761 924 996 Email: aco@unicef.org, kabul@unicef.org

US Agency for International Development (USAID)

ADDRESSES:
International: U.S. Agency for International Development Information Center, Ronald Reagan Building, Washington, D.C. 20523-1000, USA. Tel: +1 202 712 4810 Fax: + 1 202 216 3524 Web: www.usaid.gov
Afghanistan: 3B, Jami Street. Shahr-e-Naw, Kabul Tel: +93 (0)20 2200511, 31165 Mobile: +93 (0)70 275910, 276049 Email: mreabold@usaid.gov

Also try: ECHO, FAO, IOM, MSF, Oxfam, SCF, UNDP, UNESCO, UNFPA, WFP and WHO

Human rights groups

Aga Khan Development Network (AKDN)

AKDN is a family of agencies, created by his Highness the Aga Khan, which address three main areas: social development, culture, and economic development. Working in over 20 countries, the Network's underlying impulse is the ethic of compassion for the vulnerable in society and its agencies and institutions work for the common good of all citizens, regardless of origin, gender or religion. The Aga Khan Trust for Culture (AKTC) coordinates the Network's culture activities to enhance quality of life, foster self-understanding and community values, and to expand opportunities.
ADDRESSES:
International: Aiglemont, 60270 Gouvieux, France.
1-3 Avenue de la Paix, P.O. Box 2049, 1211 Geneva 2, Switzerland Tel: +41 (22) 909 72 00 Fax +41 (22) 909 72 92
Afghanistan: House No. 43, Street 13, Wazir Akbar Khan. Kabul Tel: +93 (0) 20 2301189 Mobile: +93 (0) 70 281141 Fax: (SAT): +873 682 341 599
Email: mtheuss@kbl.pactect.net Web: www.akdn.org

Amnesty International (AI)

AI is a London-based international advocacy organization which campaigns against human rights abuses worldwide. AI has published numerous papers on the human rights situation in Afghanistan.
ADDRESSES:
International Secretariat, 1 Easton Street, London WC1X 0DW, UK.
Tel: +44 (0)20 7413 5500 Fax: + 44 (0)20 7956 1157 Email: amnestyis@amnesty.org Web: www.amnesty.org
9, av. de la Gare-des-Eaux-Vives, Case postale 6224, 1211 Geneva 6, Switzerland.
Tel: +41 (22) 735 85 00 Fax: +41 (22) 700 51 46
Email: amnestygeneve@hotmail.com Web: www.amnestygeneve.ch
Afghanistan: House No. 450, Street 13, Wazir Akbar Khan, next to UNHCR Guest House, Kabul
Mobile: +93 (0)70 279363 Email: gacharya@amnesty.org, maldner@amnesty.org

Human Rights Watch

A US-based NGO which campaigns against human rights abuses.
ADDRESS:
350 Fifth Avenue, 34th floor, New York, NY 10118-3299, USA. Tel: +1 (212) 290 4700 Fax: +1 (212) 736 1300
Email: hrwnyc@hrw.org Web: www.hrw.org

International Human Rights Law Group (IHRLG)

A non-profit and non-governmental organization of human rights and legal experts engaged in human rights advocacy, litigation and training around the world. Established over 20 years ago, the Law Group started a women's rights advocacy program (WRAP) for Afghan refugee women in Pakistan in 1999.
ADDRESSES:
Afghanistan: House No. 200, 3rd, Ansari Street, Shahr-e-Naw, Kabul. Tel: +93 (0)20 290225 Fax: +93 (0)20 290336 Email: BelquisA@hrlawgroup.org
Pakistan: 98 E Abdara Road, University Town, Peshawar.
International: 1200, 8th Street NW, Suite 602, Washington DC 20036, USA.
Tel: +1 202 822 4600 Fax: +1 202 822 4606
Email: media@hrlawgroup.org Web: www.hrlawgroup.org

Lawyers' Committee for Human Rights

ADDRESS: 333 Seventh Avenue, 13th Floor, New York, NY 10001-5004, USA.
Tel: +1 212 845 5200 Fax: +1 212 845 5299 Email: nyc@lchr.org
Web: www.lchr.org

Physicians for Human Rights

ADDRESS: 100 Boylston Street, Suite 702, Boston, MA 02116, USA.
Tel: +1 617 695 0041 Fax: + 1 617 695 0307 Email: phrusa@phrusa.org
Web: www.phrusa.org

Robert F. Kennedy Center for Human Rights

ADDRESS: 1367 Connecticut Avenue NW, Suite 200, Washington DC 20036, USA.
Tel: +1 202 463 7575 Fax: + 1 202 463 6606 Email: info@rfkmemorial.org
Web: www.rfkmemorial.org/CENTER/

Schell Center for International Human Rights

ADDRESS: Yale Law School, New Haven, Connecticut 06520, USA.
Tel: +1 203 432 7129 Web: www.yale.edu Email: schell.law@yale.edu

Women-focused agencies

Afghan Institute of Training & Management (AIL)

Founded in 1995 to assist Afghan women and children, AIL is run entirely by Afghan women and is one of the largest employers of Afghan women in the country. Sectors: empowering Afghan women by expanding their educational and health opportunities and by fostering self-reliance and community participation.
ADDRESS: House 387, Masomi Street, Rd 3, Behind Cinema Baharistan, Kart-e-Parwan, Kabul. Tel: 30582 Satphone: +882 1650265266
Or contact through: Women's Learning Partnership (WLP), 4343 Montgomery Avenue, Suite 201, Bethesda, MD 20814, USA. Tel: +1 301 654 2774
Fax: + 1 301 654 2775 Email: wlp@learningpartnership.org Web: www.learningpartnership.org

APWO

ADDRESS: House No. 56, Street No. 15, Wazir Akbar Khan, Kabul. Tel: 21072

Afghan Women's Association for Rehabilitation & Development (AWARD)

ADDRESS: House No.10, Street 3, 2nd Part of Kart-e-Parwan, Kabul. Tel: +93 (0)70 282494

Afghan Women's Development Association (AWDA)

ADDRESS: House No. 30, Lane No. 4, Kolola Pushta Street, Ansari Watt, opposite to UNICA, Kabul. Tel: 32015

Afghan Women's Empowerment Program (AWEP)

ADDRESS: Taimani Watt, Golaye Masjid, Street 4, Next to Butcher Street, Shahr-e-Naw, Kabul. Tel: +93 (0)70 282056

Afghan Women's Network (AWN)

A group of Afghan women living in Pakistan and Afghanistan – active in Peshawar, Islamabad, Mazar-e-Sharif and Kabul. Many of the women previously worked in Afghanistan as lawyers, engineers, professors and doctors. They now work with NGOs, UN agencies and in schools. AWN was established in September l996.
ADDRESSES:
Afghanistan: House 193, Street 3, Qala-e-Fathullah, Kabul. Tel: +93 (0)20 220 0691 Email: awnkabul@hotmail.com, awnkabul@afghanwomensnetwork.org
Pakistan: House 86, Sector D/2, Abdara Main Road, University Town, Peshawar
Tel: +92 (91) 570 4928 Fax: +92 (91) 850670 Email: awn@brain.net.pk
Web: www.afghanwomensnetwork.org

AWNB Women's Network

ADDRESS: c/o Swiss Peace, Qua-e-Markaz Square, Opposite Malalai Maternity Hospital, Kabul
Tel: +93 (0)20 220 1061

Afghan Women's Welfare Development (AWWD)

ADDRESS: Qala-e-Fathullah, Madina Market, Street 1, House No. 25, Kabul.
Mobile: +93 (0)70 282 494

Humanitarian Organization for Orphans and Widows of Afghanistan (HOOWA)

ADDRESS: Microyan 3rd, Block No. 135, Apartment No. 23
Tel: +93 (0)20 230 0801

International Working Group on Refugee Women (IWGRW)

A Swiss-based NGO, forming part of the Special Committee of International NGOs on Human Rights (Geneva). IWGRW is active within the Afghan diaspora in Western Europe.
ADDRESS: c/o Webster University, 13-15, route de Collex, 1293 Bellevue, Switzerland.
Tel: +41 (22) 774 24 52 Fax: +41 (22) 774 30 13

National Relief Assistance (NRA)

ADDRESS: Mohd. Jan Khan Watt, 5th Floor of Ghausi Market, Opposite of Ministry of Information, Kabul. Tel: 22677, 34006, 34627

Physiotherapy & Rehabilitation Support for Afghanistan (PARSA)

ADDRESS: House No. 1, on Right Side of Street Next to Ministry of Commerce, North Side of Dar-ul-Aman Road, Kabul
Tel: +93 (0)20 2200401 Email: marymacmakin@yahoo.com

The Revolutionary Association of the Women of Afghanistan (RAWA)

RAWA has been active since the mid-1980s, campaigns for women's rights and provides education and health facilities for women and children.
ADDRESSES:
Afghanistan: PO Box 374, Quetta, Pakistan. Tel: +92 300 8551638
International: The Afghan Women's Mission, 260 S. Lake Avenue, PMB 165, Pasadena, CA 91101, USA
Fax: + 1 760 2819855, and +44 870 8312326 Email: rawa@rawa.org
Web: www.rawa.org

SWNHO

ADDRESS: Airport Main Rd, Qala-e-Khayata, Kabul. Mobile: +93 (0)70 282 494

Women's Assistance Association (WAA)

ADDRESS: Lane 1, Street No.13, House No. 563, Wazir Akbar Khan, Kabul.
Tel: 61466

Women's Commission for Refugee Women and Children (WCRWC)

ADDRESS: 122 East 42nd Street, 12th Floor, New York, NY 10168-1289, USA.
Tel: +1 (212) 551 3111 and +1 (212) 551 3088 Fax: + 1 (212) 551 3180
Email: info@womenscommission.org Web: www.womenscommission.org

Women's Unity for Rehabilitation (WUR)

ADDRESS: House No.165, Ansari Watt, Right 2nd, Between UNICEF No.1 Guest House & ANCB, Shahr-e-Now, Kabul
Mob: 070282324

Policy & research institutes

The Carter Centre Conflict Resolution Programme

453 Freedom Parkway, Atlanta, GA 30307, USA.
Tel: +1 (404) 420 5185 Fax: + 1 (404) 420 3862

Center for International Security and Arms Control – Stanford University

CISAC, Encina Hall, Stanford, CA 94305-6165, USA. Tel: +1 (650) 725 6488
Fax: + 1 (650) 724 5683 Email: andersonhsiao@stanford.edu
Web: http://cisac.stanford.edu

Centre for Peace Studies

Global Rea House, 20 Pembroke Park, Dublin 4, Ireland. Tel: +353 (1) 684914

Centre for South Asian Studies – Jawaharlal Nehru University

School of International Studies, New Mehranli Road, New Delhi, 110 067, India.

Deutsches Orient Institut

Neuer Jungfernstieg 21 D-20354 Hamburg, Germany. Tel: +49 (0)40 42825 514 Fax: + 49 (0)40 42825 509 Email: doi@doi.duei.de Web: www.doihh.de

International Institute for Strategic Studies (IISS)

Arundel House, 13-15 Arundel Street, Temple Place, London WC2R 3DX, UK.
Tel: +44 (0) 20 7379 7676 Fax: +44 (0) 20 7836 3108
Email: iiss@iiss.org Web: www.iiss.org

Mersham Center – Ohio State University

199 West, 10th Avenue, Columbus, OH 43210 2399, USA.
Tel: +1 (614) 292 1618 Fax: + 1 (614) 292 2407

Nederlands Instituut voor International Betrekkingen Clingendael

Netherlands Institute of International Relation, Clingendael 7, 2597 VH The Hague, The Netherlands, P.O. Box 93080 2509 AB The Hague.
Tel: +31 70 3245384 Fax: +31 70 3282002 Email: info@clingendael.nl
Web: www.clingendael.nl

Nizhni Novogrod State University – Centre for Peace and Conflict Resolution Research

Ulianov Street 2, Nizhni Novogrod, 603005, Russian Federation.
Tel: +7 (831) 239 0249

Panteios University of Social & Political Sciences

Institute of International Relations, 136 Syggrou Ave, GR-176 71, Athens, Greece. Tel: +30 1 9220100 and +31 1 9223227 Fax: +30 1 9223690
Email: rector@panteion.gr Web: www.panteion.gr

Radcliffe College, The Mary Ingram Bunting Institute

34 Concord Avenue, Cambridge, MA 02138, USA. Tel: +1 (617) 495 8212
Fax: + 1 (617) 495 8136 Email: bunting_fellowships@radcliffe.harvard.edu
Web: www.radcliffe.edu/fellowships/index.html

Strategic and Defence Studies Centre – Australian National University (SDSC)

Strategic and Defence Studies Centre, Australian National University, Building 6, Fellows Road, Canberra ACT 0200, Australia. Tel: +61 2 6125 9921
Fax: +61 2 6248 0816 Email: sdsc@anu.edu.au
Web: www.rspas.anu.edu.au/sdsc

School of Oriental & African Studies (SOAS)

Thornhaugh Street, Russell Square, London WC1H 0XG, UK.
Tel: +44 (0)20 7637 2388 Fax: +44 (0)20 7436 3844

Editors' Note: Contact lists have been compiled from the ACBAR Directory of Humanitarian Agencies Working for Afghans, internet searches, agency reports and returned EFG questionnaires. These lists are not exhaustive and are bound to contain some errors. Please help us keep up to date by sending your changes and corrections to the Editors.

INFORESOURCES

J. Hartley/UNICEF

Getting the news

Daily

Afgha.com
Afghan press agency with daily news, archives, links to organizations and other resources. News can be sent to your mobile phone.
http://www.afgha.com

Afghan Daily
Part of the World News Network, a well-organized website with news and features from the world's press on Afghanistan, Pakistan and the 'war on terror'.
http://www.afghandaily.com

Afghan News.net
Daily news from international wire and radio sources, plus useful links.
http://www.afghannews.net

Afghan News Network
Daily news from regional and international wire agencies, compiled by the US-based Afghan News Network.
http://www.myafghan.com

Afghanistan News.net
Daily news from a variety of media sources, plus information on weather, economy, history and travel.
http://afghanistannews.net

Afghan Online Press
Daily news compiled from wire agencies (AFP, AP, Xinhua) and both regional and international newspapers. Plus radio in Dari and Pashto via the internet, links to new books and other information about Afghanistan.
http://www.aopnews.com

Afghanistan Research Group (ARG)
Information, reports, articles and other material from ARG's work and from the internet, plus excellent external links.
http://www.bglatzer.de/arg

Afghaniyat
An efficient email listserv providing daily news, articles and comments from leading international media, experts, officials and Afghans worldwide.
Email: afghaniyat-subscribe@yahoogroups.com
Web: http://groups.yahoo.com/group/afghaniyat

Radio Free Afghanistan
Daily radio news via the internet in Dari, Pashto and English.
Email: afghan@rferl.org
Web: http://www.rferl.org/bd/af

Relief Web
Daily news on humanitarian, development, political and security issues – drawn from UN, World Bank, NGO, Red Cross/Crescent and donor reports plus wire agencies. Compiled by the UN's Office for the Coordination of Humanitarian Affairs.
http://www.reliefweb.int

Weekly

Afghan News Channel
Regular news stories compiled from international media.
http://afghan-network.net/News

Alert Net
Reuters' AlertNet provides regular news on Afghanistan's humanitarian and political situation. Weekly email alert for Afghanistan also available.
http://www.alertnet.org

IRIN
Regular media and UN reports on Afghanistan, plus interviews with key players. Provided by the UN's Integrated Regional Information Network.
http://www.irinnews.org/AsiaFP.ASP

Open Society Institute
Regular news, resource and analysis site of the Central Eurasia Project of the Open Society Institute, including special Afghanistan pages.
http://www.eurasianet.org/resource/afghanistan/index.shtml

United Nations Assistance Mission in Afghanistan (UNAMA)
UNAMA publishes a weekly press briefing on the political, military and humanitarian situations. The site also includes UN fact sheets, publications, videos and useful weblinks to all the main UN agencies.
Contact:
Spokesman/ Director of Office of Communication and Public Information
Tel: (+39-0831) 24 6123 Mobile: (+93-70) 282 168 Tie Line: (+1-212) 963-2668 Ext: 6123
Email: spokesman-unama@un.org
Web: http://www.unama-afg.org

The Washington Post
World News Search, with latest news, wire stories, background information, reports and links.
http://www.washingtonpost.com/wp-dyn/world/search

Monthly

Afghanistan Information Management Service (AIMS)
News and reports from UN, NGO and media sources, compiled by this Kabul-based UN agency.
http://www.aims.org.af

British Agencies Afghanistan Group (BAAG)
BAAG produces a reliable and well-sourced Monthly Review, available on the web or by email, which covers security, humanitarian, economic and political developments in Afghanistan.
Contact:
BAAG Project Coordinator, The Refugee Council, 240/250 Ferndale Road, London SW9 8BB, UK.
Tel: +44 (0)20 7820 3098 Fax: +44 (0)20 7840 4388
Email: Peter.Marsden@RefugeeCouncil.org.uk
Web: http://www.baag.org.uk

Email listservs for Afghanistan

Afghaniyat
Daily news, articles and comments from leading media & experts.
Email: afghaniyat-subscribe@yahoogroups.com
Web: http://groups.yahoo.com/group/afghaniyat

BBC World Service
Customized email news updates for Asia Pacific.
Web: http://www.bbc.co.uk/email/news

Human Rights Watch
Weekly Afghanistan email updates.
Email: afghanistan-subscribe@topica.email-publisher.com
Web: http://www.hrw.org/act/subscribe-mlists/subscribe.htm#afghanistan

Specialist websites

Academic & Research

http://www.areu.org.pk
Kabul-based Afghanistan Research and Evaluation Unit

http://www.columbia.edu/cu/lweb/indiv/mideast/cuvlm/Afghanistan.html
Columbia University: links to relevant web sites

http://www.crisisweb.org
Brussels-based International Crisis Group, specializing in detailed analysis and policy recommendations

http://www.institute-for-afghan-studies.org
Institute for Afghan Studies

http://www.lib.utexas.edu/maps/afghanistan.html
University of Texas at Austin: Perry-Castañeda map library

http://www.nyu.edu/its/pubs/connect/spring03/pdfs/afghan_library.pdf
New York University's Afghanistan Digital Library Project

Environment & Agriculture

http://www.adb.org/documents/others/cna_afg/agriculture/cna_afg_agri.pdf
Asian Development Bank's comprehensive needs assessment

http://www.fao.org/reliefoperations/appeals/2003/afghanistanTAPA.html
UN Food and Agriculture Organization's appeal for Afghanistan

http://www.futureharvest.org/news/afghanistan_fh1.shtml
Future Harvest Consortium's agricultural projects in Afghanistan

http://www.nationalgeographic.com/landincrisis
National Geographic's Afghanistan page, with articles, interactive maps and interviews

http://www.unodc.org/pdf/afg/afghanistan_opium_survey_2003.pdf
UN Office on Drugs and Crime: Afghanistan Opium Survey 2003

http://www.wri.org/central_asia/afghanistan.html
World Resources Institute: papers on Afghan resources, agriculture and environment

Humanitarian & Development

http://www.afghanaid.org.uk
Afghanaid

http://www.careusa.org/newsroom/specialreports/Afghanistan
Care International's special reports on Afghanistan

http://www.cdc.gov
Centers for Disease Control and Prevention

http://www.DisasterRelief.org
Joint website of American Red Cross, CNN and IBM

http://www.icbl.org/lm/2003/afghanistan.html
International Campaign to Ban Landmines, report on Afghanistan

http://www.icrc.org/eng/afghanistan
International Committee of the Red Cross

http://www.theirc.org
International Rescue Committee

http://www.msf.org
Médecins Sans Frontières

http://www.oneworld.net/southasia
Umbrella website for over 100 international and local human rights and sustainable development organizations

http://www.oxfam.org
Oxfam International

http://www.reliefweb.int
Provided by UN OCHA, covering natural disasters and conflicts

http://www.savethechildren.org
Save the Children

http://www.undp.org/afghanistan
United Nations Development Program (UNDP) in Afghanistan

http://www.unicef.org/noteworthy/afghanistan
UN Children's Agency information on Afghanistan

http://www.us-arc.org
U.S. Afghanistan Reconstruction Council

http://www.developmentgateway.org/node/134111
World Bank's Development Gateway site for Afghan reconstruction

Human Rights

http://mailman.aaas.org/mailman/listinfo/aaashran
The US-based AAAS Human Rights Action Network

http://www.amnesty.org
Amnesty International

http://www.derechos.org/saran/afg.html
Derechos: Human Rights in Afghanistan

http://www.hrw.org/asia/afghanistan.php
Human Rights Watch Afghanistan page

http://www.phrusa.org/campaigns/afghanistan
Physicians for Human Rights

http://www.unhchr.ch
UN Office of the High Commissioner for Human Rights

http://usinfo.state.gov/dhr/human_rights.html
US State Department's Human Rights Reports

Media

http://www.ainaworld.com
Aïna and the Afghan Media and Cultural Centre

http://www.bbc.co.uk/worldservice/people/highlights/010711_reach.shtml
The BBC's REACH project: Radio Education for Afghan Children

http://www.iwpr.net/afghan_index1.html
Institute for War and Peace Reporting: Afghanistan project

http://lanfiles.williams.edu/~dedwards/wamp.htm
The Williams Afghan Media Project, in conjunction with the Afghan Media Resource Center

http://www.mediaaction.org/afghansite.html
Media Action International

http://www.mediachannel.org
A media monitoring and news site, with analysis and tools for journalists, as well as up-to-date global news

http://www.nyu.edu/globalbeat
A news resource for "the global journalist", produced by New York University's Center for War, Peace and the News Media

Refugees & IDPs

http://www.aims.org.af/assistance_sectors/refugee
UN's Afghanistan Information Management Service: reports and maps on refugees and IDPs

http://www.idpproject.org
Norwegian Refugee Council's Global IDP Project

http://www.irinnews.org/AsiaFP.asp
UN's Integrated Regional Information Network: reports on refugees and IDPs

http://www.unhcr.ch
UN High Commissioner for Refugees

INFORESOURCES

http://www.refugees.org/world/countryindex/afghanistan.htm
U.S. Committee for Refugees: reports on Afghanistan

Telecommunications

http://www.afghanwireless.com
Website for the AWCC (Afghan Wireless Communication Company)

http://www.thuraya.ch
Combination GSM, GPS and Satellite mobile phones

http://www.itu.ch
International Telecommunications Union (ITU)

http://www.remotesatellite.com/index.html
Provides a short course on satphones

United Nations

http://www.aims.org.af
Afghanistan Information Management Service, operating as part of UNDP and OCHA.

http://www.irinnews.org/AsiaFP.ASP
UN's Integrated Regional Information Network, covering Africa and Asia.

http://www.reliefweb.int
Provided by OCHA, covering natural disasters and conflicts

http://www.unama-afg.org
UN Assistance Mission in Afghanistan (UNAMA) – provides weblinks to all the main UN agencies in Afghanistan.

http://www.unsystem.org
Official locator for UN Agency websites.

Women

http://www.afghan-web.com/woman
Site covering various aspects of Afghan life including women's issues

http://www.awai.org
Afghan Women's Association International

http://www.feminist.org/afghan/intro.asp
Feminist Majority Foundation's Campaign for Afghan Women and Girls

http://www.phrusa.org/campaigns/afghanistan/Afghan_report.html
Women's Health and Human Rights report, by Physicians for Human Rights

http://www.rawa.org or http://rawasongs.fancymarketing.net/index.html
RAWA! (Revolutionary Association of the Women of Afghanistan)

http://www.un.org/womenwatch
UN's internet gateway for advancement of women

http://www.wapha.org
Women's Alliance for Peace and Human Rights in Afghanistan

Libraries

ACBAR Resource and Information Centre (ARIC), Peshawar
ARIC is the best reference library on Afghanistan in the region. It contains thousands of books, agency reports, maps, journals and videos on every sector of interest in Afghanistan. The ARIC Bulletin, produced monthly, details all new acquisitions in English, Dari and Pashto and other languages. Photocopying for documents and maps is available for a small fee. A number of Nancy Hatch Dupree's books are for sale at ARIC. The *Essential Field Guide to Afghanistan* is also for sale.
ADDRESSES:
Pakistan: 2 Rehman Baba Road, U.P.O. Box 1084, University Town, Peshawar
TEL: +92 (91) 5704392; 850839; 5702531; 5702962 FAX: +92 (91) 840471
Email: aric@brain.net.pk or info@afghanresources.org
Web: http://www.afghanresources.org
Afghanistan: 12 Jami Watt, Shahr-e-Naw, Kabul
TEL: +93 (20) 2200208, +93 (0)70 281415
Email: info@acbar.org
Hours: Mondays to Thursdays: 0800-1630; Fridays: 0800-1230; Saturdays and Sundays: closed

Afghan Media Resource Centre (AMRC), Peshawar
AMRC has an enormous collection of photographs, video and film footage, newspapers and magazines. Started by Boston University School of Communications in the 1980s and funded by the US State Department to train Afghan photographers and cameramen, the majority of its work has focused on documenting the Soviet-Afghan war.
ADDRESS:
2 Canal Bank Road, University Town, Peshawar, Pakistan
TEL: +92 (91) 41691, 45256

British Council
The British Council is a developmental, educational and cultural organization with offices and libraries in over 100 countries. It promotes the exchange of ideas, expertise and knowledge between UK organizations and partners throughout the world.
ADDRESSES:
London: 10 Spring Gardens, London, SW1A 2BN, UK
TEL: +44 (0)20 7930 8466 FAX: +44 (0)20 7839 6347
Email: general.enquiries@britishcouncil.org Website: http://www.britcoun.org
Pakistan: Block 14, Civic Centre, G-6, Islamabad
TEL: +92 (51) 829041-4 FAX: +92 (51) 276683
Email: (name)@bc-isb.sdnpk.undp.org

School of Oriental and African Studies (SOAS), London
One of the principal academic and research institutions in London covering the Middle East, Central Asia and Afghanistan. Publications relating to Afghanistan can be found on the ground floor under shelf-mark 'ON'; reference works (covering encyclopaedias, dictionaries and bibliographies) are found under 'ON' in the Islamic Reading Room, also on the ground floor. A charge is made for day tickets; six month or yearly membership is available. Information about the library is on the SOAS Web Page and on the following:
ADDRESS:
Thornhaugh Street, Russell Square, London WC1H 0XG, UK.
TEL: +44 20 7898 4152
General enquiries: libenquiry@soas.ac.uk
Website: http://www.soas.ac.uk/library/index.cfm
Library Hours:
Mondays to Fridays: 0900–1700 (2045 during academic term-time); Saturdays: 0930–1700

Stifthung Bibliotheca Afghanica: The Swiss/Afghanistan Archive, Liestal
A scientific institution for documentation and research of Afghanistan's nature, culture and history (including contemporary history). For humanitarian and scientific matters use of the library is free of charge. All materials must be inspected on the library premises (there is no loaning of books). The library contains: 14,000 titles on Afghanistan/Central Asia in European languages; a further 6,000 titles in Oriental languages; extensive collection of Afghan maps in different scales; Phototheca Afghanica, a collection of over 7,000 black & white prints.
ADDRESS:
Benzburweg 5, CH-4410 Liestal, Switzerland
TEL/FAX: +41 (61) 921 9838
Email: afghannet@spectraweb.ch
Hours: by appointment with the director

Bibliography[1]

Al Qa'eda, Taliban & Fundamentalism

Holy War, Inc.: Inside The Secret World of Osama Bin Laden, Peter L. Bergen, Free Press (2001)

Taliban: A Shadow Over Afghanistan, Burchard Brentjes, Helga Brentjes, Rishi Publications (2001)

The Lessons of Afghanistan: War Fighting, Intelligence, and Force Transformation (Significant Issues Series, Vol. 24, No. 4), Center for Strategic and International Studies (2002)

Islamic Fundamentalism in Afghanistan: Its Character and Prospects, Graham E. Fuller, Rand Corp.

The Taliban: Ascent to Power, M. J. Gohari, Oxford University Press (2001)

Afghanistan's Endless War: State Failure, Regional Politics, and the Rise of the Taliban, Larry P. Goodson, University of Washington Press (2001)

Reaping the Whirlwind: Al Qa'ida and the Holy War, Michael Griffin, Pluto Press (2003)

Fundamentalism Reborn? Afghanistan and the Taliban, William Maley (Editor), Hurst & Co. (London, 1998)

The Taliban: War and Religion in Afghanistan, Revised Edition, Peter Marsden, Zed Books (2002)

Taliban Phenomenon: Afghanistan 1994-1997, Kamal Matinuddin, Oxford University Press (1999)

The Rise of the Taliban in Afghanistan: Mass Mobilization, Civil War, and the Future of the Region, Neamatollah Nojumi, Palgrave Macmillan (2002)

Taliban: Militant Islam, Oil and Fundamentalism in Central Asia, Ahmed Rashid, Yale University Press (2001)

Inside Al Qaeda: Global Network of Terror, Rohan Gunaratna, Berkley Pub Group; Reissue edition (2003)

The Fragmentation of Afghanistan: State Formation and Collapse in the International System, Barnett R. Rubin, Yale University Press, Second Edition (2002)

Ethnic & Tribal

Islam, Ethnicity and the State in Pakistan: An Overview, R.Binder, in *The State, Religion and Ethnic Politics: Afghanistan, Iran, Pakistan,* A. Banuazizi and M. Weiner (Editors), Syracuse University Press (New York, 1996)

The Most Difficult Choice, R. Breen, in *Refugees*, UNHCR (Geneva, Issue 11, October 1997)

---

[1] *Alphabetical order by author*

The State, Religion and Ethnic Politics: Afghanistan, Iran, Pakistan, Ed. Banuazizi and Weiner, Syracuse University Press (New York, 1996)

The Biggest Caseload in The World, R. Colville, in *Refugees*, UNHCR (Geneva, Issue 11, October 1997)

Afghanistan, Dupree, L., Princeton University Press (New Jersey, 1980)

Afghanistan's Population Inside and Out, Eighmy, T., US Agency for International Development (Islamabad, 1990)

Is Afghanistan on the Brink of Ethnic and Tribal Disintegration? Glatzer, B., in *Fundamentalism Reborn? Afghanistan and the Taliban*, Ed. Maley, St. Martins (New York, 1998)

The Emergence of Modern Afghanistan, Gregorian, V., Stanford University Press (Stanford, 1969)

Tribalism and Rural Society in the Islamic World (History and Society in the Islamic World), David M. Hart, Frank Cass Publishers (2000)

Paying for Taliban's Crimes: Abuses Against Ethnic Pashtuns in Northern Afghanistan, Human Rights Watch Vol. 14, No. 2 (New York, 2002)

Afghanistan under Soviet domination, Hyman, A., Macmillan (3rd edition, 1982)

The Afghan Transitional Administration: Prospects and Perils, International Crisis Group (Brussels, 2002)

Dark Side of Moon, A. Jamal, in *Refugees*, UNHCR (Geneva, Issue 11, October 1997)

Afghanistan: A nation of minorities, Javad, N., Minority Rights Group (London, 1992)

Government and Society in Afghanistan, H. Kakar, University of Texas Press (Austin, 1979)

The Pacification of the Hazaras of Afghanistan, H. Kakar, ACAS Occasional papers (New York, 1973)

Saire Dar Hazarajat, A. Laly, Ihsani (Qom, Iran, 1994)

The Hazaras of Afghanistan – An Historical, Cultural, Economic and Political Study, Dr Sayed Askar Mousavi, Curzon Press Ltd. (London, 1997)

The Struggle for Afghanistan, N. Newell and R. Newell, Cornell University Press (London, 1981)

The Kafir of the Hindu-Kush, George Robertson, Oxford University Press (1st Edition, 1896; reprinted, 1975)

The Kirghiz and Wakhi of Afghanistan: Adaptation to Closed Frontiers and War, M. Nazif Mohib Shahrani, University of Washington Press, 2nd Edition (2002)

The Ethnic Composition of Afghanistan, Wak Foundation for Afghanistan (Peshawar, 1998)

State Building and Social Fragmentation in Afghanistan, N. Shahrani, in *The State, Religion and Ethnic Politics: Afghanistan, Iran, Pakistan,* A. Banua-zizi and M. Weiner (Editors), Syracuse University Press (New York, 1996)

The Democratic Republic of Afghanistan, USSR Academy of Sciences, Institute for Oriental Studies (Moscow, 1981)

The Baluchis and The Pathans, V. Wrisling, Minority Rights Group Report (London, 1987)

General

Dictionary of Afghan Wars, Revolutions and Insurgencies, (Historical Dictionaries of Wars, Revolution and Civil Unrest, No. 1), Ludwig W. Adamec, The Scarecrow Press Inc.

Historical Dictionary of Afghanistan, Ludwig W. Adamec, The Scarecrow Press Inc. (Metuchen, NJ and London, 1997)

A Biographical Dictionary of Contemporary Afghanistan, Ludwig W. Adamec, Akademische Druck-u. Verlagsanstalt (Graz, 1987)

Afghanistan Crises, Tahir Amin, Holy Koran Publishing House

Afghanistan: Fighting for Freedom (Discovering Our Heritage), Mir T. Ansary, Dillon Press

The Tragedy of Afghanistan: A First-Hand Account, Raja Anwar, Fred Halliday, Khalid Hasan (Translator), Verso Books (London, 1988)

Afghanistan, The Definitive Account of a Country at Crossroads, George Arney, Mandarin (London, 1990)

The Politics of Social Transformation in Afghanistan, Iran, and Pakistan (Contemporary Issues in the Middle East), Ali Banuazizi and Myron Weiner (Editors), Syracuse University Press

Afghanistan, A Country Study, Sally Ann Baynard, Laurie Krieger, Robert S. Ford, Donald M. Seekins, Samuel Hayfield, United States Government

Le Royaume de L'Insolence, L'Afghanistan 1504 - 2001 (Kingdom of Insolence), Michael Barry, Flammarion (Paris, 2002)

NGO Coordination at field level, Jon Bennett, ICVA (Geneva, 1994)

The World Factbook, United States Central Intelligence Agency (Washington, annually)

Danziger's Adventures; from Miami to Kabul, Nick Danziger, HarperCollins

Bridgehead Afghanistan, Wilhelm Dietl, South Asia Books

Afghanistan: Coordination in a Fragmented State, Antonio Donini, Eric Dudley, Ron Ockwell, United Nations Department for Humanitarian Affairs (New York, 1996)

Afghanistan, Louis Dupree, Princeton University Press (2nd Edition, 1980; reprinted by Oxford University Press, 1997)

State, Revolution, and Superpowers in Afghanistan, Hafizullah Emadi, Praeger publications (New York, 1990)

Shadow Over Afghanistan, Fazel Rahman Fazel, Western Book/Journal Press

Afghanistan: Highway of Conquest, Arnold Fletcher, Cornell University Press

Afghanistan: Agony of a Nation, Sandy Gall, Bodley Head

The Road to Kabul: An Anthology, Gerald De Gaury, Book Sales

Afghanistan: Key to a Continent, John C. Griffiths, Westview Press

Conflict in Afghanistan (Flashpoint), J. Griffiths, Rourke Publishing Group

Under a Sickle Moon: A Journey Through Afghanistan, Peregrine Hodson, Ulverscroft Large Print Books

Afghanistan, Michael Howarth, Chelsea House

Asia and Pacific Review: 58 Countries, from New Zealand to China to Afghanistan, Hunter Publishing

Afghanistan: Land in Shadow, Chris Johnson, OXFAM (Oxford, 1998)

Afghanistan Venture, Paul S. Jones, The Naylor Company

Afghanistan (World Bibliographical Series, Vol. 135), Schuyler Jones, Abc-Clio

The Sewing Circles of Herat, Christina Lamb, Harper Collins (London, 2002)

Afghanistan in Pictures (Visual Geography), Lerner Publications Company

The light garden of the angel king: journeys in Afghanistan, Peter Levi, Collins

The bookseller of Kabul, Asne Seierstad Little, Brown (2003)

Caravan, Darryl Ligasan (Illustrator), Lawrence Jr. McKay, Lee & Low Books

The Land and People of Afghanistan, Lippincott-Raven Publishers

Afghanistan: A Profile, Ralph H. Magnus, Westview Press

Afghan Alternatives: Issues, Options and Policies, Editor: Ralph H. Magnus, Transaction Books (New Brunswick, NJ, 1985)

Caravans to Tartary, Sabrina Michaud, Roland Michaud, Thames & Hudson

Afghanistan, Sabrina Michaud, Roland Michaud, Thames & Hudson

Caravans: A Novel, James Albert Michener, Random House

The 3rd World: Afghanistan and Pakistan, E. Willard Miller, Vance Bibliographies

Afghanistan in Crisis, K. P. Misra, Stosius Inc./Advent Books Division

The Politics of Afghanistan, Richard Newell, Cornell University Press (1972)

Health Care in Muslim Asia: Development and Disorder in Wartime Afghanistan, Ronald W. O'Connor, University Press of America

Islam and Politics in Afghanistan, Asta Olesen, Curzon Press

Afghanistan (Country Guide Series Report from the Aacrao-Aid Project), Holly A. O'Neill, American Association of College Registrars

Adventures in Afghanistan, Louis Palmer, Octagon Press

La Nouvelle Asia Centrale (ou La Fabrication des nations), Olivier Roy, Editions du Seuil (Paris, 1997)

The Fragmentation of Afghanistan: State Formation and Collapse in the International System, Barnett R. Rubin, Yale University Press, Second Edition (2002)

The Search for Peace in Afghanistan: From Buffer State to Failed State, Barnett R. Rubin, Yale University Press

Regime Change in Afghanistan: Foreign Intervention and the Politics of Legitimacy, Amin Saikal, William Maley, Westview Press

Political Order in Post-Communist Afghanistan, Fazel Haq Saikal, William Maley, Lynne Rienner Publications

A Violation of Trust, Joseph S. Salzburg, Sovereign Books

Afghanistan of the Afghans, The Sirdar Ikbal Ali Shah, Octagon Press

Tales of Afghanistan, Amina Shah, Ishk Book Service

Kara Kush, Idries Shah, Octagon Press

Afghan Caravan, Safia Shah (Editor), Octagon Press

Superpower Detente and the Future of Afghanistan, Jasjit Singh, Eduard Shevardnadze, B.K. Shrivastava, B. Gupta, South Asia Books

Afghanistan, Alex Ullmann, Ticknor & Fields

Afghanistan: is there hope for peace? Hearings before the Subcommittee on Near Eastern and South Asian Affairs of the Committee on Foreign Relations, United States Senate, One Hundred Fourth Congress, second session, June 6, 25, 26, and 27, 1996.

War in Afghanistan, Mark Urban, St Martins Press

An Afghanistan Picture Show: Or, How I Saved the World, William T. Vollmann, Farrar Straus & Giroux

Afghanistan, Non-Alignment and the Super Powers, Mohammed Amin Wakman, Humanities Press

Pakistan & Afghanistan: Resistance and Reconstruction, Marvin Weinbaum, Westview Press

Pakistan and Afghanistan, Westview Press

Widener Library Shelflists, 19. Southern Asia: Afghanistan, Bhutan, Burma, Cambodia, Ceylon, Harvard University Press

The Bear Trap: Afghanistan's Untold Story, Mohammed Yousaf, Mark Adkin, Leo Cooper (London, 1992)

Devil's Playground, Said Yassin Zia, Morris Publications

Historical and Cultural

Mohammad Daoud, Personality, Ideas and Policies: A Study in Contemporary Afghan History, Assem Akram, Mizan Publishing, Persian Language Edition (2001)

Histoire de la Guerre d'Afghanistan, Assem Akram, Editions Balland (Paris, 1996)

Afghanistan (Cultures of the World), Sharifah Enayat Ali, Marshall Cavendish Corp.

Afghanistan of the Afghans, Shah Sirdar Ikbal Ali

Archaeology of Afghanistan: From Earliest Times to the Timurid Period, F. R. Allchin, N. Hammond (Editor), Academic Press

Buzkashi: Game and Power in Afghanistan, G. Whitney Azoy, University of Pennsylvania Press (1982)

The Central Asian Arabs of Afghanistan: Pastoral Nomadism in Transition, Thomas J. Barfield, University of Texas Press (1981)

A History of Afghanistan, Vitaly Baskakov (Translator), Firebird Publications

Among the Afghans (Central Asia Book Series), Arthur Bonner, Duke University Press

The History of the Saffarids of Sistan and the Maliks of Nimruz, Clifford Edmund Bosworth, Mazda Publications

The Later Ghaznavids: Splendour and Decay: The Dynasty in Afghanistan and Northern India, 1040-1186, Clifford Edmund Bosworth, Mazda Publications

Gemstones of Afghanistan, Gary W. Bowersox, Geoscience Press (1997)

Cabool in 1836-37 and 8, Being the Personal Narrative of a Journey to, and Residence in, that City, Sir Alexander Burnes, (London 1842. Reprinted by Ferozsons, Lahore, 1964 and by Akademische Druk-u. Verlagsanstalt, Graz, 1973)

The Road to Oxiana, Robert Byron, Macmillan (London, 1937; reprinted by Picador, London, 1981)

The Pathans: 500 BC-AD 1957, Olaf Caroe, Oxford University Press (Oxford, 1958; reprinted, Karachi, 1973)

Chroniques Afghanes, 1965-1993, Pierre Centlivres, University of Neuchatel, Switzerland (Paris, 1997)

Imageries Populaires en Islam, Pierre Centlivres & Micheline Centlivres-Demont, Georg Editeur SA (Chene-Bourg, 1997)

An Historical Guide to Kabul, Nancy Hatch Dupree (2nd Edition, Kabul, 1972)

The National Museum of Afghanistan, a pictorial guide, Nancy Hatch Dupree (Kabul, 1974)

An Historical Guide to Afghanistan, Nancy Hatch Dupree (2nd Edition, Kabul, 1977)

Heroes of the Age: Moral Fault Lines on the Afghan Frontier (Comparative Studies on Muslim Societies, No 21), David B. Edwards, University of California Press

An Account of the Kingdom of Caubul, Mountstuart Elphinstone, John Murray (London, 1815; reprinted by Akademische Druk-u. Verlagsanstalt, Graz, 1969 and by Oxford University Press, Karachi, 1972)

Afghanistan Dar Panj Qarn Akheer (lit. "English Afghanistan in the Past Five Centuries"), Mir M. Sediq Farhang, Sanai Publishing

Afghanistan (Enchantment of the World), Leila Merrell Foster, Childrens Press

Caravans and Trade in Afghanistan, Birthe Frederiken

Award Winning Low-Fat Afghani Cooking, Asad Gharwal

Afghanistan in the Course of History, Volume Two, Mir Gholam Mohammad Ghobar, Hashmat K. Gobar (2001)

The Emergence of Modern Afghanistan: Politics of Reform and -Modernization, 1880-1946, Vartan Gregorian, Stanford University Press (Stanford, 1969)

Afghanistan: Government and Politics, Verinder Grover, Deep & Deep Publications (2002)

External Influences and the Development of the Afghan State in the Nineteenth Century, Zalmay A. Gulzad, Peter Lang Publishing

Afghanistan: The Synagogue and the Jewish Home, Zohar Hanegbi, Center for Jewish Art

Traditional Textiles of Central Asia, Janet Harvey, Thames and Hudson (London, 1996)

Kabul, M. E. Hirsh, Griffin Trade Paperback (2002)

Government and Society in Afghanistan: The Reign of Amir' Abd al-Rahman Khan, Hasan Kawun Kakar, University of Texas (Austin, 1981)

Afghanistan: The Great Game Revisited, Rosanne Klass (Editor), Freedom House (New York, 1987)

The Constitutional Decade, Sabah Kushkaki, Cultural Council of Afghanistan Resistance (Language: Dari)

Life of the Amir Dost Mohammed Khan of Kabul, Mohan Lal, Oxford University Press

The 'Ancient Supremacy': Bukhara, Afghanistan and the Battle for Balkh, 1731-1901 (Islamic History and Civilization, No 15), Jonathan L. Lee, E J Brill

Permian Stratigraphy and Fusulinida of Afghanistan With Their Paleogeographic and Paleotectonic Implications, E. la Leven, Calvin H. Stevens, Donald L. Baars, Geological Society of America

Afghanistan and Afghans: History, Travels and Wars, J. Thorn, R. Lockyer, D. Smith, Deep & Deep Publications (2002)

Kabul Catastrophe: the Invasion and Retreat 1839-1842, Patrick Macrory, Prion Books Ltd. (2002)

Signal Catastrophe; The Retreat from Kabul, 1842, Patrick Macrory, Hodder and Stoughton (London, 1966)

Waqf in Central Asia: Four Hundred Years in the History of a Muslim Shrine, 1480-1889, R. D. McChesney, Princeton University Press

The Afghanistan Wars, William Maley, Palgrave Macmillan (2002)

Tournament of Shadows: The Great Game and the Race for Empire in Central Asia, Carl E. Meyer, Shareen Blair Brysac, Counterpoint Press (1999)

Afghanistan: Paradise Lost, Roland Michaud, Rizzoli International

Horsemen of Afghanistan, Roland & Sabrina Michaud, Thames and Hudson (London, 1988)

Oral Narrative in Afghanistan: The Individual in Tradition, Margaret Ann Mills, Garland Publications

Rhetorics and Politics in Afghan Traditional Storytelling, Margaret Ann Mills, University of Pennsylvania Press

Afghan Craftsmen: The Cultures of Three Itinerant Communities, (Carlsberg Foundation's Nomad Research Project), Ida Nicolaisen, Thames & Hudson

Afghan Nomads in Transition: A Century of Change Among the Zala, Khan Khel (The Carlsberg Foundation's Nomad Research Project), Ida Nicolaisen, Gorm Pedersen, Thames & Hudson

Amidst Ice and Nomads in High Asia, Edward F. Noack, National Literary Guild

Afghan Wars, 1839-1992: What Britain Gave Up and the Soviet Union Lost, Edgar O'Ballance, Brasseys Inc. (London, 1993)

Oriental Rugs: The Carpets of Afghanistan, R. D. Parsons

Reform and Rebellion in Afghanistan, 1919-1929: King Amanullah's Failure to Modernize a Tribal Society, Leon B. Poullada, Cornell University Press (Ithaca, 1973)

The Kingdom of Afghanistan and the United States: 1828-1973, Leon B. Poullada & Leila J. Poullada, Dageforde Publishing and the Center for Afghanistan Studies at the University of Nebraska at Omaha

Cultural Policy in Afghanistan, Shafie Rahel, UNESCO

Between Two Giants: Political History of Afghanistan in the Nineteen Century, Sayed Qassem Reshtia, Afghan Jehad Works Translation Centre (Peshawar, 1990)

The Savage Frontier: A History of the Anglo-Afghan Wars, D. S. Richards, Pan Macmillan (2002)

Ancient Art from Afghanistan: Treasures of the Kabul Museum, Benjamin, Jr. Rowland, Ayer Co. Publishers

Revolutions & Rebellions in Afghanistan: Anthropological Perspectives, M. Nazif Shahrani, Robert L. Canfield (Editors), University of California Institute for International Studies (Berkeley, 1984)

Dust of the Saints: A Journey to Herat in Time of War, Radek Sikorski, Paragon House

The Minaret of Djam: An Excursion in Afghanistan, Freya Stark, Transatlantic Arts

Fire in Afghanistan: 1914-1929, Rhea Stewart, Doubleday & Co. (New York, 1973)

A History of Afghanistan, Percy Sykes, Macmillan (London, 1940, reprinted by Oriental Books Reprint Corp., New Delhi, 1981)

Afghanistan: An Atlas of Indigenous Domestic Architecture, Albert Szabo, Thomas J. Barfield, University of Texas Press

Beyond the Khyber Pass: The Road to British Disaster in the first Afghan War, John H. Waller, Random House

Charles Masson of Afghanistan: Explorer, Archaeologist, Numismatist, and Intelligence Agent, Gordon Whitteridge, Aris & Phillips

Human Rights & Women

Afghanistan: No justice and security for women, Amnesty International (London, 2003)

Women in Afghanistan: The violations continue, Amnesty International (London, 1997)

Veiled Courage: Inside the Afghan Women's Resistance, Cheryl Benard, Broadway Books (2002)

With All Our Strength: The Revolutionary Association of the Women of Afghanistan, Anne E. Brodsky, Routledge (2003)

Women of Afghanistan, Isabelle Delloye, Ruminator Books (2003)

Women of the Afghan War, Deborah Ellis, Prager Trade (2000)

Repression, Resistance, and Women in Afghanistan, Hafizullah Emadi, Praeger Publishers (2002)

Afghanistan: Warlords Implicated in New Abuses, Human Rights Watch (New York, 2003)

"We Want to Live as Humans:" Repression of Women and Girls in Western Afghanistan, Human Rights Watch (New York, 2002)

Afghanistan the Forgotten War: Human Rights Abuses and Violations of the Laws of War Since the Soviet Withdrawal, Human Rights Watch

Afghanistan: Minorities, Conflict and the Search for Peace, Peter Marsden, Minority Rights Group (2001)

Women for Afghan Women: Shattering Myths and Claiming the Future, Sunita Mehta (Editor), Palgrave Macmillan (2002)

Afghanistan: A Nation of Minorities, Nassim Jawad, Minority Rights Group International (London, 1992)

Women's Health and Human Rights in Afghanistan, Physicians for Human Rights Staff, Physicians for Human Rights (2001)

Blind Chickens & Social Animals: Creating Spaces for Afghan Women's Narratives Under the Taliban, Anna M. Pont, Chronicle Books (2nd Edition, 2001)

Afghanistan: Lifting the Veil, Reuters, Pearson Technology Group, Reuters Books (1st Edition, 2002)

A Nation is Dying, Jeri Laber and Barnett R. Rubin, Northwestern University Press (1988)

The Women of Afghanistan Under the Taliban, Rosemarie Skaine, Mcfarland & Company (2001)

International Human Rights in Context, Henry Steiner and Philip Alston, Oxford University Press (Oxford, 1998)

The Universal Declaration of Human Rights

The Geneva Conventions (1949) and the **Geneva Protocols** (1977)

The International Covenant on Civil and Political Rights

The International Covenant on Economic, Social and Cultural Rights

The Convention Against Torture and Other Cruel, Inhuman or Degrading Treatment or Punishment

Humanitarian Aid & Development

Agents of Altruism: The Expansion of Humanitarian NGOs in Rwanda and Afghanistan (Non-State Actors in International Law, Politics and Governance), Katarina West, Ashgate Publishing Company (2002)

Publications by the Afghan Research and Evaluation Unit (AREU):

Afghan Elections: The Great Gamble, November 2003

How the Government Works in Afghanistan, Joint AREU/World Bank Study, October 2003

Three Villages in Alingar, Laghman: A Case Study of Rural Livelihoods, October 2003

Land and the Constitution, September 2003

100 Households in Kabul: A Study of Winter Vulnerability, August 2003

Land Rights in Crisis, by Liz Alden Wily, March 2003

Taking Refugees for a Ride? David Turton and Peter Marsden, December 2002

Strategic Coordination in Afghanistan, Nicholas Stockton, August 2002

Addressing Livelihoods in Afghanistan, Adam Pain and Sue Lautze, September 2002

Review of the Strategic Framework for Afghanistan, Mark Duffield, Patricia Gossman and Nicholas Leader, June 2002

The Public Health System in Afghanistan, Ronald Waldman and Homaira Hanif, July 2002

Publications by the British Agencies Afghanistan Group (BAAG):

BAAG Briefing Paper on the development of Joint Regional Teams (JRTs) in Afghanistan, Barbara J Stapleton (London, 2003)

BAAG Evacuation Plans, Jeanne Bryer, BAAG (London, 2003)

United Nations documents are available online at: **http://www.unama-afg.org/docs/index.html** or at **http://www.aims.org.af**

The Money Exchange Dealers of Kabul : A Study of the Hawala System in Afghanistan, World Bank (Washington DC, 2003)

Soviet Invasion

Inside the Soviet Army in Afghanistan, Alex Alexiev, Rand Corp

Afghanistan: The Soviet Invasion in Perspective, Anthony Arnold, Hoover Institution Press (Stanford, CA, 1981 & 1985)

The Fateful Pebble: Afghanistan's Role in the Fall of the Soviet Empire, Anthony Arnold, Presidio Press

Afghanistan's Two-Party Communism: Parcham and Khalq, Anthony Arnold, Hoover Institution Press (Stanford, CA, 1983)

Russian Roulette: Afghanistan Through Russian Eyes, Gennady Bocharov. (Translated by Alyona Kojevnikov), A Cornelia and Michael Bessie Book/ HarperCollins

Afghanistan-Washington's Secret War, Phillip Bonosky, International Publishers Company, 2nd Edition, 2001)

The Hidden War: A Russian Journalist's Account of the Soviet War in Afghanistan, Artyom Borovik, Atlantic Monthly Press

Afghan Communism and Soviet Intervention, Henry S. Bradsher, Oxford University Press (1999)

Afghanistan and the Soviet Union, Henry S. Bradsher, Duke University Press (Durham, 1983)

Guerrilla Strategies: An Historical Anthology from the Long March to Afghanistan, Gerard Chaliand, University of California Press

Out of Afghanistan: The Inside Story of the Soviet Withdrawal, Diego Cordovez and Selig S. Harrison, Oxford University Press (1997)

The Red Army on Pakistan's Border: Policy Implications for the United States, (Foreign Policy Report), Theodore L. Eliot (Editor), Brasseys Inc.

Before the Taliban: Genealogies of the Afghan Jihad, David B. Edwards, University of California of Press (2002)

Gorbachev's Afghan Gambit (National Security Paper, 9), Theodore L. Eliot Institute of Foreign Policy Analysis

Afghan Resistance: The Politics of Survival, Grant M. Farr and John G. Merriam (Editors), Westview Press

Afghanistan, the Soviet Union's Last War, Mark Galeotti, Frank Cass & Co.

INFORESOURCES

The Fall of Afghanistan: An Insider's Account, Abdul Samad Ghaus, Brasseys Inc.

Afghanistan: The Soviet War, Edward Girardet, Croom Helm, London and St Martins' Press (New York, 1985)

British and American Responses to the Soviet Invasion of Afghanistan, Gabriella Grasselli, Dartmouth Publishing Co.

Afghanistan: Politics, Economics and Society: Revolution, Resistance, Intervention (Marxist Regimes Series), Bhavani Sen Gupta, Francis Pinter Publishing Ltd. (London, 1986)

The Soviet-Afghan War: How a Superpower Fought and Lost, Michael A. Gress (Editor), Russian General Staff

Red Flag Over Afghanistan: The Communist Coup, the Soviet Invasion, and the Consequences, Thomas T. Hammond, Westview Press (Colorado, 1984)

The Soviet War in Afghanistan: Patterns of Russian Imperialism, Milan Hauner, University Press of America

Afghanistan and the Soviet Union: Collision and Transformation, Milan Hauner, Robert L. Canfield, Westview Press

The Soldiers' Story, Anna Heinamaa, Maija Leppanen, Yuri Yurchenko, University of California International

The Afghan Rebels: The War in Afghanistan, D.J. Herda, Franklin Watts,

Afghanistan Under Soviet Domination, 1964-83, Anthony Hyman, St Martins Press, and Macmillan (2nd Edition, London, 1984)

War in a Distant Country, Afghanistan: Invasion and Resistance, David G. Isby, Arm and Armour Press (London, 1989)

Afghanistan: The Soviet Invasion and the Afghan Response, 1979-1982, M. Hasan Kakar, University of California Press (San Diego, 1992)

Soldiers of God: With the Mujahideen in Afghanistan, Robert D. Kaplan, Houghton Mifflin Company

Untying the Afghan Knot: Negotiating Soviet Withdrawal, Riaz M. Khan, Duke University Press (Durham, 1991)

Holy War, Unholy Victory: Eyewitness to the CIA's Secret War in Afghanistan, Kurt Lohbeck, Regnery Publishing, Inc.

Soviet-American Relations with Pakistan, Iran, and Afghanistan, Hafeez Malik, St. Martin's Press

Afghanistan: Soviet Vietnam, Naomi Marcus, Marianne Clarke Trangen (Translator), Vladislav Tamarov, Mercury House

Stumbling Bear: Soviet Military Performance in Afghanistan, Scott R. McMichael, Brasseys Inc.

Holy Blood: An Inside View of the Afghan War, Paul Overby, Praeger Publications

Afghanistan, Mongolia and USSR, Ram Rahul, Vikas Publications

War Without Winners: Afghanistan's Uncertain Transition After the Cold War, Rasul Bakhsh Rais, Oxford University Press

The Soviet Withdrawal from Afghanistan: Analysis and Chronology, Tom Rogers, Greenwood Publishing Group

Soviet Intervention in Afghanistan: Causes, Consequences and India's Response, Arundhati Roy, Stosius Inc./Advent Books Division

Afghanistan: From Holy War to Civil War, Olivier Roy, Darwin Press

Islam and Resistance in Afghanistan, Olivier Roy, Cambridge University Press (2nd Edition, Cambridge, 1990)

The Fragmentation of Afghanistan: State Formation and Collapse in the International System, Barnett R. Rubin, Yale University Press, Second Edition (2002)

Soviet Policy Toward Turkey, Iran, and Afghanistan: The Dynamics of Influence, Alvin Z. Rubinstein, Praeger Publications (New York, 1982)

The Pulicharki Prison: A Communist Inferno in Afghanistan, Professor Mohammed Osman Rustar, Ehsanullah Azeri (Editor), Writers Union of Free Afghanistan

The Soviet Withdrawal from Afghanistan, Amin Saikal, William Maley (Editor), Cambridge University Press

The Afghan Syndrome: The Soviet Union Vietnam, Maj. Gen Oleg Sarin and Col. Lv Dvoretsky, Presidio Press (CA, 1993)

Soviet Expansion in the Third World: Afghanistan a Case Study, Nasir Shansab, Bartleby Press

Bibliographies

Additional bibliographies can be found in the following:

Historical Dictionary of Afghanistan, Ludwig W. Adamec, The Scarecrow Press Inc. (Metuchen, N.J. and London, 1991). Entries (47 pp) under: General; Cultural; Economic; Historical and Political; Juridical; Scientific; Social.

A Bibliography of Afghanistan, Keith McLachlan and William Whittaker, Middle East & North African Studies Press Ltd, Gallipoli House, The Cottons, Outwell, Wisbech, Cambridge, PE14 8TN (England, 1983). Entries (671pp) under: Bibliographies; General; Geology; Flora and Fauna; Water Resources; Geographical Studies; Travel; Historical Studies; History and Politics; Social Studies; Afghan Economy and Infrastructure; Agriculture and Forestry; Language and Literature; Supplement of Publications post 1979; Maps; Index.

The Fragmentation of Afghanistan: State Formation and Collapse in the International System, Barnett R. Rubin, Yale University Press, Second Edition (2002). Entries under: Books and Articles; Official Publications; Government Reports; Documents and Document Collections; News Sources.

Annotated Bibliography of Afghanistan, 3rd Edition, Donald N. Wilber, Human Relations Area Files Press, New Haven, Connecticut (USA, 1968), 252pp. Entries under: General Sources of Information and Reference Works; Geography; History; Social Organizations; Social Evolution and Institutions; Political Structure; Economic Structure; Languages and Literature; Art and Archaeology; Index.

Databases and directories

The Afghan Research and Evaluation Unit (AREU) publishes:

A to Z Guide, 2nd edition (Kabul, 2003). Information on aid agencies, documents, contact details etc.

The Agency Coordinating Body for Afghan Relief (ACBAR) publishes:

Directory of Humanitarian Agencies. Annual publication listing most NGOs working in Afghanistan (including agencies with offices in Pakistan). Contains alphabetical list of NGOs with details of sectors and areas of operations, budgets and principal donors.

Dictionaries

A Grammar of the Pukhto-Pushto or Language of the Afghans, H. G. Raverty, Laurier Books Ltd./AES (2000)

English-Pashtun Dictionary, Afghan National Islamic Council of Immigrants in America (1986)

Concise English-Afghan Dari Dictionary, S. Sakaria (Kabul, 1967)

FOR THE ROAD

J. Hartley/UNICEF

English-Dari phrasebook

The following information is taken from the Concise English-Afghan Dari Dictionary edited by S. Sakaria (Kabul, 1967), which can still be found in some Kabul bookshops. We are grateful to Gordon Adam for his help in editing this section.

PRONUNCIATION

Vowels

a as in father
e as in every
i as in ill
o as in orbit
u as in boot
aa as in market
ai as in ice
au as in our
dj as in pleasure

Consonants

Most consonants are pronounced as they are in Western tongues. A few, however, should be noted:

g is always hard, as in good.
q is not followed by ***u***, as in English; it is a somewhat more explosive, breathy sound, much as the **kh** in khaki, a Persian word long ago assimilated by English.
kh is quite a throaty, coughing sound, much as the **ch** in the Scottish loch, or the German **ch**.

GRAMMAR

Sentence Structure

In Dari, the sentence order is: SUBJECT-OBJECT-VERB, e.g.

Aan tefel khub ast	That child good is
Baks raa mekhaahad	He (she) the box wants
Khana-e-maa az erfaarat dur ast	House of us (our house) from the embassy far is

Articles

A, An and *the* are all expressed by *yak* (one) whenever it is deemed necessary. Generally, however, the article is used only when particular emphasis is placed on the subject.

Nouns

1. Plurals are formed by adding *haa*:

dars	lesson
dorshaa	lessons
tefel	child
tefelhaa	children

2. A word is attached to its modifier by adding *-e:*

dars-e-mushkel	difficult lesson
tefel-e khub	good child

3. Objective (accusative) case is indicated by *raa:*

Tefel khub ast	The child is good
Tefel raa mebinam	I see the child
Tefelhaa raa mebinam	I see the children

Prepositions

ba	to, at, into, on
baa	with, by means of
dar	in
az	from

Pronouns

1. Personal Pronouns

man	I
tu	you – intimate form
o	he, she
iin	it, this
aan	it, that
maa	we
shomaa	you – polite form for both singular and plural use
aanhaa	they

2. Possessive Pronouns. Possession is shown by adding *-e* to the thing possessed. Two forms are generally used: the formal and the shortened.

Formal		Shortened
baks-e man	my box	baks-am
ketaab-e man	my book	ketaab-am

3. Relative and Interrogative Pronouns

ki	who	-e ki, azki	whose
ki raa	whom		
che	what	kodaam	which

4. Demonstrative Pronouns

iin	this	innhaa	these
aan	that	aanhaa	those

Interrogative Adverbs

kai	when
kojaa	where
cheraa	why
chand	how many
cheqadar	how much
chetaur	how

Imperatives are usually indicated by the prefix ***be-***

raftan	to go	berau! (boro)	go away!
aamadan	to come	be'aa!	Come!
pak kardan	to clean	paak kon!	Clean (it)!

Questions

Shomaa ketaab daari?	Do you have a book?
Ketaab-e khub daari?	Do you have a good book?
Habib iin ketaab raa mekhaahad?	Does Habib want his book?
Che mekhaahed?	What do you want?
Chand daana ketaab daarand?	How many book(s) do they have?

Note: daana (piece) usually follows chand (how many).

Yes and No/Negation

bale (yes) often introduces a positive answer; ne, na-, and n' denote negation

Bale, man ketaab daaram	Yes, I have a book
Ne, ketaab na-daaram	No, I don't have any books
Bale, Habib iin ketaab raa mekhaahad	Yes, Habib wants this book
Ne Habib iin ketaab raa na–mekhaahad	No, Habib doesn't want this book

VERBS

Infinitive	to see	didan
Present	I see	man mebinam
Imperative	See!	bebin, loftan bebined
Past	I saw	man didam
Perfect	I have seen	man dida'am
Past perfect	I had seen	man dida budam
Past continuous	I was seeing	man medidam
Conjunctive	I want to see	man mekhaaham bebinam
	Perhaps I can see	shayad bebinam
	I ought to see	bayad bebinam
	I must see	man majbur hastam bebinam

THE VERB "TO BE": *BUDAN / HASTAM*

Present		**Optative**	
hastam	I am	baasham	I may be
hasti	you are	baashi	you may be
ast	he is	baashad	he may be
hastem	we are	baashem	we may be
hasted	you are	baashed	you may be
hastand	they are	baashand	they may be

USEFUL EXPRESSIONS

Greeting and Farewell

Salaam! Salaam a-laykum!	Peace! Peace to you!
Khub hasti?	Are you well? (Intimate form)
Shomaa chetaur hasted?	How are you? (Polite form)
Aaz amadan-e shomaa, khosh hastam	I am happy that you have come (lit. From your coming, I am happy)
Aaz didan-e shomaa, khosh shodam	I become happy to see you
Bubakhshed	Excuse me (*Note:* bakhshish, a present or gift)

Nam-e shomaa chist (che ast)?	What is your name?
Nam-e man Shikria ast	My name is Shikria
Famil-e shomaa khub ast?	Is your family well?
Bale, tashakor aanhaa khub hastand	Yes, thank you, they are well
Bisyaar tashakor!	Thank you very much!
Tefel-e man bisyaar mariz ast	My child is very ill
Bisyaar afsos!	(I am) very sorry!
Afsos!	Sorry!
Ba'aman-e Khoda	Goodbye (lit. Go in the safety of God)
Khodaa Haafez	Goodbye (lit. God be your protector)
Lotfan aasta gap beegee	Please speak more slowly
Man na-mefahmam	I do not understand
Lotfan tekraar ko	Repeat it, please

Driving and Directions

Lotfan aasta boro!	Please go slowly!
Lotfan zud boro!	Please go fast! Please hurry!
Rubaru	Straight ahead (lit. Face to face)
Dast-e raast	Right (lit. Right hand)
Dast-e chap	Left (lit. Left hand)
Baash! iinja baash!	Stop! Stop here!
Lotfan iinja baash	Please stop here
Sarak-e Bamiyan khub ast?	Is the road to Bamiyan good?
Baa shomaa chand nafar ast?	How many people are with you?
Che taklif/mushkil ast?	What's the trouble?

Shopping and Eating

Chand qimat?	How much (is the) price?
Qimat ast!	It is expensive!
Ne, qimat nist, arzaan ast	No, it is not expensive, it is cheap
Iin che ast? Aan che ast?	What is this? What is that?
Chist? (Che ast)?	What is it?
Kist? (Ki ast)?	Who is it?
Man yak otaq-e yak nafara mekhaaham	I want a single room
Otaq-e naan kojaast?	Where is the dining room?
Lotfan bishi	Please sit down
Loftan naan beegee	Please take food
Lotfan darwaaza raa waaz ko	Please open the door
Lotfan kelkin raa basta ko	Please close the window
Naan mehaahed?	Would you like some food?
Du, tokhme-e josh wa chai mekhaaham	I want two boiled eggs and some tea
Digar che mekhaahed?	What else do you want?
Man chai sabz mekhaaham	I want a cup of green tea
Ju'aab-e chai koja ast?	Where is the lavatory? (lit. Where is the answer to tea?)
Tashnaab kojast?	Where is the washroom?

TIMES, SEASONS, NUMERALS

waqt	time, early
naawaqt	late
baja	o'clock
saa'at	hour
daqiqa	minute
juma	Friday
shanbe	Saturday
yak shanbe	Sunday
du shanbe	Monday
se shanbe	Tuesday
chaar shanbe	Wednesday
panj shanbe	Thursday
saniya	second
roz	day
shab	night
diroz	yesterday
dishab	last night
emroz	today
emshab	tonight
fardaa	tomorrow
fardaa shab	tomorrow night
pas fardaa	day after tomorrow
har roz	every day
har shab	every night
sobh	morning
chasht	noon
baad az chasht	afternoon
hafta	week
	(*Note:* haft, seven)
maah	month
saal	year
mausem	season
bahaar	spring
taabestaan	summer
khazaan	autumn
zemestaan	winter
dafa, yak dafa	one time, once
yak dafa digar	once again
hesaab	calculation
hesaab kardan	to count
adad	numeral, number
pesh	before
baad	after
ziyaad	too much
kam-e	a little

bisyaar	many, much, very
sefer	zero
yak, awal	one, 1st
du, dowom	two, 2nd
se, sowom	three, 3rd
chaar, chaarom	four, 4th
panj, panjom	five, 5th
shash, shashom	six, 6th
haft, haftom	seven, 7th
hasht, hashtom	eight, 8th
noh, nohom	nine, 9th
dah, dahom	ten, 10th
yaazdah	eleven, 11
duaazdah	twelve, 12
sezdah	thirteen, 13
chaardah	fourteen, 14
paanzdah	fifteen, 15
shaanzdah	sixteen, 16
hafdah	seventeen,17
hajdah	eighteen, 18
nozdah	nineteen, 19
bisttwenty, 20	
bist-o yak	twenty one, 21
bist-o du	twenty two, 22
si	thirty, 30
chel	forty, 40
pinja	fifty, 50
shast	sixty, 60
haftaad	seventy, 70
hashtaad	eighty, 80
nawad	ninety, 90
sad	one hundred, 100
hazaar	one thousand, 1,000

Telling the time

Chand baja ast?	What o'clock is it?
Che waqt ast?	What time is it?

VOCABULARY

VERBS

Infinitive	Infinitive	Present
awake	bedar shodan	meshawam
bear	bordan	mebaram
beat	zadan	mezanam
become	shodan	meshawam
break	shekastan	meshkenam
bring	awordan	me'aaram
build	saakhtan	mesaazam
burst	tarqidan	metarqam
buy	kharidan	mekharam
can	tawaanestan	metawaanam
catch	greftan	megiram
come	aamadan	me'aayam
cost	arzidan	mearzam
creep	khazidan	mekhazam
cut	buridan	meboram
dig	kandan	mekanam
do	kardan	mekonam
drink	nushidan	menosham
drive	raandan	meraanam
eat	khordan	mekhoram
fall	oftaadan	me'oftam
flee	gorekhtan	megorezam
fight	jangidan	mejangam
find	yaaftan	meyaafam
fly	paridan	meparam
forget	faraamosh kardan	faraamosh mekonam
give	daadan	medeham
go	raftan	merawam
grind	maida kardan	maida mekonam
grow	ruidan	meroyam
have	daashtan	daaram
hear	shonidan	meshnawam
knit	baaftan	mebaafam
know	daanestan	medaanam
lay	maandan	memaanam
learn	amokhtan	me'aamozam
let	gozaashtan	megozaaram
light	bal kardan	bal mekonam
lose	gom kardan	gom mekonam
make	saakhtan	mesaazam
owe	qarzdaar budan	qarzdaar hastam
pay	pardaakhtan	mepardaazam
put	maandan	memaanam
read	khaandan	mekhaanam
recognize	shenaakhtan	meshnaasam
run	dawidan	medawam
say	goftan	megoyam
see	didan	mebinam

seek	paalidan	mepaalam
sell	frokhtan	mefrosham
send	frestaadan	mefrestam
set	neshastan	meshinam
shine	drokh'shidan	medrokh'sham
shut	bastan	mebandam
sing	saraa'idan	mesaraayam
slay	koshtan	mekhosham
sleep	khaabidan	mekhaabam
slide	lakh'shidan	melakh'sham
spin	residan	meresam
stand	estaadan	me'estam
steal	dozdidan	medozdam
stick	chaspidan	mechaspam
take	greftan	megiram
teach	dars daadan	dars medeham
think	feker kardan	feker mekonam
throw	andaakhtan	meandaazam
weave	baaftan	mebaafam
write	naweshtan	menawisam

EATING AND COOKING

apple	seb
apricot	zard aalu
asparagus	maarchoba
beans	lubiya
beef	gosht-e gau
beet	lablabu
boiling-water	aab-e josh
breakfast	naashtaa
bucket	satel
cabbage	karam
cardamom	hel
carrot	zardak
cauliflower	gole karam
cherry	gelaas
corn	jawaari
cucumber	baadrang
egg	tokhom
eggplant	baanjaane siyaah
flour	aard
fruit	mewa
grape	angur
icebox	yakh-chaal
kerosene	tel-e khaak
leek	gandana
lentil	daal
lettuce	kaahu
melon	kharbuza
mint	naanaa
mutton	gosht-e gosfand
okra	baamiyaa
onion	piyaaz
parsley	gashniz
peach	shaftaalu
pear	naak
peas	moshong
pepper	morch
pot	deg
potato	kachaalu
prune	aalubokhaaraa
radish	moli
raisin	keshmesh
rhubarb	rawaash
rice	brenj
sour-cherry	aalubaalu
spinach	paalak
squash	kadu
sugar cane	naishakar
tomato	baanjaane rumi
turnip	shalgham
veal	gosht-e gosaala
vegetables	tarkaari
water melon	tarbuz
wheat	gandom
yeast	kalpura

English-Pashto field vocabulary

n. noun, a. adjective, v.t. verb transitive, v.i. verb intransitive

accident	n. hadisa'h, afat	enemy	n. dushman
afraid	v.i. tarhedal	evil	a. badi, ba'a
angry	a. khafah	excellent	a. shaeh
arable	a. shud-yar	eye	n. starga'h
army	n. lashkar	face	n. makh
asleep	a. u-dah	far	a. bi-yartah
bad	a. kharab	farmer	n. zamin-dar
barley	n. aor-bushey	field	n. wand, kisht
barren(land)	a. dag	fire	n. aor, balarn
bath	n. hammam	food	n. khwarah, shuma'h, n'mara'i
beggar	n. gada	girl	n. jina'i
big	a. lo-e, ghat	goat	n. wuz, psah (markhor: wild goat)
bird	n. murgha'h	God	n. Allah
black	a. tor	gold	n. zar
blanket	n. shara'i	good	a. shaeh
blood	n. winey	government	n. daulat
boil	v.i. aeshedal	governor	n. hakim, sardar
bone	n. had	grass	n. alaf, washah
book	n. kitab	green	a. shin
bread	n. doda'i, nan	gun	n. topak
canal	n. wala'h	hand	n. las
chair	n. kursi, chauki	happy	a. khwash
child	n. wor-kaey, halak	harvest	n. fasl
cold	a. sor	headman	n. malik
cook	n. bawarchi	heavy	a. drund
corn	n. hala'h, danah	herd (cows)	n. park
cotton	n. ma-luch	home	n. astogna'h
cow	n. ghwa	horse	n. as (asp)
cup	n. kandol	hour	n. sa'at
danger	n. wera'h	hot	a. garm
dark	a. tor	husband	n. merah
daughter	n. lur	ice	n. kangal
day	n. wradz	ill	a. najor
dead	a. mar	infant	n. tandaey
dirty	a. khiran	infidel	n. kafir
donkey	n. khar	irrigate	v.t. lundawul
dog	n. spaey	journalist	n. khabar'nigar
door	n. war	journey	n. safar
dry (land)	a. wuch	kill	v.t. wajlal
early	a. sahar	lady	n. bibi, merman
earth	n. z'maka'h, zamin, mulk (land)	land	n. z'maka'h, zamin
empty	a. khali	law	n. shara, shari'at

leader	n. sardar, komand'r (mujahed)
light	a. roshna'i, rarna
mad	a. lewanaey
male	a. nar, merah
market	n. bazaar
meat	n. ghwasha'h
mountain	n. ghar, koh
mother	n. mor
much	a. der, frewan
news	n. khabar
night	n. shpa'h
noon	n. gharma'h, takkarna'h
numerous	a. der, garn, wadan
open	a. arat
ox	n. ghwayaey
pain	n. dard
pass	n. tangaey, dara'h (defile), ghashaey (mountain)
path	n. lar, wat
peace	n. sulha'h, ashti
plunder	v.t. tala'h, talanka
poor	a. khwar, tarah
quick	a. zaer
quiet	a. aram, karar
rain	n. baran
red	a. sur, surkh
rest	n. aram
rice	n. w'rijey
right (not left)	a. rast
river	n. sin, daryah
road	n. lar, rah
room	n. khuna'h, hujra'h
sad	a. zahir
safe	a. aman, salamat
salt	n. malga'h
salutation	n. salaam
sheep	n. majz (male), mejz (ewe)
shoe	n. parna'h, na'l (horse shoe)
sister	n. khor
sleep	v.i. khub ka
small	a. wor, lajz
snow	n. wawra'h
son	n. dzo-e, zo-e
state	n. daulat
storm	n. sila'i, tufan
straight	a. sam, sat
stream	n. lashtaey, wala'h
thief	n. ghal
time	n. waght
understand	v.i. pohedal
urgent	a. zarur
valley	n. dara'h
village	n. kalaey, dih
war	n. jang, jihad (religious war)
water	n. aobah, sakao
wood	n. largaey, jar (copse, small wood)
wound	n. parhar, zakhm
young	a. dzwan, halak

Sources: The Pushtu Manual (H.G. Raverty), personal notes (E.R. Girardet)

Acronyms

AACA	Afghan Assistance Coordination Authority
ACBAR	Agency Coordinating Body for Afghan Relief
AETF	Afghanistan Emergency Trust Fund
AIA	Afghan Interim Authority/Administration
AIHRC	Afghanistan Independent Human Rights Commission
ANA	Afghan National Army
ANCB	Afghan NGOs' Coordinating Bureau
AREU	Afghanistan Research and Evaluation Unit
ARIC	ACBAR Research and Information Centre
ARSG	Afghanistan Reconstruction Steering Group
ARTF	Afghanistan Reconstruction Trust Fund
ATA	Afghanistan Transitional Authority/Administration
AWCC	Afghan Wireless Communications Company
CAP	Consolidated Appeal Process
CAS	Country Assistance Strategy
CBO	Community-Based Organization
CDF	Comprehensive Development Framework
CEDAW	Convention on the Elimination of all Forms of Discrimination against Women
CIMIC	(ISAF) Civil Military Cooperation/Coordination
CJCMOTF	Coalition Joint Civil-Military Operations Task Force
CLJ	Constitutional Loya Jirga
CMOC	Civil-Military Operations Centre
CNA	Comprehensive Needs Assessments
CRC	Convention on the Rights of the Child
DAD	Donor Assistance Database
DDR	Disarmament, demobilization and reintegration
DSRSG	Deputy Special Representative of the Secretary-General
EC	European Commission
ECHO	European Commission Humanitarian Aid Office
ELJ	Emergency Loya Jirga
EPI	Expanded Programme on Immunization
FAO	(UN) Food and Agriculture Organization
FFW	Food for Work
GDP	Gross Domestic Product
GIS	Geographic Information Systems
IASC	Inter-Agency Standing Committee
ICRC	International Committee of the Red Cross
IDP	Internally Displaced Person
IFI	International Financial Institution
ILO	International Labour Organisation
IMF	International Monetary Fund
IOM	International Organization for Migration
IRIN	Integrated Regional Information Network

ISAF	International Security Assistance Force
ITAP	Immediate and Transitional Assistance Programme for Afghanistan
MACA	Mine Action Centre for Afghanistan
MAPA	Mine Action Programme for Afghanistan
MCH	Mother and Child Health
MDG	Millennium Development Goals
MoA	Ministry of Agriculture & Livestock
MoBTA	Ministry of Border & Tribal Affairs
MoC	Ministry of Communications
MoCT	Ministry of Civil Aviation & Tourism
MoD	Ministry of Defence
MoE	Ministry of Education
MoF	Ministry of Finance
MoFA	Ministry of Foreign Affairs
MoH	Ministry of Health
MoHE	Ministry of Higher Education
MoI	Ministry of Interior
MoIC	Ministry of Information and Culture
MoIWRE	Ministry of Irrigation, Water Resources and Environment
MoJ	Ministry of Justice
MoLI	Ministry of Light Industries & Food
MoLSA	Ministry of Labour and Social Affairs
MoMD	Ministry of Martyrs and Disabled
MoMI	Ministry of Mines & Industries
MoP	Ministry of Planning
MoPilgrimage	Ministry of Haj (Pilgrimage)
MoPW	Ministry of Public Works
MoR	Ministry of Reconstruction
MoRR	Ministry of Refugee & Repatriation
MoT	Ministry of Transportation
MoTr	Ministry of Trade
MoUDH	Ministry of Urban Development & Housing
MoWA	Ministry of Women's Affairs
MoWP	Ministry of Power
MRRD	Ministry of Rural Rehabilitation and Development
NATO	North Atlantic Treaty Organization
NDB	National Development Budget
NDF	National Development Framework
NGO	Non-Governmental Organization
NID	National Immunization Day
NRVA	National Risk and Vulnerability Assessment
NWFP	North West Frontier Province (Pakistan)
OCHA	(UN) Office for the Coordination of Humanitarian Affairs
OECD	Organisation for Economic Cooperation and Development
OEF	Operation Enduring Freedom
OFDA	Office for Foreign Disaster Assistance (part of USAID)

OSAGI	Office of the Special Adviser on Gender Issues and Advancement of Women
OSGA	Office of the Secretary-General in Afghanistan
P.E.A.C.E.	Poverty Eradication and Community Empowerment Initiative
PCP	Principled Common Programming
PNA	Preliminary Needs Assessment
ProMIS	Project Management Information System
PRSP	Poverty Reduction Strategy Paper
PRT	Provincial Reconstruction Team
RAMCC	Regional Air Movements Control Centre
RC/HC	Resident Coordinator/Humanitarian Coordinator
SRSG	Special Representative of the Secretary-General
SSR	Security Sector Reform
SWABAC	South-West Afghanistan and Balochistan Association for Coordination
TAPA	Transitional Assistance Programme for Afghanistan
TBA	Traditional Birth Attendant
TISA	Transitional Islamic State of Afghanistan
UF	United Front (Northern Alliance)
UN	United Nations
UNAMA	United Nations Assistance Mission in Afghanistan
UNCHS/Habitat	United Nations Centre for Human Settlements (Habitat)
UNDP	United Nations Development Programme
UNEP	United Nations Environment Programme
UNESCO	United Nations Educational, Scientific and Cultural Organization
UNFPA	United Nations Population Fund
UNHAS	United Nations Humanitarian Air Services
UNHCHR	United Nations High Commissioner for Human Rights
UNHCR	United Nations High Commissioner for Refugees
UNICEF	United Nations Children's Fund
UNIFEM	United Nations Development Fund for Women
UNJLC	United Nations Joint Logistics Centre
UNODC	United Nations Office for Drugs and Crime
UNOPS	United Nations Office for Project Services
UNSECOORD	United Nations Security Coordinator
UNSG	United Nations Secretary-General
USAID	United States Agency for International Development
UXO	Unexploded Ordnance
VAM	Vulnerability Analysis and Mapping
WFP	(UN) World Food Programme
WHO	(UN) World Health Organization

Index

A

B

C

G

H

I

J

K

L

M

N

O

P

Q

R

S

About Media Action International and *CROSSLINES*

Media Action International, Geneva, Switzerland and Media Action International (USA): First established in 1994 as the International Centre for Humanitarian Reporting (ICHR), Media Action International is a not-for-profit foundation focusing on media and public information support in humanitarian, conflict and post-conflict situations. As a highly innovative media group, it has sought to serve as a communications bridge between international aid organizations, donors, peacekeepers and local populations affected by crisis. Since merging with the Radio Partnership in 1999, MAI has implemented credible and independent public information initiatives in crisis situations ranging from the war in Kosovo and floods in Mozambique to reconstruction in Afghanistan, conflict resolution in Aceh and media training in the Ivory Coast.

Working with professional journalists and producers, MAI projects have included daily and independent humanitarian radio broadcasts over indigenous stations by local journalists in Albania and Macedonia aimed at Kosovar refugees; road shows to promote peace-building and elections in Kosovo; youth radio programmes highlighting democracy, employment, culture and other related issues in the Balkans; peace-building workshops and specialized health, environmental and other forms of reporter training in Rwanda and West Africa; the Kabul Travelling Theatre to publicise health, landmines and other forms of awareness in rural areas of Afghanistan; Youth Journalism Training with Afghan universities and Radio Education for Afghan Children in Afghanistan (REACH); as well as Lifeline Media for conflict, humanitarian and post-conflict recovery situations.

MAI has implemented numerous projects aimed at promoting more effective and critical monitoring and coordination of donor and international aid agency activities in the public domain. Donors and partners have included the Dutch government, DFID (UK), Danish government, the Swiss Development Corporation, USAID, UNICEF, UNHCR, World Vision, UNDP, ICRC and others.

Media Action International (USA) is an independent foundation based in the United States. Registered as a 501 (c) (3) not-for-profit organization, MAI USA was created in 2003 to assist in the support and implementation of credible and independent humanitarian-based public information initiatives.

***CROSSLINES*, Geneva, Switzerland.** An independent group of journalists, producers and media consultants focusing on credible information and monitoring in the public domain of the international humanitarian, development and peacekeeping industries, *CROSSLINES* has undertaken and supported various publishing and training projects including *CROSSLINES Global Report*, the *Afghanistan Monitor* and the *Essential Field Guides to humanitarian and conflict zones.*